Gary H Hall "Segullah"
Walt Zorn
Mark J. Mangano

THE
COLLEGE
PRESS
NIV
COMMENTARY

OLD TESTAMENT
INTRODUCTION

THE
COLLEGE
PRESS
NIV
COMMENTARY

OLD TESTAMENT

INTRODUCTION

MARK MANGANO, ED.

Old Testament Series Co-Editors:

Terry Briley, Ph.D.   Paul Kissling, Ph.D.
Lipscomb University   Great Lakes Christian College

COLLEGE PRESS
PUBLISHING COMPANY
Joplin, Missouri

Library of Congress Cataloging-in-Publication Data

College Press NIV commentary Old Testament introduction/
by Mark Mangano, editor.
    p.   cm.
  Includes bibliographical references.
  ISBN 0-89900-896-8
  1. Bible. O.T.–Introductions.   I. Mangano, Mark, 1958–
BS1140.3.C645 2005
221.6'1–dc22

                                            2005014466

A WORD
FROM THE PUBLISHER

Years ago a movement was begun with the dream of uniting all Christians on the basis of a common purpose (world evangelism) under a common authority (the Word of God). The College Press NIV Commentary Series is a serious effort to join the scholarship of two branches of this unity movement so as to speak with one voice concerning the Word of God. Our desire is to provide a resource for your study of the Old Testament that will benefit you whether you are preparing a Bible School lesson, a sermon, a college course, or your own personal devotions. Today as we survey the wreckage of a broken world, we must turn again to the Lord and his Word, unite under his banner and communicate the life-giving message to those who are in desperate need. This is our purpose.

ABBREVIATIONS

AAFS . . . .*Annales Academiae Scientiarum Fennicae, Series*
AASOR . . .*Annual of the American School of Oriental Research*
ABD . . . . .*Anchor Bible Dictionary*
ANET . . . .*Ancient Near Eastern Texts Relating to the Old Testament.*
       Ed. by J.B. Pritchard
AUSS . . . .*Andrews University Seminary Studies*
BA . . . . . .*Biblical Archaeologist*
BAR . . . . .*Biblical Archaeology Review*
BASOR . . .*Bulletin of the American School of Oriental Research*
BDB . . . . .Brown, Francis, S.R. Driver, and C.A. Briggs. *A Hebrew*
       and English Lexicon of the Old Testament. Oxford, 1907.
BHS . . . . .*Biblia Hebraica Stuttgartensia*
Bib . . . . . .*Biblica*
BJS . . . . . .*Brown Judaic Studies*
BKAT . . . .*Biblischer Kommentar, Altes Testament*
BRev . . . . .*Bible Review*
BSac . . . . .*Bibliotheca Sacra*
BT . . . . . .*The Bible Translator*
BWANT . .*Beiträge zur Wissenschaft vom Alten und Neuen Testament*
BZAW . . . .*Beihefte zur Zeitschrift für die alttestamentliche Wissenschaft*
CBC . . . . .*Cambridge Bible Commentary*
CBQ . . . . .*Catholic Biblical Quarterly*
CJT . . . . . .*Canadian Journal of Theology*
COS . . . . .*The Context of Scripture*
CTQ . . . . .*Concordia Theological Quarterly*
ErIsr . . . . .*Eretz-Israel*
ExpTim . . .*Expository Times*
FOTL . . . .*Forms of the Old Testament Literature*
FRLANT . .*Forschungen zur Religion und Literatur des Alten und*
       Neuen Testaments

GTJ . . . . .*Grace Theological Journal*
HAR . . . . .*Hebrew Annual Review*
HBC . . . . .*Harper's Bible Commentary*
HS . . . . . .*Hebrew Studies*
HSM . . . . .*Harvard Semitic Monographs*
HTR . . . . .*Harvard Theological Review*
HTS . . . . .*Harvard Theological Studies*
HUCA . . . .*Hebrew Union College Annual*
IB . . . .*Interpreter's Bible.* Ed. by G.A. Buttrick et al. 12 vols.
         New York, 1951–57
ICC . . . . . .*International Critical Commentary*
IDB . . . . . .*Interpreter's Dictionary of the Bible*
IEJ . . . . . .*Israel Exploration Journal*
Int . . . . . .*Interpretation*
ISBE . . . . .*International Standard Bible Encyclopedia*
ITC . . . . . .*International Theological Commentary*
JBL . . . . . .*Journal of Biblical Literature*
JBR . . . . . .*Journal of Bible and Religion*
JETS . . . . .*Journal of the Evangelical Theological Society*
JPS . . . . . .*Jewish Publication Society*
JPSV . . . . .*Jewish Publication Society Version*
JSOT . . . . .*Journal for the Study of the Old Testament*
JTS . . . . . .*Journal of Theological Studies*
KHC . . . . .*Kurzer Hand-Commentar zum Alten Testament*
LCL . . . . .*Loeb Classical Library*
LXX . . . . .*Septuagint*
MT . . . . . .*Masoretic Text*
NAC . . . . .*New American Commentary*
NCB . . . . .*New Century Bible*
NEAEHL .*The New Encyclopedia of Archaeological Explorations in the
         Holy Land.* Ed. by E. Stern. 4 vols. Jerusalem, 1993
NEASB . . .*Near East Archaeology Society Bulletin*
NIB . . . . . .*New Interpreter's Bible*
NIBCOT . .*New International Bible Commentary on the Old Testament*
NICOT . . .*New International Commentary on the Old Testament*
NIDOTTE .*New International Dictionary of Old Testament Theology
         and Exegesis*
NIV . . . . . .*New International Version*
NRSV . . . .*New Revised Standard Version*

OTG . . . . .*Old Testament Guides*
OTL . . . . .*Old Testament Library*
RB . . . . . .*Revue Biblique*
ResQ . . . . .*Restoration Quarterly*
RevExp . . .*Review and Expositor*
RSV . . . . .*Revised Standard Version*
SBL . . . . .*Society of Biblical Literature*
SBLDS . . .*Society of Biblical Literature Dissertation Series*
StudBib . . .*Studia Biblica*
SwJT . . . . .*Southwestern Journal of Theology*
TBT . . . . .*The Bible Today*
ThViat . . .*Theologia Viatorum*
TNTC . . . .*Tyndale New Testament Commentaries*
TOTC . . . .*Tyndale Old Testament Commentaries*
TWOT . . .*Theological Wordbook of the Old Testament*
TynBul . . .*Tyndale Bulletin*
VT . . . . . .*Vetus Testamentum*
WBC . . . . .*Word Biblical Commentary*
WTJ . . . . .*Westminster Theological Journal*
ZAW . . . . .*Zeitschrift für die alttestamentliche Wissenschaft*
ZBAT . . . .*Züricher Bibelkommentare: Alten Testament*

Simplified Guide to Hebrew Writing

Heb. letter	Translit.	Pronunciation guide
א	ʼ	Has no sound of its own; like smooth breathing mark in Greek
ב	b	Pronounced like English B *or* V
ג	g	Pronounced like English G
ד	d	Pronounced like English D
ה	h	Pronounced like English H, silent at the end of words in the combination āh
ו	w	As a consonant, pronounced like English V or German W
ו	û	Represents a vowel sound, pronounced like English long OO
ו	ô	Represents a vowel sound, pronounced like English long O
ז	z	Pronounced like English Z
ח	ḥ	Pronounced like German and Scottish CH and Greek χ (chi)
ט	ṭ	Pronounced like English T
י	y	Pronounced like English Y
כ/ך	k	Pronounced like English K
ל	l	Pronounced like English L
מ/ם	m	Pronounced like English M
נ/ן	n	Pronounced like English N
ס	s	Pronounced like English S
ע	ʻ	Stop in breath deep in throat before pronouncing the vowel
פ/ף	p/ph	Pronounced like English P *or* F
צ/ץ	ṣ	Pronounced like English TS/TZ
ק	q	Pronounced very much like כ (k)
ר	r	Pronounced like English R
שׂ	ś	Pronounced like English S, much the same as ס
שׁ	š	Pronounced like English SH
ת	t/th	Pronounced like English T *or* TH

Note that different forms of some letters appear at the end of the word (written right to left), as in כָּפַף (*kāphaph*, "bend") and מֶלֶךְ (*melek*, "king").

Vowels in Hebrew (except where the ו is used to represent a vowel sound), are represented by "vowel points" added to the consonant. For example: הַ (*ha*, "the"). The letter *yod* (י, *y*) also becomes a *part of* certain vowel sounds, as in the conjunction כִּי (*kî*, "that"). Originally, Hebrew was written as "unpointed" text, with just the consonants. For convenience, the different vowel points are shown below on the letter Aleph (א).

אָ	ā	Pronounced not like long A in English, but like the broad A or AH sound
אַ	a	The Hebrew short A sound, but more closely resembles the broad A (pronounced for a shorter period of time) than the English short A
אֶ	e	Pronounced like English short E

א	ē	Pronounced like English long A, or Greek η (eta)
א	i	Pronounced like English short I
א	î	The same vowel point is sometimes pronounced like אִי (see below)
א	o	This vowel point sometimes represents the short O sound
א	ō	Pronounced like English long O
א	u	The vowel point ֻ sometimes represents a shorter U sound and
א	ū	is sometimes pronounced like the וּ (û, see above)
אִי	ê	Pronounced much the same as א
אִי	ê	Pronounced much the same as א
אִי	î	Pronounced like long I in many languages, or English long E
א	ə	An unstressed vowel sound, like the first E in the word "severe"
א, א, א	ŏ, ă, ĕ	Shortened, unstressed forms of the vowels א, א, and א, pronounced very similarly to א

TABLE OF CONTENTS

Key to Contributers:
  DM — Dale Manor
  GH — Gary Hall
  MM — Mark Mangano
  RB — Randall Bailey
  WZ — Walter Zorn

INTRODUCTION

MARK MANGANO

DALE MANOR

BIBLIOGRAPHY
FOR INTRODUCTION

Alter, Robert. *The Art of Biblical Narrative*. New York: Basic Books, 1981.

Archer, Gleason L. Jr. *A Survey of Old Testament Introduction*. Chicago: Moody Press, 1978.

Aristotle. *The Poetics*. LCL. Cambridge: Harvard University Press, 1927.

Avigad, Nahman. "Samaria (City)." *NEAEHL*, 4:1300-1310. Ed. by E. Stern. New York: Simon & Schuster, 1993.

Bar-Efrat, Shimon. *Narrative Art in the Bible*. Sheffield: Almond, 1989.

Bass, George F. "A Pioneering Excavation Off Turkey: Lessons from a Bronze Age Wreck." In *Archaeology under Water: An Atlas of the World's Submerged Sites*, pp. 32-35. Ed. by K. Muckelroy. New York: McGraw-Hill, 1980.

Beckwith, Roger. "The Canon of the Old Testament." In *The Origin of the Bible*, pp. 51-64. Ed. by Philip Wesley Comfort. Grand Rapids: Tyndale House, 1992.

_____ . *The Old Testament Canon of the New Testament Church*. Grand Rapids: Eerdmans, 1985.

Berlin, Adele. *Poetics and Interpretation of Biblical Narrative*. Sheffield: Almond, 1983.

Braudel, Fernand. *The Mediterranean and the Mediterranean World in the Age of Philip II*, vol. 1. Trans. by S. Reynolds. New York: Harper & Row, 1972.

Bruce, F.F. *The Canon of Scripture*. Downers Grove, IL: InterVarsity, 1988.

Bullinger, E.W. *Number in Scripture*. Grand Rapids: Kregel, 1969; reprinted from first edition published 1894.

Bunimovitz, Shlomo, and Zvi Lederman. "Beth-Shemesh: Culture Conflict on Judah's Frontier." *BAR* 23 (1997): 42-49, 75-77.

Charlesworth, James H., ed. *The Old Testament Pseudepigrapha*. Garden City, NY: Doubleday, 1983.

Clines, David J.A. *The Theme of the Pentateuch.* JSOTSupp 10. Sheffield: Sheffield Academic Press, 1984.

Danby, Herbert. *The Mishnah.* London: Oxford University Press, 1933.

Davis, Thomas W. *Shifting Sands: The Rise and Fall of Biblical Archaeology.* New York: Oxford University, 2004.

deClaisse-Walford, Nancy L. "The Dromedary Saga: The Formation of the Canon of the Old Testament." *RevExp* 95 (1998): 493-511.

Dempster, Stephen G. *Dominion and Dynasty: A Theology of the Hebrew Bible.* New Studies in Biblical Theology 15. Downers Grove, IL: InterVarsity/Leicester, England: Apollos, 2003.

de Vaux, Roland. "On Right and Wrong Uses of Archaeology." In *Near Eastern Archaeology in the Twentieth Century: Essays in Honor of Nelson Glueck*, pp. 64-80. Ed. by J.A. Sanders. Garden City, NY: Doubleday, 1970.

Dever, William G. *Archaeology and Biblical Studies: Retrospects and Prospects.* Winslow Lectures, 1972. Evanston, IL: Seabury-Western Theological Seminary, 1974.

——————. "The Impact of the 'New Archaeology' on Syro-Palestinian Archaeology." *BASOR* 242 (1981): 15-30.

Dorsey, David A. *The Literary Structure of the Old Testament.* Grand Rapids: Baker, 1999.

Dothan, Trude. *The Philistines and Their Material Culture.* Jerusalem: Israel Exploration Society, 1982.

Fokkelman, J.P. *Reading Biblical Narrative: An Introductory Guide.* Louisville, KY: Westminster John Knox, 1999.

Fox, Michael V. *Character and Ideology in the Book of Esther.* Columbia, SC: University of South Carolina Press, 1991.

Gitin, Seymour. "Ekron of the Philistines: Part II: Olive-Oil Suppliers to the World." *BAR* 16 (1990): 32-42, 59.

——————. "Tel Miqne-Ekron: A Type-Site for the Inner Coastal Plain in the Iron Age II Period." *Recent Excavations in Israel: Studies in Iron Age Archaeology*, pp. 23-58. Ed. by S. Gitin and W.G. Dever. AASOR 49. Winona Lake, IN: ASOR, 1989.

Green, William Henry. *General Introduction to the Old Testament: The Canon.* Reprint. Grand Rapids: Baker, 1980.

Gunneweg, Jan, Isadore Perlman, and Zeev Meshel. "The Origin of the Pottery of Kuntillet 'Ajrud." *IEJ* 35 (1985): 270-283.

Guthrie, Donald. *The Pastoral Epistles.* TNTC. Grand Rapids: Eerdmans, 1978.

Harrington, Daniel J., and Anthony J. Saldarini. *Targum Jonathan of the Former Prophets.* The Aramaic Bible, vol. 10. Wilmington, DE: Michael Glazier, 1987.

Harris, R. Laird. *Inspiration and Canonicity of the Bible.* Grand Rapids: Zondervan, 1969.

Harrison, R.K. "Old Testament and New Testament Apocrypha." In *The Origin of the Bible.* Ed. by Philip Wesley Comfort. Grand Rapids: Tyndale House, 1992.

Hays, J. Daniel. "Has the Narrator Come to Praise Solomon or to Bury Him? Narrative Subtlety in I Kings 1–11." *JSOT* 28 (2003): 149-174.

Holladay, William L. *Long Ago God Spoke.* Minneapolis: Fortress Press, 1995.

Josephus. *The Life; Against Apion.* Vol. 1. LCL. Ed. by H. St. J. Thackeray. Cambridge, MA: Harvard University Press, 1976.

King, Philip J. *American Archaeology in the Mideast: A History of the American Schools of Oriental Research.* Philadelphia: ASOR, 1983.

Lake, Kirsopp. *Eusebius I.* LCL. Cambridge, MA: Harvard University Press, 1959.

Leiman, Sid Z. *The Canonization of Hebrew Scripture: The Talmudic and Midrashic Evidence.* The Connecticut Academy of Arts and Sciences. Hamden, CT: Archon Books, 1976.

Lewis, Jack P. "Jamnia Revisited." In *The Canon Debate*, pp. 146-162. Ed. by Lee Martin McDonald and James A. Sanders. Peabody, MA: Hendrickson, 2002.

_____. "What Do We Mean by Jabneh?" *JBR* 32 (1964): 125-132.

Liddell, Henry George, and Robert Scott. *A Greek-English Lexicon.* Rev. by H.S. Jones. Oxford: Clarendon Press, 1968.

Linnemann, Eta. *Historical Criticism of the Bible: Methodology or Ideology?* Trans. by R.W. Yarbrough. Grand Rapids: Baker, 1990.

Long, V. Philips. *The Art of Biblical History.* Grand Rapids: Zondervan, 1994.

Longman, Tremper III. *How to Read Proverbs.* Downers Grove, IL: InterVarsity, 2002.

Mangano, Mark. *Esther & Daniel.* The College Press NIV Commentary. Joplin, MO: College Press, 2001.

McDonald, Lee M. *The Formation of the Christian Biblical Canon.* Peabody, MA: Hendrickson, 1995.

McDonald, Lee Martin, and James A. Sanders, eds. *The Canon Debate.* Peabody, MA: Hendrickson, 2002.

Merrillees, Robert S. "Opium for the Masses: How the Ancients Got High." *Odyssey* 2 (1999): 20-29, 58.

Metzger, Bruce M., ed. *The Oxford Annotated Apocrypha.* New York: Oxford University Press, 1977.

Miller, J. Maxwell, and John H. Hayes. *A History of Ancient Israel and Judah.* Philadelphia: Westminster, 1986.

Moore, George Foot. *Judaism in the First Centuries of the Christian Era.* New York: Schocken Books, 1971 repr.

Motyer, J. Alec. *Isaiah.* TOTC. Downers Grove, IL: InterVarsity, 1999.

Muilenburg, James. "Form Criticism and Beyond." *JBL* 88 (1969): 1-18.

Murphy, Roland E. "The Old Testament Canon in the Catholic Church." *CBQ* 28 (1966): 189-193.

"Narrative, Hebrew." *ABD*, 4:1023-1027. Ed. by David Noel Freedman. New York: Doubleday, 1992.

Oulton, J.E.L. *Eusebius II.* LCL. Cambridge, MA: Harvard University Press, 1957.

Pratt, Richard L. Jr. *He Gave Us Stories: The Bible Student's Guide to Interpreting Old Testament Narrative.* Brentwood, TN: Wolgemuth and Hyatt, 1990.

Pritchard, James B. *The Water System of Gibeon.* Philadelphia: University Museum, 1961.

Renfrew, Colin, and Paul Bahn. *Archaeology: Theories, Methods, and Practices.* 3rd ed. New York: Thames & Hudson, 2000.

Roberts, David. "The Ice Man: Lone Voyager from the Copper Age." *National Geographic* 183 (1993): 36-67.

Ryken, Leland. *How to Read the Bible as Literature . . . and Get More Out of It.* Grand Rapids: Zondervan, 1984.

Sandars, N.K. *The Sea Peoples: Warriors of the Ancient Mediterranean.* Rev. ed. London: Thames & Hudson, 1985.

Sandy, D. Brent, and Ronald L. Giese Jr. *Cracking Old Testament Codes.* Nashville: Broadman & Holman, 1995.

Schneirla, William. "The Orthodox Old Testament Canon and the So-called Apocrypha." *SVTQ* ns 1 (1957): 40-46.

Schoville, Keith N. *Biblical Archaeology in Focus.* Grand Rapids: Baker, 1978.

A Select Library of Nicene and Post-Nicene Fathers of the Christian Church. Second series, vol. 4. *St. Athanasius: Select Works and Letters.* Grand Rapids: Eerdmans, 1978.

A Select Library of Nicene and Post-Nicene Fathers of the Christian

Church. Second series, vol. 6. *St. Jerome: Letters and Select Works*. Grand Rapids: Eerdmans, 1954.

Silberman, Neil Asher. *Digging for God and Country: Exploration, Archeology, and the Secret Struggle for the Holy Land, 1799–1917*. New York: Alfred A. Knopf, 1982.

Stott, John R.W. *Guard the Gospel: The Message of 2 Timothy*. Downers Grove, IL: InterVarsity, 1973.

Sundberg, Albert C. Jr. "The 'Old Testament': A Christian Canon." *CBQ* 30 (1968): 143-155.

_____ . *The Old Testament of the Early Church*. HTS 20. Cambridge, MA: Harvard University Press, 1964.

_____ . "The Protestant Old Testament Canon: Should It Be Re-examined?" *CBQ* 28 (1966): 194-203.

Tate, Marvin E. "The Old Testament Apocrypha and the Old Testament Canon." *RevExp* 65 (1968): 339-356.

Ussishkin, David. "Lachish." *NEAEHL*, 3:897-911. Ed. by E. Stern. New York: Simon & Schuster, 1993.

von Daniken, Erich. *Chariots of the Gods? Unsolved Mysteries of the Past*. London: Souvenir, 1969.

Wise, Michael, Martin Abegg Jr., and Edward Cook. *The Dead Sea Scrolls: A New Translation*. San Francisco: HarperSanFrancisco, 1996.

Wright, J. Stafford. "The Interpretation of Ecclesiastes." In *Classical Evangelical Essays in Old Testament Interpretation*. Ed. by Walter C. Kaiser Jr. Grand Rapids: Baker, 1980.

Yadin, Yigael, et al. *Hazor: The Third and Fourth Seasons, 1957–1958*. Plates. Jerusalem: The Magnes Press, 1961.

Yeivin, Zeev. "Eshtemoa." *NEAEHL*, 2:423-426. Ed. by E. Stern. New York: Simon & Schuster, 1993.

Young, E.J. *An Introduction to the Old Testament*. Grand Rapids: Eerdmans, 1977.

_____ . *Thy Word Is Truth*. Grand Rapids: Eerdmans, 1967.

Zias, Joseph, and Karen Numeroff. "Ancient Dentistry in the Eastern Mediterranean: A Brief Review." *IEJ* 36 (1986): 65-67.

INTRODUCTION

The College Press NIV Commentary Series on the Old Testament is a multivolume work, providing clear exposition of each biblical book. College Press offers in this singular volume an introduction to the entire Old Testament. An *introduction* is a type of book which treats the individual books of the Old Testament one by one, giving attention to such issues as authorship, date, and purpose.

Five men have collaborated in the writing of this volume. Dr. Randall C. Bailey, Associate Professor at the V.P. Black School of Biblical Studies, Faulkner University, in Montgomery, Alabama, contributed the chapters on the five books of the Pentateuch and the Book of Daniel. Dr. Dale W. Manor, Associate Professor at the College of Bible and Religion, Harding University, in Searcy, Arkansas, contributed the chapters on the Historical Books — Joshua, Judges, Ruth, Samuel, Kings, Chronicles, Ezra–Nehemiah, and Esther. Dr. Manor is also the Field Director of the Tell Beth-Shemesh excavations in Israel. Not surprisingly, the introductory chapter on archaeology is also his contribution.

Dr. Gary H. Hall, Professor of Old Testament and Hebrew at Lincoln Christian Seminary in Lincoln, Illinois, wrote the chapters on the prophetic material. Dr. Walter D. Zorn, also from Lincoln Christian College and Seminary, contributed chapters on Psalms, Job, and Song of Songs. Dr. Mark J. Mangano, also from Lincoln Christian College and Seminary, contributed three introductory chapters, as well as work on Proverbs and Ecclesiastes. He also served as the editor of this project.

The content of each chapter is organized according to nine headings. These headings are described below.

Bibliography. "Of making many books there is no end" (Eccl 12:12). The many books (and articles) listed in each chapter reflect important contributions to the study of that biblical book, as well as remind us that each scholar is indebted to the contributions of others ("As iron sharpens iron, so one man sharpens another" [Prov 27:17]).

Historical and Cultural Background. In order to maximize our understanding of God's Word, we must minimize the distance between the ancient world and our world. We are separated from the ancient world by culture and customs, language, and a vast expanse of time. "Background" studies are pivotal then in bridging the gap between "their" world and "our" world. In order to properly understand the message of any prophet, for example, the reader must place that prophet on the timeline of ancient Israel's history. The reader must also know how that prophetic message reflects international concerns. Are the Assyrians looming on the horizon? Or is it the Babylonians? Cultural realities are also vitally important. For example, a reader of Genesis must understand the cultural realities of adoption and surrogacy if she is to understand the roles played by Eliezer (Gen 15:2-3) and Hagar (Genesis 16) in the Abraham cycle.

Text and Authorship. The Masoretic Text of the Hebrew Scriptures (the Old Testament) was faithfully preserved by the Masoretes (hence the title), Hebrew scholars and scribes. In spite of their faithful commitment to the text as the Word of God, errors of transmission crept into the tradition. Manual copying renders any text subject to corruption. These errors are identified and classified through the practice of textual criticism. Errors typically result from the interplay between a scribe's eye, hand, and brain (and perhaps his ear). These errors are often identifiable by comparing a Hebrew manuscript with either another Hebrew manuscript (such as a Dead Sea Scroll) or a manuscript of another language. The Hebrew Old Testament, for example, was early translated into Greek. This translation is known as the Septuagint (the LXX). English translations of the Hebrew Bible factor in the considerations of textual criticism (note Isa 33:8, for example, in the NIV). Where the issue of textual criticism looms large, the authors have made note.

History of Interpretation. Each biblical book has been variously interpreted. Jonah, for example, has been read as a legend, an allegory, a parable, or an historical narrative, to list a few of the suggestions. The study of the history of any book's interpretation is essential for at least two reasons. First, the interpreter is forced to identify the proper questions to ask of a text, and then to properly answer those questions. If Jonah is an historical narrative, then what qualities does it share with other biblical examples of history writing (such as Samuel or Kings)? How does one interpret Hebrew poetry? In terms of what is commonly called *synonymous parallelism*, will the interpreter adopt a minimalist approach, where the second line is mere ballast or "stylistic" variation, or the maximalist approach, where the second line focuses, amplifies, or intensifies the author's thought? Second, the interpreter becomes keenly aware of how culture may influence interpretation. Has the "spirit of the age" led to an allegorical interpretation of the Song of Songs? Has that same spirit led to a rejection of the predictive element of prophecy? Has that spirit led interpreters to "conservative" or "liberal" interpretations, rather than correct ones?

The authors of this introduction also explore the evidence that helps answer the question of authorship. Biblical books do not come down to us with title pages, replete with an author's name, date, and copyright. The interpreter must search for internal clues and consult with external tradition to answer the question of authorship.

Structure. A working outline for the biblical book under consideration is provided in each chapter. An outline helps trace the direction of thought a book takes. This section is more than outline though. The author may investigate issues of narrative, explore the literary artistry of the text, or focus on how literary form aids the content in communicating the intended message, to name a few options.

Genre. A genre is a group of texts that may be similar in content, form, function, mood, and/or style. Genre is important for interpretation. Consider the following verse from 2 Kings 24:1. "During Jehoiakim's reign, Nebuchadnezzar king of Babylon invaded the land, and Jehoiakim became his vassal for three years. But then he changed his mind and rebelled against Nebuchadnezzar." The reader instantly recognizes the genre as historical narrative, and expects the author to convey historical or chronological information. Consider another example. "All hard work brings a profit, but mere talk leads only to poverty" (Prov 14:23). The reader quickly recognizes the genre as proverb, and expects the author to convey sage advice for a life lived wisely. These two examples point out that proper recognition of genre will suggest an appropriate reading strategy and frame the reader's expectations.

Theological Themes. Since the Bible is God's Word to us, Scripture is a treasure of truth about God, mankind, and our relationship with Him. Each book of the Old Testament contributes in unique ways to the theological worldview of Scripture.

New Testament Connections. In this section the author explores how the New Testament incorporates the Old Testament. The New Testament authors may allude to, paraphrase, or quote from the First Testament. They may reference people, places, events, words, ideas, or themes. The Old Testament points forward to the victory of God in the Messiah and the victory of God's Kingdom over all evil forces. In Jesus that victory is incarnated. His Church bears witness to the transforming and victorious presence of the Salvation of God.

Special Issues. Each author is free to add a final section to a chapter, to deal with issues raised by a specific book. Dr. Manor, for example, ended his chapter on Kings with a special section entitled, "Historical Reliability of the Records." This addition is apropos given the historical nature of the books of Kings.

This volume is written with several presuppositions about Scripture. First, the Bible is the Word of God, inspired by the Holy Spirit. "Above all, you must understand that no prophecy of Scripture came about by the prophet's own interpretation. For prophecy never had its origin in the will of man, but men spoke from God as they were carried along by the Holy Spirit" (2 Pet 1:20-21).

Second, the Bible is trustworthy and true. In the Pastorals Paul repeatedly affirms, "Here is a trustworthy saying" (1 Tim 1:15; 3:1; 4:9; 2 Tim 2:11; Titus 3:8). This is our contention for the entire Bible, as it was for Paul. He wrote, "All Scripture is God-breathed and is useful for teaching, rebuking, correcting and training in righteousness, so that the man of God may be thoroughly equipped for every good work" (2 Tim 3:16-17).

Third, the Bible is not contradictory. Even though multiple human authors contributed to the Bible, from differing periods of time, using diverse genres, the biblical message is consistent. The Bible is the witness of the Father to the Son (John 5:39) through the Holy Spirit (1 Cor 2:6-15).

Our desire in these pages is to provide a resource for your study of the Old Testament that will benefit you, whether you are preparing a Bible school lesson, a sermon, a college course, or even your personal devotions.

This volume is dedicated to the praise of God, His Son, Jesus Christ, and the Holy Spirit.

M. Mangano
April, 2005

CANON

The books of the Hebrew Bible, the Old Testament, are twenty-four in number, arranged in three divisions. The first division is the *tôrah* ("law"), comprised of Genesis, Exodus, Leviticus, Numbers, and Deuteronomy. These five books (the Pentateuch) are commonly called the "Law/Book of Moses" (cf. Mark 12:26). The second division is the *nebî'îm* ("prophets"), which is subdivided into the four Former Prophets (Joshua, Judges, Samuel, and Kings) and the four Latter Prophets (Isaiah, Jeremiah, Ezekiel and the Book of the Twelve Prophets). The third division is called the *kethûbîm* ("writings"). It is comprised of eleven books (the Hagiographa): Psalms, Proverbs, Job, Song of Songs, Ruth, Lamentations, Ecclesiastes, Esther, Daniel, Ezra–Nehemiah (counted as one book), and Chronicles. These twenty-four books are identical with the thirty-nine of the Protestant Old Testament. The difference in numbering is obvious: counting the twelve (*minor*) prophets separately and dividing Samuel, Kings, Chronicles, and Ezra–Nehemiah into two each.

These books comprise the Old Testament canon. The term *canon* denotes a list of books "recognized as worthy to be included in the sacred writings of a worshipping community."[1]

What historical textual witnesses exist that reference the list of books above, in whole or in part?

---

[1]F.F. Bruce, *The Canon of Scripture* (Downers Grove, IL: InterVarsity: 1988), p. 17. Shnayer (Sid) Z. Leiman (*The Canonization of Hebrew Scripture: The Talmudic and Midrashic Evidence* [Hamden, CT: Archon Books, 1976], pp. 14-15) has written, "A canonical book is a book accepted by Jews as authoritative for religious practice and/or doctrine, and whose authority is binding upon the Jewish people for all generations. Furthermore, such books are to be studied and expounded in private and in public." To an observant Jew of the present century, not only the Hebrew Bible, but the Mishnah, Talmud, and halakhic codes are also canonical in that they are authoritative and serve to guide him in his daily behavior. Leiman suggests that the canonicity of the Hebrew Scriptures is different in kind from the canonicity of such books as the Mishnah and Talmud. The Hebrew Scriptures are inspired, that is, composed under divine influence. Extra-biblical Jewish literature is uninspired, that is, not composed under divine influence.

TEXTUAL WITNESSES: JEWISH SOURCES

The Hebrew Bible

In the Hebrew Bible there are suggestions that certain books were already considered authoritative, if you will, canonical.

2 Kings 14:6

When Amaziah (796–767) had gained firm control of Judah, he put to death the officials who had murdered his father Joash (835–796). Amaziah did not, however, put to death the sons of the assassins. Amaziah recognized the authority of Deuteronomy 24:16 — "Fathers shall not be put to death for their children, nor children put to death for their fathers; each is to die for his own sins" — and responded accordingly.

2 Chronicles 17:9

The chronicler assumes the canonical status of the Torah during the lifetime of Jehoshaphat (872–848).

Jeremiah 26

In Jeremiah 26 certain priests and prophets suggested that the prophet Jeremiah "be sentenced to death because he [had] prophesied against [Jerusalem]" (v. 11). But some of the elders of the land defended Jeremiah by appealing to an analogous circumstance in the prophetic ministry of Micah, who two centuries earlier had also prophesied against the capital city, Jerusalem (Micah 3:12). Micah had not been put to death. In fact, King Hezekiah sought the Lord's favor and the disaster was averted. These elders reasoned that if they put to death this "present day Micah," then they would bring a terrible disaster on themselves! (v. 19). The unquestioned authority of Micah's message and ministry was assumed in this defense of Jeremiah.

Daniel 9

Daniel 9:2 reads: "I, Daniel, understood from the Scriptures, according to the word of the LORD given to Jeremiah, the prophet, that the desolation of Jerusalem would last seventy years." The reference to "seventy years" is found in Jeremiah 25:11 and 29:10. Note that Daniel refers to this material as "Scripture."

Zechariah 1

The sixth-century prophet Zechariah said, "Do not be like your forefathers, to whom the earlier prophets proclaimed: This is what the LORD Almighty says: 'Turn from your evil ways and your evil practices.' But they would not listen or pay attention to me, declares the LORD" (1:4). The message of repentance would certainly characterize the prophetic message. But Zechariah appears to have passages like Jeremiah 18:11-12; 25:5; and 35:15 specifically in mind here.

Nehemiah 8

When the returned exiles hear the Law, they weep and begin immediately to obey its commands.

> They found written in the Law, which the LORD had commanded through Moses, that the Israelites were to live in booths during the feast of the seventh month and that they should proclaim this word and spread it throughout their towns and in Jerusalem: "Go out into the hill country and bring back branches from olive and wild olive trees, and from myrtles, palms and shade trees, to make booths"—as it is written (8:14-15).

Other Jewish Writings

Baba Bathra

A tradition from no later than the second century quoted in the Babylonian Talmud, in the tractate *Baba Bathra* (14b-15a), bears witness to these divisions and their respective contents.

> Our rabbis taught: The order of the Prophets is, Joshua, Judges, Samuel, Kings, Jeremiah, Ezekiel, Isaiah, and the Twelve Minor Prophets. . . . The order of the Hagiographa is Ruth, the Book of Psalms, Job, Proverbs, Ecclesiastes, Song of Songs, Lamentations, Daniel and the Scroll of Esther, Ezra and Chronicles. . . . Who wrote the Scriptures? Moses wrote his own book and the portion of Balaam and Job. Joshua wrote the book which bears his name and [the last] eight verses of the Pentateuch.[2]

---

[2]The Babylonian Talmud, Seder Nezikin in Four Volumes, vol. 2: *Baba Bathra*, translated into English with notes, glossary and indices under the

4 Ezra

The number of books — twenty-four — is also referenced in the late first-century A.D. work *The Fourth Book of Ezra* (14:45-47):

> And when the forty days were ended, the Most High spoke to me, saying, "Make public the twenty-four books that you wrote first and let the worthy and the unworthy read them; but keep the seventy [i.e., esoteric, apocalyptic books] that were written last, in order to give them to the wise among your people.[3]

Josephus

Josephus, the famous first-century Jewish historian, counted only twenty-two books. Here is his famous quotation (*Against Apion*, I.37-42):

> It therefore naturally, or rather necessarily, follows (seeing that with us it is not open to everybody to write the records, and that there is no discrepancy in what is written; seeing that, on the contrary, the prophets alone had this privilege, obtaining their knowledge of the most remote and ancient history through the inspiration which they owed to God, and committing to writing a clear account of the events of their own time just as they occurred)—it follows, I say, that we do not possess myriads of inconsistent books, conflicting with each other. Our books, those which are justly accredited, are but two and twenty, and contain the record of all time.
>
> Of these, five are the books of Moses, comprising the laws and the traditional history from the birth of man down to the death of the lawgiver. This period falls only a little short of three thousand years. From the death of Moses until Artaxerxes, who succeeded Xerxes as king of Persia, the prophets subsequent to Moses wrote the history of the events of their own times in thirteen books. The remaining four books contain hymns to God and precepts for the conduct of human life.
>
> From Artaxerxes to our own time the complete history has been written, but has not been deemed worthy of equal credit with the

---

editorship of Rabbi Dr. I. Epstein (London: Soncino Press, 1935–48), pp. 70-71.

[3]James H. Charlesworth, ed., *The Old Testament Pseudepigrapha* (Garden City, NY: Doubleday, 1983), 1:555.

earlier records, because of the failure of the exact succession of the prophets.

We have given practical proof of our reverence for our own Scriptures. For, although such long ages have now passed, no one has ventured either to add, or to remove, or to alter a syllable; and it is an instinct with every Jew, from the day of his birth, to regard them as the decrees of God, to abide by them, and, if need be, cheerfully to die for them.[4]

The "books of Moses" are the famous five, the Pentateuch. The "thirteen books" are probably (1) Joshua, (2) Judges + Ruth, (3) Samuel, (4) Kings, (5) Chronicles, (6) Ezra + Nehemiah, (7) Esther, (8) Job, (9) Isaiah, (10) Jeremiah + Lamentations, (11) Ezekiel, (12) The Book of the Twelve Prophets, and (13) Daniel. "The remaining four books" are probably Psalms, Proverbs, Song of Songs, and Ecclesiastes — books that "contain hymns to God and precepts for the conduct of human life."

In *Baba Bathra* Ruth and Lamentations are separately mentioned, whereas in Josephus, Ruth is probably combined with Judges due to the same chronological setting ("In the days when the judges ruled") and Lamentations with Jeremiah due to the tradition that asserts the prophet's authorship of Lamentations.

TEXTUAL WITNESSES: CHRISTIAN SOURCES

The Hebrew Scriptures, *Baba Bathra*, 4 Ezra, Josephus — these are Jewish sources bearing witness upon the question of the number of books in the Hebrew canon.[5] What of Christian witnesses?

Melito

According to Eusebius's *Ecclesiastical History* (IV.xxvi.12-14), Melito, Bishop of Sardis about A.D. 170, wrote to Onesimus:

Since you often desired, in your zeal for the true word, to have extracts from the Law and the Prophets concerning the Saviour,

---

[4]Josephus, *The Life/Against Apion*, vol. 1, LCL, ed. by H. St. J. Thackeray (Cambridge, MA: Harvard University Press, 1976), pp. 177-181.

[5]See also Jubilees 2:23-24, n. y, in *The Old Testament Pseudepigrapha*, vol. 2, ed. by James H. Charlesworth. Leiman (*Canonization*, pp. 53-56) cites a number of rabbis who flourished between 170 and 350 A.D. who spoke or wrote of a canon of twenty-four books.

and concerning all our faith, and, moreover, since you wished to know the accurate facts about the ancient writings, how many they are in number, and what is their order, I have taken pains to do thus, for I know your zeal for the faith and interest in the word, and that in your struggle for eternal salvation you esteem these things more highly than all else in your love towards God. Accordingly when I came to the east and reached the place where these things were preached and done, and learnt accurately the books of the Old Testament, I set down the facts and sent them to you. These are their names: five books of Moses, Genesis, Exodus, Numbers, Leviticus, Deuteronomy, Joshua the son of Nun, Judges, Ruth, four books of Kingdoms, two books of Chronicles, the Psalms of David, the Proverbs of Solomon and his Wisdom, Ecclesiastes, the Song of Songs, Job, the prophets Isaiah, Jeremiah, the Twelve in a single book, Daniel, Ezekiel, Ezra. From these I have made extracts and compiled them in six books.[6]

Melito's list probably includes all the books of the Hebrew Bible except Esther.[7] Ezra probably includes Nehemiah, and Lamentations was probably an appendix to Jeremiah.

Origen

Origen (185–254), according to Eusebius (VI.xxv.1-2), wrote:

But it should be known that there are twenty-two canonical books, according to the Hebrew tradition; the same as the number of the letters of their alphabet. . . These are the twenty-two books according to the Hebrews: That which is entitled with us Genesis, but with the Hebrews, from the beginning of the book, *Brēsith*, that is, 'In the beginning.' Exodus, *Ouelle smōth*, that is 'These are the names.' Leviticus, *Ouïkra*, 'And he called.' Numbers, *Ammes phekōdeim*. Deuteronomy, *Elle addebareim*, 'These are the words.' Jesus the son of Nave, *Iōsoue ben noun*. Judges, Ruth, with them in one book, *Sōpheteim*. Of Kingdoms i, ii, with them one, *Samuel*, 'The called of God.' Of Kingdoms iii, iv, in one *Ouammelch david*, that is, 'The kingdom of David.' Chronicles i, ii, in one, *Dabrē iamein*,

---

[6]Kirsopp Lake, *Eusebius I*, LCL (Cambridge, MA: Harvard University Press, 1959), p. 393.

[7]Roger Beckwith (*The Old Testament Canon of the New Testament Church* [Grand Rapids: Eerdmans, 1985], p. 315) conjectures that Melito's omission of Esther reflects the Palestinian (Jewish) debate concerning its canonicity.

that is, 'Words of days.' Esdras i, ii, in one, *Ezra*, that is, 'Helper.'
Book of Psalms, *Sphar thelleim*. Proverbs of Solomon, *Melōth*.
Ecclesiastes, *Kōelth*. Song of Songs (not, as some suppose, Songs
of Songs), *Sir assireim*. Esaias, *Iessia*. Jeremiah with Lamentations
and the Letter, in one, *Jeremia*. Daniel, *Daniēl*. Ezekiel, *Ezekiēl*. Job,
Jōb. Esther, *Esthēr*. And outside these there are the Maccabees,
which are entitled *Sar bēth sabanai el*.[8]

Origen lists the books according to their Greek and Hebrew
names. Apart from Maccabees he has listed only twenty-one books.
The Book of the Twelve Prophets has apparently dropped out in the
course of transmission. His twenty-two books correspond to the
twenty-four of the Hebrew Bible, except that he has added the *Letter
of Jeremiah* to Jeremiah.

Athanasius

In 367, Athanasius, bishop of Alexandria, dealt with the canon of
the Old and New Testaments.

> There are, then, of the Old Testament, twenty-two books in num-
> ber; for, as I have heard, it is handed down that this is the num-
> ber of the letters among the Hebrews; their respective order and
> names being as follows. The first is Genesis, then Exodus, next
> Leviticus, after that Numbers, and then Deuteronomy. Following
> these there is Joshua, the son of Nun, then Judges, then Ruth. And
> again, after these four books of Kings, the first and second being
> reckoned as one book, and so likewise the third and fourth as one
> book. And again, the first and second of the Chronicles are reck-
> oned as one book. Again Ezra, the first and second are similarly
> one book. After these there is the book of Psalms, then the
> Proverbs, next Ecclesiastes, and the Song of Songs. Job follows,
> then the Prophets, the twelve being reckoned as one book. Then
> Isaiah, one book, then Jeremiah with Baruch, Lamentations, and
> the epistle, one book; afterwards, Ezekiel and Daniel, each one
> book (Letter XXXIX).[9]

He lists Ruth separately from Judges and omits Esther.

---

[8]J.E.L. Oulton, *Eusebius II*, LCL (Cambridge, MA: Harvard University
Press, 1957), pp. 73-75.

[9]*A Select Library of Nicene and Post-Nicene Fathers of the Christian Church*, second series, vol. 4: *St. Athanasius: Select Works and Letters* (Grand Rapids:
Eerdmans, 1978), p. 552.

Jerome

Jerome (c. 347–420) was a Hebrew scholar with Jewish teachers. When he speaks of the opinions of the Jews, he speaks from knowledge. In his preface to the books of Samuel and Kings (published about A.D. 391), books found in his Vulgate translation of the Old Testament, we read:

> The Hebrews have twenty-two letters. . . . Again, five are double letters, Caph, Mem, Nun, Pe, Tsade, for at the beginning and in the middle of words they are written one way, and at the end another way. Whence it happens that, by most people, five of the books are reckoned as double, Samuel, Kings, Chronicles, Ezra, Jeremiah with Kinoth, i.e. his Lamentations. As, then, there are twenty-two elementary characters by means of which we write in Hebrew all we say, and the compass of the human voice is contained within their limits, so we reckon twenty-two books, by which, as by the alphabet of the doctrine of God, a righteous man is instructed in tender infancy, and, as it were, while still at the breast. . . . And so there are also twenty-two books of the Old Testament; that is, five of Moses [Genesis–Deuteronomy], eight of the prophets [Joshua, Judges–Ruth, Samuel, Kings, Isaiah, Jeremiah, Ezekiel, the Twelve], nine of the Hagiographa [Job, Psalms, Proverbs, Ecclesiastes, Song of Songs, Daniel, Chronicles, Ezra–Nehemiah, Esther], though some include Ruth and Kinoth (Lamentations) amongst the Hagiographa, and think that these books ought to be reckoned separately; we should thus have twenty-four books of the old Law.[10]

A TRIPARTITE DIVISION?

We speak today of the "Law, Prophets, and Writings" constituting the Old Testament. Is there historical evidence suggesting that this tripartite division of Old Testament Scripture was well understood?

New Testament

The New Testament commonly refers to the entire Old Testament as "The Law and the Prophets" (Matt 5:17; 7:12; 11:13; 22:40;

---

[10]*A Select Library of Nicene and Post-Nicene Fathers of the Christian Church*, second series, vol. 6: *St. Jerome: Letters and Select Works* (Grand Rapids: Eerdmans, 1954), pp. 489-490.

Luke 13:28; 16:16,29,31; 24:27; John 1:45; Acts 13:15; 28:23; Rom 3:21b). Sometimes the whole of the Old Testament is referred to simply as the "Law" (John 10:34; 1 Cor 14:21). In Luke 24 Jesus appears among his disciples, and says, "This is what I told you while I was still with you: Everything must be fulfilled that is written about me in the Law of Moses, the prophets and the Psalms" (44). Does this one verse allude to the Law, Prophets, and Writings, the three-fold division of the Old Testament canon evident in the other sources mentioned above?[11]

Preface to Sirach

Yeshua (or Jesus) ben Sira's grandson, who translated his grand-father's work (Ecclesiasticus or Sirach) into Greek and added a preface (ca. 132 B.C.), states:

> Whereas many great teachings have been given to us through the law and the prophets and the others that followed them, on account of which we should praise Israel for instruction and wisdom; and since it is necessary not only that the readers themselves should acquire understanding but also that those who love learning should be able to help the outsiders by both speaking and writing, my grandfather Jesus, after devoting himself especially to the reading of the law and the prophets and the other books of our fathers, and after acquiring considerable proficiency in them was himself also lead to write something pertaining to instruction and wisdom, in order that, by becoming conversant with this also, those who love learning should make even greater progress in living according to the law.[12]

---

[11]In Matthew 23:35 we read, "And so upon you will come all the righteous blood that has been shed on earth, from the blood of righteous Abel to the blood of Zechariah son of Berakiah, whom you murdered between the temple and the altar" (cf. Luke 11:51). The death of Abel is recorded at Genesis 4:3-8. The death of Zechariah is found at 2 Chronicles 24:19-22. Genesis comes at the beginning of the canon, while 2 Chronicles comes at the close of the canon according to the Hebrew order. Jesus may be referencing the entire Old Testament here. 4QMMT (C 9-10), a Qumran text difficult to read due to corruption, appears to reference a tripartite canon: "the book of Moses, the books of the Prophets, and David" (Michael Wise, Martin Abegg, Jr., & Edward Cook, *The Dead Sea Scrolls: A New Translation* [San Francisco: HarperSanFrancisco, 1996], p. 363).

[12]Bruce M. Metzger, ed., *The Oxford Annotated Apocrypha* (New York: Oxford University Press, 1977), p. 128.

2 Maccabees

In 2 Maccabees 2:13-15 we read:

The same things are reported in the records and in the memoirs of Nehemiah, and also that he founded a library and collected the books about the kings and prophets, and the writings of David, and letters of kings about votive offerings. In the same way Judas also collected all the books that had been lost on account of the war which had come upon us, and they are in our possession. So if you have need of them, send people to get them for you.[13]

While there is no mention here of the Law, the Prophets and David seem to be recognized categories of Scripture. The "books about the kings" are probably Samuel and Kings. The "writings of David" probably mean primarily the Psalter.

The "Judas" here is Judas Maccabeus. The "war" in question is the Maccabean war of liberation from the persecutor Antiochus Epiphanes, whose hostility toward Scripture is mentioned at 1 Maccabees 1:56. What is meant by the term "collected"? Beckwith has suggested that, "He must have done it primarily by compiling a list. In listing the books, he would not only have grouped them in their separate sections: he must also have arranged them in some order or other within those sections."[14] If this conjecture is correct, then a tripartite division of Scripture was formalized by as early as the mid-second century B.C.

Philo

The tripartite division of Scripture may be attested by Philo of Alexandria (20 B.C.– A.D. 45). In describing a Jewish sect in Egypt, Philo says that they possessed "laws and oracles delivered through the mouth of prophets, and psalms and anything else which fosters and perfects knowledge and piety" (Philo *The Contemplative Life* 25).

Baba Bathra

This threefold division is clearly attested in *Baba Bathra* 13b, "Our Rabbis taught: It is permissible to fasten the Torah, the Prophets,

---

[13]Ibid, p. 266.
[14]Beckwith, *Old Testament Canon*, p. 153.

and the Hagiographa together. This is the opinion of R. Meir. R. Judah, however, says that the Torah, the Prophets, and the Hagiographa should each be in a separate scroll; while the Sages say that each book should be separate."[15]

ANTILEGOMENA

There was discussion in Jewish circles during the early centuries of the Christian era relative to the canonicity of Ecclesiastes, Esther, Ezekiel, Proverbs, and Song of Songs. For example, in the Mishnah, tractate "Yadaim" (Hands), we read:

> All the Scriptures render the hands unclean. The Song of Songs and Ecclesiastes render the hands unclean. R. Judah says: The Song of Songs renders the hands unclean, but about Ecclesiastes there is dissension. R. Jose says: Ecclesiastes does not render the hands unclean, and about the Song of Songs there is dissension. R. Simeon says: Ecclesiastes is one of the things about which the School of Shammai adopted the more lenient, and the School of Hillel the more stringent ruling. R. Simeon b. Azzai said: I have heard a tradition from the seventy-two elders on the day when they made R. Eleazar b. Azariah head of the college [of Sages], that the Song of Songs and Ecclesiastes both render the hands unclean. R. Akiba said: God forbid!—no man in Israel ever disputed about the Song of Songs [that he should say] that it does not render the

---

[15]Babylonian Talmud, p. 66. The following three examples also bear witness to this tripartite division of Scripture. (1) "Elisha b. Abuyah (110–135) related that R. Eliezer (80–110) said to R. Joshua (80–110): While they occupy themselves with their matters, let us occupy ourselves with ours. They sat and studied Torah, and from the Torah they went on to Prophets, and from the Prophets to the Hagiographa. Fire descended from heaven and surrounded them" [*J. Hagigah* 77b]. (2) "Sectarians asked Rabban Gamaliel (80–110): Whence do we know that the Holy One, blessed be He, will resurrect the dead? He answered them from the Torah, Prophets, and Hagiographa, yet they were not convinced" [*Sanhedrin* 90b]. (3) "Ben Azzai (110–135) was sitting and expounding Scripture, and the flame was burning around him. They asked him: Are you studying the Merkabah [Chariot] portions of Scripture? He replied: No, but I am joining passages from the Torah with parallel passages in the Prophets, and passages from the Prophets with parallel passages in the Hagiographa; and the words of the Torah glow as on the day they were given at Sinai" [*Vayyikra Rabbah* 16:4]. For these examples and others, see Leiman, *Canonization*, pp. 56-72.

hands unclean, for all the ages are not worth the day on which the Song of Songs was given to Israel; for all the Writings are holy, but the Song of Songs is the Holy of Holies (3.5).[16]

The reasons for discussion are obvious in each case. If the reader does not recognize the interpretive value of the expression "life under the sun," then Ecclesiastes is indeed a treatise in pessimism.[17] If the reader does not recognize the presence and activity of God in the Esther story,[18] though his name is never once explicitly mentioned, then this story is truly godless. If the reader assumes that Ezekiel's vision of restoration must match every detail of the Mosaic Law, then much work will be expended in harmonizing the apparent discrepancies between the prophet and the Pentateuch.[19] If the reader does not recognize that proverbs are not universally valid (their validity depends upon the right time and the right circumstance),[20] then Proverbs 26:4-5 are contradictory. If the reader wrongly assumes that human sexuality is inherently evil, then the Song of Songs is pornographic.

JAMNIA

Many scholars have advanced what has been called the "Council of Jamnia Theory." This theory suggests that Jewish authorities gathered in Jamnia[21] in about A.D. 90 to define the limits of the Hebrew Canon. For example, Albert C. Sundberg Jr. writes, "About A.D. 90,

---

[16]Herbert Danby, *The Mishnah* (London: Oxford University Press, 1933), pp. 781-782. "By declaring that the Scriptures make the hands unclean," writes Roger Beckwith (*Old Testament Canon,* p. 280), "the rabbis protected them from careless and irreverent treatment, since it is obvious that no one would be so apt to handle them heedlessly if he were every time obliged to wash his hands afterwards."

[17]J. Stafford Wright, "The Interpretation of Ecclesiastes," in *Classical Evangelical Essays in Old Testament Interpretation*, ed. Walter C. Kaiser Jr. (Grand Rapids: Baker, 1980), pp. 133-150.

[18]Mark Mangano, *Esther & Daniel*, The College Press NIV Commentary (Joplin, MO: College Press, 2001), pp. 24-27.

[19]George Foot Moore, *Judaism in the First Centuries of the Christian Era* (New York: Schocken Books, 1971 repr.), 1:247.

[20]Tremper Longman III, *How to Read Proverbs* (Downers Grove, IL: InterVarsity, 2002), pp. 48-49.

[21]Jamnia was about 15 miles south of Joppa, near the sea coast.

contemporary with the writings of Josephus, the Jewish canon of Holy Scriptures was closed by the rabbinical schools at Jamnia."[22]

This theory has come under criticism, especially in the publications of Jack P. Lewis[23] and Lee M. McDonald. Having sifted the rabbinic material, McDonald concludes: "There is evidence that a discussion was held at Jamnia on the canonical status of Ecclesiastes and the Song of Songs, but this is not enough to suggest that any binding or official decisions were made regarding the scope of the biblical canon at Jamnia."[24]

Long after Jamnia, rabbis were still discussing certain of the antilegomena. Regarding Esther, Rabbis Eleazar, Akiba, Meir, and Jose b. Durmaskith, concluded that it "was composed under the inspiration of the holy spirit" (Babylonian Talmud, tractate *Megillah*, 7a-7b).

Such continuing discussions certainly argue against the "Council of Jamnia Theory." More importantly, the conclusion of "inspiration of the holy spirit" is instructive. In the words of E.J. Young, "Apparently, no religious council in ancient Israel ever drew up a list of divine books. Rather, in the singular providence of God, His people recognized His Word and honoured it from the time of its first appearance. Thus was formed the collection of inspired writings which are known as the canonical books of the Old Testament."[25]

---

[22]Albert C. Sundberg Jr., *The Old Testament of the Early Church*, HTS 20 (Cambridge, MA: Harvard University Press, 1964), p. 72.

[23]Jack P. Lewis, "What Do We Mean by Jabneh?" *JBR* 32 (April 1964): 125-132; "Jamnia Revisited," in *The Canon Debate*, ed. by Lee Martin McDonald and James A. Sanders (Peabody, MA: Hendrickson, 2002), pp. 146-162.

[24]Lee M. McDonald, *The Formation of the Christian Biblical Canon*, rev. and expanded ed. (Peabody, MA: Hendrickson, 1995), p. 49. See the quotation from Yadaim ("Hands") in the *Antilegomena* section above.

[25]E.J. Young, *An Introduction to the Old Testament* (Grand Rapids: Eerdmans, 1977), p. 37. Gleason L. Archer Jr. (*A Survey of Old Testament Introduction* [Chicago: Moody Press, 1978], p. 77) has written: "But if, on the other hand, a sovereign God has taken the initiative in revelation and in the production of an inspired record of that revelation through human agents, it must simply be a matter of recognition of the quality already inherent by divine act in the books so inspired. When a child recognizes his own parent from a multitude of other adults, he does not impart any new quality of parenthood by such an act; he simply recognizes a relationship which already exists. So also with lists of authoritative books drawn up by ecclesiastical synods or councils. They did not impart canonicity to a single page of Scripture; they simply acknowledged the divine inspiration of religious documents which were inherently canonical from the time they were first composed."

APOCRYPHA

The books the Jews regarded as outside the canon are as follows: 1 Esdras, 2 Esdras, Tobit, Judith, the additions to Esther, the Wisdom of Solomon, Ecclesiasticus, Baruch, the Letter of Jeremiah, the additions to the Book of Daniel (the Prayer of Azariah and the Song of the Three Young Men, Susanna, and Bel and the Dragon), the Prayer of Manasseh, 1 Maccabees, and 2 Maccabees.

The use of the term "apocrypha" to mean "noncanonical" goes back to Jerome (346/347–420), who urged that the books found in the Septuagint and in the Latin Bibles that did not occur in the canon of the Hebrew Old Testament should be treated as apocryphal.[26] Harrison adds, "They were not to be disregarded entirely, since they were part of the great contemporary outpouring of Jewish national literature. At the same time they should not be used as sources for Christian doctrine, but at best for supplementary reading of an uplifting or inspirational nature."[27]

Protestant theologians have followed the tradition established by Jerome. Roman Catholic theologians and Orthodox scholars[28] have followed the tradition of Augustine (354–430), a younger contemporary of Jerome, who argued for the inclusion of apocryphal books into the canon of Scripture. At the Council of Trent, a theological council of the Roman Catholic Church organized to respond to the

---

[26]In his preface to the books of Samuel and Kings, published about A.D. 391, Jerome lists the books comprising the Old Testament. He concludes, "And so there are also twenty-two books of the Old Testament; that is, five of Moses, eight of the prophets, nine of the Hagiographa, though some include Ruth and Kinoth (Lamentations) amongst the Hagiographa, and think that these books ought to be reckoned separately; we should thus have twenty-four books of the old law. . . . This preface to the Scriptures may serve as a 'helmeted' introduction to all the books which we turn from Hebrew into Latin, so that we may be assured that what is not found in our list must be placed amongst the Apocryphal writings. Wisdom, therefore, which generally bears the name of Solomon, and the book of Jesus, the Son of Sirach, and Judith, and Tobias, and the Shepherd are not in the canon. The first book of Maccabees I have found to be Hebrew, the second in Greek, as can be proved from the very style" (*Nicene and Post-Nicene Fathers*, 6:490).

[27]R.K. Harrison, "Old Testament and New Testament Apocrypha," in *The Origin of the Bible*, ed. by Philip Wesley Comfort (Grand Rapids: Tyndale House, 1992), p. 84.

[28]William Schneirla, "The Orthodox Old Testament Canon and the So-called Apocrypha," *St. Vladimir's Seminary Quarterly* ns 1 (October 1957): 40-46.

challenges that emerged from the Protestant Reformation, in 1546, Augustine's wider canon was accepted.[29]

The New Testament quotes directly from the majority of Old Testament books. The exceptions are Joshua, Judges, Ruth, 2 Kings, 1 & 2 Chronicles, Ezra, Nehemiah, Esther, Ecclesiastes, Song of Solomon, Lamentations, Obadiah, Nahum, and Zephaniah. I think it telling that not one single book of the Apocrypha is cited as having divine authority. Jude's citations of *The Assumption of Moses* (v. 9) and *Enoch* (v. 14) does not mean he believed they were divinely inspired. Neither does Paul's citation of various Greek poets (Aratus, Menander, and Epimenides) in Acts 17:28, 1 Corinthians 15:33, and Titus 1:12 suggest divine inspiration.

Books which appear in the Septuagint (LXX) but not in the Hebrew Bible Bruce refers to as the "Septuagintal plus."[30] These books are Judith, Tobit, an expanded edition of Esther, Wisdom, Ecclesiasticus (Sirach), Baruch, the Letter of Jeremiah, an expanded version of Daniel, and the books of Maccabees. The great codices of the fourth and fifth centuries also contained these books. Codex Sinaiticus (4th century) includes in its Old Testament collection Tobit, Judith, 1 & 4 Maccabees, Wisdom of Solomon, and Sirach. Vaticanus (4th century) includes Wisdom, Sirach, Judith, Tobit, Baruch, and the Letter of Jeremiah. Alexandrinus (5th century) contains Baruch, the Letter of Jeremiah, Tobit, Judith, the books of Maccabees, Wisdom, and Sirach. Why are these books bound up along with the books of holy Scripture?

The Church considered such books as "not unworthy to be bound up along with books of holy scripture."[31] Alienation between Jew and Christian, as well as the general ignorance of Semitic languages in the church outside Palestine and Syria, could have led to the inclusion of such books in these codices.[32]

Some scholars have answered this question by devising the "Alexandrian Canon Hypothesis." It postulates that two divergent canons existed among Jews during the first century. The more

---

[29]Roland E. Murphy, "The Old Testament Canon in the Catholic Church," *CBQ* 28 (1966): 189-193; Albert C. Sundberg Jr., "The Protestant Old Testament Canon: Should It Be Re-examined?" *CBQ* 28 (1966): 194-203.

[30]Bruce, *Canon,* p. 48.

[31]Ibid., p. 69.

[32]Roger Beckwith, "The Canon of the Old Testament," in *The Origin of the Bible,* ed. Philip Wesley Comfort (Grand Rapids: Tyndale House, 1992), p. 63.

extensive canon reflects the canon of Alexandrian Jewry, while the Masoretic canon reflects the canon that obtained in Palestine. Based on the evidence of these important codices, the Church adopted the canon of Alexandrian Jewry.

The hypothesis is untenable. Since these codices are Christian and relatively late, they offer no direct evidence for the canon of Jewish Alexandria. Additionally, the only Jewish witness from Alexandria, Philo, never cites the Apocrypha!

The absence of disputes about the Apocrypha in the rabbinic sources is an eloquent fact. "They [the books of the Apocrypha] are outside of the Hebrew Bible today," writes Roger Beckwith, "and there is no sign that they were ever extruded from it, so the point on which the rabbis were universally agreed can only have been that the books which today make up the Apocrypha and Pseudepigrapha were uncanonical."[33]

THE HOLY SPIRIT

Judaism recognized the role played by the Holy Spirit as the authenticating sign of Scripture (cf. the statements of Josephus above). The classic rabbinic statement on the cessation of prophecy states: "With the death of Haggai, Zechariah and Malachi the latter prophets, the Holy Spirit ceased out of Israel" (*Tosephta Sotah* 13.2). The role of the Spirit in the production of Scripture is referenced by 2 Peter 1:21: "For prophecy never had its origin in the will of man, but men spoke from God as they were carried along by the Holy Spirit" (cf. 1 Cor. 2:6-16).

Additional rabbinic statements confirm this classic expression. "Until then [the coming of Alexander the Great and the end of the empire of the Persians] the prophets prophesied through the Holy Spirit. From then on, 'incline thine ear and hear the words of the wise'" (*Seder Olam Rabbah* 30, quoting Prov 22:17). "Rab Samuel bar Inia said, in the name of Rab Aha, 'The Second Temple lacked five things which the First Temple possessed, namely, the fire, the ark, the Urim and Thummim, the oil of anointing and the Holy Spirit [of prophecy]" (*Jer. Taanith* 2.1).[34]

---

[33]Beckwith, *Old Testament Canon*, p. 382. Note also that none of the books of the Apocrypha were embraced in Origen's Hexapla, which presumably underlined for him the limits of the Jewish canon.

[34]Quoted in Beckwith, *Old Testament Canon*, p. 370.

CONCLUSIONS

(1) In the Hebrew Bible there are suggestions that certain books were already considered authoritative, if you will, canonical.
(2) Additional Jewish sources testify to either the structure or order of the Old Testament canon.
(3) The Christian witness of Melito, Origen, Athanasius, and Jerome reflect Jewish influences.
(4) Both Jewish and Christian sources bear testimony to a threefold division of the Old Testament canon: Law, Prophets, and Writings.
(5) There was discussion in Jewish circles during the early centuries of the Christian era relative to the canonicity of Ecclesiastes, Esther, Ezekiel, Proverbs, and Song of Songs (the "Antilegomena").
(6) No religious council in ancient Israel, such as Jamnia, ever drew up a list of divine books.
(7) The absence of disputes about the Apocrypha in the rabbinic sources is an eloquent fact.
(8) Judaism and Christianity recognized the role played by the Holy Spirit as the authenticating sign of Scripture.

THE AUTHORITY OF THE OLD TESTAMENT

The question of the authority of the Old Testament for the Christian was answered by the apostle Paul in 2 Timothy 3:14-17. There Paul reminded Timothy:

> [14]But as for you, continue in what you have learned and have become convinced of, because you know those from whom you learned it, [15]and how from infancy you have known the holy Scriptures, which are able to make you wise for salvation through faith in Christ Jesus. [16]All Scripture is God-breathed and is useful for teaching, rebuking, correcting and training in righteousness, [17]so that the man of God may be thoroughly equipped for every good work.

"From infancy" Timothy had been instructed in the Old Testament Scriptures. (The New Testament was still a work in progress.) These Scriptures, Paul says, "are able to make you wise for salvation through faith in Christ Jesus." In short, the Old Testament is a manual for salvation in the Messiah.

These Scriptures are also "useful for teaching, rebuking, correcting and training in righteousness." In short, they are a manual for obtaining maturity. Paul defines maturity in Ephesians 4:13 as "attaining to the whole measure of the fullness of Christ."

This maturity equips the Christian ("the man of God") for "every good work." The Old Testament is finally, then, a manual for ministry.

A manual for salvation in the Messiah, a manual for obtaining maturity, and a manual for ministry — this is the Old Testament, the very Word of God!

A MANUAL FOR SALVATION IN THE MESSIAH

On trial before Agrippa Paul affirmed that his Bible, the Old Testament, proclaims the gospel message. "I am saying nothing beyond what the prophets and Moses said would happen — that the Christ would suffer and, as the first to rise from the dead, would proclaim light to his own people and to the Gentiles" (Acts 26:22-23).

Likewise, in the opening verses of Romans, Paul affirms that God's gospel was "promised beforehand through his prophets in the Holy Scriptures regarding his Son, who as to his human nature was a descendant of David, and who through the Spirit of holiness was declared with power to be the Son of God by the resurrection from the dead: Jesus Christ our Lord" (1:2-4).

Peter also affirms this salvific focus of the Hebrew Scriptures.

> [10]Concerning this salvation, the prophets, who spoke of the grace that was to come to you, searched intently and with the greatest care [11]trying to find out the time and circumstances to which the Spirit of Christ in them was pointing when he predicted the *sufferings of Christ* and the *glories that would follow*. [12]It was revealed to them that they were not serving themselves but you, when they spoke of the things that have now been told you by those who have preached the gospel to you by the Holy Spirit sent from heaven (1 Pet 1:10-12, italics added).

Isaiah 53 is *the* text pointing to the "sufferings of Christ." Many texts point to the "glories that would follow," but Psalm 110:1 may be the most glorious.[35]

---

[35]For a fuller and more detailed picture of the vast influence of the Old Testament upon the message of the New Testament, consult the chapters of

Isaiah 53

In four classic texts the prophet Isaiah writes of The Servant of the LORD — 42:1-4; 49:1-6; 50:4-9; 52:13–53:12. The last text includes all of chapter 53, the golden passion of the Old Testament. This chapter is easily divided into four three-verse stanzas. The first stanza, 53:1-3, depicting the Divine Sufferer, quoted below, is summarized in Luke 18:31-32: "Jesus took the Twelve aside and told them, 'We are going up to Jerusalem, and everything that is written by the prophets about the Son of Man will be fulfilled. He will be handed over to the Gentiles. They will mock him, insult him, spit on him, flog him and kill him.'"

> Who has believed our message
>   and to whom has the arm of the LORD been revealed?
> He grew up before him like a tender shoot,
>   and like a root out of dry ground.
> He had no beauty or majesty to attract us to him,
>   nothing in his appearance that we should desire him.
> He was despised and rejected by men,
>   a man of sorrows, and familiar with suffering.
> Like one from whom men hide their faces
>   he was despised, and we esteemed him not.

The second stanza, 53:4-6, depicting the Divine Substitute, quoted below, is heard again in 1 Peter 2:24-25: "He himself bore our sins in his body on the tree, so that we might die to sins and live for righteousness; by his wounds you have been healed. For you were like sheep going astray, but now you have returned to the Shepherd and Overseer of your souls."

> Surely he took up our infirmities
>   and carried our sorrows,
> yet we considered him stricken by God,
>   smitten by him, and afflicted.
> But he was pierced for our transgressions,
>   he was crushed for our iniquities;
> the punishment that brought us peace was upon him,
>   and by his wounds we are healed.

---

this introduction. Each chapter includes a section connecting the Testaments.

> We all, like sheep, have gone astray,
>> each of us has turned to his own way;
> and the LORD has laid on him
>> the iniquity of us all.

The third stanza, 53:7-9, depicting the Divine Sacrifice, quoted below, was the text the Ethiopian eunuch was reading and about which he asked Philip, "Tell me, please, who is the prophet talking about, himself or someone else?" (Acts 8:34). Philip "began with that very passage of Scripture and told him the good news about Jesus" (8:35).

> He was oppressed and afflicted,
>> yet he did not open his mouth;
> he was led like a lamb to the slaughter,
>> and as a sheep before her shearers is silent,
>> so he did not open his mouth.
> By oppression and judgment, he was taken away.
>> And who can speak of his descendants?
> For he was cut off from the land of the living;
>> for the transgression of my people he was stricken.
> He was assigned a grave with the wicked—
>> and with the rich in his death,
> though he had done no violence,
>> nor was any deceit in his mouth.

The final stanza, 53:10-12, depicts Divine Satisfaction because Jesus' death and resurrection secured the justification of sinful mankind. "He [Jesus] was delivered over to death for our sins and was raised to life for our justification" (Rom 4:25). It was God's will that Jesus should die because only the sinless can die for the sinful (Acts 2:23). "For you know that it was not with perishable things such as silver or gold that you were redeemed from the empty way of life handed down to you from your forefathers, but with the precious blood of Christ, a lamb without blemish or defect. He was chosen before the creation of the world, but was revealed in these last times for your sake" (1 Pet 1:18-20).

> Yet it was the LORD's will to crush him and cause him to suffer,
>> and though the LORD makes his life a guilt offering,
> he will see his offspring and prolong his days,
>> and the will of the LORD will prosper in his hand.

After the suffering of his soul,
> he will see the light of life and be satisfied;
by his knowledge my righteous servant will justify many,
> and he will bear their iniquities.
Therefore I will give him a portion among the great,
> and he will divide the spoils with the strong,
because he poured out his life unto death,
> and was numbered with the transgressors.
For he bore the sin of many,
> and made intercession for the transgressors.

Psalm 110:1

Psalm 110 is the psalm most quoted by the New Testament. This is so because verses 1 and 4 are keys to the New Testament's Christology. Verse 1 is important to us here.

The psalm's superscription suggests that King David authored this piece. This is confirmed by Matthew 22:43 and Acts 2:34-36. Verse 1 is then David's report of a conversation he heard between the first and second persons of the Godhead — a conversation between God the Father and his Son, centuries before that Son came in human flesh!

The verse reads, "The LORD says to my Lord: 'Sit at my right hand until I make your enemies a footstool for your feet.'" The LORD (Yahweh, the God of the patriarchs) promises David's Lord, the Messiah (see Matt 22:41-46), that He would defeat all the enemies of the Messiah's Kingdom. As Victorious Lord, he deserves all the spoils of war — authority, glory, sovereign power, worship, and dominion (Dan 7:14).

A MANUAL FOR MATURITY

Paul reminded Timothy that Scripture is useful for "teaching, rebuking, correcting and training in righteousness." Paul is here suggesting that the profit of Scripture relates to both creed and conduct. "As for our creed," writes John Stott, "Scripture is profitable for teaching the truth and refuting error. As for our conduct, it is profitable for reformation of manners and discipline in right living."[36]

---

[36]John R.W. Stott, *Guard the Gospel: The Message of 2 Timothy* (Downers Grove, IL: InterVarsity, 1973), p. 103. Donald Guthrie (*The Pastoral Epistles,*

Teaching the Truth and Refuting Error

God exists. This is truth. Both natural (Ps 19:1-6; Acts 14:17; Rom 1:18-20) and special revelation (Old and New Testaments) bear elegant witness to the existence of God. The doubt of (agnosticism) or denial of (atheism) God's existence is error. Psalm 14:1 asserts, "The fool says in his heart, 'There is no God.'"

The creation of mankind in the *Imago Dei* marks humanity as radically different from other creatures. This is truth. "Then God said, 'Let us make man in our image, in our likeness and let them rule over the fish of the sea and the birds of the air, over the livestock, over all the earth and over all the creatures that move along the ground'" (Gen 1:26). Philosophical naturalism denies this truth. Naturalism's explanation of human origins so devalues mankind that it leaves us without meaning, with moral anarchy, and with existential despair and misery. This is error.

The cosmos pulsates with the ever-present potential for direct, divine intervention. This is truth. The Old Testament is replete with examples of miraculous intervention. Though barren, Sarah conceived and bore Isaac (Genesis 21). This was a miracle. God used a series of plagues to bring about the release of his people from Egyptian slavery (Exodus 7–11). These mighty acts of God were miracles. The death of one hundred and eighty-five thousand men in the Assyrian camp was a miracle (Isa 37:36). The deliverance of Shadrach, Meshach, and Abednego from the fiery furnace (Daniel 3) and Daniel from the lions' den (Daniel 6) were miracles. Antisupernaturalism is error. It is both intellectual arrogance and moral cowardice.

God governs the cosmos justly. This is truth. The Bible consistently affirms that the righteous are vindicated by God, while the wicked are shamed and silenced by God. A brief sampling of this theme from the Psalter is evidence enough. "For the LORD watches over the way of the righteous, but the way of the wicked will perish" (1:6). "The eyes of the LORD are on the righteous and his ears are attentive to their cry; the face of the LORD is against those who do evil, to cut off the memory of them from the earth" (34:15-16) "The wicked plot against the righteous and gnash their teeth at them; but

---

TNTC [Grand Rapids: Eerdmans, 1978], p. 164) understands the Scriptures' profitability the same way. "Four spheres are now mentioned in which the usefulness of Scripture can be seen. The former two relate to doctrine and the latter two to practice."

the LORD laughs at the wicked, for he knows their day is coming" (37:12-13). "Better the little that the righteous have than the wealth of many wicked; for the power of the wicked will be broken, but the LORD upholds the righteous" (37:16-17). "The righteous will be glad when they are avenged, when they bathe their feet in the blood of the wicked. Then men will say, 'Surely the righteous still are reward-ed; surely there is a God who judges the earth'" (58:10-11). To dis-credit or deny that God judges rightly is error. It is hubris; it is self-seeking. God asks Job, "Would you discredit my justice? Would you condemn me to justify yourself?" (Job 40:8).

God's reign and rule are eternal. His kingdom is invincible (Dan 2:44-45). All enemies, including the Devil (Gen 3:15), demons, and death (Isa 25:7-8), capitulate to him. This is truth. Even Nebuchad-nezzar apprehended this truth:

> His dominion is an eternal dominion; his kingdom endures from generation to generation. All the peoples of the earth are regard-ed as nothing. He does as he pleases with the powers of heaven and the peoples of the earth. No one can hold back his hand or say to him: "What have you done?" (Dan 4:34b-35).

If God alone is invincible, then every other alliance, or object of trust, is ill-fated. It is folly. It is error. The seductions of this world — glory, wealth, wisdom, sophistication, culture, nongods — are mirages. "See, the LORD is going to lay waste the earth and devastate it; he will ruin its face and scatter its inhabitants—it will be the same for priest as for people, for master as for servant, for mistress as for maid, for seller as for buyer, for borrower as for lender, for debtor as for cred-itor. The earth will be completely laid waste and totally plundered" (Isa 24:1-3).

Truth is a term fittingly applied to God's nature (Ps 25:5; 31:5; Jer 10:10) and to his words (Ps 119:142,151,160). The above truths are a subset of this one truth. "All truth comes from God and is truth because it is related to God."[37] To deny this is error; it is folly.

Reformation of Manners and Discipline in Right Living

The famous Ten Commandments (Exodus 20 and Deuteronomy 5) are foundational to the Old Testament's covenant ethic. Of course,

---

[37]*TWOT*, I:53.

the same can be said for the New Testament. Note below how every sphere of life is infused with divine sanctity. Keeping these commandments is a discipline in right living.

Commandment(s)	Text (Exodus)	Sanctity of . . .
1-3	(1) You shall have no other gods before me. (2) You shall not make for yourself an idol in the form of anything in heaven above or on the earth beneath or in the waters below. (3) You shall not misuse the name of the LORD your God	Sanctity of Worship
4	Remember the Sabbath day by keeping it holy. Six days you shall labor and do all your work, but the seventh day is a Sabbath to the LORD your God. On it you shall not do any work.	Sanctity of Time
5	Honor your father and mother.	Sanctity of Authority
6	You shall not murder.	Sanctity of Life
7	You shall not commit adultery.	Sanctity of Marriage and Sexuality
8	You shall not steal.	Sanctity of Possessions and Personhood
9	You shall not give false testimony against your neighbor.	Sanctity of Truth and Mutual Trust
10	You shall not covet your neighbor's house. You shall not covet your neighbor's wife, or his manservant or maidservant, his ox or donkey, or anything that belongs to your neighbor.	Sanctity of Human Rights

Space does not permit comment upon each of these ethical commitments. I will comment briefly upon the sanctity of sexuality (commandment seven), the sanctity of possessions (commandment eight), and the sanctity of truth (commandment nine).

Sanctity of Sexuality

When God had finished creating man and woman, he declared his creation "very good." God's pronouncement extends to sexual differentiation (male and female) and sexual exclusivity (husband and wife). The Old Testament rejoices, then, in marriage and within marriage sexual union.

The Book of Proverbs rejoices in marriage. "A wife of noble character is her husband's crown" (12:4; 31:10). "He who finds a wife finds what is good and receives favor from the LORD" (18:22). "Houses and wealth are inherited from parents, but a prudent wife is from the LORD" (19:14).

Proverbs also rejoices in sexual intimacy and delight. "May your fountain be blessed, and may you rejoice in the wife of your youth. A loving doe, a graceful deer—may her breasts satisfy you always, may you ever be captivated by her love" (5:18-19).

Of course, the Song of Songs extols both marriage and intimacy. E J. Young has captured the value of this book:

> The Song does celebrate the dignity and purity of human love. This is a fact which has not always been sufficiently stressed. The Song, therefore, is didactic and moral in its purpose. It comes to us in this world of sin, where lust and passion are on every hand, where fierce temptations assail us and try to turn us aside from the God-given standard of marriage. And it reminds us, in particularly beautiful fashion, how pure and noble true love is.[38]

Sanctity of Possessions

Wealth is an important topic in the Book of Proverbs. A brief sampling of its teaching will set us on a disciplined path to right living.

First, ill-gotten gain is fleeting. Money may be made at the expense of truth (11:18; 20:17; 21:6), justice (29:4; contrast this with 11:1; 16:11; 20:10,23), and others (22:16; 28:24). Such wealth is "a fleeting vapor and a deadly snare" (21:6). "Dishonest money dwindles away" (13:11a). Second, money may be lost through debt (6:1-3; 22:7), greed (11:24; 28:22), hasty decisions (21:5), laziness (20:4,13; 24:30-34), mistrust (11:28), pleasure (21:17,20), socializing in the wrong circles (23:19-21), and mere talk (14:23).

Third, we have an obligation to give to God (3:9-10), to the poor (19:17), to our neighbor (3:27-28), and to family (13:22; 31:18). Fourth, wisdom is necessary in properly dealing with money (4:7; 8:20-21; 15:16,22; 17:16; 22:4; 23:4). "Blessed is the man who finds wisdom, the man who gains understanding, for she is more profitable than silver and yields better returns than gold. She is more precious than rubies; nothing you desire can compare with her"

---

[38]Young, *Introduction*, p. 336.

(3:13-15). Finally, money has limitations. It does not profit us in the day of wrath (11:4). It is fleeting: "Cast but a glance at riches, and they are gone, for they will surely sprout wings and fly off to the sky like an eagle" (23:5; cf. 27:24a). Wealth will amount to nothing at death. Classic expressions of this are found in both testaments. In Ecclesiastes 5:15 we read, "Naked a man comes from his mother's womb, and as he comes, so he departs. He takes nothing from his labor that he can carry in his hand" (cf. Job 1:21; Ps 49:10-12). In 1 Timothy 6:7 Paul writes, "For we brought nothing into the world, and we can take nothing out of it" (cf. Jas 1:10-11; Luke 12:15-21).

Sanctity of Truth

According to Proverbs 6:17-19 the LORD hates "haughty eyes, *a lying tongue*, hands that shed innocent blood, a heart that devises wicked schemes, feet that are quick to rush into evil, *a false witness who pours out lies*, and *a man who stirs up dissension among brothers*." Three of these seven are examples of the misuse of words. Words are important to the LORD!

The Hebrew word רָכִיל (*rākîl*), translated "slanderer," occurs six times in the Old Testament. God's displeasure with slander is evident throughout the entire Old Testament — the Law, Prophets, and the Writings. In the Law Leviticus 19:16 reads. "Do not go about spreading slander among your people." In the Prophets, in a context of judgment, Ezekiel 22:9 reads: "In you [Jerusalem] are slanderous men bent on shedding blood" (cf. Jer 6:28; 9:4). In the Writings, Proverbs 11:13 reads: "A gossip betrays a confidence, but a trustworthy man keeps a secret." Proverbs 20:19 adds: "A gossip betrays a confidence; so avoid a man who talks too much."

The slanderous tongue does have the power of death. This power must be tamed and then executed. The tongue also has the power of life. "The tongue has the power of life and death, and those who love it will eat its fruit" (Prov 18:21). "Reckless words pierce like a sword, but the tongue of the wise brings healing" (12:18). "An anxious heart weighs a man down, but a kind word cheers him up" (12:25). "The tongue that brings healing is a tree of life" (15:4; cf. 10:11). "A man finds joy in giving an apt reply—and how good is a timely word" (15:23). "Pleasant words are a honeycomb, sweet to the soul and healing to the bones" (16:24). "A word aptly spoken is like apples of gold in settings of silver" (25:11; cf. 10:20,32; 25:12).

A MANUAL FOR MINISTRY

The Old Testament, a manual for ministry/missions, reveals a mission-minded God. In the "covenant" passages, God reveals his concern for a lost humanity. When God calls Abram, he promises that "all peoples on earth will be blessed through" the patriarch and his family (Gen 12:3b). When God calls Israel at Mount Sinai to be his people, he declares them to be "a kingdom of priests and a holy nation" (Exod 19:6). As a "kingdom of priests" Israel was meant to mediate the Presence of the LORD to the nations that bordered her. This is why Israel is called the firstfruits of the harvest (Jer 2:3). "Firstfruits" implies a later harvest. That harvest was to be the nations! At 55:3-7 the prophet Isaiah reflects upon the mission emphasis of the covenant made with David (2 Samuel 7):

> Give ear and come to me; hear me, that your soul may live. I will make an everlasting covenant with you, my unfailing kindnesses promised to David. See, I have made him a witness to the peoples, a leader and commander of the peoples. Surely you will summon nations you know not, and nations that do not know you will listen to you, because of the LORD your God, the Holy One of Israel, for he has endowed you with splendor. Seek the LORD while he may be found; call on him while he is near.

Jeremiah 31:31-34, the famous New Covenant passage, is the longest Old Testament passage cited by the New Testament. And this for obvious reasons! The mission-minded God had taken on human flesh to achieve all that he had promised to Abraham, Israel, David, Jeremiah, and the peoples/nations of the earth!

The Psalms are replete with references to the salvation of the nations. Listen to this catalogue: "All the earth bows down to you; they sing praise to you, they sing praise to your name" (66:4). "May the nations be glad and sing for joy, for you rule the peoples justly and guide the nations of the earth. May the peoples praise you, O God; may all the peoples praise you" (67:4-5). "Among the gods there is none like you, O Lord; no deeds can compare with yours. All the nations you have made will come and worship before you, O Lord, for they will bring glory to your name. For you are great and do marvelous deeds; you alone are God" (86:8-10). "Praise the LORD, all you nations; extol him, all you peoples. For great is his love toward us, and the faithfulness of the LORD endures forever" (117:1-2).

Unfortunately Israel did not share God's commitment to the nations. This is best illustrated in the hypocrisy of Jonah. You know the story line. The LORD dispatches the prophet to Nineveh to warn her citizenry of his judgment upon their wickedness (1:2). But Jonah runs from his calling. He buys passage on a ship headed in the wrong direction. But the LORD, through a storm and a big fish, reroutes the prophet. Jonah finally does preach. The people of Nineveh repent. God relents from sending calamity. But the prophet is "greatly displeased" (4:1).

Why would a prophet of God run from his calling? Why would a prophet become "greatly displeased" when his message is heard and obeyed? Jonah answers these questions at 4:2: "I knew that you are a gracious and compassionate God, slow to anger and abounding in love, a God who relents from sending calamity." In short, Jonah knew that if the citizens of Nineveh responded appropriately, the gracious LORD would relent from destroying the wicked city. Jonah did not want to be involved in any way with the "salvation" of these pagan (and hated) Assyrians. At least Jonah was honest!

Jonah's answer reveals his hypocrisy though. His answer echoes Exodus 34:6. This context is significant. The LORD has just relented from destroying his own people for their pagan ways — idolatry (the sin of the golden calf) and sexual impurity. Surely God's people knew better! If the LORD had once (that's an understatement!) extended grace and compassion to Jonah's countrymen, a people who knew better, then sheer hypocrisy now wishes destruction upon a pagan people who "cannot tell their right hand from their left" (4:11).

If a prophet of God had run from his calling and task, then it is no surprise that the nation failed at its priestly task. Isaiah indicts Israel this way: "As a woman with child and about to give birth writhes and cries out in her pain, so were we in your presence, O LORD. We were with child, we writhed in pain, but we gave birth to wind. We have not brought salvation to the earth; we have not given birth to the people of the world" (26:17-18).

The LORD is mission-minded. But Israel did not share the mind of God. Why was this? Many answers are appropriate for this question. Worldliness is one such answer. Israel had conformed itself to the world, seeking worldly resources and securities and worshiping man-made gods. Listen to Isaiah 2:6b-8:

They are full of superstitions from the East; they practice divination like the Philistines and clasp hands with pagans. Their land is full of silver and gold; there is no end to their treasures. Their land is full of horses; there is no end to their chariots. Their land is full of idols; they bow down to the work of their hands, to what their fingers have made."

With respect to ministry/mission/evangelism, of course, the Church must have the mind of God. The Church dare not compromise its calling and task by indifference, hypocrisy, or worldliness!

CONCLUSION

The Old Testament is a manual for salvation in the Messiah, for maturity, and for ministry/mission. This has always been and will always be. This is so because God "wants all men to be saved and to come to knowledge of the truth. For there is one God and one mediator between God and men, the man Christ Jesus, who gave himself as a ransom for all men—the testimony given in its proper time" (1 Tim 2:4-6).

Paul has instructed us in the "usefulness" of divine writ, the Holy Scriptures. This timeless usefulness results from the origin of Holy Scriptures: "All Scripture is God-breathed." "What Paul wishes to assure Timothy," writes E.J. Young, "is that the Bible is the product of the Divine breath, and it is this fact of being breathed out by God that constitutes the very heart and core of the Biblical doctrine of inspiration."[39]

OLD TESTAMENT NARRATIVE

James Muilenburg's presidential address delivered to the Society of Biblical Literature on December 18, 1968, "revolutionized" the study of the Bible.[40] Leland Ryken has characterized this revolution, this new approach to the Bible, as follows:

A number of ingredients make up this new approach to the Bible: a concern with the literary genres of the Bible; a new willingness to treat biblical texts as finished wholes instead of as a patchwork

---

[39]E.J. Young, *Thy Word Is Truth* (Grand Rapids: Eerdmans, 1967), p. 23.
[40]James Muilenburg, "Form Criticism and Beyond," *JBL* 88 (1969): 1-18.

of fragments; a focus on the Bible as it now stands instead of conducting excavations in the redaction (editing) process behind the text; an inclination to use literary instead of traditional theological terms to discuss the stories and poems of the Bible; an appreciation for the artistry of the Bible; a sensitivity to the experiential, extra-intellectual (more-than-ideational) dimension of the Bible.[41]

This essay examines the artistry of Old Testament narrative. The sublime beauty of Holy Scripture should not surprise us.[42] After all God is the author! This essay is written with illustration in mind. The reader may consult the references at the beginning of this section for the technical details of theory.

Reading a narrative, or a story, minimally involves paying attention to setting, characters, and plot.[43]

SETTING

Temporal

The temporal setting of a story is vital. The story of Ruth, for example, is set "in the days when the judges ruled" (1:1). The Book of Judges, which precedes Ruth in our English Bibles, details the political calamities that befell Israel during the "days when the judges ruled." These calamitous circumstances were a direct result of Israel's covenant infidelity. This nexus of disobedience and distress is presented as a thesis statement in Judges 2 and then amply illustrated throughout the book.

> They forsook the LORD, the God of their fathers, who had brought them out of Egypt. They followed and worshiped various gods of the peoples around them. They provoked the LORD to anger because they forsook him and served Baal and the Ashtoreths. In his anger

---

[41]Leland Ryken, *How to Read the Bible as Literature . . . and Get More Out of It* (Grand Rapids: Zondervan, 1984), p. 11. For more on the tendency to read the Pentateuch as a patchwork of documents, see Randall Bailey's chapter on Genesis in this volume.

[42]Fokkelman (*Reading Biblical Narrative: An Introductory Guide* [Louisville, KY: Westminster John Knox Press, 1999], p. 27) has written that "the stories in the Bible are products of literary design, right down to the smallest detail, and usually very subtle, too."

[43]Aristotle, *The Poetics*, LCL (Cambridge: Harvard University Press, 1927), p. 25 [vi. 9-11].

against Israel the LORD handed them over to raiders who plundered them. He sold them to their enemies all around, whom they were no longer able to resist. Whenever Israel went out to fight, the hand of the LORD was against them to defeat them, just as he had sworn to them. They were in great distress (2:12-15).

One such example of this thesis is sounded at 3:7-8: "The Israelites did evil in the eyes of the LORD; they forgot the LORD their God and served the Baals and the Asherahs. The anger of the LORD burned against Israel so that he sold them into the hands of Cushan-Rishathaim king of Aram Naharaim, to whom the Israelites were subject for eight years." This same connection is sounded also at 3:12-14; 4:1-3; 6:1-6; 10:6-9; 13:1.

"In the days when the judges ruled" conditions the reader then to expect sin and suffering, disobedience and distress, chaos and curse. Ruth 1:1 mentions "a famine in the land." Famine is one of the curses for disobedience cited in Deuteronomy 28:22-24. A famine in Bethlehem at the outset of this story is wildly ironic. The name "Bethlehem" means "house of bread"! Ruth 1:3-5 describes how death left Naomi without husband or son. Such suffering! Such distress!

Amidst this backdrop of a family's pain and a nation's distress, the Lord would intervene in such loving ways to introduce the hope of Israel, the line of David (Ruth 4:13-21).

Physical

In Isaiah 7 the prophet and his son met with King Ahaz "at the end of the aqueduct of the Upper Pool, on the road to the Washerman's Field." At the time, Ahaz was facing a political crisis — King Rezin of Aram and Pekah king of Israel had joined forces to fight against him in Jerusalem (Isa 7:1). In the face of this crisis, what options did Ahaz have? He could surrender. Such an option was unlikely. He could fight the coalition alone. This seemed impractical. He could enlist an ally against the foe. Egypt to the south or Assyria to the east were possibilities. He could, of course, see the crisis as more than political. That is, it was a spiritual crisis. In such a case, he could entrust himself to the Lord and wait for his deliverance!

Isaiah oriented Ahaz toward faith, saying, "If you do not stand firm in your faith, you will not stand at all" (7:9b). Isaiah also assured Ahaz of the long-term picture, saying, "Be careful, keep calm and don't be afraid. Do not lose heart because of these two smoldering stubs of firewood — because of the fierce anger of Rezin and Aram and of the son of Remaliah" (7:4).

What option did Ahaz exercise? He chose an alliance with Assyria. In 2 Kings 16:7-9 we read,

> Ahaz sent messengers to say to Tiglath-Pileser king of Assyria, "I am your servant and vassal. Come up and save me out of the hand of the king of Aram and of the king of Israel, who are attacking me." And Ahaz took the silver and gold found in the temple of the LORD and in the treasuries of the royal palace and sent it as a gift to the king of Assyria. The king of Assyria complied by attacking Damascus and capturing it. He deported its inhabitants to Kir and put Rezin to death.

In terms of the moment, the decision was politically expedient. Ahaz had exhibited worldly savoir-faire. The power of the coalition was shattered, the political crisis was averted. But in terms of the long-range impact, the decision was monstrous folly. Enlisting the aid of Assyria made Judah vulnerable to Assyria's might. In 701 B.C. the Assyrians moved against Judah, capturing all but Jerusalem, and this only because the Lord intervened to save the capital (2 Kgs 19:35).

In terms of faith the decision was catastrophic. Without faith there are no people of God. If there are no people of God, then the external signs of such a reality — both king and kingdom — are irrelevant. J. Alec Motyer has framed the gravity of this moment:

> From the time when Ahaz disbelieved, he and David's descendants reigned as puppet kings, by courtesy first of Assyria and then of Babylon, until the fall of Jerusalem in 586 BC extinguished kingdom and monarchy altogether so that (with Christian hindsight), when Immanuel was born, the heir to David's throne was an unknown carpenter in Nazareth (Mt. 1:16)! Thus Isaiah concertinas the centuries, for when Immanuel was born he inherited only the memory of a kingdom and a non-existent crown—and it was Ahaz' fault.[44]

Isaiah 36 records that Sennacherib, king of Assyria, had captured all of the fortified cities of Judah, with Jerusalem now in his sights. The king sent his field commander to engage Jerusalem first in a bat-

---

[44]J. Alec Motyer, *Isaiah*, TOTC (Downers Grove, IL: InterVarsity, 1999), p. 78.

tle of propaganda. Notice where his war of words commences: "the aqueduct of the Upper Pool, on the road to the Washerman's Field" (Isa 36:2)!

Hezekiah, the son of Ahaz, is now king in Jerusalem. In the face of this crisis, what options does Hezekiah have? He could surrender. This hardly seems likely. He could fight the Assyrians alone. This seems impractical; he has already lost the countryside to the Assyrian menace. He could enlist an ally against the foe. Egypt to the south is a possibility. In fact, he had already done so. Note the words of the field commander: "Look now, you are depending on Egypt, that splintered reed of a staff, which pierces a man's hand and wounds him if he leans on it! Such is Pharaoh king of Egypt to all who depend on him" (36:6; cf. 37:9).

Like father, like son. Hezekiah has maneuvered as Ahaz did. Both father and son faced spiritual crises presented in the form of political/military challenge. Did Ahaz enlist the help of the Lord? No! Will Hezekiah? Let the text speak for itself:

> And Hezekiah prayed to the LORD: "O LORD Almighty, God of Israel, enthroned between the cherubim, you alone are God over all the kingdoms of the earth. You have made heaven and earth. Give ear, O LORD, and hear; open your eyes, O LORD, and see; listen to all the words Sennacherib has sent to insult the living God. . . . Now, O LORD our God, deliver us from his hand, so that all kingdoms on earth may know that you alone, O LORD, are God" (37:15-17,20).

Of course faith/trust works! Ahaz, are you listening? The Lord delivered Hezekiah and Jerusalem from the menacing Assyrians. "Then the angel of the Lord went out and put to death a hundred and eighty-five thousand men in the Assyrian camp. When the people got up the next morning — there were all the dead bodies! So Sennacherib king of Assyria broke camp and withdrew. He returned to Nineveh and stayed there" (37:36-37).

CHARACTERS

Just because a person is in the Bible does not mean that he or she is a godly or honorable person. Not everyone in the Bible is a Daniel or a Ruth! Often the author declines a direct assessment of a character. As readers we will be drawn to a particular judgment of a character based on a number of criteria. Our assessment of Jacob is based on his deception of both his impulsive brother and blind father. Our perspective on Solomon is informed by subtle reminders of his disobedience of Deuteronomy 17. We view Samson as a failed Nazirite, Mordecai and Esther are assessed in light of the absence of God's name from the Book of Esther.

Jacob

As Jacob descended the birth canal, his hand grasped his twin brother's (Esau) heel, foreshadowing his manipulative attempts to outstrip his older brother's primogeniture.

How unfortunate and unnecessary this manipulation, given that the Lord had already promised Jacob's ascendancy. The Lord had spoken to Rebekah, Jacob and Esau's mother, about her twin boys, saying, "Two nations are in your womb, and two peoples from within you will be separated; one people will be stronger than the other, and the older will serve the younger" (Gen 25:23).

Taking unfair advantage of his brother's impulsive character, Jacob bought his "famished" brother's birthright for some stew (Gen 25:29-34). Taking advantage of his father's (Isaac) blindness, Jacob seized the blessing which had been meant for Esau (Gen 27:27-29). When Esau learned of the second deception, he said, "Isn't he rightly named Jacob? He has deceived me these two times: He took my birthright, and now he's taken my blessing!" (27:36).

Solomon

Solomon is perhaps the most enigmatic character in all of the Old Testament. He is commonly perceived as a "wise" man, yet his actions betray his folly. This folly is evident in his inattention to the details of the Law.

Deuteronomy 17 provides the kings of Israel/Judah with a charter for rule. "The king, moreover, must not acquire great numbers of horses for himself or make the people return to Egypt to get more of them, for the Lord has told you, 'You are not to go back that way again.' He must not take many wives, or his heart will be led astray. He must not accumulate large amounts of silver and gold" (17:16-17).

First Kings 10:26-28 and 11:3 indict Solomon[45] for his disobedience to this charter:

---

[45]J. Daniel Hays, "Has the Narrator Come to Praise Solomon or to Bury Him? Narrative Subtlety in I Kings 1–11," *JSOT* 28 (2003): 149-174.

> Solomon accumulated chariots and horses; he had fourteen hun-
> dred chariots and twelve thousand horses, which he kept in the
> chariot cities and also with him in Jerusalem. The king made sil-
> ver as common in Jerusalem as stones, and cedar as plentiful as
> sycamore-fig trees in the foothills. Solomon's horses were import-
> ed from Egypt and from Kue—the royal merchants purchased
> them from Kue. . . . He had seven hundred wives of royal birth
> and three hundred concubines, and his wives led him astray.

Solomon's disobedience to the Law, especially in the realm of
marriage and idolatry, led to the breakup of the united monarchy.
Listen again to the author of Kings:

> The LORD became angry with Solomon because his heart had
> turned away from the LORD, the God of Israel, who had appeared
> to him twice. Although he had forbidden Solomon to follow other
> gods, Solomon did not keep the LORD's command. So the LORD
> said to Solomon, "Since this is your attitude and you have not kept
> my covenant and my decrees, which I commanded you, I will most
> certainly tear the kingdom away from you and give it to one of
> your subordinates. Nevertheless, for the sake of David your father,
> I will not do it during your lifetime. I will tear it out of the hand
> of your son. Yet I will not tear the whole kingdom from him, but
> will give him one tribe for the sake of David my servant and for
> the sake of Jerusalem, which I have chosen" (11:9-13).

Samson

God willed that Samson be a Nazirite, set apart from birth.
According to Numbers 6:1-21 a Nazirite "must abstain from wine
and other fermented drink" (v. 3), "no razor may be used on his
head" (v. 5), and "he must not go near a dead body" (v. 6). Samson
compromises each of these elements, demonstrating how the power
of uncontrolled passion can compromise a man's divine calling.

Samson married a young Philistine woman. To celebrate the
occasion, a feast was organized (Judg 14:10). The Hebrew word here
for "feast" implies "drinking"! If Samson partook of the intoxicants,
then he has violated the first element of his vow. Before the feast
had started, Samson had violated the third element of his vow; he
had scooped honey out of a lion's carcass (14:8-9). Seduced by fifty-
five hundred shekels of silver, Delilah, a woman loved by Samson
(and the only woman named in the Samson stories!), learned that

the source of Samson's great strength was the length of his hair. One night as Samson slept, she had his head shaved. "And his strength left him" (14:19). Now all three elements of the Nazirite vow were compromised. Notice what the text says at this point: "He awoke from his sleep and thought, 'I'll go out as before and shake myself free.' But he did not know that the LORD had left him" (16:20).

Mordecai and Esther

The absence of God's name from the Book of Esther implies his displeasure with the sinfulness of his people.[46] Mordecai and Esther, the heroes of the story, were not blameless. Mordecai advised Esther to conceal her identity (2:10,20) in order to become queen. Mordecai's pride led to the confrontation with Haman. Esther was willing to hide her identity to become queen and was not reluctant to indulge the king's sexual appetite (2:15-16; cf. Deut 7:3).

PLOT

The Abraham Cycle

In Genesis 12 the Lord promised Abram that one day he would become a great family/nation, that that nation would have a special relationship with him, and that that nation would have its own land. The unfolding of this threefold promise is the plot of the Pentateuch plus Joshua.[47] Genesis 12–50 focuses attention on the first element of the promise: "I will make you into a great nation" (12:2).[48]

The fulfillment of this promise is threatened first by Sarai's barrenness. "Now Sarai was barren; she had no children" (11:30; cf.

---

[46]Mangano, *Esther & Daniel*, p. 24.

[47]David J.A. Clines (*The Theme of the Pentateuch*, JSOTSupp 10 [Sheffield: Sheffield Academic Press, 1984], p. 29) has written: "The theme of the Pentateuch is the partial fulfilment — which implies also the partial non-fulfilment — of the promise to or blessing of the patriarchs. The promise or blessing is both the divine initiative in a world where human initiatives always lead to disaster, and a re-affirmation of the primal divine intentions for man. The promise has three elements: posterity, divine-human relationship, and land. The posterity-element of the promise is dominant in Genesis 12–50, the relationship-element in Exodus and Leviticus, and the land-element in Numbers and Deuteronomy."

[48]Cf. 12:2,7; 13:15; 15:4-5,13,16,18; 16:10; 17:2,4-7,16,19-20; 21:12-13,18; 22:16ff.; 26:3-4,24; 28:13-14; 35:11; 46:3.

15:2-3; 16:1). How would the Lord overcome this obstacle? How would Abram and Sarai translate God's promise in light of this physical challenge?

In the ancient world, as in our own, a couple unable to have children could adopt an heir. The adoption option seems to have been evoked by Abram in Genesis 15:2-3: "But Abram said, 'O Sovereign LORD, what can you give me since I remain childless and the one who will inherit my estate is Eliezer of Damascus?' And Abram said, 'You have given me no children; so a servant in my household will be my heir.'" Abram and Sarai viewed Eliezer as the fulfillment of the promise. Quite possibly Lot, Abram's nephew, was also seen as a possible candidate for adoption.

In the ancient world, unlike our own, a husband without an heir could take a surrogate wife. This reality is evident in the story of Hagar and Ishmael. "Now Sarai, Abram's wife, had borne him no children. But she had an Egyptian maidservant named Hagar; so she said to Abram, 'The LORD has kept me from having children. Go, sleep with my maidservant; perhaps I can build a family through her'" (16:1-2).

Another threat to the promise of progeny is found at Genesis 12:10: famine. Famine is a shortage of food. Without food, life is jeopardized. What would happen to the promise of God if either Abram or Sarai were to die due to famine? Famine threatens the family of Abram also at Genesis 26 and 42.

Abram and Sarai journeyed to Egypt for grain. While there she was taken into the Pharaoh's palace due to her beauty. Without Sarai Abram can in no way have the child promised to both! The Lord resolved this dilemma by inflicting serious diseases on Pharaoh and his household, compelling Pharaoh to release Sarai and send them on their way (12:17-20). The "wife-napping" of Sarah also occurs at Genesis 20 (cf. Gen 26:1-11).

Having left Egypt Abram returned to Bethel. There "quarreling arose between Abram's herdsmen and the herdsmen of Lot" (13:7). What could happen to the promise if the quarreling escalated to the point of forfeited life, Abraham's life? Murder is not unexpected in a book which recounts the murder of Abel by his brother Cain.

Notice what the remainder of that verse narrates. "The Canaanites and Perizzites were also living in the land at that time." Do you think these indigenous groups were happy to see an interloper like Abram grazing his flocks on their land? They could have easily banded together to fight these insurgents.

In Genesis 14 Abram engages a coalition of kings in war in order to rescue Lot. Any military maneuver poses a threat to life, Abram's life!

Barrenness, famine, wife-napping, quarreling, and war all threatened the promise of progeny. The Lord had intervened at key points in this compelling story line to preserve his promise. And so, in Genesis 21, a child is born to Abram and Sarai; his name is Isaac.

The child is born. The promise is beginning to take on definition. And then, quite unexpectedly, the Lord commands Abram, "Take your son, your only son Isaac, whom you love, and go to the region of Moriah. Sacrifice him there as a burnt offering on one of the mountains I will tell you about" (22:2).

Has the Lord really commanded the death of the son? Yes! But at the point in the narrative when Abram is about to plunge the knife into the body of his son, the Lord again intervened. "Do not lay a hand on the boy. . . . Do not do anything to him. Now I know that you fear God, because you have not withheld from me your son, your only son" (22:12). In a sense, the Lord has overcome the Lord!

The incident suggests that no thing or no one, not even the Lord himself, can abrogate the divine promise!

Genesis 23 records the death of Sarah; Genesis 25 the death of Abraham. What would happen to the promise now if Isaac dies without fathering the next generation? It is a legitimate question given the dangers with which life is fraught.

Isaac fathers Jacob and Esau, but Esau threatens to kill his brother. Jacob flees for his life to the old country. There he begins his family only to be threatened by his own father-in-law. In time Jacob returns to Palestine. Will Esau now carry out his threat to take life? Will the family survive the famine that closes the book of Genesis?

The Book of Genesis is a gripping history of God protecting and preserving the promise of family. The story is artistically brilliant, but it also teaches us that God will overcome all threats (against remarkable odds) to achieve salvation for the nations.[49]

---

[49]Exodus 1:7 summarizes the rapid growth of Abraham's family during its sojourn in Egypt: "the Israelites were fruitful and multiplied greatly and became exceedingly numerous, so that the land was filled with them."

Threats to the Promise of Family in the Abraham Cycle (11:26–25:11)

Barrenness	Gen 11:30; 16:1; 17:17; 18:11
Famine	Gen 12:10
Wife-napping	Gen 12:15; 20:2
Quarreling	Gen 13:7; 21:9
War	Gen 14:15
Near-sacrifice of Isaac	Gen 22:2
Death	Gen 23:1-2; 25:7-8

David and His Sons (2 Samuel 11–2 Kings 2)

After David had committed adultery with Bathsheba, Nathan, the prophet, came to David with a story meant to illustrate the gravity of David's heinous act. Upon hearing the story, David pronounced, "As surely as the LORD lives, the man who did this deserves to die! He must pay for that lamb four times over, because he did such a thing and had no pity" (2 Sam 12:5-6).

David had unknowingly pronounced judgment upon himself. From this point in the narrative, to the end of David's life, the text focuses on the death of four of David's sons! With the exception of the first son, know assuredly that these children die on account of their own sin, but their father's sin casts an ominous shadow over their lives.

The first son is unnamed; he is the child conceived by the adulterous affair of his parents (2 Sam 12:19). The second son to die is Amnon, murdered by a vengeful Absalom because Amnon had raped his sister (2 Sam 13:29). Absalom would die third. He had led a coup against his father; he paid the ultimate price, his life (2 Sam 18:14-15). Adonijah would be the fourth. He was struck down at the command of Solomon (1 Kgs 2:25).

Like their father before them, these three sons had transgressed a sexual taboo. Amnon had raped his half-sister (2 Sam 13:14); Absalom had sexual relations with his father's concubines (2 Sam 16:22); Adonijah had requested that Abishag be given to him as wife (1 Kgs 2:17). Abishag was the young woman who had kept David warm in his old age, "but the king had no intimate relations with her" (1 Kgs 1:1-4).

Like their father before them, David's sons combined sexual transgression with violence (David had Uriah, the husband of Bathsheba, placed on the front lines in battle so that he would lose his life). Absalom had Amnon murdered. Solomon would have Adonijah murdered.

The LORD's Centrality in the Plot of Esther

A remarkable feature of the Book of Esther is the complete absence of the name of God. It is agreed that this feature must have been intentional. This omission does not detract from the book's theological worth, rather it enhances it. The Book of Esther affirms that the God who appears hidden nevertheless remains present. According to Michael V. Fox, four types of evidence can be adduced to demonstrate God's presence and activity in the Esther story: allusions, coincidences, reversals, and themes.[50]

Various statements have been thought to allude to God. In point of fact, both Esther and Mordecai believe that their God is present. When Esther instructs Mordecai to "gather together all the Jews who are in Susa, and fast for me" (4:16), she is expressing a belief in the efficacy of prayer. (In the OT fasting is associated with praying.) Mordecai's words to Esther in 4:14 reveal his belief in the certainty of divine deliverance.

Esther 9:1 reads, "On this day the enemies of the Jews had hoped to overpower them, but now the tables were turned and the Jews got the upper hand over those who hated them." The verse provokes the question, Turned by whom? The answer is obvious: God.

The "coincidences" reported in the Book of Esther cannot be mere chance; God surely brought them to pass. The coincidences include: the timely vacancy of the queenship at the Persian court, the opportune accession of a Jew to queenship, Mordecai's discovery of the eunuchs' conspiracy, Esther's favorable reception by the king, the king's insomnia, Haman's early arrival at the palace, and Haman's reckless plea for mercy at Esther's feet.[51]

The author consistently uses the technique of reversal (peripety) to highlight the providential intervention of God. Take note of these examples.

---

[50]Michael V. Fox, *Character and Ideology in the Book of Esther* (Columbia, SC: University of South Carolina Press, 1991), p. 240.
[51]Ibid., p. 241.

3:1 After these events, King Xerxes honored Haman son of Hammedatha, the Agagite, elevating him and giving him a seat of honor higher than that of all the other nobles.

10:3 Mordecai the Jew was second in rank to King Xerxes, preeminent among the Jews, and held in high esteem by his many fellow Jews.

3:7 . . . they cast the pur (that is, the lot) in the presence of Haman to select a day and month. And the lot fell on the twelfth month, the month of Adar.

9:24-25 For Haman son of Hammedatha, the Agagite, the enemy of all the Jews, had plotted against the Jews to destroy them and had cast the pur (that is, the lot) for their ruin and destruction. But when the plot came to the king's attention, he issued written orders that the evil scheme Haman had devised against the Jews should come back onto his own head, and that he and his sons should be hanged on the gallows.

3:10 So the king took the signet ring off his finger and gave it to Haman son of Hammedatha, the Agagite, the enemy of the Jews.

8:2a The king took off his signet ring, which he had reclaimed from Haman, and presented it to Mordecai.

3:11b and do with the people as you please

8:8a Now write another decree in the king's name in behalf of the Jews as seems best to you.

4:1 When Mordecai learned of all that had been done, he tore his clothes, put on sackcloth and ashes, and went out into the city, wailing loudly and bitterly.

8:15a Mordecai left the king's presence wearing royal garments of blue and white, a large crown of gold and a purple robe of fine linen. And the city of Susa held a joyous celebration.

4:3 In every province to which the edict and order of the king came, there was great mourning among the Jews, with fasting, weeping and wailing. Many lay on sackcloth and ashes.

8:17a In every province and in every city, wherever the edict of the king went, there was joy and gladness among the Jews, with feasting and celebrating.

5:14 His wife Zeresh and all his friends said to him, "Have a gallows built, seventy-five feet high, and ask the king in the morning to have Mordecai hanged on it."

7:9-10 Then Harbona, one of the eunuchs attending the king said, "A gallows seventy-five feet high stands by Haman's house. He had it made for Mordecai, who spoke up to help the king." The king said, "Hang him on it!" So they hanged Haman on the gallows he had prepared for Mordecai.

6:6-9 When Haman entered, the king asked him, "What should be done for the man the king delights to honor?" Now Haman thought to himself, "Who is there that the king would rather honor than me?" So he answered the king, "For the man the king delights to honor, have them bring a royal robe the king has worn and a horse the king has ridden, one with a royal crest placed on its head. Then let the robe and horse be entrusted to one of the king's most noble princes. Let them robe the man the king delights to honor, and lead him on the horse through the city streets, proclaiming before him, 'This is what is done for the man the king delights to honor!'"

6:11-12 So Haman got the robe and the horse. He robed Mordecai, and led him on horseback through the city streets, proclaiming before him, "This is what is done for the man the king delights to honor!" Afterward Mordecai returned to the king's gate. But Haman rushed home, with his head covered in grief.

Finally, the presence of religious themes bears witness to God's presence. For example, the deliverance of the Jewish people from Haman's attempted genocide is clear enough, for they are the people of God's covenant. Just as God delivered his people from Egyptian servitude and this freedom is celebrated annually with the Passover, now God has delivered his people from the threat of genocide, and this is remembered annually by celebrating Purim.

Elijah and Elisha

Before Elijah was translated to heaven, Elisha asked to inherit a double portion of his predecessor's spirit (2 Kgs 2:9). Elisha did not want to excel his master — that is, to possess twice as much of the Spirit as his master had. He used terminology from inheritance laws (Deut 21:17) to make known his desire to inherit his master's prophetic ministry.[52] Elisha wants to be seen as Elijah's firstborn prophetic son.

David A. Dorsey has conjectured that the "double portion" may be understood with reference to the number of episodes devoted to Elijah — seven — and then to Elisha — fourteen.[53] A tradition in earlier Judaism says that Elisha actually outdid (twice as much) his mentor in working signs and wonders.[54] This is borne out by the text, as the following chart shows.[55]

ELIJAH	ELISHA
(1) The shutting up of heaven (I Kgs 17:1)	(1) Dividing the Jordan (2 Kgs 2:13-14)
	(2) Healing the water (2:19-22)
(2) The miracle of flour and oil (17:16)	(3) The mauling of the "young men" (2:24)
	(4) The miracle of water (3:17)
(3) The miracle of life — a dead son brought back to life (17:22-23)	(5) The miracle of the widow's oil (4:1-7)
	(6) Raising the widow's son (4:32-37)

---

[52]*Targum Jonathan of the Former Prophets* reads, "May there be a double share in the spirit of your prophecy with me" (Daniel J. Harrington and Anthony J. Saldarini, *Targum Jonathan of the Former Prophets*, The Aramaic Bible [Wilmington, DE: Michael Glazier, 1987], 10:267).

[53]David A. Dorsey, *The Literary Structure of the Old Testament* (Grand Rapids: Baker, 1999), p. 139.

[54]In the Babylonian Talmud, tractate *Sanhedrin* (47a), reference is made to the one resurrection associated with Elijah (1 Kgs 17:22-23) and the two associated with Elisha (2 Kgs 4:37 and 13:20-21).

[55]E.W. Bullinger, *Number in Scripture* (Grand Rapids: Kregel, 1969; repr. from 1st ed. published 1894), pp. 202-203.

(4) The miracle of fire — the contest on Mount Carmel (18:38)	(7) Healing the stew (4:40-41) (8) The feeding of a hundred (4:42-44)
(5) The miracle of rain (18:41-45)	(9) The healing of Naaman (5:1-19) (10) Gehazi's leprosy (5:20-27)
(6) Another miracle of fire (2 Kgs 1:10)	(11) A floating axhead (6:6-7) (12) Opening the eyes of a servant (6:17)
(7) Yet another miracle of fire (2 Kgs 1:12)	(13) The blinding of the army (6:18) (14) Opening the eyes of an army (6:20)
(8) The miracle of parted water — dividing the Jordan (2 Kgs 2:8)	(15) A prophecy of famine and siege (7:1-20) (16) A dead man raised (13:20-21)

CONCLUSION

I conclude this essay by quoting the last sentence from Robert Alter's classic volume, *The Art of Biblical Narrative*: "Subsequent religious tradition has by and large encouraged us to take the Bible seriously rather than to enjoy it, but the paradoxical truth of the matter may well be that by learning to enjoy the biblical stories more fully as stories, we shall also come to see more clearly what they mean to tell us about God, man, and the perilously momentous realm of history."[56]

THE BIBLE AND ARCHAEOLOGY[57]
Dale W. Manor

The Bible and archaeology. Visions of Indiana Jones and adventure often invade the imagination. The pursuit, however, is much more mundane, and paradoxically more important than these fanciful images. For a long time, believers have had an appreciation of archaeology as a resource to prove the Bible, but this use needs

---

[56]Robert Alter, *The Art of Biblical Narrative* (New York: Basic Books, 1981), p. 189.

[57]Because of the nature of this volume, the focus of this essay is on archaeology as it relates primarily to the Hebrew Bible.

modification as we consider more carefully the intersection of the two disciplines.

THE BIBLE

While the modern believer usually has some understanding of the nature of the Bible, for the purposes of this discussion, it is necessary to emphasize a few points that relate more directly to the issue of how archaeology and the Bible intersect. The Bible is an anthology of sixty-six books with a unifying theme that presents God's theological and ethical teachings in a variety of contexts — they are not arbitrary statements divorced from their social or cultural surroundings.

The Old Testament is the story of a people whose homeland centered in Canaan.[58] Because the primary purpose of the biblical narrative is to explain and expound God's interactions with his people, the Bible contains little about everyday life or politics, except as these impinge upon the overarching themes or story development. Furthermore, the books of the Bible were written in contexts in which the authors assumed the readers understood the circumstances of the writing, hence much of the background material is missing.[59] This background, however, is vital to a fuller understanding of the messages.

We address certain aspects of the historical context when we ask such questions as: "Who wrote the text?" "To whom was it written and when?" "What issues are of concern in the book or letter?" Likewise, attention to the language in which the text was originally written

---

[58]A number of terms apply to the region. Canaan is often used to refer to the land before the Israelites arrived. The term Palestine derives linguistically from the Philistines (פְּלִשְׁתִּי, *Pᵊlištî*) and its appropriation by Herodotus to refer to the land (*Histories* 1.105 et al.). The Bible will often refer to the land as Israel or Israel and Judah, depending upon the focus of the discussion.

[59]A modern example of this assumed familiarity might be if one were to discover a cache of letters that his/her grandfather and grandmother exchanged. The grandchild would be able to understand a good bit of the correspondence, but there would inevitably be allusions and references to events, people, and conversations that have no elaboration because they were shared experiences with an assumed familiarity between them. The young reader would be at a loss to understand some of these statements without additional investigation, and for some of them there may never be adequate explanation.

(syntax, idioms, figures of speech, and so forth) reflect our desire to read the text in light of its original historical setting.

Other information that helps to place the events, and sometimes even conversations, in perspective are environmental matters such as geography, weather patterns, wildlife and animal use, and the kind of wild and domestic vegetation that existed in the region.[60] These impact agricultural practices and daily life concerns and in turn affect the development of social customs as people sought to survive in often-harsh surroundings.[61]

Inevitably, as people congregate, they must organize to maintain social equilibrium and stability. Leaders will arise in the form of judges or kings. Inevitably, the social structures find themselves at odds with their neighbors who precipitate conflicts. Israel's demand for a king was based not only on their desire to be like their neighbors (1 Sam 8:5), but also the threats posed by the Philistines (1 Samuel 13) and the Ammonites (1 Sam 12:12). Almost inevitably, larger political powers arise (Syria, Assyria, Babylonia, Persia, Greece) which affect the balance of life as the oppressors demand subservience and tribute. Hence, in varying degrees political systems impact the daily lives of the people.

These issues would be understood by the people to whom the books were originally written, but we are separated from those events by thousands of miles, thousands of years, advances in technology, and differing cultural norms. The more we understand about the larger context of the Bible's events, the better equipped we are to understand more precisely God's expectations of them and to extrapolate his expectations of us.

---

[60]Generally, the environment and geography of the land of Canaan find parallels in Arizona and southern California. It is inaccurate to assume that their struggles for survival would characterize the same efforts of the South or the Northeast United States where rain and vegetation are much more readily abundant.

[61]The Bible occasionally speaks of early and late rains (cf. Deut 11:14; Jer 5:24; Joel 2:23) which are very distinct periods with additional rains rare outside those bounds (part of the significance of Samuel's sign in 1 Samuel 12:17-18 was that it was not the rain season). In addition, the tendency under normal circumstances is that the amount of rainfall is inconsistent from year to year, rendering their survival precarious at best.

ARCHAEOLOGY

The word "archaeology" derives from two ancient Greek words: ἀρχαῖος (*archaios*) meaning "ancient" and λόγος (*logos*) meaning "word" < "study of." Even in the ancient world, the compound word was used for "*antiquarian lore, ancient legends* or *history*"[62] as indicated in Josephus's *Jewish Antiquities.*[63]

We do not refer to ancient history as archaeology; ancient history is usually considered a study of much earlier times. In modern academic circles, archaeology is a subdiscipline of anthropology. Strictly speaking, anthropology is the study of humanity and includes essentially everything that human beings do. Anthropology is subdivided into four categories: cultural anthropology, physical anthropology, linguistics, and archaeology. Cultural anthropology studies the rules that govern human interaction with one another and how art, law, morals, religion, and custom factor into that interaction. Physical anthropology studies the physical traits and developments of people as well as their genetic connections. Linguistics attempts to trace and analyze the languages of humanity, tracing their development and how cultural and social issues may have contributed to the language developments and differentiations. Archaeology deals with the physical remains of human behavior.[64] In many ways archaeology involves all four disciplines as finds come to light that require the various anthropological disciplines to understand them. A functional definition of modern archaeology is a study of "past societies primarily through their material remains — the buildings, tools, and other artifacts that constitute what is known as the *material culture* left over from former societies."[65]

People often think of archaeology as a science. Modern archaeology tries to formulate and test hypotheses in an attempt to produce

---

[62]Henry George Liddell and Robert Scott, *A Greek-English Lexicon*, rev. by H.S. Jones (Oxford: Clarendon Press, 1968), p. 251.

[63]Josephus's word, "Antiquities," is the Greek word ἀρχαιολογία (*archaiologia*).

[64]Recent developments, however, have begun to use archaeological technique and theory to study modern human activity. By studying living cultures, we can begin to identify the patterning of the artifacts of ancient peoples — this use is part of ethnoarchaeology. For more modern application, archaeologists can study people's disposal patterns and draw inferences about human behavior that we may not otherwise reveal in verbal descriptions of what we believe or think.

[65]Colin Renfrew and Paul Bahn, *Archaeology: Theories, Methods, and Practices*, 3d ed. (New York: Thames & Hudson, 2000), p. 9.

explanatory models. To assist in this endeavor, many scientific disciplines inform the investigative process. Archaeologists rely upon botany to identify plant remains and zoology to identify animal bones and their possible uses.[66] Geography and geology are important to identify environmental factors that contribute to strategies of survival. Chemistry can help identify trace elements in vessels.[67] Physics and nuclear sciences can help date artifacts as well as identify similarities and dissimilarities in clay sources.[68] Statistics can assist in calculating probabilities and distribution and clustering of artifacts.

Archaeology, however, might be considered one of the humanities. It deals with "prehistory"[69] and history (our primary focus).

---

[66]With such investigations, archaeologists can reconstruct the basic dietary components of ancient peoples and see how they might have used the animals. A good zooarchaeologist not only can identify the species of animals in the archaeological record, but can also often identify the ages at which death occurred, the ways in which they were killed, and sometimes even the purposes for which they were killed (for sacrifices, for diet, or of natural causes). Bone analysis at the site of Tel Beth-shemesh has revealed only one possible pig bone from occupation levels of the site after the Israelites arrived, whereas contemporary Philistine sites to the west have yielded significant numbers of pig bones (Shlomo Bunimovitz and Zvi Lederman, "Beth-Shemesh: Culture Conflict on Judah's Frontier," *BAR* 23 [1997]: 48-49, and private communication). This faunal data dovetails perfectly with the Levitical kosher laws applicable to the Hebrews (Leviticus 11).

[67]Trace analysis of the contents of certain unique ceramic juglets have revealed that some of them had contained opiate derivatives (Robert S. Merrillees, "Opium for the Masses: How the Ancients Got High," *Odyssey* 2 [1999]: 20-29, 58). These juglets originally came from Cyprus implying a trade network; the juglet design may have been a kind of marketing strategy.

[68]Neutron activation permits scholars to identify clay sources from which pottery was made. This information can often reveal long-distance trade connections. Some of the storage jars at Kuntillet 'Ajrud (where the famous "May you be blessed by YHWH and his Asherah" inscription is found) are made out of clay sources that came from Judah (Jan Gunneweg, Isadore Perlman, and Zeev Meshel, "The Origin of the Pottery of Kuntillet 'Ajrud," *IEJ* 35 [1985]: 270-283).

[69]Technically, prehistory deals with the period before writing. The prehistoric era can vary significantly with the region under consideration. For Mesopotamia and Egypt, it is before ca. 3500 B.C. For the Americas, it would be before the Mayas (ca. 500 A.D.). Australia's prehistory is before 1788 A.D. when the British took over the island. Even after these respective dates, the history in these regions remains inevitably spotty. The literature without exception leaves gaps in its record — there are things that are not written down. As time passes and writing becomes more common, the gaps reduce.

Historical studies try to describe the mechanics of people's social and cultural interactions and then to explain *why* those societies and cultures behaved as they did (i.e., what forces prompted the people to behave as they did). This investigation, of course, cannot rely solely upon the hard data of antiquity extracted through the sciences, but it must try to identify the beliefs, motives, artistry, feelings, and opinions of the ancient society.

The archaeologist relies upon various academic disciplines to assist in the interpretation of the finds. But the finds themselves will be only partial collections of the activities of antiquity. Written records (texts and inscriptions), which would be valuable to reveal what the people might have thought, are rare for much of the biblical period. Given the paucity of written sources and the friability of the archaeological record,[70] archaeology remains the only avenue by which to reconstruct that world. In addition it is essentially impossible to collect, examine, and properly evaluate every piece of evidence that might have been preserved. Furthermore, the investigator will inevitably be challenged to describe the finds with exactness (e.g., how precisely do you describe the color "red"?) or to identify and explain how an artifact might have been used (without some ancient instruction manual). Much more difficult is a determination of what the ancient society thought of the artifact (e.g., the "meaning" attached to it). Regretfully, these variables inject into the archaeological enterprise an element of subjectivity that some people overlook and others exaggerate.

RELATION OF ARCHAEOLOGY AND THE BIBLE

There is an ongoing debate about whether archaeology can or does prove the Bible. Archaeologists generally no longer pursue the

---

[70]The archaeological record by nature preserves only a fraction of the entire range of human activity. While artifacts reflect some kind of mental activity, the meanings behind them are often elusive without written records to explain them. Furthermore, before the advent of extensive use of plastics and metals, much of the material of antiquity was susceptible to fairly rapid decay or recycling. The preservation of the body and weapons of the "Ice Man" (David Roberts, "The Ice Man: Lone Voyager from the Copper Age," *National Geographic* 183 [1993]: 36-67) in the Alps demonstrates an exceptional array of materials that normally is not preserved. Other examples are the tomb discoveries of Egypt, which, if they have survived plundering, are preserved largely because of the exceptional environmental contexts of their deposition.

discipline with this agenda. There were efforts by some in earlier years to do so, but the nature of the evidence is such that these expectations are unrealistic and tend to skew one's investigation. In some areas, archaeology has meshed well with the Bible,[71] but in others, significant tensions exist. Some of the tensions may arise from the presuppositions of the investigator.[72] Some of the prevailing theories of how archaeology relates (or should relate) to the Bible stand at odds with the statements in the Bible, but given the nature of academic investigation, the theories almost inevitably will change, while the text remains fairly static.

De Vaux has stated:

> Archaeology does not confirm the text, which is what it is, it can only confirm the interpretation we give it. If the results of archaeology seem to be opposed to the conclusions of text criticism, the reason may perhaps be that not enough archaeological facts are known or that they have not been firmly established; the reason may also be that the text has been wrongly interpreted. Accord

---

[71]The traditional identification of the Hittites is a classic case in point. Additionally, the general origins of the Sea Peoples (for the purposes of the Old Testament, the Philistines) have been confirmed by archaeological investigation — both sources attribute their origins to the general region of the Mycenaean/Greek world (cf. Jer 47:4; Amos 9:7 with studies of the Philistines and Sea Peoples [Trude Dothan, *The Philistines and Their Material Culture* (Jerusalem: Israel Exploration Society, 1982); and N.K. Sandars, *The Sea Peoples: Warriors of the Ancient Mediterranean*, rev. ed. (London: Thames & Hudson, 1985)]).

[72]The simple issue of whether one believes that miracles could have occurred inevitably colors the interpretation of what could and could not have happened. Modern historians tend to discount miracles in their effort to reconstruct biblical history (see explicitly J. Maxwell Miller and John H. Hayes, *A History of Ancient Israel and Judah* [Philadelphia: Westminster, 1986], p. 59; and generally Eta Linnemann, *Historical Criticism of the Bible: Methodology or Ideology?* trans. by R.W. Yarbrough [Grand Rapids: Baker, 1990]). In fairness, we must recognize that some miracles are God's timing of natural events to occur. Many of the plagues of Egypt were natural-type events, which otherwise could occasionally occur (frogs, gnats, flies disease, locust, etc.); elements of the miracles were their timing and strategic placement. Conservatives often tend to believe that all miracles are full suspensions of natural events. The believer, however, will recognize that some miracles *are* suspension of natural law (a burning bush that is not consumed; death of only the firstborn in a given night; Jesus walking on water; the resurrection, etc.).

must finally be achieved between these two means of knowing historical reality, but it can not and must not be attained by a tendentious use of archaeological facts. If biblical studies have suffered from an excess of textual criticism, the remarkable and beneficial growth and progress of archaeology must not be permitted to lead to an opposite excess.[73]

This approach assumes that the two data sources of the Bible and archaeology can somehow intersect, and probably for the believer, this assumption will drive the effort.

In many ways it is unrealistic to expect much of the archaeological enterprise to relate specifically to the events or people of the Bible. For instance, the Bible narrates that Abraham traveled and lived in the countryside. Archaeology might tell us something about nomadic living, but it is unlikely that archaeology would "prove" any specific details of his life.

If the primary concern of archaeology is not to prove the Bible is true, what contributions might we expect it to offer biblical studies? Perhaps an answer can be found in the parallels between archaeology and history. The French historian, Fernand Braudel, has suggested three levels of history. The first he calls "the long duration," which he defines as a history ". . . whose passage is almost imperceptible, that of man in his relationship to his environment, a history in which all change is slow, a history of constant repetition, ever-recurring cycles."[74] For the archaeologist this would be the historical arena of human interaction with the environment — human survival strategies, modes of production, reproduction, and technological strategies used in self-sustenance.

Braudel's second tier of history is ". . . social history, the history of groups and groupings. . . . studying in turn economic systems, states, societies, civilizations. . . ." For the archaeologist, the manifestation of this level is evident in the study of macro-social organizations such as tribes, city-states, states, and nations.

The third tier is what Braudel calls the "history of events" and discusses the specifics of human existence. This level is manifest in the

---

[73]Roland de Vaux, "On Right and Wrong Uses of Archaeology," in *New Eastern Archaeology in the Twentieth Century: Essays in Honor of Nelson Glueck*, ed. by J.A. Sanders (Garden City, NY: Dubleday, 1970), p. 78.

[74]Fernand Braudel, *The Mediterranean and the Mediterranean World in the Age of Philip II*, vol. 1, trans. S. Reynolds (New York: Harper & Row, 1972), pp. 20-21.

events, regimes, and individuals of history. For the Bible, it would be the evidence of battles, kings, and prophets. This level is perhaps the most exciting and is traditionally the arena of the "prove-the-Bible" philosophy; it would be where the confirmation of Abraham as a person would exist, but the brevity of the battle or person tends to make the nature of the evidence ephemeral and elusive.

If we use Braudel's categories, it is clear that archaeology lends itself better to the "long duration," by unearthing and providing data indicative of the everyday life of people's existence. The higher up the tiered structure one moves, the less likely is the archaeologist to find specific data that relate to individual people or events.

A major methodological understanding in any enterprise is to recognize the limited range of questions that the discipline might answer. Archaeology does not provide answers to all the questions that we might conceivably ask. The questions we pose to archaeology must respect the data base providing the answers.[75]

When we consider the full range of human existence and experience, only a fraction of that will be preserved in any way since much of it decays and is removed from the scene.[76] Of those that are preserved, written works are a significantly smaller range of representation. Artifacts and materials directly related to the Bible and its record are minuscule in proportion to the variety and volume of the archaeological record.

It is true that archaeology has discovered some remarkable finds that mesh well with the biblical texts — references to David, Ahab, Jehu, Jeremiah, Hezekiah, and others (the third tier of Braudel's thesis) — but these are few in relation to the mass of material connected with everyday life (the bottom tier). Archaeology has done a remarkable job in bringing to light the daily life situations of the periods of the Bible; finds directly related to the biblical story are regretfully few, but when they occur they can be sensational.

---

[75]The Bible tacitly implies this limited range of answers. Moses states that "The secret things belong to the Lord our God, but the things revealed belong to us and to our children forever, that we may follow all the words of this law" (Deut 29:29). In other words, while God expects people to obey what he has revealed, there are things that he has not revealed and the Bible is not the source of answers to those questions (e.g., the Bible says nothing of *why* the sky is blue).

[76]Jesus alludes to this reality when he states that "moth and rust destroy, and . . . thieves break in and steal" (Matt 6:19).

Sadly, there is often a tendency to seek a premature correspondence of archaeological finds with the Bible. Many of the claims of the discovery of Noah's ark, the ark of the covenant, the discovery of Sodom and Gomorrah, the site of the crossing of the Red Sea, the identification of Sinai, the burial box of Jesus' brother, etc. have created significant stir in conservative religious circles. Many of these deserve serious investigation, but the claims are often on very shaky foundations with minimal, if any, evidence. It is disconcerting and seriously hurts the cause of the believer to make claims that are unsubstantiated and which many times require retraction. The effect to the skeptical searcher will likely be further skepticism than faith. It is vitally important that we recognize that faith should rest in the reality of Jesus' resurrection, not in the specific identification of the site of his tomb or burial. If and when we find evidence from archaeology that meshes with the Bible, our faith may be corroborated, but it should not rest primarily upon that basis.

There is, though, an additional way in which archaeology relates to biblical studies. Some occasionally argue that, since the Bible is a book two thousand years old, it cannot relate to modern times because times have changed so much. The argument is specious in that it assumes that modern technological circumstances have vitiated the message of the Bible.[77] A study of the Bible's context demonstrates a sophistication far beyond what many people are aware. Our failure or refusal to recognize the sophistication of the ancients reflects an intellectual arrogance. This is demonstrated in the refusal of some to believe that the Egyptians built the pyramids, since we have not determined how they did it. The line of argument appears to be that since we, with our insights, do not know how they built them, then the Egyptians could not have built them. Therefore they must have been built by space aliens![78]

We will consider briefly the sophistication of the biblical world in customs, technology, trade, and government. The Bible has sev-

---

[77]One should concede that technology has complicated the application of the Bible's truths, but that does not necessarily mean its message is irrelevant. The ability of modern science to gene-splice and clone, for instance, has raised questions of concern, but perhaps the difficulty of applying the Bible's teaching is more a commentary on the obstinacy of humanity than it is on the irrelevance of the Bible.

[78]Such "reasoning" has penetrated popular "science" television programs and can trace some of its roots to Erich von Daniken's *Chariots of the Gods? Unsolved Mysteries of the Past* (London: Souvenir, 1969).

eral prohibitions against "moving the ancient landmarks" (Deut 19:14; 27:17; Prov 22:28; 23:10; Hos 5:10). Studies in archaeology and ancient customs reveal that the ancient landmarks were related to property rights. God expressed his concern for the well-being of the people and especially for the widow and orphan by prohibiting the illicit movement of the boundary markers related to the family inheritances. He also required a building code that houses be built with walls around the perimeters of their roofs to prevent people from falling off (Deut 22:8).[79]

Technology in the ancient world can be seen in the ability of the people to dig sophisticated water systems to provide for their towns. Exemplary among these are the twelfth–eighth century water shaft and system at Gibeon[80] and the 210,000 gallon capacity cistern from the tenth-century Tel Beth-shemesh.[81] Hazor preserves well-made ceramic drainage pipes from the nineteenth–eighteenth centuries B.C.[82] Very ornate ivory carvings have been found from Ahab's Samaria.[83] Surgical procedures including skull trephination[84] and dentistry fillings[85] have been preserved from the eighth and third-second centuries respectively.

Ancient trade has already been mentioned with reference to the opiate trade. But long-distance trade can be seen in the shipments of talents of copper ingots in the thirteenth–twelfth centuries B.C. and discovered in excavations of shipwrecks.[86] In addition, the Assyrians facilitated the production of an olive oil industry centered in Ekron in the seventh century B.C. which produced an estimated 1.1

---

[79]The roof was used for multiple activities. Rahab dried flax on the roof (Joshua 2). After an afternoon nap David was strolling on the roof of his palace when he saw Bathsheba (2 Sam 11:2). Saul slept on the roof when Samuel met him and initially anointed him (1 Sam 9:25-26).

[80]James B. Pritchard, *The Water System of Gibeon* (Philadelphia: University Museum, 1961), pp. 22-23.

[81]Bunimovitz and Lederman, "Beth-Shemesh," pp. 42-49, 75-77.

[82]Yigael Yadin et al., *Hazor: The Third and Fourth Seasons, 1957–1958* (Jerusalem: The Magnes Press, 1961), pl. XXX.2-3.

[83]Nahman Avigad, "Samaria (City)," *NEAEHL*, 4:1304-1306.

[84]David Ussishkin, "Lachish," *NEAEHL*, 3:908-909.

[85]Joseph Zias and Karen Numeroff, "Ancient Dentistry in the Eastern Mediterranean: A Brief Review," *IEJ* 36 (1986): 65-67.

[86]Cf. George F. Bass, "A Pioneering Excavation off Turkey: Lessons from a Bronze Age Wreck," in *Archaeology under Water: An Atlas of the World's Submerged Sites*, ed. by K. Muckelroy (New York: McGraw-Hill, 1980), pp. 32-35.

million liters of oil a year,[87] some of which was shipped to Egypt and the Aegean.[88]

Government showed significant growth as it demanded taxes. Caches of silver nuggets from the tenth–ninth centuries have been found at Eshtemoa which may have been collected for transfer to the central government. The rate was apparently 20 percent as implied by inscriptions on two of the juglets.[89]

A host of additional points could be listed. The people of the ancient world were quite sophisticated in their abilities to deal with the world around them. Admittedly, our world is far more technologically based; ultimately, however, the Bible focuses more upon the attitudes that drive people's behavior. It primarily addresses the question of sin, not technology.[90] Fair-minded people should recognize that while we may be able to steal electronically, lust using the internet, or kill with high technology equipment from long distances, the problems still spring from the heart.[91]

Archaeology and historical studies can demonstrate that the technical execution of human behavior may have evolved, but the ancients were more sophisticated than we often give them credit for being. The basic concerns of human beings, however, have been consistent: we still wrestle with questions of origins, with how to cope with our environment, with questions of survival, with concerns for family, with questions of why there is evil, with where we will go after this life. To these kinds of questions, archaeology demonstrates a basic sameness of humanity. This being the case, archaeology demonstrates that times have not changed, we have simply applied a technological veneer: the Bible is still relevant.

---

[87]Seymour Gitin, "Tel Miqne-Ekron: A Type-Site for the Inner Coastal Plain in the Iron Age II Period," *Recent Excavations in Israel: Studies in Iron Age Archaeology*, ed. by S. Gitin and W.G. Dever, AASOR 49 (Winona Lake, IN: ASOR, 1989), p. 48.

[88]Seymour Gitin, "Ekron of the Philistines: Part II: Olive-Oil Suppliers to the World." *BAR* 16 (1990): 40.

[89]Zeev Yeivin, "Eshtemoa," *NEAEHL*, 2:426.

[90]God is apparently concerned with what we actually do, and technology may complicate the application of the Bible, but the principles of God's word transcend the technical to try to change people's hearts.

[91]And so the Bible teaches: "Above all else, guard your heart, for it is the wellspring of life" (Prov 4:23). Jesus elaborates: "For from within, out of men's hearts, come evil thoughts, sexual immorality, theft, murder, adultery, greed, malice, deceit, lewdness, envy, slander, arrogance and folly. All these evils come from inside and make a man 'unclean'"(Mark 7:21-23).

BRIEF HISTORY OF ARCHAEOLOGY[92]

Even though the academic discipline of archaeology is relatively young, the interest in antiquities is itself an ancient phenomenon which can be traced back at least to the Assyrians and Assurbanipal who collected earlier written records in what we often call a library.[93]

In more modern times, a significant event occurred during Napoleon's expedition to Egypt in 1798–99, when the Rosetta Stone was discovered. Using the Greek text of the trilingual text — in hieroglyphs, Demotic,[94] and Greek — Jean François Champollion (1790–1832) was able in modern times finally to decipher the Egyptian hieroglyphs. This breakthrough paved the way to translating the previously incomprehensible hieroglyphic texts from Egypt.

Eventually the British established the Palestine Exploration Fund (1865), part of whose rationale was to respond to the implications of Darwin's *Origin of Species* and the text-critical work of Julius Wellhausen and his German colleagues. It was to be ". . . a society for the accurate and systematic investigation of the archaeology, topography, geology and physical geography, natural history, manners and customs of the Holy Land, for biblical illustration."[95] One of the first projects was to send C.R. Condor and H.H. Kitchener to Palestine to produce detailed maps of the Holy Land. From 1871–1877, they mapped some 6,000 square miles of Palestine. Their diligence produced the best maps available for the region until the advent of modern aerial cartography.

---

[92]A convenient general history of archaeology appears in Keith N. Schoville (*Biblical Archaeology in Focus* [Grand Rapids: Baker, 1978], pp. 79-93), Neil Asher Silberman (*Digging for God and Country: Exploration, Archeology, and the Secret Struggle for the Holy Land, 1799–1917* [New York: Alfred A. Knopf, 1982]), and Philip J. King (*American Archaeology in the Mideast: A History of the American Schools of Oriental Research* [Philadelphia: ASOR, 1983]). For a history of method and theory in Syro-Palestinian (i.e., "Biblical") Archaeology, see William G. Dever (*Archaeology and Biblical Studies: Retrospects and Prospects*, Winslow Lectures, 1972 [Evanston, IL: Seabury-Western Theological Seminary, 1974]; "The Impact of the 'New Archaeology' on Syro-Palestinian Archaeology," *BASOR* 242 [1981]: 15-30) and Thomas W. Davis (*Shifting Sands: The Rise and Fall of Biblical Archaeology* [New York: Oxford University, 2004]).

[93]Much of our knowledge of ancient Mesopotamian literature derives from Assurbanipal's collection.

[94]Demotic is a simplified, vernacular cursive form of the Egyptian language which developed in the seventh century B.C.

[95]From King, *American Archaeology*, p. 7.

The idea of modern archaeology can be traced to the brilliant career of British archaeologist, Sir William Matthews Flinders Petrie (1853–1942). In Egypt, Petrie developed the theory of relative chronology based on the stylistic variations of pottery. In 1890, he excavated the site of Tell el-Hesi in Palestine. His work was only six weeks in duration, but he noted that the ceramic styles changed with the stratigraphic sequence. With this observation he was able to demonstrate the legitimacy of ceramic typology and its implication for chronological sequencing. This simple, yet brilliant observation permitted archaeological investigations to be placed on a significantly firmer chronological base.

An unsuccessful entry into archaeology occurred with the establishment of the American Palestine Exploration Society in 1870. It folded, however, in 1877. Fortunately, academic archaeological interest in America precipitated the establishment in 1900 of the American Schools of Oriental Research, which today remains a premier force of archaeological, linguistic, and historical studies of the ancient east Mediterranean and Mesopotamian worlds.

Before World War I, archaeology was usually little more than treasure hunts in which the British, French, and Germans competed to fill their respective national museums. A notable exception of quality was George Reisner's excavation at Samaria (1908–1910) where he implemented systematic and careful excavation recording strategies. Among these were surveying, drawings, and photographs.

After World War I, archaeology matured significantly as the British and French imposed more stringent controls and standards on the expedition projects in their Mandate regions. The impacts of the national schools began to become apparent, although the excavation techniques themselves were still somewhat deficient. There was little concern for stratigraphic excavation and research designs were poor if they existed at all.

William Foxwell Albright (1891–1971) brought a new sophistication to archaeology with his genius ability to trace ceramic typology and, at least intuitively, to use it to trace the stratigraphy at the sites.[96] Albright's advance of archaeology did not always have an effect on the major projects of the period.

---

[96]It appears that Albright used his genius understanding of ceramic typology sometimes to create some of the stratigraphic observations that he proposed.

Significant expeditions include those at Megiddo (1921–1933, University of Chicago), Beth-shan (1921–1933, University of Pennsylvania), Jericho (1930–1936, John Garstang of British School of Archaeology in Jerusalem), Tell Beit Mirsim (1926–1932; Wm. F. Albright), and Lachish (1932–1938; aka: Tell ed-Duweir by J.L. Starkey). While these projects produced huge volumes of material, their use for historical and cultural reconstruction is limited by the lack of method and theory that characterized them.

The period after World War II, from ca. 1945–1970 is often referred to as the period of "Biblical Archaeology" in which many scholars approached the enterprise with an agenda to demonstrate the legitimacy of the Bible. Among these personalities were George Ernest Wright and his work at Shechem, Yigael Yadin and the Hazor project, and Benjamin Mazar's work in Jerusalem.

Somewhat outside this stream is the work of Kathleen Kenyon and her project at Jericho. Kenyon was not a biblical scholar in any sense of the term but had been trained strictly in archaeology at the feet of Sir Mortimer Wheeler. She did, however, introduce into the Palestinian world the technique of careful, systematic excavation and recording that permit better reconstruction of the site. Her techniques, now refined and modified, dominate essentially any project in the Levantine world.

Moving the discipline further was William G. Dever. Dever had been raised as a missionary's son and attended Milligan College and then Butler University before going to Harvard where he studied and worked with George Ernest Wright. He began to clamor for a separation of archaeology from biblical studies. He contended that for too long, archaeology had been simply a subsidiary of biblical studies and that as long as that relationship existed, the full potential of the data from the archaeology of the biblical world would be stunted. He argued that if they separated and were allowed to develop independently, the time would come when they could inform each other as equals and a greater understanding of each discipline would ensue.[97]

Part of this separation recognized that archaeology needed to become multidisciplinary in scope and not focus just on chronology or as a source to illustrate the Bible. Hence there was a need to look at the kinds of questions that archaeological circles in other parts of

---

[97]See Dever, *Archaeology*, and "'New Archaeology.'"

the world were asking, to begin to look at the larger picture of the human process, to formulate hypotheses and test them in the excavation project, and to incorporate the insights that chemistry, physics, geology, botany, zoology, etc. can contribute.

To a large extent, these goals have begun to be implemented in most excavation projects in the Middle East. As far as biblical studies are concerned, the archaeological database of information has exploded and has allowed archaeologists and biblical historians to begin to integrate the independent academic disciplines to provide a fuller picture of the world of the Old Testament — along the lines of the three-tiered proposal from Braudel. A deficiency that is now often apparent in the literature of both disciplines is a failure to know what the other is doing. Regretfully, many of the works in each arena, therefore, are written as if the other did not exist.

CONCLUSION AND PROSPECTS

The pessimism implied in the last paragraph can be remedied, and in doing so, the two disciplines can more effectively contribute to each other. The more one knows and understands about the world of the Bible, the better equipped the disciple will be to appreciate the nuances of the Bible, the richness of God's interactions with his people, and on occasions that knowledge will serve to correct our understanding.

To accomplish this greater, enhanced understanding, some strategies still need implementation:

1) It is necessary to recognize that the basic concerns and needs of humanity remain the same; the differences in humanity through time are more in technological application.
2) The disciplines of biblical studies and archaeology must continue as independent pursuits, as Dever maintains, to flourish and develop without a subservient relationship of one to the other.
3) Having affirmed that archaeology and biblical studies must remain independent disciplines, they must simultaneously maintain (and in some cases establish) cross-disciplinary communication, recognizing that neither operates in a vacuum.
4) Each discipline must understand the inevitable limitations that each brings to the enterprise of historical reconstruction. The databases within which each operates are different and each supplies information that the other does not.

5) Scholars in each discipline must be more aware of the philosophical assumptions that they bring to the investigation.
6) Archaeology must continue to develop its interdisciplinary approach. This investigation is necessary since archaeology fundamentally investigates the material remains related to any domain of human activity from which remains might be preserved. Some of the evidence can only be extracted with science-based investigation.

With this broader application, a greater insight into the world of the Bible and God's interaction with humanity will be accomplished.

PENTATEUCH

RANDALL BAILEY

BIBLIOGRAPHY FOR
THE PENTATEUCH

Albright, W.F. *From the Stone Age to Christianity.* 2nd ed. Garden City, NY: Doubleday, 1957.

—————. "Oracles of Balaam." *JBL* 63 (1944): 207-233.

—————. *Yahweh and the Gods of Canaan: A Historical Analysis of Two Contrasting Faiths.* New York: Doubleday, 1968.

Allis, O.T. *The Five Books of Moses,* 2nd ed. Philadelphia: Presbyterian and Reformed, 1949.

Anderson, B.W. *Understanding the Old Testament.* 3rd ed. Englewood Cliffs NJ/London: Prentice-Hall, 1978.

Archer, G.L. Jr. *A Survey of Old Testament Introduction.* Chicago: Moody, 1964.

Bailey, R.C. "Book Reviews." *CBQ* 55:1 (1993): 111-113.

—————. "Images of the Prophets: An Analysis of the Metaphors and Epithets Used in the Old Testament to Describe Prophets and Prophetic Activity." Ph.D. dissertation, Drew University, 1987.

Balentine, S.E. *The Torah's Vision of Holiness.* Minneapolis: Fortress, 1999.

Barnouin, M. *Les Recensements du livre des Nombres et l'astronomie babylonienne."* *BT* 27:3 (1977): 280-303.

Bimson, J.J. *Redating the Exodus.* JSOTSupp 5. Sheffield: JSOT, 1978.

Blenkinsopp, J. "The Documentary Hypothesis in Trouble," pp. 10-22. In *Approaches to the Bible.* 2 vols. Ed. by H. Minkoff. Washington, DC: BAS, 1994.

Bright, J. *A History of Israel.* 3rd ed. Philadelphia: Westminster, 1981.

Budd, P.J. *Numbers.* WBC. Waco, TX: Word, 1984.

Campbell, A., and M.A. O'Brien. *Sources of the Pentateuch.* Minneapolis: Fortress, 1993.

Carpenter, E.E. "Numbers, Book of." *ISBE²,* 3:561-567. Rev. ed. by G.W. Bromiley. Grand Rapids: Eerdmans, 1979.

Chavalas, M.W. "The Historian, The Believer, and the OT: A Study in the Supposed Conflict of Faith and Reason." *JETS* 36 (1993): 145-162.

Childs, B.S. *The Book of Exodus.* Philadelphia: Westminster, 1974.

_____ . *Introduction to the Old Testament as Scripture.* Philadelphia: Fortress, 1979.

Christensen, D.L. *Deuteronomy 1–11.* WBC. Waco: Word, 1991.

Clements, R.E. *One Hundred Years of Old Testament Interpretation.* Philadelphia: Westminster, 1976.

_____ . "Pentateuchal Problems." In *Tradition and Interpretation,* pp. 96-124. Ed. by G.W. Anderson. Oxford: Clarendon, 1979.

Damrosch, D. "Leviticus." In *The Literary Guide to the Bible,* pp. 66-77. Ed. by Robert Alter and Frank Kermode. Cambridge: Harvard University Press, 1987.

Davies, E.W. "A Mathematical Conundrum: The Problem of the Large Numbers in Numbers I and XXVI." *VT* 45 (1995): 449-469.

Dillard, R.B., and Tremper Longman III. *An Introduction to the Old Testament.* Grand Rapids: Zondervan, 1994.

Douglas, M. "The Forbidden Animals in Leviticus." *JSOT* 59 (1993): 3-23.

Driver, S.R. *A Critical and Exegetical Commentary on Deuteronomy.* 3rd ed. Edinburgh: T. & T. Clark, 1902.

Duvshani, M. "The Dynamic Character of the Book of Numbers." *Beth Mikra* 24 (1978): 27-32.

Elwell, W.A., ed. *The Concise Dictionary of Theology.* Grand Rapids: Baker, 1991.

Finegan, J. *Light from the Ancient Past: The Archaeological Background of Judaism and Christianity.* Princeton, NJ: Princeton University Press, 1959.

Fokkelman, J.P. "Exodus." In *The Literary Guide to the Bible,* pp. 56-65. Ed. by Robert Altar and Frank Kermode. Cambridge: Harvard University Press, 1987.

Freedman, D.N. "The Chronology of Israel and the Ancient Near East." In *The Bible and the Ancient Near East,* pp. 203-214. Ed. by G.E. Wright. Garden City, NY: Doubleday, 1961.

Friedman, R.E. *Commentary on the Torah.* San Francisco: HarperSanFrancisco, 2001.

Garbini, G. *History and Ideology in Ancient Israel.* New York: Crossroad, 1988.

Garstang, John. *Joshua–Judges.* New York: R.R. Smith, 1931.

Gordon, C.H. *Ugaritic Literature,* pp. 124f. Roma: Pontificium Institutum Biblicum, 1949.

Gray, G.B. *A Critical and Exegetical Commentary on Numbers.* Edinburgh: T. & T. Clark, 1903.

Hallo, W.W. "Biblical History in Its Near Eastern Setting: The Contextual Apporach." In *Scripture in Context*, pp. 1-26. Ed. by C.D. Evans, W.W. Hallo, and J.B. White. Pittsburg: Pickwick, 1980.

_____. "Leviticus and Ancient Near Eastern Literature." In *The Torah: A Modern Commentary*, pp. 740-748. New York: Union of American Hebrew Congregations, 1981.

_____. "Numbers and Ancient Near Eastern Literature." In *The Torah: A Modern Commentary*, pp. 1014-1023. New York: Union of American Hebrew Congregations, 1981.

Halpern, B. "The Exodus and the Israelite Historians." *ErIsr* 24 (1993): 89-96.

_____. "The Exodus from Egypt: Myth or Reality." In *The Rise of Ancient Israel*, pp. 86-117. Ed. by Hershel Shanks. Washington, DC: Biblical Archaeological Society, 1992.

_____. *The First Historians: The Hebrew Bible and History.* San Francisco: Harper and Row, 1988.

Harrison, R.K. "Deuteronomy." *ISBE*[2], 1:934-940. Rev. ed. by G.W. Bromiley. Grand Rapids: Eerdmans, 1979.

_____. *Introduction to the Old Testament.* Grand Rapids: Eerdmans, 1969.

Hartley, J.E. "Exodus: Historical Background" and "Exodus: Message." In *Old Testament Survey: The Message, Form, and Background of the Old Testament*, pp. 52-61, 63-79. 2nd ed. Ed. by W.S. Lasor, D.A. Hubbard, and F.W. Bush. Grand Rapids: Eerdmans, 1996.

_____. "Leviticus." In *Old Testament Survey: The Message, Form, and Background of the Old Testament*, pp. 80-98. 2nd ed. Ed. by W.S. Lasor, D.A. Hubbard, and F.W. Bush. Grand Rapids: Eerdmans, 1996.

_____. "The Pentateuch," "Genesis: Primeval Prologue," and "Genesis: Patriarchal History." In *Old Testament Survey: The Message, Form, and Background of the Old Testament*, pp. 3-14, 15-31, 32-51. 2nd ed. Ed. by W.S. Lasor, D.A. Hubbard, and F.W. Bush. Grand Rapids: Eerdmans, 1996.

Hayes, J.H. "Leviticus." In *Harper's Bible Commentary*, pp. 157-181. Ed. by J.L. Mays. San Francisco: Harper and Row, 1988.

Hendel, R. "The Exodus in Biblical Memory." *JBL* 120 (2001): 601-622.

Hubbard, D.A., and F.W. Bush. "Deuteronomy." In *Old Testament Survey: The Message, Form, and Background of the Old Testament*, pp. 111-127. 2nd ed. Ed. by W.S. LaSor, D.A. Hubbard, and F.W. Bush. Grand Rapids: Eerdmans, 1996.

_____ . "Numbers." In *Old Testament Survey: The Message, Form, and Background of the Old Testament*, pp. 99-110. 2nd ed. Ed. by W.S. LaSor, D.A. Hubbard, and F.W. Bush. Grand Rapids: Eerdmans, 1996.

Humphries, C.J. "The Number of People in the Exodus from Egypt: Decoding Mathematically the Very Large Numbers in Numbers I and XXVI." *VT* 48:2 (1998): 196-213.

Kaiser, O. "The Pentateuch and the Deuteronomistic History." In *Text in Context*, pp. 289-322. Ed. by A.D.H. Mayes. Oxford: University Press, 2000.

Kaufman, S.A. "The Structure of the Deuteronomic Law." *Maavav* 1-2 (1978–79): 105-158.

Kaufman, Y. *The Religion of Israel*. Chicago: University of Chicago Press, 1960.

Kenyon, K.M. *Archaeology of the Holy Land*. 4th ed. New York: W.W. Norton, 1979.

_____ . *Digging Up Jericho*. New York: Praeger, 1957.

Kitchen, K.A. "Exodus, The." *ABD*, 2:701-708. Ed. by David Noel Freedman. New York: Doubleday, 1992.

_____ . "The Fall and Rise of Covenant, Law and Treaty." *TynBul* 40 (1989): 118-135.

_____ . *On the Reliability of the Old Testament*. Grand Rapids: Eerdmans, 2003.

Kline, M.G. *Treaty of the Great King*. Grand Rapids: Eerdmans, 1963.

Krentz, E. *The Historical-Critical Method*. Philadelphia: Fortress, 1975.

Lambert, W.G., and A.R. Millard. *Atra-ḫasīs: The Babylonian Story of the Flood*. Oxford: Clarendon, 1969.

Laney, J.C. "The Role of the Prophets in God's Case against Israel." *BSac* 138 (1981): 313-325.

Lemche, N.P. *Ancient Israel: A New History of Israelite Society*. The Biblical Seminar 5. Sheffield: Sheffield, 1995.

Leveen, A.B. "Falling in the Wilderness: Death Reports in the Book of Numbers." *Prooftexts* 22 (2002): 245-272.

_____ . "Variations on a Theme: Differing Conceptions of Memory in the Book of Numbers." *JSOT* 27 (2002): 201-221.

Levine, B. "Leviticus, Book of." *ABD*, 4:312-321. Ed. by David Noel Freedman. New York: Doubleday, 1992.

Malamat, A."The Exodus: Egyptian Analogies." In *Exodus: The Egypt-ian Evidence*, pp. 15-26. Ed. by E.S. Frerichs and L.H. Lesko. Winona Lake, IN: Eisenbrauns, 1997.

Mayes, A.D.H. *Deuteronomy*. London/Grand Rapids: Marshall-Morgan-Scott/Eerdmans, 1981.

McBride, S.D. "Polity of the Covenant People: The Book of Deuteronomy." *Int* 3 (1987): 229-244.

McConville, J.G. "Singular Address in the Deuteronomic Law and the Politics of Legal Administration." *JSOT* 97 (2002): 19-36.

Mendenhall, G. "Ancient Oriental and Biblical Law." *BA* 17 (1954): 26-46.

_____. "The Census List of Numbers 1 and 26." *JBL* 77 (1958): 52-66.

_____. "Covenant Forms in Israelite Tradition." *BA* 17 (1954): 50-76; Repr. with corrections in *Biblical Archaeologist Reader 3*, pp. 25-53. Ed. by E.F. Campbell Jr. and D.N. Freedman. Garden City, NY: Doubleday, 1970.

Milgrom, J. *Numbers*. JPS Torah Bible Commentary. Philadelphia: JPS, 1990.

Miller, J.M., and J.H. Hayes. *A History of Israel and Judah*. Philadelphia: Westminster, 1986.

Miller, P.D. "Moses My Servant." *Int* 41 (1987): 245-255.

Monet, P. *Les Nowelles fouilles de Tanis*. Np., 1929–33.

Muilenburg, J. "The 'Office' of Prophet in Ancient Israel." In *The Bible in Modern Scholarship*, pp. 74-97. Ed. by J.P. Hyatt. Nashville: Abingdon, 1965.

Nicholson, E.W. *Deuteronomy and the Tradition*. Philadelphia: Fortress, 1967.

_____. *The Pentateuch in the Twentieth Century: The Legacy of Julius Wellhausen*. Oxford: Clarendon, 1998.

North, C.R. "Pentateuchal Criticism" In *The Old Testament and Modern Study*, 48-83. Ed. by H.H. Rowley. Oxford: Clarendon, 1951.

Noth, M. *A History of Pentateuchal Traditions*. Trans. by B.W. Anderson. Englewood Cliffs, NJ: Prentice-Hall, 1972. Originally published as *Überlieferungsgeschichte des Pentateuch*. Stuttgart, 1948.

_____. *Numbers*. Trans. by J.D. Martin. Philadelphia: Westminster, 1968.

_____. *The Deuteronomistic History*, JSOTSupp 15. Sheffield: Sheffield Academic Press, 1981. Originally published as *Überlieferungsgeschichtliche Studien*. 2nd ed. Tübingen: Max Niemeyer, 1957; 3rd ed. unaltered, 1967.

Olson, D.T. *The Death of the Old and the Birth of the New: The Framework of the Book of Numbers and the Pentateuch.* BJS 71. Chico: Scholars, 1985.

Paley, S.M. *King of the World: Ashur-nasir-pal II of Assyria 883–859 B.C.* New York: Brooklyn Museum, 1976.

Petrie, W.M.F. *Egypt and Israel.* Rev. ed. London: SPCK, 1911.

Pritchard, J.B., ed. *Ancient Near Eastern Texts Relating to the Old Testament.* 3rd ed. with Supplement. Princeton: Princeton University, 1969.

Redmount, C.A. "Bitter Lives: Israel In and Out of Egypt." In *The Oxford History of the Biblical World,* pp. 79-121. Ed. by M.D. Coogan. New York: Oxford, 1998.

Rendsburg, G.A. "The Date of the Exodus and the Conquest/Settlement: The Case for the 1100s." *VT* 42 (1992): 510-527.

Rendtorff, R. *The Old Testament: An Introduction.* Philadelphia: Fortress, 1986.

Ross, J.F. "The Prophet as Yahweh's Messenger." In *Israel's Prophetic Heritage: Essays in Honor of James Muilenburg,* pp. 88-109. Ed. by B.W. Anderson and W. Harrelson. New York: Harper and Brothers, 1962.

Rowley, H.H. *The Growth of the Old Testament.* New York: Harper and Row, 1950.

_____. *Studies in Old Testament Prophecy: Presented to T.H. Robinson on His Sixty-Fifth Birthday, August 9th, 1946.* Edinburgh: T. & T. Clark, 1950.

Sailhamer, J.H. *The Pentateuch as Narrative.* Grand Rapids: Zondervan, 1992.

Sarna, N.M. "Exodus, Book of." *ABD,* 2:689-700. Ed. by David Noel Freedman. New York: Doubleday, 1992.

_____. *Exploring Exodus: The Heritage of Biblical Israel.* New York: Schocken, 1986.

Schmidt, W.H. *Old Testament Introduction.* 2nd ed. Trans. by M.J. O'Connell and D.J. Reimer. Louisville, KY: Westminster John Knox, 1999

Shaw, C.G. "Enlightenment, The." *Encyclopedia of Religion and Ethics,* 5:310-316. New York: Charles Scribner's Sons, 1928.

Skinner, J. *Prophecy and Religion.* Cambridge: University Press, 1922.

Smith, G.A. *The Book of Deuteronomy.* Cambridge: University Press, 1918.

Soggin, J.A. *An Introduction to the History of Israel and Judah.* 2nd ed. London: SCM, 1993.

Soulen, R.N., and R.K. Soulen. *Handbook of Biblical Criticism.* 3ʳᵈ ed. rev. Louisville, KY: Westminster John Knox, 2001.

Thompson, J.A. *The Ancient Near Eastern Treaties and the Old Testament.* London: Tyndale, 1964.

Tucker, G.M. "Deut 18:15-22." *Int* 41 (1987): 292-297.

von Rad, G. *The Problem of the Hexateuch and Other Essays.* New York: McGraw-Hill, 1966.

Walton, J.H. *Ancient Israelite Literature in Its Cultural Context.* Grand Rapids: Zondervan, 1989.

_____. *Chronological Charts of the Old Testament.* Grand Rapids: Zondervan, 1978.

_____. "Deuteronomy in Exposition of the Spirit of the Law." *GTJ* 8 (1987): 213-225.

Weinfeld, M. *Deuteronomy and the Deuteronomic School.* Oxford: University Press, 1972; Repr. ed., Winona Lake, IN: Eisenbrauns, 1992.

Wellhausen, J. *Prolegomena to the History of Israel.* Merian Book Library edition, 1957; Repr. ed., Gloucester: Peter Smith, 1973.

Wenham, G.J. *The Book of Leviticus.* Grand Rapids: Eerdmans, 1979.

_____. *Exploring the Old Testament: A Guide to the Pentateuch.* Downers Grove, IL: InterVarsity, 2001.

_____. "Leviticus." *ISBE²*, 4:111-117. Rev. ed. by G.W. Bromiley. Grand Rapids: Eerdmans, 1982.

_____. *Numbers.* Downers Grove, IL: InterVarsity, 1981.

Wenham, J.W. "Large Numbers in the Old Testament." *TynBul* 18 (1967): 19-53.

Westermann, C. *Basic Forms of Prophetic Speech.* Philadelphia: Westminster, 1967.

Whybray, R.N. *Introduction to the Pentateuch.* Grand Rapids: Eerdmans, 1995.

Young, E.J. *An Introduction to the Old Testament.* Grand Rapids: Eerdmans, 1964.

GENESIS

Genesis appropriately begins "in the beginning" since it speaks of the beginning of the world, life, worship, sin, and death. This phrase (בְּרֵאשִׁית, *bᵊrē'šîth*) comprises the Hebrew title of the book. The title "Genesis," from the Greek word γενεσέως (*geneseōs*) meaning "beginning," or "generations," derives from the Septuagint. Because it is the beginning of the Bible, Genesis contains a breadth and depth that makes it both simple and complex. Dividing into two large sections, the Primeval and Patriarchal Histories, Genesis gives accounts of the creation, the first sin, the flood, and the stories of Abraham, Isaac, Jacob, and Joseph. These stories serve as introductions, not only to the Pentateuch, but to the rest of the Bible as well. This significance necessitates a somewhat larger introduction than with the other books of the Pentateuch.

HISTORICAL AND CULTURAL BACKGROUND

Genesis has many affinities with the ancient Near Eastern literature which serve as a background to the understanding of the culture and history recorded in the book. Generally speaking, the Primeval History shares a common structural pattern — "creation . . . time span . . . crisis (flood) . . . time span (modern times)"[1] — with three compositions of the early second millennium (Sumerian King List, *Atra-ḫasīs* Epic, and Eridu Genesis). More specifically, the creation narratives in chapters 1 and 2 have affinities with the Babylonian Creation Epic known as the *Enuma Elish*. The biblical account of creation out of nothing by calling matter into existence (1:1–2:4a) and the forming of man out of the dust of the ground (2:7) have affinities with similar material in the Egyptian materials. These

---

[1] K.A. Kitchen, *On the Reliability of the Old Testament* (Grand Rapids: Eerdmans, 2003), p. 447.

record how Ptah brought the world into existence by pronouncing the name of everything, whereas the potter God, Khnum, formed mankind on his potter's wheel. Similarly, in the Mesopotamian material the wild man Enkidu is formed from clay. In the Genesis account man is the climax of creation, created in God's image to rule over it in a manner similar to God's rule over the universe. In the *Enuma Elish* man is created as a slave from a god's blood so the gods will not have to work.[2]

The Tree of Life Motif, or Garden (2:9), and the Flood are common ancient Near Eastern themes. Objects "designated as 'tree,' 'sacred tree,' or 'garden' originated from a long tradition in ancient Near Eastern art," in which "a variety of animals and divine and human figures were placed on one or both sides of these symbols of vegetation as if to adore or care for them."[3] In the biblical account, the Tree of Life conveyed immortality (3:22; Prov 3:18; Rev 22:2,14, 19), while the Tree of Knowledge of Good and Evil conferred wisdom. God's decision to destroy corrupt humanity via a flood (6:5–9:17) parallels ancient Near Eastern flood stories. The two best known are *Atra-ḫasīs* and Tablet XI of the *Epic of Gilgamesh*. In the Gilgamesh account, Gilgamesh, in search of immortality, seeks out Utnapishtim, the lone survivor of the flood. *Atra-ḫasīs* records a revolt of the gods, who become tired of the excess work required of them. Mankind is created to work in their place. Soon, however, mankind multiplies and makes so much noise the gods' sleep is disturbed. After sending plague, famine, and drought, all of which are unsuccessful in keeping mankind in check, the gods determine to eradicate mankind via a flood — only *Atra-ḫasīs* survives. The general similarities are obvious (the gods/God determine(s) to destroy mankind by a flood, but representatives are saved). More specific

---

[2]For general discussions of correlations between the ancient Near Eastern and biblical materials see: Kitchen, *Reliability,* pp. 421-447; J.H. Walton, *Ancient Israelite Literature in Its Cultural Context* (Grand Rapids: Zondervan, 1989), pp. 19-44. For Mesopotamian creation materials see, E.O. Speiser, "The Creation Epic, *ANET,* pp. 60-72; id., "The Epic of Gilgamesh," *ANET,* p. 74. For Egyptian creation materials see J.A. Wilson, "The Theology of Memphis," *ANET,* p. 5; id., "A Universalist Hymn to the Sun," *ANET,* p. 368; id., "The Divine Attributes of Pharaoh," *ANET,* p. 331; id., "The Admonitions of Ipu-wer," *ANET,* p. 441.

[3]S.M. Paley, *King of the World: Ashur-nasir-pal II of Assyria, 883–859 B.C.* (New York: Brooklyn Museum, 1976), p. 22.

similarities between the Babylonian and biblical accounts include: both the ship/ark came to rest on a mountain and birds were sent out (biblical — dove and raven; Babylonian — dove, swallow, raven). Whybray has observed that such differences illustrate the theological distinctiveness of the biblical account.[4] This distinctiveness would include the monotheism of Genesis, which portrays God as desiring the best for mankind and working to save him, even when punishment is necessary.[5]

Early studies interpreted the patriarchal narratives as unhistorical, critical scholars believing they reflected the setting at the time of their writing (ninth or tenth century). However, new discoveries developed several lines of evidence which indicate a second-to-first millennium setting. (1) The names of the patriarchs, which belong to the West Semitic family of names, are rare among the Canaanites, but abundant among the Amorite population, thus pointing to the Amorites of the second millennium. (2) The account of Abraham's journey from his call in Ur to Canaan fits with the early second millennium context. (3) The nomadic lifestyle pictured in the narratives agrees with what is known of the early second millennium. (4) The narratives reflect many social, economic, and legal customs from the second and first millennia. (5) Many of the features of patriarchal religion (objects as altars, standing stones, animal sacrifice, circumcision, prayers, and oracles) picture an early era.[6] This last point is significant. The patriarchs were monotheists, worshiping in a polytheistic society. They practiced a form of "personal religion" in which the family entered into a close relationship with a deity, who blessed and protected the family. For ancient man such stories fostered a sense of the nation's, or people's place in the world.[7] For the modern interpreter these similarities indicate a common heritage

---

[4]R.N. Whybray, *Introduction to the Pentateuch* (Grand Rapids: Eerdmans, 1995), pp. 46-47.

[5]For *Atra-ḫasīs* see W.G. Lambert and A.R. Millard, *Atra-ḫasīs: The Babylonian Story of the Flood* (Oxford: Clarendon, 1969). For Gilgamesh see E.A. Speiser, "The Gilgamesh Epic," *ANET*, pp. 93-95; and Kitchen, *Reliability*, pp. 425-426.

[6]J.E. Hartley, "Genesis: Patriarchal History," in *Old Testament Survey: The Message, Form, and Background of the Old Testament*, 2nd ed., ed. by W.S. Lasor, D.A. Hubbard, and F.W. Bush (Grand Rapids: Eerdmans, 1996), pp. 41-43; Kitchen, *Reliability*, pp. 313-372.

[7]Whybray, *Introduction*, p. 36.

out of which the ancient Near Eastern grew;[8] their uniqueness points toward inspiration.[9]

TEXT AND AUTHOR

Mosaic authorship of Genesis, as well as Exodus–Deuteronomy, remained unquestioned until the rise of modern criticism in the middle of the nineteenth century. Since then two different views have crystalized: (1) those who believe Moses wrote Genesis–Deuteronomy and (2) those denying Mosaic authorship of the material.

Based on several lines of evidence, early Jewish and Christian scholars believed Moses to be the author of the Pentateuch. (1) The text indicates Moses engaged in writing activity, recording historical events, laws, and poetry (Exod 17:14; 24:4; 34:27; Num 33:2; Deut 31:22; 32). (2) There was a book of the Law associated with Moses (Josh 1:7,8), which ultimately became known as the "Book of Moses" (2 Chr 25:4; Ezra 6:18; Neh 13:1). (3) By the time of the New Testament period the Torah was connected with Moses (Matt 19:7; 22:24; Mark 7:10; 12:26; John 1:17; 5:46; 7:23). Some passages *do* seem to have been written after Moses' death (Gen 11:31; 14:14; 32:32; 36:31; 40:15; Deut 3:14; 34:1,6,10). Therefore, "Mosaic authorship" of the Pentateuch does not have to mean that Moses wrote every word.[10]

Numbers 21:14 ("Book of the Wars of the Lord") yields evidence for sources. However, authorship, sources, and inspiration are separate issues. Moses may have used sources to write the Pentateuch and other authors may have added to the Pentateuch. Similarly, one may believe in the inspiration of the original autographs and acknowledge the evidence that points to additions to Moses' work. Some, who have championed Mosaic authorship and inspiration, have allowed for the addition of others besides Moses, but this view is a far cry from the multiauthorship hypothesis propounded by source critics using the historical-critical method (HCM).

---

[8]J.E. Hartley, "Genesis: Primeval Prologue," in *Old Testament Survey: The Message, Form, and Background of the Old Testament*, 2nd ed., ed. by W.S. Lasor, D.A. Hubbard, and F.W. Bush (Grand Rapids: Eerdmans, 1996), p. 20.

[9]For a discussion of the ancient Near Eastern materials relating to the material found in Genesis see, Walton, *Ancient Israelite Literature*, pp. 45-68.

[10]R.B. Dillard and T. Longman III, *An Introduction to the Old Testament* (Grand Rapids: Zondervan, 1994), pp. 39-40; cf. O.T. Allis, *The Five Books of Moses*, 2nd ed. (Philadelphia: Presbyterian and Reformed, 1949), pp. 1-18.

HISTORY OF INTERPRETATION

Many Old Testament introductions focus[ed] on the documentary hypothesis's explanation (JEDP) for the origin of the Pentateuch. Of far greater influence has been the philosophical and theological changes brought on by the HCM's approach to the Scriptures. The presuppositions with which a scholar approaches the text determines that scholar's use and interpretation of that text. For many the HCM shifted from a faith-based approach to Scripture to a secular-based one. The following overview of the rise of the HCM and its foundational assumptions enables a fuller appreciation of the history of interpretation of Genesis and the Pentateuch.

The HCM grew out of the Enlightenment, which in its German form, *Aufklärung*, posited a tension between authoritative-traditional entities and those established by freedom and religion. Practically, the Enlightenment believed that reason could solve all problems mankind may face. The Enlightenment's impact on such documents as the Declaration of Independence illustrates its far-reaching consequences even today. In terms of religion, the Enlightenment owed much to John Locke, who, in his *Essay on Human Understanding* (1690) and *The Reasonableness of Christianity as Delivered in the Scriptures* (1695), ". . . argued that 'reason is a natural revelation.' God communicates to man through his natural powers new discoveries which reason validates by offering proofs."[11] Because Deism accepted religion only on the basis of reason, it questioned the integrity and reliableness of specific texts. However, those defending the Scriptures against deistic conclusions used reason in their arguments, shifting Bible study to a more historical approach. So Enlightenment thinking believed "there was one eternal, universally valid, internally consistent *pura doctrina sacra*," which could be found by reason, not Scripture or revelation; "Holy Scripture contains truth, but general truth that man would recognize in any case, for all truth is rational, and what is rational is capable of proof."[12] This demand for proof produced ". . . a revolution of viewpoint in evaluating the Bible. The Scriptures were, so to speak, secularized. The biblical books became historical documents to be studied and questioned like any other writing of history; rather history had become

---

[11]E. Krentz, *The Historical-Critical Method* (Philadelphia: Fortress, 1975), p. 16.

[12]Ibid., p. 17.

the criterion for understanding the Bible."[13] While many in the nineteenth century viewed these methods as theologically dangerous, others (e.g., Lightfoot, Wescott, Hort) were able to synthesize pastoral matters and historical criticism in such a way that criticism was no longer perceived as a threat.[14] Indeed, historical criticism became the generally accepted method of interpretation, which resulted in the secularization of the Bible.[15]

World War I weakened the enthusiasm in this new rationality. It questioned the optimism of a completely historical and evolutionary approach by showing that man was not evolving toward a utopia, that the historical lessons were not being learned, and that modern man could be just as cruel as ancient man. If the HCM had weakened the old positions of faith and orthodoxy had been called into question, where did the answers lie? How was the Bible to be viewed — a history book of ancient myths, or the word of God? Karl Barth and Rudolph Bultmann attempted to reconcile this dichotomy between faith and history. Barth recognized a historical/cultural gap between the so-called "superstitions" of the ancient world and the rationalism of the modern world. The exegete must break through this barrier by wrestling with the text until it speaks to the modern man. Similarly, Bultmann's existentialism made a separation between historic fact and faith, arguing faith is the decision to God's call; it is not dependent on historical knowledge, or facts.[16]

By the end of the Second World War historical criticism was firmly established without having solved the problem of the relation of faith to the method. Today historical criticism is so taken for granted that the secular historian's return to a precritical age remains an impossibility.[17] Critical scholars assume miracles and other metaphysical phenomena can be disproved or a rational explanation can be offered for them or they can be safely ignored. These presuppositions not only eliminate possible solutions, but,

---

[13]Ibid., p. 30.

[14]Ibid., p. 29.

[15]See also: C.G. Shaw, "Enlightenment, The," *Encyclopedia of Religion and Ethics* (New York: Charles Scribner's Sons, 1928), 5:310-316; W.A. Elwell, ed., *The Concise Dictionary of Theology* (Grand Rapids: Baker, 1991), pp. 155-156.

[16]For synopses of Barth and Bultmann see Elwell, *Concise Dictionary,* pp. 56-57, 76-77.

[17]M.W. Chavalas, "The Historian, The Believer, and the OT: A Study in the Supposed Conflict of Faith and Reason," *JETS* 36 (1993): 145.

when not definitely stated, can pose problems for the uninitiated. Evangelical scholars realize the HCM can supply a great deal of information that will aid in interpreting the text, but it is virtually useless with reference to divine things. God cannot be put into the proverbial test tube.

"Modern scientific history is systematic knowledge of the past; its object is man's activities in time, space, and society, expressed in coherent report (usually written). It deals with real events and real men (not abstractions), and the causes of their activities and their influence."[18] The historian claims autonomy, individual authority, self-reasoning and rational thinking, self-sufficiency, takes an atheistic/agnostic approach, seeks facts only, and believes all history is analogous. Thus the historian is *critical*. He uses his mind on the subject with which he deals. He is *positive* in that he appreciates what he discovers. He is *systematic* in the methods he uses. This view of history is essentially secular and antagonistic to faith.

Faith, on the other hand, is not necessarily validated by empirical (i.e., experiential) research, but on revelation. Thus faith is not always the result of scientific proof. If something can be proven *in fact* via research, then faith is eliminated, for "faith is *assurance* of things hoped for, a *conviction* of things not seen" (Heb 11:1, ASV, emphasis added). Chavalas illustrates these thoughts when he says, "Even if we believe that Jesus rose from the dead, the meaning (but not the evidence) behind the resurrection lies beyond the grasp of the historian."[19] Here is where the conflict, or perceived incompatibility, appears. Christianity has normally been based on supernatural metaphysics, while the HCM has been founded on a rational assessment of the probability of an event.[20] These facts indicate one must choose to be either a historian or a theologian. To choose history over theology means that we are nothing more than historians, that the Bible is nothing more than a history book, and that any lessons learned from it carry about as much weight as any other historical event. To choose theology over history means that we allow the possibility of revelation, which lies beyond historical criticism's abilities of proof, and believe the Bible contains spiritual lessons of the most significant kind.

---

[18]Krentz, *Historical-Critical Method*, pp. 34-35; cf. Chavalas, "Historian," pp. 154-155.

[19]Chavalas, "Historian," p. 158.

[20]Ibid., p. 145.

Those who deny the HCM often run the risk of accepting the criteria used by the method. Many Christian historians, attempting to adhere to both traditional theological doctrines and the dogmas of historical-critical research have functioned in a way similar to that of *theistic evolutionists* by compromising two extremes. So, theologians too must recognize their limitations, as the full quotation of Chavalas's resurrection example shows.

> The theological claims of Scripture are not to be demonstrated simply by the historical critical method, a method that the Scriptural claims transcend. Even if we believe that Jesus rose from the dead, the meaning (but not the evidence) behind the resurrection lies beyond the grasp of the historian. Biblical faith is based not solely on the historicity of the events described but on revelation. Faith only to a certain extent can bring forth objective facts to support theological claims. The problem occurs when one attempts to interpret those facts, since objective facts cannot transcend the mundane. Facts, however, can point more clearly to a particular interpretation. Yet both revelation and its theological interpretation transcend our present reality.
>
> The person who believes that faith can simply be authenticated by history or archaeology must be careful not to put his trust wholly in science rather than Scripture, a procedure that may show a misguided faith.[21]

Finally, "those who espouse the historical-critical method have also based their arguments on presuppositions — that is, on a type of 'faith.'"[22] The irony of these contradictions should be apparent. So Bible scholars must continue to wrestle with the "faith vs. history" issue. Christian historians, in reconstructing the narrative of biblical history, must go a step farther and ask whether the object of investigation includes God's actions with and for man in space and time.[23]

Based on the above, several dynamics come into play. (1) Conservative scholars can, and do, employ some of historical criticism's methods without having to deny certain principles of faith. (2) Not every tenet of these methods must be accepted by those who would employ some of its tools. (3) The more logical, philosophical view

---

[21]Ibid., p. 158.

[22]Ibid., p. 146.

[23]Cf. Krentz, *Historical-Critical Method,* p. 35.

allows for the possibility of God and does not attempt to rule him out in the interpretative process. (4) Every Bible student must first determine whether to approach the text in faith or doubt. "If an interpreter approaches the Old Testament . . . from a human vantage point, about human affairs — skepticism is warranted. A second interpreter, however, who admits the reality of God and who believes that God is the ultimate and guiding voice of the Bible will not have difficulty accepting the supernatural events of the Bible."[24]

The HCM's basic assumptions had a domino effect. The ruling out of miracle meant the text must be approached historically; this produced the Documentary Hypothesis, which divided scholarship, creating a continual evolution of new theories, resulting in its failure as a viable view for the origin of the Pentateuch. The classic theory contends for four separate documents that eventually came to be combined into one document. Several versions of this theory exist, but regardless of the view discussed "we are dealing entirely with hypotheses and not facts."[25]

Early critical scholars noted divergences in the text which seemed to indicate its composite nature. These included the following. Two of the *Divine names*, (e.g., YHWH, Elohim, El Elyon, El Shaddai) became representative of the supposed documents J (=YHWH) and E (=Elohim). *Doublets* represented a basic story retold with different characters, as observed in Abraham's and Isaac's wife-sister stories (Gen 12:10-20; 20; 26:1-11), or Joseph's separate dreams of stars and sheaves (Gen 37:5-11). Similarly, different names designated the same referent (e.g., Reuel/Jethro, Horeb/Sinai, Jacob/Israel, and Ishmaelites/Midianites). *Stylistic differences*, such as the two creation accounts (Gen 1:1-2:4a; 2:4bff.), indicated the synthesis of two traditions. *Different theologies* indicated different sources. To these scholars, J described God anthropomorphically, E focused on the religious and moral concepts, D called for centralization of worship and emphasized retribution, and P accentuated the cult and God's transcendence. Supposed observable contradictions (e.g., the duration of the flood [40 days vs. 150 days, Gen 7:2,24] and the number of animals taken into the ark [2 of each kind vs. 7 of each kind, Gen 6:19; 7:2]) illustrated the above.[26]

---

[24]Dillard and Longman, *Introduction*, p. 23
[25]Whybray, *Introduction*, pp. 26-27.
[26]Cf. R.N. and R.K. Soulen, *Handbook of Biblical Criticism*, 3rd ed. rev.

Early critical scholars exhibited great confidence in their conclusions; their later counterparts display less confidence. The '20s witnessed a consensus of opinion that the documents were chronologically arranged JEDP, with Ezekiel 40–45 between D and P, and D identified with the finding of the law book in Josiah's reign (seventh century). By the '30s J.E. McFadyen wrote: "'To a superficial observer the situation today must seem like confusion confounded. . . . Everywhere uncertainties abound, and, like the dove after the Deluge, we seem to find no solid ground anywhere for the sole of our foot.'"[27] This degeneration of confidence was paralleled by a softening of positions between liberal and conservative scholars. Critics have given ". . . a stronger emphasis on the thematic unity of the Pentateuch . . . , while conservatives have been less hesitant to speak of sources."[28]

Forerunners of Wellhausen had "suggested that Moses used sources recognizable by the generic name Elohim, as distinct from Yhwh."[29] Spinoza (1632–1677) questioned the literary unity of Genesis. Jean Astruc (1684–1766) and Richard Simon (1638–1712) argued that the Pentateuch was composed of several sources originating from different periods. The acceptance and refinement of these ideas crystalized in "a recognition of four basic literary documents, labeled . . . E^1, E^2, J and D."[30]

W.M.L. de Wette (1780–1849) identified the D source with the law book found in Josiah's reign (2 Kings 22–23). This theory "became a pivotal point . . . because it made possible a distinction between earlier legislation, which was not in accord with Deuteronomy, and later legislation, which presupposed it."[31] So the D document was thought to be easily established, but none of the other documents could be identified with any known events in Israel's history, nor could they be placed in any logical chronological order. The main

---

(Louisville, KY: Westminster John Knox, 2001), pp. 178-179; Dillard and Longman, *Introduction*, pp. 40-41; Allis, *Five Books*, pp. 23-29, 40-95, 96-16.

[27]J.E. McFadyen, *The People and the Book* (1925), pp. 183, 218; cited by C.R. North, "Pentateuchal Criticism," in *The Old Testament and Modern Study*, ed. by H.H. Rowley (Oxford: Clarendon, 1951), p. 48.

[28]Dillard and Longmam, *Introduction*, p. 39.

[29]J. Blenkinsopp, "The Documentary Hypothesis in Trouble," in *Approaches to the Bible*, ed. by Harvey Minkoff (Washington, DC: BAS, 1994), 1:11.

[30]R.E. Clements, *One Hundred Years of Old Testament Interpretation* (Philadelphia: Westminster, 1976), p. 8.

[31]Blenkinsopp, "Documentary Hypothesis," p. 12.

problems here were what to do with E^1 and E^2. Some scholars had regarded E^1 as the oldest and fundamental of the Pentateuchal sources, while Eduard Reuss (1804–1891) and others had accepted the latter. K.H. Graf (Reuss's student) argued that E^1 was actually a priestly document (P), which changed the document from the earliest to the latest document.[32]

The hypothesis, based on an evolutionary view of religion, turned the biblical chronology on its head. Biblical chronology indicates the law preceded the prophets. Popular evolutionary theories believed life evolved from the simple to the complex. Since the Pentateuch was perceived as very complex (with all of its laws and regulations), and since the culture in which the prophets lived and worked was perceived as simple, scholars argued the prophets, working in this culture and pushing an "ethical monotheism," evolved the law in the Babylonian Exile in all of its complexity.[33] Wellhausen accepted these presuppositions completely, added them to his own studies, made them seem more conclusive than either Reuss or Graf had been able to do, and ultimately published them in his *Prolegomena zur Geschichte Israels* in 1883. Israel's history showed an evolutionary movement from a monarchy to a priestly theocracy. Wellhausen, influenced by Hegelian philosophy and an evolutionary concept of religion, believed that the sources had not been composed before the mid-ninth century. They told nothing of the nature of oldest religion in Israel, but reflected the situation that had developed by the time of composition.[34] So how could Wellhausen speak of a history of religion of Israel? Wellhausen ". . . never provided a basis in Israelite social structure for evaluating political history. . . . he had produced a programmatic source analysis; but . . . his sources' claims remained unproved."[35]

Wellhausen's work was challenged by Hermann Gunkel (1862–1932), who went behind the written sources in an attempt to answer the question of the evolution of Israel's history. In doing so he pointed out cracks in Wellhausen's theories. Whereas Wellhausen regarded JEDP as original sources originating late in Israel's history, Gunkel

---

[32]Clements, *One Hundred Years*, pp. 8-9.

[33]Ibid., p. 11.

[34]J. Wellhausen, *Prolegomena to the History of Israel* (Merian Book Library edition, 1957; repr. ed., Gloucester: Peter Smith, 1973), pp. xvi-552.

[35]B.S. Halpern, *The First Historians: The Hebrew Bible and History* (San Francisco: Harper and Row, 1988), pp. 23-24.

argued they were committed to writing only after a long period of time in which they had existed orally. In this oral stage they consisted of separate individual narratives which were independently related to particular places and customs. This *Sitz im Leben* (setting in life) aided the understanding of many of the features that the written documents contained. The examination of the narratives and laws separately as individual units allowed the recovery of knowledge of a much earlier period of Israel's life than that in which the final composition of the source documents had taken place. To Gunkel, each type of narrative had a particular place and function in society. For example, several of the patriarchal stories were told to explain how certain places had come to be sanctuaries (Bethel), or why certain customs were performed (circumcision), or the like. Eventually these were put together as chains of stories relating to particular individuals (Abraham and circumcision), and ultimately became the extended sources (JEDP) of Wellhausen. The data these stories contained yielded significant information regarding the earliest spiritual life of Israel.

Hugo Gressman (1877–1927) refined Gunkel's methods and challenged Wellhausen's late dating of the Decalogue (Exod 20:2-7). He argued (a) the separate narratives, which had been pieced together in literary form, should be studied by themselves, and (b) this same method could also be used in the study of the legal collections. He thus established that the Decalogue "was older than the prophets, and represented the foundational traditions of Israelite religion."[36]

Critical scholars described E as an epic history that ran parallel to J. Prochsch argued E's disjointed narratives were spliced into J at significant points when the redactor combined these two histories. Volz modified this theory, arguing E never was a continuous document, but represented various glosses (GE) and additions to a different J. Thus J and E should both be eliminated. Genesis was actually composed by a single story writer J (SWJ). The so-called E was actually an editor (EdE) of this larger work.[37]

The strongest case for any of the documents is that found in J. But if scholars such as Volz could argue E represented glosses added to J, and if Gunkel and Gressman could emphasize that the smaller narrative units which were based in oral tradition actually made up such documents as J, then the conclusion must be reached that J, or

---

[36]Clements, *One Hundred Years*, p. 17.
[37]North, "Pentateuchal Criticism," p. 57.

any of the other documents for that matter "is in some degree composite" and that "J, and with it the documentary hypothesis as a whole, is volatilized."[38] Scholars began to multiply documents. Smend argued that the J material in the Pentateuch, and particularly in Genesis 1–11, should be separated into J^1 and J^2. Otto Eissfeldt expanded and revised this (1887–1973), arguing the material should be separated "into three continuous strands, which he designated by the sigla L (*Laienschrift* or Lay-source), J, and E, his 'L' in Genesis being roughly equivalent to what had previously been assigned to J^1."[39] When these were combined together with the priestly document (P) they produced LJEP. Others have proposed similar things. Fohrer has argued for a similar document N (*Nomadenquelle*). N was older than J or E, and which also had behind it a G^1, thus: G^1NJE(D)P. There was also a G^2 which served as a basis for JE: G^1N(G^2JE)(D)P. Julian Morgenstern proposed a document K (= Kenite). K is a kind of biography of Moses composed in 899 B.C. in connection with the reformation of King Asa. It is the oldest document in the Hexateuch. R.H. Pfeiffer proposed an S (= South of Seir). S is confined to Genesis and is very similar to Eissfeldt's L. Pfeiffer argued that it appeared in Edom in Solomon's time and has subsequently received many additions (called S^2) between 600 and 400 B.C.[40]

Like J, P was divided and ". . . carried to such lengths as to result in a return to the old fragmentary hypothesis. . . . Baentsch . . . worked with no less than seven P-sigla: P, Ps, Pss, Ph ([Lev] xvii-xxvi), Po (i-vii), Pr (xi-xv), and Rp. Any one of the secondary sources might have a second (Ph^s, Pr^s) or third (Pr^{ss}) hand, together with redactors (Rpo, Tph) and even secondary redactors (Rp^s). We even meet with refinements like Po^1, Po^2, Po^{1s}, Po^{2s}. This is surely the *reduction ad absurdum* of the analytical method and it is improbable that we shall ever see anything quite like it again."[41] Such absurdity as this justifies Paul Volz's criticism of Eissfeldt's L source being applied to the entire method. "'I see in this Synopsis the culmination of the hitherto prevailing method, and I find that it proves exactly the opposite

---

[38]Ibid., p. 59.

[39]Ibid., p. 53.

[40]For detailed discussions of the documentary issues, see North, "Pentateuchal Criticism," pp. 54-55, 59; R.E. Clements, "Pentateuchal Problems," in *Tradition and Interpretation*, ed. by G.W. Anderson (Oxford: Clarendon, 1979), p. 102.

[41]North, "Pentateuchal Criticism," p. 56.

of what it is meant to prove, for the miserable fragments of narrative which for the most part of the columns contain prove precisely that there were not four original narratives, and that this entire Pentateuchal Synopsis is nothing but the artificial creation of modern erudition.'"[42] Y. Kaufmann toppled "the whole of Wellhausen's picture of the growth of the Pentateuch,"[43] when he argued that the entire P document was itself preexilic representing a stream of tradition running parallel with D.

Engnell and the Uppsala School continued Gunkel's emphasis of the oral stage behind the documents, thus multiplying the sources even more. "Instead of sources and 'redactors' we have to reckon with units of oral tradition, complexes of tradition, and collections of tradition, together with circles of traditionists and schools within which these traditions were handed on, often through several generations."[44] Engnell placed such emphasis in the oral tradition that he rejected Wellhausenian literary criticism and argued for "a radical break with the whole method."[45]

Gerhard von Rad identified Deuteronomy 6:20-24; 26:5b-9 and Josh 24:2b-13 as short historical credos and argued these were typical of a kind of oral brief summary, or confession, which had been used in acts of worship. These confessions recorded God's saving acts in history and were used in the Feast of Weeks in Gilgal in the days of Israel's early settlement. J had taken over these and filled them with additional information from other historical sources. Von Rad's work paved the way for looking at J, not just as a document, but as an author as well. Such interest in the makeup of the authors behind the documents pushed to the forefront a traditio-historical approach in which critical scholars determined the documents could not be "defined to the last detail," but were "transmitted and woven together in the course of the religious and national history," in a manner that "cannot entirely account for the Pentateuch on the literary critical assumption of a more or less mechanical addition of purely literary works into a fixed and unalterable form," because "the bringing together of the sources by the hand of redactors, is more than a matter of arithmetic."[46]

---

[42]Ibid., p. 55.
[43]Clements, *One Hundred Years*, p. 19.
[44]North, "Pentateuchal Criticism," p. 64.
[45]Ibid., p. 65.
[46]Ibid., p. 73; cf. pp. 71-72.

Though the traditional hypothesis continues to have its support-
ers (e.g., Campbell, Schmidt, and Nicholson),[47] Noth's version of this
traditio-historical approach created a new documentary theory valid
until the 1970s.[48] Noth isolated five themes comprising the traditions of material: promise to the patriarchs; exodus from Egypt;
wanderings in the wilderness; revelation at Sinai; entry into the land.
These themes allowed the author to include a large amount of material into the overall tetrateuchal history.[49] Since Noth "the age and
character of . . . [these] narrative complexes . . . have been differently defined,"[50] with each scholar adding his or her own particular
version to the hypothesis.[51]

Regardless of the version defended, this traditio-historical approach has focused so much on the theological nature of the writing
rather than the sources, that in many cases there remains "no longer
. . . any connection with the classical documentary hypothesis."[52]
Critical scholars perceive the combining of the smaller narrative
traditions into larger ones, each with its own distinct profile. These
independent, distinct units "have been collected and shaped from
very different perspectives and leading ideas."[53] Comprehensively
this theological redaction allowed the Deuteronomic editor-redac-
tor[s] to play a significant role in the shaping of the Pentateuch as a
whole. Such "unnamed men . . . acted as its interpreters, and contributed to its growth and meaning."[54] When critical scholars do not
engage in such tradition-historical speculation they usually bracket
the historical-critical problems and deal with "religious questions."[55]

---

[47]A. Campbell and M.A. O'Brien, *Sources of the Pentateuch* (Minneapolis: Fortress, 1993), p. ix + 266 pp.; W.H. Schmidt, *Old Testament Introduction*, 2nd ed., trans. by M.J. O'Connell and D.J. Reimer (Louisville, KY: Westminster John Knox, 1999), p. xiii + 452 pp.; E. Nicholson, *The Pentateuch in the Twentieth Century: The Legacy of Julius Wellhausen* (Oxford: Clarendon, 1998), p. vi + 294 pp.

[48]O. Kaiser, "The Pentateuch and the Deuteronomistic History," in *Text in Context*, ed. by A.D.H. Mayes (Oxford: University Press, 2000), p. 289.

[49]Ibid.

[50]Ibid., pp. 289-290.

[51]Cf. North, "Pentateuchal Criticism," pp. 71-73.

[52]R. Rendtorff, *The Old Testament: An Introduction* (Philadelphia: Fortress, 1986), p. 160.

[53]Ibid., p. 161.

[54]Clements, "Pentateuchal Problems," p. 119.

[55]R.C. Bailey, "Book Reviews," *CBQ* 55 (1993): 112.

Eisegesis (reading into the text) such as this provides no answers and illustrates the need to develop a "method which takes into account both application and the critical issues."[56]

Currently critical scholars focus their attention on (a) how the overall unity of the Pentateuch came into being, and (b) how each author or redactor introduced his own layer of meaning and interpretation into it. However, identification of these layers "has proved much more difficult in practice to show the nature and scope of their work, than it has been to show what the authors of the individual source documents were seeking to achieve."[57] This being the case then, the critical scholar is farther than ever from proving any kind of documentary hypothesis, reenforcing the axiom, "the 'documentary hypothesis' . . . as its name implies, is doomed to remain hypothetical — that is to say, beyond demonstrable proof."[58] So critical scholarship today ends with the same problem with which the older hypothesis began, "How is Old Testament religion to be interpreted?" More particularly, "What is the historical value of the biblical account from Genesis through Deuteronomy?" "Is it reliable?" "What is its value as a source for the history of Old Testament religion?" These oft-repeated questions illustrate the tension that has always existed between rational historical criticism and an evangelical approach to the Old Testament.

These highlights of a long and often stormy history indicate the following for present and future studies: (1) The confidence among early scholars has ended in doubt though nothing has emerged to replace the theory of J, E, D, and P as the main documents comprising the Pentateuch. (2) The hypothesis has always raised more questions than answers. (3) Many of these questions are the same today as those with which the hypothesis began. (4) This inability to answer some questions, while raising more of the same, has caused some scholars to view the theory as no longer relevant. (5) Future research, if present patterns continue, will be on the final form of the text.[59]

---

[56]Ibid., p. 113.

[57]Clements, "Pentateuchal Problems," p. 122; cf. Kaiser, "Pentateuch and Deuteronomistic History," p. 315.

[58]W.W. Hallo, "Biblical History in Its Near Eastern Setting: The Contextual Approach," in *Scripture in Context*, ed. by C.D. Evans, W.W. Hallo, and J.B. White (Pittsburg: Pickwick, 1980), p. 4.

[59]For a detailed discussion of these issues, see: Blenkinsopp, "Documentary Hypothesis," p. 14; Rendtorff, *Introduction*, p. 159; J.E. Hartley,

Those scholars who still adhere to the hypothesis argue for something like the following.[60]

J (Yahwist), the first of the four supposed sources for the Pentateuch, derives its designation from the English spelling of the German *Jahve*. Scholars have always debated its existence, date, and nature. Many today date it in the tenth or ninth centuries B.C. in Judah. Epic in style, it supposedly describes the origin of Israel as a fulfillment of Yhwh's promises to Abraham (numerous descendants and a land of their own, Gen 12:1-4). It relates this history of the patriarchs to the captivity in Egypt, wilderness period, and conquest of Canaan. Some scholars today believe a redactor supplemented this document with an E document (R^{JE}) in the eighth century. Others argue for an older tradition behind J (e.g., Smend's J^1, Eissfeldt's L; Pfeiffer's S, etc.). J is believed to begin in Genesis 2 and continue through Numbers.

E (Elohist), the second of the four supposed sources of the Pentateuch, derives its name from the source's supposed preference for the use of the Hebrew term for God (*Elohim*). As with the other Pentateuchal documents, E's provenance, date, and extent are debated. Its location in the Pentateuch is so difficult to determine that many scholars believe it was a redactor's supplement to the older J. Stylistically, E is supposed to view God more remotely than J and emphasizes religious and moral concerns. Generally believed to have originated in the ninth or eighth centuries in Ephraim from much older traditions, it supposedly begins in Genesis and continues through Numbers.

"The Pentateuch," in *Old Testament Survey: The Message, Form, and Background of the Old Testament*, 2nd ed., ed. by W.S. Lasor, D.A. Hubbard, and F.W. Bush (Grand Rapids: Eerdmans, 1996), p. 13; Dillard and Longman, *Introduction*, pp. 45-47.

[60]For discussions of the "J (Yahwist)" see: Soulen, *Handbook*, pp. 89-90; cf. Dillard and Longman, *Introduction*, pp. 41-42; Hartley, "The Pentateuch," pp. 10-11. For discussions of the "E (Elohist)" see: Soulen, *Handbook*, pp. 50-51; cf. Dillard and Longman, *Introduction*, pp. 41-42; Hartley, "The Pentateuch," pp. 10-11. For discussions of the "D (Deuteronomic Code)" see: Soulen, *Handbook*, pp. 46-47; cf. Dillard and Longman, *Introduction*, p. 42; Hartley, "The Pentateuch," p. 11. For discussions of the "P (Priestly Code; Priestly Document; Priestly Narrative; Priestly Writer)" see: Soulen, *Handbook*, pp. 127-128; cf. Dillard and Longman, *Introduction*, p. 42; Hartley, "The Pentateuch," p. 11.

D (Deuteronomic Code), the third of the supposed sources of the Pentateuch, comprises the core of the laws (Deuteronomy 12–26) found in the Temple (2 Kings 22–23). Scholars debate the form of the law found at the time, though nearly all date it to the time of Josiah. Stylistically, the source is perceived as prosaic, wordy, preachy, etc. Wherever such material occurs in the Old Testament, scholars label it D(eutronomistic). Theologically, the source focuses on purity in worship, a central shrine, etc.

P (Priestly Code; Priestly Document; Priestly Narrative; Priestly Writer), as with the other hypothetical documents, has been debated by recent scholarship relative to its nature, date, and content. Its name derives from the Hebrew priests whose theological views and traditions it is supposed to represent. Most scholars are in agreement that P represents the last of the source material comprising the Pentateuch. Early on, however, P was perceived as the earliest of the documents rather than the latest (fifth or fourth centuries). Scholars perceive P as focusing on those areas associated with the priesthood — legal and cultic issues, genealogies, lists, dates, measurements, formulas, etc. Repetitious in nature, P describes the creation (1:1–2:4a), can stand alongside similar material such as J (2:4b-25), and summarizes the origins of the people, their institutions and laws to their settlement in the land, and emphasizes God's holiness, sovereignty, and transcendence.

Prodocumentary scholars argue redactors put together these four documents according to the following evolutionary schema: J, E, JE, D, P. At each stage a redactor added the pertinent material, each redactor being more significant than the previous because they were giving the documents their distinctive look until the completion of the Pentateuch.[61]

STRUCTURE

The Primeval History (1:1–11:32) and the History of the Patriarchs (12:1–50:26) comprise Genesis's major divisions. The Primeval History moves from the grand sweep of creation, sin, the flood, and the tower of Babel to Abraham as the ancestor of Israel out of which grew the nation. The History of the Patriarchs focuses on Abraham's family (his son, his grandson, and 12 great-grandsons) and sets the

---

[61]Dillard and Longman, *Introduction*, p. 42.

stage for the dwelling/enslavement/exodus in Egypt as recorded in the book of Exodus.

Another way of dividing Genesis involves the use of the word "generations" (תּוֹלְדֹת, *tôlᵊdōth*). Following a prologue (1:1–2:3), the book divides into ten episodes.

1. Prologue, 1:1–2:3	7. Terah, 11:*27*–25:11
2. Heaven and Earth, 2:*4*–4:26	8. Ishmael, 25:*12*-18
3. Adam, 5:*1*–6:8	9. Isaac, 25:*19*–35:29
4. Noah, 6:*9*–9:28	10. Esau, 36:*1*–37:1
5. Sons of Noah, 10:*1*–11:9	11. Esau, 36:*9*–37:1
6. Shem, 11:*10*-26	12. Jacob, 37:*2*–50:26

This use of *tôlᵊdōth* "provides a sense of unity that cuts across the hypothetical sources"[62] above and may be indicative of its use as a "catch line,"[63] in which, following ancient Near Eastern custom, the last line of a tablet was repeated as the first line of the next tablet, thus indicating the sources used by the author Moses.[64]

A close reading of Genesis, following this division, reveals that the author's literary style involves writing an overview, or overlap of the topics to be discussed, followed by a focusing in on one particular event of the overview and elaborating it. For example, Genesis 1:1 reads as a summary statement of all seven days of creation. Chapters 1:2–2:3 detail each of the seven days. Then 2:4-24 focus more specifically on the sixth day. Other passages function in a similar fashion. (1) The birth of Seth and his son, Enosh, and men beginning to call on the name of the Lord (4:25-26) overlap with the genealogy of chapter 5. (2) The births of Noah's sons Shem, Ham, and Japeth in 5:32 overlap with the details of 6:1-8. (3) The details of the building of the ark in 6:9-22 prefigure the flood itself and contrast Noah's righteousness with the wickedness of the world. Note how these are interspaced: wickedness of man and God's decision (6:1-7) vs. Noah's righteousness (6:8-10); details of the wickedness of man and instructions regarding the ark's construction (6:11-21) vs. Noah's obedience (6:22). (4) God's instructions for Noah to go into

---

[62]Ibid., p. 48.

[63]Cf. R.K. Harrison, *Introduction to the Old Testament* (Grand Rapids: Eerdmans, 1969), pp. 548ff.

[64]Numbers that are bolded and italicized indicate verses in which the term occurs. The Esau generation is mentioned twice.

the ark, taking the appropriate animals with him because the earth will be destroyed (7:1-4) followed by Noah's obedience (7:5) overlap with the flood itself and God's covenant with Noah (7:6–9:17). (5) Noah's sons' dispersal throughout the earth (9:18-19) overlaps with the cursing of Canaan (9:20-28) and the table of nations (10:1-32). (6) The genealogy of the Semites (10:21-32) overlaps with the Tower of Babel episode as is evidenced by the repetition of the scattering of Noah's descendants in 10:32b by 11:9b and the repetition and extension of Shem's genealogy (10:21-29) to Abram (11:10-26). (7) The genealogy of Terah (11:27-32) overlaps with the account of God's call of Abraham (12:1-4), as is evidenced by Acts 7:2, which indicates that God called Abram at Ur (cf. Gen 11:28) before he dwelt in Haran. As these examples illustrate, the book's structure runs counter to the classical documentary theories and highlights an orderliness to the work as a whole.

A less observed, but significant structural marker is the promise(s) in 12:1-4. These promises, first made here with Abraham, are reaffirmed and elaborated at significant points to Abraham and his descendants (Abraham — 12:2-5; 15:4,7,18-21; 17:4-8; 22:17-18; Isaac — 26:5,24; Jacob — 28:13-15; 35:11-12). Running in tension with these separated promises is the suspense of the various stories, each of which raises the question, "How will God fulfill his promises under these conditions?" (1) Immediately after the call, the role of Sarah as the future mother of the heir is endangered in Egypt when she is taken into Pharaoh's harem (12:10-13). (2) The land promise is put in jeopardy by Lot's decision (13:2-18). (3) The birth of Ishmael places the heir promise at risk (ch. 16). (4) The heir promise is placed in danger when Sarah is taken into Abimelech's harem (20:1-18). (5) The offering of Isaac places in danger the promise of a great progeny (ch. 22). (6) Similarly, finding a wife for Isaac hints at the threat of the promise of great progeny (ch. 24). (7) The Jacob-Esau rivalry puts the promise in doubt when Esau threatens to kill Jacob (27:41). (8) The Joseph story illustrates the danger to the promise when Joseph and ultimately the entire family go to Egypt, thus leaving the land of promise (chs. 37ff.). Finally, the book ends in the tension of chaos vs. faith. The last words of Genesis record the burial of Joseph in a coffin in Egypt (50:26). The book that began with the creation *ex nihilo*, moving to the promise to Abraham of a great progeny, has ended in death. Yet faith is exhibited in that while the promise is in jeopardy, Joseph reminds the family that

God has yet to complete his fulfillment of the promise. "I am about to die, but God will surely come and bring you to the land that he swore to Abraham and Isaac" (50:24).[65]

GENRE

Various genres intermesh with the structure to produce a highly sophisticated account. Chapters 1, 5, and 11 contain intensely structured texts which emphasize particular literary points, while chapters 2-4, 6-9, and 11 revel in the drama of the story. Each performs a different purpose. Chapter one moves to the apex of God's creation by issuing eight commands that can be divided into two groups of four. The first four describe the creation and ordering of the cosmos, while the second four describe the perfecting of that cosmos — man being the last of the creation. In addition, these commands contain a tripartite structure: an announcement ("and God said"), followed by the creative command ("let there be"), followed by a report of the results ("and it was so"). The genealogical lists of 5, 10, and 11:10-32 use the same structure for each generation, enabling the text to move the reader along the main point of the story — the call of Abraham. These structured lists are interspaced with the dramas of 2-4, 6-9, and 11:1-9 to show God's continual interaction with the apex of his creation — humankind — who incessantly fails due to the power and growth of sin.[66] Though created with a "unique nature and dignity . . . human beings by virtue of their divine origin," and though made in God's image, are "yet marred materially by the sin that . . . disfigured God's good work."[67]

THEOLOGICAL THEMES

Generally speaking, Genesis introduces not just the Torah, but the story of redemption, ultimately concluding in Jesus' sacrifice and the establishment of the church. The creation is pronounced as "good," which contrasts significantly with the multiplication of sin that begins in chapter 3ff. Part of this "good" creation is man, "made in the image of God," who has godlike characteristics. As God created the universe

---

[65]Whybray, *Introduction,* pp. 54-59.
[66]Cf. Hartley, "Genesis: The Primeval Prologue," pp. 18-19.
[67]Ibid., p. 22.

and is sovereign, so humankind is created in God's image and given dominion over fish, cattle, the earth, and creepers (1:26). God created the universe by calling things into existence — "Let there be light and there was light." This calling into existence had the effect of creating it and assigning its function in the world. So the image (man) is given dominion over these things by naming the animals (2:19). Man, by naming animals and woman, assigns them a function in the world. Adam did not say, "Let there be woman"; she already existed. Rather he said, "This is now bone of my bones and flesh of my flesh; she shall be called 'woman,' for she was taken out of man. For this reason a man will leave his father and mother and be united to his wife, and they will become one flesh" (Gen 2:23-24).[68] God created male and female in his image in 1:26. Adam and Eve (the image) created children in their image (5:3). The language of 5:3 is nearly identical to 1:26. All of this hints at the significance of the fall — the image of God was marred. The death of God's son would be required to restore the image (cf. Rom 5:12-15; 1 Cor 15:22).

Immediately upon the completion of creation sin enters the world, and from this point it increases continually (Adam/Eve, Cain/Abel, boast of Lamech, total depravity of man by chapter 6). God, though long-suffering and patient, ultimately destroys mankind. The account indicates that as sin grows so grows an ever-increasing severity of punishment that ultimately produces the destruction of mankind in the flood. God determines to save humankind through Noah, thus providing an escape (9:17). God's judgment against the Tower of Babel episode illustrates the nonresolution of the problem and sets the stage for God's call of Abraham. The genealogical list of Shem (11:10-22) bridges the old world with the new world of God's covenant with Abraham.

The story's focus on Abraham indicates God's new choice to deal with sin by entering into a long-term binding agreement with one of mankind's representatives. This binding agreement, covenant, sets the stage for the unfolding of the plan of redemption. God binds himself in 12:1-4 "to bless those who bless" Abraham, "curse those who curse" Abraham, and bless the entire world through Abraham. Abraham, for his part, must separate himself from his country and relatives, and go where God directs him.

---

[68]This interpretation extends Adam's speech to include verse 24; most translations assign this verse to the narrator rather than Adam's speech.

The rest of the Bible is interpreted in this light. Israel becomes the beginning of that fulfillment, which runs through Israel's history and ultimately concludes in Jesus. These blessings, however, must be read in the context of Abraham's faith. It began as a mustard seed. God had called Abraham at Ur (Acts 7:1). Abraham departed Ur but did not leave his relatives. Taking his father, Terah, and his nephew, Lot, he settled in Haran. Terah died in Haran; Abraham departed to the country God would show him. Abraham was blessed materially, but not truly blessed until he separated from his nephew Lot. Ultimately, he did separate from him and was blessed with the sons Ishmael and Isaac. Ishmael was not the child of promise and was cast out. God commanded Abraham to sacrifice Isaac, the child of promise. The sacrifice of Isaac represented the ultimate test of Abraham's faith: Abraham believed that God would prevail by raising Isaac, resulting in Abraham's being credited with righteousness due to his faith (15:6; 22; Heb 11:17-19).

At appropriate times the promises were repeated, in whole or in part, to each of the patriarchs (12:2-3; 15:18; 17:2-5; 22:17-18; 26:3-4; 28:14; 35:11), thus affirming God's covenant with Abraham. Beginning with the Joseph story the storyline changes. The previous stories portray God's interaction with the patriarchs. Here Joseph tells his brothers, in his famous "you meant it for evil, but God meant it for good" speech (Gen 50:19-20), "God overrules the wicked intentions of men and women in order to save his people, [which] runs throughout the Old Testament. . . ."[69] In each of these stories one or more of the promises are put in danger of not being fulfilled, but are ultimately accomplished due to God's grace.

NEW TESTAMENT CONNECTIONS

The "seed (offspring) of woman" in Genesis 3:15 forms a connecting link with Matthew 1, and Matthew 27–28. The offspring of the woman is fulfilled in the virgin birth (Matthew 1), while the "offspring of Satan" would refer to those under his influence, i.e., the Jewish leaders and Roman soldiers who crucified Christ, thus bruising his heel (Matthew 27). Christ then arose from the dead never to die again (Matthew 28), thus bruising Satan's head. Therefore, we all

---

[69]Dillard and Longman, *Introduction*, p. 55; cf. Whybray, *Introduction*, pp. 55ff.

live in hope of the resurrection, which reverses God's judgment on humankind, i.e., death.

Similarly, Paul refers to Genesis 15:1-6 in Galatians 3:6ff. to indicate that all people who believe the gospel are the spiritual descendants of Abraham. God told Abraham that his descendants would be as the stars in the heavens. Abraham believed God for which God credited him righteous. Paul's point is that Christians have believed and thus are the spiritual descendants of Abraham (cf. Rom 4:11).

God's call of Abraham in Genesis 12:1-3 marked the beginning of God's election of a race of people through whom the Messiah, or Jesus, would come, ultimately making Christians spiritual descendants of Abraham. As Paul states it in Galatians 3:13-14, "Christ redeemed us from the curse of the law by becoming a curse for us, for it is written: 'Cursed is everyone who is hung on a tree.' He redeemed us in order that the blessing given to Abraham might come to the Gentiles through Christ Jesus, so that by faith we might receive the promise of the Spirit." Beyond this, ". . . the book of Hebrews (11:8-19) draws our attention to Abraham's life as a struggle of faith. . . . Abraham received God's promise and then struggled in the face of obstacles to the fulfillment of that promise. So Hebrews draws an analogy with Christians. They too have received the promise of God, but daily confront obstacles. Abraham is presented as an example in order to support the Christian reader in this struggle."[70]

---

[70]Dillard and Longman, *Introduction,* p. 56.

EXODUS

The Exodus of Israel from Egypt is the central event of the Hebrew Bible. This act of redemption by God became the foundation for Israelite faith and practice reflected in the many Old Testament allusions to the Exodus as the basis for obedience to the covenant, proper ethical treatment of others, the establishment of the sovereignty of God, a national dateline marking the nation's history, and a standard for the measurement of all subsequent events. For the Christian, the Exodus serves similar functions, pointing to the important work of redemption as seen in the New Testament's record of the death, burial, and resurrection of Jesus Christ.[1]

The book of Exodus connects with Genesis in several ways. (1) The book's Hebrew title (the English title stems from the LXX and means "to go out") derives from the words, וְאֵלֶּה שְׁמוֹת (wᵉ'ēlleh šᵉmôth, "and these are the names"), which is a virtual repetition of Genesis 46:8ff., both texts detailing the sons of Israel who went down to Egypt. (2) Exodus 13:19 refers to the honoring of Joseph's instructions regarding his bones (Gen 50:22-26). (3) The polarity between light and darkness found in Genesis 1 is redefined in Exodus 8:23 in terms of God's division between Israel and Egypt. Light is associated with Israel while darkness is associated with Egypt. This light/darkness motif continues in Israel's journeys with the cloudy and fiery pillars by day and night (13:21-22; 14:19-20; 19:18; 20:18; 33:9-11; 40:34-38). (4) God's promises to Abraham to make of him a great nation (Gen 12:1-3; Gen 15:5) are fulfilled. Though numbering less than one hundred people upon their entrance into Egypt, they numbered 603,550 males over twenty years of age by the beginning of the wanderings (Num 1:46), thus

---

[1]For representative discussions of the significance of Exodus see: N.M. Sarna, *Exploring Exodus: The Heritage of Biblical Israel* (New York: Schocken, 1986), pp. 1-2; R. Hendel, "The Exodus in Biblical Memory," *JBL* 120 (2001): 601; K.A. Kitchen, "Exodus, The," *ABD* (1992): 2:701.

placing the population in the millions. The Exodus facilitated this fulfillment of God's promise. The language of Exodus 1:7 recalls Genesis 1:28, both texts emphasizing a geometric growth. Similarly, God's giving the midwives families (הַמְיַלְּדֹת, ham⁹yall⁹dōth, Exod 1:21) and Moses' birth (תֵּלֶד, tēled, Exod 2:2) are from the same semantic root as the "generations" (תּוֹלְדֹת, tôl⁹dōth) of the Genesis narratives, indicating shifts in the genealogical line and the promises to the entire nation. (5) A similar shift occurs in issues of primogeniture. The Isaac/Ishmael, Jacob/Esau, and Ephraim/Manasseh rivalries of Genesis are reworked in terms of God choosing Israel from the nations, as the tenth plague emphasized (Exod 4:22-23) and reaffirmed (Deut 7:7). (6) The death angel sent to kill Moses' uncircumcised son (Exod 4:24-26) reaffirms the importance of circumcision (Genesis 17). (7) The Sabbath commandment (Exod 20:8-11) is issued in the context of the first Sabbath (Gen 2:1-3). (8) God's revelation to Moses (Exod 3:6,15) presupposes the patriarchal history of Genesis. These are but a few of the connections with Genesis which indicate the people did grow into a great nation, were given a covenant at Sinai, and began their journey to the promised land, in accordance with the fulfillment of the promises of God to the patriarchs. So Exodus, as the sequel to Genesis, describes the deliverance of the children of Israel by God and the establishment of a new covenant between God and Israel. The rest of the Old Testament looks back on the Exodus as the primary redemptive event in Israel's history.[2]

HISTORICAL AND CULTURAL BACKGROUND

The Exodus occurred at the end of the late bronze age (ca. 1550–1200). Politically, several new empires developed in the ancient Near East during this period. The Hurrian state of Mitanni covered northwest Mesopotamia (Syria to the Zagros Mountains). Northwest of

---

[2]Cf. Dillard and Longman, *Introduction*, p. 57; Harrison, *Introduction*, p. 566; E.J. Young, *An Introduction to the Old Testament* (Grand Rapids: Eerdmans, 1964), pp. 62-63; J.E. Hartley, "Exodus: Message," in *Old Testament Survey: The Message, Form, and Background of the Old Testament*, 2nd ed., ed. by W.S. Lasor, D.A. Hubbard, and F.W. Bush (Grand Rapids: Eerdmans, 1996), p. 63; J.P. Fokkelman, "Exodus," in *The Literary Guide to the Bible*, ed. by R. Altar and F. Kermode (Cambridge: Harvard University Press, 1987), pp. 56-65; Sarna, *Exploring Exodus*, pp. 5-6.

Mitanni lay the Hittites. East of Mitanni stood Assyria. Egypt was on the rise, having just recovered from the Hyksos domination (1700–1500). With the defeat of the Hyksos, Egypt entered a period of expansion northeast into Asia. This put Egypt in conflict with Mitanni for control of Syria. After fifty years of intermittent fighting both sides agreed to cease hostilities in order to deal with the Hittites. For another fifty years Mitanni and Egypt were at peace, during which time Egypt reached the zenith of power under Amenophis III (1403–1364) who engaged in a life of luxury and building projects. The Amarna revolution occurred under Amenophis IV (1366–1317). He began the worship of Aten (the Solar Disk), proclaimed it the only true god, changed his name to Akhenaten ("the Splendor of Aten"), and built a new capital, Akhetaten, at the modern site of Tell el-Amarna. The Amarna Letters, discovered there in 1887, were written from Egyptian vassals in Syria-Palestine to Amenophis III and IV. They reveal the opulence and religious interests of Amenophis III and IV, which diverted their attention from Syria-Palestine allowing a state of anarchy to arise. The Hittites defeated Mitanni and put a vassal on the throne. Assyria took the northeastern part of the empire and Asia, ending Egyptian control of the area. Under the Nineteenth Dynasty Egypt regained control of Syria-Palestine under Rameses II (1290–1224). Rameses II completed his last years in building activities. Merneptah, who succeeded his father ca. 1220, faced an invasion by the People of the Sea from the west. He commemorated his defeat of them in the famous stele named for him, which contains the first extrabiblical reference to Israel. These interactions produced international alliances in which nations adapted each other's culture and gods. The literature of various cultures were translated as Akkadian became the international business and governmental language. The massive syllabic and ideographic cuneiform was surpassed by the Canaanite development of alphabetic writing with approximately twenty-five symbols. In addition to the above, the exceptional Ugaritic texts of Ra Shamara Ugarit produced parallels that illuminated much of Israelite culture.[3]

---

[3]Cf. Hartley, "Exodus: Historical Background," in *Old Testament Survey: The Message, Form, and Background of the Old Testament*, 2nd ed., ed. by W.S. Lasor, D.A. Hubbard, and F.W. Bush (Grand Rapids: Eerdmans, 1996), pp. 52-58; J. Bright, *A History of Israel*, 3rd ed. (Philadelphia: Westminster, 1981), pp. 108-133.

Into this context falls the knotty problem of the evidence for, and date of, the Exodus. More will be said about this under "History of Interpretation," but note here that a straightforward reading of Genesis–Exodus fits well with ancient Near Eastern culture. The Joseph story reflects Egyptian life and customs. Egypt did employ Semitic peoples. Some of the names, particularly Moses' family, are Egyptian. Subject peoples' escape from oppressors was not unique to Israel. Finally, the invention of such a background history is negligible from a social-psychological perspective.[4]

TEXT AND AUTHOR

As with the other pentateuchal books, the acceptance of Mosaic authorship of Exodus prevailed until the rise of modern criticism. The documentary theories inserted in place of Mosaic authorship all have difficulties. (1) Traditional critical scholarship argues J, E, and P may be found in Exodus. Yet, as noted in the introduction to Genesis, the distinguishing of J from E (or any other of the supposed documents) has proven difficult for scholarship. (2) Pro-documentary scholarship has failed to reach unanimity in determining (a) whether the material at the end of the book relating to the tabernacle is a separate source or redacted material, or (b) the relationship between the legal material and the narrative texts. (3) Early critical scholars thought the Decalogue originated in E, whereas modern scholarship believes the legal material to be independent compositions inserted into the narrative. (4) Some critical scholars use the Hittite treaties as models of the integration of legal and narrative (historical prologue), though recent scholarship has criticized this. (5) So critical scholarship has failed to reach a consensus regarding the book's composition and authorship.[5]

Contrary to these theories, three passages in Exodus indicate writing activity of Moses (17:14; 24:4; 34:4,27-29). Further, the New Testament affirms that Moses wrote the law (Mark 1:44; John 7:19-22; Acts 26:23). As noted when discussing Genesis, the idea of Mosaic authorship recognizes the lack of continuity of the narrative, as well as the possibility of later insertions. Mosaic authorship would involve the ancient Near Eastern practice of recording of events as

---

[4]Hartley, "Exodus: Historical Background," p. 59.
[5]Dillard and Longman, *Introduction*, p. 58.

they occurred. These "documents" would serve as a reservoir to assemble the material in a general sequence of events rather than a precise chronology.[6]

HISTORY OF INTERPRETATION

Modern scholarship has also failed to reach a consensus relative to the Exodus event. Some scholars accept the historicity of the event,[7] while others type the story as folk tradition, or the like.[8] All scholarship falls within these extremes, exhibiting varying combinations of the two. Kitchen has provided a useful summary of some of the major shifts in this continuum (e.g., Bright — no doubt there was an Exodus; Anderson — an Exodus interpreted through Israel's faith; Garbini — while the probability of the Exodus exists there is no way to verify the event; Lemche — the Exodus traditions are legendary).[9] Depending upon the position taken, scholarship has also questioned the number of people departing Egypt, the biblical description of Moses, the date and substance of the Exodus, and the tabernacle. However, for those accepting the historicity of the event, the date of the Exodus has remained the most thorny problem. For this reason the following discussion focuses on this problem. Detailed discussions of the date of the Exodus may be found in the technical literature. The following summarizes the general issues.[10]

---

[6]Harrison, *Introduction*, pp. 568-569.

[7]Cf., e.g., W.F. Albright, *Yahweh and the Gods of Canaan: A Historical Analysis of Two Contrasting Faiths* (New York: Doubleday, 1968), pp. 159, 164; Bright, *History*, pp. 120ff.; G.L. Archer Jr., *A Survey of Old Testament Introduction* (Chicago: Moody, 1964), pp. 164, 213-223; Young, *Introduction*, p. 67; Dillard and Longman, *Introduction*, pp. 58-62; Hartley, "Exodus: Historical Background," pp. 58-59.

[8]Cf., e.g., J.M. Miller and J.H. Hayes, *A History of Israel and Judah* (Philadelphia: Westminster, 1986), pp. 67-68, 78-79; J.A. Soggin, *An Introduction to the History of Israel and Judah*, 2nd ed. (London: SCM, 1993), pp. 108-139.

[9]Kitchen, "Exodus," *ABD*, 2:701-702; B.W. Anderson, *Understanding the Old Testament*, 3rd ed. (Englewood Cliffs, NJ/London: Prentice-Hall, 1978), pp. 43-45; G. Garbini, *History and Ideology in Ancient Israel* (New York: Crossroad, 1988), p. 15; N.P. Lemche, *Ancient Israel: A New History of Israelite Society*, The Biblical Seminar 5 (Sheffield: Sheffield, 1988), p. 109.

[10]Hendel ("Exodus in Biblical Memory," p. 602, esp. n. 3) has noted some of the more pertinent, recent works dealing with the historicity of the Exodus: B. Halpern, "The Exodus and the Israelite Historians," *ErIsr* 24

Dates for the Exodus range from the fifteenth to the eleventh centuries, with the fifteenth and thirteenth being the most popular centuries among scholars.[11] No direct, extrabiblical evidence weights any one of these centuries more than the others, making the extant, circumstantial evidence open to interpretation. This situation allows each scholar to exploit the data in favor of a particular century.

Traditionally the fifteenth-century date fits better with the biblical record than with the archaeological record. First Kings 6:1 states Solomon began to build the Temple 480 years after the Exodus during the fourth year of his reign (dated 967), establishing a date of 1447. Judges 11:26 records Jephthah's negotiations with the king of Ammon. Jephthah claims Israel held Moab since the entrance into the land 300 years earlier. Jephthah's date establishes the date of about 1400 for the conquest, thus corroborating the date of 1447 for the date of the Exodus. Genesis 15:13 lists the predetermined period of slavery to be 400 years, covering four generations (v. 16), which coordinates with the genealogy of Moses: Moses was the great-grandson of Levi, son of Jacob (Exod 6:1,16,18,20). Joseph's great-great-grandson, Jair, participated in Joshua's wars of conquest (Gen 50:23; Num 32:39-41; Deut 3:14; Josh 13:1; 17:1). Moses' birth occurred after the onset of the oppression, and he was 80 years old at the Exodus (2:1; 7:7; Deut 34:7), indicating that the enslavement period lasted at least this long. Finally, the MT Exodus 12:40-41 gives the figure 430 years as the time Israel spent in Egypt, but the Samaritan Pentateuch and the LXX (as well as Gal 3:17) include the length of stay in Canaan, beginning with the call of Abraham as part of this 430 year period. Thus the genealogies leave room only for about a century or so for the period in Egypt. This would allow the following chronological schema, or the like:

(1993): 89-96; id., "The Exodus from Egypt: Myth or Reality," in *The Rise of Ancient Israel*, ed. by Hershel Shanks (Washington, DC: Biblical Archaeological Society, 1992), pp. 86-117; A. Malamat, "The Exodus: Egyptian Analogies," in *Exodus: The Egyptian Evidence*, ed. by E.S. Frerichs and L.H. Lesko (Winona Lake, IN: Eisenbrauns, 1997), pp. 15-26; C.A. Redmount, "Bitter Lives: Israel In and Out of Egypt," in *The Oxford History of the Biblical World*, ed. by M.D. Coogan (New York: Oxford, 1998), pp. 79-121; Dillard and Longman, *Introduction*, p. 59.

[11]G.A. Rendsburg, "The Date of the Exodus and the Conquest/Settlement: The Case for the 1100s," *VT* 42 (1992): 510-527; cf. Harrison, *Introduction*, p. 315; Hartley, "Exodus: Historical Background," p. 58.

1. The Exodus occurred 430 years from Abraham's call, Gal 3:16-17
2. Abraham was 75 years old in Haran, leaving 430 years, Gen 12:4
3. Abraham was 100 when Isaac born, leaving 405 years, Gen 21:5
4. Isaac was 40 at marriage, leaving 365 years, Gen 22:20
5. Isaac was 60 at Jacob/Esau's birth, leaving 345 years, Gen 25:26
6. Jacob was 130 when he came to Egypt, leaving 215 years, Gen 47:9
7. Thus Israel grew into a nation during 215 years of living in Egypt.

However, the above fails to note the statement that God called Abraham "while he was in Mesopotamia, before he lived in Haran" (Acts 7:1-2). Assuming this call occurred 5 years before produces Abraham's age of 70 years at his call rather than 75. This means the period in Egypt must be adjusted to 210 years rather than 215. This figure of 70 years fits better with Scripture and Jewish tradition. Exodus 12:41 says the 430 years was "to the very day," which occurred on the first Passover. Joshua 5:11 says the people ate of the land the day after the "Passover, that very day." The phrases "to the very day" and "that very day" seem to indicate a lining up of chronology. Abraham's call, Isaac's birth, and the Passover occur on the same day; 430 years figures from the call; 400 from Isaac's birth.[12]

Scholars arguing for a fifteenth-century date pointed to Garstang's excavations at Jericho. Garstang identified a city "D," which he concluded was constructed in the fifteenth century and destroyed approximately a century later, as the "Jericho" destroyed by Joshua.[13] However, excavations by Kenyon in 1952 forced a reinterpretation of this archaeological data. Kenyon established that city "D" actually should be dated to the third millennium B.C. and that, while evidence once existed for thirteenth- and twelfth-century levels which might have been attacked by Joshua, this evidence had long since eroded away.[14]

The Amarna Tablets (discovered in 1887; consisted of 350 tablets, about 150 of which were written from Syro-Palestinian vassals to their

---

[12]Cf. Dillard and Longman, *Introduction,* p. 59; Archer, *Survey,* pp. 212-214; Harrison, *Introduction,* pp. 315-317.

[13]J. Garstang, *Joshua–Judges* (New York: R.R. Smith, 1931), p. 146.

[14]K.M. Kenyon, *Archaeology of the Holy Land,* 4th ed. (New York: W.W. Norton, 1979), pp. 208, 331-332; cf. Kenyon, *Digging Up Jericho* (New York: Praeger, 1957); cf. Harrison, *Introduction,* p. 318.

Egyptian overlords, Amenhotep III [ca. 1405–1368] and Akhenaton [ca. 1370–1353]) factor into attempts to establish the fifteenth-century date. Most of the letters complain of the Habiru, who perennially overran the country. Many scholars equated these events with Joshua's conquest. More recent research, however, indicates the Habiru should be associated with a social class, making this an internal social problem, rather than any linguistic connection with the Hebrews, which would point to an invasion by a powerful army.[15]

Traditionally the thirteenth-century date fits better with the archaeological record than the biblical record. (1) Some scholars have identified Pithom and Rameses (Exod 1:11) with Pi-Ramses built by Seti I or Rameses II in the thirteenth century. Monet's Excavations at Tanis-Avaris indicate the reconstruction of the city by Seti I, while literary artifacts mention Rameses II and his successors. Because contemporary texts mentioned the employment of Hapiru to drag the huge blocks of masonry used there, scholars identified Rameses as the Pharaoh of the oppression. Petrie's excavations at Tell el-Retabeh uncovered massive brickwork, which scholars interpreted as evidence for Pithom mentioned in Exodus 1:11, again pointing to Rameses II as the Pharaoh of the oppression. Taken together, this evidence seemed sufficient to identify the Hyksos invasion of Egypt with the Hebrew's occupation of the land of Goshen in the Nile delta (Gen 47:1,4,6,27). All of the above encouraged scholars to argue the Exodus occurred 430 years after the founding of Tanis-Avaris around 1300 B.C. (2) The "Israel stele" of Merneptah celebrates a victory over several Canaanite groups in his fifth year (1209). The stele mentions Israel by name, indicating the Exodus must have occurred earlier. (3) Evidence of Israelite settlements built upon destroyed Canaanite sites occur at Bethel, Tel Zeror, Beth Shemesh, and possibly Tell Beith Mirsim. In addition, Hazor was destroyed in the thirteenth century, possibly in the time of Joshua–Judges. Destruction of several Canaanite cities, the resettling of some cities by peoples of both similar and different cultures, and a surge of population by pastoral peoples, all over a two-century period, argue for the settlement patterns portrayed in the book of Judges. (4) Egyptian documents from the time of Merneptah and Rameses II document the use of Semites as slaves during this period. (5) The thirteenth-century date fits well with the time spent in

---

[15]Harrison, *Introduction,* pp. 318-321.

Egypt (400 years according to Gen 15:13 and 430 years according to Exod 12:40).[16]

Regardless of the century chosen, objections are raised for nearly every conclusion drawn.[17] Some of the more pertinent ones are listed here. Those arguing against a fifteenth-century date contend that "Pithom and Rameses" (Exod 1:11) should not be identified with Maskhout and Tanis because both of these were unoccupied in the fifteenth. They argue instead that Qantir contains evidence of fifteenth-century occupation, making it a better site than Tanis as Rameses; "Rameses" (1:11) results from later textual updating. Similarly, pro-thirteenth scholars have identified the thirteenth-century destructions of cities in Syria-Palestine as those destroyed by Joshua, while pro-fifteenth-century scholars counter these thirteenth-century destruction sites need not be identified with Joshua's conquest because many of the fifteenth-century destruction sites traditionally identified with Egyptian attacks on Hyksos fortifications can just as easily be identified with Joshua's conquests. In addition, those arguing for a thirteenth-century date assume the 400 and 430 years refer to the time spent in Egypt, while those who contend for a fifteenth-century date allow the 400 and 430 years to begin with Abraham's call and end with the Exodus. Finally, those arguing for a fifteenth-century date contend the 480 years of 1 Kings 6:1 is a literal figure, while those arguing for a thirteenth-century date counter it ". . . may be an 'aggregate' or 'symbolic' number . . . based on the total of twelve generations of 40 years each."[18]

---

[16]For detailed discussions relating to the dating of the exodus see: Harrison, *Introduction*, pp. 321-323; Hartley, "Exodus: Historical Background," pp. 59-60; P. Monet, *Les nouvelles fouilles de Tanis* (1929–33); Dillard and Longman, *Introduction*, pp. 59-62; J.J. Bimson, *Redating the Exodus*, JSOTSupp 5 (Sheffield: JSOT, 1978), pp. 1-351; Archer, *Survey*, pp. 164, 212-223; J. Finegan, *Light from the Ancient Past: The Archaeological Background of Judaism and Christianity* (Princeton, NJ: Princeton University Press, 1959), pp. 120-121.

[17]Cf. J.H. Walton, *Chronological Charts of the Old Testament* (Grand Rapids: Zondervan, 1978), pp. 29-30, for summaries and rebuttals for each century. See also: Dillard and Longman, *Introduction*, pp. 59-62; Bimson, *Redating*, pp. 42, 47-48, 67-80.

[18]Hartley, "Exodus: Historical Background," p. 60; cf. D.H. Freedman, "The Chronology of Israel and the Ancient Near East," in *The Bible and the Ancient Near East*, ed. by G.E. Wright (Garden City, NY: Doubleday, 1961), pp. 206-208.

The above illustrates the difficulty of the problem. Just about any position receives a counterinterpretation, indicating "the enormous amount of care that must be exercised in an attempt to interpret and correlate archaeological data with a view to elucidating and establishing the larger historical pattern."[19] The nature of archaeological data compounds the problem further: "They are not brute facts with which the biblical material must conform and that can prove or disprove the Bible. Archaeology rather produces evidence that, like the Bible, must be interpreted."[20] All in all, this writer believes the archaeological and biblical evidence harmonize best with the fifteenth-century date. Whether or not the exact date is ever known, the more important issue is the impact this event had on the nation, the results of which were the recording of the events that God used to form the nation, as entered in this book of the same name.

STRUCTURE

Scholars divide Exodus differently. Those divisions which work best are probably those which emphasize the motifs of salvation (1:1–18:27), a law (19:1–24:18), and worship (25:1–40:38), or the like.[21] An outline of Exodus follows:

The oppression in Egypt — 1:1-22
The birth, training, and call of Moses — 2:1-7:7
The plagues, the Passover, and the Exodus — 7:8–15:21
The journey to Horeb (Mount Sinai) — 15:22–18:27
The giving of the Law at Sinai — 19:1–24:18
The divine plan for the tabernacle — 25:1–31:18
The idolatry of the Israelites and Moses' intercession — 32:1–33:23
The regiving of the law — 34:1-17
The construction and erection of the tabernacle — 35:1–40:38

The content embedded in this outline produce some fascinating narrative and structural issues.

The birth story of Moses prefigures the water motif that played out in the history of the nation's salvation from Egypt. When Pharaoh decreed that all the male babies should be drowned (1:22),

---

[19]Harrison, *Introduction*, pp. 324-325.
[20]Dillard and Longman, *Introduction*, p. 61.
[21]Dillard and Longman, *Introduction*, p. 62; cf. Sarna, *Exploring Exodus*, pp. 6-7.

baby Moses was placed in an ark and hidden among the reeds of the Nile. Pharaoh's daughter rescued him, giving him his name (meaning "to draw out"). These events prefigure the rescue of Israel when it safely crossed the Sea of Reeds (Red Sea).[22]

The ten plagues occur in series, three disasters in each, with the fourth unrelated to any natural occurrences, indicating God's hand behind the event. Pharaoh is forewarned of the first two plagues in each of the series, but not of the third (7:16-24; 8:1-7,16-18[Heb 12-14],20-24[Heb 16-20]; 9:1-7,8-12,13-21; 10:3-6,21-29). In the first plague of each series God commands Moses to meet Pharaoh "in the morning" (7:15; 8:20; 9:13), while no such time command exists in the other two plagues of each series. The first plague of each series contains the command to "Station/Present yourself to Pharaoh" (Exod 7:15; 8:20; 9:13), the second contains the command "Go to Pharaoh" (9:1; 10:3), and the third contains no such instruction (8:16-19; 9:8-12; 10:21-29). The first series is brought on by Aaron, while the third series is brought on by God. Within this general structure three Hebrew words, הלך (*hlk*, "to go, come, walk," 7:15), בוֹא (*bō'*, "come in, come, go in, go," 8:1[Heb 7:26]; 9:1), and נצב/יצב (*yṣb/nṣb*, "take one's stand, be stationed by appointment," 7:15, 8:20[Heb 8:16], 9:13) dominate. They combine in a progressive format to create an intensity of action and deed. The use of *yṣb/nṣb* ("take one's stand, be stationed by appointment) in the first plague of each series yields an image of Moses' "preparing for the confrontation" (7:15; 8:20[Heb 8:16]; 9:13). The use of *bō'* ("come in, come, go in, go") in the second plague of each series yields the image of God's presence in the confrontation (8:1[Heb 7:26]; 9:1; 10:1). The absence of any similar term in the third plague of each series reflects the intensity of the situation by having this third plague proceed almost immediately, without any confrontation or discussion between the warring parties. All of this is set up by the first plague, which contains both *hlk* ("to go, come, walk," 7:15) and *nṣb* ("take one's stand, be stationed by appointment," 7:15), when God first commands Moses "Go and station yourself. . . ." (7:15). The series ends with the tenth plague, which possesses no such terms, but contains instead a short narrative detailing the purpose and significance of this last plague (11:1-3). In this way the first nine plagues build toward the climaxing tenth. The first nine plagues (all

---

[22]Sarna, "Exodus, Book of," *ABD*, 2:695.

based in natural phenomena except for the timing element in which the plague is initiated at Moses' command) build in intensity through the ninth. A brief interlude occurs before the most powerful and devastating plague (which is grounded in no natural phenomena) against Pharaoh — the death of his firstborn, and all the firstborn of Egypt (11:4).[23]

The hardening of Pharaoh's heart occurs in this same context (chs. 4–14) exactly twenty times, with the cause for the hardening being divided equally between Pharaoh and God (Pharaoh—7:13,14, 22; 8:15,19,32; 9:7,34,35; 13:5; God—4:21; 7:3; 9:12; 10:1,20,27; 11:10; 14:4,8,17), indicating a sharing of responsibility between the two beings — God demanded and Pharaoh responded.

Pharaoh's negotiations represent another perspective in the contest between God and Pharaoh. Sandwiched between the hardening accounts, they reveal a weakening on Pharaoh's side while simultaneously his heart becomes, paradoxically, harder. In the first proposal Pharaoh says, "*Who is the LORD, that I should heed him and let Israel go? I do not know the LORD, and I will not let Israel go*" (5:2, NRSV, emphasis added). In the second proposal Pharaoh no longer asks disrespectfully, "who is the LORD?" but gives in a little. Summoning Moses and Aaron he said, "*Go, sacrifice to your God within the land*" (8:25, NRSV, emphasis added). The third proposal begins by Pharaoh making a counteroffer to sacrifice in the wilderness, but not very far, coupled with a request for prayers: "I will let you *go to sacrifice* to the LORD your God *in the wilderness*, provided you *do not go very far away. Pray for me*" (8:28, NRSV, emphasis added). The fourth proposal begins with Pharaoh's sending for Moses and Aaron, acknowledging his sin and requesting prayer, and proposing to do just what God asks: "Then Pharaoh summoned Moses and Aaron, and said to them, '*This time I have sinned; the LORD is in the right, and I and my people are in the wrong. Pray to the LORD!* Enough of God's thunder and hail! *I will let you go; you need stay no longer*'" (9:27-28, NRSV, emphasis added). Prior to the fifth proposal Pharaoh's officials advise him to let the people go and recognize the land's destruction. Pharaoh responds by commanding Israel to go worship, but counters with the command to leave their children,

---

[23]Ibid., pp. 695-696. Cf. Sarna, *Exploring Exodus*, pp. 75-77, esp. Table 4.2, for the structure of the plagues; cf. Hartley, "Exodus: Message," pp. 68-70; and Young, *Introduction*, pp. 64-65.

ultimately refusing to let them go, as he drives Moses and Aaron from his presence:

> Pharaoh's officials said to him, "How long shall this fellow be a snare to us? Let the people go, so that they may worship the LORD their God; do you not yet understand that Egypt is ruined?" So Moses and Aaron were brought back to Pharaoh, and he said to them, "*Go, worship the LORD your God! But which ones are to go?*" Moses said, "We will go with our young and our old; we will go with our sons and daughters and with our flocks and herds, because we have the LORD's festival to celebrate." He said to them, "*The LORD indeed will be with you, if ever I let your little ones go with you! Plainly, you have some evil purpose in mind. No, never! Your men may go and worship the LORD, for that is what you are asking.*" And *they were driven out from Pharaoh's presence.* (10:7-11, NRSV, emphasis added).

The sixth proposal reverts to an admission of sin, requests forgiveness and prayer for the removal of the plague:

> Pharaoh hurriedly summoned Moses and Aaron and said, "*I have sinned* against the LORD your God, and against you. *Do forgive my sin just this once, and pray to the LORD your God that at the least he remove this deadly thing from me.*" So he went out from Pharaoh and prayed to the LORD. The LORD changed the wind into a very strong west wind, which lifted the locusts and drove them into the Red Sea; not a single locust was left in all the country of Egypt. *But the LORD hardened Pharaoh's heart*, and he would not let the Israelites go. *Then the LORD said to Moses, "Stretch out your hand toward heaven so that there may be darkness over the land of Egypt*, a darkness that can be felt." So Moses stretched out his hand toward heaven, and there was dense darkness in all the land of Egypt for three days. People could not see one another, and for three days they could not move from where they were; but all the Israelites had light where they lived. Then Pharaoh summoned Moses, and said, "Go, worship the LORD. Only your *flocks and your herds shall remain behind.* Even *your children may go with you*" (10:16-24, NRSV, emphasis added).

The seventh proposal gives permission for the children to go, but commands the flocks and herds be left behind: "Then Pharaoh summoned Moses, and said, 'Go, worship the LORD. Only your *flocks and your herds shall remain* behind. Even your *children may go* with you'" (10:24, NRSV, emphasis added). The eighth proposal contains the command to go, coupled with a requested blessing: "Then he summoned Moses and Aaron in the night, and said, '*Rise up, go away from my people, both you and the Israelites! Go, worship the LORD, as you said. Take your flocks and your herds, as you said, and be gone. And bring a blessing on me too!*'" (12:31-32, NRSV, emphasis added). Ultimately Pharaoh hardened his heart again, for he pursued Israel only to be drowned in the Red Sea (14).[24]

The ten plagues, the hardening of Pharaoh's heart, and the negotiations intermesh to produce a story emphasizing the growing power of God against the continually weakening Pharaoh (perceived as a God by the Egyptians), which itself radicalizes the separation of Israel from Egypt. They were totally freed, redeemed, by God and thus belonged completely to him.

The chronological displacement of several episodes indicate an emphasis of event over chronology. (1) The visit of Jethro, in which he gave Moses advice relative to the appointment of judges (18:1ff.), must have occurred after God's revelation at Sinai. In 18:5 the people were already encamped at "the mountain of God," but their arrival is not recorded until 19:1-2. Deuteronomy 1:9-17 refers to Jethro's advice (v. 9), indicating the people departed from Horeb immediately after and "implying that the former took place toward the end of the sojourn at Sinai; this is consonant with Num 11:11,28-32 which testifies to Jethro's presence in the camp in 'the second month of the second year after the Exodus,' so that the report of Exod 18:27 registering Jethro's departure must be dated after the theophany."[25] Such an arrangement contrasts the friendliness of the Midianites with the treachery of the Amalekites and provides a good transition to the giving of the law in chapter 20.

The episode of the golden calf (32:1–33:23) traverses the account of the erection of the tabernacle, highlighting the rejection of God in their midst and the insertion of a god of their own making. So, "The present arrangement of the material draws attention to this and points the way to the only legitimate expression of experiencing God — viz., through divinely authorized means and not through idols."[26]

---

[24]Cf. Young, *Introduction*, p. 66.

[25]Sarna, "Exodus," *ABD*, 2:696.

[26]Ibid.

Structural similarities between the Sinai Covenant and international treaties, observed by some scholars, include the following: (a) preamble — identified the author with his titles; (b) historical prologue — setting forth the historical relationship between the suzerain and the vassal; (c) stipulations — demanding loyalty from the vassal and specific rules describing the relationship; (d) provisions — detailing such things as the vassal's obligations, including but not limited to, the obligation to come to the suzerain's court, to provide troops for defense, the proper place for the treaty to be located and the calendar for its public reading; (e) curses and blessings — invoked on the vassal depending upon his obedience or disobedience. Some scholars have noted the above various items in Exodus and Deuteronomy.

Preamble:	"I am the LORD your God," Exod 20:2a
Historical Prologue:	"who brought you out of the land of Egypt, out of the house of slavery," Exod 20:2b; cf. Josh 24:2-13
Stipulations:	loyalty demanded in the phrase, "You should have no other gods before me," Exod 20:3; specific stipulations are seen in the other ten commandments, Exod 20:4-7
Provisions:	the law was to be kept in the ark of the covenant, Exod 25:16; cf. Deut 10:1-5; public reading of the law was to occur every seven years, Deut 31:10-13
Curses and Blessing:	pronounced, Deut 28:1-14,15-68

For those who accept it, this parallel indicates God's use of the familiar treaty pattern of the ancient Near East for theological purposes. In this treaty format, with which Moses and the people were familiar, God bound the people to him because of his past redemptive acts for them. Thus the ten commandments become, not law in the common sense, but policy stating the type of behavior demanded. The "Book of the Covenant" or "Covenant Code" (20:23–23:33) defined and applied this type of behavior contractually to everyday life in terms of God and his human community.[27]

---

[27]For discussions comparing and contrasting biblical law to ancient Near Eastern treaties see: Hartley, "Exodus: Message," pp. 72-75; G. Mendenhall, "Ancient Oriental and Biblical Law," *BA* 17 (1954): 26-46; id., "Covenant Forms in Israelite Tradition," *BA* 17 (1954): 50-76; repr. in *The Biblical Archaeologist Reader 3*, ed. by E.F. Campbell and D.N. Freedman (Garden

GENRE

A number of genres occur in Exodus, including the general categories of narrative, law, and poetry. These combine to form prophetic or theological history which reveals the nature of God in his acts: the *birth story* of Moses (2:1-10) focuses on the key issues that molded the future leader of Israel; *fragmented stories*, such as Zipporah's circumcision of her son (4:24-26), reenforce God's demand for obedience;[28] *theophanies* (God's appearance to men), such as the burning bush (ch. 3), the appearance to the people at Sinai (ch. 19), and the appearance to Moses (33:19-23) mark key episodes; *poetic elements*, such as God's revelation of his name to Moses (3:15), or the creation of the altar celebrating the victory of Amelek (17:16); *hymns*, as the one celebrating the deliverance from Egypt at the Red Sea (15:1-21); *parenetic discourse* (i.e., dialogue containing wisdom or advice), as the advice to obey God in order to maintain good health (15:26), or the advice to obey God in order to become a kingdom of priests, holy to God, and celebrated among the nations (19:3-6), or the advice to obey the angel sent before the nation (23:20-33), all reflect God's interest in the lives of the people, regardless of its significance; *judicial*, *moral*, and *ceremonial law*, commonly called the "covenant code," and emphasizing proper conduct among people (20:33–23:33); *genealogical information*, providing the family trees for key characters in the history (1:1-5; 6:14-27); *lists*, such as those providing the items necessary for the construction of the tabernacle (25:1-31; 35:4–40:33); *a census*, necessary for the establishing of a tabernacle "tax" in order to facilitate its service (30:13-16); *chronological notices*, as Moses' age when he confronted Pharaoh (7:7), the length of time in Egypt (12:40-41), the time of the nation's arrival at Sinai (19:1), or the date the tabernacle was set up (40:2); *ritual*, *cultic*, and *ceremonial laws*, necessary for the proper implementation of the daily tabernacle service and festivals (4:24-26; 12:44,48-49). All of the above, and other, similar material, weave

City, NY: Doubleday, 1970), pp. 25-53; J.A. Thompson, *The Ancient Near Eastern Treaties and the Old Testament* (London: Tyndale, 1964); R.E. Friedman, *Commentary on the Torah* (San Francisco: HarperSanFrancisco, 2001), pp. 234-235.

[28]J.H. Sailhamer, *The Pentateuch as Narrative* (Grand Rapids: Zondervan, 1992), pp. 248-249.

together into a coherent account which bridges the events of the patriarchs and the new nation developing from them.[29]

THEOLOGICAL THEMES

The book's two themes — deliverance and law — may be expanded to affirm God's sovereignty, man's failure in defying God, history's meaning and purpose, God as redeemer, a paradigm of future redemption, the reinterpretation of the religious calendar/ritual, and the ethicinizing of history.[30] However, the grouping of salvation, law, and worship, or Exodus, law, and tabernacle, or the like, forms a more succinct arrangement.[31]

NEW TESTAMENT CONNECTIONS

The three just-mentioned themes resound through the Bible, finding completion in the New Testament. The Exodus-Salvation of Israel occurred as God's greatest act in the Old Testament. Remembering his promise to Abraham (Gen 12:1-3; 15; 17), God grew Israel into a great nation, the process of which shaped the national identity. This event, with its wilderness period, became foundational to the interpretation of the Babylonian Captivity, in which the people traveled back from this second captivity, through the wilderness, to the promised land (Isa 35:5-10; 40:3-5; 43:14-21; Hos 2:14-16). Prophets such as Hosea (11:1-2) used the event to interpret Israel's disobedience. Matthew (2:15) expanded Hosea's thought to show how Jesus' life was a microcosm of Israel's history, but with this difference: Jesus, the obedient son, contrasts with Israel, the disobedient son. Both went down into Egypt (Gen 46:8ff.; Exod 1:1ff.; Matt 2:13-15). Both came out of Egypt (Exodus 12–18; Matt 2:15). Both were baptized — Israel in the Red Sea (Exodus 14; 1 Cor 10:1-6); Jesus in the Jordan River (Matt 3:13-17). Both spent time in the wilderness — Israel for forty years, where it failed miserably (Exod 16:35; Num 14:33-34; 32:13; Deut 2:7; 8:2,4; 29:5; Josh 5:6; 14:7; Hos 11:1-2); Jesus, for forty days, where he succeeded (Matt 4:2; Mark 1:13; Luke 4:2).

---

[29]Cf. Dillard and Longman, *Introduction,* p. 64; N.M. Sarna, "Exodus," *ABD,* pp. 693-694.

[30]Sarna, *Exploring Exodus,* pp. 2-3.

[31]Dillard and Longman, *Introduction,* p. 64.

The ten plagues are reinterpreted throughout Scripture as symbolic of God's wrath and grace, and ultimately heavily employed in the powerful imagery of Revelation. "The book of Revelation is saturated with the imagery from the plague tradition. . . . The plague tradition . . . theme has become both a cosmological and eschatological battle between God and Satan. No longer is the battle a glorious memory in Israel's past history, but it still lies in the future with its impending threat. The struggle with evil has taken on a new dimension of anguish and terror. The people of God do not stand carefully protected in Goshen, but are called upon to participate in the battle unto death. All the terrors of Gog and Magog, of the dragon from the deep, of the beasts from Daniel's visions, are combined into a terrifying picture of the Antichrist."[32]

The redemption of Jesus presupposed God's redemption of Israel. Luke's account of the transfiguration mentions that Moses and Elijah were "speaking of his departure, which he was about to accomplish at Jerusalem" (9:31). The Greek word here is ἔξοδον (*exodon*, "exodus"). The use of the word initiates the imagery of the Exodus story.

Jesus was crucified at the Passover (the primary feast celebrating the Exodus), becoming the Passover lamb who died for others (Matt 26:19; Mark 14:16; Luke 22:3; 1 Cor 5:7). In addition, even today Christians speak of trials and tribulations as a "wilderness period," in which they long for their exodus to their promised land (Heb 3:7–14:13). These few examples indicate that the reader with a good understanding of both the Old and New Testaments sees in the Exodus God's deliverance of Israel foreshadowing the death of Christ and the establishment of the church.[33]

In giving Israel a new law (covenant), God laid the foundation for the existence of the children of Israel as a nation. However, this temporary covenant with Israel actually foreshadowed the better and final covenant between God and his people. The work of Jesus in redemption occurred in the context of bringing to fruition that law and establishing the new covenant, as the numerous New Testament statements which speak of fulfilling the Old Testament show (e.g., Matt 1:22; 2:15; 3:15; 5:17; 8:17; 12:17; 13:35; 21:4; John 12:38;

---

[32]B.S. Childs, *The Book of Exodus* (Philadelphia: Westminster, 1974), p. 169.

[33]Cf. Dillard and Longman, *Introduction*, pp. 64-67.

13:18; 15:25; 18:9,32; 19:24,28), as well as reinterpreting Old Testament events in the context of New Testament times, events, and practices. Finally, this new covenant, written on the hearts of believers rather than tables of stones (Jer 31:31-34; Heb 8:6-13), indicates the internalizing and spiritualizing of this new agreement by those he redeemed.

The tabernacle and its worship furnishes the best example of this dynamic. Everything that was used in the tabernacle worship would be found and explained more fully in the New Testament forms and worship. The tabernacle emphasized God's holy presence in Israel. With its outer court, holy place, and most holy place, it accented the various gradations of this holiness of God. The various ceremonies involving ritual cleanness and uncleanness emphasized this gradation also. In the New Testament this presence of Holy God among his people was fulfilled (reinterpreted?) in Jesus, who "became flesh and tabernacled among us" (John 1:14). Similarly, Hebrews shows in many ways, how the ceremonies of the tabernacle prefigured the redemption Jesus accomplished as our Passover lamb, as the sacrificial lamb on the day of atonement, etc., who accomplished not a temporary redemption, "because it was impossible for the blood of bulls and goats to take away sin" (Heb 10:4), but an eternal redemption when he entered the Holy Place with his own blood (Heb 9:12).[34]

The Christian's appreciation of the work of Jesus in mankind's salvation is understood and appreciated in a ratio equal to the understanding of the messages and themes of the Exodus and the book which bears its name.

---

[34]Cf. Ibid., pp. 67-71.

LEVITICUS

"Leviticus," the Latin form of the Greek name *Levitikon*, "pertaining to the Levites," comes from the Septuagint via the Latin
Vulgate. The Hebrew title, וַיִּקְרָא (*wayyiqre'*, "and he called," derives
from the first word in the book. Leviticus is the natural sequel to
Genesis and Exodus. Several items in the book connect with the preceding material. The descriptions of the sacrifices naturally follow
the construction of the tabernacle in Exodus (25–40). Genesis portrays the fall of Adam and Eve and the promises of God to Abraham,
and Exodus describes the growth of Abraham's descendants into the
nation of Israel delivered from Egyptian bondage. Leviticus records
the prerequisites necessary for that nation to enter into the presence
of God. The people had been redeemed from Egypt, entered into a
covenant with God, and erected the place of worship (the tabernacle). Leviticus provides the necessary ritual and regulations for that
relationship. As such, it becomes important "for understanding the
overall role of law in the Bible."[1] Two key concepts highlight the
book: (1) *holiness*, or separation, shows how Israel was set apart from
other nations in order that it might properly worship the Holy God;
(2) *worship*, meaning the process by which the approach to this God
is made. This emphasis on holiness and worship presuppose the
rules necessary for their implementation.

---

[1] D. Damrosch, "Leviticus," in *The Literary Guide to the Bible*, ed. by R. Alter
and F. Kermode (Cambridge: Harvard University Press, 1987), p. 66. See
also: G.J. Wenham, "Leviticus," *ISBE²*, 4:111; Young, *Introduction*, p. 75;
Archer, *Survey*, p. 227; J.E. Hartley, "Leviticus," in *Old Testament Survey: The
Message, Form, and Background of the Old Testament*, 2nd ed., ed. by W.S. Lasor,
D.A. Hubbard, and F.W. Bush (Grand Rapids: Eerdmans, 1996), pp. 80-81;
Harrison, *Introduction*, p. 589.

HISTORICAL AND CULTURAL BACKGROUND

The events of Leviticus occur within a one-year period. Israel departed Egypt in the first month, the fifteenth day of the month (Exod 16:1), traveled to Sinai in the third month (Exod 19:1), and set up the tabernacle the first month, the first day of the month, the second year (Exod 40:17). The people departed Sinai on the twentieth day of the second month, the second year (Num 10:11). This chronology connects with the issuance of the laws of Leviticus at Sinai (7:38; 25:1; 26:46; 27:34) and gives a historical time slot for the dating of events such as those of chapter 10.

The literary context matches the chronological context, forming part of a larger narrative of instructions and regulations extending from Exodus 19:1 to Numbers 10:10. While Exodus 19–24 contain the core of the Sinai covenant, Leviticus works out this covenantal relationship: (a) the conduct of covenantal worship (1–7), (b) proper behavior of covenantal people (18–25), and (c) blessings and curses which are dependent on proper covenant keeping (26). As noted in the discussion of the book of Exodus, the Sinai Covenant may be placed in the context of ancient Near Eastern treaties. In Leviticus this covenantal relationship plays out in terms of Israel's vassal obligations to God (the overlord). Because God brought Israel out of Egypt, the nation was obligated totally to him and bound to him forever. Obedience would bring blessings, while disobedience would bring curses, both of which are rooted in a covenantal relationship (26:1-13). While blessings produced reward and disobedience yielded punishment, God was ever-ready to forgive and reinstate the broken relationship (26:13-46). Because God had brought Israel out of Egypt, Israel was obligated to keep the law (11:45; 18:3; 23:43).[2]

Recent advances in the comparative or contextual approach, developed by Hallo, have yielded significant comparisons and contrasts between Leviticus and its ancient Near Eastern counterparts. The consumption of food (chs. 1–11), purification requirements (chs. 12–16) and sanctification (chs. 17–24) interact throughout Leviticus with God, priest, and laity. "To each are assigned very specific portions of all edibles, each receive distinct roles in purification and discrete levels of holiness."[3] These areas reflect many ancient Near

---

[2]Cf. Wenham, "Leviticus," *ISBE*[2], 4:116; Hartley, "Leviticus," p. 81; Harrison, *Introduction,* p. 589.

[3]W.W. Hallo, "Leviticus and Ancient Near Eastern Literature," in *The*

Eastern practices that have been modified for Israel's use in a way similar to the ancient Near Eastern vassal treaties' adaptation to formulate the Sinai Covenant. The consumption of food echoes the ancient Near Eastern practice of the "care and feeding of the gods." Based on the assumption that gods, like men, must eat, ancient Near Eastern priests engaged in daily rituals of food preparation for the God. The animal was slaughtered. Parts of the entrails were used in the divinatory practices of the day, while other parts comprised the meal and were placed before the image of the deity, who magically consumed it. In Leviticus the care and feeding of God involved no image to consume the food magically. Rather, the animal was slaughtered, burned on the altar, and the priests and laity ate their respective portions. Chapters 1–11 detail which part of the sacrifices belonged to God, to the priests, and to the laity. This ritual transformed the "care and feeding of the gods" into a fellowship meal among the representatives of the three groups. The slaughtering of the animal to prepare this fellowship meal also served "to atone for other human transgression."[4] The laws of purification grew out of an ancient Near Eastern society "acutely sensitive to the conditions described"[5] in chapters 12–16.

> . . . [T]he Mesopotamian concern was rooted in the manic world view. That is, natural . . . phenomena were signals vouchsafed to men by the gods, 'an early warning system' of evils to come. Ritual was needed to dissipate, not the fungus, but the (greater) evil that it portended. The levitical legislation was therefore a reaction to a very deep-rooted popular prejudice shared to some extent by the Israelites. Without attempting to eradicate such a fear at one stroke, it wisely instituted a systematic set of rules for dealing with the system that inspired it.[6]

The laws of sanctification have many parallels to ancient Near Eastern laws, particularly those dealing with sexual conduct. In both systems, the adulterer and adulteress are put to death (Lev 10:10; cf. Ur-Nammu, 4; Eshnunna, 129, 133; Assyrian, 13-16, 23; Hittite, 197ff.). In both incest was forbidden (Lev 10:11-21; 18:6-18; cf. Hammurabi, 154 158; Hittite, 189 195), as was homosexuality (Lev 18:22; 20:13;

Torah: A Modern Commentary (New York: Union of American Hebrew Congregations, 1981), pp. 740-741.

[4]Ibid., p. 743.
[5]Ibid.
[6]Ibid., p. 744.

cf. Assyrian, 20), and bestiality (Lev 18:23; 20:15-16; cf. Hittite laws, 199-200). Despite these similarities, however, there were differences. Ancient Near Eastern laws were promulgated by kings, indicating their royal authority, whereas the levitical laws were issued by God and related to his holiness (20:26). Many other areas of comparison and contrast exist, but these should be sufficient to illustrate the unique nature of the levitical system from its Near Eastern counterparts.

TEXT AND AUTHOR

Unlike Exodus (cf. Exod 17:14; 24:4; 34:27), which names Moses as the author of particular sections, Leviticus nowhere names an author. Nevertheless, the evidence for Mosaic authorship is impressive and is based on four lines of evidence. (1) Thirty-six divine speeches begin with, "The Lord called/spoke" (1:1; 4:1; 5:14; 6:1,8,19,24; 7:22,28; 8:1; 10:8; 11:1; 12:1; 13:1; 14:1,33; 15:1; 16:1; 17:1; 18:1; 19:1; 20:1; 21:1,16; 22:1,17; 22:26; 23:1,9,23,26,33; 24:1,13; 25:1; 27:1). The recipients of this address are varied. Four of these times they are designated "to Moses and Aaron" (11:1; 13:1; 14:33; 15:1). One time the designation is "to Aaron" (10:8). The other thirty-one times the designations are "to Moses."[7] Such a multitude of references point, not only to Mosaic authorship, but to inspiration as well. Many of the laws (lepers outside the camp rather than the city [13:46]; accessibility of the tabernacle for offerings made [17:1-9]; those prefaced with "God is bringing you into the land" [14:34; 18:3; 23:10; 25:2], e.g.) indicate a wilderness setting and the tabernacle rather than the Temple. (2) The elaborate rituals of Leviticus, because they are found in Near Eastern cultures long before the late period, argue against the late date assigned by critical scholarship. (3) Further, the predominating issues and circumstances of the exile are missing in Leviticus. The problem of marriage with Canaanites, so important in Ezra and Nehemiah's day (Ezra 9–10; Neh 13:23-31), is not addressed. Leviticus exalts the priesthood, but the exilic priesthood opposes the reforming work of Nehemiah (Nehemiah 13). The tithe laws of the Pentateuch indicate a ratio of ten Levites to every priest (Num 18:26-31), whereas the exile seems to experience a shortage of Levites (Ezra 8:15). (4) The prophet Ezekiel cites Leviticus several times (Ezek

---

[7]Cf. Dillard and Longman, *Introduction,* p. 74.

22:26 and Lev 10:10; Ezek 20:11 and Lev 18:5; Ezekiel 34 and Leviticus 26), which indicates the material quoted (Leviticus) "was an old work whose laws were binding on Israel because they enshrined the covenant between God and His people."[8] Finally, as noted above, the similarity of the ancient Near Eastern law codes to Leviticus indicate its legislative material is "similar to the provisions enacted in the early second millennium, well before the time of Moses."[9]

HISTORY OF INTERPRETATION

With the rise of critical interpretation many scholars perceived Leviticus's emphasis on the cult as indicative of the P source. According to this theory religion evolved from the simple to the complex. The so-called "P" represents the end of this evolution. Because early worship was thought to be free of complex rituals, the ceremonies described in Exodus–Leviticus were perceived as projections into the past of late practices. References to sacrifice at the tabernacle (17:1-9) reflect enforcement of Josiah's reformation and the centralization of the worship at Jerusalem (2 Kings 23). Whereas early sacrifices were simple and joyful experiences that could be practiced anywhere (Judg 13:16ff.; 1 Sam 16:2), the sacrifices of Leviticus are highly ritualistic ceremonies designed to atone for sin. Along with centralization and ritualization of ceremonies, a rigid calendar system fixed specific dates for celebrations (ch. 23). Finally, the exaltation of the high priest in Leviticus reflects the evolution from simple to complex. These data point to the Josianic reform (seventh century) as the earliest date of completion, with a final editing in the exilic period (fifth century). So prodocumentary scholars perceive P to be the latest document and assign nearly all of Leviticus to it. The narratives (e.g., chs. 8–10, 16) derive from P while the rest of the material (chs. 1–7; 11–15; 17–26; 27) was reworked and spliced with this narrative. Kaufman modified this by arguing that, while P is Leviticus, it is pre-exilic.[10] Such theories as these must remain tentative, in spite of the confidence of many who espouse them, because "We do not know enough about the development of Hebrew language, law, and reli-

---

[8]Wenham, "Leviticus," *ABD,* 4:112. See Wenham for a detailed discussion of the just-mentioned four lines of evidence.

[9]Archer, *Survey,* p. 230.

[10]Y. Kaufman, *The Religion of Israel* (Chicago: University of Chicago Press, 1960), p. 178.

gion to make the elaborate analyses offered in some works anything more than conjecture."[11]

STRUCTURE

Three phrases serve as major structural markers for the book as a whole: "God spoke to Moses"; "You must be holy for I am holy"; "The Lord said." As already noted, "God spoke to Moses" appears in the first verse of nearly every chapter and provides a coherent, repetitive unity to the entire work. "You must be holy for I am holy" provides a major reason for specific legislation. "The Lord said," begins twelve sections, each of which ends with a statement summarizing the material.[12]

Citation, "Lord said"	Legislation	Summary	Subject
1:1–7:38	Sacrifices	7:37-38	"burnt offering," etc.
8:1–10:20	Priests	10:20	"Moses heard…."
11:1-47	Diet and Defilement	11:46-47	"law of creeping thing, clean/ unclean"
12:1-8	Childbirth	12:7b-8	"law for her who bears a child"
13:1–14:57	Cleansing	14:54-57	"the ritual for any leprous disease"
15:1-33	Discharge/ defilement	15:32-33	"ritual for discharge"
16:1-34	Ritual Day of Atonement	16:34b	"Moses did as the Lord commanded"
17:1–21:24	Holiness of Life	21:24	"Moses spoke to Aaron . . . to Israel"

---

[11]Wenham, "Leviticus," *ISBE²*, 4:112; cf. G.J. Wenham, *The Book of Leviticus* (Grand Rapids: Eerdmans, 1979). See also Dillard and Longman, *Introduction*, p. 74; Harrison, *Introduction*, pp. 591-593.

[12]Cf. J.H Hayes, "Leviticus," in *Harper's Bible Commentary*, ed. by J.L. Mays (San Francisco: Harper and Row, 1988), p. 157.

22:1–23:44	Holy Things/ Feasts	23:44	"Moses declared . . . the Lord's feasts"
24:1-23	Oil, bread, and blasphemy	24:23b	"They took the blasphemer . . . . and stoned him"
25:1–26:46	Land's Sabbath, Jubilee, Blessings & Curses	26:46	"Statues, ordinances and laws, God made"
27:1-34	Vows	27:34	"Commandments God gave to Israel"

This structure, "introduction ['God called/spoke/said . . .'] + legislation + summary statement ['Thus God said. . . .']," serves to bring the material to the forefront of the people's conscience reminding them of the divine origin of the commands — a process the prophets centuries later would emphatically use when indicating the divine origin of their oracles. In fact, the structure of the prophetic oracles presuppose the levitical structure: "The Lord said to prophet X, 'Thus you will say. . . .' + oracle + 'Thus the Lord says. . . .'" Note the similarities:

Levitical Legislation	*Prophetic Oracle*
"The Lord said/spoke. . . ."	"The Lord said/spoke to prophet X. . . ."
legislation	oracle
"Thus the Lord said"	"Thus the Lord said"[13]

Leviticus also may be divided into two major sections: 1–16 and 17–27. Chapters 1–16 reflect the rules inherent in sacrificial worship, while 17–27 contain the various laws of holiness. These may be broken down further.

    I. Function of Sacrifices and Priesthood in Worship — 1:1–16:36
      A. The laws regarding sacrifice — 1:1–7:38

---

[13]Cf. such classic works as C. Westermann, *Basic Forms of Prophetic Speech* (Philadelphia: Westminster, 1967); and J.F. Ross, "The Prophet as Yahweh's Messenger," in *Israel's Prophetic Heritage: Essays in Honor of James Muilenburg*, ed. by B.W. Anderson and W. Harrelson (New York: Harper and Brothers, 1962), pp. 88-109.

The interweaving of the narrative and legislative material gives a social-religious-political context to the entire work. The narrative detailing the installation of the priests (8:1–10:20) is inserted following the laws regarding sacrifice (1:1–7:38) and just prior to the laws of purity (11:1–15:32). The narrative describing the Day of Atonement (ch. 16) comes just after these purity laws and just before laws of holiness (17:1–21:24). The narrative portraying the execution of the blasphemer (24:10-23) occurs just after these laws of holiness and just prior to the laws referring to the land's sabbath, Jubilee, and the blessings and curses (25:1–26:46). The narrative regulating proper voluntary religious offerings (vows) completes the book (ch. 27).

Any structural markers observed in the book must take note of the logical narrative-like flow describing the prerequisites necessary to move from an unorganized theocracy to one with fully functioning cult. This "first things first" structure produces a document that begins with definitions necessary for the ritual (ch. 1) and ends with rules for the personal devotional acts known as vows (ch. 27). Because definitions were prerequisite both to the nation as a whole and to the priesthood, 1:1–6:7 address all Israel and describe the various offerings, their purpose and function, while 6:8–7:38 address Aaron and his sons (and by implication the priesthood) and describe their purpose and function in making the offerings. Once the sacrifices were defined, the priesthood could be established (8:1–10:20). Once the priesthood was in operation, purity laws could be established (11:1–15:32). The creation of purity laws set the stage for the most holy day of the Israelite calendar, the day of atonement (ch. 16). The day of atonement necessitated a discussion for the laws of holiness (17:1–26:2). Commonly called the "Holiness Code" (chs. 17–26), these chapters, due to the dominant theme of holiness, follow the pattern of the first half of the book. Leviticus 17:1-2 addresses both the nation and the priests; chapters 17:3–20:27 focus on the nation of Israel and the general laws of holiness applicable to them. Next, 21:1–26:2 address the priests and focus on the specific laws of holiness applicable to them, holy days, and festivals. Promises and warnings relative to the keeping of these laws naturally follow (26:3–46). Finally, laws regulating voluntary items of worship, vows and tithes, close the book (27:1-34).[14]

Mary Douglas's "ring" structure refines this stress on theocracy, cult, and narrative flow, emphasizing chapter 19 as the midpoint of the book's structure.[15]

27: Redeeming things/persons	26: Ending: Equity between people/ God
1–9: Things/persons consecrated	Things/Persons consecrated: 25
10: The Holy Place defiled	The Name defiled: 24
11–15: Blemish/leprosy	Feasts, Day of Atonement: 23
16: Atonement for Tabernacle	Blemish/leprosy: 21–22
17: Bridge: Summary	
18: Regulation of sex, Moleck	Regulation of sex, Moleck: 20:
19: Midpoint, Equity between people	

This structure possesses the advantage of matching "everything that has been said in the first round by a second round which enriches, completes and explains what was left unexplained before."[16] Douglas's description of this structure illustrates the interlocking of the various pericopes.

> From its opening on the theme of things dedicated to the Lord, the book's circuit runs to the mid-point, ch. 19, which is on the concept of righteousness, largely in the sense of honesty and fair dealing, and with regard for correct recognition of status. The twice repeated lists of prohibited sexual relations (chs. 18.6-19 and 20.11-22) and the references to children offered to Moleck (18.21 and 20.11-22) fulfill the convention of a flanking parallel on either side of the turn. After the turn the selec-

---

[14]For discussion of the structure of Leviticus see: Young, *Introduction,* pp. 76-78; Wenham, "Leviticus," *ISBE²,* 4:111; Hartley, "Leviticus," p. 82; Hallo, "Leviticus and ANE Literature," p. 744; Harrison, *Introduction,* p. 590; S.E. Balentine, *The Torah's Vision of Holiness* (Minneapolis: Fortress, 1999), pp. 169-170.

[15]M. Douglas, "The Forbidden Animals in Leviticus," *JSOT* 59 (1993): 9-12.

[16]Ibid., p. 9.

tions return step by step until ch. 25, which deals with things belonging to the Lord, the land (25.23), and the people (25.55). The grand peroration and conclusion is ch. 26 which matches to the mid-point, ch. 19, which has announced the meaning of righteousness in dealing from persons to persons. Now at the conclusion it is a matter of applying the same concept to the dealings of the people with their God, justice and mercy if they keep their promises and pay their dues, terrible punishments if they do not. The latch, ch. 27, locks on the beginning by speaking both of things consecrated and things belonging to the Lord. The latter are firstlings which cannot be consecrated because they belong to him already (27.26).[17]

While this structure goes "against the scholarly consensus that ch. 17 belongs with 18–26,"[18] it recognizes the resolution of the "puzzles in the first 16 chapters" in their "counterpart halves."[19] This relationship of "delayed completion,"[20] or meaning, facilitates the book's reading, something nearly impossible in the reading of the book through other structural lenses.[21]

GENRE

These just-noted structural markers, "God spoke to Moses" and "You must be holy for I am holy," give the entire work a narrative context by blending logically the rules and regulations with the *Sitz im Leben* (situation in life). The *Sitz im Leben* is the tent of meeting, which serves to place the laws into the larger framework of the events at Sinai and the Pentateuch as a whole. As Damrosch has observed, "Far from interrupting the narrative, the laws complete it, and the story exists for the sake of the laws which it frames."[22] Just how smoothly this blending is may be seen in a comparison of the last verses of Exodus (40:33-38) with the first verses of Leviticus. Verse 33b states that Moses "finished the work" of erecting the tabernacle. Verses 34-35 state "the glory of the Lord filled the tabernacle." Verses

---

[17]Ibid., p. 10.
[18]Ibid., pp. 11-12.
[19]Ibid., p. 12.
[20]Ibid.
[21]Ibid., p. 9.
[22]Dunrosch, "Leviticus," p. 66.

36-38 parenthetically describe the process by which Israel knew to move during their wanderings — when the cloud (i.e., the glory of the Lord) that filled the tabernacle moved, Israel followed. Leviticus 1:1 takes up where Exodus 40:35 leaves off. Note how succinct Exodus 40:33-35 and Leviticus 1:1-2a are when they are put together:

> He set up the court around the tabernacle and the altar, and put up the screen at the gate of the court. So Moses finished the work. Then the cloud covered the tent of meeting, and the glory of the LORD filled the tabernacle. Moses was not able to enter the tent of meeting because the cloud settled upon it, and the glory of the LORD filled the tabernacle. Yhwh called to Moses and spoke to him from the tent of meeting, saying: "Speak to the children of Israel. . . ."

When God began to dwell in the tabernacle in the center of the camp, not even Moses could enter the tent — it was holy to the Lord. So God spoke to Moses from the tabernacle in order to give instructions relative to Israel's coming into his presence.[23]

While Leviticus has traditionally been interpreted as a guidebook or manual for priests,[24] the more likely view perceives the book as instructions for the entire congregation relative to the cult. While priests play a major role in this process, details necessary for a training manual for priests are missing. No specifics are given for how the priest is to process the sacrifice, e.g., the instruments needed for the sacrificial ritual, the posture taken by the priest when performing the sacrifice, or the speech spoken during the process are all missing as instructions.[25]

THEOLOGICAL THEMES

Various theological themes have been identified by scholars. Some of the more significant ones follow. Archer has identified five principles which seem to undergird the book and supply the basis for several themes in it. (1) The redeemed nation must keep itself holy (set apart) for service to God, whose service maintained a sac-

---

[23]For discussions of the genre of Leviticus see: Wenham, "Leviticus," *ISBE*[2], 4:111; Dillard and Longman, *Introduction*, pp. 74, 76; Damrosch, "Leviticus," p. 66.

[24]E.g., Harrison, *Introduction*, pp. 590, 598.

[25]Hartley, "Leviticus," pp. 81-82.

rificial system which made atonement by the shedding of innocent blood. (2) The grace of God (his holiness?) demanded that he be approached in the manner *he* specified and not in "some kind of self-justifying personal merit." (3) Because Israel was holy to God (i.e., married to him), she must "abstain from all sexual unchastity" and "refrain from contact with corruption and decay." (4) Nothing impure or subject to decay could be presented as an offering to God. (5) The religious year was dominated by the sacred number seven, "symbolizing the perfect work of God": (a) the seventh day is a holy sabbath; (b) the seventh year made a sabbath year; (c) "seven sevens of years" were followed by a fiftieth year called "Jubilee," which resulted in the return of all lands to their original families; (d) Passover occurred on the evening of the fourteenth of Abib; (e) the Feast of Unleavened Bread lasted for seven days; (f) Pentecost was celebrated on the fiftieth day following seven sabbaths; (g) three of the most significant feasts were celebrated during the month of Tishri, which was the seventh month (Trumpets, Day of Atonment, Tabernacles); the Feast of Tabernacles was celebrated for seven days during Tishri.[26]

Holiness of God. Two recurring statements describe the inherent holiness of God and the demands it made on Israel. "You will be holy because I am holy" (11:44,45; 19:2; 20:7,26; cf. 21:8; 22:32) makes clear the relationship — a holy God *must* have a holy people. "I am the Lord your God [who brought you out of Egypt]" (11:44,45; 18:2,4,5,21,30; 19:2,3,4,10,12,14,25,31,32,34,36[36]; 20:7,24; 21:8; 22:33[33]; 23:22,43[43]; 24:22; 25:17,38[38],[42],55[55]; 26:1,13) describes the nature of the bond between God and Israel — he is the God that redeemed them from Egypt producing their eternal debt to him. Together, these two phrases, in the ancient Near Eastern treaty format, intersect throughout the legal and regulatory material, implying Israel's responsibility to be separate from the world as a people for God alone. Commands such as, "You shall not do as they do in the land of Egypt . . . and you shall not do as they do in the land of Canaan, to which I am bringing you. You shall not follow their statutes" (18:3), "You shall observe my statutes and keep them" (18:4), and "You shall observe my statutes and keep them in order to live" (18:5) are all preceded by "I am the Lord your God" (18:2). Similar patterns occur in each of the other passages cited above.

---

[26]Cf. Archer, *Survey*, pp. 228-229.

"You shall honor your father and mother, keep my sabbaths, and do not turn to idols" (19:3-4), "You shall not turn to idols or cast metal images for yourselves" (19:4), "You shall not strip your vineyard bare, or gather the fallen grapes of your vineyard; you shall leave them for the poor and the alien" (19:10) are framed by "You will be holy, for I am holy" (19:2; 20:7). These examples show that holiness must embrace the entire nation (Exod 19:6; Deut 26:19) and was foundational to the descriptions of sacrificial rituals, dietary laws, sexual purity, etc.[27]

Presence of God. God's inherent holiness and its demands for a holy people, seen in the recurring refrains "Be holy for I am holy," and "I am the Lord your God,'" served to remind Israel "that every aspect of their life — religion (chs. 21–24), sex (chs. 18 and 20), relations with neighbors (chs. 19, 25), especially their care of the latter (19:14, 32; 25:17, 36, 43), is God's primary concern to their covenant redeemer."[28] More specifically, God was present in worship. The sacrifices took place in God's presence (1:5,11) and provided "a pleasing odor for the Lord" (1:9,13,17; 2:9; 3:5). The priest who would enter God's presence to offer sacrifice (16:1; 21:17) should exercise caution to follow the most minute details (8:9,13,17) in order to avoid death. Priests dare not follow their own rules. Not recognizing this fact meant that holiness would not be maintained and death would result (8:35; 10:1-9; 16:2,13).

Sacrificial System. The sacrificial system (chs. 1–7) and the ritual importance it embraced derived from the holiness of God and his demands for a holy people. The system provided the means by which the people approached such a holy God. As such, the system functioned to ensure that the people serving such a holy God were themselves holy. Specific sacrifices provided proper ritual cleansing so Israel could abide in God's presence. The *burnt offering* (עֹלָה, '*ōlāh*, 1:1-17), whose fragrant aroma went up (עָלָה, '*ālāh*, "ascending") provided for the expiation of sin, made atonement (כִּפֶּר, *kip-pūr*, 1:4), and was probably the most frequently occurring sacrifice. The *sin offering* (חַטָּאת, *ḥaṭṭā'th*, "sin," 4:1–5:13; 6:24-30), also called "purification offering," expiated unintentional sins such as coming into contact with unclean things, or uttering rash words (cf. 5:1-6). The *guilt offering* (אָשָׁם, '*āšām*, "guilt," 5:14–6:7[Heb 5:14-26]; 7:1-

[27]Cf. Dillard and Longman, *Introduction*, pp. 76-77; Wenham, "Leviticus," *ISBE*², 4:113-115.
[28]Wenham, "Leviticus," *ISBE*², 4:113.

10), which had similarities to the sin offering, expiated for such things as deceiving a neighbor in a matter of a deposit or a pledge, or defrauding him by robbery, lying, or swearing falsely (6:1-7[Heb 5:20-26]), or the cleansing of a leper (14:1ff.). The *grain offering* (מִנְחָה, *minḥāh*, "gift," 2:1-16; 6:14-23), a composition of flour, oil, and incense, was burned as a gift to God. The *peace offering* (שְׁלָמִים, *šelemîm*, from שָׁלוֹם, *šālōm*, "peace," 3:1-17; 7:11-38) emphasized the fellowship between the worshiper(s) and God. This fellowship was covenantal in nature because the corporate meal was eaten by everyone (the Lord, 3:3-5; the priest, 7:29-36; the worshipers). The *thank offering* (תּוֹדָה, *tōdāh*, "thanksgiving," "praise," 7:12-13) offered as thanks or praise for a blessing received. The *votive offering* (נֶדֶר, *nēder*, "vow," 7:16) was offered at the fulfillment of a vow. The *freewill offering* (נְדָבָה, *nᵉdābāh*, 7:16; 35:29) was offered voluntarily from the heart. Those offerings which required the sacrifice of an animal removed sin by offering a substitute to die in the place of the sinner. They were comprised of that which sustained life, and consecrated the individual (and nation) for proper fellowship with God. Because "the life of the flesh is in the blood" (17:11) the sacrificial blood shed in these sacrifices served as the cleansing agent which could reverse the ongoing process of sin which profaned the holy and made unclean. Those offerings which did not require the sacrifice of an animal served to maintain the fellowship with God.[29]

Priesthood. Inherent in the very concept of priesthood is the idea of holiness. The holiness of God demanded that a group of people be set apart to mediate between him and the common. The ordination of Aaron and his descendants (ch. 8) set them apart to offer holy sacrifices and function in God's holy presence. Most of the laws are directed at the priests instructing them how to preserve their holiness (chs. 21–22). They in turn instructed the people so they might become holy and enter into God's presence.[30]

Purity. Cultic purity, or cleanness, as one approached God, involved the eating of proper food (ch. 11) and the separation from items and events in life that corrupted that purity, including but not

---

[29]For discussions of the sacrificial system of Leviticus see: Dillard and Longman, *Introduction*, pp. 77-79; B. Levine, "Leviticus, Book of," *ABD*, ed. by David Noel Freedman (New York: Doubleday, 1992), 4:313; Wenham, "Leviticus," *ISBE*², 4:115; Young, *Introduction*, pp. 81-83; Archer, *Survey*, pp. 231-232; Hartley, "Leviticus," pp. 96-97; Harrison, *Introduction*, p. 600.

[30]Dillard and Longman, *Introduction*, pp. 79-80.

limited to childbirth (ch. 12), skin diseases and mildew (chs. 13–14), and discharges (15). The very diagram of God's presence in Israel demanded that purity be maintained. The tabernacle, where God dwelt, was located at the center of the camp. As one went outward from here he moved toward the unclean and impure. The unclean, the impure, and the Gentiles dwelt outside the camp. Explaining the purpose of the purity laws in terms of health regulations for the nation has merit,[31] but the nullification of the dietary laws (Rom 14:14) and the spiritualization of physical circumcision (Rom 2:25-29) in the New Testament indicate that something more than proper health is in play here. Wholeness, or completeness, is the concept. Death was the ultimate uncleanness, the opposite of holiness. To be in conformity with the natural order implied cleanness, whereas non-conformity implied uncleanness. The daily ritual separated the clean from the unclean, the holy from the common and forced the concept of inner purity to the forefront of the nation's consciousness.[32]

NEW TESTAMENT CONNECTIONS

Generally speaking, these themes reach full, spiritual maturity in the New Testament. Leviticus may be designated the gospel of the Old Testament in that the rituals commanded in the book typify the gospel age. Jesus is the Christian's High Priest who offered himself as the perfect sacrifice as an atonement for sin (Heb 4:14–5:10; 9:6). This high priesthood both presupposed and contrasted with the Aaronic priesthood of Leviticus. The Aaronic priesthood and its sacrifices pointed to the supreme one, ultimately made by Christ. However, Christ's priesthood, unlike the Aaronic priesthood, but like Melchizedek's of Genesis, is without predecessor or successor, and involves Jesus' being both high priest and king. Finally, the change from the Mosaic covenant to the New Covenant demanded the change of the priesthood from the Aaronic to the Melchizedekal priesthood of Jesus, which was a greater priesthood as is indicated by the fact that the ancestor of Aaron paid tithes to Melchizedek (cf. Gen 14:18-20, Ps 110.4, Heb 5:6,10; 6:20; 7:1-17).[33]

---

[31]Cf., e.g., Harrison, *Introduction,* pp. 603-607.

[32]See also Dillard and Longman, *Introduction,* pp. 80-81; Wenham, "Leviticus," *ISBE²,* 4:113-115; Hartley, "Leviticus," pp. 94-95.

[33]For discussions of the New Testament's connections with Leviticus see

But more specifically, ***the presence of God***, articulated so well in Leviticus, finds expression in such New Testament passages as John 1:14 ("The word became flesh and tabernacled among us"), 1 Corinthians 6:19 ("your body is the temple of the Holy Spirit"), and Matthew 18:20 ("Where two or three are gathered together, there I am among them"). ***Holiness*** is exploited throughout the New Testament. Christians are holy saints called by God as he had called ancient Israel (cf. Col 1:22; 1 Pet 1:2; 2:9f.). Christians live holy lives (Col 1:22; 1 Pet. 1:15) and are made holy not by themselves, but through obedience (Rom 6:17-19), in a way similar to Israel and its obedience. Like Israel, Christians are following the injunction, "Be holy, for I am holy" (1 Pet 1:16). What are some ways we can be holy? How do we maintain our holiness? What makes us unholy? The ***sacrifices*** of Leviticus pointed to the ultimate sacrifice of Jesus. Whereas the levitical sacrifices had to be repeated, the crucifixion, with its atoning blood, occurred "once for all . . . to remove sin" (Heb 9:26), cleanses continually (1 John 1:7), and is for the whole world (1 John 2:1-2). The ***priesthood***, not only changed in terms of the high priesthood, as just noted, but with the change of the high priesthood a new priesthood was established in which every Christian becomes his or her own priest (Rom 12:1; 1 Pet 2:9; Rev 1:6). This priesthood of believers allows the Christian to enter a fellowship with God that is indescribable. The ***purity legislation*** in the New Testament, keeping oneself pure (1 Tim 5:22), prayer expressed out of a pure heart and mind (2 Tim 2:22; Titus 1:15), and the practice of a pure religion (Jas 1:27), draws upon the concepts of cleanness in Leviticus.

Dillard and Longman, *Introduction,* p. 76; Wenham, *ISBE*², 4:113, 115; Hartley, "Leviticus," pp. 97-98; Harrison, *Introduction,* pp. 612-613.

NUMBERS

"Numbers" is the English title translation of the Vulgate title, *Numeri*, which is a translation of the LXX title, *Arithmoi*. The LXX, Vulgate, and English titles arise from the censuses (chs. 1 and 26), as well as other emphases of numbers. Two Hebrew titles designate the book. וַיְדַבֵּר (*way°dabbēr*, "and he [Yahweh] said") derives from the first word in the MT, while בְּמִדְבָּר (*bamidbār*, "in the wilderness") points to the locations where the most significant events occurred. Numbers transitions from the generation that departed Egypt, only to die in the wilderness, to the new generation, born in the wilderness, who entered the promised land.[1]

HISTORICAL AND CULTURAL BACKGROUND

Though not strictly chronological, the history recorded in Numbers covers about thirty-eight years (cf. Num 1:1 with Deut 1:3). The tabernacle was erected on the first day of the first month of the second year (Exod 40:17). The events of Numbers begin one month later, on the first day of the second month of the second year (1:1). Travel from Sinai to Kadesh-barnea took eleven days (Deut 1:2). The first fourteen chapters can be placed in this period of time. The middle of the book deals with the thirty-eight years of wanderings and additional legislation (chs. 15–19). The concluding part of the book deals with the conquest of Canaan (chs. 20–36).

---

[1] For discussions of the title of Numbers see: E.E. Carpenter, "Numbers, Book of," *ISBE*[2], rev. ed. by G.W. Bromiley (Grand Rapids: Eerdmans, 1979), 3:561; Dillard and Longman, *Introduction*, p. 83; Young, *Introduction*, p. 84; Archer, *Survey*, p. 233; Harrison, *Introduction*, p. 614; D.A. Hubbard and F.W. Bush, "Numbers," in *Old Testament Survey: The Message, Form, and Background of the Old Testament*, 2nd ed., ed. by W.S. LaSor, D.A. Hubbard, and F.W. Bush (Grand Rapids: Eerdmans, 1996), p. 100; Sailhamer, *Pentateuch as Narrative*, p. 369.

Numbers is the logical sequel to Exodus–Leviticus and introduces several events in Deuteronomy. The tabernacle legislation of
Exodus was completed and the people arranged around it (Exodus
40; Numbers 2). The altar, legislated in Exodus, was dedicated (Exod
27:1-8; 38:1-7; Num 7:1-89). The culmination of God's promise to
multiply Abraham's descendants is noted (Gen 12:1-3; 15; cf. Exod
1:1-7; Numbers 2). Though not yet possessing the land, Israel was on
the move toward the fulfillment of the land promise (Gen 12:1-4;
Exod 3:17; 6:4,8; 23:20-26; etc.). The legal material of Exodus and
Leviticus is often illustrated in the events of Numbers, as for example, the enforcement of the Sabbath law (Exod 20:8-10; Lev 23:3;
Num 15:32-37). The Balaam oracles of Numbers 22–24, in which
Balaam attempted to curse Israel, but instead blessed the nation,
recall God's promise to bless those who bless Abraham's descendants and curse those who curse them (Gen 12:1-3). The book anticipates the death of Moses in Deuteronomy (Num 27:12-14; Deut
31:14-16; 34:1-12). Numbers "explains why Israel did not immediately enter the land of Canaan upon leaving Egypt,"[2] and records
"the unfaithfulness, rebellion, apostasy, and frustration, set against
the background of God's faithfulness, presence, provision, and for-
bearance."[3]

A good case can be made for the historicity of Numbers when
compared to the ancient Near Eastern material. Israel's "wanderings
formed part of a general pattern of massive migrations which swept
the whole known world in the thirteenth century B.C.E."[4] Sea Peoples
and Arameans moved throughout the area. The empires of the Hittites
in Anatolia, the Kassites in Babylonia ended, while those of Egypt
and Assyria "bent, but did not break." The Iron Age was ushered in.
The sack of Troy (1250 B.C.) probably initiated these events. Such
works as the *Illiad*, the *Odyssey*, the *Aeneid* and the epic of *Tukulti-
Ninurta* reflect these events in their heroic accounts. Numbers differs from these ancient works in that it contains "No such [heroic]
characterization"; rather it portrays "a rebellious and stiff-necked
people suspicious of its leaders, pining for the fleshpots of Egypt"

---

[2]Carpenter, "Numbers," *ISBE*[2], 3:562.

[3]Hubbard and Bush, "Numbers," p. 99. See also: Young, *Introduction,*
p. 84; Dillard and Longman, *Introduction,* pp. 84-85.

[4]W.W. Hallo, "Numbers and Ancient Near Eastern Literature," in *The
Torah: A Modern Commentary* (New York: Union of American Hebrew Congregations, 1981), p. 1015.

(cf. Exod 16:3) and reflects "a sober recital of the tribulations of migration and the harsh realities of territorial acquisition devoid of romantic embellishment."[5] More specifically, the narratives of Numbers ". . . directly reflect earthly reality, not burgeoning fantasy. Salt-tolerant reeds, water from rock, habits of quails, *kewirs*, etc. reflect *real* local conditions, requiring local knowledge (not book learning in Babylon or Jerusalem). These narratives are thus in total contrast to such texts as the 'King of Battle' tale of Sargon of Akkad, with mountains bounded with gold and boulders of lapis lazuli gemstone, and trees with thorns sixty cubits (100) feet long!"[6] Therefore, *even with these differences*, the various genres comprising Numbers are similar to those in the ancient Near East and thus reflect the ancient Near Eastern context of the thirteenth century B.C.

TEXT AND AUTHOR

Much of the book exhibits evidence of Mosaic authorship. The single reference to the writing activity of Moses (Num 3:2) indicates Moses not only wrote about the places Israel visited, but also probably wrote much of the other material, though others may also have participated in a manner similar to Jeremiah and Baruch (cf. Jer 36:4-5,8,10). Both Aaron (9:1) and Eleazer (26:1) received revelations, and Eleazar was involved with recording activity (26:63). The various genres (boundary lists [Numbers 34], narratives [22–24], poetry [10:35-36; 21:14-15,17-18,27-30], travel itineraries [33:1-49]) formed the basis of sources used to compose the book. So a good case can be made for Mosaic supervision and authorship, as well as the historical and theological accuracy of the material, as opposed to the traditional source analysis.[7]

HISTORY OF INTERPRETATION

The rise of historical criticism precipitated a three-phased period of study. In the first stage, scholars attempted to assign one or more of the supposed sources to Numbers (J, E, D, and P). To G.B. Gray,

[5]Ibid., p. 1016.
[6]Kitchen, *Reliability*, p. 311.
[7]For discussions of the evidence for mosaic authorship see: Carpenter, "Numbers," *ISBE*², 3:562; Dillard and Longman, *Introduction*, p. 84; Hubbard and Bush, "Numbers," pp. 101-102.

J, E, and P formed the compositional sources of Numbers, which included different levels of P materials. Seventy-five percent of Numbers was assigned to P, dated in the fifth century. The material not assigned to P was ascribed to J (ninth century) and E (eighth century). These conclusions presumed such things as the late dating of the supposed source documents, an elaborate cultic ritual, and a retrojection of postexilic priestly tradition into the past to justify the practices of postexilic Judaism. The supposed, simple rituals of early Israelite religion were perceived as having evolved into a complex legalism, which began with the centralization of the cult by King Josiah recorded in 2 Kings 23. The second stage of study assumed a long period of oral tradition as envisioned by Gunkel and Gressman. The third approach, envisioned by Noth, merged the former two approaches and argued that five themes (promise to the patriarchs; exodus from Egypt; wanderings in the wilderness; revelation at Sinai; entry into the land) developed orally and independently before they were committed to writing. While these approaches recognized the antiquity of the material, thus severely weakening the documentary hypothesis, more recent form-critical research confirms this conclusion, but recognizes a much shorter time period between the events and its written documentation. Many events could have been documented as the events occurred. So modern scholarship still adheres to many of these early views, though in modified format, as for example, the difficulty of identifying J and E in Numbers. Even many conservative scholars accept the existence of some type of source material, though nothing like the classical documentary hypothesis.[8]

Running in tandem with this source-critical analysis has been the tendency to question the reliability of the text. The charge that the original seventy people entering Egypt would produce 603,550 fighting men, yielding a total population of approximately 2.5 to 3 million people by the end of the Egyptian captivity, raises the most serious threat to the integrity of the text. In fact, it impacts on sev-

---

[8]For discussions of the evidence presented for documentary sources see: Hubbard and Bush, "Numbers," pp. 101-102. Carpenter, "Numbers," *ISBE²*, 3:562-563; Dillard and Longman, *Introduction*, pp. 84-85; G.B. Gray, *A Critical and Exegetical Commentary on Numbers* (Edinburgh: T. & T. Clark:, 1903), pp. xxix-xxxix; M. Noth, *Numbers*, trans. by J.D. Martin (Philadelphia: Westminster, 1968), p. 10; id., *History*, pp. 42-66; cf. Clements, "Pentateuchal Problems," p. 109; Young, *Introduction*, pp. 84-93; Harrison, *Introduction*, pp. 631-632.

eral minor ones. How could any people grow into such a large group in so short a time? How could so large a group organize in so short a time to exit Egypt, or assemble around the tabernacle? How could the wilderness support so large a population with all of its livestock and belongings (Exod 12:38)?

Some scholars have ignored the problem.[9] Of the various solutions posed, each possesses weaknesses.[10] (1) The literal interpretation accepts the biblical text as is, asserting that it emphasizes the people's fertility and the durability of their belongings (Exod 1:7; Deut 8:4), and the organization of the people into smaller groups could handle the organized march out of Egypt (Numbers 2; 10:14-20; e.g., Young and Archer).[11] Yet such figures seem to contradict such passages as Deuteronomy 7:1,7, and 9, which emphasize that the other nations were more numerous than Israel. So "every bit of available evidence biblical, extrabiblical and archaeological, seems to discourage interpreting the numbers in Numbers literally."[12] (2) The "misplaced" census theory argues the list came from the time of the Monarchy, but does not address the rapid multiplication of the nation.[13] (3) Petrie's view that the Hebrew word translated "thousands" should be translated "chieftains," "clans," "family," or "tent

---

[9]Friedman, *Commentary on the Torah*, pp. 428, 432, 519; Sailhamer, *Pentateuch*, pp. 370-371, 410-412.

[10]Several research histories of the problem have been written over the years. Two of the most recent, detailed reviews of research are: E.W. Davies, "A Mathematical Conundrum: The Problem of the Large Numbers in Numbers I and XXVI," *VT* 45:4 (1995): 449-469; C.J. Humphries, "The Number of People in the Exodus from Egypt: Decoding Mathematically the Very Large Numbers in Numbers I and XXVI," *VT* 48:2 (1998): 196-213. An older work of similar caliber may be seen in J.W. Wenham, "Large Numbers in the Old Testament," *TynBul* 18 (1967): 19-53. Nearly all traditional introductions and similar works give shorter, introductory overviews; examples of these are: Harrison, *Introduction*, pp. 631-634, 615-617; Young, *Introduction*, pp. 85-86; Archer, *Survey*, pp. 234-238; Dillard and Longman, *Introduction*, p. 84; Hubbard and Bush, "Numbers," pp. 103-106; G.J. Wenham *Numbers* (Downers Grove, IL: InterVarsity, 1981), pp. 23-25; id., *Exploring the Old Testament: A Guide to the Pentateuch* (Downers Grove, IL: InterVarsity, 2001), p. 106; Kitchen, *Reliability*, pp. 264-265.

[11]Young, *Introduction*, pp. 85-86; Archer, *Survey*, pp. 234-238.

[12]Hubbard and Bush, "Numbers," p. 105.

[13]W.F. Albright, *From the Stone Age to Christianity*, 2nd ed. (Garden City, NY: Doubleday, 1957), p. 291; G.E. Mendenhall, "The Census List of Numbers 1 and 26," *JBL* 77 (1958): 52-66; cf. B.S. Childs, *Introduction to the Old Testament as Scripture* (Philadelphia: Fortress, 1979), p. 200.

group" does not fully explain the issue.[14] In the first place, "while the term . . . can certainly designate a 'clan,' or 'subdivision of a tribe,'" there is no evidence "that the word was used to refer to a social unit as small as the 'family' or 'tent group.'"[15] In the second place, some of the figures must be interpreted literally, as for example the 22,000 Levites who served as surrogates for the 22,273 firstborn males (3:43-50).[16] (4) The view that the census figures are somehow related to specific Babylonian astrologers' calculations[17] has received support from some scholars,[18] but rests on the, as yet unproven assumption, that the biblical writers "would have the necessary arithmetical calculations," and that they "would have been sufficiently familiar with astrological lore to have realized that a correlation was supposed to exist between the numbers recorded in the census lists and the Babylonian astronomical periods."[19] (5) The view that "numerical computations rest upon some basis of reality which was quite familiar to the ancients, but which is unknown to modern scholars," allows the numbers to be used as "symbols of relative power, triumph, importance, and the like," for they are "not meant to be understood either strictly literally or as extant in a corrupt textual form,"[20] and this view most accurately describes our present knowledge — the precise value of the numbers remain a mystery.

In comparison to the above, the view that Moses could not have written the statement about his meekness (12:3) is a minor issue. Whether one attempts to defend the account's mosaic authorship by asserting that some sort of comparison is being made between Moses and his fellow Israelites,[21] or argues the statement may be a post-Mosaic gloss,[22] the issue poses no greater threat to the book's Mosaic integrity than Deuteronomy 24:5ff. does when it reports Moses' death. Scholars, rather than questioning the integrity of these passages, should recognize their historicity until they are dis-

---

[14]W.M.F. Petrie, *Egypt and Israel*, rev. ed. (London: SPCK, 1911), pp. 40ff.

[15]Davies, "Mathematical Conundrum," p. 461.

[16]Hubbard and Bush, "Numbers," p. 105.

[17]M. Barnouin, *Les Recensements du livre des Nombres et l'astronomie babylonienne*," *BT* 27:3 (1977): 280-303.

[18]Cf. Wenham, *Numbers*, p. 338; J. Milgrom, *Numbers*, JPS Torah Bible Commentary (Philadelphia: JPS, 1990), p. 338.

[19]Davies, "Mathematical Conundrum," p. 460.

[20]Harrison, *Introduction*, p. 631.

[21]E.g., Young, *Introduction*, p. 86; Archer, *Survey*, p. 238.

[22]E.g., Dillard and Longman, *Introduction*, p. 84.

proved. These accounts are in line with the ancient Near Eastern social-political-literary contexts of the thirteenth century. The book's testimony that the events and materials employed to assemble (write) Numbers were from the Mosaic period, i.e., written by Moses or at his direction, should be accepted.

GENRE

Numbers contains nearly every type of biblical literature, making it the most difficult book of the Pentateuch to survey. Milgrom's list[23] illustrates how wide-ranging the genres are: "narrative (4:1-3), poetry (21:17-18), prophecy (24:3-9), victory song (21:27-30), prayer (12:13), blessing (6:24-26), lampoon (22:22-35), diplomatic letter (21:14-19), civil law (27:1-11), cultic law (15:7-21), oracular decision (15:32-36), census list (26:1-5), temple archive (7:10-88), itinerary (33:1-49)."[24] These genres, which are similar to those found in the larger ancient Near Eastern context of the same period, served as source material to create a narrative document that illustrates the prior pentateuchal legislation, as, for example, the man gathering wood on the Sabbath (Num 15:32). The law said, "Remember the Sabbath day by keeping it holy" (Exod 20:8). The man was kept in custody "because it was not clear what should be done to him" (Num 15:34).[25]

STRUCTURE

The presence of diverse genres allows differing structures depending upon the theme emphasized. The tripartite structure takes precedence, though dual ones also occur. One tripartite division derives from a geographical emphasis.[26]

I. Preparation for leaving Sinai — 1:1–10:10
II. From Sinai to the plains of Moab — 10:11–21:35
III. Events in Moab, instructions regarding the conquest and division of the land — 22:1–36:13

---

[23]Milgrom, *Numbers*, p. xiii.

[24]Dillard and Longman, *Introduction*, pp. 85-86.

[25]See also Rendtorff, *Introduction*, p. 147; Sailhamer, *Pentateuch*, pp. 369-370; Carpenter, "Numbers," *ISBE²*, 3:562; M. Duvshani, "The Dynamic Character of the Book of Numbers," *Beth Mikra* 24 (1978): 27-32; W.F. Albright, "Oracles of Balaam," *JBL* 63 (1944): 207-233.

[26]Milgrom, *Numbers*, p. xi; Young, *Introduction*, p. 84.

A second tripartite structure gives a topical emphasis.[27]

I. Creating community at Sinai — 1:1–9:14
II. The journey's successes and failures — 9:15–25:18
III. Final preparations for entry — 26:1–35:34

A third tripartite partition yields topical and geographical emphases.[28]

I. Sinai: Preparations for departure and journey to Kadesh — 1:1–12:16
II. Kadesh: In the wilderness of Paran until the arrival in the Plains of Moab — 13:1–22:1
III. Moab: Preparation for Canaan and a backward and forward look — 22:2–36:13

A fourth tripartite arrangement emphasizes chronological themes.[29]

I. The first day of the second month to the nineteenth day of the wilderness — 1:1–10:11
II. Five months of the forty years in the wilderness — 21:10–36:13
III. Undated events during the forty years in the wilderness — 10:12–21:9

Dual structures have been used to place an emphasis on comparisons and contrasts. Olson, for example, perceives a generational division.

I. The first generation exits Egypt only to die in the wilderness — 1:1–25:18
II. The second generation, born in the wilderness, prepares to enter the promised land — 26:1–36:13.[30]

One of the most interesting dual structures notes that the juxtaposition of chapters 10 and 11 refines the thematic meaning of the two wilderness generations, creating "thematic repercussions."[31] Chapters 1–10 portray the creation of the nation in the wilderness after its deliverance from Egypt, in which the people respond with "uni-

[27]P.J. Budd, *Numbers*, WBC (Waco, TX: Word, 1984), p. xvii, cited in Dillard and Longman, *Introduction*, p. 86.
[28]Hubbard and Bush, "Numbers," pp. 100-101.
[29]Milgrom, *Numbers*, p. xiii.
[30]D.T. Olson, *The Death of the Old and the Birth of the New: The Framework of the Book of Numbers and the Pentateuch*, BJS 71 (Chico: Scholars, 1985), pp. 118-120, cited in Dillard and Longman, *Introduction*, p. 87.
[31]A.B. Leveen, "Variations on a Theme: Differing Conceptions of Memory in the Book of Numbers," *JSOT* 27 (2002): 201.

fied obedience to God's commands as mediated by Moses."[32] In this context legislation is provided "for all time — providing the means of instruction and the justification for communal celebration, an unquestioned instrument in the hands of an authority it upholds."[33] Numbers 11 begins a pericope which interrupts the harmonious picture of chapter 10 and contrasts how inadequate the people were. Because this generation failed "only their children will be able to implement God's plans, but only in a distant future."[34] Leveen speaks of this even more articulately in another article, saying, "That demise begins in chapter 11. . . . Coming after the carefully orchestrated opening chapters, 1–10, which depict the harmonious relationship between God as guide, Moses as His prophet, and the people as willing followers, chapter 11 abruptly interrupts all that preceded it. At this juncture in the journey, the actual voices of the populace are heard for the first time. They are voices raised in steady complaint."[35]

The cleavage created by this juxtaposition may be read across the book. Chapters 1–10 focus on the organization and harmony of the people as they were forged into a nation. However, all was not perfect. They were striving to arrive, but had a long way to go. This portrayal of the nation in quasi-generational terms depicts one generation as a failure and the other as a success (but not without its own failures). Israel is presented as always on the verge of going, but never arriving. Specifically, this "near success, but failure" picture may be seen in the narratives' focus on the near-fulfillment, or non-fulfillment, of the promises. The remainder of the book concentrates on the rebellious nature of the people as they move from place to place. This moving without arriving gives the book a sense of "action," which, when coupled with God's judgment against unbelief (14:39-45; 26:64-65), illuminate the message of the futility of going without God. The legal and cultic materials scattered throughout 10:11–36:13 illustrate the struggle and growth of the congregation — new laws and rules are needed as the community evolves. Seen in this way, Numbers fits quite logically, not just into the context of the Pentateuch, but Joshua–Judges as well. To

---

[32]Ibid., p. 218.

[33]Ibid.

[34]Ibid., p. 219.

[35]A.B. Leveen, "Falling in the Wilderness: Death Reports in the Book of Numbers," *Prooftexts* 22 (2002): 248.

accommodate this theological-historical emphasis chronological considerations are downplayed. For example, 1:1–10:10 deal with Israel's preparations for leaving Sinai and beginning the journey to Canaan. Within this large section of events 1:1–6:21 are placed before the events of 7:1–9:16, though they are later chronologically.

> The material in 1:1-6:21 is placed before events in 7:1-9:16 even though the events in 1:1-6:21 actually took place after 7:1-9:16 (cf. 1:1; 7:1-, 9:1,15; 10:10; Ex. 40:1,17). The sequence seems theologically, as well as literarily, acceptable, for the mustering of Israel around the tabernacle indicates the writer's concern for the central shrine of Israel. God's holiness permeates the camp and it must not be defiled (1:47-54). Before normal operations within the sphere of Yahweh's holiness can begin the congregation must be properly protected from Yahweh's holiness (1:53). Certain laws are added which are aimed at keeping the camp holy and undefiled lest Yahweh's holiness destroy the camp (5:1-6:21). The Aaronic benediction is fittingly placed at 6:22-27 because the holy congregation has been established. The dedication of the altar is subordinate to the establishment of Israel around the tabernacle (7:1-89). After the consecration of the Levites the people can keep the first Passover (9:1-14), and Israel's final preparation for moving out of the camp is described, including a specific description of how and when the people moved.[36]

THEOLOGICAL THEMES

The multifarious genres and structures extant in Numbers are brought together to portray the people in transition physically (from Egyptian bondage to Canaan, the land of promise) and spiritually (from a family of slaves to an organized theocratic nation). This transitional process allows the reciprocal testing of God and people.

> *God* tests the people to see whether they will obey him or not (Exod. 15:25; 20:20), and the *people* test *God* to see whether or not he will in fact provide for their material needs in the wilderness (17:2, 7) and to see to what extent he will suffer

---

[36]Carpenter, "Numbers," *ISBE*², 3:563-564. For discussions on the structure of the book see also: Whybray, *Introduction*, pp. 78-82; Dillard and Longman, *Introduction*, pp. 86-87.

their disobedience (Num 14:22). The many instances of their discontent, lack of faith, and rebelliousness against Moses or against God himself (Exod. 14:10-14, immediately after their departure from Egypt; Exod. 16:17:1-7; 32:1–33:6; Num. 11; 12; 13–14; 16; 10:1-13) reveals a constant change of mood in the three participants, God, Moses, and the people.[37]

Similarly, the relationship between God and Moses varies. On the one hand God and Moses communicate directly, with Moses serving as God's spokesman, while on the other Moses is frustrated and complains of the impossible position in which he is placed until he ultimately prays for death (11:11-15). He even disobeys, which keeps him out of the promised land (20:11-12). The people too are complex and described negatively. Like Moses, the generation that came out of Egypt is condemned to die in the wilderness, failing to enter the promised land (14:23). By the end of their journey, the people who just after the exodus had toyed with idolatry (Exodus 32) are fully immersed in it (Numbers 25). Out of these two general themes several other ones arise.

Holy character. The nation's holy character derives from several sources. Levitical legislation dictated the people were to be holy because God was holy (Lev 11:44,45; 19:2; 20:7,26; cf. 21:8; 22:32). Their redemption made them a holy nation (Exod 6:6; 19:5-6). God's dwelling among them, his very presence, made them holy, and passages such as Numbers 1:50-54 and chapter 5 give and repeat instructions relative to the rituals necessary to maintain such holiness. The foundation of the rituals was obedience. "The unbelief, murmuring, and rebellion of Israel as depicted by the author is in stark contrast to the characteristics that should have marked Israel (cf. chs. 11; 12; 13–14; 16; 20:1-13; 21:4-9; 25:1-4; 26:63-65)."[38] The reference in Joshua 5:3-5 stands as a testimony to the rebelliousness begun in Exodus (Exodus 5; 15:22–16:36; 17:1-7; 32; 33).

> So Joshua made flint knives, and circumcised the Israelites at Gibeath-haaraloth. This is the reason why Joshua circumcised them: all the males of the people who came out of Egypt, all the warriors, had died during the journey through the wilderness after they had come out of Egypt. Although all the people

---

[37]Whybray, *Introduction,* p. 78.
[38]Carpenter, "Numbers," *ISBE*[2], 3:564.

who came out had been circumcised, *yet all the people born on the journey through the wilderness after they had come out of Egypt had not been circumcised* (Josh 5:3-5, NRSV, emphasis added).

This passage and the events of Numbers 13–14 illustrate the people's denial of the promises to Abraham. Passages such as 14:10b-14 describe the nation's expendability and worthlessness in both generations. The generation that came out of Egypt died in the wilderness through unbelief and disobedience, which extended into the next generation who still had to be circumcised, something neglected in the wilderness.

God's patience, presence, and providence. This holy character-disobedience paradigm may be delineated further when contrasted with God's patience, presence, and providence. A holy God dwelling among his people (Exod 40:34-38; Lev 26:11f.; Num 1:47-54; 9:15-23) sanctified the obedient and destroyed the disobedient (11:1-3). This relationship, so unique to Israel (Deut 4:7-8), manifested itself in the theophany of the cloud and fire (9:15-23; cf. Exod 14:24; 16:6-7; 25:8; 29:43-46; 40:34-38). As just noted, such a holy God, dwelling among his people, demanded the nation's holiness through obedience. This obedience brought his care when the holy nation faced serious threats. Similarly, God was the holy nation's provider during this forty years (ch. 26). However, their disobedience brought wrath (1:47-54). A tension is created between these obedience-blessings and disobedience-wrath in such narratives as God's recapitulation of his decision to destroy them (14:13-19; cf. Exod 32:9-13). Taken together, these accounts point to God's sovereignty, so well illustrated in the Balaam account (23:1–24:25) and the ensuing plague (25:1-16). God's sovereign blessings are illustrated in Balaam's frustrated efforts to curse Israel, while God's sovereign wrath is illustrated in his punishment of Israel due to her illicit sexual union with Moab which led them into idolatry. "God's sovereignty extends over all history according to His covenant with Israel (24:20-25), and only He can effect blessings and curses on nations and peoples."[39]

The Land. The land of Canaan represents in Numbers both a physical and spiritual journey, or goal. It is part and parcel of the promise-fulfillment theme of the Pentateuch. Though God freely gave the land as promised (13:1f.; 14:8,23,39; 32:7-9; 33:53), Israel

---

[39]Ibid.

received the promise through faith. The lack of faith exhibited at Moab brought disaster (32:14-15), as well as causing the failure of the first attempt at taking the land (14:10-43). So the inheritance of the land depended upon a faithfulness that was revealed in obedience. Not maintaining this faith-obedience paradigm defiled the land (35:34) and endangered the nation's continued possession of it (33:56). All of the above reenforces the general lesson that God's people progress in relation to their faith and trust in him.[40]

NEW TESTAMENT CONNECTIONS

The book of Numbers is quoted only three times in the New Testament. John 19:36 quotes Numbers 9:12, observing that Jesus' death, prior to his bones being broken, typologically fit the requirements of the law; as no bone of the Passover lamb was to be broken, so our Passover Lamb, Jesus, died with unbroken bones. In 2 Timothy 2:19, Paul quotes Numbers 16:5 to make the point, as with Korah's rebellion in the days of Moses, God knows who the truly obedient are. Jesus quotes Numbers 30:2 in Matthew 5:33, making the point that his followers should always give a "yes" or "no."

However, the influence of Numbers is far greater than these three citations imply. Jude 5-7 references the rebellious generation that was destroyed in the wilderness (cf. Num 14:23-25; 26:64-65), admonishing us to persevere in our faith so that we do not lose our inheritance through unbelief. Hebrews 3:1–4:13 uses wilderness imagery from Numbers to continue this same thought to a different group of Christians, warning us to "hold onto the confidence and pride of our hope" (3:6). The implication is that we should not exhibit the tendencies of the wilderness Israel to allow doubt to destroy our faith and hope, producing unbelief and rebellion (3:12-19). Rather the Christians should continue in faith, holding to the hope of their future inheritance (4:11-13). The future of Christians (heaven) parallels Israel's Promised Land (Canaan). The Corinthian Christians reminded Paul of the wilderness Israel, which served as examples of what *not* to be (1 Cor. 10:1-11). The events recounted in Numbers "happened to them as a warning which were written for our instruction" (v. 11). The situation at Corinth, and today for

---

[40]See also Archer, *Survey*, p. 234; Harrison, *Introduction*, p. 634; Hubbard and Bush, "Numbers," pp. 106-110.

Christians, is not unlike the events reported in Numbers. God was displeased with a people who having experienced his redemptive salvation still rebelled against him (Num 14:10-35; 21:4-9; John 3:14-15; 12:32-33; 1 Cor 10:1-5). Such rebellion exhibited itself then, and exhibits itself now, in several ways. Christians are warned and instructed against idolatry (v. 7), sexual immorality (v. 8), testing God (v. 9), and complaining (v. 10). These things happened as examples to warn and instruct us (v. 11). The above illustrate the New Testament's typological use of the Old Testament events. These events occur in a historical-theological context that illustrates God's people must remain faithful in order to receive the promised covenantal blessings. Beyond this, people in this covenantal relationship can expect to receive God's providential care as did Israel in the wilderness.[41]

---

[41]Cf. Carpenter, "Numbers," *ISBE*[2], 3:567; Dillard and Longman, *Introduction*, pp. 89-90; Hubbard and Bush, "Numbers," p. 110.

DEUTERONOMY

The English title "Deuteronomy" derives from the Latin *deutero-nomii,* which itself derives from the LXX's δευτερονόμιον (*deuterono-mion*), a mistranslation of 17:18: "And when he [the king] shall be established in his government, then shall he write for himself this *repetition* of the law into a book by the hands of the priests the Levites" (emphasis added). While the Hebrew can have this nuance, the context of 17:18 indicates the more correct idea to be "copy." The king was to write for himself, not a repetition (*deuteronomion*), but a copy (מִשְׁנֶה, *mišnēh*) of the law. Even so, the book does restate and summarize many of the laws of Exodus–Numbers. The Hebrew title derives from the first words of the book, אֵלֶּה הַדְּבָרִים (*'ēlleh haddᵊbārîm,* "these are the words"), and introduces the literary form of the book — addresses of Moses at the end of his career in which he summarized the significant events of the last forty years, admonishing the nation to proper duty. These speeches were designed to ensure the nation's loyalty to God promised at Sinai.[1]

HISTORICAL AND CULTURAL BACKGROUND

Kline,[2] building on the work of Mendenhall,[3] argued Deuteronomy's structure more closely resembled the second millennium Hittite treaties than the first millennium Assyrian treaties.

---

[1] R.K. Harrison, "Deuteronomy," *ISBE*², rev. ed. by G.W. Bromiley (Grand Rapids: Eerdmans, 1979), 1:934-935; id., *Introduction,* p. 635; Archer, *Survey,* p. 239; Young, *Introduction,* p. 94; Dillard and Longman, *Introduction,* pp. 91-92; D.A. Hubbard and F.W. Bush, "Deuteronomy," in *Old Testament Survey: The Message, Form, and Background of the Old Testament,* 2ⁿᵈ ed., ed. by W.S. LaSor, D.A. Hubbard, and F.W. Bush (Grand Rapids: Eerdmans, 1996), p. 111; A.D.H. Mayes, *Deuteronomy* (London/Grand Rapids: Marshall-Morgan-Scott/Eerdmans, 1981), p. 27.

[2] M.G. Kline, *Treaty of the Great King* (Grand Rapids: Eerdmans, 1963), pp. 13ff.

[3] Mendenhall, "Covenant Forms," pp. 50-76.

Second Millennium Treaties	Deuteronomy	First Millennium Treaties
Preamble, defining the vassal's obligations to the great king	**Preamble** (Deut 1:1-5; cf. Exod 20:1; Josh 24:2)	**Preamble**, defining the vassal's obligations to the great king
Historical prologue, reciting the historical relationship between the overlord and the vassal	**Historical prologue** (Deut 1:6–3:29; Exod 20:2; Josh 24:2-13)	*Historical Prologue Missing*
Stipulations, demanding loyalty from the vassal and listing the specific rules defining the relationship	**Stipulations** (*general* – Deut 4–11; Exod 20:3-17,22-26; Josh 24:14-25; *specific* – Deut 12–26; Exod 21:23,25-31)	**Stipulations**, demanding loyalty from the vassal and listing the specific rules defining the relationship
Deposition of the treaty text in vassal's sanctuary	**Deposition** of text (Deut 31:9,24-26; Exod 25:16; 34:1,28ff.; Josh 24:26)	*Deposition of the text missing*
Provisions for the vassal's obligations, including, but not limited to, the obligation to come to the suzerain's court, the obligation to provide troops for defense, the description of the location in which to place the treaty, and the calendar for its public reading	**Provisions** for public reading, etc. (Deut 31:10-13)	**Provisions** for the vassal's obligations, including, but not limited to, the obligation to come to the suzerain's court, the obligation to provide troops for defense, the description of the location in which to place the treaty, and the calendar for its public reading
Lists of witnesses (the gods of both vassal and suzerain)	**Lists** of witnesses (Deut 31:16-30; 32:1-47; Exod 24:4; Josh 24:22,27)	**Lists** of witnesses (the gods of both vassal and suzerain)
Blessings *and* **curses** invoked on the vassal depending upon his obedience or disobedience	**Blessings** (Deut 28:1-14; Lev 26:3-13; Josh 24:19f) *and* **Curses** (Deut 28:15-68; Lev 26:13-33)	*Curses only are listed*

Deuteronomy contained a near one-to-one correspondence with second millennium Hittite treaties, while first millennium Assyrian treaties lacked the historical prologue, the requirement to deposit a copy of the treaty in the sanctuaries of both overlord and vassal, and listed only the curses imposed on the vassal for noncompliance. These facts influenced Weinfeld and Kitchen to argue for a synthesis of all ancient Near Eastern treaty forms as foundational to Deuteronomy.[4] Recently Kitchen, reexamined the issue and concluded, "The Sinai documents have an indubitable fourteenth/thirteenth century format,"[5] and "that the bulk of Deuteronomy in form and content is irrevocably tied to usage in the late second millennium is a fact that clashes horribly with the hallowed speculations about the origins and history of 'Deuteronomic' thought that have been developed across two hundred years, and in particular with the last sixty years and with the 'minimalism' of the last decade or so."[6] Deuteronomy's relationship with these second millennium treaties impacts all areas of its interpretation. The similarity of Deuteronomy to second millennium treaties fits well with its description as a covenant (29:9,12,14,21).[7]

TEXT AND AUTHOR

The text reflects "good classical Hebrew" that is "grammatically and linguistically . . . superior to *some* of the later books in the Hebrew canon."[8] The early argument that Aramaisms in the book are indicative of a seventh-century date are invalid today because scholars now recognize that Amaraic "had a long pre-history," which "overlaid in Palestine an older stratum of Canaanite at an *early* stage of its development, so that many of the alleged Aramaisms in the Hebrew Bible, on which occasionally far-reaching critical conclusions have been based, are in fact pure Canaanitisms or common

---

[4]M. Weinfeld, *Deuteronomy and the Deuteronomic School* (Oxford: University Press, 1972; repr. ed., Winona Lake, IN: Eisenbrauns, 1992), pp. 59-178; K.A. Kitchen, "The Fall and Rise of Covenant, Law and Treaty," *TynBul* 40 (1989): 118-135.

[5]Kitchen, *Reliability*, p. 289.

[6]Ibid., p. 299.

[7]Harrison, "Deuteronomy," *ISBE*², 1:937-938; id., *Introduction*, pp. 648-650; Dillard and Longman, *Introduction*, pp. 97-99; Mayes, *Deuteronomy*, pp. 30-34; Hubbard and Bush, "Deuteronomy," p. 112.

[8]Harrison, "Deuteronomy," *ISBE*², 1:938.

North-west Semitic."[9] Even the Pentateuch indicates Aramean connections (Gen 31:47; Deut 26:5). As might be expected from a book of speeches from a dying leader, Deuteronomy's rhetoric "is sometimes stern, sometimes tender, but always urgent and expansive, without ever becoming prolix or tedious."[10]

Several factors point to Deuteronomy's authenticity as a record of Moses' last speeches, formulated along the lines of thirteenth-century international treaties. The forty occurrences of his name, written in an authoritative first-person style (cf. e.g., 1:16; 3:21; 29:5), portray Moses sermonizing in preparation for Israel's upcoming occupation of the land (cf. 4:5,14; 5:31; 7:1; etc.). Specific texts in 31:1–34:12 picture Moses as the compiler of the law. "Then Moses wrote down this law and gave it to the priests, the sons of Levi, who carried the ark of the covenant of the Lord, and to all the elders of Israel" (31:9, NRSV). The Song of Moses (32:1ff.), written and taught to the Israelites (31:22) at God's command, stood as his witness against Israel (31:19). The account of Moses' death (34:1ff.), which early scholarship pointed to as evidence Moses could not have written the Pentateuch, indicates only that these last verses could not have been written by Moses. Jewish tradition confirms this idea by assigning the final eight verses of the Torah to Joshua. All of the above fits with the ancient Near Eastern tradition of recording events at, or shortly after, the time of their occurrence, as must have been the case with the death of Moses.

One of the most significant evidences for a thirteenth-century date for Deuteronomy and Mosaic authorship comes from references in Joshua, Judges, Samuel, and Kings. Harrison has isolated an impressive list of passages which indicate the principles espoused by Moses in Deuteronomy were not only "known and observed but also that they were known in written form as codified statutes."[11] (1) The spoils of Jericho were "devoted" (Josh 6:17f.; Deut 13:15-18; cf. Josh 10:40; 11:12,15; Deut 7:2; 20:16-20). (2) The punishment of Achan reflects prior legislation (Josh 7:25; Deut 13:10; 17:5). (3) When Ai was captured "only the cattle and the spoil" were taken as booty (Josh 8:27; Deut 20:14). (4) Bodies were taken down from their hanging position before nightfall (Josh 8:29; 10:26; Deut 21:23). (5) The altar on Mount Ebal was built and written upon in accor-

---

[9]Ibid.

[10]Ibid., 1:939.

[11]Ibid.; cf. id., *Introduction*, pp. 650-653; cf. Archer, *Survey*, pp. 243-250.

dance with Mosaic command (Josh 8:30-34; Deut 27:3-6,8). (6) The reading of the curses and blessings on Ebal and Gerizim was done in accordance with Moses' prior instructions (Josh 8.33-35; Deut 11:29; 27:12-26). (7) The erection of the memorial by the two-and-a-half tribes upon their return to the east side of the Jordan, and the accusation that its construction created plural sanctuaries reflects prior legislation (Josh 22:29; Deut 12:5). (8) The complete destruction of Zephath (Judg 1:17; Deut 7:2; 20:16-20), Gideon's reduction of his army (Judg 7:1-7; Deut 20:1-9), Gideon and Manoah both sacrificing on altars other than Shiloh, but only at God's direct command (Judg 6:25-27; 13:16), and Micah's desire to have a Levite for a priest (Judg 17:13; Deut 10:8; 18:1-8; 33:8-11) all indicate Deuteronomy was familiar to the people in the period of the judges. (9) In Samuel, Elkanah goes yearly to worship God at the central shrine at Shiloh, and, when this is destroyed, Samuel sacrificed at Mizpah, Ramah, and Bethlehem (7:7-9,17; 16:5) in accordance with Deuteronomy 12:10-20. (10) Solomon violated three specific commands of Deuteronomy and multiplied silver (1 Kgs 10:27), gold (1 Kgs 10:14-16,21), and wives (1 Kgs 11:1-11) in direct violation of Deuteronomy 17:17. (11) Upon his appointment as king Joash received "the crown" and "the testimony" (2 Kgs 11:12; Deut 17:18). (12) Amaziah spared his father's murderers (2 Kgs 14:6; Deut 24:16), and Hezekiah removed the high places, broke down their pillars, and cut down the Asherahs, both in accordance with Moses' instructions (2 Kgs 18:4,22; Deut 7:5; 12:3). (13) The prophets referenced Deuteronomy (fighting with priests, Hos 4:4 and Deut 17:12; removing landmarks, Hos 5:10 and Deut 19:14; returning to Egypt, Hos 8:13; 9:3 and Deut 28:68; God's dealings with Ephraim, Hos 11:3 and Deut 1:31; 32:10; God's special relationship with Israel, Amos 3:2 and Deut 7:6; 4:7f.; Israel's violation of specific laws, Amos 1:6-8 and Deut 24:12-15; 23:17; Zion being pictured as a secure dwelling place, Isa 2:2-4; 8:18; 28:16; 29:lf; cf. Micah 1:4). "[N]ot one of the four great prophets of the 8th cent. BCE — Isaiah, Micah, Amos, Hosea — ever recognized 'high places' as legitimate centers of worship."[12] The above indicates that Deuteronomy "at least [reflects] a tradition that accurately represents" Mosaic authorship, but more likely contains the "actual words of Moses."[13]

---

[12]Harrison, "Deuteronomy," *ISBE*², 1:939.
[13]Hubbard and Bush, "Deuteronomy," p. 117.

HISTORY OF INTERPRETATION

The Mosaic authorship of Deuteronomy was not doubted prior to nineteenth-century criticism. Several references *were* interpreted as isolated insertions by later editors to clarify the text (2:10-11,20-23; 3:9,11,13b-14; 10:6-9; 34), while other references describing the written nature of the material (27:3,8; 28:58; 29:21,29; 30:10,19; 31:24) indicated Moses' hand. The rise of nineteenth-century criticism triggered a history of research that goes far beyond this simple view of authorship and has yielded a tremendous amount of literature, comprising a wide range of subjects and theories. These we will only be able to highlight.[14]

Some nineteenth-century critical scholars connected Deuteronomy with a supposed "D" document, dated in the seventh century B.C. Wellhausen asserted the book "was found and published" in the eighteenth year of King Josiah for the purposes of initiating Josiah's reform and centralizing the religion in Jerusalem (2 Kings 22).[15] Several seemingly valid reasons pointed to connections between these events in 2 Kings and Deuteronomy.[16] (1) Deuteronomy 12 required the destruction of Canaanite high places and the centralization of the worship, which thing Josiah seemed to do (2 Kgs 23:4-20). (2) Passover observance in Deuteronomy 16, unlike Exodus 12, took place at the central sanctuary, which thing Josiah did (2 Kgs 23:21-22). (3) Deuteronomy 18:14-22 demanded the destruction of mediums and all forms of divination, which thing Josiah did (2 Kgs 23:24). (4) The book presented to Josiah and the reaction it produced in him (2 Kgs 22:13,19) seemed to reflect the curses of Deuteronomy 28. (5) Deuteronomy 17:18-19 required kings to rule according to the law, which Josiah seemed to do (2 Kgs 22:11). (6) The "book of the covenant" (2 Kgs 23:2) seemed confirmed as the book of Deuteronomy when scholars were able to show affinities between Deuteronomy and ancient Near Eastern treaties. (7) Material in Kings reflected the theology of Deuteronomy in such things as the place where God put his name (Deut 12:5; 2 Kgs 23:27) and divine retribution (Deut 31:24-29; 2 Kgs 22:16-20; 23:26-27).

---

[14]See also: Dillard and Longman, *Introduction*, pp. 91-92, for an extensive bibliography dealing with Deuteronomy research; cf. D.L. Christensen, *Deuteronomy 1–11* (Waco: Word, 1991), pp. xxv-lvi.

[15]Wellhausen, *Prolegomena*, pp. 402, 487.

[16]Dillard and Longman, *Introduction*, pp. 93-94.

Though at first criticized, this new explanation came to be one of the focal points of the new pentateuchal criticism, making Deuteronomy the primary document by which the other sources (J, E, and P) were dated.[17]

As the nineteenth century closed and the twentieth began, scholars continued to identify the various sources thought to comprise the book. Changes between singular and plural forms indicated earlier and later material, and/or different authors,[18] a view that continues to be a focal point of research.[19] Driver isolated perceived contradictions between material in Genesis–Numbers and Deuteronomy, which, he argued, indicated Deuteronomy originated in Josiah's day, thus reaffirming Wellhausen's position.[20] (1) Exodus allowed the father to refuse the marriage of his daughter to a man who had seduced her (Exod 22:17), whereas Deuteronomy required it (Deut 22:28-29). (2) In Exodus the institution of the Sabbath derived from creation (Exod 20:11), while in Deuteronomy the Sabbath commemorated the Egyptian servitude (Deut 5:15). (3) The purpose for the ritual killing of all animals in Leviticus is sacrificial (Lev 17:3-5), but Deuteronomy permits animals to be slaughtered away from the centralized worship shrine (Deut 12:15-17). (4) Numbers 18:21-24 and Leviticus 27:30-33 reserved the tithe for the Levites, while Deuteronomy 14:22-29 allowed a portion of the tithe to remain with the family. Von Rad refined the issue further, arguing two separate traditions (a Sinai tradition and an Exodus-Conquest tradition) had been redacted into a salvation history (*Heilsgeschichte*).[21] The Sinai materials possessed a cultic setting, which was evidence of a Levitical origin. Others (e.g., Wellhausen, and Driver)

---

[17]See: H.H. Rowley, *The Growth of the Old Testament* (New York: Harper and Row, 1950), p. 29; Clements, *One Hundred Years*, pp. 8-9; Hubbard and Bush, "Deuteronomy," p. 114.

[18]G.A. Smith, *The Book of Deuteronomy* (Cambridge: University Press, 1918).

[19]Cf. E.W. Nicholson, *Deuteronomy and the Tradition* (Philadelphia: Fortress, 1967), pp. 22-26; Mayes, *Deuteronomy*, pp. 35-37; J.G. McConville, "Singular Address in the Deuteronomic Law and the Politics of Legal Administration," *JSOT* 97 (2002): 19-36.

[20]S.R. Driver, *A Critical and Exegetical Commentary on Deuteronomy*, 3rd ed. (Edinburgh: T. & T. Clark, 1902), pp. iii-xix, xxxiv-lxv; cf. Wellhausen, *Prolegomena*, p. 487.

[21]G. von Rad, *The Problem of the Hexateuch and Other Essays* (New York: McGraw-Hill, 1966), pp. 1-78.

argued for prophetic influence,[22] while Weinfeld more recently represents those who argue for a wisdom connection.[23]

The mid-twentieth century saw the publication and subsequent influence of Noth's theory of a "Deuteronomistic History." Generally speaking, the "Deuteronomist" signifies the name Noth gave "to the author/compiler of the OT book of Deuteronomy and/or certain portions of the OT that reflect the literary and theological characteristics of Deuteronomy, whether found in Gen–Josh, or Deut–2 Kgs, the latter called the 'Deuteronomistic History.'"[24] This history, which extended to 2 Kings 25:30, with the exception of Deuteronomy 1–3 (which served as an introduction to the entire history), Noth described as essentially a unity, composed by a single author who had a definite theological plan. The author showed an interest in chronology and the relating of key events to each other (e.g., 1 Kgs 6:1 and the Exodus). At significant points in the narrative the historian introduced key speeches (Jos 12; 23; 1 Sam 12; 1 Kgs 8:14ff.), allowing these sources to "speak for themselves." This theory, by far, has enjoyed the most influence, impacting nearly every facet of biblical studies. In the last half of the twentieth century scholars turned more to synchronic interpretations, which emphasize the unity of the book. Yet these exhibit no "clear consensus on most issues," including, but not limited to, "the relationship of the book to the remainder of the Deuteronomistic History (Joshua–Kings), the relevance of the treaty parallels for genre and setting, questions of provenance (from the north, the Levites, prophets, sages?), and the issue of the relationship of the book to Josiah's reforms."[25]

Some scholars disagreed with these views, positing dates from the time of Samuel to 400 and noting that the centralization theories contradict or misinterpret several pieces of data.[26] Connecting Deuteronomy with the centralization of the worship in Jerusalem

[22]Wellhausen, *Prologemena*, p. 487; Driver, *Deuteronomy*, pp. iii-xix, xxxiv-lxv.

[23] Weinfeld, *Deuteronomy and the Deuteronomic School*, pp. 53-58; cf. Dillard and Longman, *Introduction*, pp. 94-96.

[24]Soulen, *Handbook*, p. 46; cf. M. Noth, *The Deuteronomistic History, JSOTS* 15 (1981): 6, 14, 84, 89, originally published as *Überlieferungsgeschichtliche Studien*, 2nd ed. (Tübingen: Max Niemeyer, 1957; 3rd ed. unaltered, 1967).

[25]Dillard and Longman, *Introduction*, pp. 96-97; cf. Halpern, *The First Historians*, pp. 30-31; Hubbard and Bush, "Deuteronomy," pp. 116-117; Mayes, *Deuteronomy*, pp. 81-107.

[26]Harrison, "Deuteronomy," *ISBE²*, 1:935-937; cf. id., *Introduction*, pp. 640-649.

ignores the lack of evidence in the book for such a centralization. "The place which the Lord your God shall choose" (Deut 12:5,11) is very enigmatic. The statement refers more to a place of choice rather than a specific geographical location. So, "Deuteronomy lays no emphasis whatever upon the peculiar claim of Jerusalem to be the sole place of worship."[27] Rather, Deuteronomy 14:14 indicates Jerusalem's exclusion since the "place" was to be "in one of your tribes," and Jerusalem lay outside tribal jurisdiction until David conquered it. Further, the command to build an altar and inscribe the law on it at Ebal (27:1-8) anticipates a cultic center while allowing worship at other places. Therefore, "the centralization theory of Wellhausen, so important for his general chronology, rests upon a misreading and misunderstanding of the Hebrew text."[28] Jerusalem seems to be a second choice, being occupied by Hurrians, Hyksos, and Jebusite rulers from 2000 to David's capture of it. Further, Josiah abolished idolatry only in Jerusalem and Judah since the centralization had already been accomplished by Solomon. Finally, there seems to be no way positively to identify the law found in Josiah's day with any major part of Deuteronomy. While part of the book may have been included, other abstracted parts of the law may have been found that day. Doubts such as these indicate the impossibility of equating the law scroll of Josiah with Deuteronomy exclusively, indicating this theory raises more problems than it solves, especially in light of the book's affinity to second-millennium treaties.[29]

STRUCTURE

Beyond the general structure identified in ancient Near Eastern treaties,[30] scholars have observed the book comprises three discourses, followed by three short appendices.[31]

---

[27]J. Skinner, *Prophecy and Religion* (Cambridge: University Press, 1922), p. 167; cf. H.H. Rowley, *Studies in Old Testament Prophecy: Presented to T.H. Robinson on His Sixty-Fifth Birthday, August 9th, 1946* (Edinburgh: T. & T. Clark, 1950), p. 166.

[28]Harrison, "Deuteronomy," *ISBE*², 1:936.

[29]See also: Mayes, *Deuteronomy*, p.103; Archer, *Survey*, pp. 91-95; Kaiser, "Pentateuch and Deuteronomistic History," pp. 309-314.

[30]Harrison, "Deuteronomy," *ISBE*², 1:935; Dillard and Longman, *Introduction*, p. 99; Hubbard and Bush, "Deuteronomy," pp. 112-113.

[31]Harrison, "Deuteronomy," *ISBE*², 1:938; cf. id., *Introduction*, pp. 653-662.

I. *1:1–4:43* rehearses God's past dealing with Israel
  A. When and where he delivered them — 1:1-5
  B. The nation's experiences from Horeb to Moab — 1:6–3:29
  C. Exhortations to fidelity in the context of the threat of
     idolatry — 4:1-40
  D. Appendix listing the three cities of refuge on the east side
     of the Jordan — 4:41-43
II. *4:44–26:19* are exhortative and legal
  A. Introductory superscription, laws, testimonies and judg-
     ments — 4:44-49
  B. Exposition of the ten commandments — 5:1–11:32
  C. Special laws dealing with "worship, purity, tithes, the
     three annual feasts, the administration of justice, kings,
     priests, prophets, war, and the private and social life of
     the people" — 12:1–26:19
III. *27:1–31:30* is comprised of predictive and threatening mate-
   rials discussing blessings and curses depending upon obedi-
   ence or disobedience
  A. Directions to write these laws on Mount Ebal — 27:1-10
  B. They are to be ratified by the reading of the blessings and
     curses from the respective mountains, Gerizim and Ebal
     — 27:11-26
  C. Warnings against disobedience — 28:1–29:1
  D. Exhortations to accept the terms of the covenant — 29:2–
     30:20
  E. The farewell of Moses and the commissioning of Joshua —
     31:1-30
IV. *32:1–34:12* comprise three appendices
  A. Moses' Song —32:1-52
  B. Moses' Blessing — 33:1-29
  C. Moses' Death — 34:1-12

GENRE

This synthesis of second-millennium Near Eastern treaties and
sermonic-speeches, which move from reflections on lessons learned
from the past to commentary on the Decalogue, to exhortations
(warnings and blessings, etc.) regarding the future, reenforce Deuteronomy as a written document. Further, the significance of the
minor genres still shines through. Deuteronomy as *constitution*
derives out of the treaty genre and defined Israel's covenant life. As

such the book seems foundational to western constitutionalism.[32] Deuteronomy as an *exposition* or *commentary* on the decalogue[33] points to the hortatory nature of the book. Deuteronomy as *direct address* revealed in its three-speeches structure, synthesize these other genres and allow the reader to enter into a living world of care, concern, urgency, etc., that only comes when the dying impart their words to the next generation.[34]

THEOLOGICAL THEMES

The key theological themes of Deuteronomy which have influenced the religious thought of ancient Israel, Judaism, and Christianity may be described in terms of several overarching concepts. The *credal-like* statement of Leviticus's motto, "You shall be holy for I am holy" (Lev 11:44,45; 19:2; 20:7,26), is restated in Deuteronomy, but with an *election emphasis*, "For you are a people holy to the LORD your God; the LORD your God has chosen you out of all the peoples on earth to be his people, his treasured possession" (7:6, NRSV). This holiness of God reflects God's *unique character*, "Hear, O Israel: the LORD our God, the LORD is one" (6:4), which itself placed upon Israel the specific responsibility to "love the LORD your God with all your heart and with all your soul and with all your strength" (6:5), and made the nation holy (as just noted), reflecting the nation's *unique character* among the nations. The uniting of these two, *a unique God with his unique people*, produced a unique relationship defined by the word *covenant*. This covenant, based not on fear but love, provided the highest privileges in terms of covenant blessings and required specific responsibilities. The holy life lived (7:6, 14:2; 18:13; 26:19) expressed itself in kindness toward "the needy, the poor, the orphan, the widow, the Levite, the stranger (10:18f., 17–21, 26:12), to the animal creation (25:4),"[35] and required

---

[32]S.D. McBride, "Polity of the Covenant People; the Book of Deuteronomy," *Int* 3 (1987): 229-241.

[33]S.A. Kaufman, "The Structure of the Deuteronomic Law," *Maavav* 1-2 (1978–79): 105-158; J.H. Walton, "Deuteronomy in Exposition of the Spirit of the Law," *GTJ* 8 (1987): 213-225; cf. Dillard and Longman, *Introduction,* p. 100.

[34]See also, Dillard and Longman, *Introduction,* pp. 99-101.

[35]Harrison, "Deuteronomy," *ISBE²*, 1:935, cf. 1:939-940.

parents to teach the covenant to their children (4:9; 6:7,20-25; 11:19-21; 31:13). These lofty ideals were not without the necessary *divine retribution*. The covenant in Deuteronomy ties God's promised gift of the land to the condition of Israel's obedience and faithfulness (4:25; 6:18; 8:1; 11:8-9,18-21; 16:20). Obedience brought the promise of keeping the land as well as prosperity; disobedience brought disaster, death, and the loss of the land (4:25-31; 11:26-28). This tension of grace and law sets the stage for the unfolding of the rest of the nation's history. Israel was at a crossroads. The uniqueness and holiness of God as he entered into a relationship of love with his people (covenant), meant they must love him in return, be unique, be holy, resist idolatry, remain faithful to the covenant, and accept that obedience brought reward while disobedience brought punishment. In short, Israel must remember — not forget — God. Would the nation's actions produce threat or promise?[36]

NEW TESTAMENT CONNECTIONS

The prophet like Moses. Of the many citations of Deuteronomy in the New Testament, perhaps the most far-reaching for Israel was Deuteronomy 18:14-24. This passage promised that God would send a "prophet like Moses," indicating Moses' historic function as mediator between nation and deity. Moses reminded Israel of God's appearance at Horeb, which so disturbed the people they requested him to stand in their place (4:10-14; 5:22-31). When he did so and related the words of God to the people, he became their prophet, indeed, the model for all of Israel's prophets to follow (18:14-22). The promise of a "prophet like Moses" indicated God's continued care for the nation. In contrast to this promise stood 34:10, which observed, "There has not arisen a prophet like Moses in Israel." The tension between the expectation of "a prophet like Moses" and the reality of none having arrived set the stage for a long succession of prophets, each of which, while recognizing that up to that point there had not been a prophet like Moses (34:10-12), might have thought of himself as that prophet. These "prophets like Moses" exhorted the people to be faithful to the covenant (13:1-5) and

---

[36]See also: Dillard and Longman, *Introduction,* pp. 102-105; Hubbard and Bush, "Deuteronomy," pp. 119-125; Mayes, *Deuteronomy,* pp. 55-81; Archer, *Survey,* p. 241.

expected their prophecies to be fulfilled (18:21-24). In this sense, Deuteronomy 18:14-24 became the fountainhead of Israelite prophecy. As God revealed his word to Moses, so he revealed his word to his prophets (cf. Amos 3:7). These "prophets like Moses" became "Yahweh's messengers, his covenant mediators, intercessors for the people, [and] speakers for God," who were "sent from the divine king . . . to reprove and pronounce judgment upon Israel for breach of covenant."[37] When they proclaimed this message they preached the creative word of God, which did not return to him empty (Isa 55:11). God's word in their mouths gave them the authority "over nations and over kingdoms, to pluck up and to pull down, to destroy and to overthrow, to build and to plant" (Jer 1:9b-10).[38]

The "servant-prophet" epithet illustrates this connection. The epithet, "my servant Moses," or the like (Deut 34:5; cf. Exod 14:31; Num 12:7-8; Josh 1:1-2,7,13,15; 8:31,33; 9:24; 11:12,15; 12:6; 13:8; 14:7; 18:7; 22:2,4-5; 1 Kgs 8:53,56; 2 Kgs 18:12; 21:8; 1 Chr 6:49; 2 Chr 1:3; 24:6,9; Neh 1:7-8; 9:14; 10:29; Ps 105:26; Isa 63:11; Dan 9:11; Mal 4:4), resounds throughout the biblical record. The individual prophets, Ahijah (1 Kgs 14:18; 15:29), Elijah (1 Kgs 18:36; 2 Kgs 9:36; 10:10), and Jonah (2 Kgs 14:25) are all designated as "servant(s) of the Lord," or the like. As a group, the prophets are designated "my/his/your servants the prophets" ("my servants" – 2 Kgs 9:7; 17:13; Jer 7:25; 26:5; 29:19; 35:15; 44:4; Ezek 38:17; Zech 1:6; "his servants the prophets" – 2 Kgs 17:23; 21:10; 24:2; Jer 25:4; Amos 3:7; Dan 9:10; "your servants the prophets" – Ezra 9:11 and Dan 9:6). This "servant-prophet" epithet presupposes a special relationship with YHWH. Deuteronomy 32:36 observed that "YHWH would vindicate his people and have compassion on his servants," while verse 43 noted, "he avenges the blood of his servants." In language closely resembling Deuteronomy 32:43, Jehu was anointed (2 Kgs 9:7) so "that I may avenge on Jezebel the blood of *my servants the prophets*, and the blood of the *servants of the Lord*" (emphasis added). Inherent in the servant-prophet's relationship with YHWH

---

[37]J. Muilenburg, "The 'Office' of Prophet in Ancient Israel," in *The Bible in Modern Scholarship*, ed. by J.P. Hyatt (Nashville: Abingdon, 1965), p. 97.

[38]For discussions of the relationship between the prophets and Moses see: Young, *Introduction*, pp. 100-101; Dillard and Longman, *Introduction*, pp. 103-104; J.C. Laney, "The Role of the Prophets in God's Case against Israel," *BSac* 138 (1981): 313-325; G.M. Tucker, "Deut 18:15-22," *Int* 41 (1987): 292-297; P.D. Miller, "Moses My Servant," *Int* 41 (1987): 245-255.

was his punishment of the prophet's adversaries. Similarly, fulfilled prophecy characterized the servant-prophet's relationship to YHWH. In language reminiscent of Deuteronomy 18:14-24, 2 Kings 10:10 says, "Know then that there shall fall to the earth nothing of the word of the LORD, which the LORD spoke concerning the house of Ahab; for the LORD has done what he said through *his servant Elijah*" (NRSV, emphasis added). This and other passages (1 Kgs 14:18; 15:29; 2 Kgs 9:36; 14:25) emphasize not the fulfillment of the word of the prophets, but the fulfillment of the word of the Lord which he spoke through *his servant the prophet*. The servant-prophet served as the vehicle through which YHWH made known his word, which, when fulfilled, indicated these servant-prophets stood in the tradition of "a prophet like Moses" (Deut 18:15-22). The "prophet like Moses" had YHWH's words in his mouth and spoke according to YHWH's commands (v. 18). If a prophet spoke presumptuously – the thing does not come to pass – he was not considered to be "a prophet like Moses." Connecting prophecy with the epithet in accounts of fulfilled prophecy inferred that a particular prophet was "a prophet like Moses," "a servant of YHWH," in a sense similar to Moses' servanthood. Elijah's speech at Mount Carmel illustrates this fact. "O LORD, God of Abraham, Isaac, and Israel, let it be known this day that you are God in Israel, that *I am your servant*, and *that I have done all these things at your bidding*" (1 Kgs 18:36, NRSV, emphasis added). Elijah wanted YHWH to show not only that he was God in Israel as opposed to Baal, but that Elijah was YHWH's faithful "servant" sent with a particular commission ("I have done all these things at thy word") as opposed to the prophets of Baal. The other passages where "my/his/your servants the prophets" is used have the same connotation. The prophets faithfully carried out their commissions. Like Moses, who had been "faithful in all my [YHWH's] house" (Num 12:7), so these had been faithful in their commissions. YHWH sent the servant-prophets to warn the people of their evil deeds but they refused to heed the warnings or keep his commandments (2 Kgs 17:13). Israel's exile occurred because it followed the sins of Jeroboam I which the servant-prophet predicted (2 Kgs 17:22,23); similarly, God sent his warnings against Judah *via* his servant-prophets (2 Kgs 21:10ff.). These took the form of punishing invasions against Jehoiakim predicted by the servant-prophets (2 Kgs 24:2). In Jeremiah the servant-prophet epithet takes on a special intensity. YHWH sent again and again the servant-prophets commissioned to speak his word (7:25; 25:4; 26:5; 29:19; 35:15; 44:4). So the servant-prophets stood in the mainstream of a tradition which considered them in a special relationship with their Lord, YHWH, and which expected them faithfully to carry out the commission for which he had selected them, which emphasized YHWH's word mediated through them. The above indicates, while "no prophet has risen in Israel like Moses" (Deut 34:10), there was a steady stream of prophets who were similar to Moses. As he was faithful in his servanthood, so they were faithful in theirs. As he had stood ready to do YHWH's bidding, so did these servant-prophets. Israel's continually looking for the "prophet like Moses," God's faithful servant, ultimately evolved into that of the ideal servant (Isa 42:1-4; 49:1-6; 50:4-9; 52:13–53:12), which pointed to Christ. The people's question to John whether he was the "prophet like Moses" (18:15-19; John 1:21) indicates their anticipation of the appearance of just such a prophet. Ultimately Christians understood that Jesus was the "prophet like Moses," mediator and lawgiver, who faithfully carried out the commission given him (Deut 5:27; 18:15-19; 34:11-12; John 6:14; Acts 3:22; 7:37; Heb 4:14-16).[39]

Other areas of contact with the New Testament include the following. Jesus summarized the entire old covenant in a single sentence (Mt. 22:37; cf. Deut 6:5). He stated that he and the father were one, echoing the *Shema* (6:4; John 10:30; 17:21-23). He quoted from Deuteronomy to answer Satan during the temptation (Matt 4:4,7,10; cf. Deut 8:3; 6:16,13). The central sanctuary of Deuteronomy became a heavenly sanctuary for the new Israel (Heb 12:18-24). As the nation of Israel was God's treasure (Deut 7:6; 14:2; 26:18), so the church is his treasure (Eph 1:14; Titus 2:14; 1 Pet 2:9). God is a consuming fire for the church as he was for ancient Israel (Deut 4:24; Heb 12:29). No wonder "the early church saw in itself the recreation of an ideal Israel. Just as Israel was portrayed in Deuteronomy as a unity having one God, one people, one land, one sanctuary, and one law, so the church is exhorted to a similar unity, for there is one body, one Spirit, one hope, one Lord, one faith, one baptism, one God and Father of all (Eph 4:4-5). Jesus prayed that his people might

---

[39]Cf. R.C. Bailey, "Images of the Prophets: An Analysis of the Metaphors and Epithets Used in the Old Testament to Describe Prophets and Prophetic Activity" (Ph.D. dissertation, Drew University, 1987), pp. 161-162, 169, 174-179; Tucker, "Moses My Servant," p. 253.

be one (John 17:11)."[40] All of the above indicates that Deuteronomy is an Old Testament book whose influence is immeasurable.[41]

[40]Dillard and Longman, *Introduction,* p. 106, cf. p. 105.
[41]Cf. Hubbard and Bush, "Deuteronomy," pp. 126-127; Tucker, "Moses My Servant, p. 255.

BOOKS OF
HISTORY

DALE MANOR

BIBLIOGRAPHY FOR
THE BOOKS OF HISTORY

Aharoni, Yohanan. "New Aspects of the Israelite Occupation in the North." In *Near Eastern Archaeology in the Twentieth Century: Essays in Honor of Nelson Glueck*, pp. 254-267. Ed. by J.A. Sanders. Garden City, NY: Doubleday, 1970.

_____ . "Nothing Early and Nothing Late: Re-writing Israel's Conquest." *BA* 39 (1976): 55-76.

Ahlström, Gösta W. *Who Were the Israelites?* Winona Lake, IN: Eisenbrauns, 1986.

Albright, William F. "Archaeology and the Date of the Hebrew Conquest of Palestine." *BASOR* 58 (1935): 10-18.

_____ . *The Archaeology of Palestine*. Gloucester, MA: Peter Smith, 1971.

_____ . *The Biblical Period from Abraham to Ezra*. New York: Harper & Row, 1963.

_____ . "The Israelite Conquest of Canaan in the Light of Archaeology." *BASOR* 74 (1939): 11-23.

Alt, Albrecht. "The Settlement of the Israelites in Palestine." In *Essays on Old Testament History and Religion*, pp. 175-221. Trans. by R.A. Wilson. Garden City, NY: Doubleday, 1967.

Baldwin, Joyce G. *Esther*. TOTC 12. Leicester: Inter-Varsity Press, 1984.

_____ . *1 & 2 Samuel*. TOTC 8. Leicester, England: Inter-Varsity Press, 1988.

Batten, Loring W. *The Books of Ezra and Nehemiah*. ICC. Edinburgh: T. & T. Clark, 1913.

Beller, David. "A Theology of the Book of Esther." *ResQ* 39 (1997): 1-15.

Ben-Tor, Amnon, and Maria Teresa Rubiato. "Excavating Hazor, Part 2: Did the Israelites Destroy the Canaanite City?" *BAR* 25 (1999): 22-39.

Benzinger, I. *Jahvist und Elohist in den Königsbüchern*. BZAW II, 2. Berline-Stuttgart-Leipzig: Töpelmann, 1921.

Berg, Sandra B. *The Book of Esther: Motifs, Themes, and Structure.* SBLDS 44. Missoula, MT: Scholars Press, 1979.

Betlyon, John W. "Coinage." *ABD*, 1:1076-1089. Ed. by D.N. Freedman. New York: Doubleday, 1992.

Bewer, Julius A. *The Literature of the Old Testament.* Rev. ed. New York: Columbia University, 1933.

Bimson, John J., and David Livingston. "Redating the Exodus." *BAR* 13 (1987): 40-53, 66-68.

Biran, Avraham. *Biblical Dan.* Jerusalem: Israel Exploration Society, 1994.

Blenkinsopp, Joseph. *Ezra–Nehemiah: A Commentary.* OTL. Louisville, KY: Westminster/John Knox, 1988.

Block, Daniel I. *Judges, Ruth.* NAC 6. Nashville: Broadman & Holman, 1999.

Boling, Robert G. *Judges: A New Translation with Introduction and Commentary.* AB 6A. Garden City, NY: Doubleday, 1975.

Boling, Robert G., and G. Ernest Wright. *Joshua: A New Translation with Notes and Commentary.* AB 6. Garden City, NY: Doubleday, 1982.

Bowman, Sheridan. *Radiocarbon Dating.* Berkeley: University of California, 1990.

Braun, Roddy. *1 Chronicles.* WBC 14. Waco, TX: Word Books, 1986.

Bright, John. *A History of Israel.* 3rd ed. London: SCM Press, 1981.

Brueggemann, Walter. "Samuel, Book of 1–2: Narrative and Theology." *ABD*, 5:965-973. Ed. by D.N. Freedman. New York: Doubleday, 1992.

Budd, Philip J. *Numbers.* WBC 5. Waco, TX: Word Books, 1984.

Budde, Karl. *Die Bücher Samuel erklärt.* KHC 8. Tübingen and Leipzig: J.C.B. Mohr, 1902.

Bunimovitz, Shlomo. "Socio-Political Transformations in the Central Hill Country in the Late Bronze-Iron I Transition." In *From Nomadism to Monarchy: Archaeological and Historical Aspects of Early Israel*, pp. 179-202. Ed. by I Finkelstein and N. Na'aman. Jerusalem: Israel Exploration Society, 1994.

Bush, Frederic W. *Ruth, Esther.* WBC 9. Dallas, TX: Word Books, 1996.

Campbell, Edward F. Jr. "The Hebrew Short Story: A Study of Ruth." In *A Light unto My Path: Old Testament Studies in Honor of Jacob M. Myers*, pp. 83-101. Ed. by H.N. Bream, R.D. Heim, and C.A. Moore. Gettysburg Theological Studies 4. Philadelphia: Temple University Press, 1974.

_____. *Ruth*. AB 7. Garden City, NY: Doubleday, 1975.

Childs, Brevard S. *Introduction to the Old Testament as Scripture*. Philadelphia: Fortress, 1979.

Clines, David J.A. *Ezra, Nehemiah, Esther*. NCB. Grand Rapids: Eerdmans, 1984.

Cogan, Mordechai. "Chronology." *ABD*, 1:1002-1011. Ed. by D.N. Freedman. New York: Doubleday, 1992.

_____. "Cyrus Cylinder (2.124)." *COS*, 2:314-316. Ed. by W.W. Hallo and K.L. Younger Jr. Leiden: Brill, 2003.

_____. *1 Kings*. AB 10. New York: Doubleday, 2000.

Cogan, Mordechai, and Hayim Tadmor. *2 Kings*. AB 11. New York: Doubleday, 1988.

Cross, Frank Moore. *Canaanite Myth and Hebrew Epic*. Cambridge, MA: Harvard, 1975.

_____. "The History of the Biblical Text in the Light of the Discoveries in the Judaean Desert." *HTR* 57 (1964): 281-299.

_____. "A Reconstruction of the Judean Restoration." *JBL* 94 (1975): 4-18.

Cundall, Arthur E. "Judges — An Apology for the Monarchy?" *ExpTim* 81 (1970): 178-181.

Cundall, Arthur E., and Leon Morris. *Judges and Ruth: An Introduction and Commentary*. TOTC 7. Downers Grove, IL: InterVarsity, 1968.

Davies, Philip R. *In Search of "Ancient Israel."* JSOTSupp 148. Sheffield: JSOT Press, 1992.

de Miroschedji, Pierre. "Susa." *ABD*, 6:242-245. Ed. by D.N. Freedman. New York: Doubleday, 1992.

deVaux, Roland. *Ancient Israel*, vol 1: *Social Institutions*. New York: McGraw-Hill, 1965.

_____. *Ancient Israel*, vol 2: *Religious Institutions*. New York: McGraw-Hill, 1965.

_____. *The Early History of Israel*. Trans. by D. Smith. Philadelphia: Westminster, 1978.

_____. "Israel (Histoire de)." In *Dictionnaire de la Bible, Supplément*, 4:764-769. Paris: Letouzey et Ane, 1928–.

Dever, William G. "The Middle Bronze Age: The Zenith of the Urban Canaanite Era." *BA* 50 (1987): 148-177.

_____. *What Did the Biblical Writers Know and When Did They Know It? What Archaeology Can Tell Us about the Reality of Ancient Israel*. Grand Rapids: Eerdmans, 2001.

_____. *Who Were the Early Israelites and Where Did They Come From?* Grand Rapids: Eerdmans, 2003.

_____. "Will the Real Israel Please Stand Up? Archaeology and Israelite Historiography: Part I." *BASOR* 297 (1995): 61-80.

DeVries, Simon J. *1 Kings.* WBC 12. Waco, TX: Word Books, 1985.

de Wette, Wilhelm Martin Lebrecht. *BEAT.* 2 vols. Halle: Schimmelpfennig, 1806-1807.

Dietrich, Walter. *Prophetie und Geschichte: Eine redaktionsgeschichtliche Untersuchung zum deuteronomistischen Geschichtswerk.* FRLANT 108. Göttingen: Vandenhoeck und Ruprecht, 1972.

Dillard, Raymond B. "Reward and Punishment in Chronicles: The Theology of Immediate Retribution." *WTJ* 46 (1984): 164-172.

_____. *2 Chronicles.* WBC 15. Waco, TX: Word Books, 1987.

Dillard, Raymond B., and Tremper Longman III. *An Introduction to the Old Testament.* Grand Rapids: Zondervan, 1994.

Dothan, Trude. "Philistines, Archaeology." *ABD,* 5:328-333. Ed. by D.N. Freedman. New York: Doubleday, 1992.

Drews, Robert. *The End of the Bronze Age: Changes in Warfare and the Catastrophe ca. 1200 B.C.* Princeton: Princeton University, 1993.

Emerton, J.A. "Did Ezra Go to Jerusalem in 428 B.C.?" *JTS,* ns 17 (1966): 1-19.

Fensham, F. Charles. *The Books of Ezra and Nehemiah.* NICOT. Grand Rapids: Eerdmans, 1982.

Finkelstein, Israel. *The Archaeology of the Israelite Settlement.* Jerusalem: Israel Exploration Society, 1988.

_____. "Ethnicity and Origin of the Iron I Settlers in the Highlands of Canaan: Can the Real Israel Stand Up?" *BA* 59 (1996): 198-212.

_____. "The Great Transformation: The 'Conquest' of the Highlands Frontiers and the Rise of the Territorial States." In *The Archaeology of Society in the Holy Land,* pp. 349-365. Ed. by T.E. Levy. New York: Facts on File, 1995.

_____. *Shiloh: The Archaeology of a Biblical Site.* Monograph Series of the Institute of Archaeology 10. Tel Aviv: Tel Aviv University, 1993.

Finkelstein, Israel, and Neil Asher Silberman. *The Bible Unearthed: Archaeology's New Vision of Ancient Israel and the Origin of Its Sacred Texts.* New York: Touchstone, 2002.

Flanagan, James W. "Samuel, Book of 1–2: Text, Composition, and Content." *ABD,* 5:957-965. Ed. by D.N. Freedman. New York: Doubleday, 1992.

Freedman, David Noel. "The Chronicler's Purpose." *CBQ* 23 (1961): 432-442.

Freedman, David Noel, and David F. Graf, eds. *Palestine in Transition: The Emergence of Ancient Israel.* Sheffield: Almond, 1983.

Gerleman, G. *Esther.* BKAT 21. Neukirchen: Neukirchener, 1982.

Goetze, Albrecht. "Treaty between Hattusilis and Ramses II." *ANET*, pp. 201-203. Ed. by J.B. Pritchard. Princeton: Princeton University, 1969.

Goodman, William R. "Esdras, First Book of." *ABD*, 2:609-611. Ed. by D.N. Freedman. New York: Doubleday, 1992.

Gordis, Robert. "Love, Marriage, and Business in the Book of Ruth: A Chapter in Hebrew Customary Law." In *A Light unto My Path: Old Testament Studies in Honor of Jacob M. Myers*, pp. 241-264. Ed. by H.N. Bream, R.D. Heim, and C.A. Moore. Gettysburg Theological Studies 4. Philadelphia: Temple University, 1974.

Gottwald, Norman K. *The Tribes of Yahweh: A Sociology of the Religion of Liberated Israel, 1250–1050 B.C.E.* Maryknoll, NY: Orbis, 1979.

Graham, M. Patrick, Kenneth G. Hoglund, and Steven L. McKenzie, eds. *The Chronicler as Historian.* JSOTSupp 238. Sheffield: JSOT Press, 1997.

Grasham, William W. "The Theology of the Book of Esther." *ResQ* 16 (1973): 99-111.

Gray, John. *1 & 2 Kings.* 2nd, fully rev. ed. OTL. Philadelphia: Westminster Press, 1970.

Gunkel, Herman. "Ruth." In *Reden und Aufsätze*, pp. 65-92. Göttingen: Vandenhoek & Ruprecht, 1913.

Hackett, Jo Ann. "There Was No King in Israel." In *The Oxford History of the Biblical World*, pp. 132-164. Ed. by M.D. Coogan. New York: Oxford University, 1998.

Haley, John W. *An Examination of the Alleged Discrepancies of the Bible.* Reprint, Nashville: Gospel Advocate, n.d.

Hallo, W.W. "The First Purim." *BA* 46 (1983): 19-29.

Hallo, W.W., and K.L. Younger, eds. *COS.* 3 vols. Leiden: Brill, 1979–2003.

Halpern, Baruch. "Erasing History: The Minimalist Assault on Ancient Israel." *BRev* 11 (1995): 26-35, 47.

_____ . *The First Historians: The Hebrew Bible and History.* San Francisco: Harper & Row, 1988.

Hals, R.M. *The Theology of the Book of Ruth.* Philadelphia: Fortress, 1969.

Handy, Lowell K., ed. *The Age of Solomon: Scholarship at the Turn of the Millennium*. Leiden: Brill, 1997.

Harrison, Roland K. *Introduction to the Old Testament*. Grand Rapids: Eerdmans, 1969.

Hasel, G.F. "Chronicles, Books of." *ISBE*[2], 1:666-673. Rev. ed. by G.W. Bromiley. Grand Rapids: Eerdmans, 1979.

Hasel, Michael G. "'Israel' in the Merneptah Stele." *BASOR* 296 (1994): 45-61.

Herzog, Chaim, and Mordechai Gichon. *Battles of the Bible*. 2nd ed. Toronto: Stoddart, 1997.

Hicks, John Mark. *1 & 2 Chronicles*. College Press NIV Commentary. Joplin, MO: College Press, 2001.

Hill, Andrew E., and John H. Walton. *A Survey of the Old Testament*. 2nd ed. Grand Rapids: Zondervan, 2000.

Hobbs, T.R. *2 Kings*. WBC 13. Waco, TX: Word Books, 1985.

Hoffmeier, James K. "The Annals of Thutmose III." *COS*, 2:7-13. Ed. by W.W. Hallo and K.L. Younger Jr. Leiden: Brill, 2000b.

——————. *Israel in Egypt: The Evidence for the Authenticity of the Exodus Tradition*. New York: Oxford University, 1997.

——————. "The (Israel) Stela of Merneptah." *COS*, 2:40-41. Ed. by W.W. Hallo and K.L. Younger Jr. Leiden: Brill, 2000a.

Hoffmeier, James K., and Alan Millard, eds. *The Future of Biblical Archaeology: Reassessing Methodologies and Assumptions*. Grand Rapids: Eerdmans, 2004.

Holladay, Carl R. "Eupolemus." *ABD*, 2:671-672. Ed. by D.N. Freedman. New York: Doubleday, 1992.

Holladay, William L., ed. *A Concise Hebrew and Aramaic Lexicon of the Old Testament*. Grand Rapids: Eerdmans, 1988.

Holloway, Steven W. "Kings, Book of 1-2." *ABD*, 4:69-83. Ed. by D.N. Freedman. New York: Doubleday, 1992.

Hopkins, David C. *The Highlands of Canaan: Agricultural Life in the Early Iron Age*. Sheffield: Almond, 1985.

Hubbard, Robert L. Jr. *The Book of Ruth*. NICOT. Grand Rapids: Eerdmans, 1988.

Ishida, Tomoo, ed. *Studies in the Period of David and Solomon and Other Essays*. Winona Lake, IN: Eisenbrauns, 1982.

Japhet, Sara. "Sheshbazzar and Zerubbabel — Against the Background of the Historical and Religious Tendencies of Ezra–Nehemiah." *ZAW* 94 (1982): 66-98.

_____ . "The Supposed Common Authorship of Chronicles and Ezra–Nehemiah Investigated Anew." *VT* 18 (1968): 330-371.

Johnston, Gordon H. "פָּחַד." *NIDOTTE,* 3:599-608. Ed. by W.A. VanGemeren. Grand Rapids: Zondervan, 1997.

Jones, Gwilym H. *1 and 2 Kings.* 2 vols. NCB. Grand Rapids: Eerdmans, 1984.

Joüon, Paul. *Ruth: Commentaire philologique et exégétique.* 1924. Repr. Rome: Institut Biblique Pontifical, 1953.

Kalimi, Isaac. "History of Interpretation: The Book of Chronicles in Jewish Tradition from Daniel to Spinoza." *RB* 105 (1998): 5-41.

Katzenstein, H.J. "Philistines, History." *ABD,* 5:326-328. Ed. by D.N. Freedman. New York: Doubleday, 1992.

Keil, C.F. *The Books of the Chronicles.* Trans. by A. Harper. Biblical Commentary on the Old Testament. Reprint. Grand Rapids: Eerdmans, n.d.

Keil, C.F., and F. Delitzsch. *Commentary on the Old Testament in Ten Volumes.* Vol. 2: *Joshua, Judges, Ruth, I & II Samuel.* Repr. Grand Rapids: Eerdmans, n.d.

Kirkpatrick, Patricia. *The Old Testament and Folklore Study.* JSOTSupp 62. Sheffield: JSOT, 1988.

Kitchen, Kenneth. "Egyptians and Hebrews, from Ra'amses to Jericho." In *The Origin of Early Israel – Current Debate: Biblical, Historical and Archaeological Perspectives,* pp. 65-131. Ed. by S. Ahituv and E.D. Oren. Beersheba: Ben Guryon University, 1998.

_____ . *On the Reliability of the Old Testament.* Grand Rapids: Eerdmans, 2003.

Klein, Ralph W. "Chronicles, Book of 1-2." *ABD,* 1:992-1002. Ed. by D.N. Freedman. New York: Doubleday, 1992.

_____ . *1 Samuel.* WBC 10. Waco, TX: Word Books, 1983.

Knoppers, Gary N. *1 Chronicles 1–9.* AB 12. New York: Doubleday, 2004.

_____ . *Two Nations under God: The Deuteronomistic History of Solomon and the Dual Monarchies,* vol. 1: *The Reign of Solomon and the Rise of Jeroboam.* HSM 52. Atlanta: Scholars Press, 1993.

_____ . *Two Nations under God: The Deuteronomistic History of Solomon and the Dual Monarchies,* vol. 2: *The Reign of Jeroboam, the Fall of Israel, and the Reign of Josiah.* HSM 53. Atlanta: Scholars Press, 1994.

Koch, Klaus. "Ezra and the Origins of Judaism." *JSS* 19 (1974): 173-197.

Leith, Mary Joan Winn. "Israel among the Nations." In *The Oxford History of the Biblical World*, pp. 276-316. Ed. by M.D. Coogan. New York: Oxford University, 1998.

Lemche, Niels Peter. *Early Israel: Anthropological and Historical Studies on the Israelite Society before the Monarchy.* Leiden: Brill, 1985.

_____ . *The Israelites in History and Tradition*. Louisville, KY: Westminster John Knox, 1998.

Lemche, Niels Peter, Thomas L. Thompson, William G. Dever, and P. Kyle McCarter Jr. "Face to Face: Biblical Minimalists Meet Their Challengers." Interview by Hershel Shanks. *BAR* 23 (1997): 26-42, 66.

Lichtheim, Miriam. *Ancient Egyptian Literature*, vol. 3: *The Late Period*. Berkeley: University of California, 1980.

Linafelt, Tod, and Timothy K. Beal. *Ruth, Esther.* Berit Olam. Collegeville, MN: The Liturgical Press, 1999.

Long, Jesse C. Jr. *1 & 2 Kings.* College Press NIV Commentary. Joplin, MO: College Press, 2002.

Long, V. Philips. *The Art of Biblical History.* Grand Rapids: Zondervan, 1994.

Longman, Tremper III. "Form Criticism, Recent Developments in Genre Theory, and the Evangelical." *WTJ* 47 (1985): 46-67.

Malamat, Abraham. "Charismatic Leadership in the Book of Judges." In *Magnalia Dei: The Mighty Acts of God: Essays on the Bible and Archaeology in Memory of G. Ernest Wright*, pp. 152-168. Ed. by F.M. Cross, P.D. Miller, W.E. Lemke. Garden City, NY: Doubleday, 1976.

_____ . "Israelite Conduct of War in the Conquest of Canaan according to the Biblical Tradition." In *Symposia: Celebrating the Seventy-Fifth Anniversary of the Founding of the American Schools of Oriental Research (1900–1975)*, pp. 35-55. Ed. by F.M. Cross. Cambridge, MA: American Schools of Oriental Research, 1979.

Manor, Dale W. "A Brief History of Levirate Marriage as It Relates to the Bible." *ResQ* 27 (1984): 129-142.

Marincola, John, rev. Herodotus, *The Histories.* Trans. by A. de Selincourt. Rev. with Introduction and Notes by J. Marincola. London: Penguin Books, 2003.

Mattingly, Gerald. L. "The Exodus-Conquest and the Archaeology of Transjordan: New Light and an Old Problem." *GTJ* 4 (1983): 245-262.

Mayes, Andrew D.H. *Israel in the Period of the Judges.* Naperville, IL: A.R. Allenson, 1974.

Mazar, Amihai. "The 'Bull Site' — An Iron Age I Open Cult Place." *BASOR* 247 (1982): 27-42.

McCarter, P. Kyle Jr. *1 Samuel.* AB 8. Garden City, NY: Doubleday, 1980.

McKenzie, John L. *The World of the Judges.* Englewood Cliffs, NJ: Prentice-Hall, 1966.

Meinhold, A. "Die Gattung der Josephgeschichte und des Estherbuches: Diasporanovelle II." *ZAW* 88 (1976): 72-93.

Mendenhall, George E. "The Hebrew Conquest of Palestine." *BA* 25 (1962): 66-87.

_____ . *The Tenth Generation: The Origins of the Biblical Tradition.* Baltimore: Johns Hopkins University, 1973.

Merling, David. "Large Numbers at the Time of the Exodus." *NEASB* 44 (1999): 15-27.

Meyers, Eric M. "The Persian Period and the Judean Restoration: From Zerubbabel to Nehemiah." In *Ancient Israelite Religion: Essays in Honor of Frank Moore Cross,"* pp. 509-521. Ed. by P.D. Miller Jr., P.D. Hanson, and S.D. McBride. Philadelphia: Fortress Press, 1987.

_____ . "Synagogue (Introductory Survey)." *ABD*, 6:251-260. Ed. by D.N. Freedman. New York: Doubleday, 1992.

Millard, Alan. "The Babylonian Chronicle (1.136-137)." *COS*, 1:467-468. Ed. by W.W. Hallo and K.L. Younger Jr. Leiden: Brill, 2003.

Miller, J. Maxwell, and John H. Hayes. *A History of Ancient Israel and Judah.* Philadelphia: Westminster Press, 1986.

Montgomery, James A., and Henry Snyder Gehman. *The Book of Kings.* ICC. Edinburgh: T. & T. Clark, 1951.

Moore, Carey A. *Daniel, Esther, and Jeremiah: The Additions.* AB 44. Garden City, NY: Doubleday, 1977.

_____ . *Esther.* AB 7B. Garden City, NY: Doubleday, 1971.

_____ . "Esther, Book of." *ABD*, 2:633-643. Ed. by D.N. Freedman. New York: Doubleday, 1992.

_____ . "On the Origins of the LXX Additions to the Book of Esther." *JBL* 92 (1973): 382-393.

Moore, George F. *A Critical and Exegetical Commentary on Judges.* Edinburgh: T & T Clark, 1895.

Moore, Michael S. *"Haggo'el*: The Cultural Gyroscope of Ancient Hebrew Society." *ResQ* 23 (1980): 27-35.

Moran, William L., ed. and trans. *The Amarna Letters*. Baltimore: The Johns Hopkins University, 1992.

Myers, Jacob M. *I Chronicles*. AB 12. Garden City, NY: Doubleday, 1965a.

───────────. *II Chronicles*. AB 13. Garden City, NY: Doubleday, 1965b.

───────────. *Ezra–Nehemiah*. AB 14. Garden City, NY: Doubleday, 1965.

Na'aman, Nadav. "The 'Conquest of Canaan' in the Book of Joshua and in History." In *From Nomadism to Monarchy: Archaeological and Historical Aspects of Early Israel*, pp. 218-281. Ed. by I. Finkelstein and N. Na'aman. Jerusalem: Israel Exploration Society, 1994.

Nelson, R.D. *The Double Redaction of the Deuteronomistic History*. JSOTSupp 18. Sheffield: Sheffield Academic Press, 1981.

Niditch, Susan. "Legends of Wise Heroes and Heroines." In *The Hebrew Bible and Its Modern Interpreters*, pp. 445-463. Ed. by D.A. Knight and G.M. Tucker. Chico, CA: Scholars Press, 1985.

Nielsen, Kirsten. *Ruth: A Commentary*. OTL. Louisville, KY: Westminster John Knox, 1997.

Noth, Martin. *The Deuteronomistic History*. 2nd ed. JSOTSupp 15. Sheffield: JSOT Press, 1991.

───────────. *The History of Israel*. 2nd ed. New York: Harper & Row, 1960.

───────────. *Überlieferungsgeschichtliche Studien: Die sammelnden und bearbeitenden Geschichtswerke im Alten Testament*. Tübingen: Max Niemeyer, 1943 (part of which is trans. into English as *The Chronicler's History*. JSOTSupp 50. Sheffield: JSOT Press, 1987).

O'Connell, R.H. *The Rhetoric of the Book of Judges*. VTSupp 63. Leiden: Brill, 1996.

Paton, Lewis Bayles. *The Book of Esther*. ICC. Edinburgh: T. & T. Clark, 1908.

Payne, J. Barton. "Validity of Numbers in Chronicles." *NEASB* 11 (1978): 5-58.

Peters, Melvin K.H. "Septuagint." *ABD*, 5:1093-1104. Ed. by D.N. Freedman. New York: Doubleday, 1992.

Pfeiffer, Robert H. *Introduction to the Old Testament*. New York: Harper & Brothers, 1948.

Porten, Bezalel. "Elephantine Papyri." *ABD*, 2:445-455. Ed. by D.N. Freedman. New York: Doubleday, 1992.

_____ . "The Passover Letter (3.46)." *COS*, 3:116-117. Ed. by W.W. Hallo and K.L. Younger Jr. Leiden: Brill, 2003.

_____ . "Request for Letter of Recommendation (First Draft) (3.51)." *COS*, 3:125-130. Ed. by W.W. Hallo and K.L. Younger Jr. Leiden: Brill, 2003.

Pritchard, James B., ed. *Ancient Near Eastern Texts Relating to the Old Testament.* 2nd ed. with Supplement. Princeton: Princeton University, 1969.

Rainey, Anson F. "Israel in Merneptah's Inscription and Reliefs." *IEJ* 51 (2001): 57-75.

Reich, Ronny, and Eli Shukron. "Reconsidering the Karstic Theory as an Explanation to the Cutting of Hezekiah's Tunnel in Jerusalem." *BASOR* 325 (2002): 75-80.

Rosenberg, Stephen. "The Siloam Tunnel Revisited." *Tel Aviv* 25 (1998): 116-130.

Rowley, Harold Henry. "The Chronological Order of Ezra and Nehemiah." In *The Servant of the Lord and Other Essays on the Old Testament*, pp. 129-159. London: Lutterworth, 1952.

Rozenberg, Martin S. "The Sofetim in the Bible." *ErIsr*. Nelson Glueck Memorial Volume, 12 (1975): 77*-86*.

Sack, Ronald H. "Nabonidus (Person)." *ABD*, 4:973-976. Ed. by D.N. Freedman. New York: Doubleday, 1992.

Sakenfeld, Katharine Doob. *Ruth*. Int. Louisville, KY: John Knox, 1999.

Saley, Richard J. "The Date of Nehemiah Reconsidered." In *Biblical and Near Eastern Studies: Essays in Honor of William Sanford LaSor*, pp. 151-165. Ed. by G.A. Tuttle. Grand Rapids: Eerdmans, 1978.

Sandmel, Samuel. *The Hebrew Scriptures: An Introduction to Their Literature and Religious Ideas.* New York: Alfred A. Knopf, 1968.

_____ . "Ruth." In *The Hebrew Scriptures: An Introduction to Their Literature and Religious Ideas*, pp. 489-583. New York: Alfred A. Knopf, 1963.

Sasson, Jack M. *Ruth: A New Translation with a Philological Commentary and a Formulist-Folklorist Interpretation.* 2nd ed. Sheffield: Sheffield Academic Press, 1995.

Schneider, Tammi J. *Judges*. Berit Olam. Collegeville, MN: Liturgical Press, 2000.

Schoville, Keith N. *Ezra–Nehemiah*. College Press NIV Commentary. Joplin, MO: College Press, 2001.

Schultz, Samuel J. "Mystic Numbers." *NEASB* 10 (1977): 29-35.

Shea, William H. "Esther and History." *AUSS* 14 (1976): 227-246.

Shenkel, James D. *Chronology and Recensional Development in the Greek Text of Kings*. HSM 1. Cambridge, MA: Harvard University, 1968.

Smend, Rudolf. "Das Gesetz und die Völker: Ein Beitrag zur deuteronomistischen Redaktionsgeschichte." In *Probleme biblischer Theologie*: Gerhard von Rad zum 70 Geburtstag, pp. 494-509. Ed. by H.W. Wolff. Munich: Chr. Kaiser Verlag, 1971.

_____ . "JE in den geschichtlichen Büchern des Alten Testament, herausgegeben von H. Holzinger." *ZAW* 39 (1921): 204-215.

Smith, James E. *1 & 2 Samuel*. College Press NIV Commentary. Joplin, MO: College Press, 2000.

Soderlund, Sven K. "Septuagint." *ISBE*², 4:400-409. Fully rev. Ed. by G.W. Bromiley. Grand Rapids: Eerdmans, 1988.

Soggin, J.A. *Judges*. Trans. by J. Bowden. OTL. Philadelphia: Westminster, 1981.

Stager, Lawrence E. "The Archaeology of the Family in Ancient Israel." *BASOR* 260 (1985): 1-35.

_____ . "Forging an Identity: The Emergence of Ancient Israel." In *The Oxford History of the Biblical World*, pp. 90-131. Ed. by M.D. Coogan. New York: Oxford University, 1998.

Stern, Ephraim. *Archaeology of the Land of the Bible*, vol. 2: *The Assyrian, Babylonian, and Persian Periods (732–332 B.C.E.)*. New York: Doubleday, 2001.

_____ . "Between Persia and Greece: Trade, Administration and Warfare in the Persian and Hellenistic Periods (539–563 BCE)." In *The Archaeology of Society in the Holy Land*, pp. 432-445. Ed. by T.E. Levy. New York: Facts on File, Inc., 1995.

Sutter, David E. "Artaxerxes (Person)." *ABD*, 1:463-464. Ed. by D.N. Freedman. New York: Doubleday, 1992.

Talmon, Shemaryahu. "'Wisdom' in the Book of Esther." *VT* 13 (1963): 419-455.

Thiele, Edwin R. *The Mysterious Numbers of the Hebrew Kings*. Rev. ed. Grand Rapids: Eerdmans, 1983.

Thompson, Thomas L. *Early History of the Israelite People from the Written and Archaeological Sources*. Leiden: Brill, 1992.

_____ . *The Mythic Past: Biblical Archaeology and the Myth of Israel*. New York: Basic, 1999.

Tischler, N.M. "Ruth." In *A Complete Literary Guide to the Bible*, pp. 151-164. Ed. by L. Ryken and T. Longman III. Grand Rapids: Zondervan, 1993.

Tzaferis, Vassilios. "Crucifixion — the Archaeological Evidence." *BAR* 11 (1985): 44-53.

Ungnad, A. "Keilinschriftliche Beitrage zum Buch Esra und Ester." *ZAW* 58 (1940–41): 240-244.

——————— . "Keilinschriftliche Beitrage zum Buch Esra und Ester." *ZAW* 59 (1942–43): 219.

Van Alstine, George A. "Dispersion." *ISBE*[2], 1:962-968. Fully rev. Ed. by G.W. Bromiley. Grand Rapids: Eerdmans, 1979.

van Dijk-Hemmes, Fokkelien. "Ruth: A Product of Women's Culture?" In *A Feminist Companion to Ruth*, pp. 134-139. Ed. by A. Brenner. Sheffield: Sheffield Academic Press, 1993.

Vaughn, Andrew G., and Ann E. Killebrew. *Jerusalem in Bible and Archaeology: The First Temple Period.* Atlanta: SBL, 2003.

Viejola, Timo. *Das Königtum in der Beurteilung der deuteronomistischen Historiographie: Ein redaktionsgeschichtliche Untersuchung.* AASFS B 198. Helsinki: Suomalainen Tiedeakatemia, 1977.

von Rad, Gerhard. *Das Geschichtsbild des chronistischen Werkes.* BWANT 54. Stuttgart: Kohlhammer, 1930.

——————— . *Old Testament Theology.* Trans. by D.M.G. Stalker. 2 vols. New York: Harper & Row, 1962.

Weeks, Kent R. *The Lost Tomb.* New York: William Morrow, 1998.

Weinfeld, Moshe. *Deuteronomy and the Deuteronomic School.* Oxford: Clarendon Press, 1972. Reprint, Winona Lake, IN: Eisenbrauns, 1992.

Weippert, Manfred. *The Settlement of the Israelite Tribes in Palestine: A Critical Survey of Recent Scholarly Debate.* Naperville, IL: Allenson, 1971.

Wenham, J.W. "Large Numbers in the Old Testament." *TynBul* 18 (1967): 19-53.

Wente, Edward F. "Rameses (Place)." *ABD*, 5:617-618. Ed. by D.N. Freedman. New York: Doubleday, 1992a.

——————— . "Rameses II." *ABD*, 5:618-620. Ed. by D.N. Freedman. New York: Doubleday, 1992b.

Whitelam, Keith W. *The Invention of Ancient Israel: The Silencing of Palestinian History.* London: Routledge, 1996.

Williamson, H.G.M. *Ezra, Nehemiah.* WBC 16. Waco, TX: Word Books, 1985.

Wilson, John A. "Treaty between the Hittites and Egypt." In *ANET*, pp. 199-201. Ed. by J.B. Pritchard. Princeton: Princeton University, 1969.

Wilson, John, and Vassilios Tzaferis. "Banias Dig Reveals King's Palace." *BAR* 24 (1998): 54-61, 85.

Wiseman, Donald J. "Studies in Aramaic Lexicography." *JAOS* 82 (1962): 290-299.

Woods, Clyde M. "An Introduction to Esther." Unpublished M.A. Thesis. Memphis, TN: HGSR, 1959.

Wright, J. Stafford. "The Historicity of the Book of Esther." In *New Perspectives on the Old Testament*, pp. 37-47. Ed. by J.B. Payne. Waco, TX: Word, 1970.

Yadin, Yigael. "The Transition from a Semi-Nomadic to a Sedentary Society in the Twelfth Century B.C.E." In *Symposia: Celebrating the Seventy-Fifth Anniversary of the Founding of the American Schools of Oriental Research (1900–1975)*, pp. 57–68. Ed. by F.M. Cross. Cambridge, MA: American Schools of Oriental Research, 1979.

Yamauchi, Edwin. "The Archaeological Background of Nehemiah." *BSac* 137 (1980): 291-309.

_____ . *Persia and the Bible*. Grand Rapids: Baker, 1996.

Young, Edward J. *An Introduction to the Old Testament*. Rev. ed. Grand Rapids: Eerdmans, 1964.

Younger, K. Lawson Jr. *Judges/Ruth*. NIV Application Library. Grand Rapids: Zondervan, 2002.

Zenger, Erich. *Das Buch Ruth*. ZBAT 8. Zurich: Theologischer, 1986.

Zertal, Adam. "Israel Enters Canaan — Following the Pottery Trail." *BAR* 17 (1990): 28-49, 75.

Zevit, Ziony. "Archaeological and Literary Stratigraphy in Joshua 7–8." *BASOR* 251 (1983): 23-35.

Zias, Joseph, and Eliezer Sekeles. "The Crucified Man from Giv'at ha-Mivtar: A Reappraisal." *IEJ* 35 (1985): 22-27.

JOSHUA

The title of the book of Joshua derives from its main human character — Joshua. In the Pentateuch, his name was originally Hoshea (הוֹשֵׁעַ, *hošēaʻ*, meaning "salvation," or "deliverance"), but for some unexplained reason, Moses changed it to Joshua (יְהוֹשֻׁעַ, *yᵊhôšuaʻ*, meaning "YHWH is salvation [deliverance]" Num 13:16), which emphasizes YHWH as the source of salvation and deliverance. The latter is the name that adheres through the remainder of the Bible.

TEXT AND AUTHOR

The authorship of Joshua has traditionally been ascribed to Joshua the son of Nun who acceded to leadership upon Moses' death (Deut 31:1-8; Josh 1:1-9). He was groomed to this end by the Lord and Moses, and the decree of transition was indicated in the Pentateuch (Deut 31:7-8,23). A number of parallels of Joshua's leadership with that of Moses emphasize Joshua's legitimacy as leader. God informs Joshua that he would be with Joshua just as he had been with Moses, if (as Moses had been) Joshua will be strong and courageous (Josh 1:5). The people's declaration that they would obey Joshua just as they had obeyed Moses reveals a continuity of leadership (Josh 1:16-17). Similar to the crossing of the Sea of Reeds, the crossing of the Jordan River on dry land even though it was flood season would further enhance his legitimacy in the eyes of the people (Joshua 3 and Exodus 14).

Joshua would have witnessed the majority of the events narrated in the book, and he would be the most logical one to record at least the main issues. Indeed, a statement regarding Rahab implies that she was still alive while some of the narration was recorded (Josh 6:25).[1]

---

[1] The NRSV removes the chronological significance of this reading by rendering it: "Her family has lived in Israel ever since." The Hebrew more explicitly says "And she lived in the midst of Israel unto this day."

One may reasonably infer that Joshua did not record his own death and burial (Josh 24:29-30), and fundamentally the same issues are implied in this appendix as would apply to the narration of Moses' death at the end of Deuteronomy (ch. 34).

Having said that, however, the book gives no necessary indication that it was written by Joshua nor that all of it had to be recorded in a short time in relation to his life. It may well have been put together at a significantly later date, but there is little information necessarily to indicate when.

The date of the composition, therefore, is open to debate. If one assumes Joshua composed the book, the date would depend upon when the Exodus/Conquest occurred, which would therefore be either in the early fourteenth century B.C. or late thirteenth century. The issue of the date of Moses/Joshua is a matter of intense scrutiny and debate with little resolution in sight.[2]

It is possible that the book takes its current form later in Israelite history. The text seems to imply that it was basically put together before David took the throne. The book identifies Jerusalem as Jebus (Josh 18:27), and Judges implies that the city was still outside the political control of the Israelites (Judg 19:10–12). David finally captured Jebus/Jerusalem after he had reigned seven years in Israel (2 Samuel 5).

STRUCTURE

The narrative of Joshua flows smoothly as the Israelites camp at Shittim from which they transition to Canaan where they conquer the land in a series of military engagements. After taking general control of the land, Joshua oversees the division of the land among the tribes. The book ends with a series of speeches, after which Joshua's death is narrated.

    I. Israel Conquers Canaan — 1:1–12:24
       A. God speaks with Joshua — 1:1-9
       B. Israel prepares to cross the Jordan — 1:10–2:24
          1. Joshua commands to prepare — 1:10-11
          2. Joshua reminds the two-and-a-half tribes of their obligations — 1:12-18
          3. The spies reconnoiter Jericho — 2:1-24

---

[2]See further discussion below.

GENRE

The book of Joshua presents itself as a historical record, and it is in the section normally referred to as the historical books. As might be anticipated, however, its historicity has come under fire as critical scholarship has developed.

In the heyday of source criticism, scholars attempted to trace elements of the Documentary Hypothesis (J,E,D,P) into the remainder of the historical books. A partial issue perpetuating the search was the recognition that the land promises of the Pentateuch had not come to fruition without the narrative of Joshua — hence some argued for a "hexateuch."

Judges 1 was usually assigned to the J (Yahwist) source, and since the narratives of Judges and Joshua seemed to be at odds with each other,[3] it was suggested that Joshua 1–12 reflected the work of an E (Elohist) source. Since Joshua 13–22 was concerned more with administrative issues and in particular with Levitical cities and cities of refuge, it was assumed that this section belonged to the P (Priestly) source. The language of the book reflects Deuteronomic phraseology and themes and hence was believed to reflect at least some Deuteronomic Theology editing.

Such a source critical approach to Joshua dominated the research of the book so extensively that the cohesiveness of the storyline and theology became lost in the constant shuffle of sources and assumed redactions. The source critical approach to Joshua is now largely abandoned and approaches that recognize its theme and essential unity tend to dominate the scholarship.

An alternative approach began to rise which sought to trace the story units with particular locales (*Ortsgebundenkeit*). This emphasis tended to look at the book and its stories as etiologies to explain situations that later Israelites encountered. Among them would be how the forefathers captured Jericho, or how they took Ai (interestingly, a name meaning "ruin"[4]). Noth's work (1960) divided the narrative into regional concerns with chapters revolving around the tribes of Benjamin (Joshua 1–9), Ephraim (10), Galilee (11), etc. Somewhat corroborating this local compositional approach is the difficulty that scholars have had in finding archaeological confirmation of the battles and conflicts in the Joshua narrative.[5]

The introduction of etiological explanations moved the proposed composition of the book away from the time of Joshua himself to a period significantly removed from him or the events narrated. Again, partially driving this proposal to a late composition was the difficulty of corroborating the narrative with archaeological evidence. The dates most commonly suggested for the composition of the book were anywhere from the seventh century B.C. to the Postexilic period, although there are no intrinsic reasons to push the dates that far from Joshua's time.

---

[3]See further discussion below.
[4]Although, this definition is debated; see Ziony Zevit, "Archaeological and Literary Stratigraphy in Joshua 7-8," *BASOR* 251 (1983): 23-35.
[5]See further discussion below.

THEOLOGICAL THEMES

In the Hebrew, Septuagint, and English Bibles, Joshua has always immediately followed the Pentateuch. The story line requires this placement since the Pentateuch leaves the Israelites just on the edge of their new inheritance.

The book of Joshua is vitally important to the theme of the Bible and in particular as part of God's promise to Abraham. God had promised Abraham that he would have a direct male descendant (Gen 17:15-22). Isaac was the son of promise, and the promise was accomplished in Abraham's lifetime (Genesis 21). Another promise was that Abraham's descendants would become a great nation and numerous (Gen 12:2; 15:4-5). This promise was more specifically to unfold when a famine forced Jacob and his sons to descend into Egypt where the Israelites became numerous (Exod 1:7-12) and were eventually forged into a nation with God as their king (Exodus 24). Another major promise was that the descendants would inherit the land of Canaan where Abraham walked (Gen 13:14-18; 17:4-8). The appropriation of this promise is much of the story line of the Pentateuch as the Israelites make their way from bondage in Egypt to the borders of the land of promise. However, the Pentateuch ends with the Israelites encamped at Shittim across the Jordan river from their destination.[6]

It is perhaps striking that the issue of circumcision as a physical ceremony does not appear in the narrative from Genesis until its reappearance in Joshua.[7] Joshua notes that the ceremony had been neglected during the years of wandering (5:5-6). Its reinstatement implies a continuity of the Israelites, who had just crossed the Jordan into the land of promise, as heirs of the Abrahamic covenant; God had chosen Abraham and his offspring through Isaac as his special people who would receive the land (cf. Gen 17:8-19).

Similarly, the celebration of the Passover in Joshua (5:10) reflects another continuity of the people with the Pentateuchal episodes.

---

[6]Another promise with multiple levels of fulfillment is that Abraham and Sarah would be progenitors of kings (Gen 17:6,16). This promise is certainly unfulfilled in the Pentateuch and remains so in Joshua; it is ultimately fulfilled through Jesus, the King.

[7]The sole exception is the cryptic episode of Zipporah circumcising Moses' children in Exodus 4. The word appears in Deuteronomy (10:16; 30:6) where it serves as a metaphor of repentance.

The Exodus Passover was when God "brought the Israelites out of the land of Egypt" (Exod 12:51), and he had directed, "When you come to the land that the Lord will give you, as he has promised, you shall keep this observance" (Exod 12:25). Israel's arrival in the land of promise affirms the fulfillment of God's promise.

As a correlate to the Passover celebration, the miraculous provision of manna ceased (Josh 5:12). Manna was the supernatural source of sustenance that God had provided for Israel during their years of wandering. It was a necessary provision because of the scarcity of food resources to sustain the population (Exodus 16; Numbers 11), but now that the Israelites had arrived at the land flowing with milk and honey (Exod 3:8; Josh 5:6), the supernatural provision was no longer necessary.

Even the capture of Jericho serves as a point of continuity with the Pentateuchal story. God had consistently commanded the Israelites to give him the first of everything. The Passover had required the firstborn of everyone, but the Israelites could redeem the firstborn with the substitutional death of a lamb (Exodus 12). Otherwise the first of the families, flocks, and fields were all his (Exod 13:2; 23:16-17; 34:26). Everything associated with the capture of Jericho was to belong to the Lord — all animals, people, and artifacts were to be dedicated to destruction (Josh 6:17-19) as a kind of whole burnt offering to God. Only the precious metals — gold, silver, bronze and iron (Josh 6:19) — were saved and became part of the treasury of the Lord. This offering of first fruit recognized that the land was God's, but he had given it to Israel, just as the Lord had promised.

Another theme hinted at in the book is the grace of YHWH to receive God-fearing Gentiles into his fold. This comes to the fore with the accommodation of Rahab into the citizenry of Israel (Josh 6:22-25). Her declarations emphasize a faith in YHWH and his abilities to deliver the land into Israel's possession (Josh 2:8-11) — a tacit continuity of the land promise issue itself. One might consider the deliverance of the Gibeonites as a manifestation of grace (Joshua 9), although their reprieve derives more from Israel's failure to consult the Lord than an explicit statement from the Lord.

The book of Joshua is a vital link from the Patriarchs and Moses to the presence of the Israelites in the land. While the book emphasizes God's fulfillment to bring Israel into the land of promise, the Israelites fail to follow through with God's expectations in purging the land of its inhabitants. It is this failure that becomes the focus to one degree or another through the remainder of the Hebrew Bible. The New Testament book of Hebrews picks up on this theme, pointing out that even though Joshua ("YHWH is salvation") brought Israel into the land, there remained another promise that was greater. The leader into that greater promise would be Jesus, the Greek pronunciation of the Hebrew name, Joshua (see Heb 4:1-11).

NEW TESTAMENT CONNECTIONS

As one reads through the New Testament, Rahab appears in the genealogy of Jesus (Matt 1:5). Most scholars identify the Rahab of Matthew's genealogy with Rahab the prostitute of Joshua 2. If Matthew's genealogy is complete, it would indicate that Rahab was the great-great grandmother of David and mother-in-law through Boaz of Ruth.[8] Rahab appears in the New Testament as an example of faith (Heb 11:31) as well as one who acted upon her faith (Jas 2:25).

Perhaps more important, however, is the parallel established in the New Testament in the repetition of Joshua's name, meaning "YHWH is salvation," translated into Greek as "Jesus" (cf. Matt 1:21). Furthermore, the Hebrew writer argues strongly for a parallel of the functions of Joshua and Jesus as the ones leading God's people into their final place of real rest (Heb 4:1-11).

SPECIAL ISSUES

CONNECTIONS OF JOSHUA WITH JUDGES

One area of controversy is how to correlate the apparent discrepancy of the nature of the events narrated in the book of Joshua with the tone of Judges. A superficial reading of Joshua can leave the impression of a wholesale *blitzkrieg* into Canaan in which Israel destroys the entire Canaanite population and their cities and immediately assimilates the land under their own domination. Judges, on the other hand, notes the reticence of Israel to take the land and emphasizes their tentativeness to settle in the land and the frequent tensions they experience with the Canaanite residents.

---

[8]A chronological implication of Matthew's genealogy is that there would be only five generations inclusively from the entrance into Canaan to the birth of David.

A full resolution of this tension is outside the parameters of this discussion, but important to keep in mind is the purpose of each book's narrative — each has a particular point to make. As noted earlier, Joshua accentuates the fulfillment of God's promises. Without Joshua, the Pentateuch promises are empty. A careful reading of Joshua, however, notes several statements that the land had not been totally subjugated, but that work remained to be done (see Josh 13:1-7 and in particular the severe warning Joshua gives against intermarrying with the Canaanites that remain among them; Joshua 23). Joshua's point is that God has fulfilled his promise and given Israel the land.

Judges, on the other hand, notes the covenant failure of Israel to follow the Lord. Joshua directed them to drive out the remaining population (Joshua 23), and Judges makes explicit that they failed to do so, leaving themselves open to the temptations and distractions of the resident Canaanite religion and their eventual apostasy from the Lord.

Scholars will often argue that we must respect the genre and setting of the literature of antiquity. When it is convenient, however, they often undermine its integrity to impose the "scientific" rigors of western evaluation and make more of the apparent differences than is necessary.

DATE OF THE EVENTS

Determining the dates of the events of Joshua has been challenging. A simple reading of the text of the Bible appears at first glance (depending upon which part one reads) to yield a fairly straightforward chronology. If one begins with the statement in 1 Kings 6:1 and assumes an accession date for Solomon of ca. 970 B.C., the Exodus would have occurred ca. 1446 B.C. with the conquest (i.e., Joshua) commencing about 1406 B.C. This fifteenth-century date is often referred to as the "early date." On the other hand, if one begins with the statement in Exodus 1:11 that the Israelites were involved in the construction of the store city of Rameses, who is consistently placed in the thirteenth century B.C. (ca. 1279–1213 B.C.), the conquest would have occurred sometime at least toward the end of Rameses' reign. The thirteenth-century date for the Exodus/Conquest is often referred to as the "late date."

Israel is certainly in the land by ca. 1207 B.C. since Merneptah mentions having conducted a campaign into Canaan and had encountered Israel.[9] Both date theories (i.e., the early date and the late date) have their strengths and weaknesses.[10]

The early-date theory is easy to grasp from the standpoint of a straightforward reading and calculation of the data given in 1 Kings 6:1. It also fits more easily into a straightforward reading of the chronology data of Judges (although the Judges data do not fit easily with either scenario, see further discussion in "Judges"). As far as the archaeological picture is concerned, the site of Jericho at least has some meager remains to corroborate the existence of a city to conquer, but no evidence of fortifications on the scale implied in the Bible have come to light.

Weaknesses of the early date, however, are numerous given our current understanding of the data and those weaknesses occur from the perspectives of the Bible, history, and archaeology.

In the fifteenth century, Thutmose III was the king of Egypt for most of the century (ca. 1479–1425) and apparently had Canaan in an ironclad hold as indicated, not only from his statements of some twenty military campaigns into Canaan, among which was a significant campaign against a Canaanite coalition at Megiddo,[11] but also from excavation data in Canaan which appear to confirm his claims.[12] When God lists the peoples in Canaan that the Israelites would need to displace, he never mentions the Egyptians among them (cf. Gen 15:19-21; Exod 3:8; 3:17; 23:23; 32:2; 34:11; Deut 7:1; 20:17; Josh 3:10; and then as narrative events, Josh 9:1; 11:3; 12:8; 24:11; Judg 3:5). A hundred years later, Amenhotep IV's reign (aka:

[9]See James K. Hoffmeier ("The (Israel) Stela of Merneptah," *COS*, 2:40-41.) for translation of the stele. There are, however, significant debates among the scholars of exactly how to understand the claim and in particular the identity and nature of the reference to "Israel." See for instance Gösta W. Ahlström (*Who Were the Israelites?* [Winona Lake, IN: Eisenbrauns, 1986], pp. 37-43), Michael G. Hasel ("'Israel' in the Merneptah Stele," *BASOR* 296 [1994]: 45-61), and Anson F. Rainey ("Israel in Merneptah's Inscription and Reliefs," *IEJ* 51 [2001]: 57-75).

[10]The data discussed here derive from the possible permutations given the current data available. The picture could change dramatically with some discovery forcing a reevaluation and reassessment. A maxim of archaeology which is often forgotten is that "Lack of evidence does not prove lack of existence."

[11]James K. Hoffmeier, "The Annals of Thutmose III," *COS*, 2:7-13.

[12]William G. Dever, "The Middle Bronze Age: The Zenith of the Urban Canaanite Era," *BA* 50 (1987): 174-177.

Akhenaten; ca. 1352–1336 B.C.) appears essentially to control the region as implied in the flurry of correspondence known as the Tell el-Amarna correspondence.[13] The nature of the correspondence implies that the Egyptians had controlled the area for some time before his accession.

Joshua's reference to the presence of the Philistines as a powerful force to be overthrown (Josh 13:2-3) is difficult to mesh with the early date. The preponderance of evidence of the migrations of the Sea Peoples, of whom the Philistines were a part, points to a date in the thirteenth–twelfth centuries B.C.[14] Admittedly, the Patriarchal narratives refer to the presence of Philistines in the area (Genesis 20–21, 26), but their presence is not presented as some powerful force. Perhaps they were in Canaan as a trading outpost from the Greek mainland.

From an archaeological standpoint, there is no evidence of an influx of new population, either ethnically or numerically in the early-date period, nor is there any evidence of a departure of a population from Egypt. While there is some meager evidence of occupation at Jericho, there is none for Ai, which was the second site that the Israelites attacked and destroyed (Joshua 8).

The reference to the Israelites working at Rameses (Exod 1:11) additionally poses a problem for the early-date scenario. The site, however, was continually occupied from the time of the Hyksos until the time of Rameses,[15] and one may legitimately argue that the reference to Rameses in Exodus is an editorial clarification similar to the reference to Dan in the Genesis 14 narrative, which did not receive the name of Dan until the time of the Judges (Judg 18:29).

The late-date scenario (i.e., the thirteenth century) begins with the reference in Exodus 1:11 where the Israelites help build the store cities. The late-date hypothesis has a number of strengths to commend it from the standpoint of the Bible, history, and archaeology.

---

[13]For the correspondence, see William L. Moran, ed. and trans., *The Amarna Letters* (Baltimore: The Johns Hopkins University, 1992). While some may equate the 'Apiru (Habiru) of the Amarna correspondence with the Hebrews, the connection is weak. At best, one might argue that the Hebrews were a part of a larger social grouping known in the wider ancient world as 'Apiru.

[14]See surveys by H.J. Katzenstein ("Philistines, History," *ABD*, 5:326-328) and Trude Dothan ("Philistines, Archaeology," *ABD*, 5:328-333) for convenient overviews of the Philistines.

[15]Edward Frank Wente, "Rameses (Place)," *ABD*, 5:617-618.

From the standpoint of the Bible, the argument takes the remark in Exodus at face-value.[16] Additionally, it would accommodate Joshua's statement of the presence of the Philistines in the area as a force with whom to contend (Josh 13:2-3).

Historically, the late date puts the Exodus in the context of Rameses II's reign. No doubt, he was a powerful monarch, marching through the land of Canaan during the first half of his reign to campaign into northern Syria against the Hittites. The Hittites and Egyptians ended their conflict with a treaty.[17] Normally, however, rapid movements through the land of Canaan would occur along the coastal plain rather than inland where the Israelites would eventually begin their occupation. Given this scenario, however, the traipsing through Canaan would have occurred before and immediately after the Israelites left Egypt and not after their settlement in the land. Israel would therefore have posed no challenge to Egyptian movements during Rameses' reign since they were probably in the process of wandering.

The recent rediscovery of the tomb of Rameses II's family[18] offers some interesting implications. Some evidence indicates that Egypt was a matrilineal society in which the legitimacy of the monarch depended upon the mother. If this is the case, it is possible that the tomb (KV 5), which was designed to hold the remains of dozens of people, may have been built to accommodate the deaths of multiple children within a short period. Given God's declaration of the death of the firstborn of the land of Egypt (cf. Exod 11:5), perhaps the firstborn would not have been only the firstborn of Rameses as the father, but of each of his wives.[19]

On the ground, corroboration of the late date Exodus/Conquest may be found in the sudden increase in both population and settlements in the land of Canaan,[20] particularly in the middle part of the

---

[16]The problem of 1 Kings 6:1 and its reference to the passage of 480 years will be discussed briefly below.

[17]Albrecht Goetze, "Treaty between Hattusilis and Ramses II," *ANET*, ed. by J.B. Pritchard (Princeton: Princeton University, 1969), pp. 201-203; and John A. Wilson, "Treaty between the Hittites and Egypt," *ANET*, pp. 199–201.

[18]Kent R. Weeks, *The Lost Tomb* (New York: William Morrow, 1998).

[19]I am indebted to my colleague, Janet Fortner of the Department of History at Harding, for this suggestion.

[20]See for instance Lawrence E. Stager ("Forging an Identity: The Emergence of Ancient Israel," in *The Oxford History of the Biblical World*, ed. by

country, the area around Galilee, and Transjordan, which are the areas where the Bible describes the Israelites as having had greater success in their initial settlements. Furthermore, the site of Hazor in northern Israel shows evidence of extensive destruction from this period,[21] which fits the description in the Bible of the thorough destruction of the site at the hands of the Israelites (Josh 11:10-13).

The thirteenth-century setting for the Exodus and Conquest, however, is not without its problems. Among them are the facts that neither Jericho nor Ai have preserved evidence of occupation for the time period.[22] Additionally, Egypt yields no evidence of the departure of a large population.

For most Bible students, the more likely challenge is the statement in 1 Kings 6:1 which states that the Temple construction began 480 years after Israel came out of Egypt. Simple arithmetic puts the date to ca. 1446 instead of during the time of Rameses II. Advocates

---

M.D. Coogan [New York: Oxford University, 1998], pp. 97-100). The increases indicated in the archaeological data, however, do not mesh well with the significantly higher data implying some 2.5 million people involved in the Exodus/Conquest indicated in the Bible. While there is no easy resolution to this discrepancy, the word normally rendered "thousand" in the Hebrew Bible (אֶלֶף, 'eleph), may legitimately and alternatively be rendered "clan" or "tribe" (cf. e.g., Judg 6:15; 1 Sam 10:19). Such a possibility could dramatically reduce the number of people involved in the Exodus/Conquest (note statements in Deuteronomy indicating that Israel was not particularly large numerically compared with other peoples; 7:7,17; 9:1; 11:23). In modern times, it was not until within the last forty years that the population of Canaan approached and exceeded 2.5 million. For discussions of this problem, see Philip J. Budd (*Numbers*, WBC 5 [Waco, TX: Word Books, 1984], pp. 6-9) and David Merling ("Large Numbers at the Time of the Exodus," *NEASB* 44 [1999]: 15-27).

[21]Amnon Ben-Tor and Maria Teresa Rubiato, "Excavating Hazor, Part 2: Did the Israelites Destroy the Canaanite City?" *BAR* 25 (1999): 22-39.

[22]The problems at Jericho are all the more difficult since there are no suitable sites in the area that could be alternative locations for Joshua's Jericho. The effects of erosion and the hazards of excavation, however, should caution against arguing too much (cf. the implications in John Wilson and Vassilios Tzaferis, "Banias Dig Reveals King's Palace," *BAR* 24 [1998]: 54-61, 85). On the other hand, there are legitimate questions about the identity of Ai — most scholars identify it with the site of et-Tell. There are, however, significant issues relative to its geographic setting, as well as the nature of the finds at the site, to warrant searching for an alternative location for Joshua's Ai (John J. Bimson and David Livingston, "Redating the Exodus," *BAR* 13 [1987]: 40-53, 66-68).

of the late-date scenario do not disregard the number, but instead understand it in some kind of symbolic or figurative way rather than arithmetically. Numbers in the Bible are not necessarily always arithmetic, nor do we necessarily always use numbers arithmetically. When we speak of the lines at the store being a mile long, we do not mean so literally, but our point is understood. Although the Bible speaks of twelve tribes of Israel, we know that arithmetically there were thirteen.[23] Similarly, the Bible speaks of twelve apostles, but depending upon how one defines apostle, there were at least fourteen, with thirteen of them living at the same time.[24] Given the statement in Exodus (1:11) that the event apparently occurred in the time of Rameses, how might one alternatively understand the number 480?

Among other combinations, the number 480 is the result of the factors of 12 and 40. A careful reading of Chronicles, in combination with Exodus, reveals that there were twelve generations from the Exodus to the high priest who presided under Solomon's Temple construction (see 1 Chr 6:3-10 and Exod 6:16-25 which imply that Phinehas was alive when the Exodus commenced). If twelve generations are involved, it is possible that the number 40 rather than reflecting an arithmetic number, could have become a metaphor for a generation. Some Egyptian sources indicate that a reasonable time for a man to have a child would be in his twenties.[25] If one rounds the number to 25 years for a generation and multiplies the 25 years times 12 generations, the result is 300 years. Adding 300 years to the fourth year of Solomon's reign as the time

---

[23]The tribe of Joseph was replaced with his two sons, Manasseh and Ephraim (Gen 48:3-6). Levi was removed from the typical list, probably because the tribe was not allotted a contiguous land allotment, but was scattered through the territories of the other Israelites.

[24]While Jesus chose twelve to be his apostles (Matt 10:1-4), the term seems to adhere as an accommodation of the total number of special appointments, including eventually Matthias and Paul. In Matthew 19:29 Jesus notes that the twelve apostles would judge the twelve tribes of Israel — a statement that must be accommodative rather than arithmetic. In similar fashion, John notes that Thomas was one of the twelve (20:24), but at the point of the discussion, Judas had killed himself and Matthias had not been appointed. The same issue holds true with Paul's statement of Jesus' appearance first to Cephas, then to the twelve (1 Cor 15:5), Judas was apparently dead at the time (cf. Matt 27:3-5).

[25]Miriam Lichtheim, *Ancient Egyptian Literature*, vol. 3: *The Late Period* (Berkeley: University of California, 1980), p. 168.

the Temple construction began, the result is 1266 B.C. — well embedded in the reign of Rameses. Corroborative of this date is the fact that many of the construction projects of Rameses were conducted in the early part of his reign.[26]

THEORIES OF ISRAEL'S EMERGENCE

With the advent of critical scholarship and its tendencies to question the historical reliability of the Bible, new theories have emerged by which to explain the emergence of the ancient Israelites. Four major theories dominate the discussion.

Pan-Canaanite Conquest

The traditional theory which is derived from the Bible is the Conquest theory which posits a fairly straightforward consideration of the biblical account of a conquest of the land, followed by a somewhat erratic settlement period. From the modern perspective, the dominant personalities involved in affirming this approach are the inimitable William F. Albright and Yigael Yadin. Albright and Yadin operated somewhat in the infancy of archaeology (more accurately, probably in the adolescence of archaeology), and because of some of their methodological weaknesses and presuppositional differences with them, many scholars abandoned their conclusions, seeking alternative explanations.

Peaceful Infiltration

Albrecht Alt and his successor, Martin Noth, proposed and developed the peaceful infiltration theory to explain Israel's presence. Essentially, it argued that there was no pan-Canaan conquest, but the Israelites migrated into the region peacefully, settling in the open areas between the resident Canaanite towns. They eventually intermarried with the Canaanite population and took over under the banner of Yahwism to bind them into a national entity.

A major weakness of this approach is that it based its model on the romanticism of the Bedouin desert tribes. It finds little corroboration in the archaeological record nor would it account for the huge increase in population evident from the archaeological survey work.

---

[26]Edward Frank Wente, "Rameses II," *ABD*, 5:618-619.

Peasant Revolt

An alternative theory emerged under the general work of two scholars: George Mendenhall and Norman Gottwald. While the two authors would argue for little similarity in their theories, most recognize that their similarities are far greater than the dissimilarities. As the term implies, the theory posits that the Israelites essentially were resident Canaanites, who became disenchanted with their Canaanite overlords and rose up in rebellion against them, eventually establishing themselves as the dominant culture, using Yahwism as the rally banner of rebellion and equality.

Corroborating this theory somewhat are the data from the Amarna correspondence, which reveal an apparently disenfranchised population which had retreated from the dominance of the Canaanite cities and had taken up residence in the countryside. The texts refer to these people as the 'Apiru. The correspondence furthermore reveals that the Egyptians demanded tribute from the Canaanite lords, probably putting the general population into oppression.

This theory finds significantly more corroboration in the archaeological and literary record than the Peaceful Infiltration theory. The theory, however, fails to address the reality of other egalitarian type settlements outside the domain of what is understood as Israelite,[27] which appear to have not been Yahwistic. Additionally, the appeal to the Amarna correspondence reflects neither the early- nor late-date scenarios.

Both of these theories suffer with difficulties in describing exactly how and why Yahwism would have come into the mix at all. Furthermore, from where did the idea of Yahweh come?

Symbiotic Theory

The symbiotic theory is probably the dominant one among current nonconservative scholars. Its major architect was the rising Israeli archaeologist, Israel Finkelstein. Essentially, his argument is that the Israelites were really Canaanites, who for unexplained reasons left the land for a while, eventually to return from their desert, pastoralist wanderings with a new religion called Yahwism. The precipitating reason for their departure is unknown, but could have been because of environmental stresses, disease and/or plague,

---

[27]Stager, "Forging," p. 104.

famine, or warfare. Their departure would not necessarily require abandonment of all family connections, but some of them may have remained behind in the cities, maintaining ties with their migrating kin. Eventually the pastoralists returned home and settled down again with their newfound faith.

Interestingly, the primary materials upon which Finkelstein relies in his reconstruction are the remains from the central part of the country where there is little evidence of conflict and cultural change. There are other possible explanations for this continuity (see below).

Problematic with all these last three scenarios is the implication of how peripheral is the entire Exodus narrative and its paradigm of God's deliverance and its repeated reiteration throughout the pages of the Hebrew Bible. In other words, if there were no exodus, why does the image remain so dominant?

Eclectic Theory

Probably more relevant is an approach that blends the above theories in varying degrees. Starting with the integrity of the narrative of Joshua, it would appear that there was a conquest by a group of people entering from outside of Canaan. Admittedly, there is difficulty in tracing this group back to Egypt,[28] but it is known that the Egyptians were inclined not to present themselves literarily in a negative light.[29] Additionally, if the numbers of Israelites involved in the Exodus was significantly reduced from the traditional tally (see above, n. 20), perhaps the departure of the Hebrews would not have been as significant a departure from the standpoint of the Egyptians as we would assume.[30]

Tracing Israel's passage through the desert has been a challenge as people have assumed that one should be able to trace the presence of some 2.5 million people who traveled for 40 years. Surely,

---

[28]However, see James K. Hoffmeier, *Israel in Egypt: The Evidence for the Authenticity of the Exodus Tradition* (New York: Oxford University, 1997).

[29]Wente, "Rameses II," p. 619.

[30]Pharaoh's statement in Exodus 1:9 which notes that the Israelites were more numerous and powerful than the Egyptians could be understood as a hyperbole to legitimate their oppression. Alternatively, he may have perceived the Israelites as part of the larger Canaanite world and hence their possible alignment with a possible Canaanite threat. The more pertinent issue is his fear that Israel might align with any potential enemies who might attack Egypt (cf. Exod 1:10).

we should be able to find remains of people, artifacts, etc. This, of course, assumes the huge number as well as an assumption that the nature of their travels and camps would duplicate ours. Dever notes that tracing Bedouin presence is difficult at best.[31] Furthermore, why should we assume that ceramics should be found in the desert to such a degree? Ceramics are too easily broken to be suitable for such extensive migratory travel. More appropriate would be the use of metals, wood, and skins — all of which are either easily recycled or are friable. Additionally, the Bible implies that there was some kind of miraculous intervention of preservation when Deuteronomy notes that neither their clothes nor sandals wore out (8:4; 29:5). If such preservation was a reality, then why should such preservation not extend to other artifacts they might carry?

Israel's settlement starts mainly in the central part of the country, which interestingly does not involve any significant military campaign. There was a campaign in the south (Joshua 6–10) and one in the north from the Jezreel Valley northward (Joshua 11), but Joshua notes no military engagement in the central part of the country, especially north of Gibeon and south of the Jezreel Valley. Instead, the text implies that Israel passed through the region unopposed (cf. Joshua 8 and Israel's passage from Jericho to Mount Ebal and back to Jericho and then Joshua 11 when they pass through Canaan from Jericho to the north unopposed).

Given the frequent references to Shechem and the Patriarchal connections there, it is possible that the residents in the central part of the country were relatives of the Israelites and hence, not candidates for extermination.[32] We tend to assume that when the sons of Jacob descended into Egypt (Genesis 41–50), they all remained there and none returned to Canaan after the famine ended. The famine lasted no more than five years after Jacob and the family went to Egypt (Gen 45:5-6). Why should we necessarily assume none returned to Canaan? The Bible does not explicitly say they did not, nor does it say they did. It is true that descendants of some of each of the Patriarchal sons left Egypt in the Exodus (cf. Numbers 2), but some may have returned to Canaan and eventually received their wandering kin under Joshua's leadership.

---

[31]William G. Dever, *Who Were the Early Israelites and Where Did They Come From?* (Grand Rapids: Eerdmans, 2003), p. 73.

[32]See similar argument by Dever, ibid., pp. 61-62.

If this scenario is workable, then in a way Finkelstein's thesis takes on some credibility[33] as the sons of Jacob, having left Canaan because of a famine (Genesis 41–50), return to the land after several hundred years to a people to whom they were related. This hypothesis would explain why no military campaign occurs in the middle part of the country and why Israel passes through with such ease. It would also explain in part the continuity of the material culture as Israel coming from the desert and being unfamiliar with ceramic technology, would learn the technology and designs of their kin already in the land.

Additionally, a peaceful accommodation would occur in some areas as indicated by the treaty drawn up with the Gibeonites (Joshua 9). Furthermore, both Joshua and Judges indicate a mix of populations, probably usually relatively peaceful, but punctuated by occasional skirmishes and rebellions, evidence of which appears in destruction levels at some of the towns.

Crucial to the database is the fact that the Bible notes that only four cities were physically destroyed in the conquest period: Jericho (Joshua 6), Ai (Joshua 8), Hazor (Joshua 11:11-13), and Jerusalem (Judg 1:8). Dever and others who argue from the list in Joshua 13 that these cities were all destroyed read too much into the statement. God's intent was not physically to destroy the cities, but to allow the Israelites to take up residence in them after having killed the population. He made this explicit in Exodus 23:29-30 and Deuteronomy 6:10-12 when he indicated he would not drive the Canaanites out all at once and that Israel would appropriate and inherit houses, fields, and cisterns they had not worked to develop. To accomplish this, the military engagements described in Joshua were typically in the open country, away from the cities, permitting the destruction of the bulk of the population while leaving the cities intact.[34]

---

[33]Finkelstein would almost certainly not agree with this scenario; I am only appropriating certain elements of his thesis into the biblical narrative.

[34]See Abraham Malamat, "Israelite Conduct of War in the Conquest of Canaan according to the Biblical Tradition," in *Symposia: Celebrating the Seventy-Fifth Anniversary of the Founding of the American Schools of Oriental Research (1900–1975)*, ed. by F.M. Cross (Cambridge, MA: American Schools of Oriental Research, 1979), pp. 46-53.

JUDGES

HISTORICAL AND CULTURAL BACKGROUND

The book of Judges paints a dismal picture of Israel's history, especially after the fairly glowing and optimistic successes narrated in Joshua. This sudden shift in tone has fueled much discussion and debate regarding the nature of the two books and how to correlate their records.[1]

Judges is the seventh book in the Hebrew Bible and is the second in the section known among the Hebrews and Jews as the "Former Prophets" and among most English speakers as the "Historical Books." The book's title in the Hebrew Bible is שֹׁפְטִים (šôphᵊṭîm) and translates to κριτάι (kritai) in the Septuagint. Both words legitimately translate into English as "judges." The verb form of "judge" applies to people who take various leadership roles of the Israelites during times of crisis. The period is one of transition from the stable guidance of the founding leaders of Moses and Joshua to the establishment of the monarchy. The period of chaos that characterizes Judges has been likened to the so-called "Intermediate Periods" of Egypt and Mesopotamia.[2]

The book's use of the term "judge" is somewhat foreign to most Westerners. It is clear that the people were not judges in the sense that people came to them to arbitrate disputes. Deborah is the only person in the book who is described as having functioned in an adjudicative capacity of some kind (4:4-5). Interestingly, no one in the book is specifically called by the noun "judge" (שֹׁפֵט, šōphēṭ), except, YHWH whom Jephthah calls "the Judge" (הַשֹּׁפֵט, haššōphēṭ; 11:27). The verb form, however, applies to most of the people in the book.

---

[1]Discussion of this topic appears in the chapter on Joshua as well as additional concerns below.

[2]Kenneth A. Kitchen, *On the Reliability of the Old Testament* (Grand Rapids: Eerdmans, 2003), pp. 203-204.

Some have suggested that the judges were charismatic leaders. However, this definition is deficient. Most Americans would infer that the judges had magnetic personalities to whom people are attracted, but this concept of charismatic would be erroneous – it appears that Samson was a significant loner and perhaps such a social boor that it was necessary to hire people to be his wedding party (14:10-11).

If by charismatic one means God's impartation of power to do the necessary task, then the term applies.[3] The Greek word χάρισμα (*charisma*) means basically "gift," and it was God's gift that led the people into their particular roles.

This call to leadership by God sometimes appears in story fashion (cf. Gideon and Samson); other times it is indicated by the phrase "the spirit of the Lord" (רוּחַ יְהֹוָה, *rûaḥ YHWH*) coming upon the person (cf. Othniel [3:10]; Gideon [6:34]; Jephthah [11:29]; Samson [13:25; 14:6; 14:19; 15:14]).[4] Other indications are the simplified summaries of "the Lord raised up" (Ehud), which as an introductory reference (2:16) applies to all the personalities in the book who are described as having judged.

Functionally, the term "judge" applies to those whose authority was personal and not by heredity which typified the later monarchy. Alternatively, God had established a hereditary kind of judiciary with the high priest and his access to the Urim and Thummim (Exod 28:30; Num 27:21; 1 Sam 28:6; Ezra 2:63; Neh 7:65). Additionally, the Levites were to serve in instructive and judicial capacities among the Israelites (Deut 21:5; 33:8-10). The priests and Levites served in judicial capacities along with the local judges to administer justice (cf. Deut 17:9; 19:17).

Somewhat enigmatic is how to understand the references to various judges about whom no warlike activities of any kind appear (e.g., Tola, Jair, Ibzan, Elon, Abdon). Perhaps their abilities were exercised in their mental or moral qualities in arbitrating local disputes and applying the Mosaic law to their environs.[5] Probably the

---

[3]See further note in "New Testament Connections" below.

[4]One should not equate the "spirit of the Lord" coming upon the person with the same dynamic as the baptism of the Holy Spirit narrated in the book of Acts (Acts 1:5; 2:1-4). The fact that the "spirit of the Lord" came upon Samson several times implies that the phenomenon was not an abiding condition, but was episodic.

[5]Arthur E. Cundall and Leon Morris, *Judges and Ruth: An Introduction and Commentary*, TOTC 7 (Downers Grove, IL: InterVarsity, 1968), p. 16.

best comprehensive definition that accommodates the nuances of the personalities and their behaviors narrated in the book derives from the verb and means to "exercise authority, rule, govern."[6] Such a definition would mesh well with the fact that the noun "judge" (*šōpēt*) does not apply directly to anyone in the book except the Lord himself (11:27), while the verb applies to the people — Othniel (3:10), Deborah (4:4), Tola (10:2), Jair (10:3), Jephthah (12:7); Ibzan (12:8,9), Elon (12:11), Abdon (12:13,14), and Samson (15:20; 16:31), while at the same time not implying approval of the flaws of the people involved.

TEXT AND AUTHOR

Early Jewish tradition attributed the composition of the book to Samuel.[7] There is little evidence to bring to the discussion by which to make a determination. Samuel is certainly a candidate for authorship. The tenor of the book, however, seems to favor the appointment of a king (cf. 21:25), whereas Samuel appears antagonistic to a king other than Yahweh (cf. 1 Sam 8:6-18; 12:1-18). Alternatively, it is Samuel who anoints Saul to the kingship (1 Samuel 10) and eventually anoints David as well (1 Samuel 16). Regardless of who the human author was, he apparently used written sources of some kind which he then placed into a theological framework to emphasize Yahweh's displeasure with Israel's unfaithfulness and the attempt to bring them back to him (further discussion of sources follows below).

The beginning of the span of time involved in the events narrated in Judges depends upon the question of the date of the Exodus/ Conquest which was addressed in the discussion of Joshua (see previous chapter). If one subscribes to an early date for the Exodus/ Conquest, the date range of the events spans from ca. 1400–1050 B.C. If one subscribes to a late date Exodus/Conquest, the span would be from ca. 1220–1050 B.C.

The closing end of the narrative in either scenario would be near the birth of Samuel and his activity leading to the initiation of the Monarchy. Admittedly, the compressed time span poses some challenges, which will be addressed in the section on Special Issues (below).

---

[6]Martin S. Rozenberg, "The *Sofetim* in the Bible," *ErIsr,* Nelson Glueck Memorial, vol. 12 (1975): 86*.

[7]*Baba Bathra* 14b, 15a

The time of composition seems fairly contemporary with the events that are narrated and the book seems to have been put together fairly early in the Monarchy. This inference is drawn to a large extent on the basis of the recurring phrase declaring that "in those days Israel had no king. . ." (17:6; 18:1; 19:1; 21:25). The structure seems more to be an explanation of why they needed a king, looking back from a period when the monarchy had begun rather than as a plea to explain why they needed a king.

A composition fairly early in the Monarchy is further implied by the fact that, according to the book of Judges, Jerusalem was still under Jebusite control (19:10-12). The fact is narrated as if it were still Jebusite. David apparently did not capture the city until after the seventh year of his reign (2 Sam 5:5-10).

The narration about Jonathan's sons being priests at Dan until the captivity (Judg 18:30) poses a problem for the chronology of composition. It is often assumed that the captivity under consideration was that of Tiglath-Pileser III in ca. 732 B.C., which is alluded to in summary fashion in 2 Kings 15:29.

However, more likely the phrase refers not to the Assyrian captivity, but to the capture of the ark by the Philistines when they took it into their custody during the priesthood of Eli (1 Samuel 4–5) and accompanying repercussions because of Israel's unfaithfulness. The Psalmist later would remember the event of the ark's capture as an episode in which Yahweh allowed his tabernacle to be destroyed and sent "his might into captivity" (Ps 78:60-61);[8] such a departure of Yahweh from Israel's protection may have precipitated the capture of the territory by alien northern peoples and necessitated Saul's later campaign against the kings of Zobah (cf. 1 Sam 14:47).[9] This understanding meshes well with the declaration in Judges 18:31 that they served idols while "the house of God was in Shiloh." According to current understanding, the destruction of Shiloh was ca. 1050 B.C.[10] and would allow the historical implications of the text to stand as composed soon after the Monarchy was established.

---

[8]The NIV adds the phrase "the ark of" to the text of Psalms.

[9]For a fuller discussion of this historical reconstruction, see C.F. Keil and F. Delitzsch, *Commentary on the Old Testament in Ten Volumes*, vol. 2: *Joshua, Judges, Ruth, I & II Samuel* (repr., Grand Rapids: Eerdmans, n.d.), pp. 440-442.

[10]Israel Finkelstein, ed., *Shiloh: The Archaeology of a Biblical Site*, Monograph Series of the Institute of Archaeology 10 (Tel Aviv: Tel Aviv University, 1993), p. 9.

STRUCTURE

The book of Judges opens with an overall thesis of Israel's failure to follow through with the Lord's instructions. The author then provides a series of personality vignettes to demonstrate the implications of Israel's failure and God's presence in the form of the deliverers. He then offers representative events that further demonstrate the degradation and chaos of Israel which, according to the author, was a consequence of the lack of a king (Judg 17:6; 18:1; 19:1; 21:25).

The book may be outlined as follows:

I. Background for Judges Revealed — 1:1–3:6
    A. Judah and Simeon conquer their land — 1:1-21
    B. Israel does not purge the land — 1:22-36
    C. Israel breaks covenant — 2:1-5
    D. Joshua dies and is buried — 2:6-10
    E. Israel apostatizes — 2:11-15
    F. Judges deliver Israel; Israel apostatizes again — 2:16-23
    G. Canaanite nations test Israel — 3:1-6

II. Judges Deliver Israel from Oppression — 3:7–16:31
    A. Othniel delivers Israel — 3:7-11
    B. Ehud delivers Israel — 3:12-30
        1. Moab punishes Israel's sin — 3:12-14
        2. Ehud assassinates Eglon — 3:15-25
        3. Israel defeats Moab — 3:26-30
    C. Shamgar delivers Israel — 3:31
    D. Deborah and Barak deliver Israel — 4:1–5:31
        1. Canaanites punish Israel — 4:1-3
        2. Deborah summons Barak — 4:4-10
        3. Israel routs Canaanites — 4:11-16
        4. Jael assassinates Sisera — 4:17-22
        5. Israel subdues Jabin — 4:23-24
        6. Deborah sings in victory — 5:1-31
    E. Gideon delivers Israel — 6:1–8:35
        1. Midian punishes Israel — 6:1-6
        2. A prophet speaks to Israel — 6:7-10
        3. The Lord calls Gideon — 6:11-24
        4. Gideon destroys altar of Baal — 6:25-35
        5. Gideon tests God — 6:36-40
        6. Israel defeats Midian — 7:1–8:21
        7. Gideon refuses kingship — 8:22-23
        8. Gideon makes golden ephod — 8:24-28

GENRE

Compared with some of the other books of the Hebrew Bible, the Hebrew text of Judges is quite well preserved. The literary issues, however, tend to focus upon the traditional disputes of source criticism. Conclusions regarding these questions largely revolve around the presuppositions that modern scholars bring to the discussion. Early critical scholarship sought to identify the preconceived strands of material usually called J and E, then to JE, which were later compiled with Deuteronomistic revisions. As good a basic discussion as any of these lines of reasoning may be found in the commentary by G.F. Moore.[11] Somewhat revelatory, however, are his frequent comments regarding the tentativeness of the source critical enterprise.

Such plodding attempts at source critical analysis of the biblical texts have significantly faded — perhaps because there are no firm points of reference by which to fragment the text into the minutiae imagined by many scholars. Most scholars now concede that the biblical writers often used sources in their compositions. The Hebrew Bible refers to archival records either as sources from which data have been drawn, to corroborate the reliability of the narrative, or to urge readers to investigate the events. Note references to the "book of the annals of Solomon" (1 Kgs 11:41); the "book of the

---

[11]George F. Moore, *A Critical and Exegetical Commentary on Judges* (Edinburgh: T. & T. Clark, 1895), pp. xv-xxxvii.

annals of the kings of Israel" (1 Kgs 14:19; 15:31; 16:5,14,20,27; 22:39; 2 Kgs 1:18; 10:34; 13:8,12; 14:15,28; 15:11,15,21,26,31); the "book of the annals of the kings of Judah" (1 Kgs 14:29; 15:7,23; 22:46; 2 Kgs 8:23; 12:20; 14:18; 15:6,36; 16:19; 20:20; 21:17,25; 23:28; 24:5); to records by Samuel, Nathan, and Gad (1 Chr 29:29); and to the book of Jashar (Josh 10:13; 2 Sam 2:18). The New Testament implies similar sources as Luke begins his narrative indicating his research (cf. Luke 1:1-4). Such sources do not necessarily imply mere human composition — God could easily have directed the writers to the sources for their information.

The trend is to see the historical books, Judges included, as history — certainly not history according to the strictures of modern academic criteria, but history nonetheless with a line of argumentation and a point.[12] The core of the book consists of the narration of the various judges with an introduction that sets up the problem. The appendix of chapters 17-21 presents episodes of examples of the type of degeneration that characterized the anarchy of the period and which precipitated the need for the various oppressions and judges.

The theme of the book is summarized in the last verse of the book: "In those days Israel had no king; everyone did as he saw fit" (21:25). It was a period of political and social anarchy in which not only was there no earthly king, but the Lord himself generally was not recognized as their leader (cf. 1 Sam 8:7; 12:12).

After a brief introduction of the declining successes of the tribes to accommodate their land allotments (1:1-2:10), the thesis of Israel's historical cycle of apostasy, oppression, repentance, and deliverance (2:11-3:6) sets the stage for the representative vignettes of the judges (3:7-16:31) and similar events of chaos (17:1-21:25). Ultimately, in the book, Israel does not learn the lessons of their unfaithfulness.

The author appears to present the book as an apology to legitimate the establishment of the monarchy[13] as he tacitly implies that Israel's degeneration has developed because there was no king in

---

[12]A good discussion of the historiographic perspective of the biblical writers can be found in Baruch Halpern, *The First Historians: The Hebrew Bible and History* (San Francisco: Harper & Row, 1988).

[13]Arthur E. Cundall, "Judges — An Apology for the Monarchy?" *ExpTim* 81 (1970): 178-181. R.H. O'Connell (*The Rhetoric of the Book of Judges*, VTSupp 63 (Leiden: Brill, 1996) specifically argues that the book is a legitimation of David's reign as opposed to Saul's.

Israel (Judg 17:6; 18:1; 19:1; 21:25). The narrative flows well into the book of Samuel since the events of Samuel develop out of the period of the Judges, and especially since Samuel is the last judge of Israel (1 Sam 7:15-17) before the formation of the monarchy.

THEOLOGICAL THEMES

The theology of Judges emphasizes Israel's failure to keep covenant with Yahweh. Yahweh had decreed repeatedly through Moses that when Israel entered the promised land they were to purge the inhabitants of the land and to demolish their places of worship (cf. e.g., Exod 23:20-32; Deut 7:1-6; 12:1-32). Similar injunctions came from Joshua as well (Joshua 23), but with Joshua's death, Israel's incentive died, and they failed to follow through with God's instruction. Instead, they allowed the resident Canaanite populations to remain. As God had predicted, Israel was distracted by the foreign deities and turned aside to worship them (Judges 2), hence breaking faith with Yahweh and bringing upon themselves some of the punishments that God had promised would come (Leviticus 26; Deuteronomy 28; Joshua 23). The punishments were designed to try to bring the people of Israel to their senses and recognize the need to worship and serve Yahweh, but their repentance was typically short-lived and they quickly returned to their unfaithfulness.

This cycle of punishment follows the thesis of Deuteronomistic History laid out quite systematically in the book of Deuteronomy. Some of the concerns of Deuteronomistic Theology do not appear in Judges, but the stage is set for the theological fulfillment in the events of Judges. The book exposes Israel's weakness leading to their desire for an earthly monarch to lead them in battle (cf. 1 Sam 8:19-21; 12:12) and the accompanying problems that the king would bring (cf. Deut 17:14-20; 1 Sam 8:10-18). Deuteronomy and Judges lay the cause of this weakness fundamentally to a failure of Israel to devote themselves exclusively to Yahweh by allowing the Canaanite gods and peoples to distract them into apostasy (Deut 30:15-20; 31:1-29; Judges 2).

The core component of adulterated worship of YHWH in combination with Baal and Asherah is a theme that threads throughout the entire Deuteronomic History (i.e., Deuteronomy, Joshua, Judges, 1–2 Samuel and 1–2 Kings). Noth's premise was that Deuteronomy could not have spoken so eloquently and accurately of what happened in Israel and Judah's history unless it were written after the events had occurred.[14] Interestingly, Josiah's reforms of 2 Kings 22–23 seem almost like a checklist of efforts to bring Israel into compliance with what is laid out in Deuteronomy, hence many scholars argue that Deuteronomy is essentially a product of the mid-to-late seventh century B.C.[15] A significant presupposition of this line of reasoning is that there could be no such thing as predictive prophecy nor inspiration in the sense that conservative believers usually understand it. Because of this presuppositional difference, many conservatives have uncritically rejected the idea of a Deuteronomistic History simply because of the premise that it was a late development.

This rejection, however, is premature. A careful consideration of the warnings in Deuteronomy[16] indeed can be traced through the Historical Books (excluding Ruth), but this does not necessarily imply strictly late authorship of Deuteronomy. Alternatively, the believer should understand that Moses in Deuteronomy is warning Israel of what will happen if they fail to follow the Lord and that the books of Joshua through 2 Kings narrate how the warnings unfolded. Rather than being written after the fact, Deuteronomy *predicts* what would happen and serves as the thesis by which to read the narratives of the Historical Books.

NEW TESTAMENT CONNECTIONS

There are few direct references to the book of Judges in the New Testament. Paul's sermon in Antioch of Pisidia simply recognizes that there were judges between the period of the conquest and the arrival of Samuel (Acts 13:20). Some have noted similarities of the angelic announcement to Mary (Luke 1:31) with the angelic revelation to Samson's mother (Judg 13:3), and the angelic blessing on Mary (Luke 1:42) which sounds similar to Deborah's blessing of Jael

---

[14]Martin Noth, *The Deuteronomistic History*, 2nd ed. (Sheffield: JSOT, 1991).

[15]See the discussion on Deuteronomy in this volume.

[16]E.g., expunging of high places and other places of worship (Deut 12:1-3); demands of centralized worship (Deut 12:4-28); warnings about kings and their behaviors (Deut 17:14-17); rewards for obedience (Deut 28:1-14); punishment for disobedience (Deut 28:15-68).

(Judg 5:24).[17] However, it seems stretched necessarily to argue a connection with the Judges narrative. The argument fails to recognize that there are limited ways to communicate ideas — inevitably there will be similar phrases used in communication.

The most obvious place where Judges appears in the New Testament is in the list of what is commonly called the "heroes of faith" in Hebrews 11:32.[18] The Hebrew writer simply lists Gideon, Barak, Samson, and Jephthah with no elaboration of exactly how he meant the allusion to be interpreted. Unquestionably, they are noted as examples of faith, but that does not necessarily mean that the personalities should be imitated in all aspects of their lives. Block proposes a strategy by which to fit the flaws of the people into our understanding:

> The message is that if anything positive was accomplished during the dark days of the judges, it was the work of God. The human tools available within Israel were raw, and their characters reveal many flaws. But God's work had to be done; again and again the nation needed deliverance from external enemies. Despite defects of personality and lack of nerve, the deliverers stepped out against overwhelming odds. This was either the mark of folly or of faith. The author of Hebrews is correct in casting his vote with the latter. Empowered by the Spirit of God, the deliverers charged into battle.[19]

SPECIAL ISSUES

Three main issues complicate our discussion: the claimed contradiction of the accounts of Joshua and Judges (addressed briefly in the introduction to Joshua above), the organization of the book, and the chronological scheme.

At first glance, the book of Judges appears to present the narrative as a sequential succession of persons and events. Upon closer

---

[17]See Daniel I. Block, *Judges, Ruth*, NAC 6 (Nashville: Broadman & Holman, 1999), pp. 69-70.

[18]The reference in Hebrews 11:33 of some who "shut the mouths of lions" may allude to Samson, but since Samson has already been mentioned explicitly, it seems more likely that the reference would be primarily to Daniel (Dan 6:16-22).

[19]Block, *Judges, Ruth*, p. 70.

scrutiny, however, it is possible that some of the people ruled contemporaneously. There is no evidence in the book necessarily to imply that any of the judges ruled over the entire range of Israelite territory — a careful reading reveals that the judges typically were rather regional in influence.[20]

Organizationally, it is clear that elements of Judges overlap Joshua. While the opening statement affirms "after the death of Joshua . . ." (1:1), suddenly Joshua appears again in 2:6 dismissing Israel from a meeting at Bochim. Furthermore, the narration of Othniel's accommodation of Kiriath-sepher in 1:12-15 and his role in 3:7-11 overlap his appearance in Joshua 15:13-19.

Additionally, the appendix stories seem to reconnect with elements appearing earlier in Judges. Dan's migration northward in Judges 18:1 seems to elaborate on the move summarized in Judges 1:34 when Dan fails to secure his allotment. In addition, the statement that Jonathan, grandson of Moses, served as the priest for the Danites in their northern city (Judg 18:30) implies that the episode must have come fairly early in the sequence of Judges, even though the narration is almost at the end of the book.[21]

Furthermore, in the narrative in which Benjamin nears extinction, Phinehas son of Eleazar, son of Aaron, appears as priest before whom Israel inquires regarding their successes against Benjamin (20:27). This is the same Phinehas who was instrumental in investigating the eastern tribes' construction of the memorial altar at the Jordan as narrated in Joshua (22:13).

The arrangement of these episodes in a thematic way rather than as sequential events should caution the reader against too rigidly forcing the text into a preconceived chronological pattern. Hence, and especially given the discussion of the date of the span of the period of the judges, the question inevitably arises of whether to begin

---

[20]Ehud operated in the area of Jericho (Judges 3); the oppression from which Deborah and Barak delivered Israel focused upon the area north of the Jezreel Valley (Judges 4–5) and Gideon's seemed to focus upon the eastern Jezreel Valley and southward into Ephraim (Judges 6–7); Jephthah was east of the Jordan (Judges 11) and Samson operated in the territories of Dan, Philistia, and western Judah (Judges 13–16).

[21]The Masoretic text reads "Manasseh" instead of "Moses." "Moses," however, appears in some LXX texts and the Vulgate. The connection through Gershom strongly implies that it should be Moses instead — Moses had a son named Gershom while on his way to Egypt to begin his divine mission (Exod 2:22).

the span's calculation with a literal interpretation of the data from 1 Kings 6:1 and its affirmation that the Temple's construction began 480 years after Israel left Egypt or with the statement in Exodus 1:11 which narrates that Israel was involved in the construction of the store city of Rameses. The first calculation would yield a date for the beginning of the events of Judges sometime in the early fourteenth century B.C., whereas the latter would yield a beginning date sometime in the late thirteenth or early twelfth centuries B.C.

Neither date meshes well with the data in Judges if it is calculated on a superficial level and as sequential historical narratives. Admittedly, the data mesh more easily with the early date Exodus/ Conquest thesis rather than the late one. If one adds the numbers together in Judges relative to the duration of the periods of oppression and the periods of judgeships, the sum is 410 years (3:8,11,14,30; 4:3; 5:31; 6:1; 8:28; 9:22; 10:2,3,8 12:7,9,11,14; 13:1 15:20 [16:31]). To this number, one must add the 40 years wandering (Num 14:33-34; 32:13; Josh 5:6; 14:7-10), the duration of Joshua's reign (unknown), the duration of Eli's work (40 years; 1 Sam 4:18), the duration of Samuel's work before Saul was anointed (unknown), the duration of Saul's reign (not given in the Hebrew text),[22] the duration of David's reign (40 years; 2 Sam 5:4); and the four years of Solomon's reign until the construction of the Temple (1 Kgs 6:1) for a total of 574 *plus* the variable unknowns. This calculation for the Exodus would place the event well before 1540 B.C. — a date to which essentially no one subscribes.

The fact that the Judges narration reveals that the deliverances were always local or at most only a few tribes and were never pan-Israelite, legitimately permits a reduction of the extreme chronology. Some of the oppressions and judgships may have been simultaneous rather than sequential. Moore notes fairly, however, that the "most serious objection to the synchronistic hypothesis in any form is, that the chronology of the book is, on the face of it, continuous . . . ."[23] However, the prospect of a simultaneous judgship is implied in Judges 5:6-7 with Deborah and Shamgar. Furthermore, it is possible that the oppressions of the Ammonites and Philistines (Judg 10:6-8) may

---

[22]The Hebrew Bible in 1 Samuel 13:1 does not preserve the numeric datum of the duration of Saul's reign. The number "forty" for Saul's reign derives from Paul's remark in the sermon in Acts 13:21.

[23]Moore, *Commentary on Judges,* p. xl.

have been the setting not only for Jephthah's work, but also for Samson's (see possible allusion in 1 Sam 12:11-12).

Contributing to the impression to make the narrative episodes sequential is the Hebrew phrase normally rendered "The Israelites again did what was evil . . ." (cf. 3:12 et al.: וַיֹּסִפוּ בְּנֵי יִשְׂרָאֵל לַעֲשׂוֹת; *wayyōsiphû bᵊnê yiśrā'ēl la'ăśôth*). The phrase, however, can legitimately be rendered, "And the sons of Israel added to do evil . . ." (i.e., "And the sons of Israel did more evil . . ."), as if the sin is compounded and not necessarily sequential,[24] demonstrating the chaos of what life was like without a king to guide them and their refusal consistently to follow God.

The chronological scheme is further curious in the recurrence of the number "forty" (Judg 3:11; 5:31; 8:28; 13:1) and its double — eighty (Judg 3:30) — and its half — twenty (Judg 4:3: 15:20 [repeated in 16:31]). The number forty had perhaps evolved idiomatically to refer to a generation rather than to a numeric value. Admittedly, sorting through the difficulties of when it might be idiomatic rather than arithmetic is challenging. This suggestion is not to argue that the Bible is wrong, but instead that maybe sometimes we are at a loss of how to understand how it says what it says.

The fact of the organizational scheme of Judges, the fact that judges were all local or regional and never pan-Canaan, and the difficulty of sorting through the chronological challenges should alert the reader to the need for some flexibility in chronological reconstructions. More data, either of an interpretive nature, or of unequivocal extrabiblical control is necessary to make the system more precise, and those data may remain permanently elusive.

---

[24]Admittedly, it can be understood "did again . . ."; but see BDB, p. 415, for the hiphil of יָסַף.

RUTH

"Ruth" transliterates the Hebrew (רוּת) and Greek (Ρούθ) titles of the book and takes its title from the principal character of the book. Ruth follows the book of Judges in the Septuagint and almost all English versions, however, in most Hebrew Bibles, it follows the book of Proverbs in the Jewish section of Scripture known as the Writings (כְּתוּבִים, *kᵉthûbîm*; also known as the Hagiographa). This placement may be because it is with a series of books read at special Jewish festivals — in this case at the Feast of Weeks (i.e., Pentecost) celebration which celebrates the first harvest.

HISTORICAL AND CULTURAL BACKGROUND

During the chaos and anarchy of Judges (Ruth 1:1), Ruth presents a relatively serene portrait of rural life, although with a crisis twist. Internationally, not only was Israel suffering with chaos, albeit for a different reason, the remainder of the Mesopotamian and Mediterranean basin were experiencing similar cultural throes. The Hittites, Egypt, Babylonia, and Assyria were all in decline. Greece was fracturing under the pressure from the Dorians, and the Sea Peoples (among whom were the Philistines) were disrupting the Mediterranean basin. The causes for this upheaval are multiple and may include environmental stresses including a series of earthquakes. The loss of influence of the superpowers of the ancient world, however, allowed a number of smaller states to emerge in their vacuum. Among them were the Syrians, Phoenicians, Edomites, Ammonites, and of course, the Israelites. Israel is trying to carve its independence in the midst of the chaos.

TEXT AND AUTHOR

The Hebrew text of Ruth is well preserved. The main difficulties focus on the passage in 2:7 and the question of how to understand the presence of the genealogy at the end of the book (4:18-22).

The author of the book is not identified, although early Jewish tradition attributes it to Samuel. The last chapter includes David in a brief genealogy (4:18-22), but David is not identified as the king in the list. Samuel was the prophet who anointed David to the office (1 Samuel 16), but he died before David actually occupied the throne (cf. 1 Sam 25:1).

Several modern scholars have suggested that the narrative may derive from an initial oral stage and was the product of a guild of women storytellers,[1] however, ultimately, the human author and gender are unknown.

Since the authorship is unknown, the date of composition is also uncertain. If Samuel composed the book, then it would likely have been before ca. 1010 B.C. when David acceded to the throne. Samuel, however, anointed David well before he took office (1 Samuel 16). The book mentions David as if the reader would readily identify him. This leaves the impression that it was written, or at least the final genealogy attached, after David took the throne (ca. 1010 B.C.). If this is the case, it is odd that the genealogy does not identify David as "the king," alternatively, it may have not been necessary to do so since the audience apparently knew who David was.

Some have inferred from the reference to the custom of the sandal exchange as a rite of earlier time (Ruth 4:7) that the text was written down significantly after the events occurred. While such an inference may be valid, the term "earlier times" (לְפָנִים, l°phānîm) sometimes refers to a single generation's separation (cf. Job 42:11). Alternatively, the term could have been a later gloss to clarify the practice for future generations.[2]

The scholarly arguments for when the book was composed range widely from roughly the time of David to as late as the late Postexilic period.[3] The criteria depend on a number of variables all of which are ultimately subjective and depend on one's presuppositions of

---

[1]Cf. Fokkelien van Dijk-Hemmes, "Ruth: A Product of Women's Culture?" in *A Feminist Companion to Ruth*, ed. by A. Brenner (Sheffield: Sheffield Academic Press, 1993), p. 136; N.M. Tischler, "Ruth," in *A Complete Literary Guide to the Bible*, ed. by L. Ryken and T. Longman III (Grand Rapids: Zondervan, 1993), pp. 151-164; Robert L. Hubbard Jr., *The Book of Ruth*, NICOT (Grand Rapids: Eerdmans, 1988), p. 24.

[2]Cundall and Morris, *Judges & Ruth*, p. 234.

[3]Erich Zenger, *Das Buch Ruth*, ZBAT 8 (Zurich: Theologischer, 1986), p. 28.

issues such as the nature of the theology of the work, the social and legal institutions of the narrative (e.g., the use of the sandal ceremony in 4:7), the purpose and intent of the book (e.g., whether it is a polemic against Ezra/Nehemiah marital reforms or not),[4] supposed parallels with other stories of the Hebrew Bible and the assumed dates that are ascribed to their composition (e.g., with the Joseph stories, Esther, Tobit, and Judith), and the nature of the language (e.g., Aramaisms).[5]

The identification of Aramaisms in the book used to be a heavily weighted criterion for dating the composition late.[6] There is evidence that Aramaic influences may have occurred as early as the Middle Babylonian and Middle Assyrian periods (i.e., as early as ca. 1400 B.C.).[7] The presence of Aramaisms are not now recognized as sufficient evidence intrinsically to demand a late composition.[8]

In contrast, some have argued that the Hebrew reflects an early developmental stage. The challenge is to determine if the usage is archaic or dialectal[9] or archaizing.[10] Alternatively, some argue that the overall linguistic features point to a composition sometime in the transition from Standard Biblical Hebrew and Late Biblical Hebrew – the exile serving as the basic demarcation.[11]

Another theory proposes that Ruth was an oral composition which was reduced to writing much later. Niditch, however, argues that this thesis falters on the fact that the formulaic patterns one

---

[4]Cf. Julius A. Bewer, *The Literature of the Old Testament*, rev. ed. (New York: Columbia University, 1933), pp. 282-284.

[5]See Frederic W. Bush, *Ruth, Esther*, WBC 9 (Dallas: Word Books, 1996), p. 18.

[6]Cf. Paul Joüon, *Ruth: Commentaire philologique et exégétique* (1924; repr. Rome: Institut Biblique Pontifical, 1953), pp. 11-13.

[7]See Donald J. Wiseman, "Studies in Aramaic Lexicography," *JAOS* 82 (1962): 290-299.

[8]Jack M. Sasson, *Ruth: A New Translation with a Philological Commentary and a Formalist-Folklorist Interpretation*, 2nd ed. (Sheffield: Sheffield Academic Press, 1995), p. 244.

[9]Edward F. Campbell Jr., *Ruth*, AB 7 (Garden City, NY: Doubleday, 1975), p. 25.

[10]Robert Gordis, "Love, Marriage, and Business in the Book of Ruth: A Chapter in Hebrew Customary Law," in *A Light unto My Path: Old Testament Studies in Honor of Jacob M. Myers*, ed. by H.N. Bream, R.D. Heim, and C.A. Moore, Gettysburg Theological Studies 4 (Philadelphia: Temple University, 1974), p. 245.

[11]Bush, *Ruth, Esther*, pp. 20-30.

would expect in an oral composition are insufficient in number to indicate such an origin.[12] Kirkpatrick presses the argument and affirms that the phrases and structures do not even necessarily indicate an oral origin.[13]

It seems possible that there may have been some minor alterations to the text or changes made in textual transmission that could account for some of these variations, but there is no overwhelming reason to ascribe a late composition to the book.

STRUCTURE

The outline of the book is simple, with each chapter essentially serving as its own unit:

I. Ruth enters Judah — 1:1-22
II. Ruth meets Boaz — 2:1-23
III. Ruth proposes marriage to Boaz — 3:1-18
IV. Boaz marries Ruth — 4:1-22

GENRE

The evaluation of genre intrinsically affects how one interprets a piece.[14] A straightforward reading of the text leaves the impression it is a historical narrative. Some have argued that the book is a novella[15] or folktale.[16] In either case the issue of historicity is essentially irrelevant. Hubbard proposes it is a short story which allows for historical background and rooting.[17] One wonders if modern scholarship has often imposed categories on biblical studies that were totally foreign to the writers of the Bible.[18]

---

[12]Susan Niditch, "Legends of Wise Heroes and Heroines," in *The Hebrew Bible and Its Modern Interpreters*, ed. by D.A. Knight and G.M. Tucker (Chico, CA: Scholars Press, 1985), pp. 455-456.

[13]Patricia Kirkpatrick, *The Old Testament and Folklore Study*, JSOTSupp 62 (Sheffield: JSOT, 1988), pp. 116-117, 51-65.

[14]Tremper Longman III, "Form Criticism, Recent Developments in Genre Theory, and the Evangelical," *WTJ* 47 (1985): 61-65.

[15]Herman Gunkel, "Ruth," in *Reden und Aufsätze* (Göttingen: Vandenhoek & Ruprecht, 1913), pp. 84-85.

[16]Sasson, *Ruth*, p. 216.

[17]Hubbard, *Ruth*, pp. 47-48.

[18]Cf. Longman, "Form Criticism," pp. 53-54.

It seems best to understand the book as a short story[19] albeit one with a point and implied lesson. The objections leveled against its being history remain unpersuasive. The circumstances, language, and customs (and need to explain what had been practiced) point to a historical basis. In all fairness, the narrations of how known personalities have had events of extraordinary circumstances contribute to their development are well enough known and dramatic enough to warn against *ipso facto* dismissing the narrative as some fiction or folklore. An odd twist of the book which strengthens a historical conclusion is that David is described as the descendant of a Moabite woman. Why connect his genealogy with a Gentile Moabite woman if it is fiction? Hubbard has pointed out ". . . a writer would hardly invent the idea, particularly if he wanted to honor David. In sum, while the skill of the storyteller is quite evident, the heart of the story is historical."[20]

THEOLOGICAL THEMES

As is true of most of the books, several purposes come into play. One reveals how a Moabitess became part of the genealogy of David (4:18-22). Another takes a cue from the genealogy at the end: some have argued that it is to show the legitimacy of David's position on the throne.[21] Hubbard has noted that the point is that "if the same divine providence which guided Israel's ancestors also provided David, Yahweh has indeed appointed him king."[22] However, the tone of the book is not argumentative, and it is difficult to understand why the discussion of Ruth would serve as any significant legitimizing element to the throne;[23] to the contrary, such foreign connections might significantly detract from his legitimacy.

A third inference is to demonstrate how to treat foreigners living among the Israelites. The Law has explicit legislation about treatment of foreigners and sojourners (Exod 22:21; 23:9; Lev 19:33-34; Deut 10:17-19). Admittedly, Israel did not always accommodate the foreigners and poor among them (cf. Isa 1:23; 10:1-2; Mal 3:5).

---

[19]Bush, *Ruth, Esther,* pp. 41-42.

[20]Hubbard, *Ruth,* p. 48.

[21]Kirsten Nielsen, *Ruth: A Commentary,* OTL (Louisville, KY: Westminster John Knox, 1997), p. 29.

[22]Hubbard, *Ruth,* p. 42.

[23]Katharine Doob Sakenfeld, *Ruth,* Int. (Louisville, KY: John Knox, 1999), p. 3.

Because of the almost isolationist policies of Ezra (Ezra 9), some have inferred that the book was written in the Postexilic period as a polemic against his efforts. While some aspects of the book might apply to those circumstances, the tone of the book is not polemic.

An additional reality of the book, if not a purpose, demonstrates that the time of the judges was not total despair and spiritual darkness. The narrative serves as an excellent transition to the books of Samuel and especially as David comes into the scene. Linafelt suggests that it bridges from the chaos and anarchy of Judges to the stability of David[24] (cf. Ruth 1:1 with 4:17, 22); he notes that ". . . nowhere else in the Bible is a genealogical list used at the end of a narrative; they are always used to introduce a story that follows."[25] While this observation has some merit, neither are genealogical lists usually followed by an interlude of several chapters (i.e., 1 Samuel 1–16) until the main point of concern is introduced — David.

Probably the most important theme that characterizes the book of Ruth is the underlying emphasis on Yahweh's kindness (חֶסֶד, *ḥesed*). Although Yahweh is explicitly active in only one passage of Ruth (4:13), the reflective reader notes that Yahweh is at work behind the scenes. The Hebrew word *ḥesed* appears three times in the book, noting the Lord's kindness and that of people to one another (cf. 1:8; 2:20; 3:10).

God's *ḥesed*, however, is shown in more subtle ways. Naomi's family has left Judah because of the famine, and they have sought refuge in Moab. While in Moab, not only does Naomi lose her husband, but her two sons as well — she is left destitute of support. She expresses bitterly her feeling of God's betrayal in her demand that the townsfolk no longer call her Naomi, but Mara; she believes she has returned empty (1:20-21).

She sees her redemption beginning to materialize when Ruth returns with the plentiful harvest from her gleaning (2:20), realizing apparently that the Lord indeed is still concerned. As the story closes and her full redemption is found in the birth of her grandson, who will be her provider, the women of the town point out to her that the Lord had not left her without a kinsman-redeemer (4:14), and then they affirm, "Naomi has a son" (4:17). She had thought

[24]Tod Linafelt and Timothy K. Beal, *Ruth, Esther*, Berit Olam (Collegeville, MN: The Liturgical Press, 1999), pp. xix-xxv.
[25]Ibid., p. xx.

Yahweh was her enemy, but finally came to see that he was really in the shadows. The theme is Yahweh's *ḥesed* to Naomi as provided through Ruth.

NEW TESTAMENT CONNECTIONS

The only reference to Ruth in the New Testament is in Jesus' genealogy (Matt 1:5). Theologically, however, Ruth, as a God-fearing Gentile (cf. Ruth 1:16-17), is incorporated into the people of God. She is an example of the peoples of the earth being blessed because of Abraham's descendants (Gen 12:1-3) and foreshadows the fullness of God's promise to welcome the nations into his fold through Jesus (Isa 9:1-2; Rom 1:16-17).

Additionally the theological connection is the implied providence of God to work quietly behind the scenes in a *ḥesed* sort of way for those who respect and honor him (cf. Rom 8:28).

SPECIAL ISSUES

Two main issues rise in the consideration of the book of Ruth: one is the kinsman-redeemer relationship and procedure narrated in chapter four and the other is the purpose of the genealogy at the end of the same chapter.

The kinsman-redeemer (גֹּאֵל, *gō'ēl*) relationship in chapter 4 has captured the discussion of many. The procedures have their roots in the legislation of Leviticus 25:25-55. Complicating the study, however, is the fact that the events of Ruth do not mesh perfectly with the legislation since the deceased relative's wife is not specified as an object of the kinsman-redeemer action. We are not able to address this question with certainty, but society may have perceived the legitimacy of such action as necessary in some cases of redemption.[26]

A correlate question is: "How does the levirate marriage fit the kinsman-redeemer legislation?" The legislation says nothing of taking the wife of a deceased to raise up children in the deceased's name. Mosaic law indeed had legislation for such a provision, but not in the kinsman-redeemer laws. The brother of the deceased was

---

[26]Cf. Raymond B. Dillard and Tremper Longman III, *An Introduction to the Old Testament* (Grand Rapids: Zondervan, 1994), p. 132; Hubbard, *Ruth*, p. 52.

so designated (Deut 25:5-10), and the levirate laws do not list near kinsmen as potential suitors.

Naomi had alluded to levirate practice (Ruth 1:11-13), but her reference seems to be more hypothetical than legal. If she were to marry a husband and produce sons, the sons would not have been normally considered brothers to her deceased sons. More likely she is not pleading the legal issues of levirate marriage, but expressing the futility of their plight as widows and that she had absolutely nothing to offer her daughters-in-law.

In evaluating this question, one must note that the narrative is not particularly concerned with laying out the legal technicalities of the law. Instead it reflects the application of the spirit of the law for the social setting of the time — a striking contrast to the anarchy narrated for the period of the judges. Additionally, the primary concern in the narrative is the preservation of the family through the kinsman-redeemer relation — the levirate happens to be incidental to the execution of the plan.[27]

Since the genre of the text seems to be history rather than legal, one should not necessarily expect strict narration of all the legal nuances. It is reasonable to assume that the original readers would understand the permutations of how the traditions/laws should be applied. It is clear, though, that elements of the custom changed over time as implied in the need to explain that the shoe exchange was part of the transaction (Ruth 4:7).

The genealogy of chapter four is the other focus of discussion. The date of the genealogy's attachment to the book is widely disputed. Some believe it was attached quite late, others argue that it was part of the original composition. Sakenfeld observes a stylization in the genealogy, with Boaz number seven in the sequence and David as number ten; she then notes the peculiarity of beginning the genealogy with Perez rather than Judah, the ancestor of their tribe.[28] She suggests that the genealogy may then be historically based.[29] While probably ancient, it is difficult to determine when it might have been added.

---

[27]See Michael S. Moore, "*Haggo'el*: The Cultural Gyroscope of Ancient Hebrew Society," *ResQ* 23 (1980): 27-35; Dale W. Manor, "A Brief History of Levirate Marriage as It Relates to the Bible," *ResQ* 27 (1984): 129-142.

[28]Sakenfeld, *Ruth*, pp. 3-4.

[29]Ibid., p. 3.

Hubbard notes that the genealogy's placement at the end of the book serves as a kind of chiasm with the genealogical structure of 1:1-5.[30] The presence of artistic literary structure does not necessarily imply fiction. As noted earlier, it seems odd to trace the lineage of the great king of Judah to a foreign woman if there was no historical basis to the lineage.

---

[30]Hubbard, *Ruth*, pp. 16-17.

SAMUEL

The books of 1–2 Samuel were originally a single book as implied by the Masoretic note at 1 Samuel 28:24 which indicates that this verse is the middle of the composition. The books were known as "Samuel" (שְׁמוּאֵל) in Hebrew and almost all modern English Bibles reflect the Hebrew title of the books; the Septuagint entitles them First and Second Βασιλείων (*Basileiōn*) meaning "kingdoms" and what we normally call First and Second Kings in turn in the Septuagint are Third and Fourth Kingdoms.

The Hebrew title derives from the principal character in the first of the two books. Samuel is the prophet who anoints the first two monarchs who are in turn the subjects of the first two books. Samuel, however, does not appear in the second volume at all. In some ways, the Septuagint titles are more appropriate — the sequence of First and Second Samuel and First and Second Kings is a continuous narrative of over four hundred years of the Monarchy from its inception to its ultimate demise in 586 B.C.

HISTORICAL AND CULTURAL BACKGROUND

The chronology of the events of 1–2 Samuel can be calculated in relation to the known date of Ahab's battle at Qarqar against Shalmaneser II of Assyria (853 B.C.). This permits one to date the events of 1–2 Samuel to ca. 1100–970 B.C. with David's accession in approximately 1010 B.C.

During this period, the Levant is relatively dormant as far as wide-scale international turmoil is concerned. The Hittites have essentially vanished, and neither the Assyrians nor Egyptians are active in the area. Israel's major encounter is with the Philistines who have only recently arrived and begun to settle along the southern Levantine coast. Other Sea Peoples are settling in scattered towns.[1]

---

[1]Among other Sea Peoples are the Tjekker who occupied Dor (see *COS*

God may have used this political lull as a context to plant his fledgling ragtag group of tribes[2] in the region and to permit them to germinate from a tribal organization into a monarchy. The threats from the Philistines (1 Samuel 4–8) and the Ammonites (1 Sam 12:12) served as catalysts to precipitate Israel's request for a king and statehood.

TEXT AND AUTHOR

A casual reading of most good English Bibles will reveal difficulties with the Hebrew manuscript of Samuel. Numerous footnotes will reveal obscurities in the Hebrew as well as emendations taken from other sources such as the Septuagint, the Old Latin and Vulgate, and the Dead Sea Scrolls. A couple of examples will suffice to demonstrate the challenge. A comparison of different versions' readings of the duration of Saul's reign in 1 Samuel 13:1 highlights this challenge. Of the major translations, the RSV and NRSV reflect most clearly the problem of missing data: "Saul was . . . years old when he began to reign and he reigned . . . and two years over Israel." The KJV reading, reflected as well in the NKJV, is confusing: "Saul reigned one year and when he had reigned two years over Israel . . ." and the narrative continues as an event that occurred two years into Saul's reign. The ASV adds the age of forty years when he began to reign and continues the narrative as if the events that unfold occur after he had reigned two years. The NIV and NASB (1995) state that Saul was thirty when he acceded to the throne and that he reigned forty-two years.[3]

Use of the Dead Sea Scrolls data is dramatically reflected in the emendation to 1 Samuel 10:27 by the NRSV, which adds material

---

1:90). Cf. Judges 1:27 which notes that the Israelites were unable to take the city. Although the text says that the inhabitants were Canaanites, "Canaanite" may be a generic attribution rather than ethnically specific.

[2]The reference to Israel in the Merneptah Stele (ca. 1207 B.C.) indicates that the people of Israel were a people without designation as a country or kingdom.

[3]The original NASB reads differently: Saul was forty and reigned thirty-two years. Surveys of different approaches to this verse may be found in P. Kyle McCarter Jr., *1 Samuel*, AB 8 (Garden City, NY: Doubleday, 1980), pp. 222-223; and James E. Smith, *1 & 2 Samuel*, College Press NIV Commentary (Joplin, MO: College Press, 2000), pp. 171-173.

that almost triples the length of the verse. The addition derives from the Samuel manuscript "a" from the fourth cave of Qumran (abbreviated: 4QSam[a]). Admittedly the addition is not attested in any other manuscript tradition,[4] but the question arises whether this reading precedes all the other translations and Hebrew manuscripts.[5]

In summary, the Masoretic Text, which essentially dates from the tenth century A.D., and the Septuagint diverge significantly in a number of places. Prior to the discovery of the Dead Sea Scrolls, the pressing questions, therefore, were: 1) do the Septuagintal readings reflect divergent Hebrew originals; 2) do the Septuagintal readings reflect a more correct Hebrew text that otherwise has become more corrupt; or 3) since most scholars understand that the Septuagint translators sometimes paraphrased the Hebrew text, are the differences mainly the result of these translational processes?[6]

While the answers remain elusive, the discovery of the Dead Sea Scrolls has added another question. Fragments of three manuscripts of Samuel were found in cave 4 — one dating from the third century B.C. and two from the first century B.C., and these provide evidence that there may have been another, similar textual background. McCarter notes that there are a number of other textual witnesses to consider in the evaluation of the Samuel text.[7]

While this survey may appear discouraging, some perspective will help. Our modern Bibles of Samuel divide it into approximately 1472 verses. Smith points out that there is no dispute about the overwhelming majority of the text, and notes that the NIV chose the Dead Sea Scrolls readings in only about fifty places.[8] These fifty

---

[4]It appears, however, that Josephus had access to a manuscript with this information (cf. *Ant.* 6.68-71), but Josephus is not a typical manuscript tradition.

[5]The discovery of the Dead Sea Scrolls moved the Hebrew manuscript evidence almost a millennium closer to the Old Testament autographs.

[6]The bulk of this information is condensed from McCarter, *1 Samuel,* pp. 5-7.

[7]See conveniently ibid., pp. 8-11, for evaluations of various Hebrew, Greek, Latin, Syriac, and other sources. Additionally, good surveys of the challenges, developments and directions of study may be found in McCarter, *1 Samuel,* pp. 5-11, and Ralph W. Klein, *1 Samuel,* WBC 10 (Waco, TX: Word Books, 1983), pp. xxv-xxviii.

[8]See Smith, *1 & 2 Samuel,* p. 24, 24 n 9. The Preface to the New American Bible advocates extensive use of the variant texts, and they have only adopted just over four hundred emendations (ibid., p. 24 n. 9).

places involve usually only a word or two and not entire verses. The integrity of the text is still significant, and one need not allow these variations to be unsettling — a fair and careful noting of the footnotes in most good study Bibles will alert the astute reader to the issues.

Determining the authorship of the books of Samuel has been similarly difficult. Conclusions regarding authorship are often controlled by the presuppositions of the investigators and questions they might have as they approach the text.[9]

The Bible provides no explicit information of the authorship of Samuel. Early rabbinic tradition proposed that he was Samuel,[10] but this conclusion seems unlikely since his death is narrated in 1 Samuel 25:1, obviating his composition of the second volume. In fairness, Samuel may have composed and recorded some of the events to which he was witness, but that leaves a good bit of the first volume and all of the second for someone else to write. The Bible explicitly states that Samuel, Nathan, and Gad — prophets contemporary with David — all wrote of David's reign (1 Chr 29:29; for Samuel it would probably have been the period from David's coronation in 1 Samuel 16 until Samuel's death).

Since Samuel likely did not write the entire work and since he appears only in about the first fourth of the books that bear his name, one may wonder why they might bear his name. Nothing in the text reveals the reason for such a name, but as the narrative stands, Samuel served as the major figure in the transition from Israel's loose tribal organization to the establishment of the monarchy, anointing not only Israel's first king, but more importantly, the monarch of dynastic promise. These kings, Saul and David, are the only ones discussed in Samuel.

Since it is unknown who wrote Samuel, it is therefore impossible to determine exactly when it was written. In its present form, it was likely put together after David's death, which is narrated early in 1 Kings. Its composition and/or recasting, however, could have been significantly later.

---

[9]See, for instance, this admission with his discussion in James W. Flanagan, "Samuel, Book of 1–2: Text, Composition, and Content," *ABD*, 5:957-958.

[10]Babylonian Talmud, *Baba Bathra* 14b-15.

HISTORY OF INTERPRETATION

With the advent and popularization of Wellhausen's documentary approach to Scripture, Samuel came under scrutiny similar to that which had been applied to the Pentateuch. Because of a number of apparently repetitious narratives,[11] scholars of the nineteenth and early twentieth centuries tended to approach Samuel with the same strategy of source-critical analysis, dividing it into extensions of the J and E documents that dominated liberal Pentateuchal studies.[12] The assumption was that the books were put together in the Exilic period.

The inevitable result of such approaches tends to destroy the integrity of the narrative and usually so fragments the text that it becomes almost meaningless. Furthermore finding much evidence and agreement in tracing the supposed sources remains elusive at best.

A more profitable approach was championed by Martin Noth who argued that the books of Deuteronomy and Joshua through Kings were written as a single composition during the Exile to trace God's displeasure with Israel and Judah in their apostasy which led ultimately to their exile.[13] This thesis is known as the "Deuteronomistic History." In it, Deuteronomy served as the theological premise which was traced through Israel's demise in the tribal and monarchical history until her exile. He would argue that the composition used earlier sources, but that these were put together by the exilic author to explain their demise.[14]

While subscribing to the basic tenets of Noth's Deuteronomistic Theology, von Rad[15] and Cross[16] note, however, a positive element

---

[11]See, e.g., two announcements of the end of Eli's house (1 Sam 2:31-36; 3:11-14), David is introduced to Saul twice (16:18-21; 17:55-58), twice David escapes Saul's murderous attempts (18:10-11; 19:8-10), and twice David refuses to kill Saul (24, 26), et al.

[12]Among others, see Karl Budde, *Die Bücher Samuel erklärt*, KHC 8 (Tübingen and Leipzig: J.C.B. Mohr, 1902).

[13]See pages 1-110 of Noth's *Überlieferungsgeschichtliche Studien* (1943) which was translated into English as *The Deuteronomistic History* (1981; 2nd ed., JSOTSupp 15 [Sheffield: JSOT Press, 1991]).

[14]A modern commentary that subscribes to a single author to the Deuteronomistic History is T.R. Hobbs, *2 Kings*, WBC 13 (Waco, TX: Word Books, 1985), p. xxiv.

[15]Gerhard von Rad, *Old Testament Theology*, trans. by D.M.G. Stalker (New York: Harper & Row, 1962), 1:334-347.

[16]Frank Moore Cross, *Canaanite Myth and Hebrew Epic* (Cambridge, MA: Harvard, 1975), pp. 276-277.

in the Deuteronomistic History in the form of the abiding Davidic covenant. Cross argues for a two-stage composition with the first in the seventh century leading into the rise of Josiah's reign and the latter in the sixth century Exile.[17] Typically, Europeans who subscribe to a multiple stage development of the Deuteronomistic History would argue for no production before Jerusalem's destruction in 587 B.C.[18]

A refinement of the Deuteronomistic History which accommodates von Rad's and Cross's view of a positive element is the "Prophetic History."[19] The premise is that sections of the historical books were derived from blocks of material written by the prophets; these were reworked into a prophetic history to trace the origins, development, and expectations of Israel's Monarchy. The expectation of the Monarchy was

> . . . a concession to a wanton demand of the people. Beyond this purely negative purpose, however, the history was written to set forth according to a prophetic perspective the essential elements of the new system by which Israel would be governed. The prophet, whom the example of Samuel showed to be capable of ruling alone, would continue to be the people's intercessor with Yahweh. The king would now be head of the government, but he would be subject not only to the instruction and admonition of the prophet acting in his capacity as Yahweh's spokesman but even to prophetic election and rejection according to the pleasure of Yahweh. Anyone who would become king, therefore, would have to be (like David) a man of Yahweh's own choosing.[20]

---

[17]Ibid., pp. 274-289; see also R.D. Nelson, *The Double Redaction of the Deuteronomistic History*, JSOTSupp 18 (Sheffield: Sheffield Academic Press, 1981).

[18]Walter Dietrich, *Prophetie und Geschichte: Eine redaktionsgeschichtliche Untersuchung zum deuteronomistischen Geschichtswerk*, FRLANT 108 (Göttingen: Vandenhoeck und Ruprecht, 1972); Rudolf Smend, "Das Gesetz und die Völker: Ein Beitrag zur deuteronomistischen Redaktionsgeschichte," in *Probleme biblischer Theologie*, Gerhard von Rad zum 70 Geburtstag, ed. by H.W. Wolff (Munich: Chr. Kaiser Verlag, 1971), pp. 494-509; Timo Viejola, *Das Königtum in der Beurteilung der deuteronomistischen Historiographie: Ein redaktionsgeschichtliche Untersuchung*, AASF, Series B 198 (Helsinki: Suomalainen Tiedeakatemia, 1977).

[19]McCarter, *1 Samuel*, pp. 18-23, provides a good survey of the Prophetic History theory.

[20]Ibid., p. 21.

The fact that the historical books refer to books authored by the prophets (cf. 1 Chr 29:29) implies prophetic influence. Additionally, the traditional Hebrew attribution of the books of Joshua, Judges, Samuel, and Kings as the "Former Prophets"[21] previews the development of such a theory. For the books of Samuel, the dominant personalities in the direction of the Monarchy were prophets — Samuel and Nathan.[22] These prophets were significant players in the major blocks of material normally identified for the books of Samuel: the story of Samuel (1-7), the story of Saul (8-15), and the narrations of David (1 Samuel 16 through 2 Samuel 24). The inference hence is that the stories used in the construction of the narrative could be significantly older than the final composition, but these have been reworked to such a degree that they cannot be firmly dated.

A different track notes that the literary development of the books fundamentally escapes tracing, but ultimately it is the theological message of the books as they stand that demands attention.[23] The fragmentation of the text into sources loses its meaning. Baldwin further notes that with the absence of a significant corpus of similar ancient literature with which to compare the Bible, we should be cautious about making sweeping pronouncements.[24]

Elements of all these theories have their strengths and each has its weaknesses, and especially so given the presuppositions the modern investigator brings to the study. While the text as it stands is the starting point for our study, the Hebrew Bible itself indicates occasional use of sources. We should not, however, assume that the whole narrative simply arose *tabula rasa* in the Exile. The narrative

---

[21]The books of Isaiah, Jeremiah, Ezekiel, and the twelve "minor" prophets are traditionally called the "Latter Prophets" in Hebrew circles.

[22]Prophets continue to be major players in the political directions of the monarchy as seen in the activities of Ahijah, Elijah, Elisha, Micaiah, as well as many of the literary prophets.

[23]Joyce G. Baldwin, *1 & 2 Samuel*, TOTC 8 (Leicester, England: Inter-Varsity Press, 1988). This is essentially the position of Walter Brueggemann, "Samuel, Book of 1-2. Narrative and Theology," *ABD*, 5:965-973. See additionally, Jesse C. Long Jr., *1 & 2 Kings*, College Press NIV Commentary (Joplin, MO: College Press, 2002), pp. 22-30, and sources cited there. Long provides a good, concise discussion of the approach of literary analysis, using Kings as the basis of his discussion, but the principles are more widely applicable.

[24]Baldwin, *1 & 2 Samuel*, pp. 15-16.

drew from sources, which in turn had significance for the times in which they were written.

Furthermore, there is a significant element of legitimacy to the basic constructs of the concept of a Deuteronomistic History. Barring any divine guidance, supernatural intervention, or inspiration,[25] the precision of the statements in Deuteronomy[26] which are traced through the Deuteronomistic History would dictate that Deuteronomy was composed late (i.e, seventh century), and hence the historical records reflect the thesis of Deuteronomy. Alternatively, if one accepts a Mosaic composition of Deuteronomy, it is just as feasible to see the Deuteronomistic History as a fulfillment of the theses that Moses delivered to Israel before his death and which the prophets were attempting to communicate to Israel. Smith observes, "The 'Deuteronomic' spirit is the prophetic spirit. A succession of pre-exilic prophets, some of whom may have been contemporaries of the events they relate, would have produced works stamped with the theology of Moses."[27]

STRUCTURE

I. Samuel Judges Israel — 1 Sam 1:1–12:25
   A. Samuel's birth and childhood — 1:1–2:36
   B. Samuel's call — 3:1–4:1a
   C. The ark narrative — 4:1b–7:17

---

[25]Modern secular historiography is loathe to admit supernatural intervention into its interpretive scheme. J. Maxwell Miller and John H. Hayes (*A History of Ancient Israel and Judah* [Philadelphia: Westminster Press, 1986], p. 59) note: "While modern historians do not necessarily reject the idea of divine involvement in history, it is a presupposition of modern historiography that the general cause and effect aspects of history are explainable without reference to unique disruptions in natural conditions (such as the waters of the Red Sea rolling back or the sun standing still) or any kind of overt divine involvement in human affairs. In short, modern historians have trouble with miracles."

[26]While not subscribing to all the presuppositions of his book, Moshe Weinfeld (*Deuteronomy and the Deuteronomic School* [Oxford: Clarendon Press, 1972; repr., Winona Lake, IN: Eisenbrauns, 1992], pp. 320-359) supplies a helpful compilation of Deuteronomic phrases and wording that is reflected in much of the remaining Hebrew Bible, demonstrating that Deuteronomy serves as an important statement with which the biblical writers deal.

[27]Smith, *1 & 2 Samuel*, p. 17.

1. Israel takes the ark into battle — 4:1b-22
2. Philistines capture the ark — 5:1-12
3. Philistines return the ark to Israel — 6:1–7:2
4. Samuel upbraids Israel at Mizpah — 7:3-17
   D. Samuel and Saul — 8:1–12:25
1. Israel requests a king — 8:1-22
2. Samuel privately anoints Saul — 9:1–10:16
3. Samuel presents Saul to Israel — 10:17-27
4. Saul proves self as king — 11:1-15
5. Samuel delivers farewell address to Israel — 12:1-25
II. Saul Reigns in Israel — 13:1–31:13
   A. Saul tarnishes his kingship — 13:1–15:35
1. Saul illicitly sacrifices before Philistine battle — 13:1-22
2. Jonathan rallies victory over Philistines — 13:23–14:46
3. Saul battles surrounding nations — 14:47-52
4. Saul defies the Lord by saving Amalekite king — 15:1-35
   B. David's fortunes rise — 16:1–19:17
1. Samuel anoints David — 16:1-13
2. David enters Saul's court to calm his spirit — 16:14-23
3. David defeats Goliath — 17:1-58
4. Jonathan and David make pact — 18:1-5
5. Saul conspires to have David killed — 18:6-30
6. Jonathan, Michal, and Samuel protect David — 19:1-17
   C. Saul pursues David — 20:1–30:31
1. David and Jonathan renew pact — 20:1-42
2. Ahimelech unknowingly helps David's flight — 21:1-9
3. David finds refuge in Gath — 21:10-15
4. David at Adullam and Moab — 22:1-5
5. Saul kills priests who helped David — 22:6-23
6. David rescues Keilah from Philistines — 23:1-14
7. David eludes Saul in the wilderness — 23:15-29
8. David spares Saul's life — 24:1-22
9. Nabal refuses to help David and dies; David marries Abigail — 25:1-44
10. David spares Saul's life a second time — 26:1-25
11. David seeks refuge in Gath — 27:1–28:2
12. Saul seeks counsel through a medium before battle with Philistines — 28:3-25
13. Philistines refuse David's help in war against Saul — 29:1-11
14. David pursues Amalekites who destroyed Ziklag — 30:1-31

GENRE

While the books of Samuel are historical, they are not history in our modern, traditional sense of the term. We usually define history based on social, political, and economic criteria. Clearly, neither the books of Samuel, nor any of the historical books of the Bible, focus on these issues. They are "theological" history, concentrating on God's activity and Israel's responses to him. This is not to deny its accuracy.

The Bible has become increasingly the target of severe skepticism of its historical usefulness. Major advocates of these salvos are from the pens of Niels Peter Lemche,[28] Thomas L. Thompson,[29]

---

[28]Niels Peter Lemche, *Early Israel: Anthropological and Historical Studies on the Israelite Society before the Monarchy* (Leiden: E.J. Brill, 1985); id., *The Israelites in History and Tradition* (Louisville, KY: Westminster John Knox, 1998).

[29]Thomas L. Thompson, *Early History of the Israelite People: From the Written*

Philip Davies,[30] and Israel Finkelstein and Neil Asher Silberman.[31] The cry is that the existences of Saul, David, Solomon, and the United Monarchy are at best only legendary figures in the historical construct of Israel and that the stories we have were formulated in the Postexilic period. Being such late compositions, we cannot rely upon anything they have to say in an effort to reconstruct a histori-cal reality for anything prior to the time of Hezekiah, and for most of the authors, even Hezekiah would be illusional.[32]

Thompson's summary characterizes the group:

There is no evidence of a United Monarchy, no evidence of a capital in Jerusalem or of any coherent, unified political force that dominated western Palestine, let alone an empire of the size the legends describe. We do not have evidence for the exis-tence of kings named Saul, David or Solomon, nor do we have evidence for any temple at Jerusalem in this early period.[33]

The overwhelming prejudice of these authors is clear when sur-veying their responses to the discovery of the stele at Dan which mentions the "house of David." The inscription derives from the ninth century B.C., less than a century after Solomon died. The skeptical scholars either write it off as a forgery or argue that it refers to "house of Dod," an obscure deity for whom there is little evidence, or some other unidentified entity.

Such historical cynicism has not gone unchallenged. A host of scholars, many nonbelievers, have decried such extremes[34] and

---

and Archaeological Sources (Leiden: E.J. Brill, 1992); id., *The Mythic Past: Biblical Archaeology and the Myth of Israel* (New York: Basic Books, 1999).

[30]Philip R. Davies, *In Search of "Ancient Israel,"* JSOTSupp 148 (Sheffield: JSOT Press, 1992).

[31]Israel Finkelstein and Neil Asher Silberman, *The Bible Unearthed: Archae-ology's New Vision of Ancient Israel and the Origin of Its Sacred Texts* (New York: Touchstone, 2002).

[32]Keith W. Whitelam, *The Invention of Ancient Israel: The Silencing of Palestinian History* (London: Routledge, 1996), has gone so far as to argue that the formation of Israelite history occurred in the Postexilic period, its study in the academic world has served as a juggernaut to suppress a legiti-mate Palestinian history, and that the pursuit has been to a large extent politically driven.

[33]Thompson, *Early History*, p. 164.

[34]Very useful is William G. Dever's work (*What Did the Biblical Writers Know and When Did They Know It? What Archaeology Can Tell Us about the*

demonstrated that the arguments are ill-founded or driven by methodological and/or ideological agendas.

THEOLOGICAL THEMES

Samuel demonstrates Israel's development from the perspective of God's work to unfold his plan to establish the Davidic line through whom the Messiah would ultimately come (cf. 2 Samuel 7). The narratives trace the transition from the theocracy of the "people's choice" of kings (cf. 1 Sam 8:18) to "God's choice" (1 Sam 13:14). Furthermore, the narrative demonstrates that the transition from Saul to David was the result of Saul's rebellion against the Lord and that David had nothing to do with Saul's demise. It emphasizes God's ability to implement his plan in spite of the weak and faulty character of people, including the flaws that David brought to the monarchy.

The story line demonstrates a prophetically based Deuteronomistic History. Deuteronomy had warned of the ways of kingship (Deut 17:14-20). Israel eventually asked for a king (1 Sam 8:6,19-20), and Samuel dutifully warned Israel of the effects such leadership would bring (1 Sam 8:10-18).

Deuteronomy 12 emphasized that when Israel entered the land and the Lord had given them rest from their enemies (12:10), he would designate a place for offerings. While David prematurely planned to build a permanent home for the Lord (2 Samuel 7), the Lord forbade him, but through a theophany designated where the Temple should be built by David's son, Solomon (2 Samuel 24; cf. 1 Chr 21:28–22:1; 2 Chr 3:1). In the meantime, David's mission was to secure the land militarily (cf. 2 Samuel 8, 10).

The warnings of blessings and cursings emphasized in Deuteronomy (28) find reflection in Samuel's speech to Israel as Saul enters his kingship (1 Sam 12:6-18). Saul, however, served his own interests, refusing to follow the Lord's instructions which resulted in, first the termination of his dynasty (1 Sam 13:13-14) and soon after,

---

Reality of Ancient Israel [Grand Rapids: Eerdmans, 2001]) which demonstrates that the biblical texts reflect many indications of periods earlier than the Postexilic period. Other works that are valuable are those of Kitchen (*Reliability*) and a collection of essays edited by James K. Hoffmeier and Alan Millard (*The Future of Biblical Archaeology: Reassessing Methodologies and Assumptions* [Grand Rapids: Eerdmans, 2004]).

rejection of his kingship (1 Sam 15:23-26). David received similar promises of blessings and curses when the Lord directed David not to build the Temple, but the Lord decreed that he would establish David's dynasty (2 Sam 7:7-16).

NEW TESTAMENT CONNECTIONS

Of foremost consideration in the New Testament is the fulfillment of the Davidic dynastic covenant to establish a throne of one of David's descendants forever (2 Sam 7:11-16). The sentiments expressed in Hannah's song for a child and a righteous, anointed king is reflected in Mary's song of exultation upon the announcement that she would bear the one who would sit on David's throne (Luke 2:30-33,46-55). For one to sit on David's throne, he would be a messiah — an "anointed one."[35] It is to this coronation event that Peter refers on Pentecost when he declares, "God has made this Jesus, whom you crucified, both Lord and Christ" (Acts 2:36).

The New Testament writers were careful to note that Jesus was of the proper lineage to claim David's throne (cf. Matt 1:1-20; 12:23; Luke 1:27-32; 2:4; Acts 2:25-36; Rom 1:3; Titus 2:8; Rev 22:16). Peter even emphasizes that all the prophets beginning from Samuel had spoken of these events (cf. Acts 3:24).

---

[35]The Hebrew term *messiah* (מָשִׁיחַ) translates into Greek as *christos* (Χριστός). The Samuel narrative often mentions the "Lord's anointed," alerting the reader that there is something special about the person so anointed (see 1 Sam 16:3,6,12-13; 24:6; 26:9,11,16,23; 2 Sam 1:14,16; 19:21).

KINGS

Similar to the books of Samuel, Kings was considered a single book by the Hebrews, indicated by the Masoretic marginal comment at 1 Kings 22:6 indicating it is the midpoint of the book. Its name in Hebrew is "Kings" (מְלָכִים, *mᵊlākîm*). Greek tradition considered the book to be a continuation of Samuel and, therefore, entitles it "Kingdoms" (Βασιλείων, *Basileiōn*), and designates our 1–2 Kings as the third and fourth installments of Kingdoms.

HISTORICAL AND CULTURAL BACKGROUND

The narrative of Kings begins about 970 B.C. with the accession of Solomon. The diminished political and military strength of the great Mesopotamian and Egyptian empires has permitted a number of smaller states to emerge in their vacuum. Among these are Phoenicia, Edom, and especially Syria.[1] The narrative of Kings opens with some continuing collaboration between Phoenicia and Israel (1 Kings 5) and some political contact between Solomon and Egypt in the form of Solomon's marriage to Pharaoh's daughter (1 Kgs 9:16)[2] and a passing, but significant, invasion of Judah and Israel by Shishak of Egypt soon after Solomon's death (1 Kgs 14:25-28).

Upon Solomon's death, the kingdom fractured (1 Kings 12), with a number of contributing factors. The Bible focuses on Solomon's unfaithfulness to Yahweh, in part manifest in Solomon's compromising marriages to foreign wives and his accommodation into Israel of their religious practices (1 Kgs 11:1-13). Additionally, the

---

[1]The term Syria derives from the Greeks. The more accurate term from the ancient eastern sources is Aram.

[2]A discussion of some of the implications of this arrangement is found in Malamat's article in Tomoo Ishida, ed., *Studies in the Period of David and Solomon and Other Essays* (Winona Lake, IN: Eisenbrauns, 1982), and in Kitchen, *Reliability*, pp. 107-116.

text makes it clear that Solomon had fallen into the traps against which Deuteronomy (17:14-20) and Samuel (1 Sam 8:10-18) had warned — Solomon had financially strained the Israelites (1 Kgs 4:22-28). After Solomon's death, the northern tribes simply asked that the taxes be lowered (1 Kgs 12:1-15), but Solomon's son, Rehoboam, refused, and the northern tribes seceded and crowned Jeroboam, son of Nebat, as their king (1 Kgs 12:20).

Even though Jeroboam had been promised a dynasty if he followed the Lord (1 Kgs 11:26-39), he apparently did not trust him, but sought to consolidate the secession on his own terms. He initiated four major changes to Israel's identity — he changed their gods (two golden calves), changed their places of worship from Jerusalem to Dan and Bethel (as well as other high places throughout the country), changed their priests, and established a special festival (1 Kgs 12:25-33). In doing so, Jeroboam shifted the ideological identity from a focus on Yahweh to, at best, a syncretism with the idolatrous worship that otherwise was latent in the land from the time of the Judges. Ultimately the kingdom of Israel became pluralistic in philosophy and materialistic in pursuit (as implied in Amos and Hosea).

Ahab's marriage to Jezebel opened a new chapter as Israel adopted a more international expression (1 Kgs 16:29-34). God commissioned Elijah and Elisha to try to bring Israel back to her senses (1 Kings 17–2 Kings 8), but failing to heed their pleas, he used the rising power of Syria/Aram to try to urge Israel back to faithfulness (1 Kings 20–2 Kings 13). Eventually, both Aram and Israel became objects of the rising threat of multiple Assyrian campaigns which quickly overpowered both and ended Israel's political identity with her deportation in 721 B.C. (2 Kings 17). While Assyria's threat was still on the horizon, God raised up the literary prophets — Amos, Hosea, Micah, Isaiah — to try to persuade Israel and Judah to repent.

All the while, Judah vacillated in her faithfulness to the Lord, but remained fairly free of foreign interference. However, with the demise of Israel, Judah still failed to learn her lesson and found herself in the sights of Assyria as the Lord used Assyria to try to jar Judah into faithfulness (cf. Isa 10:5-6). Hezekiah took note and attempted to reform Judah's worship and devotion to God (2 Kings 18-20). His efforts succeeded in delivering Jerusalem and the Temple from foreign occupation. The Assyrians essentially bypassed Jerusalem and extended their reach into Egypt.

In the meantime, however, Hezekiah's efforts were short-lived when Manasseh and Amon sponsored wholesale apostasy (2 Kings 21). A brief, but brilliant return to the Lord occurred with Josiah, who initiated extensive reform (2 Kings 22–23). His efforts were aborted when he died in a battle attempting to derail Egypt's reinforcements to Assyria when the Babylonians threatened to terminate Assyria (2 Kgs 23:28-30).

Upon Josiah's death, Judah quickly reverted to idolatry and Yahweh permitted Nebuchadnezzar, who had defeated the Assyrians in Carchemish, to move quickly southward and subjugate Judah (2 Kings 24). Judah's obstinate idolatry and political rebellion, however, precipitated Babylonia's final surge, in 587/586 B.C., to destroy the ideological symbols of Judah's identity — the holy city of Jerusalem and the Temple of Yahweh (2 Kgs 25:1-17).

TEXT AND AUTHOR

The Masoretic Text (MT) of Kings is better preserved than Samuel, although our ancient witnesses are few. The Dead Sea Scroll collection has yielded scant fragments,[3] but these generally reflect readings similar to the MT.[4] Difficulties, however, arise in places when comparing the Hebrew manuscripts with the Septuagint readings. The issues of textual preservation are essentially the same as those that confront the manuscripts of Samuel.[5]

The authorship of the books of Kings is unclear. Jewish tradition ascribes it to Jeremiah: "Jeremiah wrote his own book, the Book of Kings, and Lamentations,"[6] but there is no explicit statement to warrant this conclusion. It is clear that the book in the form in which we have it was finalized after the exile of 587/586 B.C. and even after 561 B.C. when Jehoiachin was released from prison to live under house arrest by Evil-merodach of Babylon (2 Kgs 25:27-30). Theoret-

---

[3]Steven W. Holloway, "Kings, Book of 1–2," *ABD*, 4:73.

[4]Mordechai Cogan, *1 Kings*, AB 10 (New York: Doubleday, 2000), p. 85.

[5]See the discussion of text in the chapter on Samuel. John Gray (*1 & 2 Kings*, 2nd, fully rev. ed., OTL [Philadelphia: Westminster Press, 1970], pp. 43-53) offers a good summary of the textual witnesses and issues. The question of chronological structuring in Kings is difficult (see discussion below), but James D. Shenkel (*Chronology and Recensional Development in the Greek Text of Kings*, HSM 1 [Cambridge, MA: Harvard University, 1968]) argues that some of the difficulties may arise from reliance upon variant manuscripts.

[6]*Baba Bathra* 15a.

ically, Jeremiah could have been involved in the composition since his life extended into the period of the exile and he narrates Jehoiachin's release (Jer 52:31-34).

The book of Kings, however, explicitly refers the reader to several sources for documentation. The first of these is in 1 Kings 11:41 which mentions the "book of the annals of Solomon" (סֵפֶר דִּבְרֵי שְׁלֹמֹה, *sēpher dibrê šᵊlōmōh*). Once the kingdom divides, frequent references appear to the "book of the annals of the kings of Judah" (1 Kgs 14:29; 15:7,23; 2 Kgs 8:23; 12:19; 14:18; 24:5; lit., סֵפֶר דִּבְרֵי הַיָּמִים, *sēpher dibrê hayyāmîm*; "book of the deeds of the days of . . .") and the "book of the annals [deeds of the days] of the kings of Israel" (1 Kgs 14:19; 15:31; 16:20; 2 Kgs 1:18; 10:34; 13:8,12).

These books have not survived, but they were running diaries of the events that occurred in the reign of a king. We do not know the exact purposes of these diaries, but they apparently served as information sources for the interpretive narrative in the Bible. Cogan suggests that "they were likely based on firsthand source material: records of wars, tribute payments, royal projects, and so forth."[7] Kitchen points out that such diary records were used by Egypt, Mesopotamia, and essentially all other ancient peoples, but these original "day books" have not been preserved in any other ancient countries either.[8] It is possible that some of the passages in Kings that find almost verbatim parallel in the prophets could have derived from a common source or alternatively, one rely upon the other (cf. Isaiah 36-39 with 2 Kgs 18:13-20:19; and Jeremiah 52 with 2 Kgs 24:18-25:21).

Additionally, some references in Kings imply personnel and/or sources from which other information might have come. Elihoreph and Ahijah are cited in 1 Kings 4:3 as secretaries (סֹפְרִים, *sōphᵊrîm*) and Jehoshaphat is identified as the recorder (הַמַּזְכִּיר, *hammazkîr*)[9]

---

[7]Cogan, *1 Kings*, p. 91.

[8]Kitchen, *Reliability*, pp. 63-64. It is to such a collection that the Bible refers when Xerxes cannot sleep and directs that the "book of the chronicles, the record of his reign" (lit., "the remembrances of the deeds of the days . . .") be read to him. This prompts him to inquire if Mordecai had been honored (Esth 6:1).

[9]James A. Montgomery and Henry Snyder Gehman (*The Book of Kings*, ICC [Edinburgh: T. & T. Clark, 1951], pp. 30-31) suggest that the מזכיר was specifically the one who kept the equivalent of the "Book of the Days."

during Solomon's reign.[10] Later, during Hezekiah's reign, Shebna is the secretary and Joah is the recorder (2 Kgs 18:18,37). These terms reflect the same offices that had existed during David's reign (cf. 2 Sam 8:16-17; 20:24-25), implying that their roles were well established. Surely the roles involved some kind of official record-keeping.

Additional record-keeping is implied in the specificity of the dates of various events narrated in Kings. Among these are notations relative to the construction of the Jerusalem Temple (1 Kgs 6:37-38) and the narration of Shishak's attack on Israel and Judah (1 Kgs 14:25). Beginning with 2 Kings 14, there is a series of references to international contacts, particularly with the Assyrians who campaigned into Israel and Judah. These can be fairly securely identified with specific campaigns mentioned in Assyrian records. Finally, the destruction of the Temple in Jerusalem is specifically dated to the nineteenth year of Nebuchadnezzar (2 Kgs 25:8). While these latter dates might have been in the memories of some of the people, it is important to remember that the chronological span of the books of Kings is almost 400 years!

The prophets likely served as another source from whom to draw information, particularly in view of their constant emphasis on Israel's and Judah's relationship to Yahweh. The Chronicler specifically apprised his readers that information about the events and kings could be found in the writings of some of the prophets (1 Chr 29:29; 2 Chr 9:29; 12:15; 20:34; 26:22; 32:32). The books of Kings refer to a number of prophets: Nathan (1 Kings 1), Ahijah (1 Kgs 11:29-38; 14:1-18), Jehu son of Hanani (1 Kgs 16:1-4,7), Elijah (1 Kings 17–19; 21; 2 Kgs 1:1–2:18), Elisha (2 Kgs 2:19-25; 2:2–9:13; 13:14-21), Micaiah son of Imlah (1 Kgs 22:2-38), Jonah (2 Kgs 14:25), Isaiah (2 Kings 19–20), Huldah (2 Kgs 22:13-20), and several unnamed prophets (1 Kgs 13:1-32; 20:13-14,22,28,35-43; 2 Kgs 21:10-15). For many of these, the text of Kings does not indicate that the prophets wrote anything; furthermore, it is peculiar that Kings has no citations for most of the literary prophets at all.

HISTORY OF INTERPRETATION

Following the introduction of Julius Wellhausen's classic expres-

---

[10]Interestingly, Jehoshaphat is retained in this role from the reign of David (2 Sam 20:24).

sion of source analysis, Kings also came under its scrutiny well into the twentieth century as Benzinger and Smend attempted to trace the "J" and "E" documents into Kings.[11] Scholarship pursued this line of reasoning until finally the fragmentation of the text essentially became its own undoing. While most modern scholars concede that sources of some kind were used in the composition (as implied in the text of Kings), "These sources have been subject to sustained editing and literary adaptation, which result in a creative and unique literary composition whose very complexity continues to baffle those who would surgically isolate the original sources from the document. . . ."[12]

As with Samuel and the earlier historical books, Noth's development of the idea of a Deuteronomistic History significantly advanced the interpretation and understanding of the text (see further discussion in Samuel in "History of Interpretation"). A number of passages in Kings imply an exilic composition (cf. 1 Kgs 4:25; 9:6-9; 11:9-13; 2 Kgs 17:19-20; 20:17-18; 21:11-15; 22:15-20; 23:26-27; 24:2-4; 24:18–25:30), and the fact that there is no reference to the Cyrus decree of 539 B.C. (which permitted Judah's return to her homeland) implies a composition before that event.

The prophetic elements, however, are frequent with the writer constantly measuring the various kings against their conformity or nonconformity to the will of Yahweh — especially as it was delineated in Deuteronomy.

Complementary with the prophetic frame of reference is the literary approach to the book which respects the book as it stands and seeks to determine the meaning of the narrative as it would have been understood by the exiled community. Both Holloway and J. Long have set forth the application of these approaches noting the stylistic and literary constructs that accentuate the message and cause the source-analysis approach to pale in significance.[13]

---

[11]I. Benzinger, *Jahvist und Elohist in den Königsbüchern*, BAZW II, 2 (Berline-Stuttgart Leipzig: Töpelmann, 1921); R. Smend, "*JE in den geschichtlichen Büchern des Alten Testament, herausgegeben von H. Holzinger*," *ZAW* 39 (1921): 204-215.

[12]Holloway, "Kings," 4:71.

[13]Holloway, "Kings," 4:76-79; Long, *1 & 2 Kings*, pp. 22-34. A general introduction to literary analysis of the historical books may be found in V. Philips Long, *The Art of Biblical History* (Grand Rapids: Zondervan, 1994).

STRUCTURE

Kings has a tripartite division – the first part is of Solomon's reign, followed by the division of the kingdom into the northern kingdom of Israel and the continuation of the southern Davidic kingdom of Judah. The third section narrates the history of the kingdom of Judah after Israel was sent into exile.

I. Solomon Rules over All Israel – 1:1–11:43
   A. Solomon secures the throne and David dies – 1:1–2:46
   B. Solomon reigns as king – 3:1–11:43
     1. Solomon displays wisdom – 3:1–4:34
     2. Solomon builds the Temple and his palace – 5:1–7:51
     3. Solomon dedicates the Temple – 8:1-66
     4. Episodes of Solomon's reign – 9:1–10:29
       a. God makes covenant with Solomon – 9:1-9
       b. Solomon creates tension with Hiram – 9:10-14
       c. Solomon employs forced labor – 9:15-28
       d. Queen of Sheba visits Solomon – 10:1-13
       e. Solomon displays his economic splendor – 10:14-29
     5. Solomon's wives lead him into apostasy and God condemns him – 11:1-43
II. The Monarchy Divides into Israel and Judah – 1 Kgs 12:1–2 Kgs 17:41
   A. Solomon's kingdom splits – 12:1–14:31
     1. Ten tribes rebel against Rehoboam – 12:1-20
     2. Rehoboam tries to reunite kingdom, but God forbids him – 12:21-24
     3. Jeroboam reigns in Israel – 12:25–14:20
       a. Jeroboam establishes religious apostasy – 12:25-33
       b. Man of God from Judah condemns Jeroboam – 13:1-34
       c. Ahijah prophesies Jeroboam's son will die – 14:1-16
       d. Jeroboam dies – 14:17-20
     4. Rehoboam reigns in Judah – 14:21-31
       a. Judah apostatizes from the Lord – 14:21-24
       b. Shishak plunders the Jerusalem Temple – 14:25-28
       c. Rehoboam dies – 14:29-31
   B. Histories of Israel and Judah alternate – 1 Kgs 15:1–2 Kgs 17:41
     1. Abijam and Asa reign in Judah – 15:1-24
     2. Nadab, Baasha, Elah, Zimri, Omri, and Ahab reign in Israel – 15:25–16:34

3. Elijah prophesies in Israel — 1 Kgs 17:1–2 Kgs 2:11
   a. God sustains Elijah with aid of ravens and a widow — 17:1-24
   b. Elijah challenges prophet of Baal at Carmel — 18:1-46
   c. Jezebel's threats cause Elijah to flee to Horeb — 19:1-18
   d. Elijah summons Elisha to follow him — 19:19-21
   e. God delivers Ahab from a Syrian invasion — 20:1-22
   f. God delivers Ahab from a second Syrian invasion — 20:23-34
   g. God condemns Ahab for sparing Ben-Hadad — 20:35-43
   h. Elijah condemns Ahab for seizing Naboth's vineyard — 21:1-29
   i. Ahab and Jehoshaphat of Judah ally in war against Syria — 22:1-40
      (1) Micaiah prophesies Ahab's death — 22:1-28
      (2) Ahab dies in battle against Syria — 22:29-40
   j. Jehoshaphat reigns in Judah — 22:41-50
   k. Ahaziah reigns in Israel — 1 Kgs 22:51–2 Kgs 1:16
   l. Jehoram/Joram succeeds Ahaziah — 1:17-18
   m. Elijah taken up into heaven — 2:1-11
4. Elisha prophesies in Israel — 2:12–8:29
   a. Elisha begins his ministry — 2:12-25
   b. Jehoram/Joram campaigns against Moab — 3:1-27
   c. Elisha performs miracles — 4:1–8:6
      (1) Widow's oil increases — 4:1-7
      (2) Shunammite woman has son — 4:8-17
      (3) Elisha raises Shunammite woman's son from dead — 4:18-37
      (4) Elisha purifies poisonous stew — 4:38-41
      (5) Elisha feeds a hundred men on meager fare — 4:42-44
      (6) Elisha heals Naaman — 5:1-27
      (7) Elisha recovers lost axe head — 6:1-7
      (8) Elisha reveals Syrian battle plans to Jehoram — 6:8-10
      (9) Elisha strikes Syrians blind — 6:11-23
      (10) Elisha prophesies deliverance of Samaria — 6:24–7:20
      (11) Gehazi narrates Elisha's activities — 8:1-6
   d. Elisha anoints king of Syria — 8:7-15

      5. Jehoram and Ahaziah reign in Judah — 8:16-29
      6. Jehu reigns in Israel — 9:1–10:36
        a. Elisha instructs servant to anoint Jehu as king — 9:1-13
        b. Jehu assassinates Jehoram/Joram of Israel — 9:14-26
        c. Jehu assassinates Ahaziah of Judah — 9:27-29
        d. Jehu massacres the house of Ahab and relatives of Ahaziah — 9:30–10:17
        e. Jehu massacres worshipers of Baal — 10:18-36
      7. Athaliah reigns in Judah — 11:1-20
      8. Jehoash reigns in Judah — 11:21–12:21
      9. Jehoahaz and Jehoash/Joash reign in Israel — 13:1-25
     10. Amaziah reigns in Judah — 14:1-22
     11. Jeroboam son of Joash reigns in Israel — 14:23-29
     12. Azariah/Uzziah reigns in Judah — 15:1-7
     13. Zechariah, Shallum, Menahem, Pekahiah, and Pekah reign in Israel — 15:8-31
     14. Jotham and Ahaz reign in Judah — 15:32–16:20
     15. God brings Assyria to destroy Israel because of her sins — 17:1-23
     16. Foreigners settle in Samaria — 17:24-41
  III. Kingdom of Judah Survives Alone until Babylonian Capture — 18:1–25:30
    A. Hezekiah reigns in Judah — 18:1–20:21
      1. Hezekiah seeks to restore proper worship — 18:1-8
      2. Assyrians threaten Judah — 18:9-37
      3. Isaiah assures Hezekiah that Jerusalem will survive — 19:1-37
      4. Hezekiah becomes ill and fraternizes with Babylonians — 20:1-21
    B. Manasseh reigns in Judah — 21:1-18
      1. Manasseh leads Judah back into idolatry — 21:1-9
      2. Prophets predict Jerusalem will fall — 21:10-18
    C. Amon reigns in Judah — 21:19-26
    D. Josiah reigns in Judah — 22:1–23:30
      1. Josiah sponsors renovation of Temple — 22:1-20
      2. Josiah leads renewal of covenant with God — 23:1-3
      3. Josiah purges country of false worship — 23:4-25
      4. God's anger over Manasseh's sin lingers — 23:26-27
      5. Josiah dies in battle against Egyptians — 23:28-30
    E. Pharaoh captures Jehoahaz — 23:31-35
    F. Nebuchadnezzar captures Jehoiakim — 23:36–24:7

G. Nebuchadnezzar captures Jehoiachin and takes him to
Babylon — 24:8-16

H. Nebuchadnezzar places Zedekiah on the throne —
24:17–25:21

  1. Zedekiah rebels against Nebuchadnezzar — 24:17–25:7
  2. Nebuchadnezzar destroys Jerusalem and the Temple —
  25:8-21

I. Nebuchadnezzar appoints Gedaliah as governor — 25:22-27

J. Evil-merodach liberates Jehoiachin from prison — 25:27-30

GENRE

As with the other books of history (Joshua through Esther) Kings
is often considered a historical book, but its emphasis is not on standard social, political, and economic issues but upon God's activities
among his people and how they respond to his expectations. Typical
modern historical emphasis tends to look more at international political activity. The references to Omri in Assyrian records indicate that
he was a formidable king,[14] but only fourteen verses narrate anything
about him in Kings (16:15-28). With all the emphasis in the Bible on
Ahab, Kings does not mention his defeat at the hands of Shalmaneser III of Assyria in 853 B.C.[15] Little is made in the Bible of the territorial expansion and rise in wealth during the reign of Jeroboam
son of Joash (cf. 2 Kgs 14:25). For social and economic issues, one
must turn more to the literary prophets — Amos, Hosea, Micah,
Isaiah, Jeremiah, and Ezekiel — for major insight, but even their
emphasis is on the spiritually degrading overtones of the wealth and
not an elaboration on any grandeur that might have existed.

Hezekiah's engineering feat of the tunnel receives only a fleeting
reference in 2 Kings 20:20, whereas the modern world is quite
impressed with the construction techniques of the enterprise and continues to debate exactly how it was accomplished so successfully.[16]

---

[14]Shalmaneser cites Omri as the forebearer of Ahab (Younger in *COS*
2:113A, ii.86b-102) and several times erroneously cites him as the ancestor
of Jehu (Younger in *COS* 2.113C, 1"-27"; *COS* 2.113D, iii.45b-iv.15a; *COS*
2:113E, 21-30a; and *COS* 2.113F). Mesha refers to Omri's capture of Moab
in his own stele on which Mesha attributes his recapture of the land to
Chemosh (see Smelik in *COS* 2.23).

[15]Ahab was part of a coalition of kings who lost in a battle at Qarqar,
which is dated to 853 B.C. (see Younger in *COS* 2.113A, ii.86b-102).

[16]See conveniently Stephen Rosenberg, "The Siloam Tunnel Revisited," *Tel*

Contrary to these kinds of modern historical concerns, the book of Kings, along with the remainder of the historical books of the Bible, are really about religion. Issues of the Temple and its construction dominate the opening chapters of Kings. A heavy focus then evaluates the kings on whether they deal with the illicit high places or not. After the kingdom splits, the northern kings are regularly measured against Jeroboam the son of Nebat, who serves as the benchmark of evil in moving Israel away from Yahweh. Occasional kings in Judah turn to the Lord in faithfulness, but the episodes are too erratic to have an abiding effect. Even the reigns of Hezekiah and Josiah — the only kings who attempt to rid the country of the high places and force the people to offer their sacrifices only at the Temple — are insufficient to stem the tide of destruction.

The narrative is history, but with a spiritual and prophetic emphasis.[17]

THEOLOGICAL THEMES

The above discussion on genre makes it clear that there is a strong theological component to Kings. The opening chapters of Kings emphasize the construction of the Temple and God's acceptance of it as the place where he chooses his name to dwell (cf. Deut 12:1-14; 1 Kgs 8:10-13,29; 9:3). This, then, voids the legitimacy of any sacrifices offered at the high places scattered through the land.

With Israel's exile, though, she is separated from her designated site of worship. Kings is a theodicy addressed primarily to the exiled people to explain how Yahweh could permit the Temple to be destroyed and the exile to occur. The premise is stated prophetically after Solomon dedicated the Temple and Yahweh appears to him. Warning Solomon that if Israel fails to follow him, God affirms: ". . . I will cut off Israel from the land I have given them and will reject this temple I have consecrated for my Name. Israel will then become a byword and an object of ridicule among all peoples. And though this temple is now imposing, all who pass by will be appalled

---

Aviv 25 (1998): 116-130; and Ronny Reich and Eli Shukron, "Reconsidering the Karstic Theory as an Explanation to the Cutting of Hezekiah's Tunnel in Jerusalem," *BASOR* 325 (2002): 75-80, for theories and bibliographies.

[17]Simon J. DeVries (*1 Kings,* WBC 12 [Waco, TX: Word Books, 1985], pp. xxix-xxxv) has a good discussion of historiography in his introduction.

and will scoff and say, 'Why has the LORD done such a thing to this land and to this temple?'" (1 Kgs 9:7-8). God's faithfulness is ironically demonstrated in his fulfillment of his promise to send them into exile if they failed to obey him (cf. 2 Kgs 21:14-15; 24:2).

The failure is demonstrated repeatedly in the narrative as the curses come upon the people to try to move them to repentance. These are prophesied in Deuteronomy, but the seeds of the exile are sown by Solomon himself and they germinate with the breach by Jeroboam. Hobbs summarizes:

> More than a political disaster, the loss of temple, city, land, and the king was a serious religious and theological crisis for the exiles. Each of the items lost represented a form of the concrete assurance of God's election of Israel and his presence with her. The land was a gift of God. The city was the dwelling-place of God (Pss 2; 48). The king was a living representation of God's grace (Pss 110; 132; 2 Sam 7). All were now lost, and with them the visible symbols of the ordering of Judean society under God. Without such centers the people lacked cohesion, and without a land it could be argued that the people lacked an identity.[18]

However, with their demise and expulsion from the land, and even the cessation of the earthly Davidic throne, even in exile there is hope. God has not forgotten his promise to establish a house for David (2 Samuel 7). Even though the earthly institution of kingship cannot deliver as evidenced by the failure of Josiah's efforts, hope glimmers with Jehoiachin's survival at the end of Kings (25:27-30).[19]

NEW TESTAMENT CONNECTIONS

Perhaps foremost is the demonstration of God's faithfulness to remember his covenant to establish David's house (2 Samuel 7). The kingdom, however, would be of a different dimension than David's. Each of the Gospels refers to the Davidic (and hence, Messianic)

---

[18]Hobbs, *2 Kings*, p. xxxiv.

[19]Interestingly, Jeremiah indicates that Jehoiachin (called Coniah in Jeremiah) would not have another son reigning "on the throne of David and ruling again in Judah" (22:30). The statement does not preclude a descendant reigning on the heavenly throne, in the "kingdom not of this world" (cf. John 18:36; Acts 2:34-36).

claim of Jesus' lineage.[20] When the Gospel begins to spread beyond the borders of Judea, the same declaration of Jesus' heritage is affirmed among the Jewish communities (Acts 2:25-35; 13:22-37; 15:13-17).

Part of the justification of Jesus' claims to fulfill the prophesies taps into the narratives surrounding Elijah. Malachi prophesied that Elijah would prepare the way for the Messiah (Mal 4:5-6), and Luke affirms in the episode where Zechariah is informed of the imminent birth of John that John would have the spirit of Elijah (Luke 1:17). The New Testament writers will emphasize this connection, even as the Jewish authorities inquire of John the Baptist if he might be the Elijah (John 1:19-20) – an identity that Jesus affirms (Matt 11:13-14). John is described with similarly distinctive dress with Elijah (cf. 2 Kgs 1:7-8 and Matt 3:4), and both Elijah and John find their archnemeses in women – Jezebel against Elijah (1 Kgs 18:2,10,14) and Herodias against John (Matt 14:3-12).

The prophetic transition from Elijah to Elisha is paralleled with the authority transition from John to Jesus, and both take place in the vicinity of the Jordan (cf. 2 Kgs 2:9-14 and Matt 3:13-17). Perhaps the most powerful presence of Elijah is at the Transfiguration with Moses and Jesus as they discussed Jesus' departure (Matt 17:1-13; Mark 9:2-8; Luke 9:28-36).

Jesus himself refers to Elijah's activities in his discussion of the receptivity of his message among the Palestinian Jews (Luke 4:25-26), and Jesus' activities were often confused with the people's perception of what Elijah might do (Matt 16:14; Mark 6:14-15; 8:27-29; Luke 9:7-8). And at Jesus' crucifixion, some thought that Jesus had summoned Elijah to assist him (Matt 27:46-49; Mark 15:35-36).

Paul cites Elijah's presence at Horeb where Elijah complained that no one was left to serve Yahweh but him. God, though, revealed that numerous people had not bowed to Baal (cf. 1 Kgs 19:9-18 and Rom 11:2-5). James cites Elijah as an example of how God hears the prayer of a common person (5:16-18).

Elisha, too, plays an important role in the New Testament narrative. Dillard and Longman suggest that Jesus' answer to John's

---

[20]See for instance: Matthew 1:1,6,17,20; 9:27; 12:23; 15:22; 20:31; 21:9,15; Mark 10:47-48; 11:10; Luke 1:27,32,69; 2:4; 3:31; 18:39; and John 7:42. Perhaps John does not emphasize the lineage angle so heavily because by the time he writes, that issue is recognized.

inquiry of Jesus' identity (Matt 11:2-3) is couched in an allusion of the transition from Elijah to Elisha:

> Elisha had restored sight to the blind (2 Kings 6:18-20), cured leprosy (chap. 5), restored the dead to life (4:32-37; 8:4-5; 13:21), and brought good news to the destitute (1-7 [sic]; 7:1-2; 8:6). This list conflates the miracles of Elisha with those of the promised Servant of the Lord (Isa. 61:1-3). Jesus was in effect telling John, "Elijah's successor has come. I am the one you are looking for."[21]

Jesus additionally cites the cure of the foreigner, Naaman, at the mediation of Elisha as an indictment of Nazareth's lack of faith (Luke 4:22-27).

SPECIAL ISSUES

CHRONOLOGY

Most people find the storyline of Kings confusing as the account bounces back and forth between events in Israel and Judah. Inevitably, the transitions from each king to the next does not coincide with the shifts in the other country. The author, therefore, will coordinate the accession year of one king with the time the king in the other country has reigned. This usually takes the form of a formula (with some variation): "In the x year of the reign of PN (proper name) king of Judah/Israel, PN began to reign and he was y years old when he began to reign and he reigned z years" (cf. 2 Kgs 8:16-17). Sometimes the mother of Judah's monarch is given (cf. 1 Kgs 22:42; 2 Kgs 15:2). Usually the faithfulness of the king of Judah is evaluated, whereas the king of Israel is usually measured against the sins of Jeroboam son of Nebat.

If one has a firm date from which to begin calculation, it would seem that the chronological reconstruction should be fairly straightforward, but this is not the case. For instance, Jehu killed Ahaziah of Judah and Joram of Israel (2 Kgs 9:21-29), after which he acceded the throne in Israel and Athaliah took the throne in Judah (11:1-3), hence both accede the throne about the same time. Careful calculation of the years of reign from Jehu and Athaliah to the destruction

---

[21] Dillard and Longman, *Introduction*, p. 167.

of Samaria at the end of Hoshea's reign (Israel) and in the sixth year of Hezekiah's reign in Judah (18:10) yields two different sums: 165 years elapsed for Judah and 143 years and 7 months for Israel — a disparity of some 22 years.

Edwin Thiele is credited with a significant breakthrough in making sense of the chronological data, although his resolutions are disputed and some are open to alternative explanations.[22] Part of the confusion rests on the question of whether the year the king acceded the throne is considered one of his years of reign or not (normally, the monarchy did not change at the change of the year). Additionally, there is some evidence of co-regencies when a monarch and his son might overlap their reigns.[23] Furthermore, it is possible that the kingdoms adopted different modes of reckoning over the course of their 250–350-year existence.

With chronology defined largely on the duration of a king's reign and not against an ongoing standard that transcends the kings, the calculation becomes difficult. Our chronological attributions tend to be relative rather than absolute. An absolute date would be a specific indication, such as July 4, 1776; a relative date would indicate a period of approximation in relation to the specific, either before or after.

The Bible does not give absolute dates, nor are there many indications of such from the ancient world. The best we can do is glean information that we can replicate or test in some way, such as a solar eclipse that was noted in the ancient world, or observations of constellations that we might duplicate in a planetarium. Fortunately, we have at least one absolute date from which to operate: June 15, 763 B.C. — it was the occasion of a solar eclipse in Assyria.[24] The Assyrians named their years after individuals who served in the government, and these are called *līmu* or eponym lists. Since it is possible to determine the date of the eclipse and the sequence of years are

---

[22]Edwin R. Thiele, *The Mysterious Numbers of the Hebrew Kings*, rev. ed. (Grand Rapids: Eerdmans, 1983).

[23]Some evidence of this possibility can be seen in the transition from David to Solomon. David is alive when Solomon is coronated (the question of David's successor is the issue of dispute in 1 Kings 1–2). The coronation occurs in 1 Kings 1:28-40, but David's death is not narrated until 1 Kings 2:10-12; the text does not say how long David continued to live after Solomon was coronated.

[24]See Millard, "The Babylonian Chronicle (1.136)," *COS* 1:467-468.

named over a span that covers 910–612 B.C., we are able to determine when an Assyrian king lived and the dates of his campaigns. Some of these campaigns involve Israel and Judah.

Additional insight and corroboration derive from the Babylonian Chronicle[25] and various Egyptian records, particularly as they encounter the Mesopotamian cultures. Some of the dates that are widely recognized are the following (all dates B.C.):

853   Shalmaneser III engages a coalition of kings including Ahab at Qarqar[26]

841   Jehu pays tribute to Shalmaneser III portrayed on the Black Obelisk[27]

738/37 Menahem pays tribute to Tiglath-Pileser III[28]

701   Sennacherib invades Judah[29]

598/97 Nebuchadnezzar captures Jerusalem[30]

587/86 Nebuchadnezzar captures Jerusalem and destroys the Temple (calculated from 2 Kgs 25:8)

Occasionally scholars appeal to archaeology to try to establish dates, but absolute dates can only be determined with some inscriptional evidence identifying a fixed point. Otherwise, ceramic typology in conjunction with soil stratigraphy is a helpful means by which to establish relative dates, but this strategy relies upon some fixed points from which to determine the variations in style.

Another frequently mentioned dating technique is carbon-14 dating, but the variable on this usually permits no more precise dating than ceramic typology. It can be helpful in refining or corroborating dates, but rarely will it be more precise.[31]

HISTORICAL RELIABILITY OF THE RECORDS

In recent years, the historical reliability of the Bible has come under increasing scrutiny and skepticism by many who argue that

---

[25]Ibid., 1.137.

[26]Younger, in *COS* 2:113A.

[27]Ibid., 2:113F.

[28]Ibid., 2:117B.

[29]Cogan, in *COS* 2:119B.

[30]Millard, in *COS* 1:137.

[31]A good, succinct orientation to how carbon-14 dating applies to archaeology and which explains well its value and drawbacks is in Sheridan Bowman, *Radiocarbon Dating* (Berkeley: University of California, 1990).

the persons of David and Solomon are essentially fictional, that Jerusalem was not a capital of a kingdom before Hezekiah, and that the Temple did not exist prior to Hezekiah. These arguments are based in part upon the difficulty of finding monumental architecture associated with the time period under consideration. The city gates of Megiddo, Hazor, and Gezer, which have traditionally been attributed to Solomon's sponsorship (cf. 1 Kgs 9:15) have found scholars who argue that they derive from at least a century after Solomon. No remnants of the Solomonic Temple have been found, and the impression is that the population of the area of Judah was minimal, hence the inference that Jerusalem was of no political significance.[32] Scholars sometimes argue that the Bible has an agenda (as if other historical accounts do not), and they assume that all the biblical texts are late compositions, and they conclude, therefore, that the Bible cannot be historically reliable — it is just an ideologically driven construct.[33]

Such scholars, however, have not gone unchallenged. Although his work significantly pre-dates the compositions of the skeptics, Ishida devotes an entire collection of essays to the period of the United Monarchy.[34] Many of the scholars in the volume had no agenda to prove the Bible or its historicity.

While he should not be considered a conservative scholar (nor would he desire to be), Dever has taken the radical skeptics to task and systematically exposed major weaknesses in their approaches.[35] Most valuable is his demonstration of what the Bible would have looked like had it been written *de novo* in the Postexilic period. From a more conservative standpoint, but from the perspective of an Egyptologist, Kitchen lays out a methodology of getting at, and evaluating the data.[36]

---

[32]According to all evidence, Solomon's Temple rested on the site now occupied by the Dome of the Rock, the third most holy site for the Islamic religion. It therefore rests on one of the most contested hills in one of the most contentious cities in the world. It would be maniacal to consider an archaeological excavation to try to identify the remains of a Hebrew religious site.

[33]Strong advocates of these positions with occasional differences among them are Lemche, *Early Israel*; id., *Israelites in History*; Thompson, *Early History*; id. *The Mythic Past*; Davies, *In Search of "Ancient Israel"*; and Finkelstein and Silberman, *The Bible Unearthed*.

[34]Ishida, *Studies*.

[35]Dever, *What Did the Biblical Writers Know?*

[36]Kitchen, *Reliability*.

A recent collection of essays by conservative scholars offers some sobering and refreshing insights into a conservative approach to the biblical texts.[37]

---

[37]Hoffmeier and Millard, *Future of Biblical Archaeology*. For convenient presentations from the spectrum of interpretations, see the interview by Shanks in Niels Peter Lemche, Thomas L. Thompson, William G. Dever, and P. Kyle McCarter Jr., "Face to Face: Biblical Minimalists Meet Their Challengers," *BAR* 23 (1997): 26-42, 66; essays in Lowell K. Handy, ed., *The Age of Solomon: Scholarship at the Turn of the Millennium* (Leiden: Brill, 1997); and essays in Andrew G. Vaughn and Ann E. Killebrew, *Jerusalem in Bible and Archaeology: The First Temple Period* (Atlanta: Society of Biblical Literature, 2003).

CHRONICLES

The Hebrew title of Chronicles translates to "the events of the days . . ." (דִּבְרֵי הַיָּמִים, *dibrê hayyāmîm*). The Septuagint identifies it as "the things omitted" or "the things passed over" (παραλειπόμενων; *paraleipomenōn*). Our title, Chronicles, derives from Jerome who described the book as containing "the chronicle of the whole of sacred history."[1]

The book was originally one volume in Hebrew, but the Septuagint divided it, likely because of the additional length required by the addition of vowels in Greek and the grammar necessary to render the equivalent Greek nuances from Hebrew. The marginal *Masora* notation identifies 1 Chronicles 27:25 as the midpoint of Chronicles.

Chronicles was apparently intended to be a continuous work with Ezra and Nehemiah, although this does not necessarily imply one author for the three books. Chronicles narrates the history of Israel from the establishment of Israel's Davidic monarchy to the demise of the kingdom into captivity and offers the returned people an explanation of their prospective relationship with God. Ezra and Nehemiah focus on Israel's release from captivity and the eventual reestablishment of the Temple and the attendant rituals and organization.

HISTORICAL AND CULTURAL BACKGROUND

The narrative of Chronicles spans the same chronological range as 2 Samuel and 1 and 2 Kings, however it does not simply repeat the story. The northern kingdom of Israel is largely ignored except as her history intersects that of Judah and her interests. Chronicles addresses a different audience in a different setting; it, therefore, has a different purpose than the Deuteronomistic History of Samuel and Kings.

---

[1]Dillard and Longman, *Introduction*, p. 169.

The Samuel and Kings narrative was primarily addressed to an audience of exiled Israelites who were wondering how they got to such a place and if there might be any hope beyond their exile. The date of the composition in its final form was about 550 B.C. while Israel was still in captivity. Chronicles, however, addresses a liberated Judah who has returned from exile to her land and is trying to make sense of her relationship with God.

Samuel and Kings had explained why Israel was in exile and only offered hope for deliverance. Chronicles offers the hope of restoration and God's accommodation of Israel back into a state of chosenness. This restored relationship, however, was contingent upon Israel's reform from earlier rebellion and the need to comply with God's law. This included reinstituting the ritual and ceremonial restoration of the Temple and the levitical system. Part of the focus is a messianic historiography of God's faithfulness to his promise to David and the enduring dynastic fulfillment, although the dynastic element retains a futuristic orientation for the returned exiles. The emphasis, then, is that God desires to have them back; he is still at work; he will keep his promise. While it does not consume much space and, in a sense, not much is made of it in the text, the Cyrus decree (2 Chr 36:22-23) is vivid indication of God's care to permit his people to return home.

TEXT AND AUTHOR

The Hebrew text of Chronicles is fairly well preserved. The Septuagint largely follows the Masoretic Text.[2] The Qumran discoveries have been of little help to refine the textual base since only a small fragment of one manuscript copy has been identified in the collection: 2 Chronicles 28:27–29:3.[3]

Chronicles is known, however, from a number of translations, among them are the Syriac Peshitta, Armenian, and Old Latin, but these are of limited value. Another source is the partial copy of Chronicles preserved in 1 Esdras which includes 2 Chronicles 35 and 36 and is attached to a continuous narrative with portions of

---

[2]Roland K. Harrison, *Introduction to the Old Testament* (Grand Rapids: Eerdmans, 1969), pp. 1169-1170; Gary N. Knoppers, *1 Chronicles 1–9*, AB 12 (New York: Doubleday, 2004), p. 56.

[3]Knoppers, *1 Chronicles 1–9*, p. 54.

Ezra and Nehemiah, but this, too, is in Greek. Knoppers notes that the Greek of the Apocryphal Chronicles is elegant and idiomatic Greek, whereas the Greek of the Septuagintal Chronicles, if translated back into Hebrew, appears to follow the Masoretic Text quite closely.[4] The relationship of the two sources to each other is a subject of significant debate,[5] but the evidence is limited and of little specific value except to raise questions.

The authorship of Chronicles is anonymous, but Jewish tradition attributes it to Ezra.[6] Attempts at authorial identification tend to revolve around the cultic, priestly, and levitical themes and the perceived continuity of Chronicles with the books of Ezra and Nehemiah. Ezra was of a priestly family (Ezra 7:1-6), and given his upbringing and the emphasis in Ezra and Nehemiah upon the stated themes, he is a reasonable candidate to propose.[7] Myers grants the viability of Ezra's authorship based largely on the similarity of themes and language.[8]

Evidence usually proposed for compositional unity is: 1) the transitional overlap of Cyrus's decree from Chronicles to Ezra; 2) 1 Esdras (ca. 150 B.C.) seems to present the books as a unit; 3) the similarity of vocabulary and grammar between the books; and 4) common theological emphasis.[9] A number of modern scholars, however, have continued to propose a single authorial composition of Chronicles, Ezra, and Nehemiah, but do not propose the author was necessarily Ezra.[10]

While the books exhibit a continuity in their conceptual sequence, these points do not necessarily imply single authorship. Dillard and

---

[4]Ibid., p. 56.

[5]Ibid. pp. 55-61.

[6]Babylonian Talmud, *Baba Bathra* 15a. A detailed discussion of authorship may be found in Knoppers, *1 Chronicles 1-9*, pp. 73-89.

[7]Cf. C.F. Keil, *The Books of the Chronicles*, trans. by A. Harper, Biblical Commentary on the Old Testament (repr., Grand Rapids: Eerdmans, n.d.), pp. 22-27.

[8]Jacob M. Myers, *I Chronicles*, AB 12 (Garden City, NY: Doubleday, 1965a), pp. lxxxvi-lxxxvii.

[9]These main points are taken from Dillard and Longman, *Introduction*, p. 171.

[10]Among these are Martin Noth (*Überlieferungsgeschichtliche Studien: Die sammelnden und bearbeitenden Geschichtswerke im Alten Testament* [Tübingen: Max Niemeyer, 1943], part of which is trans. into English as *The Chronicler's History*, JSOTSupp 50 [Sheffield: JSOT Press, 1943]), David J.A. Clines (*Ezra, Nehemiah, Esther*, NCB [Grand Rapids: Eerdmans, 1984], pp. 9-12), and Joseph Blenkinsopp (*Ezra-Nehemiah: A Commentary*, OTL [Louisville, KY: Westminster/John Knox, 1988], pp. 47-54).

Longman respond to the points above, noting how they are too simplistic.[11] The continuity of Chronicles to Ezra implied by the repetition of the Cyrus decree may have been a device by which to signal the uniting of two otherwise separate sources. Harrison notes that the repetition of the catch-line of Cyrus's decree was a common Mesopotamian literary style and that it was likely unknown to the later rabbinic writers.[12] The device does not necessarily imply unity of composition, but certainly implies unity of series. Ezra begins with the conjunction "and" (ו, *waw* in Hebrew), which is usually reserved for use in books that represent a continued thought (cf. Exodus, Leviticus, Numbers, Joshua, Judges, Samuel, Kings),[13] although it does not necessarily imply a continuation of the same author.[14]

As far as the combination of Chronicles with Ezra and Nehemiah in 1 Esdras is concerned, the combination may have just as easily occurred by consensus some time after Chronicles, Ezra, and Nehemiah were already written. It is unclear if 1 Esdras, composed ca. 150 B.C., reflects the original compositional understanding or a later perceived connection of the themes of the books.

While similarities exist in vocabulary and grammar, differences occur as well. The similarities may derive from the common pool of vocabulary and grammar dominant at the time. Additionally, though, the differences exist because of the different emphasis of the Chronicles as opposed to Ezra and Nehemiah. The former deals with the history of God's people prior to their exile, while the latter address explicitly the people in their contemporary state and concerns. Japhet has argued that if the author were the same for Chronicles and Ezra/Nehemiah, there are unexpected linguistic differences between them.[15]

There are undoubtedly some similarities in the theological issues of Chronicles with Ezra/Nehemiah, but the differences must not be

---

[11]Dillard and Longman, *Introduction*, pp. 171-172.

[12]Harrison, *Introduction*, p. 1169.

[13]Several of these are introduced with the common Hebrew word, וַיְהִי (*wayᵉhî*, traditionally rendered: "and it came to pass . . ."). Ezra, however, begins straightforwardly "And in the first year of Cyrus, king of Persia . . ." (1:1).

[14]The books of Esther and Ezekiel, however, utilize an initial "and" (*waw*), but these do not necessarily imply a continuation of thought.

[15]Sara Japhet, "The Supposed Common Authorship of Chronicles and Ezra–Nehemiah Investigated Anew," *VT* 18 (1968): 330-371.

ignored. Such emphasis differential appears especially in regard to the attitudes toward non-Israelites and the unfaithful.

Chronicles seems to seek a reunion of all Israel, including the northern remnants. Significant examples of this are Hezekiah's invitation to participate in the Passover (2 Chronicles 30); Josiah's acceptance of financial assistance from northerners (2 Chr 34:8-9); and the participation in the Passover celebration by all Judah and Israel during Josiah's reign (2 Chr 35:16-19).

Ezra/Nehemiah, on the other hand, seems to emphasize the need for isolationism. Zerubbabel refused to accept northern help to rebuild the Temple (Ezra 4:1-5). Ezra roundly denounced mixed marriages (Ezra 9–10), and Nehemiah advocated segregationist policies toward foreigners (Nehemiah 9, 13). One may argue that the demand for theological repentance implied the need for such denunciations and isolationism, but Ezra and Nehemiah seem to banish foreigners under any circumstances.

The consensus now is that the books of Chronicles and Ezra/Nehemiah are a continued thematic discussion, but most likely Chronicles was written by someone other than Ezra. If Ezra did not write Chronicles,[16] then the question is: "When was it written?" There is relatively little in the book from which to infer an answer, but certain parameters can be established.

Given the record of Cyrus's liberating decree at the end of Chronicles (36:22-23), the earliest date for the composition of the book (as we have it preserved) is ca. 539/538 B.C. Another indication is the reference to the daric coin (1 Chr 29:7) which is assumed to be named after Darius I,[17] who reigned ca. 522–486 B.C. But then the chronology would have to be of such duration that the coin become widely used for readers to recognize its legitimacy.[18]

A datum that suggests an even later *terminus ad quem* is the genealogical reference in 1 Chronicles 3:10-24, which lists at least two generations beyond Zerubbabel. Zerubbabel was one of the

---

[16]According to the traditional dating of Ezra, he arrived in Jerusalem in the seventh year of Artaxerxes I (Ezra 7:8) which would equate to ca. 458 B.C.

[17]John W. Betlyon, "Coinage," *ABD*, 1:1082.

[18]Given the assumption that the daric is named after Darius I, the use of the term in 1 Chronicles 29:7 is a retrofit of a denominational equivalent for the amount of gold contributed during David's reign for the Temple's construction.

leaders in the return from the exile (Ezra 2:2; Hag 1:1). Since the return from the exile could not occur before 538 B.C., two generations beyond Zerubbabel could push the compositional date into the fifth century B.C. Furthermore, the text in the Chronicles genealogy is difficult to decipher exactly, and there may be six generations represented, which would push the date even further.

The latest date for the composition of Chronicles would be ca. 200 B.C. Two major evidences for this inference are the citation of Chronicles in 1 Esdras, which was composed ca. 150 B.C.[19] The other ancient source citing Chronicles are writings by Eupolemus, a Jewish historian who lived in the middle of the second century B.C.[20]

The consensus of most conservative scholars is that Chronicles was written from ca. 450–350 B.C. If not by Ezra, it was written apparently by someone who shared some of his concerns relative to the need for a reformed people of God.

The writer makes it clear that he has consulted and apparently incorporated a number of sources in his research and composition.[21] These derive from canonical biblical sources as well as nonbiblical ones. From the Bible, the Chronicler utilized parts of the Pentateuch, sections of Joshua through Kings,[22] some of the prophets, Ezra and Nehemiah, and Psalms.

Among the extrabiblical sources, the Chronicler refers his readers to various books of prophets whose works have not been preserved. Among these are works by Samuel, Nathan, Gad (1 Chr 29:29), Ahijah and Iddo (2 Chr 9:29), Shemaiah and Iddo (2 Chr

---

[19]For discussions of 1 Esdras, see Harrison, *Introduction,* pp. 1196-1197; and William R. Goodman, "Esdras, First Book of," *ABD,* 2:609-611.

[20]Eupolemus was of the priestly family and is mentioned in 1 Maccabees 8:17 and 2 Maccabees 4:11. For further discussion of Eupolemus, see conveniently Carl R. Holladay, "Eupolemus," *ABD,* 2:671-672.

[21]A detailed discussion of the prospective sources used by the Chronicler appears in Knoppers, *1 Chronicles 1–9,* pp. 66-71, 118-128).

[22]Some of Samuel and Kings appear duplicated verbatim, but it is not clear if the Chronicler worked from those books specifically or if both the Chronicler and the Samuel/Kings author(s) may both have worked from a common, now missing, third source. On the basis of some of the Qumran materials, Cross suggests that the variations in details between Samuel/Kings and Chronicles may result from a manuscript of Samuel/Kings that differed from the Masoretic text (Frank Moore Cross Jr., "The History of the Biblical Text in the Light of the Discoveries in the Judaean Desert," *HTR* 57 [1964]: 281-299).

12:15), Jehu (2 Chr 20:34), and the "records of the seers" (2 Chr 33:19). The citations to the records of Isaiah may extend to a larger corpus of his (2 Chr 26:22; 32:32). Two references have caused scholars to wonder if the author used commentaries on the lives of the kings: the Chronicler notes references to "annotations of the prophet Iddo" (2 Chr 13:22) and "annotations on the book of the kings" (2 Chr 24:27). The Hebrew word (מִדְרָשׁ) rendered "annotations" in the NIV transliterates to *midrash*, which is usually understood to be a commentary. The author has taken other sources and tailored them to his point.

This selectivity and arrangement is not unique in the Bible. Similar selectivity of contents and emphasis are indicated in the New Testament as Luke indicates his investigation of the veracity of the events about which he writes (Luke 1:1-4) and John specifically notes that he has deliberately chosen certain events from the life of Jesus to make a specific point (John 20:30-31).

Additional materials that the Chronicler used were genealogical lists and laments (2 Chr 35:25; not a reference to the book of Lamentations).

HISTORY OF INTERPRETATION

In many ways, Chronicles has historically been a sort of hand-maid to the books of Samuel and Kings. This perception may in part have occurred because the Chronicles begin with what many people perceive as a burden wading through chapters of genealogies before the narrative sections begin. Furthermore, the book has a particularly strong emphasis on priestly concerns and typically limited narratives of the lives of the kings. The book received minimal attention from the early Christian communities until the nineteenth century.

Chronicles was generally assumed to be historically reliable until deWette argued it was not.[23] His conclusion, however, was fundamentally based upon the presupposition that the levitical system developed late in Israel. His premise was that with its bias toward levitical concerns, Chronicles was written late and it is, therefore, historically unreliable. Somewhat corroborating his conclusion are the large numbers that sometimes appear in Chronicles when com-

---

[23]Wilhelm Martin Lebrecht de Wette, *Beiträge zur Einleitung in das Alten Testament* (Halle: Schimmelpfennig, 1806–1807).

pared with those in Samuel and Kings.[24] This conclusion of limited historical value still lingers in some academic circles; Holloway has stated:

> 1 and 2 Chronicles is also a theological history of the Chosen People, beginning with Adam and concluding with Cyrus' Edict to the Judahite exiles. Because its synoptic narrative of the Divided Monarchy provides details "missing" in 1–2 Kings, generations of historians have selectively utilized it to create a conflated or harmonized image of "sacred history." More so than DTR, the Chronicler altered his sources and introduced *midrašim* to "rectify" his historical datum according to the exigencies of his theological program; the historical value of Chronicles is slender, and should be used with great caution for the purposes of historical reconstruction.[25]

However, other studies have revealed much more reliability of historical reconstruction and presentation than many skeptical scholars are willing to concede. Klein wrestles with these concerns in his article, but he seems unwilling fully to concede that there is more reliability than traditionally thought.[26] Archaeological studies, particularly under Albright, moved the discussion to a reliability of the narrative. However, this again has shifted to skepticism in many circles of academia. Often driving the conclusions are the presuppositions that the modern authors bring to the text and an almost unwillingness to look at and examine strategies by which the narratives may be harmonized.

Most scholars would likely agree, however, that the issues that are ultimately important are to determine the theological concerns. These should be the primary foci of discussion.

STRUCTURE

I. Genealogies of the Israelites — 1 Chr 1:1–9:44
II. United Monarchy — 1 Chr 10:1–2 Chr 9:31
   A. Saul and his sons die in battle — 10:1-14
   B. David reigns over Israel and Judah — 11:1–29:30

---

[24]See brief discussion below.
[25]Holloway, "Kings, Book of 1-2," *ABD*, 4:79.
[26]Ralph W. Klein, "Chronicles, Book of 1-2," *ABD*, 1:992-1002.

G. Athaliah seizes the throne of Judah — 22:10–23:7
H. Joash reigns in Judah — 23:8–24:27
    1. Joash is crowned — 23:8-11
    2. Athaliah is executed — 23:12-21
    3. Joash repairs the Temple — 24:1-14
    4. Joash apostatizes — 24:15-22
    5. Joash dies — 24:23-27
 I. Amaziah reigns in Judah — 25:1-28
    1. Amaziah slaughters Edomites — 25:1-16
    2. Israel defeats Judah — 25:17-24
    3. Amaziah is killed — 25:25-28
J. Uzziah reigns in Judah — 26:1-23
    1. Uzziah builds up military — 26:1-15
    2. Uzziah's pride leads to demise — 26:16-23
K. Jotham reigns in Judah — 27:1-9
L. Ahaz reigns in Judah — 28:1-27
    1. Ahaz worships other gods — 28:1-4
    2. Aram and Israel defeat Ahaz — 28:5-7
    3. Oded, the prophet, intervenes for Judah — 28:8-15
    4. Ahaz petitions for help from Assyria — 28:16-21
    5. Ahaz dies — 28:22-27
M. Hezekiah reigns in Judah — 29:1–32:33
    1. Hezekiah cleanses the Temple — 29:1-19
    2. Hezekiah restores Temple Worship — 29:20-36
    3. Hezekiah sponsors an all-Israel Passover — 30:1-27
    4. Hezekiah destroys rival high places — 31:1-10
    5. Hezekiah reorganizes priests and Levites — 31:11-21
    6. Sennacherib threatens Hezekiah — 32:1-23
    7. Hezekiah falls ill — 32:24-26
    8. Hezekiah's greatness expands — 32:27-33
N. Manasseh reigns in Judah — 33:1-20
    1. Manasseh leads Judah into sin — 33:1-9
    2. Manasseh repents of sin — 33:10-17
    3. Manasseh dies — 33:18-20
O. Amon reigns in Judah — 33:21-25
P. Josiah reigns in Judah — 34:1–35:27
    1. Josiah initiates religious reforms — 34:1-7
    2. Book of the Law discovered in the Temple — 34:8-21
    3. Josiah inquires of the Lord — 34:22-28
    4. Israel renews covenant with the Lord — 34:29-33
    5. All Israel celebrates Passover — 35:1-19

GENRE

Similar to the other historical books of the Hebrew Bible, Chronicles should not be considered a historical document defined according to modern historiographic criteria. This is not to deny a historical framework. On the contrary, as suggested above, the historicity of the accounts should be accepted, but we must attempt to respect the modes and conventions of expressions of the age. History is not just the listing of one fact after another; there is inevitably a focus, and the Chronicler has refined the historical drama significantly to preach to the restored Israelite community about their plight and expectations before the Lord who has led them back home from exile. Hence, the theology of the book cannot be ignored. Chronicles may be considered "Didactic History."

THEOLOGICAL THEMES

Several themes are interwoven into the didactic narrative of Chronicles. A major one is that even though Israel has been the recipient of God's displeasure and anger to send them into exile, Israel is still chosen by Yahweh! Over fifteen times the text speaks of God choosing (בָּחַר, *bāḥar*) significant components that define Israel as his! Among these are: he has chosen Judah as the leading tribe (1 Chr 28:4); David as his king (1 Chr 28:4; 2 Chr 6:6); Jerusalem as the city to place his name (2 Chr 6:5-6,34,38; 12:13; 33:7); Solomon as David's successor (1 Chr 28:6; 29:1); and the Solomonic Temple as the house for his name (1 Chr 28:10; 2 Chr 7:12,16). With the returned exiles, Haggai, Zechariah, and Zerubbabel will labor to reestablish the place where God caused his name to dwell, but Israel needs to seek the Lord according to his dictates.

The Chronicler will often speak of God's relation to those who seek him with their hearts. Regretfully, the modern Christian community often mistakenly caricatures the Old Testament as a rigid set of rules and regulations in which the hearts of the worshipers did not need to be engaged. Such a stereotype is grossly inaccurate. It is true, however, that the worshipers of old may have deluded themselves into such false senses of security — the prophets often derided Israel and Judah for such self-deceit (cf. Isa 1:10-20; Hos 6:1-6; Amos 5:21-24; Micah 6:6-8). Chronicles reminds and summons the returned exiles to seek the Lord with the heart[27] (cf. 1 Chr 16:10-11; 22:19; 28:9; 2 Chr 7:12-14; 11:16; 15:12,15; 19:3; 22:9; 30:19; 31:21).

Conversely, the text will note that God would abandon those who would forsake him (1 Chr 28:9; 2 Chr 15:2). While there is an almost deuteronomistic emphasis of blessings and cursings in Chronicles in some of these statements for the returned exiles (cf. 2 Chr 21:12-15; 33:7-8), the message was one of hope yet with warning! Dillard refers to this as a "theology of immediate retribution"[28] (1 Chr 28:8-9; 2 Chr 12:5-6) in which one should not infer that punishment will always be deferred — it may have an immediate impact.

Another theme with which the Chronicler was concerned was a "messianic historiography" which emphasized God's fulfillment of a dynastic concern for David's family.[29] When David expressed his determination to build the Temple, the Lord vetoed his desire, and vowed, in turn, to establish David's kingdom through one of his offspring (1 Chr 17:1-15) who is later identified as Solomon (1 Chr 22:6-10). Later monarchs are heirs because of the Lord's vow to David (cf. 2 Chr 21:7; 23:3).

A specific correlate ensconced in the Davidic dynastic promise is the sanctioning of the Temple construction. It was in the context of David's desire to build the Temple that the Lord revealed his intent to establish David's dynasty (1 Chronicles 17), however, the Temple itself would be constructed by David's son, Solomon (1 Chr 17:12; 28:2-6). The Temple is where the Lord would cause his name to dwell (2 Chr 6:3-42; 33:7-8).

For the newly returned exiles, the reconstruction of the Temple was of great importance; it was a manifestation of God's presence

---

[27]Not all the passages cited will include the word "heart," but a fair reading of the context and tone of the passages denotes such.

[28]Raymond B. Dillard, "Reward and Punishment in Chronicles: The Theology of Immediate Retribution," *WTJ* 46 (1984): 164-172.

[29]Dillard and Longman, *Introduction*, p. 174.

among them. Its reconstruction was the focus of Zerubbabel, who descended from David and Solomon (1 Chr 3:1-19; Ezra 3:1-3; Haggai; Zech 4:8-10). He was encouraged and assisted by the prophetic work of Haggai and Zechariah. This reconstruction of the Temple would easily be seen as a step by God toward reestablishing his ties with his people. The last concern to return was the monarchy!

NEW TESTAMENT CONNECTIONS

The anticipated reestablished messiahship was not fulfilled by Zerubbabel, nor by any other earthly king. This fulfillment awaited the coming of the king whose kingdom is not of this world (cf. John 18:36-37). The real temple was established by Jesus and is the one in which God's spirit dwells among his people (1 Cor 3:16). Induction into God's presence can only occur for one who honestly seeks the Lord (cf. Matt 6:33; John 4:23-24; Heb 11:6).

For those who do not seek the Lord, there will be deferred judgment (cf. 2 Thess 1:7-10; Rev 6:9-11), but there may also be more immediate retribution (cf. Acts 5:1-10; 1 Tim 5:24). The believer, however, realizes that not all suffering is necessarily connected directly with one's personal sin (John 9:1-3; Luke 13:1-5).

It would be difficult to identify many New Testament allusions that refer explicitly to Chronicles; however, Jesus' reference to the death of the priest, Zechariah (cf. 2 Chr 24:20-22), indicates familiarity with the book (Matt 23:34-35). Most understand the reference to the deaths of Abel to Zechariah to refer to the scope of the righteous who were killed or executed in the span of the Hebrew Bible's arrangement. Chronicles is the last book of the Hebrew Bible, which would span the deaths through the range of the Old Testament corpus — Genesis through Chronicles.[30]

SPECIAL ISSUES

The main issue that challenges the reader of Chronicles is the disparity between some of the numbers expressed in Chronicles as compared with the narratives elsewhere in the Hebrew Bible, par-

---

[30]For the English reader, the same effect would be expressed as Genesis through Malachi, since in English Bibles Malachi is the last book instead of Chronicles.

ticularly in Samuel and Kings. One example is the narrative relative to the price David paid for the place where he offered the sacrifice to curtail the Lord's anger. Samuel reveals that David paid fifty shekels of silver for the threshing floor of Araunah (2 Sam 24:24), whereas Chronicles states it was six hundred shekels of gold (1 Chr 21:25).[31] Another example is the difference in the census that was taken which precipitated the need for the Araunah sacrifice. The Samuel narrative reveals an army of 800,000 men of Israel with 500,000 from Judah (2 Sam 24:9), but 1 Chronicles 21:5 tallies 1,100,000 men of Israel and 470,000 men of Judah.

As a preliminary observation and one which should help keep the discussion in perspective, Payne notes that "of the 213 numbers that appear in Chronicles and that are paralleled elsewhere in Scripture, 194 agree with their parallels and no more than 19 exhibit some measure of difference."[32] Of the nineteen, some are lower and some are higher than their parallels elsewhere. This agreement calculates to 91.07 percent.

Differences, however, persist, and dealing with these differences can be challenging. Several explanations may be relevant.

Wenham offers a series of possibilities relative to the largeness of some of the numbers, some of which can be legitimately traced. He notes that there are difficulties in the state of the text and recognizes that sometimes the problem is our misunderstanding because of separation from the composition in time and culture.[33] Hence the problem may not always be in the text. One must, however, recognize the deterioration of text transmission through the centuries and millennia. Wenham lists various kinds of textual corruptions that can occur such as the inadvertent addition of extra zeros, accidentally deleting a digit, and a number entirely dropping out of the text.[34] In addition, the meaning of the number normally rendered

---

[31]The difference in the price paid may actually be the difference between the purchase of the cattle and the threshing floor in Samuel and the larger area which eventually became the entire Temple complex. While this is a reasonable explanation for the difference in this case, there are more intractable examples.

[32]J. Barton Payne, "Validity of Numbers in Chronicles," *NEASB* 11 (1978): 24.

[33]J.W. Wenham, "Large Numbers in the Old Testament," *TynBul* 18 (1967): 20-21.

[34]Ibid., pp. 21-24; see Wenham's article for additional reasons and examples.

"thousand" may sometimes translate differently.[35] Hebrew, of course, did not originally have the vowels represented, and so the three-consonant cluster of אלף (*'lp*) can have different meanings, depending upon how the vowels are arranged. Among the options are: "cattle," "thousand," "family," "clan," "tribal chief."[36] Of course, the context of usage will not permit all of these as options, but conceptual variations can come into play.

Some have suggested that the literary convention of the time and culture may have permitted legitimate use of extreme hyperbole to make a point.[37] Alternatively, Cross has concluded, based upon his study of the Dead Sea Scrolls collections, that the author may have had a different Hebrew manuscript before him than that from which the Masoretic text derives.[38]

The believer must face the difficulty that the differing data present, but Payne's observation should help keep the topic in perspective. Some of the concerns may be more perceived than real, given we are so separated by time and cultural norms from the original context of Chronicles' composition.[39]

[35]Ibid., pp. 24-25.

[36]BDB, pp. 48-49; William L. Holladay, ed., *A Concise Hebrew and Aramaic Lexicon of the Old Testament* (Grand Rapids: Eerdmans, 1988), pp. 17-18.

[37]Harrison, *Introduction*, p. 1165.

[38]Cross, "History," pp. 281-299.

[39]While no longer fashionable, John Haley's work, *An Examination of the Alleged Discrepancies of the Bible*, is still useful. The work is quite dated (ca. 1874) and many of the explanations facile, but there are still numerous valuable insights that many scholars either overlook or refuse to recognize.

EZRA-NEHEMIAH

The names of the books, Ezra (עֶזְרָא) and Nehemiah (נְחֶמְיָה) derive from the main characters in the respective books. They are considered one book in the Hebrew canon and the Babylonian Talmud cites the combined work simply as Ezra.[1] Even though they recognized a difference between the two books, the Masoretes considered them a unit as indicated by their marginal notes which cite Nehemiah 3:32 as the middle verse of the composition. By the time of Origen (third century A.D.) and Jerome (fourth century A.D.) they were separated into their respective identities.

Even though Ezra/Nehemiah was considered one volume by the Hebrews, the almost verbatim repetition of the genealogical lists in Ezra 2 and Nehemiah 7 seems to indicate that the books were originally separate compositions (see further below).

The Hebrew Bible places Ezra/Nehemiah in the section of Scripture known as the Writings (כְּתוּבִים, k°thûbîm), sometimes called the Hagiographa ("Sacred Writings"). Ezra/Nehemiah generally appears immediately before Chronicles, but in some traditions, Chronicles heads the Writings section with Ezra–Nehemiah terminating it.

In the Septuagint, the arrangement is along historical lines in two major sweeps. The Deuteronomistic History from Deuteronomy through Kings has Ruth embedded in its proper chronological sequence immediately after the book of Judges. The series of history books beginning with Chronicles through Ezra, Nehemiah, and Esther are arranged chronologically and were written in the postexilic period and with postexilic concerns.[2]

---

[1] *Baba Bathra* 15a.

[2] A good, brief discussion of the placement of Ezra/Nehemiah in the various versions may be found in Harrison, *Introduction*, p. 1136.

291

HISTORICAL AND CULTURAL BACKGROUND

The background for Ezra/Nehemiah is strongly embedded in the Babylonian conquest and exile under Nebuchadnezzar. The Babylonians made three forays into Judah with varying degrees of impact. The first was soon after the death of Josiah, when the Babylonians in 605 brought Jerusalem under their auspices and at which time they took Daniel into exile (2 Kgs 24:1; Dan 1:1). Because of Judah's persistent insubordination and attempts to align with Egypt, Nebuchadnezzar came a second time in 597 B.C. and captured Jehoiachin, taking him to Babylon as an in-house hostage (2 Kgs 24:10-16). He also took into exile a large number of crafts-men and artisans as well as the military pool (2 Kgs 24:16) and Ezekiel (cf. Ezek 1:1-2). In addition to taking the king into exile, a compounding ideological blow was the plundering of many of the vessels and goods from the Temple (2 Kgs 24:13). He put Jehoiachin's uncle on the throne, changing his name to Zedekiah, but Zedekiah eventually rebelled against the Babylonian overlords, precipitating their return a third time (2 Kgs 24:17–25:2).

This third campaign was most severe. Nebuchadnezzar laid siege to the city and destroyed the fortifications; furthermore, he burned the Temple and plundered the remaining goods associated with it (cf. 2 Kgs 25:8-17; Jer 52:12-23). Contrary to the Assyrian policy which often involved replacement populations from other coun-tries, the Babylonians did not import other people into Judah. They did, however, leave some residents in the land of Judah to work the fields (cf. 2 Kgs 25:12; Jer 52:16). Lamentations gives a good descrip-tion of the depressed state in Judah after the Temple's destruction and the decimation of the populace.

The people in exile were centered at this point in Babylon, at least as far as the correspondence and narrative is concerned. Ezekiel was the local prophet in charge through whom God's primary commu-niques were delivered. Psalm 137 reflects the deep sorrow of those in Babylon as they reflected on their demise. Jeremiah, however, admonished the people to make the best of their surroundings and build houses, plant gardens, continue with their daily lives, and seek the welfare of where they were (Jer 29:3-9). He informed them that seventy years of separation were on the horizon (Jer 25:11-12; 29:10).[3]

---

[3]Exactly how to understand this number is a challenge and open to

Apparently a good many of the exiles took Jeremiah's advice, because the evidence indicates not all the exiles returned when given the opportunity.[4]

For the remaining population in Judah, the deprivation of the Temple inevitably curtailed any proper sacrificial system. There are hints in the Bible, however, that some kind of ritual continued at the site as people brought incense to burn at the Temple (Jer 41:5), probably more a reference to the site than to a structure.

Some of the people of Judah refused to stay in the land, but fled to Egypt, forcibly taking Jeremiah with them (Jer 41:17–43:7) where some of Jeremiah's prophetic indictments occurred (Jer 43:8–44:30). The exiles settled in the regions of Migdol, Tahpanhes, Memphis, and Pathros (Jer 44:1), which indicates that they had become rather widespread. Extrabiblical evidence of a southward migration is indicated in the collection of Elephantine letters at the first cataract of the Nile (known in the NIV as Aswan; cf. Isa 49:12; Ezek 29:10; 30:6). A settlement of Jews occurred here as early perhaps as 540 B.C., and correspondence from the site has been dated to ca. 495 B.C. Some of the correspondence refers to the presence of a Temple to Yahweh (Yaho in the correspondence) when Cambyses went to Egypt ca. 525 B.C.[5]

While the Hebrews were in Babylonian exile, the dominant political power began to founder. Nabonidus, who was the last Babylonian king, was little interested in affairs of state, but was significantly distracted by religious pursuits in Teman of Arabia and in Harran as he apparently pursued the worship of Sin.[6] It appears that Nabonidus's distractions were sources of irritation with the Marduk

---

debate. One interesting observation is that a 71-year span existed from the destruction of the Temple in 586 B.C. to its rededication in 515 B.C.

[4]Two biblical examples of this would be Daniel, who continued his prophetic career well into the period after Cyrus's decree (Dan 6:28), and Esther's family, which was still in Persia during the early fifth century B.C. (Esth 1:1). Esther further indicates that Jews were widely scattered in the empire (Esth 3:8,13; 9:1-19). This dispersion is the context of the development of the Diaspora (see George A. Van Alstine, "Dispersion," ISBE[2], fully rev. ed., ed. by G.W. Bromiley [Grand Rapids: Eerdmans, 1979], 1:962-963).

[5]Bazelel Porten, "Request for Letter of Recommendation (First Draft) (3.51)," COS, 3:125-130.

[6]Ronald H. Sack, "Nabonidus (Person)," ABD, 4:975.

priesthood in Babylon, which may have been seen as threats to Marduk's supremacy.[7]

In the meantime, Cyrus was consolidating the Persian and Median peoples under his rule. With Nabonidus distracted by other concerns, Cyrus was able to position himself to take over the Babylonian empire with relative ease. By the time Nabonidus returned to Babylon, his power base had dissolved and Cyrus was able to take advantage of the deterioration and take over. Cyrus claims to have entered Babylon without a battle[8] and presented himself as the savior of the resident temples and decreed that they be subsidized.

Cyrus was viewed as a savior for Israel as well. The Lord refers to him as his "anointed" (Isa 45:1), who would be instrumental in rebuilding the Temple (Isa 44:28; 45:13). Cyrus's decree, permitting captive peoples to return to their homelands, was seen as the fulfillment of this prophecy. While the decree that was discovered in Babylon in 1879[9] does not read exactly like the decree recorded in 2 Chronicles 22:23 and Ezra 1:2-4, there is no question but that the essence of the decree is valid — Cyrus was a savior to permit the Israelites to return to their homeland and to repatriate the plundered Temple goods (cf. Ezra 1:7-11).

As far as restoring the worship of Yahweh in Jerusalem was concerned, the first item of business was to rebuild the broken down altar (Ezra 3:3). The major concern for rebuilding the altar, as indicated in the text, was the Jews' fear of the residents of the land (Ezra 3:3). Their next goal was to rebuild the Temple itself, which inevitably required more preparation and time. They needed to secure the necessary building materials and to establish the work shifts. Once the foundations of the Temple were laid, the returnees were challenged by the people of the land who bribed officials to thwart their work (Ezra 4:4-5). These were essentially the Samaritan authorities under Tattenai, the governor of the region (Ezra 5:3-5). They successfully stalled the reconstruction until 515 B.C. when the

---

[7]Cyrus accuses Nabonidus of eliminating Marduk's worship and says that Marduk summoned Cyrus to reinstate the proper worship (see Mordechai Cogan, "Cyrus Cylinder (2.124)," *COS*, 2:314-316).

[8]The battles had occurred earlier and elsewhere. Cyrus claims that no battle occurred (cf. ibid.) and the assessment is repeated in the Babylonian Chronicle (A. Millard, "The Babylonian Chronicle (1.137)," *COS*, 1:467-468).

[9]See Cogan, "Cyrus Cylinder," 2:314-316.

prophets Haggai and Zechariah inspired and urged Zerubbabel to finish the work.

The conflict with Tattenai was symptomatic of many of the conflicts that the returned exiles experienced as the more established residents of the northern territory of Samaria viewed the construction of the Temple as a threat to their power and influence. Eventually, however, a full political and economic break occurred between Judah (known as *yehud* in Hebrew) and Samaria. This is exemplified by the presence of numerous stamps in Israel known as *yhd* stamps which differentiate the region from Samaria. From Samaria has come a stamp mentioning an "Isaiah son of Sanballat, *peḥa* ('governor') of Samaria."[10]

Once the Temple was rebuilt, though, no significant progress occurred in rebuilding Jerusalem until Ezra and Nehemiah arrived, each of whom had distinct roles in Judah. The edict of Artaxerxes recorded in Ezra 7:12-26 notes a fourfold mission for Ezra: 1) to lead to Jerusalem exiled Jews who wished to return (Ezra 7:13), 2) to inquire regarding the status of Judah and Jerusalem (7:14; 10:6-7), 3) to gather and deliver goods for the Temple ritual and administration (7:15-20), and 4) to install magistrates and judges to teach and administer justice and God's law (7:25-26).

Nehemiah's roles were not as many, but were equally important. His consisted of orchestrating the reconstruction of Jerusalem's walls (Neh 2:7-8) and apparently to serve as governor (פֶּחָה, *peḥāh*; Neh 5:14; 12:26; הַתִּרְשָׁתָא, *hattîršāthā'*; 8:9; 10:2) of Judah. Of course, he encounters significant opposition from magistrates already in the region — Sanballat, Tobiah, and Geshem (Neh 2:9-10; 4:1-5; 6:1-14).

Yamauchi has suggested that Ezra's presence in Judah would have been additionally valuable as someone sympathetic with Persian ideals since there was political unrest in the region because of agitation from Egypt.[11] Meyers similarly notes that the arrival of Nehemiah with an armed contingent would serve to stabilize this extremity of the empire in the face of Egyptian rebellions.[12] This addition-

---

[10]Ephraim Stern, *Archaeology of the Land of the Bible: The Assyrian, Babylonian, and Persian Periods (732–332 B.C.E.)* (New York: Doubleday, 2001), 2:548-552.

[11]Edwin Yamauchi, "The Archaeological Background of Nehemiah," *BSac* 137 (1980): 294.

[12]Eric M. Meyers, "The Persian Period and the Judean Restoration: From Zerubbabel to Nehemiah," in *Ancient Israelite Religion: Essays in Honor of*

al political concern is not out of the question, but the Bible's emphasis is upon the religious issues; the international political concerns are irrelevant to the theological/didactic purpose of the books.

Corroborating Yamauchi's and Meyer's suggestions, Stern notes the existence of a series of fortresses in southern Canaan/Palestine. Specifically, Arad has yielded an ostracon with a Persian term that applies to a Persian military unit.[13] Some of this military unrest with Egypt is part of the larger conflict in which the Persians were engaged with the Greeks. There is evidence that parts of the southeastern Levantine region was allied with the Athenians[14] who less than a half century before Ezra's and Nehemiah's arrival had been a major object of Persia's military focus.[15]

The Exile had a number of effects on the Jews. With the deprivation of the Temple, its ritual and personnel, and the implied ideological definition that they had served, the exiles finally concluded that they were at odds with Yahweh. Jeremiah's exhortation to pray for the welfare of their seventy-year exiled locale (Jer 29:3-9) pointed to an eventual return, but in the meantime, what were they to do? Being cut off from the Temple and its ritual, the exiles began to gravitate toward more emphasis upon prayer and study. This apparently is the clouded origins of the synagogue, although the exact origins are unclear.[16] There is perhaps an allusion to an incipient synagogue setting in Ezekiel 33:30-33, as Ezekiel communicates the word of Yahweh to the exiles.

The Israelite dispersion, especially when Aramaic was emerging as the dominant political and economic language of the world, contributed to the demise of the prevalence of Hebrew among the Jews. Although Aramaic is similar to Hebrew, the dispersed Hebrews eventually lost their familiarity with the mother tongue and adopted their new socially contextualized language. From the destruction of

---

Frank Moore Cross," ed. by P.D. Miller Jr., P.D. Hanson, and S.D. McBride (Philadelphia: Fortress Press, 1980), pp. 514-517.

[13]Ephraim Stern, "Between Persia and Greece: Trade, Administration and Warfare in the Persian and Hellenistic Periods (539–563 BCE)," in *The Archaeology of Society in the Holy Land*, ed. by T.E. Levy (New York: Facts on File, Inc., 1995), p. 432.

[14]Yamauchi, "Archaeological Background," p. 294.

[15]These in particular would be the defeats of the Persians at Marathon (490 B.C.) and the sea battle at Salamis (480 B.C.).

[16]Eric M. Meyers, "Synagogue (Introductory Survey)," *ABD*, 6:252.

the Temple (ca. 586 B.C.) to Ezra's reading of the law (Neh 8:1-8; ca. 445 B.C.), some 140 years elapsed. When Ezra read the law to the people, some question exists of what is meant by the statement "making it clear and giving the meaning" (Neh 8:8). Some suggest it refers to a commentary or midrash on what was read, while others suggest that it was a translation of the Hebrew into Aramaic.[17]

This loss of familiarity with the Hebrew mother tongue probably precipitated the eventual production of the Septuagint. Most scholars do not subscribe to the almost-apocryphal story of the letter of Aristeas, but recognize that part of the impetus for the production of the Septuagint was a need-based circumstance of the dispersed Jewish community in the Greek world.

TEXT AND AUTHOR

Several books appeared in the ancient world by the name of Ezra (Esdras), but our concern is only with Ezra/Nehemiah of canonical ascription. The Hebrew text is fairly well preserved and its syntax and structure are appropriate for postexilic Hebrew,[18] however, as might be suspected with a postexilic production in the Persian period, many Persian words and expressions appear in the text.

The translations, however, are problematic. Significant variations exist between the Vaticanus and Alexandrinus productions, both of which tend to be shorter than the MT. The Vaticanus is the shorter of the two.[19] Some scholars think Sinaiticus is the best of the three.[20] Myers notes that the Vulgate reflects the Hebrew text closely.[21]

Both books have significant blocks that are written in the first person. It is natural, therefore, to infer that Ezra and Nehemiah were the authors of their respective books. Ezra was a priest and a scribe (Ezra 7:1-6), and Nehemiah is presented as an able administrator. There is some question as to whether the third person sec-

---

[17]The Palestinian Jews of the first century A.D. predominantly spoke Aramaic rather than Hebrew, which serves as part of Paul's argument for his boasting in the flesh (Phil 3:5) — he was one who knew Hebrew, the mother tongue!

[18]Jacob M. Myers, *Ezra–Nehemiah*, AB 14 (Garden City, NY: Doubleday, 1965), p. lxiii.

[19]Ibid, p. lxv.

[20]Ibid.

[21]Ibid., p. lxvi.

tions were written by Ezra and Nehemiah, but Koch has noted that there are some literary conventions that would see those sections as personal compositions as well.[22] The tone of the book sounds as if it were written in Palestine/Judah, where the bulk of the activity occurs. Corroborating this inference would be the governorship of Nehemiah as he worked in the region to stabilize it both politically and religiously.

The questions of dates focus upon two major concerns: when did the events take place, and when were the books put together? The dates of Nehemiah's activities are fairly secure, especially with the discovery of the Elephantine correspondence. These refer to Johanan, Eliashib, and Sanballat in extrabiblically dated correspondence, which has therefore corroborated the traditional dating of Nehemiah's work.[23] The Bible states that his first trip to Judah commenced in the twentieth year of Artaxerxes (Neh 2:1; = ca. 445 B.C.) and his last recorded activity was in the thirty-second year of the reign of Artaxerxes (= 433 B.C.), when he had returned to Persia (Neh 13:6). He states, however, that he returned to Judah sometime after this (Neh 13:6-7), but does not say how long he stayed (if not until his death). Artaxerxes I reigned from 465–425 B.C.

References in the Elephantine correspondence on a letter dated specifically to the seventeenth year of Darius (= ca. 407) cite "Delaiah and Shelemiah sons of Sanballat governor of Samaria"[24] who would have been the Sanballat who opposed Nehemiah (Neh 2:9-10; 4:7-8; 6:1). The information places Sanballat significantly earlier than the date of the letter.[25] The dating of Sanballat from the Elephantine letter dovetails with the data provided in Nehemiah for his arrival (Neh 2:1).[26]

---

[22]Klaus Koch, "Ezra and the Origins of Judaism," *JSS* 19 (1974): 177-178. Interestingly, the Cyrus Decree itself presents a mixture of first and third person perspective (see Cogan, "Cyrus Cylinder," pp. 314-316).

[23]Richard J. Saley ("The Date of Nehemiah Reconsidered," in *Biblical and Near Eastern Studies: Essays in Honor of William Sanford LaSor*, ed. by G.A. Tuttle [Grand Rapids: Eerdmans, 1972], pp. 151-165) continues to suggest dating the events in the fourth century B.C. instead of the fifth, but his arguments do not carry much weight.

[24]Porten, "Request," p. 130.

[25]The Elephantine correspondence does not refer to Nehemiah or Ezra.

[26]Intriguing is the reference to a Hananiah who visits the Elephantine community in 419/418 B.C. (see Bazelel Porten, "The Passover Letter (3.46)," *COS*, 3:116-117). He visits the community to investigate some activities and

The date of Ezra's activities are more challenging, and the proposals surround three possibilities. Ezra traveled to Judah in the seventh year of Artaxerxes (Ezra 7:8). The question, however, is which Artaxerxes? Three kings by that name reigned in the span of the Persian empire: Longimanus (465–425 B.C.), Mnemon (405–358 B.C.), and Ochus (359–339 B.C.). Since the last of these is out of the chronological range of Nehemiah, he should be excluded from consideration.

The simplest assessment, since Ezra and Nehemiah worked together (Neh 8:9), is to identify the first Artaxerxes as the one under whom Ezra worked, which would yield an exodus date of 458 B.C.[27] However, some historical questions arise if Ezra is placed this early such as the reference to the existence of a wall to which Ezra refers in his prayer when he arrives (Ezra 9:9).

An alternative date takes as its cue the second Artaxerxes (405–358 B.C.) and yields a date of 398 B.C. This would resolve the problem of the reference to a wall (Ezra 9:9) and would also help alleviate the assumption of some scholars that neither Ezra nor Nehemiah refer specifically to each other in their speeches.[28] An additional concern is Ezra's connection with a man named Jehohanan son of Eliashib (Ezra 10:6) who later is identified in the succession of high

---

give instructions on how properly to observe the Passover. Nehemiah 7:2 mentions Nehemiah's brother, named Hananiah (Hanani is a variant spelling) into whose care Nehemiah leaves the administration of Jerusalem. Regretfully, Hananiah was a common name of this period (as indicated in 7:2 by reference to another Hananiah), and it is impossible to make a certain connection between Nehemiah's brother and the Elephantine correspondence. William F. Albright (*The Biblical Period from Abraham to Ezra* [New York: Harper & Row, 1963], p. 94), however, suggests an identity.

[27]A number of scholars subscribe to this date; among them are Frank Moore Cross ("A Reconstruction of the Judean Restoration," *JBL* 94 [1975]: 4-18), Roland de Vaux ("Israel (Histoire de)," in *Dictionnaire de la Bible, Supplément* [Paris: Letouzey et Ané, 1928–], 4:764-769), and Koch ("Ezra," pp. 173-197).

[28]Among the scholars who propose this reconstruction are Harold Henry Rowley ("The Chronological Order of Ezra and Nehemiah," in *The Servant of the Lord and Other Essays on the Old Testament* [London: Lutterworth, 1952], pp. 129-159) and J.A. Emerton ("Did Ezra Go to Jerusalem in 428 B.C.?" *JTS*, ns 17 [1966]: 1-19). The conclusion of this assumption creates another problem: how to explain the appearance of Nehemiah and Ezra together in the narrative portions of Nehemiah. The assumption usually proposes that the texts are manipulated at a later date to make the people appear to be contemporary.

priests (Neh 12:22-23); this would place Ezra quite late. An Eliashib is noted as the high priest in Nehemiah 3:1, and for either his son (or grandson) to be high priest when Ezra associates with him would tend to be late.[29]

Several assumptions are usually made in this analysis which are not necessarily valid. One is that Ezra 10:6 refers to Jehohanan as the high priest, which the text does not say; he may have simply had quarters in the Temple area where he spent the night, perhaps as an attendant. Second, there are a number of people in the text during this period who are named Jehohanan or something similar; most of the names have variant readings (see for instance a citation in Nehemiah 12:13 and then again another in 12:22-23).[30] Third, even if Jehohanan were high priest for the Ezra 10:6 event, it would not be beyond reason to assume Ezra might still be alive in ca. 407 B.C. The priestly role was designated in Numbers as 30 to 50 years of age (Num 4:3; 8:24 indicates a 25-year-old accession age), but this relates to the Tabernacle/Temple rituals. Ezra would likely have been at least 30 when he began his journey to Israel (Ezra 7:1-7), but his role was significantly broader than his ritual roles; it is conceivable that he might still be alive in 407 B.C. which would make him ca. eighty-one years old.[31] The Bible notes that Eli was 98 when he died (1 Sam 4:15) and Aaron was 123 (Num 33:39). Perhaps the demands in the effort to rebuild the Temple and reinstitute its worship required a younger age for induction into the levitical work; Ezra 3:8 refers to Levites from age twenty and older. If Ezra were twenty when he left Persia, he would have been only about seventy in 407 B.C.!

A third date proposal has been offered that attempts to recognize that Ezra and Nehemiah were contemporaries and still place them in the reign of Artaxerxes I. Bright following Albright has proposed that the text of Ezra is corrupt and that the number "thirty" has dropped out of the text, leaving only the "seven."[32] If his pro-

---

[29]Loring W. Batten, *The Books of Ezra and Nehemiah*, ICC (Edinburgh: T. & T. Clark, 1913), p. 29.

[30]The Elephantine letters refer to Jehohanan who was high priest in Jerusalem (Porten, "Request," p. 128). The letter is dated to 407 B.C.

[31]While not a definite source of confirmation, Josephus states that Ezra died an old man and was buried in Jerusalem (*Ant* 11.5.5).

[32]John Bright, *A History of Israel*, 3rd ed. (London: SCM Press, 1981), pp. 391-402; Albright, *Biblical Period*, p. 93, n. 193. The deletion of a number is similar to the problem in the Hebrew text for Saul's reign as recorded in 1 Sam 13:1, which preserves only a partial number.

posal is valid Ezra's return would have been in ca. 428 B.C. after the wall was built and would permit the two men to have been contemporaries. A major problem with this reconstruction is that there is absolutely no hint of manuscript evidence for it from the Hebrew texts or the translations.

A resolution of the problem is outside the purview of this discussion, but the principle enunciated by Williamson seems relevant ". . .we believe that this clear statement of the text as it stands should be given the greatest possible weight."[33] Each proposal raises its own historical problems, and as far as reading the text in a straightforward manner, there is no intrinsic challenge to demand that the chronological scheme implied in the text should be overturned. Hence, given the data, a reasonable time frame for the activities and recording of the events narrated in Ezra/Nehemiah would be ca. 400 B.C.[34] Williamson argues that the bulk of Ezra/Nehemiah was composed by 400 B.C., but that the preface material consisting of Ezra 1–6 was added ca. 300 B.C.[35]

Clearly the events of the introductory material of Ezra 1–6 hark from a significantly earlier time than the lives of Ezra or Nehemiah. A number of sources can reasonably be identified in the structure of the books. Among them are: 1) a list of inventory returned to the Temple (Ezra 1:9-11); 2) lists of genealogies and census records (Ezra 2:2-70; Neh 7:5-73; 12:1-26); 3) official correspondence and historical documents consisting of Cyrus's decree in Aramaic (Ezra 6:3-5) and the correspondence between Tattenai and Darius (Ezra 5:7-17), some of which is in Aramaic (Ezra 4:6–6:18; 7:12-26); 4) speeches and prayers (Ezra 9:6-15; Neh 1:5-11; 9:1-37); and 5) the Memoirs of Ezra (chs. 7–10, some of which is in the first person, some in third

---

[33]H.G.M. Williamson, *Ezra, Nehemiah,* WBC 16 (Waco, TX: Word Books, 1985), p. xliii.

[34]So affirm a number of scholars; among them Myers (*Ezra–Nehemiah,* p. lxx), Clines (*Ezra, Nehemiah, Esther,* pp. 13-14), and Sara Japhet just a little later ("Sheshbazzar and Zerubbabel — Against the Background of the Historical and Religious Tendencies of Ezra–Nehemiah," *ZAW* 94 [1982]: 89, n. 55).

[35]Williamson's argument (*Ezra, Nehemiah,* pp. xxxv-xxxvi) operates on the assumption that the preface material is partly intended to serve as a polemic against the Samaritan temple that was built on Mount Gerizim during the late fourth century B.C. (see Josephus, *Ant* 11.7-8). It is to the ruins of this temple that the woman at the well alludes in her conversation with Jesus (John 4:20-21).

person) and the Memoirs of Nehemiah (Neh 1:1–7:5). Hill and Walton have suggested that Ezra and Nehemiah drafted their individual memoirs ca. 440–420 B.C., after which the Chronicler combined them and interwove the narrative material to which he added the introductory material relative to the work of Sheshbazzar and Zerubbabel.[36] The critical element would be when the Chronicler accomplished his work.

STRUCTURE

   I. First Exiles Return to Judah – Ezra 1:1–2:70
     A. Cyrus frees captives – 1:1-4
     B. Israelites prepare to return home – 1:5-10
     C. Zerubbabel leads Israel home – 2:1-70
  II. People Rebuild Altar and Temple – 3:1–6:22
     A. Israel rebuilds altar – 3:1-7
     B. Israel begins to rebuild Temple – 3:8-13
     C. Adversaries oppose Temple reconstruction – 4:1–6:22
        1. Zerubbabel refuses help of adversaries – 4:1-5
        2. Adversaries write Artaxerxes and stop work – 4:6-24
        3. Haggai and Zechariah inspire resumption of Temple construction – 5:1–6:22
           a. Prophets urge to resume work – 5:1-2
           b. Tattenai inquires regarding authority for Temple construction – 5:3-5
           c. Tattenai writes Darius to stop work – 5:6-17
           d. Darius investigates and authorizes work – 6:1-12
           e. Israel finishes Temple reconstruction – 6:13-15
           f. Israel rededicates Temple and festivals – 6:16-22
 III. Ezra Returns to Judah to Instruct Judah – 7:1–10:44
     A. Ezra seeks to teach God's laws – 7:1-10
     B. Ezra receives commission from Artaxerxes – 7:11-28
     C. Ezra lists exiles who return with him – 8:1-14
     D. Ezra selects Temple servants – 8:15-20
     E. Ezra returns to Judah – 8:21-36
        1. Ezra fasts and seeks God's favor – 8:21-23
        2. Ezra distributes Temple wealth among priests – 8:24-30
        3. Ezra arrives in Jerusalem – 8:31-36

---

[36]Andrew E. Hill and John H. Walton, *A Survey of the Old Testament*, 2nd ed. (Grand Rapids: Zondervan, 2000), p. 269.

E. Nehemiah makes provisions for Levites — 12:44-47

F. Nehemiah executes further reforms — 13:1-31

   1. Israel separates Ammonites and Moabites from ranks — 13:1-3

   2. Nehemiah casts Tobiah's furnishings out of the Temple — 13:4-9

   3. Nehemiah insists Levites receive portions — 13:10-14

   4. Nehemiah enforces Sabbath law — 13:15-22

   5. Nehemiah enforces separation from foreign wives — 13:23-31

GENRE

The books of Ezra/Nehemiah are clearly historiographic, but with a significant didactic application. The goal is not simply to trace the return from Exile and the efforts of the returnees to rebuild the altar and Temple. The focus is didactic as Ezra and Nehemiah challenge the fledgling community to a proper worship of Yahweh along with the restoration of the security of Jerusalem's walls. References to other real people, such as Sanballat and Jehohanan (see discussions above), who come into the narrative and who have been identified in extrabiblical sources, demonstrate a credible historical base.

THEOLOGICAL THEMES

Ezra/Nehemiah focuses on several important theological themes. The emphasis at the beginning on the return from Exile is vital. The implied theological significance is that God is loyal and has not forgotten his people — he is a covenant keeper, still working behind the scenes even through non-Israelite peoples (see Ezra 1:1-4; 10:2; Neh 9:32; 13:6). However, not only does God sanction his work through the Persian monarchy, but he continues to work among his people (Ezra 7:6,9-10,27-28).

The reconstruction of the Temple was an important theological affirmation. It fulfilled God's prophetic declarations that he would see to its reconstruction (Isa 44:28; 45:1,13). A major correlate with the rebuilding of the Temple, however, was the inevitable need to bring the people back to a full covenant renewal in part to prevent a repeat of the recent devastating exile. Their apathy to rebuild the walls (Nehemiah 1–3) was symptomatic of a larger neglect of serious devotion to the Lord's will. The people therefore needed to be reoriented to the Law (Neh 8:1-2).

As the people listened to the declaration and explanation of the Law, it served as their directive to restore proper worship. This was explicitly indicated in their celebration of the Feast of Booths as they read of its prescription (Neh 8:12-18). The Sabbath observance also resulted from their reorientation to the Law (Neh 10:31; 13:15-22) as well as did the restoration of priestly and levitical lines (Neh 13:12-14,28-29) and the realization that foreigners should be excluded from the Temple (Neh 13:1-3). The deliberate exclusion of the offer from the Samaritans to assist in the rebuilding of the Temple (Ezra 4:1-3) fits this theological framework. Ezra's (10:6-44) and Nehemiah's (13:23-27) insistence upon ethnic purity echoed the injunctions the Lord had delivered in the Law not to intermarry with the Canaanites of their earlier history (cf. Deut 7:2-3). Part of the restoration of God's will involved addressing the social injustices that the Jerusalem residents were inflicting on each other (Neh 5:1-13; cf. Exod 22:25; Lev 25:36).

NEW TESTAMENT CONNECTIONS

Surprisingly, neither Ezra nor Nehemiah are mentioned in the New Testament. The impact of their activities, however, resonate throughout it. Ezra's determination, as a levite and a scribe, to dedicate himself "to the study and observance of the Law of the LORD, and to teaching its decrees and laws in Israel" (Ezra 7:10) serves as the foundation of the emergence of the scribal school that plays so prominently in the activities of the first century A.D.

While there was a need for the ethnic exclusivity which Ezra and Nehemiah demanded, there was a real danger of overextending it to look with arrogance and disdain upon other peoples. There is no intrinsic reason to attribute these intents to Ezra or Nehemiah, but their reforms easily led to the attitudes that characterized the Pharisees of Jesus' time. The obsession that developed by the first century A.D. regarding clean and unclean (cf. Matt 15:1-9; Mark 7:1-9,17-23) had so stifled the perspectives of many of the Jews that they had difficulty seeing how to relate to the nations. Peter wrestled with such issues to the extent that the Lord had to provide several special lessons to help him see that the gospel was for all peoples (Acts 10–11; cf. Gal 2:11-14). The attitude apparently placed under a bushel the idea that they were to be a "light to the nations" (Isa 42:6-7; 51:4; 2:1-4; 9:2-7; Micah 4:2-5; Luke 2:31-32).

The episodes of Ezra/Nehemiah also help flesh out some of the background of the Samaritan conflicts that appear in the New Testament. Ezra/Nehemiah does not specifically address the construction of the Gerizim Temple, but their conflicts with the family of Sanballat played into the history eventually contributing to the construction of the rival temple in Samaria (although a later Sanballat is under consideration; see Josephus, *Ant.* 11.8.2, 4; 13.9.1). The Gerizim temple's ruins served as a springboard for Jesus to inform the woman at the well that the time was coming when geographical issues would be irrelevant in one's devotion to the Lord — worship in spirit and truth would transcend it (John 4:20-24).

SPECIAL ISSUES

A number of issues have ignited debates relative to Ezra/Nehemiah. Some of these are addressed above. One that is not are references to a number of people who appear in Ezra 4, but who are out of chronological order (as we would typically consider it). The narrative introduces the efforts of some during the time of Cyrus (4:5) to curtail the construction of the Temple which is accomplished until the reign of Darius (4:5,24). The awkwardness is the introduction of an accusation made during the reign of Xerxes (aka Ahasuerus; 4:6; 485–465 B.C.) which is followed by a letter to Artaxerxes who reigned 465–425 B.C. and in whose reign Ezra arrived on the scene in Judah (7:7). The introductions of Xerxes and Artaxerxes in the flow of the narrative is disruptive. If it is removed, the narrative would flow nicely from verse 5 immediately to verse 24.

Taking the text as it stands, it is best to consider the injected statements relative to Xerxes and Artaxerxes to be further examples of ongoing attempts to harass the returned exiles and create trouble for them. Sanballat, Tobiah, and Geshem are extensions of the harassments.

It is often noted that the books of Nehemiah and Ezra do not cite each other in the first person as interacting with one another. While this might be unusual, similarly contemporary authors in the Bible are not cross-referenced. Neither Amos nor Hosea refer to each other, although they both prophesied in the northern kingdom of Israel. Micah does not note Isaiah. As a matter of fact none of the eighth-century prophets refer to each other. Similarly, even though Haggai and Zechariah worked together to rally the Israelites to rebuild the Temple (Ezra 5:1; 6:14), neither refers to the other in his respective book. Perhaps too much is made of this point. The circles of concern for the two individuals were different. Ezra focused upon ritual and religious concerns while Nehemiah's work concentrated upon administrative issues. Furthermore, the narrative portions of the books do reflect contemporaneity. Nehemiah cites Ezra twelve times in his book and Nehemiah 8:9 makes it clear that they worked together.

Another question is how to identify the Law of Moses from which Ezra read. The identity of this hinges strongly on how one understands the composition of the Pentateuch. If the Pentateuch is understood to be a postexilic composition, the Law of Moses from which Ezra reads is usually identified as part of the Priestly Code or, at most, part of the Pentateuch before it was fully put together.[37] Indeed, much of modern scholarship argues that Ezra was the one who compiled the Pentateuch.[38] Williamson, however, addresses the compositional identity questions well[39] and concludes that in all probability it would have been "fully identical with, our Pentateuch."[40]

---

[37]See, for instance, Gerhard von Rad, *Das Geschichtsbild des chronistischen Werkes,* BWANT 54 (Stuttgart: Kohlhammer, 1930), pp. 38-41.

[38]Samuel Sandmel, *The Hebrew Scriptures: An Introduction to Their Literature and Religious Ideas* (New York: Alfred A. Knopf, 1968), pp. 328-329.

[39]Williamson, *Ezra, Nehemiah*, pp. xxxvii-xxxix.

[40]Ibid., p. xxxix.

ESTHER

The English title of the book of Esther transliterates the name of the heroine of the book as found in the Hebrew text (אֶסְתֵּר, 'estēr). This name, in turn, may be either a transliteration of the Akkadian word Ishtar, the Babylonian goddess of love, or a transliteration of the Persian word for star (stara). Her original Hebrew name, according to the text was Hadassah (Esth 2:7; הֲדַסָּה, hădassāh), meaning "myrtle."

HISTORICAL AND CULTURAL BACKGROUND

The events of the book are set in the period of the Persian empire after Cyrus the Great had conquered Babylon and decreed that the captive peoples could return to their homelands. The first migration of the Jews had returned to Palestine ca. 537 B.C. under the leadership of Sheshbazzar and Zerubbabel (cf. Ezra 1:8–2:2). The Persians had expanded their territorial holdings under the leadership of Darius I (reigned ca. 521–486 B.C.). He had engaged the Greeks in battle at Marathon in 490 B.C. suffering a significant defeat. Upon his death, his son, Xerxes (reigned 485–465 B.C.)[1] acceded to the throne and attempted to continue his father's expansionist policies. Xerxes was persuaded to attempt to conquer the Greek mainland and, as occurred with his father, he too was soundly defeated at the battles of Thermopylae and Salamis (480 B.C.) and ultimately at Plataea (479 B.C.).

The periods immediately before and after the events narrated in Esther found the Jews as objects of oppression, although in varying degrees of intensity. In Palestine, Zerubbabel's attempts to rebuild the Temple in Jerusalem (ca. 536 B.C.) took on international dimensions

---

[1]Xerxes is the Greek name by which the king is known. The usual transliteration from Hebrew is Ahasuerus.

as Tettanai corresponded with the monarchy regarding the Jews' goals (cf. Ezra 4:1-5). Other accusations were made against the Jews in the reigns of Xerxes (Ezra 4:6) and Artaxerxes (Ezra 4:7-16) and then into the time of Nehemiah's attempts to rebuild the walls of Jerusalem (Nehemiah 4, 6; 465-425 B.C.). Soon after this, Jews in Egypt were in occasional conflicts at Elephantine, which resulted in the destruction of their Temple at the site and their desire to rebuild it.[2]

TEXT AND AUTHOR

Contrary to the typical discussions of the other historical books, controversies over sources usually do not consume the discussion of Esther. Some have argued that the last section, 9:20-10:3, which specifically discusses the institution of the Purim celebration was added from another source.[3] Most readers would easily detect a shift in the nature of the narrative from the dramatic presentation of the storyline to an almost-methodical, plodding narrative — how much of this difference should be attributed to source derivation or simply a difference in the nature of the discussion is open to question.

The Hebrew text of Esther is well preserved with few places that deserve serious considerations relative to text critical concerns. Paton notes that the Hebrew manuscripts of Esther are the most commonly preserved of any portion of the Old Testament,[4] however, none of these derive from earlier than the eleventh century A.D. The likely reason for the preservation of so many manuscripts is that families wanted copies of the scroll to use in their private celebrations of Purim. No copies of the book have been identified in the Qumran collection. While the lack of discovery may be simply accident of preservation, it is likely that the separatist Qumran community may have considered the book of Esther unsuitable as Scripture because it preserves no reference to God, Esther compromises her Jewishness by marrying into the royal court of the Gentiles, and they apparently did not celebrate Purim.

The status of the Greek manuscripts, however, is significantly different. These usually are expansionistic, adding over a hundred

---

[2]Bezalel Porten, "Elephantine Papyri." *ABD*, 2:445-455.

[3]See Lewis Bayles Paton, *The Book of Esther*, ICC (Edinburgh: T & T Clark, 1908), pp. 57-60; however, Bush argues that the section should include 9:18-10:3 (*Ruth, Esther*, pp. 279, 281-282).

[4]Paton, *Esther*, p. 5.

additional verses. These appear to reflect an early reading as inferred not only from the antiquity of the language styles, but also from Josephus's apparent use of the Septuagint as the basis of his narration of Esther in *Antiquities* 11.184-296. There is little question, however, that these are additions to the text and are of little concern for canonical consideration.[5] The Greek additions appear somewhat contrived to inject God into the narrative. Moore implies that the addition of the verses disrupts the flow of thought that otherwise stands intact in Hebrew.[6]

The text gives no real evidence of who the author might be. The Babylonian Talmud suggests that the "Great Synagogue" put it together.[7] Pfeiffer somewhat cynically suggests that ". . . it was popular enthusiasm that forced the Synagogue to canonize the Book of Esther and to give official sanction to the celebration of Purim."[8]

Alternatively, Mordecai has been suggested as the author, based in part upon the statement in 9:20 which indicates that he recorded various events connected with the narrative. The statement, however, is of minimal significance relative to authorship of the book. The third-person description of Mordecai in 10:3 seems to dictate against his composition of the narrative.

Regardless, the author appears to have been at minimum extensively familiar with Persian backgrounds and customs. He may have incorporated writings of Mordecai (9:20) as well as the "book of the annals of the kings of Media and Persia" (10:2). He could also have drawn from oral tradition as the story was passed on.

---

[5]If the additions are removed from one of the Greek versions, known as the AT text, the Greek reflects a fairly close reading with the Masoretic Text. For detailed discussions of the Greek texts, see Clyde M. Woods, "An Introduction to Esther," unpublished M.A. Thesis (Memphis, TN: Harding College Graduate School of Bible and Religion, 1959), pp. 13-29; Carey A. Moore, "On the Origins of the LXX Additions to the Book of Esther," *JBL* 92 (1973): 382-393; id., *Daniel, Esther, and Jeremiah: The Additions*, AB 44 (Garden City, NY: Doubleday, 1977), pp. 161-165; and Bush, *Ruth, Esther*, pp. 279-294. Discussions of other versions, which are of little value for text critical concerns, may be found conveniently in Paton, *Esther*, pp. 5-47; and Woods, "Introduction," pp. 5-11.

[6]Carey A. Moore, *Esther*, AB 7B (Garden City, NY: Doubleday, 1971), p. LXIII.

[7]*Baba Bathra* 15a.

[8]Robert H. Pfeiffer, *Introduction to the Old Testament* (New York: Harper & Brothers, 1948), p. 746.

The time lag from the dates of the events to their composition has been a matter of debate. Scholarship has often equated the Hebrew style with that of Chronicles,[9] but the date of Chronicles is increasingly being dated to ca. 400 B.C. If a ca. 400 B.C. date is reasonable, it would place the composition of Esther in fairly close proximity to the end of the events narrated.

The earliest possible date of composition would be in the reign of Xerxes himself (ca. 485–465 B.C.). The latest date that most scholars recognize is the time of Josephus, since he appears to have used at least a Greek version of the book in his *Antiquities* (11.184-296; ca. 90 A.D.). Between these two dates are some datum issues that might help narrow the range.

Esther is not noted in the list of heros in Ecclesiasticus (early second century B.C.), but Ezra is not cited either. Her lack of appearance in the list, while damaging, is by no means devastating.

Some have argued that the date of composition of the book was during the Maccabean revolt in which Haman symbolized Antiochus Epiphanes and his attempts to remove Jewish influence from the land,[10] hence the date would be in the second century B.C. Somewhat corroborative of this is the reference to Mordecai's day (2 Macc 15:36), but this more likely indicates awareness of the story of Esther rather than a date of composition. Such a late date of composition is largely based on the presupposition that the book could not have been written earlier nor reflect any historical accuracy.

Significantly, there are no Greek loan words in the book, which likely would not have come into significant play until the Greek period ca. 330 B.C. Given the pervasiveness and power of Alexander's campaigns and the accompanying Hellenism, this lack of Greek influence is important. If Esther was simply a composition of the second century B.C., the lack of Greek influence borders on brilliant. This datum point seems to push the date of composition earlier than 330 B.C., and there is no intrinsic reason to move the date of Esther later than ca. 400 B.C.

STRUCTURE

I. Xerxes' Court Faces Intrigue — 1:1–2:23
    A. Xerxes hosts grand banquet — 1:1-9

---

[9]Paton, *Esther*, p. 62; Pfeiffer, *Introduction*, p. 741.
[10]Paton, *Esther*, pp. 61-62; Pfeiffer, *Introduction*, pp. 740-742.

B. Xerxes vanquishes Vashti — 1:10-22
   1. Vashti refuses to appear before Xerxes' audience — 1:10-12
   2. Xerxes banishes Vashti as queen — 1:13-22
C. Esther becomes new queen — 2:1-18
   1. Servants search for new queen — 2:1-4
   2. Esther becomes candidate for queen — 2:5-11
   3. Xerxes chooses Esther as queen — 2:12-18
D. Mordecai reveals plot to assassinate Xerxes — 2:19-23
II. Haman Becomes Hostile to the Jews — 3:1-9:19
  A. Xerxes promotes Haman — 3:1-2a
  B. Mordecai refuses to bow to Haman — 3:2b-6
  C. Haman plots to destroy the Jews — 3:7-15
  D. Mordecai appeals to Esther for help — 4:1-17
  E. Esther intervenes for her people — 5:1-14
   1. Esther plans banquet for Xerxes and Haman — 5:1-8
   2. Haman plots death of Mordecai — 5:9-14
  F. Jews escape extermination — 6:1-9:15
   1. Haman's plot to kill Mordecai fails — 6:1-14
   2. Haman becomes victim of his own plot — 7:1-10
   3. Mordecai receives Haman's position — 8:1-2
   4. Esther pleads for her people's deliverance — 8:3-14
   5. Jews escape hostilities — 8:15-9:10
   6. Haman's sons are executed — 9:11-15
  G. Jews rejoice with escape — 9:16-19
III. Jews institute Purim — 9:20-10:3
  A. Purim established as festival — 9:20-28
  B. Esther issues decree regarding Purim — 9:29-32
  C. Mordecai increases in influence in court — 10:1-3

GENRE

The book purports to be history in narrating the events that precipitated the celebration of the feast of Purim. As is customary, however, it is not typical history as modern scholarship defines it. The book appears almost as a modern short story with narrative tensions, irony, and reversal replete through the book.

The first word of the Hebrew of Esther is וַיְהִי (wayᵊhî), "and it was . . ." which is typical phraseology of Hebrew historical narrative. Furthermore, the book essentially invites investigation with its appeal similar to those of Kings in which the reader is referred to "the book of the annals of the kings of Media and Persia" (Esth 10:2).

The overall tenor of the book reflects accurately the state of affairs characteristic of the Persian empire during Xerxes' reign. Among these, the reader may note some of the Persian practices such as the use of hanging and impaling as forms of capital punishment (cf. Esth 2:23; 5:14; 7:10 with Herodotus 3.125, 159; 4.43); and an extremely efficient postal system (cf. Esth 3:13; 8:10 with Herodotus 8.98-99). Furthermore Xerxes was known to have hosted lavish parties (Esth 1:4-7 perhaps reflected in Herodotus 7.118-120) and to have retreated into sexual indulgence after his defeat at the hands of the Greeks (Esth 2:16 compared with his pursuits as described by Herodotus 9.108-109). This last point dovetails perfectly with Xerxes' campaign against Greece and his defeats at Thermopylae and Salamis which occurred in his sixth year (480 B.C.; cf. Esth 2:16). In general, the personality of ambition, greed, and lust reflected in Esther (1:12; 5:3; 6:6-7; 7:7-8) is reflected in similar episodes in Herodotus (7.3-9; 9.108-113).[11] Marincola summarizes his personality: "The tale of Xerxes' passion for Masistes' wife gives us our last view of the hybristic king and in it he appears partly as the tyrant ruled by lust and partly as the hapless victim of his own passion, who is unable to control his desires or the machinations of the one who uses him."[12]

The excavation of the palace in Susa has reflected the grandeur and luxury implied in Esther 1:5-6. De Miroschedji notes: "This fabulous palace is the setting of the story of Esther. . . . Several notations allow us to suppose that its writer had some topographic familiarity with the palace excavated by the archaeologists."[13] The royal palace covered ca. 12.5 acres of which the house of the king covered ca. 9.5 acres with the remaining three acres reserved for official use.[14]

The weight of this kind of corroboration has prompted many to consider the narrative as history. Pfeiffer, however, notes correctly

---

[11]The assembly by Xerxes to consider his attack against Greece (Herod 7.8-20) dovetails interestingly with the banquet held as recorded in Esther 1. The Esther narrative gives no indication that part of the "party" may have been to plan an attack against Greece, but the timing is intriguing.

[12]John Marincola, rev., Herodotus, *The Histories*, trans. by A. de Selincourt, rev. with Introduction and Notes by J. Marincola (London: Penguin Books, 2003), p. 681.

[13]Pierre de Miroschedji, "Susa," *ABD*, 6:244-245.

[14]Ibid., p. 244.

that ". . . the correct reproduction of local color and the lack of glaring inconsistencies and supernatural happenings, do not necessarily prove that the incidents related actually occurred."[15] Paton reveals part of the driving force behind many who deny the book's historicity: "The rationalists, who denied supernatural revelation, took a free attitude toward the Biblical books, and had no hesitation in questioning their historical character, if they found reason for so doing."[16]

The skeptics have offered a list of concerns that they believe undermine the book's historical credibility. While it is not possible in the scope of this article to respond to all of the concerns, it is remarkable that some of the charges that the book is unhistorical are still made in spite of a number of conservative scholars' responses to the charges.[17]

Paton and Moore both affirm a historical problem with the statement that implies that Mordecai was taken from Canaan along with Jeconiah in 597 B.C. (cf. Esth 2:5-6).[18] This would make Mordecai at least 120 years old when the narrative of Esther unfolds. Conservative scholars, however, have noted that the relative pronoun that opens verse 6 can legitimately refer to Kish instead of Mordecai.[19]

Similarly, Esther notes the existence of 127 provinces in the Persian empire (Esth 1:1; 9:30), whereas Herodotus states that there were twenty satrapies (Herod 3.89). The word in Esther is not "satrapy," and from Ezra 2:1 it appears that a satrapy could consist of a number of provinces.[20] Herodotus indicates (3.91) that the

---

[15]Pfeiffer, *Introduction*, p. 737; cf. similarly Carey A. Moore, "Esther, Book of," *ABD*, 2:638.

[16]Paton, *Esther*, p. 111.

[17]Credible responses to many of these concerns appear in the works by J. Stafford Wright ("The Historicity of the Book of Esther," in *New Perspectives on the Old Testament*, ed. by J.B. Payne [Waco, TX: Word, 1970], pp. 37-47) and William H. Shea ("Esther and History," *AUSS* 14 [1976]: 227-246). It often appears that the liberal/skeptical scholars take little note of what their conservative counterparts are doing or writing. Sometimes the presuppositions that undergird the investigation will dictate this blindness, but as is the case with several of these examples, the data can simply and fairly be understood differently without intrinsically implying a supernatural intervention.

[18]Paton, *Esther*, p. 73; Moore, "Esther," p. 638.

[19]Wright, "Historicity," p. 38; Edward J. Young, *An Introduction to the Old Testament*, rev. ed. (Grand Rapids: Eerdmans, 1964), pp. 355-356.

[20]See also Gordon H. Johnston, "פֶּחָה," *NIDOTTE*, 3:599-608.

"province" which included Syria contained Phoenicia, the part of Syria known as Palestine, and Cyprus.

More problematic is the issue of Xerxes' wife. Herodotus informs us that her name was Amestris (7.61, 114; 9.112), and attempts to identify her with either Vashti or Esther have been less than satisfactory.[21] Having a wife, in and of itself, did not preclude Xerxes having a large harem. Furthermore, Herodotus makes it clear that Xerxes was inclined to pursue relationships that were inappropriate (Herod 9.108-109). Harrison observes ". . . that Herodotus spoke of Amestris as 'wife of Xerxes,' and not as 'queen of Persia,' and it may be that she was in fact a favorite concubine or even chief of the *harîm*, who had been appointed by Xerxes to accompany him on his campaign. Whatever the nature of the situation, her behavior on that occasion furnished sufficient grounds for the monarch to consign her to obscurity on their return to Persia."[22]

Further complicating the wife issue is Herodotus's statement that the king was supposed to marry only a Persian from one of the select families of Persia (3.84). Amestris apparently was not from one of those families, but was the daughter of one of Xerxes' generals (Herod 7.61).

In fairness, there are difficulties in identifying outside the Bible the existence of the other major characters in the book. However, a cuneiform inscription found at Borsippa, and apparently from the reign of Xerxes, refers to a high official at the court of Susa whose name was Mordecai (= Mardukâ).[23] Whether this refers to the Mordecai of Esther is not certain, but the name, date, and position referred to in the inscription are intriguing and should caution against a wholesale dismissal of identification.

The reference to the irrevocability of Persian law (Esth 1:19; 8:8; cf. Dan 6:8,12,15) has posed a significant problem, since no such reference has been identified in Persian law. The closest reference to such a practice is not so much a written law, but perhaps the pride of the monarch to make a promise in the presence of numerous wit-

---

[21]See Wright, "Historicity," and Shea, "Esther and History." One hopes that Amestris's reputation for cruelty (Herod 7.114; 9.108-113) would not have characterized Esther.

[22] Harrison, *Introduction*, p. 1096.

[23]A. Ungnad, *"Keilinschriftliche Beitrage zum Buch Esra und Ester,"* ZAW 58 (1940–41): 240-244; *"Keilinschriftliche Beitrage zum Buch Esra und Ester,"* ZAW 59 (1942–43): 219.

nesses and the embarrassment which would ensue should he renege on his promises (cf. Herod 9.109).

Woods has summarized the methodological problems well: "While it is not to be expected that Esther and Herodotus, both fragmentary accounts, should agree perfectly in all things, it should be noticed that these accounts are congruous in many respects."[24] The presuppositional perspectives of the investigators will inevitably color the conclusions. It seems more reasonable to assume the accounts are historically viable and to approach them as working hypotheses and reconstructions until sufficient data come to light to force different explanations.

Alternatively, however, many believe the book of Esther is fiction,[25] although Moore argues that scholars are now more inclined to see it as a combination of fiction and history.[26] With Paton's and Pfeiffer's affirmation that the book was written during the Maccabean revolt, it seems odd that a fictional account which is assumed to have been written to affirm Jewish patriotism would incorporate foreign names for the heroine/hero (Esther and Mordecai) for the story, especially in a time when the Jews were objects of such virulent persecution.[27]

Talmon has identified Esther as "a *historicized wisdom-tale* . . . an *enactment* of standard 'Wisdom' motifs."[28] According to him, this would explain the absence of references to God, the Torah, and other distinctively Hebrew practices. Somewhat corroborative of his thesis is the fact that the book appears in the Hebrew Bible with the Hagiographa and not with the Hebrew section of the Prophets. However, Esther's placement is with other books read at the special feasts: Song of Songs, Ruth, Lamentations, and Ecclesiastes. Furthermore, Ezra, Nehemiah, and Chronicles are historical books which share a place in the Hagiographa. Dillard and Longman have observed, however, that wisdom motifs do not "invalidate historical foundation; it is a truism that 'we learn from history.'"[29]

---

[24]Wood, "Introduction," p. 60.

[25]Paton, *Esther*, and Pfeiffer, *Introduction*.

[26]Moore, *Esther*, p. L.

[27]In fairness, another Jew named Mordecai appears in Ezra (2:2 = Neh 7:7).

[28]Shemaryahu Talmon, "'Wisdom' in the Book of Esther," *VT* 13 (1963): 426.

[29]Dillard and Longman, *Introduction*, p. 193.

Another approach has suggested that the book of Esther, as well as the Joseph stories of Genesis, are "diaspora novellas" intended to provide Jews in exile a model for a general lifestyle in a pagan environment.[30] Such affirmations, however, do not necessarily require denial of historicity. Additionally, Dillard and Longman have pointed out that the circumstances of the two episodes are quite different in strategic approach: "There is no personal enemy corresponding to Haman threatening the Jews in the Joseph story; Joseph reveals his identity to his brothers, not to a king or in the presence of an enemy."[31]

A similar parallel has been identified between Esther and Exodus by Gerleman.[32] Among other similarities, Gerleman emphasizes the foreign court motif, the threat of survival, the achieved victory, and the establishment of a celebratory festival. These parallels, however, do not establish the book of Esther as fiction as opposed to history. The parallels are somewhat artificial since the analysis fails to recognize the differences in the narratives.[33] One that does not substantiate Gerleman's thesis is the very different attitude toward the Gentile monarchs. Moses operates in opposition to the monarchy, while Esther and Mordecai work within it; the goal of the Exodus was to escape oppression rather than change it; and in Exodus the oppressive king is portrayed as dead, whereas Mordecai sought to preserve Xerxes.

THEOLOGICAL THEMES

Beleaguering is the lack of reference in Esther to a number of significant Hebrew religious concepts and laws — not the least of which are any references to God! Additionally, there are no references to prayer, the Torah (law), or the Sabbath. Baldwin has suggested that the book reflects two conflicting worldviews.[34] Haman represents the chance-based strategy of relying upon the פּוּר (pûr,

---

[30]A. Meinhold, "*Die Gattung der Josephgeschichte und des Estherbuches: Diasporanovelle II*," *ZAW* 88 (1976): 72-93.

[31]Dillard and Longman, *Introduction*, p. 194.

[32]G. Gerleman, *Esther*, BKAT 21 (Neukirchen: Neukirchener, 1982).

[33]Sandra B. Berg, *The Book of Esther: Motifs, Themes, and Structure*, SBLDS 44 (Missoula, MT: Scholars Press, 1979), p. 6-8.

[34]Joyce G. Baldwin, *Esther*, TOTC 12 (Leicester: Inter-Varsity Press, 1984), pp. 37-38.

"lot") to decide his actions. On the other hand, Mordecai and Esther represent human responsibility working in concert with divine direction and intervening providence. For the believer, the book demonstrates in a grand way God's providence — he cares deeply for his people (cf. Ps 37:1-17). The subtlety of Haman's wife's statement about the Jews when Mordecai's plans start to disintegrate is telling: "Since Mordecai, before whom your downfall has started, is of Jewish origin, you cannot stand against him—you will surely come to ruin!" (6:13). For God's redemptive plan to come to fruition, it was necessary that Xerxes' edict of Jewish extermination be countered. Providence is demonstrated not only to neutralize Xerxes' decree, but to exalt God's people in spite of Haman's original intent.

This preservation is part of another underlying theme of God's commitment to his covenant with Abraham. Yahweh had declared to Abraham: "I will make you into a great nation and I will bless you; I will make your name great, and you will be a blessing. I will bless those who bless you, and whoever curses you I will curse; and all peoples on earth will be blessed through you" (Gen 12:1-3). With this preservation in a foreign land, however, the book of Esther reveals an independence that does not demand servitude to the Gentile world; instead the Jews could remain loyal to Judaism.[35]

An additional important theme is the justification for the celebration of the feast of Purim. The word Purim means "lots" (singular פּוּר, *pûr*; plural פּוּרִים, *pûrîm*) and derives, according to Esther, from Haman's strategy to determine the day on which to exterminate the Jews (Esth 9:24). Instead of a day of extermination, it became a day of deliverance worthy of celebration.

The etymology of the word *pûr* has clarified many of the challenges to the appropriation of the term for a Jewish feast. Hallo has demonstrated the legitimacy of the name's application to the celebration. He published the inscription from the only surviving *pûr* (lot) from the ancient world by which the Assyrians determined the eponym of the years of their monarchs' reigns.[36] The word for "lot"

---

[35]Dillard and Longman, *Introduction*, p. 197; see further in William W. Grasham, "The Theology of the Book of Esther," *ResQ* 16 (1973): 99-111; and David Beller, "A Theology of the Book of Esther," *ResQ* 39 (1997): 1-15.

[36]William W. Hallo, "The First Purim," *BA* 46 (1983): 19-29. The Assyrian form of the word *pûr* appears twice on the cube and indicates that the item was used for casting lots. It is instructive to note that of the probably hundreds of such items that one would expect to have been used in the ancient

appears twice on the cube and was used in a ceremony by which the year's name was given (= ca. 824 B.C.). This discovery provides etymological and ceremonial legitimacy to the name of the feast.

But what of the legitimacy of the feast for the Jews? This question is largely based upon the scholars' presuppositions relative to the historicity of the event. Pfeiffer, operating on the assumption that Esther is a product of the Maccabean age affirms:

> . . . the author of the book invented in toto the festival of Purim and also its name, as well as the story of Esther which explained its origin. The success of this brilliant hoax is due to the fact that the story and the festival expressed so exactly the popular feelings in the reign of Hyrcanus: Hurrah for the Jews! Death to the heathen! Moreover, the masses never object to joyous banquets, riotous merrymaking, and Mardi Gras revelry.[37]

Others will argue that the feast is an accommodation and adaptation from pagan festivals.[38] A pagan origin to Purim would go a long way to explain the seemingly worldly celebration indicated in the Megilla 7b which suggested that the celebrants drink to the point of inability to distinguish between "cursed be Haman" and "blessed be Mordecai." Furthermore, some would argue that the Babylonian name of the festival gives legitimacy to such an adaptation.

It is not surprising that the Jews would accept a "lot" terminology to refer to the festival. Proverbs 16:33 states that "The lot is cast into the lap, but its every decision is from the LORD." While the Hebrew word in Proverbs is different (גּוֹרָל, *gôrāl*) it is the same that is used in Esther 9:24 to explain the Hebrew equivalent of the Mesopotamian term *pûr*. Furthermore, it was Haman of Mesopotamia

---

world, this is the only one thus far to have survived and be identified! The paucity of discovery in an archaeological setting of such a common item should serve to caution against arguing that something did not exist for lack of physical evidence. The situation is similar to the evidence associated with the crucifixion; of the thousands of people who were crucified by the Romans, the only archaeological evidence found of such practices is one heel bone with a nail penetrating it (Vassilios Tzaferis, "Crucifixion — the Archaeological Evidence," *BAR* 11 [1985]: 44-53; Joseph Zias and Eliezer Sekelis, "The Crucified Man from Giv'at ha-Mivtar: A Reappraisal." *IEJ* 35 [1985]: 22-27). In fairness to Hallo, even with the discovery of the Assyrian *pûr*, he does not argue for a historical authenticity of Esther (23).

[37]Pfeiffer, *Introduction*, p. 745.

[38]Moore, "Esther," pp. 637-638.

who had cast lots to determine the date! It is ironical to use the name of the mechanics of the choice to name the celebration of deliverance. If the Jews adapted a celebration from a pagan background to give it a new interpretation, such an approach is not at all foreign to religious expression.[39] Woods, however, asks: "If Esther does not record the true origin of Purim, how did the book and the feast get together? If the feast existed prior to the book, how did the true explanation for the origin of the feast disappear? On the other hand, if the story came first and is unhistorical and late, how did the observance of the feast get started?"[40]

NEW TESTAMENT CONNECTIONS

Not only does manuscript evidence of the book of Esther not appear in the Qumran community, it is not cited or alluded to in the New Testament. That, however, does not necessarily mean it has no connection with the New Testament.

The connection to the New Testament is more conceptual than specific. Assuming a providential component to the events narrated in Esther, the fact that God works behind the scenes to preserve his people in the Old Testament and to work to fulfill his promise to Abraham, Christians can take assurance that he, too, is concerned with our welfare.[41] Similarity exists as well in the provision of Esther "for such a time as this" (Esth 4:14) and God's sending his Son to the world "when the time had fully come" (Gal 4:4). Resonating from the Jews' deliverance, God has promised that he will not allow us to be tempted beyond what we are able to endure (1 Cor 10:13), and Christians understand that this world is not our home; we are aliens on our way to a world where our real citizenship rests (cf. 1 Pet 2:11; Phil 3:20). Depending on where we live, our world is becoming at minimum more apathetic toward the faith if not outright antagonistic and hostile toward it. As the world becomes more philosophically pluralistic, the dedicated Christian will increasingly become the object of hatred, just as our Savior (John 15:18-23) and

---

[39]Although, not the best of parallels, some might note the adaptation of pagan festivals into Easter and Christmas.

[40]Woods, "Introduction," p. 57.

[41]This does not necessarily mean that he will preserve us individually or wholesale, but certainly he knows our sufferings and will carry us ultimately to the place which Jesus has prepared (cf. John 14:1-3).

Paul (2 Tim 3:12) warned. We are admonished and encouraged, however, to remain firm in his word and are assured that victory will indeed occur (Rev 2:10).

SPECIAL ISSUES

The book of Esther struggled to find acceptance into the canon of God's word. Maimonides (A.D. 1135–1204) considered Esther of greatest importance in the Hebrew canon only after the Pentateuch, however, the book did not always enjoy this level of praise. The fact that Esther is the only one of the canonical books of the Hebrew Bible that has not been identified in the manuscripts at Qumran has raised questions. Its absence may be the result of accident of preservation. More likely the Qumran community, which was ethnically quite exclusive, was probably inclined to reject the book because of their perception of the heroine's cooperation with the Gentiles as well as the fact that the book does not have any of the expected Jewish features such as God, the Law, Sabbath, or prayer. Furthermore, there is no evidence that the Qumran community observed Purim anyway.

There is no explicit statement in Josephus where he lists the book as part of the canon, but it likely was considered part of the collection of twenty-two books (*Against Apion* 1.38-41). Moore points out that in the Jewish community, the book was disputed into the fourth century A.D., although no specific reasons are offered for the questions.[42]

The Christian community wrestled with the book as well. It was generally accepted in the Church in the west, part of its acceptance based on the fact perhaps that the Septuagint preserved it, which in turn was the basis of the Scripture tradition in the West. While generally accepted by the Eastern Churches, its receptivity was not as readily given as in the West. Interestingly, the early Church Fathers, for whatever reason, did not write commentaries on the book.[43]

With the Reformation, Martin Luther's view of the book is quite harsh, although it did not permanently sway the view by the Christian community away from accepting the book. Paton, however, perpetuates Luther's cynicism and declares: "There is not one

---

[42]Moore, "Esther," p. 635.
[43]Bush, *Ruth, Esther*, p. 276.

noble character in this book. . . . Morally Est. [*sic*] falls far below the general level of the OT., and even of the Apocrypha. The verdict of Luther is not too severe: 'I am so hostile to this book that I wish it did not exist, for it Judaizes too much, and has too much heathen naughtiness' (*Tischreden*, *W. A.* xxii. 2080)."[44] Paton further affirms: "The book is so conspicuously lacking in religion that it should never have been included in the Canon of the OT., but should have been left with Judith and Tobit among the apocryphal writings."[45]

Fortunately, Luther's and Paton's views have not held sway. Most believers can see the glory of God's work behind the scenes and can affirm in New Testament phraseology: "And we know that in all things God works for the good of those who love him, who have been called according to his purpose" (Rom 8:28).

---

[44]Paton, *Esther*, p. 96.
[45]Ibid. p. 97.

THE PSALMS
AND WISDOM
LITERATURE

WALTER ZORN

MARK MANGANO

BIBLIOGRAPHY FOR
THE PSALMS &
WISDOM LITERATURE

Alden, R.L. *Job*. NAC 11. Nashville: Broadman & Holman, 1993.

Allen, Leslie C. *Psalms 101–150*. WBC. Waco: Word Books, 1983.

Allen, Ronald B. *And I Will Praise Him: A Guide to Worship in the Psalms*. Grand Rapids: Kregel, 1992.

Andersen, F.I. *Job*. TOTC. Downers Grove, IL: InterVarsity, 1976.

Anderson, A.A. *The Book of Psalms*. 2 vols. NCB. Grand Rapids: Eerdmans, 1972.

Anderson, Bernhard W. *Out of the Depths: The Psalms Speak for Us Today*. 3rd ed. with Steven Bishop. Louisville, KY: Westminster John Knox Press, 2000.

Archer, Gleason L. Jr. "The Linguistic Evidence for the Date of Ecclesiastes." *JETS* 12 (1969): 167-181.

———. *A Survey of Old Testament Introduction*. Chicago: Moody Press, 1978.

Bartholomew, Craig C. "Towards a Post-liberal Agenda for Old Testament Study." In *Make the Old Testament Live*. Ed. by Richard S. Hess and Gordon J. Wenham. Grand Rapids: Eerdmans, 1998.

Bellinger, W.H. Jr. *Psalms: Reading and Studying the Book of Praises*. Peabody, MA: Hendrickson Publishers, 1990.

Bergant, Diane. *The Song of Songs*. Berit Olam. Collegeville, MN: Liturgical Press, 2001.

Berry, Donald K. *An Introduction to Wisdom and Poetry of the Old Testament*. Nashville: Broadman & Holman, 1995. See pp. 141-156.

Bland, Dave. *Proverbs, Ecclesiastes, Song of Solomon*. The College Press NIV Commentary Series. Joplin, MO: College Press, 2002.

Bloom, Harold, ed. *The Song of Songs* Modern Critical Interpretations. New York: Chelsea, 1988.

Blumenthal, D.R. "Where God Is Not: The Book of Esther and the Song of Songs." *Judaism* 173 (1995): 80-90.

Brenner, Athalya. *The Song of Songs*. OTG. Sheffield: Sheffield Academic Press, 1989.

Brown, William P. *Character in Crisis: A Fresh Approach to the Wisdom Literature of the Old Testament*. Grand Rapids: Eerdmans, 1996. See pp. 50-119.

_____. *Seeing the Psalms: A Theology of Metaphor*. Louisville, KY: Westminster John Knox Press, 2002.

Broyles, Craig C. *The Conflict of Faith and Experience in the Psalms: A Form-Critical and Theological Study*. JSOTSupp 52. Sheffield: Sheffield Academic Press, 1988.

_____. *Psalms*. NIBCOT. Peabody, MA: Hendrickson, 1999.

Brueggemann, Walter. *The Message of the Psalms: A Theological Commentary*. Minneapolis: Augsburg, 1984.

_____. *The Psalms and the Life of Faith*. Ed. by Patrick D. Miller. Minnapolis: Fortress Press, 1995.

Bullock, C. Hassell. *Encountering the Book of Psalms: A Literary and Theological Introduction*. Grand Rapids: Baker, 2001.

Burns, Camilla. "Human Love: The Silent Voice of God." *TBT* 36 (1998): 159-163.

Buttenwieser, Moses. *The Psalms Chronologically Treated, with a New Translation*. New York: KTAV, 1969.

Carr, David McLain. *The Erotic Word: Sexuality, Spirituality, and the Bible*. Oxford: Oxford University Press, 2003.

Carr, G. Lloyd. "The Old Testament Love Songs and Their Use in the New Testament." *JETS* 24 (1981): 97-105.

_____. *The Song of Solomon: An Introduction and Commentary*. TOTC. Leicester, UK: Inter-Varsity; Downers Grove, IL: Inter-Varsity, 1984.

Ceresko, A.R. *Job 29–31 in the Light of Northwest Semitic*. Rome: Biblical Institute Press, 1980.

Childs, Brevard S. *Introduction to the Old Testament as Scripture*. Philadelphia: Fortress Press, 1979.

Clifford, Richard J. *Psalms 1–72*. Abingdon Old Testament Commentaries. Nashville: Abingdon, 2002.

_____. *Psalms 73–150*. Abingdon Old Testament Commentaries. Nashville: Abingdon, 2003.

Clines, David J.A. *Job 1–20*. WBC 17. Dallas: Word Books, 1989.

Cole, Robert L. *The Shape and Message of Book III (Psalms 73–89)*. JSOTSupp 307. Sheffield: Sheffield Academic Press, 2000.

Cooper, Jerald D. "New Cuneiform Parallels to the Song of Songs." *JBL* 90 (1971): 157-162.

Coupland, Douglas. *Life after God.* New York: Pocket Books, 1994.

Craigie, Peter C. *Psalms 1–50.* WBC. Waco: Word Books, 1983.

Crenshaw, James L. "Job, Book of." *ABD*, 3:858-868. Ed. by David Noel Freedman. New York: Doubleday, 1992.

_____. *The Psalms: An Introduction.* Grand Rapids: Eerdmans, 2001.

Crow, Loren D. *The Songs of Ascents (Psalms 120–134) Their Place in Israelite History and Religion.* SBLDS 148. Atlanta: Scholars Press, 1996.

Currid, John D. "The 'Instruction of Amenemope' and the Book of Proverbs." *Ancient Egypt and the Old Testament,* pp. 205-216. Grand Rapids: Baker, 1997.

Curtis, John Briggs. "On Job's Response to Yahweh." *JBL* 98 (1979): 498-511.

Dahood, Mitchell. *Psalms I, Psalms II, Psalms III,* AB. Garden City, NY: Doubleday, 1966.

Davidson, Robert. *Ecclesiastes and the Song of Solomon.* Daily Study Bible Series. Louisville, KY: Westminster John Knox, 1986.

Day, J. *Psalms.* OTG. Sheffield: Sheffield Academic Press, 1992.

De Jong, Stephan. "God in the Book of Qohelet: A Reappraisal of Qohelet's Place in Old Testament Theology." *VT* 47 (1997): 154-167.

Delitzsch, Franz. *Proverbs, Ecclesiastes, Song of Solomon.* Trans. by M.G. Easton. Vol. 6 of *Commentary on the Old Testament in Ten Volumes.* Repr., Grand Rapids: Eerdmans, 1975.

Dhorme, Édouard. *A Commentary on the Book of Job.* Trans. by Harold Knight. Nashville: Thomas Nelson, 1967.

Dick, M.B. "The Legal Metaphor in Job 31." *CBQ* 41 (1979): 37-50.

Dorsey, David A. "Literary Structuring in the Song of Songs." *JSOT* 46 (1990): 81-96.

Driver, S.R., and G.B. Gray. *A Critical and Exegetical Commentary on the Book of Job.* ICC. Edinburgh: T. & T. Clark, 1921.

Duvall, J. Scott, and J. Daniel Hayes. *Grasping God's Word.* Grand Rapids: Zondervan, 2001.

Eaton, J.H. *Job.* OTG 5. Sheffield: JSOT, 1985.

_____. *Psalms of the Way and the Kingdom: A Conference with the Commentaries.* JSOTSupp 199. Sheffield: Sheffield Academic Press, 1995.

Eaton, M.A. *Ecclesiastes: An Introduction and Commentary.* TOTC. Downers Grove, IL: InterVarsity, 1983.

Ellison, H.L. *A Study of Job: From Tragedy to Triumph*. Grand Rapids: Zondervan, 1971.

Falk, Marcia. *Love Lyrics from the Bible: A Translation and Literary Study of the Song of Songs*. Bible and Literature Series 4. Sheffield: Almond, 1982.

Fløysvik, Ingvar. *When God Becomes My Enemy: The Theology of the Complaint Psalms*. Saint Louis: Concordia Academic Press, 1997.

Fohrer, Georg. *Introduction to the Old Testament*. Trans. by David E. Green. Nashville: Abingdon, 1968.

Fokkelman, J.P. *Reading Biblical Poetry: An Introductory Guide*. Louisville, KY: Westminster John Knox, 2001.

Follis, Elaine R., ed. *Directions in Biblical Hebrew Poetry*. JSOTSupp 40. Sheffield: Sheffield Academic Press, 1987.

Forman, C.C. "Koheleth's Use of Genesis." *JSS* 5 (1960): 256-263.

_____ . "The Pessimism of Ecclesiastes." *JSS* 3 (1958): 336-343.

Fox, Michael V. "Frame-Narrative and Composition in the Book of Qoheleth." *HUCA* 48 (1977): 83-106.

_____ . *Proverbs 1–9*. AB. Vol. 18A. Garden City, NY: Doubleday, 2000.

_____ . *The Song of Songs and the Ancient Egyptian Love Songs*. Madison, WI: University of Wisconsin Press, 1985.

Freedman, David Noel, with Jeffrey C. Geoghegan and Andrew Welch. *Psalm 119: The Exaltation of Torah*. Biblical and Judaic Studies. Vol. 6. Winona Lake, IN: Eisenbrauns, 1999.

Freedman, Noel M. "The Spelling of the Name 'David' in the Hebrew Bible." *HAR* 7 (1983): 89-104.

Frye, J.B. *The Legal Language of the Book of Job*. Ph.D. Dissertation, University of London, 1973.

Fyall, R.S. *Now My Eyes Have Seen You: Images of Creation and Evil in the Book of Job*. Downers Grove, IL: InterVarsity, 2002.

Garrett, Duane A. *Proverbs, Ecclesiastes, Song of Songs*. NAC 14. Nashville: Broadman, 1993.

Garrett, Duane, and Paul R. House. *Song of Songs/Lamentations*. WBC 23B (Nashville: Thomas Nelson, 2004).

Gerstenberger, Erhard S. *Psalms, Part I with an Introduction to Cultic Poetry*. FOTL, Vol. XIV. Grand Rapids: Eerdmans, 1987.

_____ . *Psalms, Part 2, and Lamentations*. FOTL, Vol. XV. Grand Rapids: Eerdmans, 2001.

Gillingham, S.E. *The Poems and Psalms of the Hebrew Bible*. The Oxford Bible Series. Oxford: Oxford University Press, 1994.

Glatzer, Nahum, ed. *The Dimensions of Job*. New York: Schocken, 1969.

Gledhill, Tom. *The Message of the Song of Songs: The Lyrics of Love*. The Bible Speaks Today. Leicester, UK: Inter-Varsity; Downers Grove, IL: InterVarsity, 1994.

Glickman, S.C. *A Song for Lovers: Lessons for Lovers in the Song of Solomon*. Leicester, UK: Inter-Varsity, 1976.

Glueck, Nelson. *Ḥesed in the Bible*. Trans. by Alfred Gottschalk. Cincinnati: The Hebrew Union College Press, 1967.

Good, E.M. *In Turns of Tempest: A Reading of Job with a Translation*. Stanford: Stanford University Press, 1998.

Gordis, R. *The Book of God and Man: A Study of Job*. Chicago: University of Chicago Press, 1963.

_____ . *The Book of Job: Commentary, New Translation, and Special Notes*. New York: Jewish Theological Seminary of America, 1978.

_____ . *Koheleth – The Man and His World*. 3rd ed. New York: Schocken Books, 1968.

_____ . *The Song of Songs and Lamentations: A Study, Modern Translation, and Commentary*. 2nd ed. New York: Ktav, 1974.

Goulder, Michael D. *The Psalms of the Return: Book V, Psalms 107–150*. JSOTSupp 258. Sheffield: Sheffield Academic Press, 1998.

_____ . *The Song of Fourteen Songs*. JSOTSupp. 36. Sheffield: JSOT Press, 1986.

Grabba, L.L. *Comparative Philology and the Text of Job*. SBLDS 34. Missoula, MT: Scholars Press, 1977.

Gray, John. *The Biblical Doctrine of the Reign of God*. Edinburgh: T & T Clark, 1979.

Greenberg, M., J.C. Greenfield, and N.H. Sarna. *The Book of Job, a New Translation according to the Traditional Hebrew Text*. Philadelphia: JPS, 1980.

Gunkel, Hermann. *The Psalms, a Form-Critical Introduction*. Trans. by Thomas M. Harner, with an introduction by James Muilenburg. Philadelphia: Fortress Press, 1967.

Habel, Norman. *The Book of Job*. CB. Cambridge: Cambridge University Press, 1975.

_____ . *The Book of Job*. OTL. Philadelphia: Westminster, 1985.

Haney, Randy G. *Text and Concept Analysis in Royal Psalms*. Studies in Biblical Literature 30. New York: Peter Lang, 2002.

Harrison, R.K. *Introduction to the Old Testament*. Grand Rapids: Eerdmans, 1969.

Hartley, J.E. *The Book of Job*. NICOT. Grand Rapids, Eerdmans, 1988.

Holladay, William L. *The Psalms through Three Thousand Years: Prayerbook of a Cloud of Witnesses*. Minneapolis: Fortress Press, 1993.

Horine, Steven C. *Interpretive Images in the Song of Songs: From Wedding Chariots to Bridal Chambers*. Studies in the Humanities 55. New York: Lang, 2001.

Howard, David M. Jr. "Editorial Activity in the Psalter: A State-of-the-Field Survey." In *The Shape and Shaping of the Psalter*, pp. 52-70. Ed. by J. Clinton McCann. JSOTSupp 159. Sheffield: Sheffield Academic Press, 1996.

——————. *The Structure of Psalms 93–100*. Biblical and Judaic Studies Volume 5. Winona Lake, IN: Eisenbrauns, 1997.

Interpretation 55 (July 2001). The entire issue is devoted to Ecclesiastes.

Jaki, Stanley L. *Praying the Psalms: A Commentary*. Grand Rapids: Eerdmans, 2001.

Janzen, J. Gerald. *Job*. Int. Atlanta: John Knox Press, 1985.

Johnston, Robert K. "'Confessions of a Workaholic': A Reappraisal of Qoheleth." *CBQ* 38 (1976): 14-28.

Kaiser, Walter C. *Ecclesiastes: Total Life*. Chicago: Moody, 1979.

——————. *Proverbs: Wisdom for Everyday Life*. Grand Rapids: Zondervan, 1995.

Keel, Othmar. *The Song of Songs*. Continental Commentaries. Trans. by F.J. Geiser. Minneapolis: Fortress, 1994.

——————. *The Symbolism of the Biblical World: Ancient Near Eastern Iconography and the Book of Psalms*. Trans. by Timothy J. Hallett. Winona Lake, IN: Eisenbrauns, 1997.

Keller, Phillip. *A Shepherd Looks at Psalm 23*. Grand Rapids: Zondervan, 1970.

Kidner, Derek. *The Proverbs: An Introduction and Commentary*. Downers Grove, IL: InterVarsity, 1964.

——————. *Psalms 1–72: An Introduction and Commentary*. TOTC. Downers Grove, IL: InterVarsity, 1973.

——————. *Psalms 73–150: A Commentary*. TOTC. Downers Grove, IL: InterVarsity, 1975.

_____. *A Time to Mourn and a Time to Dance: Ecclesiastes and the Way of the World*. The Bible Speaks Today. Downers Grove, IL: InterVarsity, 1976.

_____. *The Wisdom of Proverbs, Job and Ecclesiastes: An Introduction to Wisdom Literature*. Downers Grove, IL: InterVarsity, 1985.

Kinlaw, Dennis F. "Songs of Songs." In *The Expositor's Bible Commentary*, 5:1201-1243. Ed. by F.E. Gaebelein. Grand Rapids: Zondervan, 1991.

Knight, George A.F., and Friedemann W. Golka. *Revelation of God: A Commentary on the Song of Songs and Jonah*. ITC. Grand Rapids: Eerdmans, 1988.

Koptak, Paul E. *Proverbs: From Biblical Text – to Contemporary Life*. The NIV Application Commentary. Grand Rapids: Zondervan, 2003.

Kramer, S.N. "'Man and His God': A Sumerian Variation on the 'Job Motif.'" In *Wisdom in Israel and in the Ancient Near East*. Festschrift for H.H. Rowley, pp. 170-182. Ed. by M. Noth and D. Winton Thomas. VTSupp 3. Leiden: Brill, 1969.

Kraus, Hans Joachim. *Psalms 1–59*. Trans. by William C. Oswald. Minneapolis: Augsburg, 1988.

_____. *Psalms 60–150: A Commentary*. Minneapolis: Augsburg, 1989.

_____. *Theology of the Psalms*. Minneapolis: Augsburg, 1986.

Lambert, W.G. *Babylonian Wisdom Literature*. Oxford: Oxford University Press, 1960.

Landy, Francis. *Paradoxes of Paradise: Identity and Difference in the Song of Songs*. Bible and Literature Series 7. Sheffield: Almond, 1983.

Leslie, Elmer. *The Psalms, Translated and Interpreted in the Light of Hebrew Life and Worship*. Abingdon: Abingdon-Cokesbury, 1949.

Leupold, H.C. *Exposition of the Psalms*. Grand Rapids: Baker, 1959.

Lewis, C.S. *Reflections on the Psalms*. New York: Harcourt, Brace & World, Inc., 1958.

Limburg, James. *Psalms*. Westminster Bible Companion. Louisville, KY: Westminster John Knox Press, 2000.

_____. "The Root *ryb* and the Prophetic Lawsuit Speeches," *JBL* 88 (1969): 291-304.

Longman, Tremper III. *The Book of Ecclesiastes*. NICOT. Grand Rapids: Eerdmans, 1998.

_____. *How to Read Proverbs*. Downers Grove, IL: Inter-Varsity, 2002.

_____. *How to Read the Psalms*. Downers Grove, IL: Inter-Varsity, 1988.

_____. *The Song of Songs*. NICOT. Grand Rapids: Eerdmans, 2001.

Lucas, Ernest C. *Exploring the Old Testament: A Guide to the Psalms & Wisdom Literature*. Downers Grove, IL: InterVarsity, 2003.

Mariaselvam, A. *The Song of Songs and Ancient Tamil Love Poetry*. Rome: Editrice Pontifico Istituto Biblico, 1988.

Mattingly, Gerald L. "The Pious Sufferer: Mesopotamia's Traditional Theodicy and Job's Counselors." In *The Bible in the Light of Cuneiform Literature: Scripture in Context*, 3:305-348. Ed. by W.W. Hallo et al. Ancient Near Eastern Texts and Studies 8. Lewiston, NY: Mellen, 1990.

Mays, James L. *The Lord Reigns: A Theological Handbook to the Psalms*. Philadelphia: Westminster, 1994.

_____. *Psalms*. Int. Louisville, KY: John Knox Press, 1989.

McCann, J. Clinton. "The Book of Psalms." *NIB*, 4:639-1280. Nashville: Abingdon, 1996.

_____, ed. *The Shape and Shaping of the Psalter*. JSOTSupp 159. Sheffield: Sheffield Academic Press, 1993.

_____. *A Theological Introduction to the Book of Psalms: The Psalms as Torah*. Nashville: Abingdon, 1993.

McCann, J. Clinton Jr., and James C. Howell. *Preaching the Psalms*. Nashville: Abingdon, 2001.

McCutchan, Stephen P. *Experiencing the Psalms: Weaving the Psalms into Your Ministry and Faith*. Macon, GA: Smyth & Helwys, 2000.

McKenna, D.L. *Job*. Communicator's Commentary. Waco, TX: Word, 1986.

Meek, Theophilus J. "The Song of Songs." In *IB*, 5:91-148. Ed. by G.A. Buttrick. Nashville: Abingdon, 1956.

_____. "Song of Songs and the Fertility Cult." In *The Song of Songs: A Symposium*, pp. 48-79. Ed. by W.H. Schoff. Philadelphia: Commercial Museum, 1924.

Miles, J. Jr. "Gagging on Job, or the Comedy of Religious Exhaustion." In *Studies in the Book of Job*. Semeia 7. Ed. by R. Polzin and D. Robertson. Missoula, MT: SBL, 1977. See pp. 71-126.

Miller, Patrick D. Jr. *Interpreting the Psalms*. Philadelphia: Fortress Press, 1986.

Mitchell, David C. *The Message of the Psalter: An Eschatological Programme in the Book of Psalms.* JSOTSupp 252. Sheffield: Sheffield Academic Press, 1997.

Moore, R.D. "The Integrity of Job." *CBQ* 45 (1983): 17-31.

Motyer, Alec. *The Story of the Old Testament.* Grand Rapids: Baker, 2001.

Mouser, William E. *Walking in Wisdom: Studying the Proverbs of Solomon.* Downers Grove, IL: InterVarsity, 1983.

Mowinckel, Sigmund. *The Psalms in Israel's Worship.* Two Volumes in One. Grand Rapids: Eerdmans, 2004 ed.; First published: Oxford: Basil Blackwell, 1962.

Moyise, Steve, and Maarten J. Menken, eds. *The Psalms in the New Testament.* London/New York: T & T Clark International, 2004.

Muilenburg, James. "Form Criticism and Beyond." *JBL* 88 (1969): 4.

Murphy, Roland E. *Ecclesiastes.* WBC 23a. Dallas: Word, 1992.

——————. *The Gift of the Psalms.* Peabody, MA: Hendrickson, 2000.

——————. *Proverbs, Ecclesiastes, Song of Songs.* Peabody, MA: Hendrickson, 1999.

——————. *The Song of Songs.* Hermeneia. Minneapolis: Fortress, 1990.

——————. *Wisdom Literature: Job, Proverbs, Ruth, Canticles, Ecclesiastes and Esther.* FOTL. Vol. 13. Grand Rapids: Eerdmans, 1981.

Nasuti, Harry P. *Tradition History and the Psalms of Asaph.* SBLDS 88. Atlanta: Scholars Press, 1988.

Newsom, C.A. *The Book of Job.* NIB. Vol. 4. Nashville: Abingdon, 1996.

Nougayrol, J. *Ugaritica,* 5:264-273. Paris: Imprimerie Nationale, 1968.

Parrish, V. Steven. *A Story of the Psalms: Conversation, Canon, and Congregation.* Collegeville, MN: Liturgical Press, 2003.

Parsons, Greg W. "Guidelines for Understanding and Proclaiming the Book of Ecclesiastes, Part 1." *BSac* 160 (2003): 159-173.

——————. "Guidelines for Understanding and Proclaiming the Book of Ecclesiastes, Part 2." *BSac* 160 (2003): 283-304.

Patrick, D. "The Translation of Job 42:6." *VT* 26 (1976): 369-371.

Perdue, Leo G. *Proverbs.* Int. Lousville, KY: John Know Press, 2000.

——————. *Wisdom in Revolt: Metaphorical Theology in the Book of Job.* JSOTSupp 112. Sheffield: Almond, 1991.

Perdue, Leo, and W. Clark Gilpin, eds. *The Voice from the Whirlwind: Interpreting the Book of Job.* Nashville: Abingdon Press, 1992.

Polzin, R., and D. Robertson, eds. *Studies in the Book of Job.* Semeia 7. Missoula MT: Scholars, 1977.

Pope, Marvin H. *Job.* AB. Vol. 15. 3rd ed. New York: Doubleday, 1973.

_____. *The Song of Songs.* AB 7C. Garden City, NY: Doubleday, 1977.

Porter, Stanley E. "The Message of the Book of Job: Job 42:7b as Key to Interpretation?" *EvQ* 63 (1991): 291-304.

Pritchard, James B., ed. *Ancient Near Eastern Texts Relating to the Old Testament.* 3rd edition with Supplement. Princeton: Princeton University Press, 1969.

Provan, Iain. *Ecclesiastes/Song of Solomon.* NIV Application Commentary. Grand Rapids: Zondervan, 2001.

_____. "The Terrors of the Night: Love, Sex, and Power in Song of Songs 3." In *The Way of Wisdom: Essays in Honor of Bruce K. Waltke,* pp. 150-167. Ed. by J.I. Packer and S.K. Soderlund. Grand Rapids: Zondervan, 2000.

Rabin, C. "The Song of Songs and Tamil Poetry." *Studies in Religion* 3 (1973): 205-219.

Reardon, Patrick Henry. *Christ in the Psalms.* Ben Lomond, CA: Conciliar Press, 2000.

Reichert, Victor E. *Job with Hebrew Text and English Translation, Commentary.* Soncino Books of the Bible. New York: Soncino Press, 1946.

Reid, Stephen Breck, ed. *Psalms and Practice: Worship, Virtue, and Authority.* Collegeville, MN: The Liturgical Press, 2001.

Reitman, James S. "The Structure and Unity of Ecclesiastes." *BSac* 154 (1997): 297-319.

Richter, H. *Studien zu Hiob, Der Aufbau des Hiobbuches dargestellt an den Gattungen des Rechtslebens.* Berlin: Evangelische Verlagsanstalt, 1959.

Roberts, J.J. "Job's Summons to Yahweh: The Exploitation of a Legal Metaphor." *ResQ* 16 (1973): 159-165.

Rogerson, J.W., and J.W. McKay. *Psalms 1–50, Psalms 51–100, Psalms 101–150.* Cambridge: Cambridge University Press, 1977.

Rotherham, J.B. *Studies in the Psalms.* 2 vols. Joplin, MO: College Press, 1980 (repr.).

Rowley, H.H. *Job*. NCBC. Rev. ed. Repr.: Grand Rapids: Eerdmans, 1980.

Sakenfeld, Katharine Doob. *The Meaning of HESED in the Hebrew Bible: A New Inquiry*. Eugene, OR: Wipf and Stock, 1978.

Sanders, Paul, ed. *Twentieth Century Interpretations of the Book of Job*. Englewood Cliffs, NJ: Prentice-Hall, 1968.

Sarna, Nahum M. *On the Book of Psalms: Exploring the Prayers of Ancient Israel*. New York: Schocken Books, 1995.

Schaefer, Konrad. *Psalms*. Berit Olam Series. Ed. by David W. Cotter. Collegeville, MN: Liturgical Press, 2001.

Scholnick, S.H. *Lawsuit Drama in the Book of Job*. Ph.D. Dissertation, Brandeis University, 1975.

_____ . "The Meaning of *Mišpāt* in the Book of Job." *JBL* 101 (1982): 521-529.

_____ . "Poetry in the Courtroom: Job 38–41." In *Directions in Hebrew Poetry*, pp. 185-204. Ed. by Elaine Follis. Sheffield: JSOT, 1987.

Seybold, Klaus. *Introducing the Psalms*. Trans. by R. Graeme Dunphy. Edinburgh: T & T Clark, 1990.

Sheppard, Gerald. *Wisdom as a Hermeneutical Construct: A Study in the Sapientializing of the Old Testament*. BZAW 151. Berlin: de Gruyter, 1980.

Shires, Henry M. *Finding the Old Testament in the New*. Philadelphia: Westminster Press, 1974.

Smith, James E. *The Wisdom Literature and Psalms*. Joplin, MO: College Press, 1996.

Snaith, John G. *Song of Songs*. NCB. Grand Rapids: Eerdmans, 1993.

Snaith, N. *The Book of Job: Its Origin and Purpose*. London: SCM Press, 1968.

Spangenberg, Izak J.J. "Irony in the Book of Qohelet." *JSOT* 72 (1996): 57-69.

Stadelmann, L. *Love and Politics: A New Commentary on the Song of Songs*. New York and Mahweh, NJ: Paulist Press, 1990.

Stevenson, W.B. *Critical Notes on the Hebrew Text of the Poem of Job*. Aberdeen: Aberdeen University Press, 1951.

Stuhlmueller, Carroll. *Psalms I, Psalms II*. 2 vols. Wilmington, DE: Michael Glazier, 1983.

_____ . *The Spirituality of the Psalms*. Collegeville, MN: Liturgical Press, 2002.

Sutherland, Robert. *Putting God on Trial: The Biblical Book of Job*. Victoria: Trafford Publishing, 2004.

Swindoll, C.R. *Living on the Ragged Edge: Coming to Terms with Reality*. Waco: Word, 1985.

Tate, Marvin E. *Psalms 51–100*. WBC. Dallas: Word Books, 1990.

Terrien, Samuel. *The Psalms: Strophic Structure and Theological Commentary*. Grand Rapids: Eerdmans, 2003.

Terrien, S.L., and P. Scherer. "Job." *IB*, 3:877-1198. Nashville: Abingdon, 1954.

Tesh, S. Edward, and Walter D. Zorn. *Psalms*. Vol. 1. The College Press NIV Commentary. Joplin, MO: College Press, 1999.

Tesh, S. Edward. "Theodicy." In Walter D. Zorn. *Psalms*, 2:51-56. The College Press NIV Commentary. Joplin, MO: College Press, 2004.

Thomason, B. *God on Trial: The Book of Job and Human Suffering*. Collegeville, MN: Liturgical Press, 1997.

Tournay, Raymond Jacques. *Seeing and Hearing God with the Psalms: The Prophetic Liturgy of the Second Temple in Jerusalem*. Trans. by J. Edward Crowley. JSOTSupp 118. Sheffield: Sheffield Academic Press, 1991.

_____ . *Word of God, Song of Love: A Commentary on the Song of Songs*. Trans. by J.E. Crowley. New York and Mahweh, NJ: Paulist Press, 1988.

Travers, Michael E. *Encountering God in the Psalms*. Grand Rapids: Kregel, 2003.

Tur-Sinai, N.H. *The Book of Job: A New Commentary*. Jerusalem: Kiryath Sepher, 1957.

Van der Toorn, Karel. "Did Ecclesiastes Copy Gilgamesh?" *BRev* 16 (2000): 22-30, 50.

Verheij, Arian. "Paradise Retried: On Qohelet 2:4-6." *JSOT* 50 (1991): 113-115.

Vicchio, S.J. *The Voice from the Whirlwind: The Problem of Evil and the Modern World*. Westminster, MD: Christian Classics, 1989.

Wakeman, M.K. *God's Battle with the Monster: A Study in Biblical Imagery*. Leiden: E.J. Brill, 1973.

Walsh, Carey Ellen. *Exquisite Desire: Religion, the Erotic, and the Song of Songs*. Minneapolis: Fortress, 2000.

Waltke, Bruce K. *The Book of Proverbs, Chapters 1–15*. NICOT. Grand Rapids: Eerdmans, 2004.

Ward, W. *Out of the Whirlwind: Answers to the Problem of Suffering from the Book of Job*. Richmond: John Knox, 1958.

Watts, J.D.W., J.J. Owens, and M.E. Tate. "Job." *Broadman Bible Commentary*. Nashville: Broadman, 1971. See pp. 22-151.

Webb, Barry G. *Five Festal Garments*. Downers Grove, IL: InterVarsity, 2000.

Weiser, Artur. *The Psalms*. OTL. Philadelphia: Westminster Press, 1962.

Weiss, M. *The Story of Job's Beginning*. Jerusalem: Magnes Press, 1983.

Westermann, Claus. *The Living Psalms*. Trans. by J.R. Porter. Grand Rapids: Eerdmans, 1989.

_____ . *Praise and Lament in the Psalms*. Trans. by Keith R. Crim and Richard N. Soulen. Atlanta: John Knox Press, 1981.

_____ . *The Psalms: Structure, Content & Message*. Trans. by Ralph D. Gehrke. Minneapolis: Augsburg, 1980.

_____ . *The Structure of the Book of Job: A Form-Critical Analysis*. Trans. by C.A. Muenchow. Philadelphia: Fortress Press, 1981.

Whybray, R. Norman. *Ecclesiastes*. OTG. Sheffield: Sheffield Academic Press, 1989.

_____ . "Qoheleth, Preacher of Joy." *JSOT* 23 (1982): 87-98.

_____ . *Reading the Psalms as a Book*. JSOTSupp 222. Sheffield: Sheffield Academic Press, 1996.

White, J.B. *A Study of the Language of Love in the Song of Songs and Ancient Egyptian Love Poetry*. Missoula, MT: Scholars Press, 1975.

Williams, R. "Theodicy in the Ancient Near East." *CJT* 2 (1956): 14-26. Repr. in *Theodicy in the Old Testament*. Ed. J.L. Crenshaw. Issues in Religion and Theology 4. London: SPCK; Philadelphia: Fortress, 1983. See pp. 42-56.

Wilson, Gerald H. *The Editing of the Hebrew Psalter*. SBLDS 76. Chico, CA: Scholars Press, 1985.

_____ . "Evidence of Editorial Divisions in the Hebrew Psalter." *VT* 34 (1984): 337-352.

_____ . *Psalms*. Vol. 1. The NIV Application Commentary. Grand Rapids: Zondervan, 2002.

_____ . "Shaping the Psalter: A Consideration of Editorial Linkage in the Book of Psalms." In *The Shape and Shaping of the Psalter*. JSOTSupp 159. Sheffield: Sheffield Academic Press, 1993.

_____ . "The Shape of the Book of Psalms." *Int* 46 (1992): 129-142.

_____ . "Understanding the Purposeful Arrangement of Psalms in the Psalter: Pitfalls and Promise." In *The Shape and Shaping of the Psalter*. JSOTSupp 159. Sheffield: Sheffield Academic Press, 1993.

_____ . "The Use of 'Untitled' Psalms in the Hebrew Psalter." *ZAW* 97 (1985): 404-413.

Wink, Walter. *Unmasking the Powers: The Invisible Forces That Determine Human Existence*. Philadelphia: Fortress Press, 1986.

Witherington, Ben III. "Jesus the Sage: The Wisdom of God." *The Jesus Quest: The Third Search for the Jew of Nazareth*, pp. 161-196. 2nd ed. Downers Grove, IL: InterVarsity, 1997.

Wolfers, D. *Deep Things out of Darkness: The Book of Job*. Grand Rapids: Eerdmans, 1995.

Wright, Addison G. "The Riddle of the Sphinx: The Structure of the Book of Qoheleth." *CBQ* 30 (1968): 313-334.

_____ . "The Riddle of the Sphinx Revisited: Numerical Patterns in the Book of Qoheleth." *CBQ* 42 (1980): 38-51.

_____ . "Additional Numerical Patterns in Qoheleth." *CBQ* 45 (1983): 32-43.

Wright, J. Stafford. "The Interpretation of Ecclesiastes." In *Classical Evangelical Essays in Old Testament Interpretation*, pp. 133-150. Ed. by Walter C. Kaiser Jr. Grand Rapids: Baker, 1972.

Yancey, Philip. *The Bible Jesus Read*. Grand Rapids: Zondervan, 1999.

Zenger, Erich. *A God of Vengeance? Understanding the Psalms of Divine Wrath*. Trans. by Linda M. Maloney. Louisville, KY: Westminster John Knox Press, 1996.

Zerafa, P. *The Wisdom of God in the Book of Job*. Rome: Herder, 1978.

Zorn, Walter D. *Psalms*. Vol. 2. The College Press NIV Commentary. Joplin, MO: College Press, 2004.

Zuck, Roy B., ed. *Learning from the Sages: Selected Studies on the Book of Proverbs*. Grand Rapids: Baker, 1995.

_____ . *Reflecting with Solomon: Selected Studies on the Book of Ecclesiastes*. Grand Rapids: Baker, 1994.

_____ . *Sitting with Job: Selected Studies on the Book of Job*. Grand Rapids: Baker, 1992.

JOB

HISTORICAL AND CULTURAL BACKGROUND

The author of Job has set the story in the context of the patriarchal period (c. 2000–1700 B.C.). Job himself is a patriarch who watches over a large family and acts as personal priest who sacrifices for them. He lives in the "land of Uz," a large territory east of the Jordan River which includes Edom in the south and Aramean lands in the north. Job is probably located in Edom. His wealth is determined by his number of livestock (sheep, camels, oxen, and donkeys) and servants to take care of his holdings. His large family often celebrate life (harvests?) by holding regular feasts. "Yahweh" is his God, the same God who revealed himself to Moses (Exodus 3). He is a monotheist who believes in a personal God who is sovereign and can give and take life and possessions. Job is an "Adam-like" figure who has only one wife. But what is important for the entire story of Job to have a meaningful message is the fact that he is "blameless and upright," one who "feared God and shunned evil" (Job 1:1). He is the "perfect" man who benefits from God's blessings, both materially and spiritually. This is how life ought to be for the righteous.

But the story doesn't end there. Job loses everything including his health, all because *the satan* (the adversary) has challenged Yahweh God as to Job's motivation for his faithfulness. (Special note: Yahweh God instigated the whole affair by saying to *the satan*: "Have you considered my servant Job?") *The satan* was certain Job would curse God if he lost everything. Even Job's wife plays the role of *the satan* and advises the same. Job's response is remarkable: "Shall we accept good from God, and not trouble?" (Job 2:10b). It is important as the story unfolds that the reader understand: "In all this, Job did not sin in what he said" (Job 2:10c). The rest of the story is the working out of this *theodicy* through long and torturous dialogues (with Job and his three friends, plus one young man, Elihu, who sets the stage for the speeches of God).

There are parallels to Job in ancient Near Eastern literature (as there is to Prov 22:17–24:22; cp. Egyptian "Instruction of Amenemope"). Indeed, the ancient Near East cultures were concerned about similar issues of calamity, human suffering, and its relationship to the gods.

There are at least three Egyptian texts that can be compared to Job. 1) **"The Protests of the Eloquent Peasant"** (c. twenty-first century B.C.).[1] Like Job this ancient text has a prose prologue and epilogue with nine semipoetic speeches in between. It is the story of a peasant who is robbed of his donkeys loaded with goods. His complaints to the local authorities are dismissed, so he complains to the chief steward who forces him to return and speak nine times. Each time he speaks more vehemently and vociferously. Finally, the chief steward awards him the property of the one who had robbed him. This story used very long speeches in the mouth of the poor peasant to discuss the injustice of it all, just like Job. In contrast, Job complained more to his God than to his so-called friends and became more confident of his integrity toward the end.

2) **"The Admonitions of Ipu-wer"** (c. fourteenth century B.C., original c. twenty-first century B.C.).[2] This is a fragmentary piece (missing both the beginning and end of the manuscript), but enough is there to discern it as a complaint by Ipu-wer, an Egyptian sage, to the Pharaoh for neglecting the chaos in the kingdom (Sixth Dynasty of the Old Kingdom). The whole social order is at stake and the complaint is toward the only person who can make a difference if he would. By contrast Job's complaint is about the justice of God.

3) **"A Dispute over Suicide"** (c. toward the end of the third millennium B.C.; i.e., c. 2100–2000 B.C.). This text is set in a period of hard times in Egypt which brings despair to the "hero" of the story. He contemplates suicide and has a long, drawn-out discussion with his soul (*ba*). He is fearful that his soul will not accompany him in this kind of death. Like Job, he wishes that the gods would come to his aid: "Pleasant would be the defense of a god for the secrets of my body."[3] While Job despairs of life and wishes he were dead, he does not really contemplate suicide, plus his view of life is higher

---

[1]James B. Pritchard, *Ancient Near Eastern Texts Relating to the Old Testament*. 3rd edition with Supplement (Princeton: Princeton University Press, 1969), pp. 407-410.

[2]Ibid., pp. 441-444.

[3]Ibid., p. 405.

than that of the Egyptian in despair. The discussion of the downcast Egyptian is a soliloquy whereas Job is a dialogue between Job and three friends. They have suffering and despair in common.

Mesopotamian documents also have been discovered that deal with suffering as in Job. 1) A Sumerian poem called **"Man and His God"** (c. 2000–1700 B.C.)[4] reveals how an upright and wealthy man is afflicted by a severe illness. He laments his situation, begging for his family members to join him. He appeals to his personal god for help. After the man confesses that he has sinned, the god restores the man's health by driving out the sickness demon. This upright man would have upheld the "three friends of Job," noting that all people are sinners and deserve punishment by God. However, the poem never raises the problem of divine justice as Job does.

2) Perhaps the best parallel to Job is found with the Akkadian poem **"I Will Praise the Lord of Wisdom"** (c. second millennium B.C.).[5] It is also called "The Poem of the Righteous Sufferer" or "The Babylonian Job." A man of high standing and rank in the community is suddenly and unexpectedly struck with unbelievable suffering. He appeals to his god and goddess but to no avail. He turns to divination with the same result. Then convinced of his own righteousness, he could not find the source of his suffering. After a year of lamenting he has three dreams that detail how the god Marduk sends conjurors to perform rites of exorcism in order to heal the sufferer. He concludes by praising Marduk's ability to "revive in the grave." Like Job, he laments his sufferings, he languishes when the gods do not respond, and recognizes human limitations to understanding the human condition. However, unlike Job, he never addresses the problem of theodicy (God's justice).

3) A later Akkadian work, known as **"The Babylonian Ecclesiastes,"** is also entitled "A Dialogue about Human Misery" (c. 1000 B.C.).[6] This twenty-seven-stanza poem is in the form of an acrostic with eleven verses in each stanza that start with the same letter (very much like Psalm 119, which has eight verses for each Hebrew letter). The sufferer's name is Shaggil-kinam-ubbib. He enters into dialogue

---

[4]See S.N. Kramer, "'Man and His God,' A Sumerian Variation on the 'Job' Motif," in *Wisdom in Israel and in the Ancient Near East*, Festschrift for H.H. Rowley, ed. by M. Noth and D. Winton Thomas, VTSupp 3 (Leiden: Brill, 1969), pp. 170-182.

[5]*ANET*, pp. 434-437.

[6]Ibid., pp. 438-440.

with his friend about human suffering (his suffering in particular) and the absence of divine justice. The gods are remote and do not respond. The sufferer is an orphan and has experienced nothing but trouble and difficulty all his life. The friend responds by accusing his suffering friend of trying to break the laws of the gods. But the sufferer is adamant and retorts: "[People] extol the word of a prominent man, expert in murder, [but] they abase the humble, who has committed no violence." The anomalies of life simply do not give any true answers to his suffering. He seeks answers from Ninurta, Ishtar, and the king as well as his friend. Though the subject matter can be compared with Job, the shortness of the poem and the approach to the problem differs significantly from Job.

4) Finally, an **Akkadian text found at Ugarit** (Ras Shamra)[7] testifies to another poem of a sufferer who finds it difficult to get any answers from the divine realm. His family counsels him to capitulate to his fate. The sufferer emerges from his lamenting to praise his god, Marduk. He appeals for mercy from the very god that afflicted him. Since this theme can be found in early Canaanite culture we can conclude that the author of Job had such texts (and stories) available to him. This is not to say that the author of Job *copied* these stories, but rather the themes and approaches were there. Job itself is much more complicated, more complex and lengthy, and more profound in its approach to the problem of theodicy than these stories. We agree with Hartley in his conclusion to these parallels: "This comparison of parallel literature with the book of Job shows that the author may have been influenced by the rich literary tradition of the ancient Near East about suffering, but more in format than in substance."[8]

TEXT AND AUTHOR

The text of Job as represented in the Masoretic Text (Hebrew text) is in general a good text. However, there are some problems in its interpretation for several reasons. There are over a hundred words not found anywhere else in the Hebrew Scriptures (*hapax legomena*) and thus many passages are unintelligible even to ancient translators (see LXX). While the Septuagint (LXX) sought an accu-

---

[7] J. Nougayrol, *Ugaritica* V (Paris: Imprimerie Nationale, 1968): 264-273.
[8] John E. Hartley, *The Book of Job*, NICOT (Grand Rapids: Eerdmans, 1988), p. 11.

rate translation, it resorted to paraphrasing or guessing at obscure words and phrases. Astonishingly over 350 lines (*stichoi*) of the Masoretic Text are missing in the LXX. It seems to be an attempt at a "responsible" abridgment of the lengthy speeches of the poetic section, particularly in the third cycle of speeches and Elihu's speech (chs. 22–37). Additionally, there has been some kind of disturbance in the Masoretic Text in the third cycle of speeches with seemingly omissions of expected speeches by Bildad and Zophar.[9] The discovery of Ugaritic has helped explain a few obscure passages (see Pope), but much more remains to be discovered to uncover the obscure words and phrases of the Hebrew text of Job.

The book of Job is not attributed to an author. But something of the character of the author may be deduced from the content of the book itself. He probably came from the group called "sages" — wise men of ancient Israel. As Hartley expressed it, these wise men "advocated a disciplined way of life, promising that faithful adherence to their teaching would bring prosperity and a long life (e.g., Proverbs 4). Although they paid little attention to cultic ceremony or redemptive history in their writings, they had a deep religious commitment based on a high ethical monotheism. They taught that the fear of Yahweh was the beginning of wisdom (Prov 1:7; 9:10)."[10]

These sages would have been well-read, well-traveled, and may have been conversant in several languages (cf. 2 Kgs 18:26,28). Such wisdom was not uncommon, even among kings (see for Solomon, 1 Kgs 4:29-34). Job's author knew about mining techniques (e.g., Job 28:1-11) and a great deal about nature, both the animal kingdom and biology (e.g., Job 14:7-10). His vocabulary was extensive, using five different words for the "lion" (4:10-11), thirteen different words for precious gems (28:15-19), five words for "gold," and six different words for "traps" (18:8-10). He knew ancient cultures around him, especially Egypt. Parallel phrases and words with the literature of Ugarit confirms this assessment. Motifs and images that can be

---

[9]As a possible solution to the problem, chapter 24 could be attributed to Zophar as a response to Job in chapter 21. To Bildad's speech in 25:1-6 should be added 26:5-14. Job 27:13-23 could be added to Bildad at 25:6; or if chapter 24 is not attributed to Zophar, then 27:13-23 should be given to Zophar (Habel). The third cycle somehow has lost continuity with the right speakers for the right content in the speeches. Perhaps the trailing off of thought into chaos is deliberately done by the author of Job.

[10]Hartley, *The Book of Job*, p. 15.

traced back to Canaanite myths and legends show that the author is "comfortable" with this literature and tradition. He sets his story in patriarchal history and outside the boundaries of ancient Caanan, i.e., in Edom. The use of "Yahweh," God's personal name, is restricted primarily to the prologue and epilogue (the exceptions are 12:9; 38:1; 40:1,3,6; 42:1) while archaic names for God are used in the dialogue (poetic) portion of the book. This is in line with patriarchal use of God's name.[11] He certainly is in line with those who questioned why God would allow the righteous to suffer and the wicked to prosper (see Psalms 10, 12, 13, 49, 73, 88, 109). This is the great passionate goal of the Book of Job, and its author skillfully presents his inspired approach to the answer.

Much more could be said about the author from the contents of the book, but the bottom line is that no one knows the real author of this great book. We can say he was educated, wise, and spiritually mature to the degree that he could produce such a book.

Not knowing the author of Job makes it difficult to determine the date as well. There are no historical events or markers mentioned in the text of Job that would give away such a matter. Scholars have suggested dates from the time of the patriarchs to the postexilic era.[12]

Usually the postexilic period is chosen because of the "suffering" of the Hebrew people in Babylonian captivity. But the "suffering" of Job is of an innocent individual while the "suffering" of Israel in exile is by a rebellious and sinful nation. The two cannot be compared or paralleled. In fact, Job is a counterargument against the normal view of retribution for sin. Some have tried to argue that "Aramaisms" in the book suggest a late date, but now Ugaritic studies and more understanding of the early influence of Aramaic in Hebrew argues against such a late date. In addition, Job's story is located in Edom. After the exile Edom becomes the archetype of Israel's enemies and thus it hardly seems logical that Job would emerge from that scenario. Early dates for Job are often argued because there are early ancient "Job-like" stories in Egyptian and

---

[11]This is true if we take for granted that God's personal name was not revealed until Moses' day (Exodus 3, 6). On the other hand, *Yahweh* could have been used by the Patriarchs in a restricted sense and without understanding the "meaning" of the name. Scholars debate this issue.

[12]Hartley, *The Book of Job*, p. 17. Hartley places Job in the seventh century B.C. (p. 20).

Mesopotamian cultures (see above). But none of these help locate a date for the book. The truth is that it is impossible to date the book or determine its author.[13]

HISTORY OF INTERPRETATION

The earliest interpretation of Job that is extant is *Testament of Job*, probably from Alexandria in the first century B.C. It is typical of such "testaments" where the "last words" of famous persons are given to us. It reveals more to us the concerns of first century B.C. Hellenistic thought: Jewish mysticism and magic, angelology, speculations concerning *the satan*, cosmological dualism, zeal against idols, and an interest in women. In the end a "chariot" takes Job into heaven.[14]

Apparently the Book of James of the New Testament considered the "epilogue" of Job to be important in its interpretation for he wrote: "As you know, we consider blessed those who have persevered. You have heard of Job's perseverance and have seen what the Lord finally brought about. The Lord is full of compassion and mercy" (Jas 5:11). He is referring, of course, to Job's restitution by God in the end.

Early rabbinic interpreters of Job were not as gracious, accusing Job of sinning in his heart, talking too much, and later, even of being a rebel or one who lacked the love of God. Crenshaw recounts a Jewish legend which explains why all this suffering happened to Job: "God turned Job over to Samael (Satan) to keep him occupied while the Jewish people escaping from Egypt crossed the Red Sea, then God rescued Job from the enemy power at the last moment."[15]

The interpretations given by the early Catholic church fathers were much more positive. Gregory the Great wrote thirty-five books of sermons on Job. Augustine saw the book as an example of "God's grace." Thomas Aquinas, influenced greatly by Greek philosophy, used the book of Job as a discussion on the metaphysical problem of divine providence. Even the Protestant, Calvin, wrote 159 sermons on Job, defending his view of divine providence.

---

[13]See Robert Alden, *Job*, NAC (Nashville: Broadman & Holman, 1993), 11:25-29.

[14]See article on "Job, Book of" by James L. Crenshaw in *ABD*, ed. by David Noel Freedman (New York: Doubleday, 1992), 3:858-868. A brief discussion on "History of Interpretation" is given on pp. 866-867.

[15]Ibid., p. 866.

With the emergence of the Renaissance (seventeenth and eighteenth centuries) interpreters reverted to seeing Job as a rebel and an example of the plight of all humanity. More modern interpreters have interpreted Job through their own intellectual and religious understandings. Both religious and secular interpreters have a tendency to reflect their own times in the book.

Goethe's *Faust* and Archibald MacLeish's *J.B.* are good examples of how Western literature has been influenced by Job. Ever since the Holocaust of World War II, Job has been a primary interest in the writings of some of the survivors (e.g., Elie Wiesel). Even philosophies such as existentialism and Marxism have used Job to support their own causes. With "reader-response criticism" at the forefront, many different groups read Job in light of their own "worldviews," such as feminism, vegetarianism, materialism, and so-called "Christian" reading.[16]

The fact is the Book of Job has been the object of study from the earliest of times. A "reasonably comprehensive bibliography" has been collected and presented by David Clines.[17] Such a list is a commentary on the Book of Job itself. Only the Psalms have produced more literature through the centuries.

STRUCTURE

The overall structure of Job mimics an ancient literary form which has a prologue (chs. 1 and 2) and epilogue (42:7-17) in prose while an extended dialogue and monologue (3:1–42:6) in poetry make up the main (middle) portion of the book. While some scholars have attempted to separate the two literary forms as originally two different stories,[18] modern scholarship has for the most part interpreted the book according to its canonical form. Thus, a simple literary structure according to its overall genre can be seen:

> Prologue: 1:1–2:13 – Prose
> Dialogue/Monologue: 3:1–42:6 – Poetry
> Epilogue: 42:7-17 – Prose

---

[16]See David J.A. Clines, *Job 1–20*, WBC (Dallas: Word Books, 1989), 17:xlvii-lvi.

[17]Ibid., pp. lxiii-cxv.

[18]Georg Fohrer, *Introduction to the Old Testament*, trans. by David E. Green (Nashville: Abingdon, 1968), p. 325.

Another approach to the structure is to consider the "introductions" or "conclusions" to the drama. There are narrative markers that lie outside the narrative itself which give the reader necessary information. At the end of Job's first test it is stated: "In all this, Job did not sin by charging God with wrongdoing" (1:22). Also at the end of his second test, it repeats: "In all this, Job did not sin in what he said" (2:10b). At the end of chapter 31 the information: "The words of Job are ended" (31:40c) is given along with 32:1a: "So these three men stopped answering Job." As Habel expressed it: "These prose markers provide clear evidence of the author's intention to construct the narrative as three movements (1:1–2:10; 2:11–31:40; 32:1–42:17), each with its own appropriate introduction of key characters."[19]

The first division gives all the essential characteristics of Job as "blameless and upright, a man who fears God and shuns evil" (vv. 1b; 8b; 2:3). This information is necessary for the discourse on "divine retribution" and "theodicy" that follows. In the second division, 2:11-13 introduces Job's three friends who will eventually assail Job's character as described in the first division. Chapter 32:1-5 concludes the three friends' debate with Job and introduce Elihu's angry accusations toward Job (in four speeches — chs. 32–37). This is probably an "interruption" and a "delay tactic" by the narrator before God reveals himself to Job (chs. 38–41).

In the first division God afflicts Job, but Job never knows about the heavenly exchange between God and the Satan (the readers know!). God is the topic throughout the dialogues of Job and his three friends, the second division. The three friends insist that Job's sufferings are caused by God, which would validate the doctrine of divine retribution. Job rejects his friends' accusations and challenges God to appear in "court" to confirm his innocence. Job seeks an audience with God in order to validate his integrity.

The third division has the buffoonery of the young man, Elihu, exposed in four speeches, adding nothing really new to the debate. Elihu only exacerbates the situation by condemning Job's insistence of integrity and restating the doctrine of divine retribution (34:11). He does add that God uses suffering as a form of discipline and that he will rescue anyone who turns to him in repentance. He accuses Job of pride (33:12). Elihu talks about God as if he really knows God (37:14,23-24). He declares that God governs the world justly.

---

[19]Norm Habel, *The Book of Job*, OTL (Philadelphia: Westminster, 1985), p. 27.

Finally, God himself speaks to Job in a storm (38:1) and in two speeches reveals how little Job, the human being, understands the Creator of the universe, much less the decisions made in the council of God. God challenges Job. Job is left speechless (40:3-5). After a second speech by God, Job makes a final response to God (42:1-6). What is interesting is that, even though the readers know about the heavenly scene, the problem of Job's sufferings still remains. But it ends well. Job has a new vision of God and of himself regardless of how one interprets verse 6 (42:1-6).

In the epilogue God declares Job as "right" and his friends as "foolish" (42:7-8). The priestly work of Job (1:5) must now be exercised for his guilty friends (42:8-10). This act opens the way for God to bless Job double what he had before (42:12-15). A life fully lived for God, 140 years (2×70 years!), concludes the book (42:16-17).

Perhaps readers can best be served with a content outline to Job, based on its structure of prologue, dialogues, monologues, and epilogue:

 I. Prologue — 1:1–2:13
  A. Job's Integrity — 1:1-5
  B. Job's Double Testing — 1:6–2:10
  C. Introduction of Job's Three Friends — 2:11-13
 II. Dialogues — 3:1–27:23
  A. Job's Lament — 3:1-26
  B. First Cycle of Speeches — 4:1–14:22
   1. Eliphaz — 4:1–5:27
   2. Job's Reply — 6:1–7:21
   3. Bildad — 8:1-22
   4. Job's Reply — 9:1–10:22
   5. Zophar — 11:1-20
   6. Job's Reply — 12:1–14:22
  C. Second Cycle of Speeches — 15:1–21:34
   1. Eliphaz — 15:1-35
   2. Job's Reply — 16:1–17:16
   3. Bildad — 18:1-21
   4. Job's Reply — 19:1-29
   5. Zophar — 20:1-29
   6. Job's Reply — 21:1-34
  D. Third Cycle of Speeches — 22:1–27:23
   1. Eliphaz — 22:1-30
   2. Job's Reply — 23:1–24:25
   3. Bildad — 25:1-6 + 26:5-14?

The ending section of the third cycle of speeches (25:1–27:23) of Job's three friends has been corrupted or confused in its original form. The outline above reflects an attempt (cf. Habel) to restore the material according to the pattern set by the first two cycles. This would possibly make the poem of chapter 28 Job's final reply (a debatable suggestion). On the other hand, the confusion may have been a deliberate attempt by the original author to show the deterioration of the dispute between Job and his friends. Confusion certainly abounds at the end of this third cycle.

---

[20]Some commentators include this poem as part of Job's reply at the end of his dialogue with his three friends. Others separate it out as part of the narrator's "interlude" at this juncture of the book. Either way the poem has significance to the overall interpretation of the book by declaring that true "wisdom" can only be found with God. He alone knows where it is (28:23). Therefore, God speaks in the poem to mankind and says, "The fear of the Lord—that is wisdom, and to shun evil is understanding" (28:28).

GENRE

Claus Westermann described the Book of Job as a dramatized lament. He saw the speeches of Job's three friends and God as disputations in the midst of Job's laments (Job 3 and 29–31 are labeled by Westermann as laments encompassing the speeches, 4–27). Hartley criticized this approach by declaring that "dramatized lament" is only a descriptive term and not a literary genre.[21] Certainly the Book of Job includes lament, but one could argue, not a pure form of lament.

H. Richter has identified the Book of Job as a lawsuit. Hartley has described how this idea works in Job:

> The various sections of the book correspond to different stages of a lawsuit. The first section is the procedure to reach a settlement through a pre-trial hearing (chs. 4–14). Since this attempt fails, a formal trial follows (chs. 15–31). The friends' silence after Job's oath of innocence means that they have conceded their case and Job has won. Deeply disturbed by this state of affairs, Elihu enters and appeals the decision (chs. 32–37). Finally, God appears as litigant (chs. 38–41). Under his questioning, the defendant Job withdraws his complaint so that reconciliation between God and himself is achieved (42:1-6).[22]

John Hartley, himself, considers the Book of Job to be *sui generis* ("without kind"). He does not label the book with any one genre, rather it is made up of many genres to form "an epic and a wisdom disputation." Certainly whatever the genre(s), it addresses the issue of the "righteous sufferer" and "theodicy" (the justice of God).[23]

In spite of Hartley's reticence there is a growing consensus among recent scholars that sees the Book of Job as a lawsuit drama.[24]

---

[21]Hartley, *The Book of Job*, p. 38.

[22]Ibid., pp. 37, 38.

[23]Hartley's nuanced approach to the genres of Job can be found in his commentary in *The Book of Job*, pp. 38-50.

[24]The German work is seminal: H. Richter, *Studien zu Hiob, Der Aufbau des Hiobbuches dargestellt an den Gattungen des Rechtslebens* (Berlin: Evangelische Verlagsanstalt, 1959). English works include: Michael Brennan Dick, "The

Sutherland exclaims: "In fact, *The Book of Job* consists of a number of overlapping and interlocking trials. God puts Job on trial. Satan puts God on trial. God puts Job on trial a second time. Job's friends put Job on trial. Job puts his friends on trial. Everything builds to the climactic moment when Job puts God himself on trial and refuses to acquit him."[25] God's response to Job, however, causes him to "refuse" and "retract" the lawsuit (42:6).

The key to understanding Job as a legal drama is 31:35: "Oh, that I had someone to hear me! I sign now my defense—let the Almighty answer me; let my accuser put his indictment in writing." Job demands a "face to face" courtroom encounter with God as plaintiff to charge him formally with any specific offenses (which Job cannot fathom) or with God as defendant to answer Job's charge of unlawful seizure of his property (9:12a; 10:3a) and personal well-being. Job's friends do not help this situation at all, for they are so steeped in the traditional wisdom of divine retribution that they cannot think of Job in any other context. Job, at first, is reluctant to put God on trial (9:32-35), for he himself is on trial by God (10:2,3). Yet, he wishes to have God in court (13:3). Eventually, Job cries out for a "defender" or "arbiter": "I know that my Redeemer lives, and that in the end he will stand upon the earth. And after my skin has been destroyed, yet in my flesh I will see God; I myself will see him with my own eyes— I, and not another. How my heart yearns within me!" (19:25-27; cp. 16:18-21). And that is precisely Job's problem: God is the one he wants to accuse, and yet he must appeal to God as his only arbiter! Job has no neutral arbiter and must appeal to God alone. In any case, Job cannot find God even to present his case before him (23:1-

---

Legal Metaphor in Job 31," *CBQ* 41 (January 1979): 37-50; S.H. Scholnick, "Lawsuit Drama in the Book of Job" (unpub. Ph.D. Dissertation, Brandeis University, 1975); id., "The Meaning of *Mišpāṭ* in the Book of Job," *JBL* 101 (1982): 521-529; id., "Poetry in the Courtroom: Job 38–41," in *Directions in Hebrew Poetry*, ed. Elaine Follis (Sheffield: JSOT, 1987), pp. 185-204; J.J.M. Roberts, "Job's Summons to Yahweh: The Exploitation of a Legal Metaphor," *ResQ* 16 (1973): 159-165; B. Thomason, *God on Trial: The Book of Job and Human Suffering* (Collegeville, MN: Liturgical Press, 1997); J.B. Frye, *The Legal Language in the Book of Job* (West Yorkshire, UK: British Thesis Service, 1973); and Robert Sutherland, *Putting God on Trial: The Biblical Book of Job* (Victoria, BC: Trafford, 2004). Norman C. Habel also supports this approach to Job in his discussion on "The Narrative Plot" in his *Job*, pp. 25-35.

[25]Sutherland, *Putting God on Trial*, p. 12.

7). Before his so-called friends Job anticipates his final strategy by declaring inviolable his integrity and righteousness (27:2-6). Finally, Job gives a public declaration of innocence (chs. 29–31), which is a legal appeal of a defendant for a formal judicial hearing. Job describes his past blessings from God as he himself acted as a "good" judge (ch. 29). By contrast he laments his present condition (ch. 30), even perhaps anticipating Elihu's speeches (30:1). The "Oath of Innocence" (31:35-37) is preceded and followed by a series of self-curses if Job has participated in any such vile acts (31:1-34,38-40). God must now show himself and either charge Job with wrong or vindicate him.

But the long awaited "face to face" encounter with God is delayed by Elihu's speeches (and as far as Job is concerned his oath may never be answered!). Elihu is well aware of Job's desire for litigation (32:9: "what is right" = "litigation" from מִשְׁפָּט, *mišpāṭ*). He chastises Job for his arguments (34:4-6,23; 35:2; 37:19). But in the process Elihu has in a way prepared Job for the sudden encounter with Yahweh, ironically not expected by either one (37:23).

God answers Job's request "out of the storm" (chs. 38–41). "Brace yourself like a man; I will question you, and you shall answer me" (38:3; cp. 40:7). Here the metaphor for "belt-wrestling" is used to prepare Job for his *contest* with God. God will now enter into court with Job (40:2; cp. 10:2; 13:6; 19; 23:6; 31:35; 33:13).

The key to understanding God's response to Job is the use of the word *mišpāṭ*. Whereas most of the usages in Job refer to the "judging" aspect of the word (jurisprudence), with God it refers to his "ruling" over the universe (sovereignty). Thus, God declares his "justice" before Job (40:8), and Job accepts it (42:2). God is Creator and Sovereign over everything in the universe. He is King and he claims ownership over everything, even over Job and all that he has. Job declares his ignorance and is humbled (42:3). What Job sought from God, a "face to face" encounter, he received: "My ears had heard of you but now my eyes have seen you" (42:5).

Most translations have Job "repent" in the end, such as the NIV: "Therefore I despise myself and repent in dust and ashes" (42:6). In light of the above discussion a more appropriate translation would be: "Therefore I refuse and retract (my case), (being) upon dust and ashes." Job is alive! He has not been destroyed by the Almighty God. His "Oath of Innocence" stands. "Job's action marks his return to normal life; he changes his mind about pressing his suit and assuming the posture of a plaintiff among the dust and ashes. His conflict with God is over and Yahweh is acknowledged as Lord."[26]

The drama is not over. The epilogue is essential to the story. There is still conflict between Job and his three friends. (Elihu has discreetly disappeared from the story!) Morever, God is angry with Job's friends because they have not spoken what is right (נְכוֹנָה, nᵉkônāh, "trustworthy, true words," 42:7). Ironically, Job now must act as mediator ("redeemer") for his friends (42:8,9). "After Job had prayed for his friends, the LORD made him prosperous again and gave him twice as much as he had before" (42:10). This statement seems to belie the whole story of Job in that divine retribution, whether the punishment of the wicked or the rewarding of the righteous, is a false measuring device for human experience or for God's character. But the point is made that just as God as King and Sovereign over the universe has every right to give and take, to curse and bless according to his own designs, so now God has the right to "double" Job's possessions. "The LORD blessed the latter part of Job's life more than the first" (42:12).

Because Job was sinless (1:1,8,22; 2:3,10), the evil that befell him was not punishment for sin. Because Job had no character flaw, the evil that befell him was not for correction or character development. Job maintained his innocence through attacks based on the principle of "divine retribution" by his wife, his three older friends, and the young man, Elihu. Even in God's presence Job maintained his innocence but not without confessing his ignorance to how God works in the universe. He is humbled but exhilarated at surviving his "vision" of God. Job no longer has a "case" against God. Not only does God double Job's possessions but he gives him more children to replace those he had lost. While not "doubling" the number of children, Job's three daughters are described as being most beautiful (were the first three daughters less beautiful?) and receiving equal inheritances with their brothers (42:14,15).

The "core plot" of the story of Job is: "the best man on earth suffers the worst calamities, which poses a test of faith in its most extreme form."[27] Can a free human being love God in a "disinterested" way? Job has answered that question in this great epic we

---

[26]Habel, *Job*, p. 34.
[27]Philip Yancey, *The Bible Jesus Read* (Grand Rapids: Zondervan, 1999), p. 53.

have defined as a "legal drama." Job became a prototype of the
Christ, who in spite of his perfection suffered a horrible death for
the purpose of a greater victory in the universe for all people.

THEOLOGICAL THEMES

THEODICY

No one questions the fact that the Book of Job is a theodicy.[28] "It
is a most provocative theodicy, for it is the story of the most righteous man on earth putting God on trial for crimes against humanity and refusing to acquit him."[29] The "justice of God" is in the final
analysis outside the purview of human beings. But one can seek an
approach to the answer.

In the first place, we ask why there is evil in the world. It is the
only possible world to live in for humans to have a completely self-
less love for God. If human beings thought for a moment that love
for God would bring rewards in a retributive way, then such "love"
would turn into selfishness. Humans would only serve God for what
they could get out of him. Many do that now because of their belief
in this idea. This partly explains why the "prayer of Jabez" phenomenon became a "cottage industry" in such a short time. Such here-
sies will continue. But evil must be allowed in a world where human
beings of freewill have the opportunity to love God in spite of their
circumstances.

This reasoning sounds harsh, especially for the righteous person
who suffers horrible wrongs. Job never knew of the heavenly scenes
of the exchanges between God and *the satan*. For God to reveal this
to Job would have defeated his very purpose for his creation of the
world and mankind.

God expects human beings to challenge him for such evil in the
world. Undeserved suffering will often destroy character rather than
build it up. Humans have a right to know as well as a need to know
why evil pervades their lives. Certainly there are times when punishment seems to be the acceptable answer. And there are situations
in which character development is the result of evil. Examples

---

[28]See the late S. Edward Tesh's excursus on "Theodicy" in Walter D. Zorn,
Psalms, The College Press NIV Commentary (Joplin, MO: College Press,
2004), 2:51-56.
[29]Sutherland, *Putting God on Trial*, p. 10.

abound. But human beings are in danger of sinning if they go beyond their knowledge in blaming God or too quickly acquit God of instigating evil in the world.

Only at the final judgment, when there is a general resurrection, will there be a final reckoning of one's life. At that time God will reveal his purposes in the world for each individual as well as the nations (Isaiah 60; Revelation 21–22). It is enough for humans to love God with complete selflessness. On this basis will we be judged.

Human freewill is taken seriously in Job. Being "tainted" by one man's sin (Adam) is not entertained by the Book of Job. When "divine retribution" is held up by the three friends, Job repudiates it in his case. Elihu insinuates that God is disciplining Job for his sins and that he should not question God in the matter. But just as Elihu considers God to be "beyond our reach," the Almighty speaks to Job "out of the storm" (37:23; 38:1). Indeed, God does discipline his children (Deut 8:5; Prov 3:11,12; Heb 12:4-11), but that is not what is happening with Job.

THE SATAN

For most Christians, and even the general populace, "Satan" is the name of a personal, spirit being — a fallen angel who is the epitome of evil. But "Satan" in the Hebrew Scriptures is a descriptive term, not a name. He is הַשָּׂטָן (ha-śāṭān), "the accuser." In Job he is presented as a "servant of God" (Job 1:6-12; 2:1-10). There are only two other places in the Hebrew Scriptures where this term is used. In 2 Samuel 24:1 Yahweh's anger burned against Israel, and so he incited David against her by carrying out a census (to tax and conscript an army). But in the retelling of this story in Chronicles after the exile "the satan" is the one who incites David: "Satan rose up against Israel and incited David to take a census of Israel" (1 Chr 21:1). "Satan furthers God's will by visiting wrath on disobedient mortals, and in so doing carries out the will of God."[30] He is a provoking agent on David so that David himself might impose a suffocating bureaucratic order (the census) over his people. This is all in the will of God, but a will that is full of his wrath (2 Sam 24:1).

In Zechariah 3:1 there is a scene where Joshua the high priest is

---

[30]Walter Wink, *Unmasking the Powers: The Invisible Forces That Determine Human Existence* (Philadelphia: Fortress Press, 1986), p. 12.

standing before the angel of Yahweh. *The satan* is standing at his right side to accuse him. Of what is *the satan* accusing Joshua? He has on "filthy clothes" (v. 3) which represents all the sin of God's people that apparently brought them into exile. Now God is going to re-dress Joshua with clean garments (v. 4, "rich garments," NIV), and when God's servant, the Branch, is sent, God will through him "remove the sin of [the] land in a single day" (v. 9). *The satan* acts as prosecuting attorney against Israel and his accusations demand strict justice. Without God's grace and the "removal of sin in a sin-gle day," the burden would have been crushing and unbearable for the people of God. "The Adversary merely reiterates what the accus-ing conscience of the people has been affirming all along. The guilt is real, and it is deserved. Only God's undeserved grace causes the case to be quashed."[31] That is why Yahweh rebukes the adversary twice (v. 2).

In Job there is a similar scene except that Job is truly "blameless and upright, a man who fears God and shuns evil" (Job 1:8). The adversary doesn't think so, but would he have paid any attention to Job had God not said: "Have you considered my servant Job?" (v. 8a). The adversary asserts that the "hedge" of blessing God has put around Job is why Job lives a blameless life. Job is good because God is good to him. The adversary insinuates God is wrong about Job and that Job is righteous only for what he can get out of it. We should note that when the afflictions come upon Job, two of them clearly come from God's controlling realm: the "fire of God" and "a mighty wind." But is not God also sovereign over tribes and nations — the "Sabeans" and the "Chaldeans"?

In the second round God says to the adversary: "You incited me against him to ruin him without any reason" (Job 2:3), meaning these things could not have happened to Job without God's permis-sive will. Just so, when the adversary is given permission again with one restriction, he afflicts Job with "painful sores from the soles of his feet to the top of his head" (2:7). And that is the last we see or hear of the adversary. However, one can discern that Job's wife, three friends, and Elihu play the role of "adversary" in the midst of long conversations which quickly plunge to the level of pure accu-sations. This reminds one of Jesus' encounter with Peter when Peter repeats what surely was the tempter's mind about Jesus' impending

---

[31]Ibid.

passion. When Peter argued that this death would never happen to Jesus, Jesus replied: "Get behind me, Satan! You are a stumbling block to me; you do not have in mind the things of God, but the things of men" (Matt 16:23).

In whatever way we study Job, it forces us to consider the role of the adversary (*the satan*) and in both the divine and human realm. "This adversary is merely a faithful, if overzealous, servant of God, entrusted with quality control and testing. Satan, in fact, prompts God and humanity (in the person of Job) to explore the problem of evil and righteousness at a depth never before plumbed — and seldom since."[32]

MY REDEEMER LIVES

Job 19:25-27 is a theological minefield. No matter how you interpret it, it could "blow up" in your face! Popular interpretations have easily applied this text to the Messiah and the resurrection. In the NIV it reads:

> I know that my Redeemer lives, and that in the end he will stand upon the earth. And after my skin has been destroyed, yet in my flesh I will see God; I myself will see him with my own eyes—I, and not another. How my heart yearns within me!

The context indicates that Job is seeking justice (19:7) and vindication of his integrity by an arbiter (see 5:1; 9:33-34; 16:18-21). He so wants his integrity known that he wishes his "oath of innocence" (31:35-37) might be "inscribed with an iron tool on lead or engraved in rock forever!" (19:24). Job desired an arbiter with God, but he knows that only God Himself can help him. Thus, he calls him "my Redeemer" (גֹּאֲלִי, *gō'ălî*). A "goel" is a Defender, Protector, or Vindicator — "a person who defended or avenged the cause of another, or who provided protection or legal aid for a close relative who could not do so for himself" (cf. Lev 25:23-25,47-55; Num 35:19-27; Prov 23:10-11; Jer 50:34).[33] Job not only wants the world to

---

[32]Ibid., p. 14. For an interesting, informative, but controversial discussion on *the satan*, see pp. 9-40.

[33]See Roy B. Zuck, "The Certainty of Seeing God: A Brief Exposition of Job 19:23-29," in *Sitting with Job*, ed. by Roy B. Zuck (Grand Rapids: Baker, 1992), p. 280.

read about his innocence, he wants God to stand upon the earth ("dust") and declare his innocence so the world can hear.

"And after my skin has been destroyed" probably refers to his death, that is, after his skin has all peeled away resulting in death. "Yet in my flesh I will see God." The Hebrew literally reads: "And from my flesh I shall see God," that is, "from, or out of, my flesh shall I see God." What Job seems to be saying is that even though his flesh is consumed by the ravaging boils and disease that he has, he will still see God! "He would have the satisfaction of seeing God himself, and of hearing the sentence in his favour. That expectation he deemed worthy of a permanent record, and wished it transmitted to future times, that in his darkest days and severest trials — when God overwhelmed him, and man forsook him, he still firmly maintained his confidence in God, and his belief that he would come forth to vindicate his cause."[34]

This interpretation may not satisfy those who insist on it referring to a Messiah and the resurrection of the body after death. But the context seems clear that *goēl* is referring to Job's vindicator, God himself. To get resurrection of the body from the phrase, "from my flesh," is pushing the Hebrew text as well as violating the context of Job's view of death throughout the book (cf. Job 7:9,21; 10:21,22; 14:7,9,11,12; 16:22). It is true that the Messiah would be a "Redeemer" and Christianity would clearly teach the resurrection of the body (at Messiah's second coming), but these truths must be found in the New Testament, not here in Job.

There are other theological themes that could be developed from Job, but these three are presented as examples of what the Book of Job offers us, and occasionally does not offer us.

NEW TESTAMENT CONNECTIONS

Besides the Book of Job itself "Job" is referred to in only two other places in the Bible. Ezekiel lists "Noah, Daniel [Danel], and Job" (Ezek 14:14,20) as the epitome of righteous men who alone would be saved in the midst of the sinful nation of Judah. In the New Testament only James speaks of Job: "You have heard of Job's perseverance and have seen what the Lord finally brought about. The Lord is full of compassion and mercy" (Jas 5:11). James seems to

---

[34]Albert Barnes' "Job 19:25-29," in *Sitting with Job*, p. 289.

linger on the epilogue of Job to show how God restored all he had and more. It may seem strange that James would emphasize the "patience" of Job when that is not our impression of Job when we read the book itself. Nevertheless, Job did persevere and God was compassionate and merciful to him in the end. James's emphasis is that "the Lord's coming is near" (Jas 5:8b). Be patient in suffering.

SPECIAL ISSUES

Through the years critical scholars have questioned various aspects of the text of Job as to authorship and development. We will only list and describe briefly these literary problems.[35]

1. **The relationship between the narrative prologue-epilogue (chs. 1–2; 42:7-17) and the poetic speeches (chs. 3:1–42:6)**. Critical scholars have offered various opinions as to this relationship, mainly suggesting that the narrative has been shaped to fit an existing poetic dialogue from another source. They have been combined because of their similar themes. But as has already been pointed out, there are Egyptian and Mesopotamian texts similarly structured with prose-poetry-prose. These are integrated into a whole and artistically presented for an epic story. Such is Job. Without the prologue's insistence on Job's righteousness and integrity, the dialogue on the subject of divine retribution would make little sense. Job does not reject divine retribution but rather the misapplication of this principle to himself. The epilogue confirms that God seeks the ultimate good for his servants and that a proper understanding of divine retribution is quite acceptable.

2. **Problems with the Third Cycle of Speeches (chs. 22–27)**. As already mentioned, there has been some confusion in the latter part of this cycle. Bildad's third speech is unusually short (25:1-6) in comparison to the other speeches, and Zophar's expected speech seems to be missing. Also Job's response seems to be extremely long (chs. 26–28). Besides these phenomena, parts of Job's speech in chapter 24 (vv. 18-24) are unintelligible and counter to Job's complaint in 24:1-17. Attempts have been made by many scholars to reconstruct the cycle based on the two previous ones. No reconstruction has been satisfactory. A simple solution is offered: Eliphaz (ch. 22), Job (chs. 23–24, this leaves ch. 24 a problem), Bildad (25:1-6; 26:5-14),

---

[35]See Hartley, *The Book of Job*, pp. 20-33.

Job (26:1-4; 27:1-12), Zophar (27:13-23), Job (ch. 28). Some scholars see the confusion as deliberate by the author — an attempt to demonstrate the deterioration of the disputation of the three friends of Job. The latter suggestion solves very little.

3. **The Wisdom Poem (ch. 28).** The wisdom poem is usually portrayed as if Job is the one reciting it (NIV quotation marks) or that it is an intrusion into the story of Job. On the other hand, it may be the deliberate insertion of a wisdom poem by the author of Job to do two things: 1) close out the dialogues of Job and his three friends; 2) delay and highlight Job's "oath of innocence" as recorded in chapters 29-31. The poem is highly stylized and artistically constructed with three stanzas (vv. 1-11; vv. 12-19; vv. 20-28) and seven sections (vv. 1-6; vv. 7-8; vv. 9-11; vv. 12-20; vv. 21-22; vv. 23-27; and v. 28). The key idea of the poem is that wisdom is hidden from the eyes of every living thing (v. 21) and only God knows the source of wisdom, for he created it (v. 23). Therefore, true wisdom for mankind is to fear God and shun evil (v. 28). Job is headed in the right direction when he seeks to see God "face to face" in order to be vindicated in his integrity. In this way the poem prepares for Job's "oath of innocence" and his final encounter with God in the storm (chs. 38-41). I consider it not a part of Job's speeches but rather an "interlude" by the author of the Book of Job.

4. **The Elihu Speeches (chs. 32–37).** Many have questioned the authorship of the Elihu speeches, proposing that they have come from a later hand and have been interposed in the text of Job by the final editor of the book. In other words, chapters 32–37 are not integral to Job. After all, Elihu is not mentioned in the prologue or epilogue. He is not anticipated in the dialogues of chapters 3–27. He seems to "interrupt" the anticipated appearance of Yahweh when Job finishes announcing his "oath of innocence" (chs. 29–31). But a more positive view can be offered. Elihu comes as an angry young man who wants to be successful in contrast to the three older friends of Job. Habel describes Elihu as a "brash youth who tends to make a fool of himself as a legal official. . . . Elihu presents the case of the earthly arbiter, the answer of orthodoxy given in a trial situation. . . . Thus the Elihu speech is a deliberate foil and anticlimax which retards the plot and heightens the surprise appearance of Yahweh as a celestial participant."[36] But Elihu is a poor arbiter for Job and him-

---

[36]Habel, *Job*, OTL, pp. 36-37.

self does not anticipate God's appearance when he concludes: "The Almighty is beyond our reach and exalted in power" (37:23a). Elihu thinks he knows more about God than he really does, and poor Job must listen to his brashness as he had done with the three friends, though Job will not respond.

5. **The Yahweh Speeches (chs. 38–41).** A few critical scholars attempt to show contradictions between the two speeches (38:1–40:2; 40:6–41:34). Others reformulate the two speeches in order to make one. But the majority of scholars maintain the integrity of the two speeches. As Habel expressed it: "The twofold appearance of Yahweh in the whirlwind (38:1; 40:6) corresponds to his two appearances before the council of heaven (1:6; 2:1). His twofold incitement by the Satan is balanced by a dual challenge issued to Job."[37] The first speech answers Job's accusation that God does not rule the world with justice. The second speech is designed to overwhelm Job with the fact that God is an all-powerful ruler of the cosmos and thus Job should capitulate his case. However disappointed we may be with Yahweh's speeches to Job, he does not and cannot reveal the heavenly council's challenge with *the satan* without losing the *bet*.

6. **Job's Response in 42:6.** There is much debate as to how to interpret Job's second response to Yahweh's second speech. Is Job repentant or rebellious? Most scholars support the view that in some way Job is repenting, no matter how one construes the wording of the Hebrew. By contrast J.B. Curtis has argued that Job is rebellious and totally rejects Yahweh's message.[38] He translated Job 42:6: "Therefore I feel loathing contempt and revulsion (toward you, O God); and I am sorry for frail man." B. Lynne Newell has demonstrated that this approach is unjustified.[39] She interprets (and translates) 42:6 in the following way: "Therefore I will have nothing more to do with (i.e., despise and reject) the sins of which you charged me which I committed by my speaking without understanding, and I repent upon dust and ashes."[40] Job's sin is accusing God of being unjust while justifying himself and exalting himself as a "rival god." All this occurs during his intense suffering, not before. I have suggested a more nuanced translation above in relationship to Job's

---

[37]Ibid., p. 33.

[38]John B. Curtis, "On Job's Response to Yahweh," *JBL* 98 (1979): 497-511.

[39]B. Lynne Newell, "Job: Repentant or Rebellious?" in *Sitting With Job*, pp. 441-456.

[40]Ibid., p. 455.

"oath of innocence": "I refuse and retract (my case), (being) upon dust and ashes." In other words, Job does "repent" in a fashion. He changes his mind about his case or trial against Yahweh. He knows now that he has indeed darkened the counsel of God (38:2; 42:3). But he did "see" God. The theophany had its desired effect. Job is overwhelmed, and he knows now that he must not pursue his "oath of innocence" in a courtroom trial. Thus, he "repents" of it. He "changes his mind."

7. **The Epilogue (42:7-17).** A few scholars have attempted to dismiss the epilogue as not belonging to the original story of Job. They argue that God restores Job's possessions and his family, thus supporting the principle or doctrine of divine retribution — the very doctrine Job repudiates in the dialogues (chs. 3–27). But the argument is ill-stated. The Book of Job does not reject divine retribution. Rather, it corrects the misguided application of the doctrine as presented in the speeches of Job's three friends. They were wrong. Job was right (42:7). Thus, God has every right to restore Job as a caring father would any child. What triggers Job's restoration is his prayer for his friends. Perhaps that should teach us about our troubling relationships and how we should deal with them. Job can teach us beyond the subject of suffering.

PSALMS

The Book of Psalms is one of the most important books in the Old Testament. It was at the center of the worship and study in ancient Israel. Since the Book of Psalms is all poetry, it spoke to the heart and emotions of those who shared in its message in both song and meditation. Most of the individual psalms were originally put to music. Perhaps at a later time technical terms were added to its titles. At least one technical term (*Selah*) is found in the text of the Psalms. The historical and cultural background of the Psalms begins with King David and does not end until the postexilic period, over 500 years of development. Almost half of the Psalms are attributed to David (73), but other authors are mentioned and many psalms remain anonymous. The Psalms exhibit a variety of genres or types (ex.: hymns, laments, royal, wisdom, etc.). While the structure of the Psalms is clearly divided into five "books," the reason for that division is not so clear. Many theories have been offered. Critical approaches by scholars to the Psalms, both past and present, have shed a great deal of light on the meaning and message of the Psalms. Because of the canonical form of the Psalms and the special arrangements of certain psalms, particularly at the "seams" of the "book" divisions, the theological emphases of the final editors can be discerned. Additionally, the New Testament use of the Psalms gives rich insights into the apostles' understanding of its theology and "messianic" applications.

HISTORICAL AND CULTURAL BACKGROUND

It is clear that many of the psalms are individual productions. Evidence for this appraisal is in the headings or superscriptions that appear with many of the psalms. Fifteen of these headings are historical in nature and have been traditionally considered to be reliable indications of the situations out of which the psalm arose (see

Psalms 3; 7; 18; 30; 34; 51; 52; 54; 56; 57; 59; 60; 63; 102; and 142). For example, Psalm 51 has the heading: "For the director of music. A psalm of David. When the prophet Nathan came to him after David had committed adultery with Bathsheba." This is taken to mean that David wrote this great penitential psalm after suffering remorse and being condemned by Nathan for his double sin of adultery and murder. Others understand the superscription to mean a psalm written "in relationship to" David's sin. This is a possibility, but which interpretation is accurate is difficult to discern.

Not all the historical headings seem to fit as well as Psalm 51 (cp. Psalms 30; 34). Surely David could have written the psalms attributed to him (73 psalms), for he was skillful on the lyre (1 Sam 16:14-23; 18:10). He produced laments over Saul and Jonathan (2 Sam 1:19-27) and Abner (2 Sam 3:33-34) and organized musicians at the sanctuary in Jerusalem (1 Chr 6:31-32; 16:4-7; 25:1; 2 Chr 23:18). Later Jewish tradition has David "editing" all the psalms (an impossibility!). Nevertheless, by the first century B.C. David's name became attached to all the Psalms (e.g., Heb 4:7 attributes the words of Ps 95:7-8 to David, even though that psalm is not connected to any name or group).

Other collections were probably written by individuals, who also wrote on behalf of the community of worshipers ("of/to/for the sons of Korah" — Psalms 42–49; 84–85; 87–88 and "of/to/for Asaph" — Psalms 50; 73–83). The collection, the songs of "ascents" (Psalms 120–134), probably came from individual hands but have been adapted for communal use (for pilgrimages to Jerusalem).

It must be noted that songs of praise and thanksgiving among the people of Israel date from their earliest history. Exodus 15:1-18 recorded the song that was sung to celebrate God's deliverance of his people from the Egyptians. Since Moses kept a diary of the progress of the people (Num 33:2), we may believe that he also preserved the song. By the time of David we find a group composed of Asaph and his brothers, who were specially appointed to sing of thanksgiving to God (1 Chr 16:7). The song that they were to sing (16:8-16) is composed of Psalm 105:1-15, plus a variant of Psalm 96:1-13, and an added doxology from Psalm 106:47-48. In 2 Samuel 22 we find Psalm 18.[1] Thus from Exodus, from Chronicles, and from

---

[1]Other duplications in the Psalms include: Psalm 53 = Psalm 14; Psalm

Samuel we have evidence that some psalms were preserved, with variations, independently of any formal collection.

Higher critical scholars in the last half of the nineteenth century repudiated the above "traditional" view on the premise that any advanced concept of religion must necessarily be late. They postulated that it was under the priestly direction that the Psalms were written (or that old ones were rewritten) for liturgical use in the worship of the Temple — late compositions to accompany advanced Judaism. With the Psalms evaluated by this "Hegelian" presupposition, most of the Psalms were deemed postexilic — basically a product of the second century B.C. While many today still attempt to late-date most of the Psalms, several factors are now known that must modify the "higher critical" view.

First of all, there is difficulty in harmonizing the contents of the Psalms to a late setting. For example, since there were no Jewish kings at any time during this period (the Persian and Hellenistic periods), why were royal psalms and others with references to the king included? Why were disclaimers against sacrifice (cf. Ps 51:16) included if the priestly circles controlled the composition of the Psalms?

Secondly, there have been archaeological discoveries in the twentieth century that necessitated a reevaluation of the basic assumptions under which the higher critics labored. Ugaritic literature has demonstrated that supposedly late phraseology and style of the Psalms are not late at all. They were common currency in Palestine more than three hundred years *before* the time of David and six hundred years *before* the literary prophets. The Qumran discoveries (1948) revealed that the sectarians wrote thanksgiving hymns or psalms of their own, but with a form and content unlike that of the Psalms of the Hebrew Scriptures. In addition, it is apparent that the community possessed the collection of biblical psalms known to us, albeit Books 4 and 5 were not yet in their canonical order. This is evidence that the collection had been made before the time of the Maccabees (165 B.C.), perhaps as much as two centuries before.

The evidence that demands an earlier date for many of the psalms includes: (1) the contrast in style, structure, theme, and theology of the later hymns of Qumran as compared to the Psalms, (2) the absence of any reference to historical events of a late period,

---

40:13-17 constitutes the whole of Psalm 70; and parts of two Psalms (57:7-11 and 60:5-12) make up Psalm 108.

except the ones mentioned in Psalms 89; 126; and 137 (the Baby-lonian captivity), (3) the lack of concern with eschatology that seems to have been characteristic of later Judaism, (4) the evidence in prophetic literature of the prophets' acquaintance with Psalms (or of mutual acquaintance), (5) the discovery in other ancient literature of psalms of an individualistic and personal nature, indicating that this type is not a later development as had been supposed, and (6) the spelling of David's name. There were two spellings — *dwd* and *dwyd*. The latter spelling is almost exclusively found in Chronicles, Ezra, and Nehemiah, the latest books of the Hebrew Scriptures. This is also the spelling at Qumran. The shorter spelling appears in the earlier books, and it is *only this* form that is found in the Psalms.[2]

The "late" direction in the study of the origins of the Psalms had been provided by Hermann Gunkel (1862–1932) in his form-critical approach to the subject. Gunkel reasoned that an examination of the character of the Psalms should provide clues to their purpose and thus to the situation in life that called them into being. In his study he noted that many of the psalms fell into one of a few recog-nizable types (genres; see below). Through the study of songs of a similar type, the distinguishing characteristics of this particular lit-erary form could be delineated. Acquaintance with these character-istics — structure, theme, components, formalized vocabulary, mood — would in turn help in the identification of other literature of a sim-ilar genre when it is encountered.

Convinced that form analysis and generic classification of the Psalms was a sound approach, Sigmund Mowinckel (1884–1965) gave the study new dimensions. In his view, all of the Psalms (with a few possible exceptions) were related to the cult, and were to be interpreted in terms of the ritual performed regularly at the sanctu-ary (or sanctuaries). The Psalms were, in short, originally cultic poems composed especially for repeated use in cultic ritual. Even psalms of an individual nature, such as Psalm 3, were said to be cul-tic formularies, prepared for communal use.

By far the most important cultic celebration, according to Mowinckel, was an annual New Year's Festival kept in the autumn in the Temple. Some forty psalms — hymns, psalms about the king, and even some complaint songs — were recognized as having their life

---

[2]See Noel M. Freedman, "The Spelling of the Name 'David' in the Hebrew Bible," *HAR* 7 (1983): 89-104.

situation within the framework of this comprehensive celebration. The basic theme of the festival was acted out in a ceremony of enthronement of Yahweh as universal king.

As a matter of fact, within the Hebrew scriptures there is no unequivocal evidence of any Enthronement Festival, and many scholars consider the argument from analogy to be insufficient to establish the case. That many psalms are related to worship, reflecting a cultic origin, seems obvious. Even Mowinckel recognized that some, just as obviously, did not seem for that purpose. The didactic psalms, specifically, are viewed by many scholars as not only outside the cult but actually anticultic in outlook. The truth is that the history and the scope of the Psalms are too extensive for one to restrict them in their origin to the cultic situation alone.

The contribution to the study of Psalms (their historical and cultural backgrounds) made by Gunkel and Mowinckel should not be minimized. The former, with deep insight, perceived the Psalms as literary documents arising from specific life situations and pursued his research in that direction. Mowinckel directed his attention to the cultic setting, which he believed to lie at the heart of their origin. One development, largely as a result of his work, was the recognition that the golden age of the Psalms was in the time of the Hebrew monarchy and not in the Maccabean period. Furthermore, as a result of his emphasis, insights have been gained into the nature of Israelite worship and the uses made of the Psalms. Several scholars, however, believe that Mowinckel depended too greatly upon comparative religion for many of his conclusions. The fact is firmly established that the origin of many of the psalms is to be sought in acts of worship in Israel. But to say that all of the psalms arose as forms of liturgy to accompany ritual is to overstate the case. That they were used in worship seems obvious. That they were a necessary complement to ritual is not so clear.

In pursuing the life situation, Erhard Gerstenberger, a major Psalm scholar, recommends that one continue to seek clues from form analysis. Yet he recognizes the flexibility that exists in the use that may be made of forms. *They* may be standardized (theoretically), but life situations are not. Furthermore, the language that sprang from one life situation may be utilized in quite different situations by other persons, so the form of expression does not of necessity indicate identical situations.

In the continued quest for the setting and significance of the

Psalms, Gerstenberger would augment the consideration of form by (1) a concern with philology and lexicography, (2) statistical counts of vocabulary to reveal specific typical usages, (3) research in the field of comparative literature, (4) form-critical study of Near Eastern cuneiform materials and utilization of archaeological discoveries, and (5) attention to the insights to be gained from the study of present day anthropology, specifically with reference to rites, feasts, and ritual activities. (Just how much is to be learned about the rites and practices of ancient Israel by analogy with the cultic practices of the twenty-first century might be questioned.)[3]

Were there psalms for special religious celebrations? Apparently so. Psalm 67, for example, could well have been written for use at the harvest festival, since it speaks of the earth "yielding her increase" as evidence of God's blessing. And are there psalms of an intensely personal nature and application? Again, yes. Gunkel, Mowinckel, and others have shown that in form, development, and vocabulary the Psalms exhibit similarities to ancient cultic literature, literature produced for purely cultic use. But this does not preclude the possibility that the psalmist might utilize such forms to express his own individual thoughts and feelings. In so doing he would express himself in a style and idiom that were universally used in the offering of praise to deity, and do so without respect to any liturgical use the language might have served in other situations.

Whether for liturgy or for private devotion, the Psalms have enhanced the worship of humankind for three millennia. Written over a period of several hundred years by the providence of God, we have a collection of songs for all seasons. Actually, the Psalms had their origin in hearts awakened to the grace and beneficence of God, inspired by the divine righteousness, mercy, and power. Under these circumstances the thoughts and emotions of the psalmist could not be contained but must issue forth in songs of hymns of praise, petition, and thanksgiving. The result is a hymn book, or book of devotions, that is timeless in its relevance.

---

[3]See Erhard S. Gerstenberger, *Psalms Part 1 with an Introduction to Cultic Poetry*, FOTL, vol. XIV (Grand Rapids: Eerdmans, 1988); and *Psalms, Part 2, and Lamentations*, FOTL, vol. XV (Grand Rapids: Eerdmans, 2001).

TEXT AND AUTHOR

By comparing the duplicated psalms (see footnote 1 above) one can come to the conclusion that there are irregularities in the original Hebrew text (compare Psalm 14 and 53; Psalm 18 with 2 Samuel 22; etc.). Also, there seem to be, at least at the surface, some difficulties with the acrostic Psalms 9 and 10 as well as with some of the other acrostics in the Psalms. The propensity to use *Elohim* in place of *Yahweh* in the "Elohistic Psalter" (Psalms 42–83) indicates serious "changes" and "editing" of previously written material. There are, of course, the usual variant readings due to "look-alike letters" and all the other reasons for copyists' errors. In spite of these factors the Masoretic Text (Hebrew text) remains superior to all other texts, including the Septuagint (LXX) and the secondary versions.[4] Since the LXX includes some curious readings, its use by the authors of the New Testament offers challenging evaluation for both the original Hebrew and Greek version (LXX) of the Psalter.

By the first century A.D. the entire Psalter was considered "Davidic" (see above). However, only 73 of the 150 Psalms in the Hebrew scriptures have "David" as the author, and several of these can be interpreted as "dedicated to," or "for" David instead of "by," meaning authorship. Solomon is mentioned in Psalms 72 and 127. Yet here it is more likely that Psalm 72 is viewing David as the author (see Ps 72:20) and he is writing "for Solomon," who is being enthroned as the next king (an idealized view!). Psalm 127 is clearly postexilic, but the content of the psalm, "building a house (temple?)," probably suggested the title "to Solomon." Similarly Moses is attached to Psalm 90, perhaps to give to Book 4 (Psalms 90–106) a "Mosaic" flavor in terms of the wilderness wanderings from beginning to end (cp. Psalms 105 and 106) and its relevance to the postexilic Israelites.

Either authorship or influence is given to the "sons of Korah" (Psalms 42-49; 84-85; 87-88) and Asaph (Psalms 50; 73-83). Heman the Ezrahite is connected to Psalm 88 while Ethan the Ezrahite is mentioned with Psalm 89. There are at least 49 "orphan" psalms with no authorship inscriptions. Only six of these have some inscriptions (nonauthorship information) connected to them

---

[4]See R.K. Harrison, *Introduction to the Old Testament* (Grand Rapids: Eerdmans, 1969), p. 999.

(Psalms 66; 67; 92; 98; 100; and 102).[5] Perhaps the untitled Psalms 66 and 67 should be considered "Davidic." Certainly part of Psalm 71 (vv. 1-3) comes from a Davidic psalm (Ps 31:1-4).

Given the above, it is easy to see how later Jewish teaching would attribute all the Psalms to David in some fashion. Certainly his influence over the Psalms in the first two books, as well as the "framing" of the Psalter with "David" psalms (Psalms 138–145), account for this. Clearly the sons of Korah, and especially Asaph, had much to do with the final editing of the Psalter. The orphan psalms indicate that there may have been many unknown authors of the Psalms. Providentially they have been preserved and placed in the Psalter so as to structure it for a purpose.

HISTORY OF INTERPRETATION

A brief historical survey of Psalms study will help the student understand the direction that such study has taken in the last twenty-five years. Scholars at the end of the nineteenth and beginning of the twentieth centuries began in earnest what we call "critical" studies. They were concerned about "the historical backgrounds of the biblical materials and often included radical reconstruction of the biblical text. Representative of this period and the approach that predominated are the works of Briggs (1906), Cheyne (1891, 1904), Ewald (1880), Perowne (1890), and Wellhausen (1898)."[6]

Gunkel (1926, 1933) and Mowinckel (1922, 1962) built on these critical scholars in their groundbreaking work. As already discussed above, Gunkel concentrated on the literary forms of the Psalms (genres) and tried to get back to the *Sitz im Leben* (situation in life) for each form or genre. This approach has been refined by many scholars since, and the end product can be seen with such classifications as presented by W.H. Bellinger Jr. (see below). Mowinckel, on the other hand, went beyond Gunkel and sought a cultic (worship) setting for each psalm.[7] He emphasized that the Psalms grew

---

[5]Psalm 10 is part of an acrostic with Psalm 9, a "Davidic" psalm. Psalm 33 is closely connected to Psalm 32, again a "Davidic" psalm. Thus, both Psalms 10 and 33 could be considered under David's authorship. Psalm 43 should be considered one psalm with Psalm 42, "of the sons of Korah."

[6]David M. Howard Jr., *The Structure of Psalms 93–100* (Winona Lake, IN: Eisenbrauns, 1997), p. 1.

[7]See S. Edward Tesh and Walter D. Zorn, *Psalms, Vol. I*, College Press NIV

out of a cultic setting in Israel's early monarchy at the harvest and New Year festival ("Enthronement of Yahweh" New Year Festival). Since the festival was only a conjecture at best, scholars have either dismissed or modified much of Mowinckel's work. However, it is evident that many of the psalms did have a cultic setting, and in that regard Mowinckel's contribution is still relevant. A whole generation of scholars followed these two giants in Psalms studies, each giving critique and opinions about genres and their cultic settings.[8] But even Gunkel recognized his approach had its limitations and did not address the Psalms in their final form and literary setting. As McCann has written: "It is precisely this recognition that eventually invited the movement beyond a method that aims at appreciating the *typical* and the *original* to methods that aim at appreciating the *individual* and the *final*."[9] This need led scholars in recent years to develop what is known as rhetorical and canonical criticism.[10]

We will arbitrarily call the last twenty-five years or so of the twentieth century "modern scholarship"[11] on the Psalms. Since approxi-

---

Commentary (Joplin, MO: College Press, 1999), p. 34, for a brief critique of Mowinckel's approach.

[8]See Howard, *Structure*, p. 2, where he lists the following scholars: "Anderson (1972), Buttenwieser (1938), Calès (1936), Craigie (1983), Drijvers (1964), Kidner (1973, 1975), Kissane (1954), Kraus (1978, 1988–89), Leslie (1949), McCullough and Taylor (1955), Nötscher (1947), Oesterley (1937, 1939), Sabourin (1969), Schmidt (1934), Weiser (1962), Kraus (1978), and Gerstenberger (1988). Dahood's work (1966–70) represented a major departure from these approaches, because he paid attention to Ugaritic materials, but he likewise had brief sections on forms and showed no real interest in the Psalter's organization."

[9]J. Clinton McCann Jr., "The Book of Psalms," *NIB* (Nashville: Abingdon Press, 1996), 4:652.

[10]See James Muilenburg, "Form Criticism and Beyond," *JBL* 88 (1969): 4. *Rhetorical criticism* (as applied to the Psalms) is the study of the literary features of each individual psalm in order to understand its unique poetic and creative form. *Canonical criticism*, by contrast, is the study of the final shape and form of all the psalms as the "final editors" have given them to us. As one author has expressed it: "The discovery that the Psalter has something of an overall literary shape has opened up all sorts of new directions in study of the psalms." See Craig G. Bartholomew, "Towards a Post-liberal Agenda for Old Testament Study," *Make the Old Testament Live*, ed. by Richard S. Hess and Gordon J. Wenham (Grand Rapids: Eerdmans, 1998), p. 39.

[11]Detailed review of recent scholarly work on the Psalms can be found in the following: David M. Howard Jr., *The Structure of Psalms 93–100*, Biblical and Judaic Studies (Winona Lake IN: Eisenbrauns, 1997), 5:1-19; also by

mately 1980 a major shift in Psalms studies has taken place. This shift was anticipated by Westermann's brief chapter "The Formation of the Psalter" (1961/62).[12] Westermann observed seven characteristics of the canonical form of the Psalter: 1) the predominant genre of lament psalms are found mostly in the first half of the Psalter; 2) the second half of the Psalter is predominantly made up of collections of psalms of praise; 3) the superscriptions to the Psalms identify most of the individual laments as belonging somehow to David while community psalms appear mainly in the Korah and Asaph collections as well as the "ascents" psalms; 4) the psalms of praise usually function to close a collection, hence the doxologies at the end of the various books (Ps 41:13; 72:19; 89:52; 106:48; and Psalm 150); 5) the Royal Psalms have a collection of their own but are scattered throughout the Psalter as a "frame," "having taken on a secondary messianic interpretation"; 6) the Psalter does not contain a clearly discernible collection of liturgies (hence a purpose for the Psalter can be discerned apart from a worship background!); 7) two distinctions were made in the editing process: first, individual psalms were separated from community psalms; and secondly, lament psalms were distinguished from the psalms of praise.[13]

Brevard S. Childs is credited with advocating a "canonical approach" to the entire Old Testament.[14] His conclusion was that the editor(s) of the final form of the Psalms was governed by "eschatological" concerns; i.e., using so-called Royal psalms in such a way as to be "a witness to the messianic hope which looked for the consummation of God's kingship through his Anointed One."[15] The placement of Psalm 2 solidified this for Childs. Thus, as several have

---

Howard, "Editorial Activity in the Psalter: A State-of-the-Field Survey," in *The Shape and Shaping of the Psalter*, ed. by J. Clinton McCann, JSOTSupp 159 (Sheffield: Sheffield Academic Press, 1993), pp. 52-70; and Norman Whybray, *Reading the Psalms as a Book*, JSOTSupp 222 (Sheffield: Sheffield Academic Press, 1996), pp. 15-35, chapter one, "Recent Views on the Composition of the Psalter."

[12]See Claus Westermann, *Praise and Lament in the Psalms* (Atlanta: John Knox Press, 1965, 1981), pp. 250-258. This chapter first appeared as *"Zur Sammlung des Psalters," ThViat* 8 (1961/62, 1962): 278-284.

[13]Westermann, *Praise and Lament*, pp. 257-258.

[14]See Brevard S. Childs, *Introduction to the Old Testament as Scripture* (Philadelphia: Fortress, 1979). For his discussion on the Psalms refer to pp. 504-525.

[15]Childs, *Introduction*, p. 517.

observed,[16] Psalms 1 and 2 formed an introduction to the Psalter, certainly to Books 1 & 2, as they are framed by the royal psalms of Psalms 2 and 72. The Book of Psalms was to be read as "a word of God to men" and not just "words of men to God" (prayers).[17] Therefore, God's people were to read the Psalms as "Torah" with a theologically framed message about hope for a renewed Davidic dynasty and king.[18]

These ideas were further developed by one of Childs' students, Gerald H. Wilson, in his doctoral dissertation published in 1985 that has since become a *groundbreaking* work for subsequent Psalm scholars.[19] With few exceptions most Psalm scholars today agree with the overall approach of Wilson's work.[20] He did a comparative study of Psalms with ancient Sumerian Temple Hymns, the Catalogues of Hymnic Incipits and Qumran Psalms manuscripts. The editorial techniques found in these enabled Wilson to find similar editorial work on the final form of the Psalms.

Perhaps Wilson's most insightful contribution came with his analysis of the placement of the "royal" psalms in Books 1–3 and how Books 4 and 5 relate to the "discussion" of kingship and the Davidic covenant: Psalms 2; 41; 72; and 89. (See below on "Structure" for the five "books.") Psalm 2 introduces the idea of the Davidic covenant with reminiscence of 2 Samuel 7:14. While Psalm 2 establishes the Davidic dynasty by a covenant of God, Psalm 41 gives assurances of God's divine protection and security in the face of David's enemies, though it is not a "royal" psalm. The establishment of David's dynasty

---

[16]See especially Gerald Sheppard, a student of Childs, in his *Wisdom as a Hermeneutical Construct: A Study in the Sapientializing of the Old Testament,* BZAW 151 (Berlin: de Gruyter, 1980), p. 142.

[17]This was an emphasis made by Joseph Reindl in 1981, who, perhaps, encouraged the "canonical" work of Childs and subsequent scholars.

[18]For a complete development of this point see J. Clinton McCann Jr., *A Theological Introduction to the Book of Psalms: The Psalms as Torah* (Nashville: Abingdon Press, 1993).

[19]Gerald Henry Wilson, *The Editing of the Hebrew Psalter,* SBLDS 76 (Chico, CA: Scholars Press, 1985).

[20]See Norman Whybray, *Reading the Psalms as a Book,* who gives an excellent overview of Wilson's work (pp. 20-22) and subsequent scholarly works on the canonical shape and purpose of the Psalms (pp. 23-33). Whybray himself is skeptical of Wilson's and other's conclusions about the final form of the Psalter (See pp. 41, 85, 93, 94, 99, particularly 118-124.). His criticisms have not persuaded many scholars from accepting the results of such scholars as Wilson, Mays, Howard, and McCann.

(Psalm 2) and its security (Psalm 41) are now passed on to his son (Psalm 72, attributed to Solomon), whose reign in some respects is a climax of the Davidic dynasty. Books 1 and 2, thus, highlight in a positive manner the Davidic rule. But with the addition of Book 3 a new perspective is given: the covenant with David and his dynasty has been broken and has failed (Ps 89:38,39,44). Psalm 89 concludes with the anguished cry of the Davidic descendants (Ps 89:46): "How long?" The people of the kingdom are in exile and long for the restoration of the Davidic dynasty and the honoring of God's eternal covenant (2 Sam 7:16). Books 4 and 5 are an answer to this dilemma and probably account for their unique content and composition in contrast to Books 1–3. Book 4, with its high number of "untitled" psalms (10 out of 17 psalms, NIV), seems to have been used editorially at this juncture as the "center" message of the Psalter as a whole. Wilson wrote concerning Book 4:

> In my opinion, Pss 90–106 function as the editorial "center" of the final form of the Hebrew Psalter. As such this grouping stands as the "answer" to the problem posed in Ps 89 as to the apparent failure of the Davidic covenant with which Books One–Three are primarily concerned. Briefly summarized the answer given is: (1) YHWH is king; (2) He has been our "refuge" in the past, long before the monarchy existed (i.e., in the Mosaic period); (3) He will continue to be our refuge now that the monarchy is gone; (4) Blessed are they that trust in him![21]

While Book 5 is rather lengthy (44 Psalms) and complex in structure and collections (Davidic 108–110; 122; 124; 131; 133; 138–145; "Hallelujah" psalms 111–118; 135; 146–150; "songs of ascents" 120–134; and the one great "Torah" psalm, 119), it presents the "Davidic" psalms as an inclusio for the final book (Psalms 108–110; 138–145; Psalms 146–150 being a fitting climax to the entire Psalter). The exiles must mimic their great Davidic Messiah who in times past relied upon God's trustworthiness (Psalm 107) and who trusted in God's Torah (Psalm 119). "Ps 145 stands as the 'climax' of the fifth book of the Psalter, with the final *hallel* (Ps 146–150) drawing its impetus from 145:21."[22] Thus the exiled people of God are encouraged to "meditate" upon the Psalms as God's Torah (Psalms

---

[21]Wilson, *Editing*, p. 215.
[22]Ibid., p. 225.

1 and 119), to become a "people of the Book"! They must rely upon God as their king and their refuge, not human princes who will undoubtedly disappoint.

Subsequent studies by Wilson have only served to refine the conclusions of his groundbreaking dissertation.[23] Other scholars, such as J. Clinton McCann and David M. Howard, while accepting Wilson's basic thesis, have either extended his ideas (McCann) or added more detailed analyses (Howard).[24] The scholarly discussions on this subject are continuing into the new millennium.

STRUCTURE

The Psalms are divided into five "Books" or collections: Book 1 (Psalms 1–41); Book 2 (Psalms 42–72); Book 3 (Psalms 73–89); Book 4 (Psalms 90–106); and Book 5 (Psalms 107–150). These divisions were created by including a doxology at the end of each "book" with the exception of Book 5, which ends with a series of "hallelujah"

---

[23]See Gerald H. Wilson, "Shaping the Psalter: A Consideration of Editorial Linkage in the Book of Psalms," in *The Shape and Shaping of the Psalter*, ed. J. Clinton McCann, JSOTS 159 (Sheffield: JSOT Press, 1993), pp. 72-82. Also in the same volume, "Understanding the Purposeful Arrangement of Psalms in the Psalter: Pitfalls and Promise," pp. 42-51. Other relevant articles by Wilson include the following: "The Shape of the Book of Psalms," *Int* 46 (1992): 129-142; "The Use of Royal Psalms at the 'Seams' of the Hebrew Psalter," *JSOT* 35 (1986): 85-94; "The Use of 'Untitled' Psalms in the Hebrew Psalter," *ZAW* 97 (1985): 404-413; finally before his published dissertation: "Evidence of Editorial Divisions in the Hebrew Psalter," *VT* 34 (1984): 337-352.

[24]See J. Clinton McCann Jr., "Books I–III and the Editorial Purpose of the Hebrew Psalter," in *The Shape and Shaping of the Psalter*, ed. J. Clinton McCann, pp. 93-107. McCann suggested that by studying carefully the beginning books in the "seams" such as Psalms 1-2, 42-44, and 73-74 one discerns that the first three Books of the Psalter reflect the laments and hope of the exiled community just as much as the last two Books. The need for reorientation of the exiled community away from the Davidic/Zion theology was their only avenue for renewed hope. Yet the problem and its solution would return to the Davidic covenant and his kingly role in Book 5 (Psalms 108–110 and 138–145). McCann follows Nasuti in his *Tradition History and the Psalms of Asaph* (SBLDS 898 [Atlanta: Scholars Press, 1988]) that the Asaphites of both the pre- and postexile era are prime candidates as the "editors" of our present canonical Psalter (see pp. 105-107 of the above chapter by McCann).

hymns (Psalms 146–150, perhaps Psalm 150 being a conclusion to Book 5 and the entire group for the whole Psalter):

Ps 41:13 — "Praise be to the LORD, the God of Israel, from everlasting to everlasting. Amen and Amen."

Ps 72:18-20 — "Praise be to the LORD God, the God of Israel, who alone does marvelous deeds. Praise be to his glorious name forever; may the whole earth be filled with his glory. Amen and Amen. This concludes the prayers of David son of Jesse."

Ps 89:52 — "Praise be to the LORD forever! Amen and Amen."

Ps 106:48 — "Praise be to the LORD, the God of Israel, from everlasting to everlasting. Let all the people say, 'Amen!' Praise the LORD."

The division between Books 4 and 5 seems to be arbitrary since there is a chiastic relationship in terms of content with Psalms 101 through 110. However, it makes sense to close Book 4 with two psalms about the "wilderness wanderings" of Israel, used as an inclusio with Psalm 90, a "Moses" psalm, to begin Book 4. Thus Book 4 becomes an "answer" to the dilemma of the end of Book 3, the failure of the Davidic dynasty (Psalm 89) and the subsequent exile into Babylonia. The answer is: Yahweh was Israel's King during the wilderness wanderings, and he is still King during exile (Psalm 93; 96–99) and even postexile when there was no king on the throne. (See "History of Interpretation" above.)

Why do the Psalms divide into five books? No one really knows and we can only theorize or speculate. Books 1 and 2 at one time constituted two early collections of David's psalms (Ps 72:20: "This concludes the prayers of David son of Jesse"). A group of "sons of Korah" psalms (Psalms 42–49) make up part of Book 2. One "Asaph" psalm is included in Book 2 (Psalm 50). Book 3 seems to be deliberately collected to express the anguish of the loss of land, Temple, and king (Psalms 73–89), while *the answer* is given in Book 4 (Psalms 90–107). Creating a Book 5 certainly would mimic the Torah (Pentateuch). Adding Psalms 1 and 2 about "Torah" and "the kingdom" to the front of the first Davidic collection (Psalms 3–41) would suggest that even the Psalms can be studied as "God's word to man" as well as "man's word, song, or prayers to God." The Psalms become part of the authoritative canon for the life of the community of Israel. This is likely done by the end of the fifth century B.C. when the Chronicles were completed.

The Psalms move from mainly individual lament (predominantly Davidic psalms) to communal lament and then to individual and communal praise. This movement corresponds with the overall message of the Psalter where Book 5 hints that God will one day restore David's throne to its "rightful" place (see Psalms 110; 132). Book 5 is much larger than the other books because it contains other collections not easily divided (Psalms 111–118, the "Egyptian Hallel"; Psalms 120–134, songs of "ascents"; Psalms 146–150, the "hallelujah" psalms; and Psalm 119, the "great" psalm on Torah). For this reason it also contained the most "orphan" psalms that could be strategically placed to enhance the overall message of the Book. The large number of "Davidic" psalms in Book 5 (Psalms 108–110; 122; 124; 131; 133; 138–145) is probably to give the whole Psalms collection a "Davidic" flavor or influence. As stated above, by the first century all the Psalms were considered "Davidic."

Besides the above comments about the structure of the Psalms, there is one peculiarity that must be noted. The separate books are distinguished by the preference that is shown in the choice of the term that is used to indicate God, whether Yahweh or Elohim. The following chart indicates both characteristics of the various groups of Psalms.[25]

BOOK	PSALMS	ASCRIBED TO	PSALMS	OCCURRENCES OF	
				YAHWEH	ELOHIM
1	1–2	Not ascribed			
	3–41	David	1–41	278 times	49 times
	(10; 33)	(Not ascribed)*			
2	42–49	Sons of Korah			
	50	Asaph	42–72	32	198
	51–71	David			
	72	Solomon			

---

[25]This chart should take the place of the chart on p. 41 of *Psalms*, Volume One, by Tesh/Zorn in this NIV Commentary Series. Unfortunately the chart on p. 41 of Volume One is incorrect, including footnote 47. It is amazing how many other commentaries and introductory books on Psalms include similar errors. When in doubt, we should count them, and so I did. References to *El* and *Eloah*, variations on God's name, are not included in the chart and would not necessarily change the statistical point of the chart. The new chart includes the use of *elohim* when referring to pagan gods.

BOOK	PSALMS	ASCRIBED TO	PSALMS	OCCURRENCES OF	
				YAHWEH	ELOHIM
3	73–83	Asaph	73–83	13	45 + 2 "gods"
	84; 85; 87; 88	Sons of Korah			
	86	David	84–89	31	15 + 1 "gods"
	89	Ethan			
4	90	Moses			
	101; 103	David	90–106	105	19 + 5 "gods"
	14 Orphan Psalms				
5	107–150	15 David			
		1 Solomon	107–150	237	28 + 3 "gods"
		28 Orphan Psalms			

*Psalms 9 and 10 show signs of being a single acrostic psalm at one time and Psalms 33–34 belong together as "forgiveness" and "rejoicing" belong together.

Psalms 42–83 are called the "Elohistic Psalter" because they prefer the use of *Elohim* for God's name in place of *Yahweh*. Book 1 uses "Yahweh" 278 times over against only 49 for "Elohim." However, Psalms 42–83 (Book 2 and part of Book 3, "Asaph" psalms) use "Yahweh" only 45 times while "Elohim" is used 243 times. The rest of the Psalms revert back to the predominance of "Yahweh." No one knows why.[26] Later Judaism of the Second Temple period substituted *Adonai* ("Lord") for Yahweh, but this does not explain the use of Elohim for Yahweh in these particular psalms. The fact that later psalms (exilic and postexilic) use "Yahweh" readily enough does not help us understand the phenomenon.

GENRE

"Genre" refers to the *type* of a particular psalm. But we want to broaden that idea to include the fact that all the psalms are in the form of *poetry* (a literary genre) and most were set to music for their use in worship or personal meditation. Also, the *titles and technical terms* used at the beginning of most of the psalms give information

---

[26]See Tesh/Zorn, *Psalms, Vol. I,* p. 47. Two guesses by Kirkpatrick and Weiser are offered for this phenomenon, but neither of these proposals explains why Yahweh is retained in those cases where the name still stands in this group of Psalms. These name changes remain a mystery to the biblical scholars, especially when there are examples of the reverse, where Elohim is changed to Yahweh within the Elohistic Psalter.

that sometimes affects the understanding of its genre. Finally, the *genres* of the Psalms refers to the many different types of psalms included in the Psalter.

POETRY AND MUSIC

The poetic nature of the Psalms may seem elusive to some because there is virtually no rhyming of words to be found in Hebrew verse and no *precise* meter. Yet there is a certain rhythm of stressed syllables delineating the thought pattern. A verse may consist of a single line but usually will have two or more, each of which is called a stich (*stichos*). (Some use the terms *cola/colon*.) The following is an example of a two-line verse, a distich.

> For Í — knów — my tránsgressions,
> And my sín — is always — befóre me.

This verse from Psalm 51:3 (NIV) is said to employ 3+3 meter. The translation obscures the fact that there are only six terms in the Hebrew, three in each stich. Yet the pattern of accented ideas is evident even in the English. Note that the two lines of the verse are separated by a simple pause, ending in a complete stop.

Another common meter, often used in laments and called *Qinah*, is 3+2. For example:

> O Lórd, — heár — my práyer;
> Lísten — to my cry for mércy (Ps 143:1)

In addition there may be found 2+2, 4+4, 3+2+2, 2+2+2, and other metric variations, with a mixture appearing sometimes within a single literary unit. The morphology of the Hebrew language lends itself to the above accentual patterns, but it should be noted that the number of unaccented syllables is variable. Thus Hebrew poetry seeks to present a *balance of ideas* in successive lines rather than a *balance of sound* or *uniformity in the number of syllables* per verse. The end result is the beautiful achievement of a rhythm of thought patterns, striking in its effect.

To a degree the rhythm of the Hebrew text is lost in translation and may entirely disappear in the English. Unmistakable, however, is the balance between verse members mentioned above. This is called *parallelism*, where the second line of the verse corresponds *in some way* to the first. The balance is not restricted to, nor does it necessarily require, a correspondence of meaning. But words, phrases, ideas, parts of speech, and grammatical structure of the first member of the verse may find their *complement* or *completion* in the second. Parallelism has often been defined as saying the same thing over again in different words, but this is unduly to simplify and to restrict its significance.

Scholars have discovered a number of different types of parallelism among which the following are examples:

First, the *synonymous*, in which the thought of the first line is repeated, with variation, in the second:

> I will extol the LORD at all times;
> His praise will always be on my lips (Ps 34:1).

The *antithetic*, in which the thought of the first is contrasted:

> For the LORD watches over the way of the righteous,
> But the way of the wicked will perish (Ps 1:6).

The *synthetic*, in which the second line enhances the first:

> Oh, that I had the wings of a dove!
> I would fly away and be at rest (Ps 55:6).

Most scholars have abandoned the term *synthetic* as meaningless for a third category. Other terms are used to be more descriptive of this category. For instance, the *climactic* is where the succeeding line moves beyond the first to a heightened emphasis. For example:

> If an enemy were insulting me, I could endure it;
> If a foe were raising himself against me, I could hide
>   from him.
> But it is you, a man like myself, my companion, my close
>   friend (Ps 55:12,13).

The *stairlike* parallelism is found when a word or phrase of the first line is repeated in the second as a steppingstone to the finished statement:

> Ascribe to the LORD, O mighty ones,
> Ascribe to the LORD glory and strength (Ps 29:1).

Emblematic consists of a figurative comparison:

> As the deer pants for streams of water,
> So my soul pants for you, O God (Ps 42:1).

Inverted, or *chiastic*, in which there is an inversion of the order of words in the parallel lines:

> Have mercy on me, O God, *according to your unfailing love*;
> *According to your great compassion* blot out my transgressions
>   (Ps 51:1).

The italicized words indicate the chiastic arrangement, which is after the pattern ABBA. Psalm 1:6, previously quoted, is also chiastic.

These examples do not exhaust the variety of parallelisms that exists in Hebrew poetry. The manner of expression in Hebrew is so varied that scholars have been able to point out numerous other types and subtypes. It is clear we must not attempt to make Hebrew poetry conform to modern English conventions.

Each psalm can be said to have *stanzas* or *strophes*, dividing the verses into *thought forms*, much like we do in narrative with paragraphs. But stanzas or strophes can be so varied in the Psalms that it is impossible for scholars to agree on the structure of a psalm. However, proper attention to grammar, connecting words, and structure of the psalm can usually produce a fair and accurate assessment for the psalm stanzas or strophes.

For example, Psalm 73 can be divided into the following strophes: Strophe One (vv. 1-3); Two (vv. 4-12); Three (vv. 13-17); Four (vv. 18-20); and Five (vv. 21-28). The central strophe, vv. 13-17, is a key strophe and v. 15 is central to it. It was when the psalmist came to his "senses" that everything began to change and reverse his thinking. The psalm is perfectly balanced: the first three lines are devoted to the righteous while the next nine lines to the wicked. In the latter half there is a reversal, only three lines are devoted to the wicked (vv. 18-20) and nine lines to the righteous psalmist (vv. 21-28). Thus the psalm has a pattern of ABCBA. Many psalms, however, are not so neatly divided or structured.

A characteristic of poetry in general is the use that is made of figures of speech and other literary devices. In fact this may be the most important characteristic of the Psalms (Ryken). These are found in great variety and abundance in the Psalms. Among such are the following:

Allegory — a figurative treatment of one subject under the image of another: "You brought a *vine* [Israel] out of Egypt; you drove out the nations and planted it" (Ps 80:8).

Metaphor — a comparison not to be taken literally but made to suggest a resemblance: "Since you are my rock and my fortress, for the sake of your name lead and guide me" (Ps 31:3).

Simile — the expressing of a resemblance, usually with the use of the words "like" or "as": "The righteous will flourish *like* a palm tree, they will grow *like* a cedar of Lebanon" (Ps 92:12).

Metonymy — the use of one word when another with which it is associated is really meant: "You prepare a *table* before me" (meaning *food*, Ps 23:5).

Hyperbole — an obvious exaggeration for emphasis: "Streams of tears flow from my eyes, for your law is not obeyed" (Ps 119:136).

Synecdoche — in which a part is put for the whole or the whole for a part: "You love every harmful word, O you deceitful tongue!" ("tongue" meaning *the person*, Ps 52:4).

Apostrophe — addressing either one not present, inanimate objects, or imaginary persons: "Tremble, O earth, at the presence of the Lord, at the presence of the God of Jacob" (Ps 114:7).

Personification — attributing characteristics of persons to inanimate objects: "Then all the trees of the forest will sing for joy" (Ps 96:12).

Irony — in which the actuality is the opposite of what is anticipated: "But their idols are silver and gold, made by the hands of men. They have mouths, but cannot speak, eyes, but they cannot see" (Ps 115:4,5). Or, "Their tombs will remain their houses forever, their dwellings for endless generations, though they had named lands after themselves" (Ps 49:11). Also, "The stone the builders rejected has become the capstone" (Ps 118:22).

Anaphora — repetition for emphasis or for dramatic effect: "All the nations surrounded me, but in the name of the LORD I cut them off. They surrounded me on every side, but in the name of the LORD I cut them off" (Ps 118:10,11).

Litotes — an understatement to increase the effect, or an emphasis of an idea by denying its opposite: "a broken and contrite heart, O God, you will not despise: (meaning "you will welcome") (Ps 51:17).

Assonance — a correspondence in the sound of words in terms of their vowels and used in repetition or dominance of a single vowel sound. This can only be appreciated in the original Hebrew text. (See for examples Ps 48:7a, the "*ā*" sound and Ps 113:8, the "*î*" sound.)

Alliteration — the repetition of letters or syllables having similar sounds: "Pray for the peace of Jerusalem" (שַׁאֲלוּ שְׁלוֹם יְרוּשָׁלָ͏ִם; *ša'ălû š°lôm Y°rûšālā(y)im*) (Ps 122:6).

Acrostic — in which a group of verses begin each with a successive letter of the Hebrew alphabet. Psalm 34 is an example of a simple one verse, one letter acrostic while Psalm 119 is more elaborate with eight verses per Hebrew letter. The acrostic psalms include the following variations: half verse segments (Psalms 111–112); single verse (Psalms 25; 34; 145); two verses (Psalms 9–10; 37); and eight verses (Psalm 119). In addition Psalms 33; 38; 103 have 22 lines each, no doubt because the Hebrew alphabet has 22 letters.

The poetic nature of the psalms allowed them to be sung easily, both for individual uplift and for corporate worship. Many psalms may not have been originally composed for singing and music (e.g., Psalms 1; 19; 119, the *torah* psalms; and Psalm 73, a *wisdom* psalm or psalm about *theodicy*). But even if a psalm was not composed originally for corporate or individual singing, it could be adapted. Some psalms invite the worshiper to sing with the accompaniment of musical instruments (see Psalms 68; 81; 137; 148; 150).

The musical instruments mentioned in the Psalms are classified in three groups: 1) percussions, 2) winds, and 3) strings. Percussions include a) the tambourine (Ps 81:2; 149:3; 150:4) and b) cymbals (Ps 150:5). Usually the tambourine was used by women in a victory procession (Ps 68:24-25). Wind instruments included a) the horn (*shofar*, probably not used for accompaniment but rather for announcing events, feasts, or moments in worship, Ps 47:5; 81:3; 98:6; 150:3); b) the trumpet (Ps 98:6); and c) the flute (Ps 150:4). Stringed instruments included a) lyre (*nevel*, with a sounding-box shaped as a jar, Ps 33:2; 81:2; 92:3; 144:9; 150:3) and b) another type of lyre (*kinnor*, a rounded sounding-box, the most popular lyre, Ps 33:2; 71:22; 92:3; 98:5; 137:2; 149:3; 150:3). Some lyres could have as many as ten strings (Ps 144:9).[27]

Of course, singing the psalms (with or without the instruments) seems to have been popular in Israelite worship. It seems reasonable to assume that individuals such as David sang psalms for their own enjoyment (e.g., Psalm 23) as well as for corporate worship (1 Chr 15:16; 2 Chr 35:15). But in corporate worship we do not know exactly how the congregation sang. There were singers in the Temple (Ps 68:25; 87:7), and there is good evidence that *antiphonal singing* was popular (see Ps 118:1-4; 129; and 136; cp. 1 Sam 18:7).

TITLES AND TECHNICAL TERMS

Jewish circles gave the title תְּהִלִּים סֵפֶר (*sēpher tᵊhillîm*, "Book of Praises") to the psalms. The term "praise" (תְּהִלָּה, *tᵊhillāh*) is used twenty-eight times in the Psalms and thus became a natural word for

---

[27]See C. Hassell Bullock, *Encountering the Book of Psalms* (Grand Rapids: Baker, 2001), pp. 30-34. Also for a visual look at ancient musical instruments see Othmar Keel, *The Symbolism of the Biblical World: Ancient Near Eastern Iconography and the Book of Psalms* (Winona Lake, IN: Eisenbrauns, 1997), pp. 335-356.

a title (e.g. Ps 40:3). But only one psalm is designated *tehillah* (Psalm 145), and not all psalms, by any means, fall under the category of praise hymns. Therefore, *sēpher tᵉhillîm* is inaccurate as a title for the whole, so far as content is concerned.

Another biblical term that came to be applied to the Psalms is תְּפִלּוֹת (*tᵉphillôth*, "prayers"). This title is drawn from Psalm 72:20, which states: "This concludes the prayers of David son of Jesse." This notation apparently marks the end of an early collection of psalms, and the designation may be the title that was given to this group earlier. It is true that only Psalm 17 among them is entitled "a prayer of David." Yet the element of petition occurs frequently. In the broader significance of *tephillah* as communication of man with God (see 1 Sam 2:1), the title becomes more meaningful.

In Psalm 33, a congregational hymn, worshipers are exhorted to "praise the LORD with the harp; make music to him on the ten-stringed lyre" (v. 2). The word *psaltery*, from ψαλτήριον (*psaltērion*) in the Greek translation of the Old Testament, indicates a stringed instrument plucked with the fingers. However, the term was also used to indicate the composition that was played or the song that was accompanied by such instruments. In this sense, Codex Alexandrinus used *psalterion* as the title for the Psalms. From the Greek into the Latin into English, the word came to be widely used to designate the book, and thus it became known as *The Psalter*.

In other Greek manuscripts the word ψάλμοι (*psalmoi*) became the title. From *psalmos*, denoting the music of a stringed instrument or a song sung to such accompaniment, *psalmoi* is thus similar to "psalter" in its significance. This is the term used in the New Testament. In Luke 24:44 Jesus speaks of "the Law of Moses, the Prophets and the Psalms." And in Acts 1:20 Peter says, "It is written in the book of Psalms." The Greek was a translation of the Hebrew מִזְמוֹר (*mizmôr*), a word appearing in the titles of fifty-seven of the Psalms and indicating singing and making music in praise of God. In view of the original nature of the hymns as praise sung to musical accompaniment, the designation, *Psalms*, appears suitable also.

שִׁיר (*šîr*, "song") is one other Hebrew term used to identify thirty psalms. It is not used as a title for the Psalter, yet it is significant in that it reflects the lyric nature of the Psalms. The Psalms were written (at least most of them) to be sung. Expressing the religious sentiments, aspirations, and changing moods of the human spirit, the Psalms reflect the music of the soul that has been stirred by

God's self-disclosure in nature, in historic act, and in word. The book of Proverbs has poetry that is quite similar in style to that of the Psalms, but its nature is different. It is *didactic* rather than *lyric*. Its purpose is to give instruction, to teach, whereas the Psalms are designed to give glory to God and expression to the deepest feelings of one who would live in fellowship with him (even though we recognize a few psalms as *didactic* in nature, e.g., Psalms 1 and 37). Neither the lyrics nor the music of the ancient Hebrews approximated contemporary, Western music. But the Psalms, from their lyric nature, were admirably fitted to the expression of one's spiritual longings and to the singing of praises to God.

Scholarship of the late nineteenth century A.D. (Wellhausen et al.) designated the Psalms as "the Hymn Book of the Second Temple." This view of the Psalms suggested that all earlier composition of psalms were adapted and rewritten for use in the postexilic Temple services, while the majority were produced by Temple personnel to be thus used by priests and people. Therefore, the Psalms as we have them (their canonical form) can be no later than the fourth century B.C.

While there is some truth to the above (cp. the possible rewriting and arranging of Psalms 120–134, a group of psalms where each is titled "a song of ascents"), it is a mistake to conclude that the Psalms necessarily owe their origin primarily to this period and circumstance. As a matter of fact, the participation of the populace in the Temple ritual seems to have been slight. Furthermore, at least some of the psalms are such as likely would *not* be recited at a sacerdotal service: "Sacrifice and offering you did not desire . . . burnt offerings and sin offerings you did not require" (Ps 40:6; see also Ps 50:13,14). These psalms, apparently, were not composed for the Temple liturgy. Moreover, the didactic psalms along with a few socalled "wisdom" psalms (e.g., Psalm 73) may have been *recited* in a learning experience and *not necessarily sung*! It is clear that some psalms are better suited to private rather than to public use. It would seem, therefore, that the designation "Hymn Book of the Second Temple" is a misnomer.

Technical terms can be found in the superscriptions to the Psalms. All except 34 of the Psalms have titles or superscriptions of one kind or another. Although probably not original, these superscriptions as titles existed at least 250 years or more before the Christian era, with an earlier date more likely.

The Hebrew Bible and early translations numbered the super-

scriptions as a part of the text, designating them as "verse one" of
the psalm, or in some cases as "verses one and two" (as in Psalm 60,
for example). In modern translations they appear simply as headings
before verse one. In the New English Bible they are omitted altogether!

These superscriptions are of five general types. (1) **References to
persons** are found in the majority. Among these, the name of David
is most prominent, appearing in 73 of the psalms, primarily in
Books 1–2, and 5, only once in Book 3 and twice in Book 4. Psalms
72 and 127 refer to Solomon. Eleven have reference to the sons of
Korah, twelve to Asaph, and one each to Moses, Heman, and Ethan.
"Jeduthun" is mentioned in Psalms 39; 62; and 77; but scholars
debate whether this is a name or a musical term. Most consider it
another name for Ethan (1 Chr 15:17,19; cf. 1 Kgs 4:31). It is difficult to determine authorship by these names. The Hebrew preposi-
tion, ל (lᵉ), may indicate "by" (authorship), but it could also mean
"belonging to," as belonging to a particular collection or group of
psalms or it may indicate relationship, "about" or "pertaining to" or
"for" someone, or "on his behalf."

(2) **References to historical occasions** appear in 15 psalms, all
of which are ascribed to David except Psalm 102, and all of which
are found in Books 1 and 2 except 102 and 142. That it was not
unusual, even from early times, to provide titles indicating the occasion of a song, is indicated by the examples found in 2 Samuel 22:1
and in Isaiah 38:9.

(3) **References to the type of poem** are found for many of the
psalms. The most common term is "Psalm" (mizmôr), appearing 57
times, chiefly in relationship to David. "Song" (šîr) appears 30 times,
often in combination with mizmôr, as in Psalm 30: "A Psalm of David,
a song." Thirteen of the psalms have the designation מַשְׂכִּיל (maśkîl),
a term whose root meaning is "to be wise" or "to have insight." Sometimes the reference is to skill in the performance of some task. Does
this mean that the psalm is designed to inform, to make one wise? Or
is it of such erudite nature as to require deep meditation? Some propose that the musical setting is such that a skillful musician is needed for its presentation. There is no consensus among scholars in this
regard, and for this reason the term is left *untranslated* in many
English versions (transliterating it *maschil* or *maskil*).

מִכְתָּם (miktām) appears in the title of six of the psalms of David.
The root of this word appears to be כְּתֶם (ktm), meaning "golden."

Or the word could be related to כתב (*ktb*), "to inscribe," in keeping with the LXX (εἰς στηλογραφίαν, *eis stēlographian*). Another suggestion is "to cover," on the basis of analogy with the Akkadian *katamu*, incorporating the idea of atonement. But again, in view of the uncertainty, many versions leave the term untranslated.

Psalm 7 is designated a שִׁגָּיוֹן (*šiggāyōn*) of David. The apparent root, שׁגה (*šgh*), signifies "to go astray," "to wander." The term may be descriptive either of the poem or of the musical accompaniment, but its significance is not clear. Five psalms bear the title, "A Prayer," and one is designated "Praise."

(4) **Titles with a musical reference** are quite numerous. These may refer to persons: "To the chief musician," occurring fifty-five times, *alamoth* (sopranos?), and *sheminith* (basses?). Or there may be musical directions, indicating a familiar melody to be used with the psalm indicated. These terms include: *Gittith, Muthlabben, Jeduthan, Aijeleth Shahar, Shoshannim, Yoneth elem rechokim, Mahalath, Mahalath Leannoth, Shushan-eduth,* and *Al-tashchith.* Other terms indicate musical instruments: (*Nehiloth*, flutes) and (*Neginoth*, stringed instruments).

(5) **References to the use of the Psalms in worship** appear in some titles: "For the Sabbath Day" (Psalm 92, NIV); "A Petition" (Psalm 38, NIV); "For the memorial offering (Psalm 38, RSV); "For giving thanks" (Psalm 100, NIV) or "A Psalm for the thank offerings," (Psalm 100, RSV); "For the dedication of the temple" (Psalm 30, NIV), and the aforementioned group, each titled, "A song of ascents" (Psalm 120–134, NIV). While some of these psalms may have had their origin in individual composition, they, nevertheless, were used for the liturgy in some fashion. But these psalms are not numerous so as to designate the entire Psalter in this way.

One final note on technical terms: the use of *Selah* in the text. Although the word does not appear in the titles of the Psalms, it is inserted seventy-one times in the text, almost exclusively in Books 1, 2, and 3 (only four times in Book 5: Psalm 140; 143). It is also found three times in Habakkuk, chapter 3. Because of the numerous musical references in the headings of the psalms in which *Selah* (סֶלָה, *selāh*) appears, it would seem that the term has musical significance. Believed to be derived from a Hebrew root, סלל (*sll*), meaning "lift up," it has been proposed that: (1) a pause is indicated, (2) there is to be a lifting up of voices (in volume?), or (3) there is to be an instrumental interlude. However, the meaning is still uncertain.

GENRES

It was Gunkel who focused upon the literary forms of the Psalms, especially as the form was related to function. Of these, he identified five basic types, or genres, as follows:

1. *Hymns of Praise* (with subtypes: Enthronement Psalms, honoring God as King, and Songs of Zion)
2. *Laments of the Community*
3. *Royal Psalms* (pertaining to an earthly monarch)
4. *Laments of the Individual*
5. *Individual Songs of Thanksgiving*

In addition, Gunkel recognized seven categories of a minor nature:

6. *Psalms Pronouncing Blessings and Cursings*
7. *Pilgrim Songs*
8. *National Songs of Thanksgiving*
9. *Historical Recital*
10. *Psalms of the Law*
11. *Prophetical Psalms*
12. *Wisdom Psalms*

Gunkel looked upon the Psalms as formalized liturgical literature designed to accompany ritual. This approach must, of necessity, subordinate the personal role of the individual composer, assuming that the psalm is composed for general use. Gunkel did recognize the majority of the Psalms to be privately composed, but by individuals who would fashion their work according to preexistent types. The premise is valid to a degree, but it could lead to a generalization of types where differentiations should be noted (and accepted). Even so, Gunkel's work has set the pattern utilized by many subsequent scholars and should be noted.

Since Gunkel's classifications were published, many classifications of the Psalms have been made, but none has met with universal acceptance. Great variety is characteristic of the Psalms, and some individual psalms include elements of more than one "type" within a single unit. In view of such variety, it is little wonder that many categories have been suggested and that, through various, sometimes arbitrary and subtle distinctions that number has, from time to time, been extended. One who would attempt to fit the Psalms into a neat system of types is confronted with problems. Nevertheless, it is advantageous to see the relationships that do exist, and to consider the situation in life that would be suggested by the employment, by the psalmist, of a particular type. With this in mind, and with attention given to the literary form, content, formalized vocabulary, as well as to the life situation, Bellinger has given the Psalms reader helpful genre classifications so that one may read a particular genre as a group:[28] The four main genres that Bellinger identifies are Praise, Lament, Royal, and Wisdom Psalms.

The psalms included in the last two categories are: Wisdom (1; 32; 37; 49; 73; 78; 112; 119; 127; 128; 133)[29] and Royal (2; 18; 20; 21; 45; 72; 89; 101; 110; 132; 144). He further divides the Laments into 2 subcategories: Individual (3; 4; 5; 6; 7; 9–10; 11; 13; 16; 17; 22; 25; 26; 27; 28; 31; 35; 36; 38; 39; 40; 42–43; 51; 52; 54; 55; 56; 57; 59; 61; 62; 63; 64; 69; 70; 71; 77; 86; 88; 94; 102; 109; 120; 130; 140; 141; 142; 143) and Community (12; 14; 44; 53; 58; 60; 74; 79; 80; 83; 85; 90; 106; 108; 123; 126; 137). The primary genre of Praise Psalms is subdivided even further: General Hymns (29; 33; 68; 100; 103; 105; 111; 113; 114; 115; 117; 134; 135; 139; 145; 146; 147; 149; 150), Creation Psalms (8; 19; 65; 104; 148), Enthronement Psalms (47; 93; 95; 96; 97; 98; 99), Zion Psalms (46; 48; 76; 84; 87; 122), Entrance Liturgies (15; 24), Hymns with Prophetic Warnings (50; 81; 82), Trust Psalms (23; 91; 121; 125; 131), and Thanksgiving Psalms, both Individual (30; 34; 41; 66; 92; 116; 118; 138) and Community (67; 75; 107; 124; 129; 136).

Psalms of Praise (Hymns) were songs of devotion directed toward Yahweh in recognition of his majesty, his power, and his goodness, songs that would glorify God as God. The form generally reflects a threefold pattern of development.[30] A great variety of psalms are found in this category (see Bellinger's list above).

Laments of the Individual share basically the nature of the *communal laments*. There is a distinction, of course, due to the different circumstances out of which the psalms grew and to the purpose for which they were intended. The laments of the community were occasioned by some great threat of disaster to the nation. These psalms

---

[28]W.H. Bellinger Jr., *Psalms: Reading and Studying the Book of Praises* (Peabody, MA: Hendrickson, 1990), p. 23.

[29]James L. Crenshaw has rejected the idea of a "wisdom" psalm. He wrote: "My own research in the Psalter leads me to question the very category of wisdom psalms." See his *The Psalms: An Introduction* (Grand Rapids: Eerdmans, 2001), p. 94.

[30]See Tesh and Zorn, *Psalms, Vol. I*, pp. 54-66, in this Commentary Series for a discussion on the forms of each genre. Not all genres have set forms. Here we will simply describe the various genres.

would have been used in public assembly, sung by the congregation, perhaps on special days of prayer and fasting. The individual lament, on the other hand, is the outcry of a *single person*, a soul overwhelmed by trouble and misfortune, laying bare his heart before the LORD, who alone is able to deliver him. The difficulty of laments, both individual and community, is the identification of the "enemy." Perhaps, as Longman suggests, "The psalms are purposefully vague in reference to historical events so that they can be used in a variety of situations."[31] Laments will often end in praise, a hymn, or a blessing — either for answered prayer or its anticipation (e.g., Ps 22:22-31). Over one-third of all of the Psalms fall into the class of laments, forty-eight are individual in nature and seventeen communal.

Royal Psalms are so designated because of their *content*, not because they constitute an independent literary genre. The latter may vary, according to the occasion of the psalm. It may reflect the nature of the hymn of praise (Psalm 18), or of the song of thanksgiving (Psalm 21). Psalm 72 is a prayer on behalf of the king. Psalm 45 is designated a love song in its title. More particularly, it appears to be a royal wedding song. The determining factor for a royal psalm is the prominence of the king as the central figure.

Wisdom Psalms, which some would deny as a category (Crenshaw), nevertheless can be discerned by a style manifested in two general forms, the gnomic statement or proverb, expressing in short form a universal truth, and the short essay. An example of the latter is Psalm 1, which draws a bold contrast between the blessedness of godliness and the despair of the ungodly. How to realize true success in life is the thrust of Psalm 1, just as it is of other wisdom writings in the Scriptures. Psalm 73 is a counterpoint to Psalm 1: a lament over why the wicked prosper and the righteous suffer. It is a redefinition of the meaning of how God is "good" to Israel (and thus to me)! Psalm 37, aphoristic in style, also takes note of the seeming prosperity of the wicked, but then advises patience, asserting that such prosperity will be of short duration: "Do not fret because of evil men . . . for like the grass they will soon wither" (37:1,2). Psalm 33 is a praise hymn (Bellinger categorizes it as a *general hymn*), yet it contains pithy sayings that would fit nicely in the book of Proverbs. The Great Psalm, Psalm 119, is placed in wisdom's category because

---

[31]Tremper Longman III, *How To Read The Psalms* (Downers Grove, IL: InterVarsity, 1988), p. 27.

of its praise of Torah. Wisdom psalms will often highlight the "fear of God" theme and sometimes include the word "Happy!" (אַשְׁרֵי, 'ašrê; cf. Ps 127:5; 128:1). Sometimes when a praise psalm (Psalm 145) is in the form of an acrostic, it is categorized as "wisdom" (Wilson does so, but Bellinger categorizes it as a general hymn).

No two scholars are going to agree on the genres of the Psalms and their categorizations. By reading each group together, one may discern for oneself whether the categorization is appropriate. While one scholar will deny a particular category (such as Crenshaw for "wisdom"), another scholar will use that very category as a major understanding of the structure of the Psalms (Wilson). Common sense and flexibility of opinions must be applied to the genres of the Psalms.

THEOLOGICAL THEMES

The canonical shape of the Psalter certainly "adds" to its theological themes. McCann wrote:

> The canonical form of the Psalter reminds us that the Psalms were not preserved to serve as a source for reconstructing the liturgical history of ancient Israel and Judah, although they may be used in such a task (as form critics do). Neither were the Psalms treasured as examples of beautiful poetry, although they are (as rhetorical critics recognize). Rather, the Psalms have been preserved and treasured because they have served to instruct the people of God about God, about themselves and the world, and about the life of faith.[32]

Thus the "wisdom" frame of the Psalms suggests that we read it and meditate upon it in private devotion in order for it to instruct us about the "righteous life" (Psalm 1). The "royal" frame instructs us about the mystery and work of God's king and kingdom. With the *failure* of the Davidic dynasty (Psalm 89), the final editing of the Psalter sought an *eschatological orientation* in the Psalter (i.e., the placement of Book 4 with its emphasis on the fact that "Yahweh reigns!"). Book 5 gives strong hints of a coming "Messiah" in terms of a final victory over all Israel's enemies and the ingathering of God's people in the last days (cf. Psalms 110; 132; 144).[33]

---

[32] McCann, *Theological Introduction*, pp. 20-21.
[33] See David C. Mitchell, *The Message of the Psalter: An Eschatological Programme in the Book of Psalms* (Sheffield: Sheffield Academic Press, 1997).

The Psalms as a book is a veritable gold mine for teaching us about God as Creator, Sovereign King, and Savior. While mankind is great (Psalm 8), he is also a sinner (Psalm 51). The need for God's presence in the life of the believer is stressed (cp. Psalm 139). The worldview of the Psalms emphasizes that there is only one God who has judged all the pagan gods (Psalm 82), and that his reign from heaven is eternal and he will judge the world in righteousness and truth (cf. Psalms 93; 96–99). One day a "priest-king" will come and lead a *nation of priests* to a final victory over all God's enemies (cf. Psalms 110; 132).

Thus all of creation and all nations are to give God praise, honor, and glory (cf. Psalms 146–150). Even if God's reign cannot be discerned in this life and life is threatened on earth, God allows the believer to *speak up* with words of *imprecation* (e.g., Ps 35:5,6; 58:6,10; 59:13; 69:23,24; 109:9,10; 137:8,9). *Righteous indignation* should be carefully monitored so that it not lead us into a deeper sin.

And so the Psalms not only give us doctrinal teaching about all aspects of God, his people, and the world, but also it plumbs the depths of human emotions from praise and thanksgiving to lament and cursing. In the end the psalmist would have everyone who breathes say: "Praise the LORD!" (Ps 150:6b).

We can only touch the "hem of the garment" with regard to the theological themes found in the Psalms. There has yet to be written a comprehensive study of such themes for the Psalter.

NEW TESTAMENT CONNECTIONS

Psalms is the most quoted and alluded to Old Testament book in the New Testament, followed by Isaiah and Deuteronomy. In 70 cases there are formula introductions (e.g., Mark 12:36; Acts 1:16), 60 cases in which psalms are quoted without an introductory formula (e.g., Heb 1:13), and an additional 220 instances where there are identifiable citations and references.[34] From the New Testament perspective all the Psalms are from "David" (see above).

Psalms were certainly sung by Christians in the New Testament era (cp. Mark 14:26//Matt 26:30; Acts 16:25; 1 Cor 14:15; 14:26; Eph 5:19; Col 3:16; and Jas 5:13). Even Jesus' own words concerning Jerusalem and her rejection of God's Messiah (Luke 19:43-44) are reminiscent of the imprecatory words of Psalm 137:9.

---

[34]Henry M. Shires, *Finding the Old Testament in the New* (Philadelphia: Westminster Press, 1974), p. 126.

The most important psalms quoted in the New Testament are Psalms 110:1; 2:7; 8:4-6; and 118:22. Psalms that are used multiple times include the following: Psalms 2; 22; 33; 34; 35; 39; 50; 69; 78; 89; 102; 105; 106; 107; 110; 116; 118; 119; 135; 145; 147. Several times the New Testament will quote a "grouping of psalms text" with a few other supporting texts: Romans 3:10-18; 15:9-12; Hebrews 1:5-13. The Psalms are so pervasive in the New Testament that only five books (Galatians, Philemon, 2 and 3 John, and Jude) "show no direct dependence on the Psalter. All the rest draw upon Psalms for their own purposes and in their own way."[35]

The author of the Book of Hebrews uses the Psalms almost exclusively as his theological support for his major themes. To establish the place of "divinity" and "royal exaltation" for the Son (Heb 1:3), he uses Psalm 2:7 and Psalm 110:1 as "inclusios" on the subject. Psalms 104:4; 45:6,7; and 102:25-27 are utilized (cf. Heb 1:5-13). To speak to the place of "humanity" in the mission of the Son, he quoted Psalm 8:4-6 (Heb 2:6-8). This discussion is supported by Psalm 22:22. Jesus' superiority over Moses and Joshua is carefully crafted by the use of Psalm 95:7-11, an exhortation to remain faithful so as not to forfeit the "promised rest" (Hebrews 3–4). Similar to chapter one, the Hebrews author combines Psalm 2:7 with Psalm 110:4 to expound on Genesis 14:18-20 and the uniqueness of Jesus' High Priesthood (Hebrews 5–7). While Jeremiah 31:31-34, a major text, is used to discuss the new covenant as given by Jesus (Hebrews 8), the author uses Psalm 40:6-8 as the very "words" of Jesus to exemplify the perfect sacrifice offered by him. "And by that will, we have been made holy through the sacrifice of the body of Jesus Christ once for all" (Heb 10:10). In the final chapter of miscellaneous exhortations he refers to Psalm 118:6,7 (Heb 13:6). Harold Attridge makes this conclusion concerning Hebrews use of Psalms:

> Hebrews uses Psalms in many and diverse ways, as a structuring element for the discourse as a whole, articulating its major segments and serving as an essential ingredient in its innovative Christology, as evidence along the way for various contentions that the homilist wants to make about the person and work of Christ and the kind of response required of his followers.[36]

---

[35]Ibid., p. 130.

[36]Steve Moyise & Maarten J.J. Menken, eds., *The Psalms in the New Testament* (London/New York: T & T Clark International, 2004), p. 212.

Psalms was a *living* word to the New Testament authors (Heb 4:12, reference to Ps 95:7-11). It gave the early Christians a vocabulary and a way to worship God with traditional and inspired language. Knowing the Psalms, its vocabulary, style, content, and theology, will enable one to understand the deeper nuances of the New Testament's message about Christ and the Church.

PROVERBS

The Book of Proverbs shares the skills we need to wise up and live a blessed life before our God and the family of mankind. This book shares the wisdom of God and the experiences of his people. British Prime Minister Lord John Russell wrote that in proverbial sayings we have "the wisdom of many and the wit of one." Miguel de Cervantes, a Spanish novelist of the 1500s, wrote, "Proverbs are short sentences, drawn from long experience."[1]

HISTORICAL AND CULTURAL BACKGROUND

The student of Scripture knows that the proverb[2] is scattered throughout the Bible — in the historical narratives (Judg 8:2,21; 1 Sam 10:12; 24:13), Psalms (34:11-14), prophets (Jer 13:12-14; Ezek 12:22-23; 16:44; 18:2-3), gospels (Mark 10:25,31; Luke 4:23), and the epistles (Jas 1:19-20; 1 Pet 4:8). The major collection of proverbial wisdom is, of course, the Book of Proverbs.

Wisdom and its literature was an international enterprise. This is a working assumption of the Old Testament. The prophets, for example, reminded Israel/Judah that wisdom was commonplace amongst the nations, but their wisdom was seductive, for it led foreign nations to pride, and it led God's people to live apart from him (Isa 19:11-15; Ezek 28:6-10).

Mesopotamian (Sumerian and Akkadian), Egyptian, and Northwest Semitic literature is replete with wisdom topics and attitudes, many of which have invited comparison with Proverbs.[3] Such comparisons are to be expected given the international reality of wis-

---

[1]Cited in Roy B. Zuck, ed., *Learning from the Sages: Selected Studies on the Book of Proverbs* (Grand Rapids: Baker, 1995), p. 15.

[2]The transliteration of the Hebrew word for "proverb" is *māšāl*. The transliteration of the Hebrew title of the book is *mišlê*.

[3]A convenient summary of Mesopotamian and Egyptian wisdom texts can

dom, as observed by the writer of 1 Kings 4:30: "Solomon's wisdom was greater than the wisdom of all the men of the East, and greater than all the wisdom of Egypt."

The most celebrated comparison is made between Proverbs 22:17–24:22 and the Egyptian Amenemope Instruction, written in the thirteenth or twelfth century B.C. The similarities remind us that all cultures reflect upon the world around them. "A man can still think validly and talk wisely, within a limited field, without special revelation."[4] The difference is obvious: biblical wisdom reflects the all-encompassing relationship between the LORD and his people, whereas international wisdom is pragmatic and secular.

The purpose of the volume is outlined in 1:2-6, with the book's motto following in verse 7. The book was compiled, according to verse 2, so that the reader may know what wisdom is, and to be able to see into the heart of life. Wisdom enables one to live right before God and to be just and fair before mankind (v. 3). Wisdom gives us a sense of purpose, instead of the youthful folly of impulsiveness (v. 4). The young (v. 4) and the experienced alike (v. 5) benefit from the guidance of this book. Wisdom unlocks many of the riddles and mysteries of life (v. 6).

The motto of the book comes at verse 7: "The fear of the LORD is the beginning of knowledge." The primary factor, then, in the life of wisdom is the fear of the LORD. "Wisdom is, in fact," writes Motyer, "the Lord revealing himself as a way of life for his people to practice."[5]

Wisdom (9:3) calls out, inviting all to enter her house (9:4) and to enjoy her cuisine (9:2,5). The woman or man who embraces Lady Wisdom will enjoy wisdom's promise: "For through me your days will be many, and years will be added to your life" (9:11).

---

be found in Ernest C. Lucas, *Exploring the Old Testament: A Guide to the Psalms & Wisdom Literature* (Downers Grove: IL, InterVarsity, 2003), pp. 88-89.

[4]Derek Kidner, *The Proverbs: An Introduction and Commentary* (Downers Grove, IL: InterVarsity, 1964), p. 17. Proverbs 22:24 says, for example, "Do not make friends with a hot-tempered man, do not associate with one easily angered." The Amenemope parallel reads, "Do not associate to thyself the heated man, nor visit him for conversation" (11:13-14). A convenient list of additional parallels can be found in *ANET*, p. 424, n. 46. This invaluable and standard resource also contains a translation of the Amenemope Instruction. The above translation is from it. The reader may consult John D. Currid, "The 'Instruction of Amenemope' and the Book of Proverbs," *Ancient Egypt and the Old Testament* (Grand Rapids: Baker, 1997), pp. 205-216.

[5]Alec Motyer, *The Story of the Old Testament* (Grand Rapids: Baker, 2001), p. 157.

Folly also calls out (9:15), inviting all to enter her house (9:16) and to enjoy her cuisine (9:17). The person who embraces Dame Folly will be doomed to her curse: "But little do they know that the dead are there, that her guests are in the depths of the grave" (9:18).

TEXT AND AUTHOR

Any outline of the content of Proverbs assists in the discussion of authorship. Here is a basic outline:

1:1-7	Title, Introduction, and Motto (6 proverbs)
1:8-9:18	A Father's Exhortation to His Sons (249 proverbs)
10:1-22:16	Proverbs of Solomon (375 proverbs)
22:17-24:22	Sayings of the Wise (70 proverbs)
24:23-34	Further Sayings of the Wise (12 proverbs)
25:1-29:27	Further Proverbs of Solomon, edited by Hezekiah (137 proverbs)
30:1-33	Sayings of Agur (33 proverbs)
31:1-9	Sayings of King Lemuel (8 proverbs)
31:10-31	An Acrostic Tribute to the Noble Woman (22 proverbs)

Solomon, Agur, and Lemuel (with due thanks to his mother) are the named contributors to the volume. Of the 912 proverbs collected in this book, Solomon is credited with 512 (56%), Agur with 33 (4%), and Lemuel 8 (1%). If the first two sections (1:1-7 + 1:8-9:18) are also considered Solomonic, as some are wont to do, then Solomon contributes 84%.

The number of proverbs found in 10:1-22:16, namely 375, is the numerical equivalent of the letters comprising the name of Solomon. The number of proverbs edited by Hezekiah's men is one more than the numerical equivalent of Hezekiah's name, fully spelled.

In light of 1 Kings 4:32 Solomon's contribution to this book is quite expected. There the author numbered Solomon's proverbial output at 3,000! Proverbs 1:1 may suggest that Solomon is the main contributor and perhaps the initiator of the anthology.

The sections attributed to both Agur and Lemuel are as good as anonymous since nothing is known of these two men.

Solomon is a figure of the tenth century B.C., whereas Hezekiah, who may have served as compiler or editor, reigned from 715-686 B.C.

GENRE

A proverb is brief — short and to the point. A proverb wastes no words. In boxing terms, a proverb is a quick jab. The fifteenth chapter, for example, contains thirty-three proverbs, totaling 487 words in the NIV translation. This is an average of fifteen (15) words per proverb. The shortest verse in this chapter is verse 12 (only ten English words): "A mocker resents correction; he will not consult the wise."

A proverb is easily recalled. The following examples easily roll off of the tongue. "Plans fail for lack of counsel, but with many advisers they succeed" (15:22). "Pride goes before destruction, a haughty spirit before a fall" (16:18). "Wine is a mocker and beer a brawler; whoever is led astray by them is not wise" (20:1).

A proverb has been popularly accepted as a general truth. In other words, proverbs are generalizations drawn from experience. Mouser reminds us that "the exceptional, the unusual, the unprecedented, all these are beyond the range of proverbial wisdom."[6]

Confusing a proverb with either a law or a promise is a basic interpretive mistake. Reading the proverbs as inflexible laws is troublesome. Consider the classic example: "Do not answer a fool according to his folly, or you will be like him yourself. Answer a fool according to his folly, or he will be wise in his own eyes" (26:4-5). "Do not answer a fool" and "Answer a fool" cannot both be true at the same time! The interpreter needs skill in knowing when to apply the one and then the other. In this same light, consider the following pairs of well-known contemporary proverbs. "Haste makes waste" vs. "He who hesitates is lost"; "Absence makes the heart grow fonder" vs. "Absence makes the heart to wander"; "Many hands make light work" vs. "Too many cooks spoil the broth."

A proverb is not a promise either. Has a Christian parent claimed Proverbs 22:6 as a promise from God only to be disap-

---

[6]William E. Mouser Jr., *Walking in Wisdom: Studying the Proverbs of Solomon* (Downers Grove, IL: InterVarsity, 1983), p. 12. In *Grasping God's Word* (Grand Rapids: Zondervan, 2001), by J. Scott Duvall and J. Daniel Hays, one reads, "Proverbs presents the rational, ordered norms of life. The many proverbs in the book are not universals (i.e., things that are always true), but rather norms of life (i.e., things that are normally true). God has set in place an ordered, rational world, and it all makes sense. If you work hard, you will prosper; if you don't, you will be poor. Wise, righteous, hardworking people can expect a blessed, prosperous life while foolish, sinful, lazy people can expect a hard life" (p. 378).

pointed in God or plagued by doubt in one's parenting skills or commitment to one's child?[7]

The Book of Proverbs features a number of types. One type is the "*better*" proverb. For example, "Better a poor man whose walk is blameless than a rich man whose ways are perverse" (28:6). One better proverb is found twice in the whole collection: "Better to live on a corner of the roof than share a house with a quarrelsome wife" (21:9; 25:4). The other "better" sayings are found at 12:9; 15:16,17; 16:8, 16,19,32; 17:1,12; 19:1,22; 21:19; 22:1; 25:6-7; 27:5,10 (cf. 3:14; 8:19).

Consider the **beatitudes**. "Blessed is the man who finds wisdom, the man who gains understanding" (3:13); "Blessed is the man who listens to me, watching daily at my doors, waiting at my doorway" (8:34); "He who despises his neighbor sins, but blessed is he who is kind to the needy" (14:21); "Whoever gives heed to instruction prospers, and blessed is he who trusts in the LORD" (16:20); "The righteous man leads a blameless life; blessed are his children after him" (20:7); "Blessed is the man who always fears the LORD, but he who hardens his heart falls into trouble" (28:14); "Where there is no revelation, the people cast off restraint; but blessed is he who keeps the law" (29:18; cf. 3:18,33; 5:18; 8:32; 10:6-7,22; 11:11,26; 20:21; 22:9; 24:25; 27:14; 28:20; 30:11; 31:28).

The **"abomination"** saying also features prominently in the volume. The LORD abhors/detests a perverse man (3:32; 11:20), the way and thoughts of the wicked (15:8,9,26), the proud of heart (16:5), lying lips (12:22), dishonest scales (11:1; 20:10,23), and dishonest legal proceedings (17:15). Proverbs 6:16-19 is perhaps the best known of this type: "There are six things the LORD hates, seven that are detestable to him: haughty eyes, a lying tongue, hands that shed innocent blood, a heart that devises wicked schemes, feet that are quick to rush into evil, a false witness who pours out lies and a man who stirs up dissension among brothers."

This last example is a bridge to the **"numerical sayings,"** which also occur at 30:15b-16,18-19,21-23,24-28,29-31. Using an x/x+1 format, these numerical sayings focus attention on the final item listed (the x+1 item). For example, the author (Agur) highlights the fourth item in the three-four format of 30:18-19. "There are three things

---

[7]Dr. Gary Hall (Christian Standard [May 10, 1992]: 10-11 [394-395 in bound vol.]) has argued successfully that Prov 22:6 is a warning, not a promise. The Hebrew text should be translated: "Dedicate (begin) a child to (on) his way [his own sefish way], and when/even as he grows old, he will not depart from it."

that are too amazing for me, four that I do not understand: the way of an eagle in the sky, the way of a snake on a rock, the way of a ship on the high seas, and the way of a man with a maiden."

The **acrostic** at 31:10-31 celebrates the woman of noble character. Hints about the value of such a woman have been shared throughout the volume. For example: "A wife of noble character is her husband's crown" (12:4); "He who finds a wife finds what is good and receives favor from the LORD" (18:22); "Houses and wealth are inherited from parents, but a prudent wife is from the LORD" (19:14).

The antithesis of the noble woman is also met along the way. "Better to live on a corner of a roof than share a house with a quarrelsome wife" (21:9; 25:24; cf. 21:19). "A quarrelsome wife is like a constant dripping on a rainy day; restraining her is like restraining the wind or grasping oil with the hand" (27:15-16).

The noble woman/wife receives both her husband and her children's praise: "Her children arise and call her blessed; her husband also, and he praises her" (31:28). Her network of social involvements, her "city," also blesses her: "Give her the reward she has earned, and let her works bring her praise at the city gate" (31:31). But above all, she receives the praise of the LORD. In this Word of God, we hear: "She is worth far more than rubies . . . a woman who fears the LORD is to be praised" (31:10b,30b).

The **admonition** abounds in proverbs. Consider 4:23: "Above all else, guard your heart, for it is the wellspring of life." The first "Sayings of the Wise" section features three admonitions to be wise: 22:17-19; 23:12; 24:13-14.

The proverbs exhibit imagery and parallelism, the features common to Hebrew poetry.[8] Imagery is well understood. Parallelism is more elusive. Three types of parallelism are common in Proverbs: antithetic, synonymous, and progressive.

In antithetic parallelism the second half of a sentence expresses a contrast to the first half. Consider the following examples: "A wise son brings joy to his father, *but* a foolish son grief to his mother" (10:1); "A gentle answer turns away wrath, *but* a harsh word stirs up anger" (15:1); "Lazy hands make a man poor, *but* diligent hands bring wealth" (10:4).

In synonymous parallelism the second half of a sentence repeats the thrust of the first half, but in different words. Consider these three examples from Proverbs 19: "A false witness will not go unpunished, and he who pours out lies will not go free" (v. 5).

---

[8]Review parallelism in the previous chapter on Psalms.

"Many curry favor with a ruler, and everyone is the friend of a man who gives gifts" (v. 6). "A false witness will not go unpunished, and he who pours out lies will perish" (v. 9).

In progressive parallelism the second half expands what has been said in the first half. Proverbs 10:18 is a good example: "He who conceals his hatred has lying lips, and whoever spreads slander is a fool."

THEOLOGICAL THEMES: THEOLOGY PROPER

The holiness of God is presented in Proverbs. "The fear of the LORD is the beginning of wisdom, and knowledge of the Holy One is understanding" (9:10; cf. 30:3). He is also omnipresent. "The eyes of the LORD are everywhere, keeping watch on the wicked and the good" (15:3; cf. 5:21). He is omnipotent. "By wisdom the LORD laid the earth's foundations, by understanding he set the heavens in place; by his knowledge the deeps were divided, and the clouds let drop the dew" (3:19-20). He is omniscient. "Death and Destruction lie open before the LORD—how much more the hearts of men!" (15:11).

The LORD is sovereign. "The LORD works out everything for his own ends—even the wicked for a day of disaster" (16:4; cf. 19:21). God possesses wisdom (3:19-20) and justice: "Many seek an audience with a ruler, but it is from the LORD that man gets justice" (29:26). He "gives grace to the humble" (3:34). He protects the righteous (2:7-8). He "hears the prayer of the righteous" (15:29).

NEW TESTAMENT CONNECTIONS

Note the following New Testament usage of the Book of Proverbs.

Proverbs 3:4 (LXX)	"Then you will win favor and a good name in the sight of God and man."	Romans 12:17; 2 Corinthians 8:21
Proverbs 3:11-12	"My son, do not despise the LORD's discipline and do not resent his rebuke, because the LORD disciplines those he loves, as a father the son he delights in."	Hebrews 12:5-6; Revelation 3:19

Proverbs 3:34 (LXX)	"He mocks proud mockers but gives grace to the humble."	James 4:6; 1 Peter 5:5
Proverbs 4:26	"Make level paths for your feet and take only ways that are firm."	Hebrews 12:12-13
Proverbs 10:12	"Hatred stirs up dissension, but love covers over all wrongs."	1 Peter 4:8
Proverbs 11:31 (LXX)	"If the righteous receive their due on earth, how much more the ungodly and the sinner!"	1 Peter 4:18
Proverbs 22:8 (LXX)	"He who sows wickedness reaps trouble, and the rod of his fury will be destroyed."	2 Corinthians 9:7
Proverbs 23:31 (LXX)	"Do not gaze at wine when it is red, when it sparkles in the cup, when it goes down smoothly!"	Ephesians 5:18
Proverbs 24:12c	"Will he not repay each person according to what he has done?"	Matthew 16:27; Romans 2:6; 2 Timothy 4:14
Proverbs 25:21-22	"If your enemy is hungry, give him food to eat; if he is thirsty, give him water to drink. In doing this, you will heap burning coals on his head, and the LORD will reward you."	Romans 12:20
Proverbs 26:11	"As a dog returns to his vomit, so a fool repeats his folly."	2 Peter 2:22

WISDOM & JESUS[9]

Luke records that as a child Jesus "was filled with wisdom" (2:40, 52). Jesus, accordingly, will participate in the wisdom tradition, as is evident from the following truths: "A man's life does not consist in the abundance of his possessions" (Luke 12:15b; Matt 6:21); "For where your treasure is, there your heart will be also" (Luke 12:34); "If a blind man leads a blind man, both will fall into a pit" (Matt 15:14); "Unless a kernel of wheat falls to the ground and dies, it remains only a single seed. But if it dies, it produces many seeds" (John 12:24).

Like Proverbs, Jesus confronts us with two paths: life or death. "Enter through the narrow gate. For wide is the gate and broad is the road that leads to destruction, and many enter through it. But small is the gate and narrow the road that leads to life, and only a few find it" (Matt 7:13-14).

The "great" Solomon is synonymous with the wisdom tradition. Jesus is presented as "one greater than Solomon" (Luke 11:31). The greatness of Jesus is understandable from within the wisdom movement. Wisdom resides with God (Job 28; Prov 3:19-20), but that is who Jesus is!

For this reason Paul can say that in Christ "are hidden all the treasures of wisdom and knowledge" (Col 2:3). Or, again, Jesus "has become for us wisdom from God—that is, our righteousness, holiness, and redemption" (1 Cor 1:30). Jesus Christ is "the power of God and the wisdom of God" (1 Cor 1:24).

---

[9]For a convenient summary of Jesus and sapiential literature, see Ben Witherington III, "Jesus the Sage: The Wisdom of God," *The Jesus Quest: The Third Search for the Jew of Nazareth*, 2nd ed. (Downers Grove, IL: InterVarsity, 1997), pp. 161-196.

ECCLESIASTES[1]

Douglas Coupland, who popularized the expression Generation X, shares in his 1994 publication *Life after God* how life is without religion or belief. At the end of this autobiographical search, he writes, "Now — here is my secret. I tell it to you with an openness of heart that I doubt I shall ever achieve again, so I pray that you are in a quiet room as you hear these words. My secret is that I need God — that I am sick and can no longer make it alone. I need God to help me give, because I no longer seem to be capable of giving; to help me be kind, as I no longer seem capable of kindness; to help me love, as I seem beyond being able to love."[2]

Coupland's search for meaning leads him to God. His book is a timely message for a modern (or postmodern) generation seemingly beyond God. The Book of Ecclesiastes traces an ancient man's quest for meaning. That quest, too, ended with God. "Now all has been heard; here is the conclusion of the matter: Fear God and keep his commandments, for this is the whole duty of man" (12:13).

HISTORICAL AND CULTURAL BACKGROUND

A pessimism literature existed in the ancient Near East. In the Egyptian "Song of the Harper" (c. 2100 B.C.) the lyricist is troubled by man's transience, and so calls upon the guests at a feast to surrender themselves to pleasure.

Let thy desire flourish,
In order to let thy heart forget the beatifications for thee.
Follow thy desire, as long as thou shalt live.
Put myrrh upon thy head and clothing of fine linen upon thee,

---

[1]The Hebrew title for the book is Qoheleth. This title is used throughout this chapter for the author or the revered wise man of the book.

[2]Douglas Coupland, *Life after God* (New York: Pocket Books, 1994), p. 359.

Being anointed with genuine marvels of the god's property.
Set an increase to thy good things;
Let not thy heart flag.
Follow thy desire and thy good.
Fulfill thy needs upon earth, after the command of thy heart,
Until there come for thee that day of mourning.[3]

The Babylonian *Counsels of a Pessimist* (uncertain date, anywhere between the nineteenth and seventh centuries B.C.) sounds the same tone:

Whatever men do does not last for ever,
Mankind and their achievements alike come to an end.[4]

The Babylonian *Dialogue of Pessimism* (c. 1300 B.C.) advances the propriety of an action and then its opposite, suggesting the utter absurdity of reality. For example, "I am going to love a woman. . . . The man who loves a woman forgets sorrow and fear. . . . No, slave, I will by no means love a woman. . . . Woman is a pitfall — a pitfall, a hole, a ditch. Woman is a sharp iron dagger that cuts a man's throat."[5] The dialogue concludes with the noble asking his slave, "What, then, is good?" The slave responds, "To have my neck and your neck broken. And to be thrown into the river is good."[6]

The Epic of Gilgamesh also touches upon this theme of futility. In the third tablet, we read:

Who, my friend can scale heaven?
Only the gods live forever under the sun.
As for mankind, numbered are their days;
Whatever they achieve is but the wind![7]

In the tenth tablet Gilgamesh is encouraged to forget about his quest for immortality and enjoy his present circumstances.

Gilgamesh, whither rovest thou? The life thou pursuest thou shalt not find. When the gods created mankind, death for mankind they set aside, life in their own hands retaining. Thou, Gilgamesh, let full be thy belly, make thou merry by day and by night. Of each day make thou a feast of rejoicing, day

---

[3] *ANET*, p. 467.
[4] W.G. Lambert, *Babylonian Wisdom Literature* (Oxford: Oxford University Press, 1960), p. 109.
[5] Ibid., p. 147.
[6] Ibid., p. 149.
[7] *ANET*, p. 79.

and night dance thou and play! Let thy garments be sparkling fresh, thy head be washed; bathe thou in water. Pay heed to the little one that holds on to thy hand. Let thy spouse delight in thy bosom! For this is the task of mankind![8]

The Book of Ecclesiastes would contend that, if you confine your perspective to this world alone, then all the claims of the pessimist are true. Qoheleth does also echo that joy can be found in life's simple pleasures: food, drink, and relationships (2:24; 3:12-13,22; 5:18-19; 8:15; 9:7-9).[9]

HISTORY OF INTERPRETATION

Qoheleth has been viewed as a hedonist, a pessimist, a skeptic, or an agnostic. "The Book of Ecclesiastes," writes J. Stafford Wright, "might be called the black sheep of the Bible."[10] Since no single label can express the complexity of the author's thoughts, the interpreter must remember that the canonicity of the book suggests that the author is a man of faith!

Apparent contradictions and unorthodox statements have baffled interpreters. Plumptre has gone so far as to say that the book "comes before us as the sphinx of Hebrew literature, with its unsolved riddles of history and life."[11] Listen to the tension in the following verses. "Although a wicked man commits a hundred crimes and still lives a long time, I know that it will go better with God-fearing men, who are reverent before God. Yet because the wicked do not fear God, it will not go well with them, and their days will not lengthen like a shadow" (8:12-13). How can the wicked "live a long time" and yet their days "not lengthen like a shadow?" Consider another tension. "And I declared that the dead, who had already died, are happier than the

---

[8]Ibid., p. 90.

[9]Qoheleth has "demonstrated that it is possible for men to bear the shafts of evil that threaten the human condition if they cultivate a sense of reverence for the mystery and miracle of life and strive to discover intimations of meaning in its beauty" (Robert Gordis, *Koheleth – The Man and His World*, 3rd ed. [New York: Schocken Books, 1968], p. 120).

[10]J. Stafford Wright, "The Interpretation of Ecclesiastes," in *Classical Evangelical Essays in Old Testament Interpretation* (Grand Rapids: Baker, 1972), p. 133.

[11]Quoted in A.G. Wright, "The Riddle of the Sphinx: The Structure of the Book of Qoheleth," *CBQ* 30 (1968): 313.

living, who are still alive" (4:2). Compare this with 9:4: "Anyone who is among the living has hope—even a live dog is better off than a dead lion." Which is better, life or death?

How does the reader respond to these conundrums? Do we throw up our hands as despairing skeptics? Or does dissatisfaction with our wisdom turn us in search of someone who will provide a satisfying key to the riddles of life?[12]

What, then, is the purpose of Ecclesiastes? "It is an essay in apologetics," writes Michael A. Eaton. "It defends the life of faith in a generous God by pointing to the grimness of the alternative."[13]

TEXT AND AUTHOR

TEXT

The Hebrew text has been well preserved. The fragments from Qumran support the Masoretic Text. The LXX translation is very literal, whereas the Latin Vulgate is a freer translation. The Syriac Peshitta generally agrees with the Masoretic Text.[14] The Aramaic Targum is so periphrastic that it is of little value for the textual criticism of the book.[15]

AUTHORSHIP

This question of authorship has effectively scattered the academic community rather than drawn it together. All are agreed that the name of the author is not mentioned in the book. And that is the extent of the consensus! From that point, either one argues for or against Solomonic authorship.

Certain internal clues raise the possibility of Solomonic authorship. He was most certainly a "son of David, king in Jerusalem" (1:1). This possibility is supported by the reference to great wisdom (1:16; cf. 1 Kgs 4:29-34) and to great wealth (2:4-11; cf. 1 Kgs 10:14-29). Who other than the matchless Solomon can be so described?

---

[12]"For all who are disillusioned and frustrated by life," writes Parsons, "the book commends joy in God's daily provisions and commands fearful obedience to Him" ("Guidelines for Understanding and Proclaiming the Book of Ecclesiastes, Part 2," *BSac* 160 [2003]: 304).

[13]Michael A. Eaton, *Ecclesiastes*, TOTC (Downers Grove, IL: InterVarsity, 1983), p. 44.

[14]Lucas, *Exploring*, p. 147.

[15]Roland E. Murphy, *Ecclesiastes*, WBC (Waco: Word, 1992), p. xxvi.

Hugo Grotius (d. 1645) has been acclaimed as the first to deny that Solomon was the author.[16] In more recent times, the majority of commentators have followed suit, positing a postexilic date.[17] This late date is suggested due to apparent linguistic similarities between Ecclesiastes and exilic and postexilic works like Ezra, Esther, Nehemiah, Chronicles, and Malachi.

Aramaisms represent one of these linguistic similarities.[18] But since Aramaisms may be expected in biblical Hebrew from as early as the tenth century, "they are of comparatively little significance for dating."[19]

Archer concludes, "In weighing the force of the linguistic argument, it should be carefully observed that a comprehensive survey of all the data, including vocabulary, morphology, syntax, and style, yields the result that the text of Ecclesiastes fits into no known period in the history of the Hebrew language."[20] Archer suggests then that the uniqueness of this book reflects "a conventional style peculiar to the genre to which Ecclesiastes belonged."[21] Similarly, Eaton opines "that a particular style was adopted for pessimism literature."[22]

Derek Kidner suggests that the reference to wisdom in 1:16 rules out Solomon, since he had only one Israelite predecessor — his father, David![23] Kidner proposes that the author uses this royal title (1:1) as "a means of dramatizing the quest he describes in chapters one and two. He pictures for us a super-Solomon (as he implies by the word 'surpassing' in 1:16) to demonstrate that the most gifted

---

[16]Murphy, *Ecclesiastes,* p. liii.

[17]In his book, *Five Festal Garments* (Downers Grove, IL: InterVarsity, 2000), Barry G. Webb writes, "The only point on which there is anything approaching consensus is that it is a relatively late work" (p. 83).

[18]A collection of these Aramaisms may be found in Eaton, *Ecclesiastes,* p. 18, n. 3.

[19]Eaton, *Ecclesiastes,* p. 18. Eaton adds, "Our conclusion must be that the language of Ecclesiastes does not at present provide an adequate resource for dating" (p. 19).

[20]Gleason L. Archer Jr., *A Survey of Old Testament Introduction* (Chicago: Moody Press, 1978), p. 481. Consult also Archer, "The Linguistic Evidence for the Date of Ecclesiastes," *JETS* 12 (1969): 167-181.

[21]Archer, *Survey,* p. 482.

[22]Eaton, *Ecclesiastes,* p. 19.

[23]Archer has written, "We can confidently assert that there were many more kings before Solomon in Jerusalem than just his father David. Jerusalem had been a royal city for many hundreds of years, even back to the time of Melchizedek, Abraham's contemporary" (*Survey,* p. 485).

man conceivable, who would outstrip every king who ever occupied the throne of David, would still return empty-handed from the quest for self-fulfillment."[24] If Solomon is not the author, then we are reading an example of "royal fiction."

Provan, who distinguishes between the author and the speaker, suggests that the speaker "becomes a king within the world of the text (takes on the Solomonic guise), in order to persuade his hearers of truths about the world as it is confronted by the wealthy, the powerful, and the wise — among whose ranks certainly number kings like Solomon."[25]

How is the reader to understand the title "Teacher" (1:1,12)? The Hebrew is קֹהֶלֶת (*Qoheleth*), an active participle, feminine singular, denoting an office. The term suggests then one who addresses an assembly. The Septuagint rendered this word as Ἐκκλησιαστής (*ekklēsiastēs*), from which, of course, our English title comes.

Eaton opines that an editor is presenting in his own words and style the teaching of a revered wise man. The wise man is Qoheleth, the Teacher. The editor is an "unnamed and unknown admirer or disciple working at a date and location that cannot be precisely determined."[26]

In the main body of the book, we hear the Teacher speaking in the first person (1:12; 2:1; 6:1; 9:1; etc.). At three points the Teacher is spoken of in the third person: "The words of the Teacher, son of David, king in Jerusalem" (1:1); "'Look,' says the teacher, 'this is what I have discovered'" (7:27a); "Not only was the Teacher wise, but also he imparted knowledge to the people. He pondered and searched out and set in order many proverbs. The Teacher searched to find just the right words, and what he wrote was upright and true" (12:9-10). Many recent commentators believe that the third person voice at the beginning of the book (1:1) and the end (12:9-10) point to the presence of an editor or frame narrator.[27]

---

[24]Derek Kidner, *A Time to Mourn and a Time to Dance: The Message of Ecclesiastes* (Downers Grove, IL: InterVarsity, 1976), p. 22.

[25]Iain Provan, *Ecclesiastes/Song of Solomon*, The NIV Application Commentary (Grand Rapids: Zondervan, 2001), p. 27. Provan thinks that Qoheleth is the speaker of most of the words in the book. The author is the person who has passed on to us the words of Qoheleth. Webb is of the same opinion. He writes, "The words of the Teacher are framed and interpreted for us by the voice of the frame narrator, who is the author of the book" (*Five Festal Garments*, p. 84).

[26]Eaton, *Ecclesiastes*, p. 22.

[27]Michael V. Fox, "Frame-Narrative and Composition in the Book of Qoheleth," *HUCA* 48 (1977): 83-106.

If Solomon is not the author, then the date of the book must be left undecided.

STRUCTURE

The phrase "under the sun," which occurs twenty-nine times in Ecclesiastes and nowhere else in the Old Testament, is key to unlocking this book. The phrases "under heaven" (1:13-14; 3:1) and "on earth" (5:2; 8:16) seem to be synonymous. These three phrases suggest the futility of man's search for meaning apart from God. If man lives his life apart from God, solely in the context of this world ("under the sun"), he will profit nothing and will reap dissatisfaction. "Qoheleth is addressing the general public whose view is bounded by the horizons of this world; he meets them on their own ground, and proceeds to convict them of its inherent vanity."[28]

The vanity or futility of this world is, of course, the motto of the book. From beginning (1:2) to end (12:8), the book echoes the despair inherent in life lived apart from God. The word translated "vanity" by the KJV and "meaningless" by the NIV is the Hebrew word הֶבֶל (hebel).[29] It occurs thirty-eight times in this book. In addition to this futility, man also experiences misery or adversity (2:21; 5:13,16; 6:1; 7:14; 8:6; 9:12; 10:5,13; 11:10; 12:1).

Many commentators have concluded that the book shows no order or overall progression of thought. This negative assessment ignores the witness of the Book itself: "Not only was the Teacher wise, but also he imparted knowledge to the people. He pondered and searched out and set in order many proverbs. The Teacher searched to find just the right words, and what he wrote was upright and true" (12:9-10).

Addison G. Wright has pressed for a positive assessment of the book's unity. First, he sees a continuity of thought from 1:12 to 6:9. This movement is signaled by the ninefold repetition of the expression "a chasing after the wind" (1:14,17; 2:11,17,26; 4:4,6,16; 6:9).

---

[28]G.S. Hendry, quoted in Derek Kidner, *The Wisdom of Proverbs, Job & Ecclesiastes: An Introduction to Wisdom Literature* (Downers Grove, IL: Inter-Varsity, 1985), p. 93.

[29]The word has a basic meaning of "breath" or "vapor." *Hebel* (also transliterated *hevel*) is "a judgment," writes Webb," a condition, imposed on the world, and on human beings in particular, by God. It is a manifestation of the fall and, positively, of God's rule as creator and judge" (*Five Festal Garments*, p. 104). The name Abel (Gen 4) is in Hebrew *hebel*.

This expression never again appears in the remaining chapters. Each occurrence marks a unit of thought: 1:12-15; 1:16-18; 2:1-11; 2:12-17; 2:18-26; 3:1–4:6; 4:7-16; 5:1–6:9. "In these chapters Qoheleth is reporting the results of his investigation of life undertaken to 'understand what is best for men to do under the heavens during the limited days of their life' (2:3). He begins with a double introduction (1:12-15; 1:16-18), and then evaluates pleasure-seeking (2:1-11), wisdom (2:12-17), and finally the results of toil in four sections (2:18–6:9). The evaluation repeated at the end of each section is that it is a vanity and a chase after wind."[30]

Second, 6:10-12 introduces the second half of the book. These verses conclude with two questions. "Who knows what is good for a man in life?" and "Who can tell him what will happen under the sun after he is gone?" Wright has noted that the words "do not know" and "no knowledge" occur at 9:1,5,10,12; 10:14,15; 11:2; and three times in 11:5-6. These repetitions serve as markers establishing the following units of thought: 9:1-6; 9:7-10; 9:11-12; 9:13–10:15; 10:16–11:2; 11:3-6.

Chapters seven and eight are divided into four sections — 7:1-14; 7:15-24; 7:25-29; and 8:1-17 — based on the repetition of the idea "not find/who can find" in 7:14,24,28 (twice), and 8:17 (three times).[31]

A poem on youth and old age (11:7–12:8) and an epilogue (12:9-14) round out the book.

Wright has also noted that each half of the book — 1:1–6:9 and 6:10–12:14 — consists of 111 verses. Note also that 2:1–6:9 is 93 verses, as is 6:10–11:6. The inclusio at 1:2 and 12:8 says, "Vanity of vanities, all is vanity." The sum for the numerical value of the Hebrew consonants of this expression — הבל הבלים הכל הבל (hbl hblym hkl hbl) — is 216, the very number of verses stretching from 1:1 to 12:8.[32]

The ending formulae ("a chasing after the wind," "do not know," and "not find/who can find") and these numerical patterns suggest that the book is a deliberately and carefully structured composition. The following outline reflects many of the compositional observations of A.G. Wright (who has been followed by Roland Murphy) outlined above.

---

[30]A.G. Wright, "Sphinx: Structure," p. 321.

[31]Ibid., pp. 322-323.

[32]Addison G. Wright, "The Riddle of the Sphinx Revisited: Numerical Patterns in the Book of Qoheleth," *CBQ* 42 (1980): 38-51.

I. Prologue — 1:1-11
  A. Superscription — 1:1
  B. Inclusion — 1:2 and 12:8
  C. Poem on the Futility of Toil — 1:3-11
 II. Part I — 1:12-6:9
  A. Double Introduction — 1:12-15 + 16-18
  B. The Futile Pursuit of Pleasure — 2:1-11
  C. The Futile Pursuit of Wisdom — 2:12-17
  D. The Futility of Toil — 2:18-23
  E. Hope for Meaning from the Hand of God — 2:24-26
  F. Time and Toil — 3:1-4:6
  G. Alienation and Ambition — 4:7-16
  H. God Is in Heaven — 5:1-7
  I. Riches Are Meaningless — 5:8-6:9
III. Part 2 — 6:10-11:6
  A. Introduction — 6:10-12
  B. Man Cannot Find Out What Is Good for Him to Do — 7:1-8:17
  C. Man Does Not Know What Will Come after Him — 9:1-11:6
 IV. Poem on Youth and Old Age — 11:7-12:7
  V. Inclusion — 12:8
 VI. Epilogue — 12:9-14

GENRE

Ecclesiastes is a distinguished member of the Wisdom Books of the Old Testament. Fearing God is the essence of this genre. In Ecclesiastes man is commanded five times to fear God (3:14; 5:7; 7:18; 8:12-13; 12:13).

There are no exact parallels to Ecclesiastes in the ancient Near East. The wisdom autobiography of Mesopotamia is the closest literary parallel. This genre consists of an autobiographical introduction, an autobiographical narrative, and wisdom admonitions on how to behave. Longman sees 1:12 as the introduction; 1:13-6:9 as the narrative; and 6:10-12:7 as the admonition. Longman writes, "The advice offered by Qohelet is firmly rooted in his own personal experience. His experience is the soil out of which his wisdom grows."[33]

---

[33]Tremper Longman III, *The Book of Ecclesiastes*, NICOT (Grand Rapids: Eerdmans, 1998), p. 19.

Ancient kings wrote bombastically of their accomplishments on impressive monuments. These inscriptions immortalized their names and achievements (only if the inscriptions survived the casualties of time and were later discovered by archaeologists!). The Book of Ecclesiastes subverts this genre. "Solomon's impressive works are systematically recounted, only to have hebel written over them all."[34]

The genre of the subunits of Ecclesiastes may be identified as: the reflection (1:13-15,16-18; 2:1-11,12-17), the proverb (1:15,18; 4:5-6; 7:1-12), the anecdote (4:7-8,13-16; 9:13-16; 10:5-7), and the wisdom instruction (5:1-3).[35]

THEOLOGICAL THEMES

Forty times Ecclesiastes used the word Elohim, God, and no other name, to speak of deity (thirty times the noun has the definite article, "the God"). God is in heaven (5:2), and, therefore, not subject to the verdict of vanity which shrouds life "under the sun." God is sovereign. He has planned the timing of all things (3:1-8). God is presented as judge of human actions. "For God will bring every deed into judgment, including every hidden thing, whether it is good or evil" (12:14; cf. 3:17; 8:13; 11:9). God is holy (5:1-2). He is beneficent (2:24-26; 3:13; 5:18-19; 6:2). He is inscrutable. "As you do not know the path of the wind, or how the body is formed in a mother's womb, so you cannot understand the work of God, the Maker of all things" (11:5; cf. 3:11; 8:17; 9:1).[36]

Twelve times in this book God is said to "give" (1:13; 2:26 [twice]; 3:10,11; 5:18,19; 6:2; 8:15; 9:9; 12:7,11). Five times the text says that

---

[34]Webb, *Five Festal Garments,* p. 93. A. Verheij has compared Ecclesiastes 2:4-6 with the Creation Narrative. After the completion of creation in Genesis, "God saw all that he had made, and it was very good" (1:31). For Solomon the result of his effort is the opposite to what God is said to have seen ("Paradise Retried: On Qohelet 2:4-6," *JSOT* 50 [1991]: 113-115).

[35]Longman, *Ecclesiastes,* p. 20.

[36]Stephan de Jong has shown that Qohelet's main theme ("human limitation in relation to God") is an important Old Testament theme. De Jong points out that this theme is common to the Wisdom Books (Proverbs, Job). Consequently, "the core of Qohelet's book as well as its theological building blocks are typical of the Old Testament" ("God in the Book of Qohelet: A Reappraisal of Qohelet's Place in Old Testament Theology," *VT* 47 [1997], p. 166).

mankind has a joyful "lot" from God (2:10; 3:22; 5:18,19; 9:9). "Ecclesiastes is thus an exploration of the barrenness of life without a practical faith in God. Intermingled with its pessimism are invitations to
a different outlook altogether, in which joy and purpose are found
when God is seen to be 'there' and to be characterized supremely by
generosity."[37]

Qoheleth affirms that God has "set eternity in the hearts of men"
(3:11). In other words, we have a capacity for eternal things, and cannot be complete until we come to know the Eternal One. This capacity is now evident in reverence before God (8:12) and in fear and
obedience to his commandments (12:13).

Mankind's inherent uncertainty about life is voiced a number of
times in the book (2:19; 3:21; 6:12; 8:1,7; 10:14; see also the above
section on "Structure"). This uncertainty renders the quest for
meaning a chasing after the wind! Man's mortality also compromises this quest (2:16; 3:2,19; 4:2; 5:16; 7:1,17,26; 8:8; 9:3-5; 12:1-7), as
does his depravity (2:26; 5:6; 7:20,26; 8:12; 9:2,18). Qoheleth has
noted that mankind's sin is both extensive (manifest throughout the
human race) and intensive (corrupting every aspect of man's being).[38]
"There is not a righteous man on earth who does what is right and
never sins" (7:20). "The hearts of men, moreover, are full of evil and
there is madness in their hearts while they live, and afterward they
join the dead!" (9:3).

These limitations — inherent uncertainty, mortality, and depravity — lead to frustration or vexation. "As a man comes, so he departs,
and what does he gain, since he toils for the wind? All his days he
eats in darkness, with great frustration, affliction, and anger" (5:16-
17; cf. 1:18; 2:23; 7:3,9 [twice]; 11:10).

NEW TESTAMENT CONNECTIONS

Qoheleth sees a shroud of frustration over our world. Paul
echoes this same verdict in Romans 8:20-21. "For the creation was
subjected to frustration, not by its own choice, but by the will of the
one who subjected it, in hope that the creation itself will be liberated from its bondage to decay and brought into the glorious freedom

---

[37]Eaton, *Ecclesiastes,* p. 45.
[38]James S. Reitman, "The Structure and Unity of Ecclesiastes," *BSac* 154
(1997): 303.

of the children of God." The Greek word translated "frustration" here is ματαιότης (*mataiotēs*), the very word used in the Septuagint for the word "vanity" or "meaningless."

Qoheleth asks, "What does man gain from all his labor at which he toils under the sun?" (1:3). The Hebrew word for "gain" in this question is יִתְרוֹן (*yithrôn*). This word appears in the Old Testament only in Ecclesiastes, and it appears here ten times (2:11,13 [twice]; 3:9; 5:9,16; 7:12; 10:10,11). Wisdom may be better than folly (2:13), and a king may profit momentarily from the harvest of the fields (5:9), but ultimately the verdict of vanity will overshadow every human endeavor. "As a man comes, so he departs, and what does he gain, since he toils for the wind?" (5:16; cf. 2:11). In short, there is no true profit or advantage to be gained "under the sun." Jesus framed the same truth, when he said, "What good is it for a man to gain the whole world, yet forfeit his soul? Or what can a man give in exchange for his soul?" (Mark 8:36-37).

Paul told the Athenians that God "gives all men life and breath and everything else" (Acts 17:25). This resonates with Qoheleth's emphasis upon God's goodness. Paul adds that God "determined the times set for them [mankind] and the exact places where they should live" (Acts 15:26). Qoheleth would approve (3:1-8). Paul also warns the Athenians that God "has set a day when he will judge the world with justice" (Acts 17:31). Qoheleth again approves (11:9; 12:14).

The Hebrew noun translated by the NIV as "gladness," "happiness," or "pleasure" (2:1,2,10,26; 5:19; 7:4; 8:15; 9:7) and the corresponding verb (3:12,22; 4:16; 5:18; 8:15; 10:19; 11:8,9) remind us that the enjoyment of life must be basic to our worldview. The Septuagint translated this idea into the Greek as εὐφροσύνη (*euphrosynē*). This idea and this Greek word are on Paul's lips in Acts 14:16-17: "In the past, he [God] let all nations go their own way. Yet he has not left himself without testimony. He has shown kindness by giving you rain from heaven and crops in their seasons; he provides you with plenty of food and fills your hearts with joy (*euphrosynēs*)."[39]

"What does man gain from all his labor at which he toils under the sun?" (1:3). With this question, Qoheleth introduces the futility

---

[39]Robert K. Johnston, "'Confessions of a Workaholic': A Reappraisal of Qoheleth," *CBQ* 38 (1976): 20. Qoheleth teaches that enjoyment is dependent upon the hand of God. "Man's pleasure depends on God's good pleasure, and the divine action cannot be neatly categorized or programmed by man (2:24b-26)" (p. 25).

of labor/toil, a theme which he will revisit time and time again. The word translated here as "labor" or "toil" occurs either as a noun or a verb multiple times in this book (1:3; 2:10,11,18,19,20,21,22,24; 3:13; 4:4,6,8,9; 5:14,15,17,18; 6:7; 8:15,17; 9:9; 10:15).

With the gospel comes a new kind of work in which Christians participate. It is the "work of Christ" (Phil 2:30) or the "work of the Lord" (1 Cor 15:58; 16:10). This work "partakes of the power of the resurrection and the life of the world to come, precisely because it is not our work, but God's. And to the extent that we are engaged in it, in whatever form, we can be sure that this, at least, is not futile. For in this work, the future, in which there is no longer any hebel, is already breaking in."[40]

Paul writes, "If anyone else thinks he has reasons to put confidence in the flesh, I have more: circumcised on the eighth day, of the people of Israel, of the tribe of Benjamin, a Hebrew of Hebrews; in regard to the law, a Pharisee; as for zeal, persecuting the church; as for legalistic righteousness, faultless" (Phil 2:4-6). He considers these reasons "rubbish" (2:8). Qoheleth would agree. Paul considers all these pursuits "loss for the sake of Christ" (2:7; cf. 2 Corinthians 11).

SPECIAL ISSUES

INFLUENCES

Commentators have argued for Mesopotamian, Egyptian, and Hellenistic influence upon Qoheleth.[41] It should go without saying, however, that he was thoroughly Hebraic in his thoughts. C.C. Forman contends that "the early chapters of Genesis represent the most important single influence in the ideas of Ecclesiastes regarding the nature and destiny of man, the character of human existence, and the fact of God."[42] Notice the following points of contact between Genesis and Ecclesiastes.

---

[40]Webb, *Five Festal Garments,* p. 108.

[41]See, for example, Murphy, *Ecclesiastes,* pp. xlii-xlv. Karel van der Toorn argues that Ecclesiastes was influenced by Greek thought. The occasional incorporation of sayings from Egypt and Mesopotamia testifies to Qoheleth's cosmopolitan outlook ("Did Ecclesiastes Copy Gilgamesh?" *BRev* 16 [2000]: 22-30, 50).

[42]C.C. Forman, "Koheleth's Use of Genesis," *JSS* 5 (1960): 263.

"And the LORD God formed man from the dust of the ground" (Gen 2:7a).	"All go to the same place; all come from dust, and to dust all return" (Eccl 3:20). "And the dust returns to the ground it came from, and the spirit returns to God who gave it" (12:7).
"The LORD saw how great man's wickedness on the earth had become, and that every inclination of the thoughts of his heart was only evil all the time" (Gen 6:5).	"There is not a righteous man on earth who does what is right and never sins" (Eccl 7:20). "This only have I found: God made mankind upright, but men have gone in search of schemes" (Eccl 7:29; cf. 8:11; 9:3).
"The LORD God said, 'It is not good for the man to be alone, I will make a helper suitable for him'" (Gen 2:18).	"Enjoy life with your wife, whom you love" (Eccl 9:9; cf. 4:9-12).
"Cursed is the ground because of you; through painful toil you will eat of it all the days of your life" (Gen 3:17).	"What does a man get for all the toil and anxious striving with which he labors under the sun? All his days his work is pain and grief; even at night his mind does not rest. This too is meaningless" (Eccl 2:22-23).

LITURGICAL USE

The Song of Songs, Ruth, Lamentations, Ecclesiastes, and Esther comprise "the Scrolls." These five books were adopted as lectionary readings for five of the major festivals in Judaism: Passover (Song of Songs), the Feast of Weeks (Ruth), the Ninth of Ab (Lamentations), the Feast of Tabernacles (Ecclesiastes), and the Festival of Purim (Esther).

The Feast of Tabernacles lasts seven days and celebrates the end of the agricultural year (Deut 16:13). At the same time, it recalls the period of Israel's wilderness wanderings (Lev 23:42-43). Barry Webb has noted how the reading of Ecclesiastes during this celebration kept the nation anchored. "For in the wilderness the Israelites learned about their human frailty: that their lives were a mere breath, and that to fear God and keep his commandments constituted the whole meaning of their existence. It was a lesson they needed to hear again in the context of harvest celebration, lest being able to eat and drink and find satisfaction in their work should be mistaken for an accomplishment rather than a gift, and lead them away from God rather than to him."[43]

MISOGYNY

A superficial reading of Ecclesiastes 7:26,28 suggests that Qoheleth was a misogynist, a hater of women. A closer examination eliminates this misunderstanding. The antecedent of "the woman" in verse 26 is "folly" (v. 25). Additionally, when one examines the parallelism of Hebrew numbers and recognizes the use of hyperbole (Job 9:3; 33:23), it becomes clear that Qoheleth was demonstrating the scarcity of good people, whether man or woman.[44]

---

[43]Webb, *Five Festal Garments,* pp. 106-107.

[44]Greg W. Parsons, "Guidelines for Understanding and Proclaiming the Book of Ecclesiastes, Part 2," *BSac* 160 (2003): 292-293. Here the formula seems to be x and x-1 (1 in 1,000 compared with 0 in a thousand = not at all).

SONG OF SONGS

HISTORICAL AND CULTURAL BACKGROUND

The *Song of Songs* of the Hebrew Bible is unique among the different types of biblical literature. Its unique title indicates from a Hebrew perspective that it is "the greatest of songs." It is love poetry. Love poetry as a genre is found throughout the ancient Near East in Egypt, Mesopotamia, ancient Sumer, and at Ugarit (ancient Phoenicia). In both content and form Egyptian love poetry comes closer to the Song of Songs than any others.

EGYPTIAN LOVE POETRY

Michael V. Fox has given the best English language scholarly attention to Egyptian parallels for the Song of Songs.[1] These Egyptian love songs date from the nineteenth and twentieth dynasties (c. 1305–1150 B.C.) and thus predate the period of Solomon (c. 970–930 B.C.). There are four collections: Chester Beatty Papyrus 1, Papyrus Harris 500, the Turin Papyrus, and the Cairo Love Songs.

Unlike Mesopotamian love poetry, in Egypt deities are only occasionally addressed. They seem to be for purely secular entertainment, nothing more. Features that are similar to Song of Songs include the following: 1) they are about ordinary young people; 2) they pine for each other in terms of "lovesickness"; 3) the female is referred to as a "sister," common in ancient culture; 4) the male wishes to be a "doorkeeper"; 5) fragrances are often mentioned in relationship to lovemaking; 6) the female voice is either exclusive or dominates the song; 7) separation from each other must be over-

---

[1] Michael V. Fox, *Song of Songs and the Ancient Egyptian Love Songs* (Madison, WI: University of Wisconsin Press, 1985). Also see J.B. White, *A Study of the Language of Love in the Song of Songs and Ancient Egyptian Love Poetry* (Missoula, MT: Scholars Press, 1975).

come; 8) a lush garden or field is most often the metaphor for the sexuality of the female; 9) a tree is used as a "prop" for lovemaking; and 10) descriptions of the bodies of both male and female are sometimes given. These similarities and others make it evident that Egyptian long songs had some influence over Song of Songs. But there are differences.

The differences can be significant: 1) the Egyptian songs are not really dialogues between two lovers, rather they are individual love songs perhaps sung antiphonally; 2) the male and female are very young, not adults; 3) sometimes only the female voice is heard; 4) there are adolescent fantasies and vows of thank offerings not found in Song of Songs; 5) some of the love poetry describes a brothel (Chester Beatty I group C), suggestive of the warnings in Proverbs 7, but not found in Song of Songs; 6) there is little mystery or profound imagery used in the Egyptian poems in comparison to the Song of Songs: and 7) the "boy" and "girl" in the Egyptian poetry are not married whereas it can be argued that the "union" of the female and male in Song of Songs is in the context of married bliss, not a sexual encounter between two single adults. These differences are enough to show that the Song of Songs is not simply a "copy" of Egyptian love poetry but certainly the genre has influenced the form and content of the Song of Songs.

MESOPOTAMIAN LOVE POETRY

Of lesser importance to the Song of Songs is the love poetry found among the ancient Mesopotamian cultures. While there is some similarity in terms of wording and form, "Mesopotamian love poetry almost always concerns the love affairs of the gods and tends to be hymnic or liturgical."[2] Sumerian love songs also deal with kings and their consorts (harems) or with the goddess Inanna. The closest song parallel to the Song of Songs would be *Message of Ludingirra to His Mother* (a copy dated c. 1800–1600 B.C.). It technically is not a love song but it includes descriptive praise for the "mother," which may be the goddess Inanna instead of another human. However, the description is very much like the *wasf* (Arabic meaning "description") found in Song of Songs (4:1-7; 5:10-16; 7:1-6).

---

[2]Duane Garrett and Paul R. House, *Song of Songs/Lamentations*, WBC 23B (Nashville: Thomas Nelson, 2004), p. 47.

TAMIL LOVE POETRY

Rabin (see bibliography) has attempted to show similarities between Indian love poetry and the Song of Songs. He highlights three main areas of similarities: 1) the woman is the chief character and speaker in the Song of Songs; 2) the role of nature in the poetic similes and reference to the phenomena of growth and renewal as a background to the lovers' relationship; and 3) the dominant note of the woman's speeches is longing rather than desire.[3] While these similarities are noted, they are not as strong as the Egyptian love poetry in terms of possible influence on Song of Songs. Longman's evaluation is appropriate: "We are not suggesting any kind of direct borrowing of songs between these cultures, but there was likely an awareness of love songs from other countries, at least among the elite, similar to the awareness of wise sayings from abroad (1 Kings 4:29-34)."[4] Human love and sexuality is universal and one should expect some similarities between the one extant love song of Israel and such songs from the surrounding cultures. They have increased our ability to appreciate some of the metaphors used for the descriptions of love and desire between the sexes.

TEXT AND AUTHOR

The Masoretic Text (Hebrew Text) is well-attested without major problems. The versions support it as well. Whatever problems are encountered are due to the terseness of the poetry, unusual vocabulary for the subject matter, and its genre. There have been four manuscripts found at Qumran, dating c. 30 B.C. to A.D. 70. Cave 4 divulged three manuscripts while Cave 6 produced only one insignificant manuscript. Clearly the Song of Songs was part of the Hebrew canon long before the Christian era.

Authorship must take into account the superscription to the book: "Song of the Songs which (belongs) to Solomon." Against most critical scholarship, due weight should be given to this title, although it is difficult to *interpret*. As with the Psalms, interpreting

---

[3]As summarized by Lucas, *Exploring*, 3:184. See also A. Mariaselvam, *The Song of Songs and Ancient Tamil Love Poetry* (Rome: Editrice Pontifico Istituto Biblico, 1988).

[4]Tremper Longman III, *Song of Songs*, NICOT (Grand Rapids: Eerdmans, 2001), p. 54.

the ל (l^a) can have a variety of meanings: 1) it could be *by Solomon*, meaning authorship; 2) *To Solomon*, meaning dedicated to Solomon; 3) *Concerning Solomon*, the subject matter of the book; or 4) *Solomonic*, in the literary and wisdom tradition of Solomon. Those who late-date the Song of Songs on linguistic or other grounds usually take the second or fourth view. The traditional view regards Solomon as the author (view one) and even considers Solomon the subject of the poems (view three).

Besides the superscription, Solomon's name is mentioned in the book six times (1:5; 3:7,9,11; 8:11,12). The first reference is to the "tent curtains of Solomon." It could be read as "Salma," a variant reading, and thus have nothing to do with Solomon. Song of Songs 3:7,9, and 11 are about Solomon: "Look! It is Solomon's carriage" (v. 7), "King Solomon made for himself the carriage" (v. 9), and "look at King Solomon wearing the crown" (v. 11). The context implies a wedding procession by King Solomon (literally), but it could also be a metaphorical reference to the male lover. He is being referred to as her "king" coming to her, riding in "Solomon's carriage." The only other context is at the end of the Song of Songs — 8:11,12. The female lover says: "Solomon had a vineyard in Baal Hamon; he let out his vineyard to tenants. Each was to bring for its fruit a thousand shekels of silver. But my own vineyard is mine to give; the thousand shekels are for you, O Solomon, and two hundred are for those who tend its fruit." It seems to be a parody against Solomon's "thousand" lovers (1 Kgs 11:3). The female lover says her "own vineyard" (her body) is hers to give. Solomon can have a "thousand shekels of silver" (wives and concubines?) but "my lover" will have my body!

These references to Solomon and their contexts seem to preclude Solomon as author, although it is possible for authors to speak "against" themselves. It is also possible to date the song to the tenth century B.C. since in 6:4 "Tirzah" and "Jerusalem" are mentioned as parallelisms for beauty and loveliness. Tirzah was destroyed by King Omri (885–874 B.C., 1 Kgs 16:23-24). There are no other signposts to help date the song.

Jewish tradition (*Midrash Rabbah*) attributes three books to Solomon: Song of Songs (from a youthful Solomon before his large harem), Proverbs (Solomon as a mature adult), and Ecclesiastes (Solomon in his old age). Though the tradition itself is strong, the attribution is speculative.

Perhaps it is best to keep the authorship an open question. An early date during Solomon's time for the song is not impossible nor is it impossible that Solomon could have written some of the songs within the Song of Songs. However, consistency of theme, style, language, and chiastic form suggest a single author. Who that might have been is unclear.

HISTORY OF INTERPRETATION

While the Song of Songs was interpreted originally as what it was, a love song, it very early began to be interpreted as an allegory of the love relationship between Yahweh God and Israel (Jewish interpreters) or Christ and the Church/the soul (Christian interpreters). Since there were no safeguards for allegorical interpretations, outlandish views on every aspect of the Song began to be expressed.[5] The early Roman Catholic church's repressed views of sex and the elevation of celibacy for priests spurred the allegorical approach. Allegory is also used in songs that we sing that refer to Christ as "the rose of Sharon, a lily of the valleys" (2:1) or "his banner over me is love" (2:4b).

In the last two centuries scholars have almost abandoned the allegorical approach. Recognition of love poems in the surrounding cultures of Egypt and Mesopotamia has allowed for a more realistic and literal view of the Song of Songs. But even this approach has its variations. First, there is the "three-character interpretation." This interpretation presents the Song as a drama that highlights the love of a maiden for her shepherd-boy-lover over against Solomon's "attempt" at winning her heart for his harem. One version has the woman already in Solomon's harem and she is trying to escape. Solomon is foiled in his attempt to either "win" her or "keep" her as she escapes to be with her true lover — the shepherd-boy. Few accept this interpretation, since at many points it is arbitrary in its interpretations. The reading is more eisegesis than exegesis.

F. Delitzsch (1813–1890) argued strongly for the "two-character" interpretation. He saw the song as Solomon's devotion to his one true love. (Apparently this was before the harem was developed!) Goulder thinks that the Song of Songs is a tract against racism — the marriage of Solomon to an Arabian princess. All of these dramatic interpreta-

---

[5]See Garrett and House, *Song of Songs/Lamentations*, pp. 59-76.

tions have their problems, for much must be read into the text. These interpretations become no better than the allegorizations.

More modern interpretations have attempted to "reinterpret" the Song of Songs as a fertility text from pagan myths. This approach has hardly gained a hearing, thanks to some solid criticisms by H.H. Rowley. Others claim that the Song of Songs was an ancient Israelite *epithalamium*, a series of songs to be sung over the course of a wedding ceremony. This approach came from nineteenth-century Syria, but it no longer holds any sway among scholars. Marvin Pope has argued for a "funerary" background, partly on the basis of the mention of "death" in the song. His theory is completely off the mark, and even Pope has not argued beyond his original proposal. A good example of a "feminist reading" of the Song of Songs is presented in *Exquisite Desire* by Carey Ellen Walsh.[6] While her study has many good insights into the metaphorical language of the Song of Songs, it is more a "reader-response" approach. It is not a commentary as such, but well worth the reading.

STRUCTURE

For many scholars Song of Songs exhibits no organizational structure. It is just an anthology of love poems placed together without dramatic effect or appeal. Each song is to be sung or read in its own right — and then the singer or reader moves on to the next song. On the other hand, others argue for a "macrostructure" to the Song of Songs. Duane Garrett has offered an interesting structure for those who would wish to see some in the Song. He writes: "I suggest that the Song of Songs is a unified work with chiastic structure and is composed of thirteen individual songs, or *cantos*, for presentation by a male and a female soloist with a chorus."[7] The following is his chiastic structural outline:

Superscript (1:1)
A   I. Chorus and soprano: the entrance (1:2-4)
B   II. Soprano: the virgin's education I (1:5-6)
C   III. Soprano and chorus: finding the beloved (1:7-8)
D   IV. Tenor, chorus, and soprano: the first song of
                        mutual love (1:9-2:7)

[6]See Carey Ellen Walsh, *Exquisite Desire: Religion, the Erotic, and the Song of Songs* (Minneapolis: Fortress Press, 2000).
[7]Garrett and House, *Song of Songs/Lamentations*, pp. 31, 32.

E	V. Soprano and tenor: the invitation to depart (2:8-17)
F	VI. Three wedding-night songs (3:1-5; 3:6-11; 4:1-15)
Fa	a. Soprano: the bride's anxiety (3:1-5)
Fb	b. Chorus: the bride comes to the groom (3:6-11)
Fc	c. Tenor: the flawless bride I (4:1-15)
G	VII. Soprano, tenor, and chorus: the consummation (4:16–5:1)
F'	VIII. Three wedding-night songs (5:2-16; 6:1-3; 6:4-10)
Fa'	a. Soprano, tenor, and chorus: the bride's pain (5:2-8)
Fb'	b. Chorus and soprano: the bride recovers the groom (5:9–6:3)
Fc'	c. Tenor and chorus: the flawless bride II (6:4-10)
E'	IX. Soprano, chorus, and tenor: leaving girlhood behind (6:11-13)
D'	X. Tenor and soprano: the second song of mutual love (7:1–8:4)
C'	XI. Chorus and soprano: claiming the beloved (8:5-7)
B'	XII. Chorus and soprano: the virgin's education II (8:8-12)
A'	XIII. Tenor, chorus, and soprano: the farewell (8:13-14)

This chiastic outline is based on the fact that there are four hundred lines of poetry in the Song and 4:16 begins at line 200. Thus, at the "center" of the Song is the "dramatic sexual union" of the man and woman whom Garrett calls the "tenor" and the "soprano" respectively. The "chorus" represents the "girls of Jerusalem." Thus, the Song of Songs is interpreted here as truly a song and not necessarily a drama.

GENRE

It seems best to view the Song of Songs as what it originally was: a love poem with love lyrics expressed between a woman and a man. It is the "plain sense" of the text. Longman comments: "The Song is an anthology of love poems, a kind of erotic psalter."[8] Walsh says: "The Song is essentially a book about how badly two people love and

---

[8]Longman, *Song of Songs*, p. 43.

want each other."[9] The above structural outline adheres to this genre. All other interpretations have proven unsuccessful at best, especially the allegorical. But seeing a "drama" in the Song of Songs must also be questioned. Reading the Song as a love poem forces one to consider how such poetry is formed for that genre. How do lines of poetry make up a stanza? How do the images and metaphors convey meaning? How far did ancient cultures, particularly this song, describe desire, longing, and lovemaking? These and many more questions must be asked of the Song.

THEOLOGICAL THEMES

No one should be embarrassed that Song of Songs is in the Bible. God created human sexuality and human love. "Male and female he created them" (Gen 1:27c). And then God blessed them and said to them: "Be fruitful and increase in number" (Gen 1:28a). The natural desire for love between a man and a woman is a gift from God. It goes beyond the purpose of reproduction, though that is included. Sexual love is simply one way in which men and women can express deep intimacy, especially when lovemaking is accompanied by the essential foreplay as described in the Song of Songs. The Song concentrates on the emotions of love, not the mechanics, and thus avoids the label of pornographic.

Besides sexual intimacy, this love is mutual: "My lover is mine and I am his" (2:16; cf. 6:3). It is also exclusive: "Place me like a seal over your heart, like a seal on your arm; for love is as strong as death, its jealousy unyielding as the grave" (8:6a). The Hebrew concept of love in this manner is always "married love." The ideal has always been one man, one woman where love and marriage go together (Gen 2:24,25).

The breaking of this covenant-love relationship is the prophet's way of describing Israel's breaking of covenant relationship with God by worshiping other gods or by personal and social sins that break God's laws (Hos 2:2; 3:1-3; 4:1-3; Jer 2:13,20-22; 5:7-9; etc.).

James Smith has taught that Songs fights two concepts: 1) asceticism — that sex is bad — and 2) lust — that sex is everything.[10] This

---

[9]Walsh, *Exquisite Desire*, p. 42.

[10]James E. Smith, *The Wisdom Literature and Psalms* (Joplin, MO: College Press, 1996), p. 831.

truth strikes at both the Church and our society. "If the Church tends to understand sex and even human love as taboo, society at large in our time treats it as an idol."[11]

Song of Songs teaches us that "real sex" is good and wonderful, but it is not everything. While human love is "as strong as death" (8:6b), we must subordinate ourselves to the one stronger than death, the Lord Himself! But when two lovers commit themselves to God and to one another in holy marriage, it can be "a little heaven on earth." God has created us for this heavenly bliss. If we miss it, it is our fault.

---

[11]Longman, *Song of Songs*, p. 61.

MAJOR PROPHETS

GARY HALL

RANDALL BAILEY

BIBLIOGRAPHY FOR
THE MAJOR PROPHETS

Achtemeier, Elizabeth. *The Community and Message of Isaiah 56–66: A Theological Commentary.* Minneapolis: Augsburg, 1982.

Ackroyd, Peter R. *Exile and Restoration.* London: SCM Press, 1968.

Albright, W.F. *From the Stone Age to Christianity.* Garden City, NY: Doubleday, 1957.

Alexander, J.A. *The Prophecies of Isaiah.* Reprinted by Grand Rapids: Zondervan, 1953, 1971; original 1846–47.

Allen, Leslie C. *Ezekiel 20–48.* WBC. Dallas: Word, 1990.

Allis, Oswald T. *The Unity of Isaiah.* Philadelphia: Presbyterian and Reformed, 1950.

Althann, Robert. *A Philological Analysis of Jeremiah 4–6 in the Light of Northwest Semitic.* Rome: Biblical Institute, 1983.

Archer, G.L. Jr. "Modern Rationalism and the Book of Daniel." *BSac* 136 (1979): 129-147.

—————. *A Survey of Old Testament Introduction.* Chicago: Moody, 1964.

Baltzer, Klaus. *Deutero-Isaiah.* Hermeneia. Trans. by Margeret Kohl. Minneapolis: Fortress, 2001.

Barton, G.A. "Daniel, a Pre-Israelite Hero of Galilee." *JBL* 60 (1941): 213-225.

Barton, John. *Isaiah 1–39.* OTG. Sheffield: Sheffield Academic Press, 1995.

Beasley-Murray, G.R. "The Interpretation of Daniel 7." *CBQ* 45 (1983): 44-58.

Beaulieu, P.-A., trans. "Nabonidus' Rebuilding of E-Lugal-Galga-Sisa, The Ziggurat of Ur." In *The Context of Scripture*, 2.123B:313 314. 3 vols. Ed. by W.W. Hallo (Leiden: Brill, 1979–2003).

Bergant, Dianne. *Lamentations.* Nashville: Abingdon, 2003.

Berlin, Adele. *Lamentations: A Commentary.* Louisville, KY: Westminster John Knox, 2002.

Blenkinsopp, Joseph. *Ezekiel.* Louisville, KY: John Knox, 1990.

_____. *Isaiah 1–39*; *Isaiah 40–55*; *Isaiah 56–66*. AB. New York: Doubleday, 2000, 2002, 2003.

Block, D.I. *The Book of Ezekiel.* 2 vols. NICOT. Grand Rapids: Eerdmans, 1997–98.

Bracke, William M. *Jeremiah 30–52 and Lamentations*. Louisville, KY: Westminster John Knox, 2000.

Bright, John. "The Date of the Prose Sermons of Jeremiah." *JBL* 70 (1951): 15-35.

_____. *Jeremiah*. AB. Garden City, NY: Doubleday, 1964.

_____. "The Prophetic Reminiscence: Its Place and Function in the Book of Jeremiah." *Biblical Essays, Proceedings: Die ou Testamentiese Werkgemeenskap*, pp. 11-30. Potchefstroom, South Africa: Pro Rege-Pers Beperk, 1966.

Broome, Edwin C. Jr. "Ezekiel's Abnormal Personality." *JBL* 65 (1946): 277-292.

Brownlee, W.H. *Ezekiel 1–19*. WBC. Waco: Word, 1986.

_____. *The Meaning of the Dead Sea Scrolls for the Bible*. New York: Oxford, 1964.

Brueggemann, Walter. *Isaiah 1–39*. Louisville, KY: Westminster John Knox, 1998.

_____. *Jeremiah*. Grand Rapids: Eerdmans, 1998.

Bulman, J.M. "The Identification of Darius the Mede." *WTJ* 35 (1972–73): 247-267.

Carr, David. "Reaching for Unity in Isaiah." *JSOT* 57 (1993): 61-80.

Carroll, R.P. *From Chaos to Covenant*. New York: Crossroad, 1981.

_____. *Jeremiah*. Sheffield, England: JSOT Press, 1989.

_____. *Jeremiah: A Commentary*. OTL. Philadelphia: Westminster, 1986.

Carson, D.A. "Matthew." In *The Expositor's Bible Commentary*. Ed. by Frank E. Gaebelein. Grand Rapids: Zondervan, 1984.

Charlesworth, J.H., ed. *The Old Testament Pseudepigrapha: Apocalyptic Literature and Testaments*. Vol. 1. Garden City, NY: Doubleday, 1983.

Childs, Brevard. *Isaiah*. OTL. Louisville, KY: Westminster John Knox, 2001.

Christensen, Duane. "In Quest of the Autograph of the Book of Jeremiah: A Study of Jeremiah 25 in relation to Jeremiah 46–51." *JETS* 33 (1990): 145-153.

Clements, R.E. *Isaiah 1–39*. NCB. Grand Rapids: Eerdmans, 1980.

_____ . *Jeremiah*. Atlanta: John Knox Press, 1988.

Colless, B.E. "Cyrus the Persian as Darius the Mede in the Book of Daniel." *JSOT* 56 (1992): 113-126.

Collins, J.J. *Apocalypse: The Morphology of a Genre*. Semeia 14. Missoula, MT: Scholars, 1979.

_____ . "Apocalyptic Genre and Mythic Allusions in Daniel." *JSOT* 21 (1981): 83-100.

_____ . *Daniel with an Introduction to Apocalyptic Literature*. Grand Rapids: Eerdmans, 1984.

Conrad, E.W. *Reading Isaiah*. Minneapolis: Fortress, 1991.

Cooke, G.A. *The Book of Ezekiel*. Edinburgh: T. & T. Clark, 1970 repr.; 1936.

Cooper, Lamar Eugene Sr. *Ezekiel*. Nashville: Broadman and Holman, 1994.

Coxon, P.W. "The Syntax of the Aramaic of *Daniel*: A Dialectal Study." *HUCA* 48 (1977): 107-122.

Craigie, Peter, Page Kelley, and Joel Drinkard. *Jeremiah 1–25*. WBC. Waco: Word, 1991.

Davies, P.R. "Eschatology in the Book of Daniel." *JSOT* 17 (1980): 33-53.

Day, J. "The Daniel of Ugarit and Ezekiel and the Hero of the Book of Daniel." *VT* 30 (1980): 174-184.

Dearman, Andrew. *Jeremiah/Lamentations*. The NIV Application Commentary. Grand Rapids: Zondervan, 2002.

Della Vida, G.L. "The Phoenician God Satrapes." *BASOR* 87 (1942): 29-32.

Diamond, A.R., Kathleen M. O'Connor, and Louis Stulman. *Troubling Jeremiah*. Sheffield: JSOT Press, 1999.

Dillard, R.B., and Tremper Longman III. *An Introduction to the Old Testament*. Grand Rapids: Zondervan, 1994.

Dobbs-Allsopp, F.W. *Lamentations*. Int. Louisville, KY: Westminster John Knox, 2002.

_____ . "Tragedy, Tradition, and Theology in the Book of Lamentations." *JSOT* 74 (1997): 29-60.

Dressler, H.H.P. "The Identification of the Ugaritic Dnil with the Daniel of Ezekiel," *VT* 29 (1979): 152-161.

Driver, S.R. *An Introduction to the Literature of the Old Testament*. New York: Meridian Books, 1956; a recent printing of the second edition from 1897.

Duguid, Iain M. *Ezekiel*. Grand Rapids: Zondervan, 2000.

Duhm, B. *Das Buch Jeremia*. Tübingen, 1901.

Eichrodt, Walter. *Ezekiel*. OTL. Philadelphia: Westminster, 1970.

Eissfeldt, Otto. *The Old Testament: An Introduction*. Trans. by Peter R. Ackroyd. New York: Harper and Row, 1965.

Ellison, H.L. *Ezekiel: The Man and His Message*. Grand Rapids: Eerdmans, 1956.

Flamming, James. "The New Testament Use of Isaiah." *SwJT* 11 (1968).

Fox, D.E. "Ben Sira on OT Canon Again: The Date of Daniel." *WTJ* 49 (1987): 333-350.

Fredenburg, Brandon. *Ezekiel*. College Press NIV Commentary. Joplin, MO: College Press, 2002.

Fretheim, Terence E. *Jeremiah*. Macon, GA: Smith and Helwys, 2002.

_____ . "The Repentance of God: A Study of Jer. 18:7-10." *HAR* 11 (1987): 81-92.

Gammie, J.G. "A Journey through Danelic Spaces: The Book of Daniel in the Theology and Piety of the Christian Community." *Int* 39 (1985): 144-156.

Ginsberg, H.L. "Aramaic Studies Today." *JAOS* 42 (1942): 229-238.

_____ . "The Composition of the Book of Daniel." *VT* 4 (1954): 246-275.

Goldingay, John. *Isaiah*. NIBCOT. Peabody, MA: Hendrickson, 2001.

Good, E.M. "Apocalyptic as Comedy: The Book of Daniel." *Semeia* 32 (1985): 41-70.

Gooding, D.W. "The Literary Structure of the Book of Daniel and Its Implications." *TynBul* 32 (1981): 43-79.

Gottwald, Norman. *The Hebrew Bible: A Socio-Literary Introduction*. Philadelphia: Fortress, 1985.

Grayson, A.K. *Babylonian Historical-Literary Texts*. Toronto: University of Toronto, 1975.

Greenberg, Moshe. *Ezekiel 1–20; Ezekiel 21–37*. AB. New York: Doubleday, 1983; 1997.

Gwaltney, W.C. "The Biblical Book of Lamentations in the Context of Near Eastern Lament Literature." In *Scripture in Context II: More Essays on the Comparative Method*, pp. 191-211. Ed. by W.W. Hallo, J.C. Moyer, and L.G. Perdue. Winona Lake, IN: Eisenbrauns, 1983.

Hals, R.M. *Ezekiel*. Grand Rapids: Eerdmans, 1989.

Hanson, Paul D. *The Dawn of Apocalyptic*. Philadelphia: Fortress, 1975.

_____ . *Isaiah 40–66*. Int. Louisville, KY: John Knox, 1995.

Harrison, R.K. *Introduction to the Old Testament*. Grand Rapids: Eerdmans, 1969.

_____ . *Jeremiah and Lamentations*. TOTC. Downers Grove, IL: InterVarsity, 1973.

Hartman, L.P., and A.A. DiLella. *The Book of Daniel*. Garden City, NY: Doubleday, 1978.

Hasel, G.F. "The Book of Daniel: Evidences relating to Persons and Chronology." *AUSS* (1981): 37-49.

Hayes, John H., and Stuart A. Irvine. *Isaiah, the Eighth-century Prophet*. Nashville: Abingdon, 1987.

Heim, K. "The Personification of Jerusalem and the Drama of Her Bereavement in Lamentations." In *Zion, City of Our God*, pp. 129-169. Ed. by R.S. Hess and G.J. Wenham. Grand Rapids: Eerdmans, 1999.

Hillers, Delbert. *Lamentations*. AB. New York: Doubleday, 1972.

Holladay, W.L. *The Architecture of Jeremiah 1–20*. Lewisburg, PA: Bucknell University, 1976.

_____ . "Had Ezekiel Known Jeremiah Personally?" *CBQ* 63 (2001): 31-34.

_____ . *Jeremiah*. Hermeneia. 2 vols. Philadelphia: Fortress, 1986, 1989.

_____ . *Jeremiah: Spokesman Out of Time*. Philadelphia: Pilgrim Press, 1974.

_____ . "Prototype and Copies: A New Approach to the Poetry-Prose Problem in the Book of Jeremiah." *JBL* 79 (1960): 351-367.

_____ . "Style, Irony and Authenticity in Jeremiah." *JBL* 81 (1962): 44-54.

House, Paul R. *Old Testament Theology*, chs 11, 12. Downers Grove, IL: InterVarsity, 1998.

Howie, Carl Gordon. *The Date and Composition of Ezekiel*. Philadelphia: SBL, 1950.

Huey, F.B. Jr. *Jeremiah, Lamentations*. Nashville: Broadman and Holman, 1993.

Humphreys, W.L. "A Life-Style for Diaspora: A Study of the Tales of Esther and Daniel." *JBL* 92 (1973): 211-223.

Hyatt, J.P. "Jeremiah." *IB*. Vol. 5. Ed. by G.A. Buttrick et al. New York: Abingdon-Cokesbury Press, 1951–57.

Janzen, J. Gerald. *Studies in the Text of Jeremiah.* Cambridge: Harvard University Press, 1973.

Joüon, P. "Trois noms de personnages bibliques à la lumière des textes d'Ugarit." *Biblia* 19 (1938): 280-285.

Kaiser, Otto. *Isaiah 1–12; Isaiah 12–39.* OTL. Philadelphia: Westminster, 2nd ed., 1984, 1974.

Keown, Gerald, Pamela Scalise, and Thomas Smothers. *Jeremiah 26–52.* Waco: Word, 1995.

King, Philip J. *Jeremiah: An Archaeological Companion.* Louisville, KY: Westminster/John Knox, 1993.

Kitchen, K.A. "The Aramaic of Daniel." In *Notes on Some Problems in the Book of Daniel.* Ed. by D.J. Wiseman et al. London: Tyndale, 1965.

_____. *On the Reliability of the Old Testament.* Grand Rapids: Eerdmans, 2003.

Klein, R.W. *Ezekiel, the Prophet and His Message.* Columbia, SC: University of South Carolina Press, 1988.

Koch, K. "Dareios der Meder." In *The Word of the Lord Shall Go Forth*, pp. 289-299. Ed. by C.L. Myers and M. O'Connor. Winona Lake, IN: Eisenbrauns, 1983.

_____. "Is Daniel Also among the Prophets?" *Int* 39 (1985): 117-130.

Kutsko, John F. *Between Heaven and Earth: Divine Presence and Absence in the Book of Ezekiel.* Winona Lake, IN: Eisenbrauns, 2000.

LaSor, William S., David A. Hubbard, and Frederic W. Bush, eds. *Old Testament Survey: The Message, Form, and Background of the Old Testament.* 2nd ed. Grand Rapids: Eerdmans, 1996.

Lenglet, A. "La structure littéraire de Daniel 2–7." *Bib* 53 (1972): 169-190.

Levenson, Jon. *Theology of the Program of Restoration of Ezekiel 40–48.* Missoula, MT: Scholars Press, 1976.

Levine, B.A., and A. Robertson, trans. "The Prayer of Nabonidus." In *COS*, 1.89:285-286. 3 vols. Ed by W.W. Hallo. Leiden: Brill, 1979-2003.

Lewy, J. "*Nāḫ et Rušpān.*" In *Mélanges syriens offerts à M. René Dussaud I,* pp. 273-275. Paris: Geuthner, 1939.

Lind, Millard. *Ezekiel.* Scottdale, PA: Herald Press, 1996.

Lipiński, E. "Review of André Lacoque, *Le Livre de Daniel.*" *VT* 28 (1978): 233-239.

Longman, T. III. *Fictional Akkadian Autobiography.* Winona Lake, IN: Eisenbrauns, 1991.

Lundbom, Jack. *Jeremiah 1–20; 21–36*. AB. New York: Doubleday, 1999, 2004.

Margalioth, R. *The Indivisible Isaiah*. New York: Yeshiva University, 1964.

McConville, J.G. *Judgment and Promise: An Interpretation of the Book of Jeremiah*. Winona Lake, IN: Eisenbrauns, 1993.

McKane, William. *A Critical and Exegetical Commentary on Jeremiah*. 2 vols. Edinburgh: T. and T. Clark, 1986, 1996.

McKenna, J.E. "Daniel." In *Old Testament Survey: The Message, Form, and Background of the Old Testament*, pp. 566-582. 2nd ed. Ed. by W.S. LaSor, D.A. Hubbard, and F.W. Bush. Grand Rapids: Eerdmans, 1996.

Merrill, Eugene H. "Ezekiel." In *A Biblical Theology of the Old Testament*. Ed. by Roy B. Zuck. Chicago: Moody Press, 1991.

Mickelsen, A.B. *Daniel and Revelation: Riddles or Realities?* Nashville: Thomas Nelson, 1984.

Motyer, J. Alec. *Isaiah: An Introduction and Commentary*. TOTC. Downers Grove, IL: InterVarsity, 1999.

_____. *The Prophecy of Isaiah: An Introduction and Commentary*. Downers Grove, IL: InterVarsity, 1993.

Mowinckel, Sigmund. *Zur Komposition des Buches Jeremia*. Kristiana, 1914.

Nicholson, E.W. *Preaching to the Exiles*. New York: Schocken Books, 1970.

Noth, M. "Noah, Daniel and Hiob in Ezechiel 14." *VT* 1 (1951): 251-260.

Osborne, G.R. *The Hermeneutical Spiral: A Comprehensive Introduction to Biblical Interpretation*. Downers Grove, IL: InterVarsity, 1991.

Oswalt, John N. *The Book of Isaiah, Chapters 1–39; Chapters 40–66*. NICOT. Grand Rapids: Eerdmanns, 1986, 1998.

Payne, J.B. "Eighth Century Israelitish Background of Isaiah 40–66." *WTJ* 29 (1966–67): 179-190; *WTJ* 30 (1967–68): 50-58, 185-193.

Perdue, Leo, and Brian Kovacs. *Prophet to the Nations: Essays in Jeremiah Studies*. Winona Lake, IN: Eisenbrauns, 1984.

Peterson, Eugene. *Run with the Horses*. Downers Grove, IL: InterVarsity, 1983.

Provan, Ian. *Lamentations*. Grand Rapids: Eerdmans, 1991.

Rendtorff, R. *The Old Testament: An Introduction*. Philadelphia: Fortress, 1986.

Renz, Thomas. "Proclaiming the Future: History and Theology in Prophecies against Tyre." *TynBul* 51 (2000): 17-58.

_____. *The Rhetorical Function of the Book of Ezekiel*. Leiden: Brill, 1999.

Rhodes, A.B. "The Book of Daniel." *StudBib* 6 (1952): 436-450.

_____. "The Kingdoms of Men and the Kingdom of God." *Int* 15 (1961): 411-430.

Rosenbloom, Joseph. *The Dead Sea Isaiah Scroll*. Grand Rapids: Eerdmans, 1970.

Rosenthal, F. *Die aramaistische Forschung seit Th. Nödeke's Veröffentlichungen*. Leiden: Brill, 1964 repr.; 1939).

Rowley, H.H. *The Aramaic of the Old Testament: A Grammatical and Lexical Study of Its Relations with Other Early Aramaic Dialects*. London: Oxford University Press, 1929.

_____. "The Bilingual Problem of Daniel." *ZAW* 50 (1932): 256-268.

_____. "The Composition of the Book of Daniel: Some Comments on Professor Ginsberg's Article." *VT* 5 (1955): 272-276.

_____. *Darius the Mede and the Four World Empires in the Book of Daniel*. Cardiff: University of Wales, 1934.

_____."The Unity of the Book of Daniel." *HUCA* 23 (1950–51): 233-273. Reprinted in *The Servant of the Lord and Other Essays*, pp. 237-268. London: Lutherworth, 1952.

Schaeder, H.H. *Irainische Beiträge*. Halle, Saale: Max Niemeyer, 1930–.

Seitz, Christopher R. *Isaiah 1–39*. Int. Louisville, KY: John Knox, 1993.

Shanks, Hershel. "Destruction of Judean Fortress Portrayed in Dramatic Eighth-Century B.C. Pictures." *BAR* 9 (March/April, 1984): 48-65.

Shea, W.H. "Daniel 1-6." *AUSS* 23 (1985): 277-295.

_____. "Darius the Mede: An Update." *AUSS* 20 (1982): 229-247.

Smith, S. *Babylonian Historical Texts relating to the Downfall of Babylon*. London: Methuen and Co., 1924.

Soulen, R.N., and R.K. Soulen. *Handbook of Biblical Criticism*. 3rd ed. rev. Louisville, KY: Westminster John Knox, 2001.

Spiegel, S. "Noah, Danel and Job: Touching on Canaanite Relics in the Legends of the Jews." *Louis Ginzberg Jubilee Volume*, pp. 305-355 [English Section]. New York: American Academy for Jewish Research, 1945.

Stohlmann, Stephen. "The Judean Exile after 701 B.C.E." In *Scripture in Context II: More Essays on the Comparative Method*, pp. 147-175. Ed. by W.W. Hallo, J.C. Moyer, and L.G. Perdue. Winona Lake, IN: Eisenbrauns, 1983.

Stuart, Douglas. *Ezekiel*. WBC. Dallas: Word, 1989.

Talmon, S. "Daniel." In *The Literary Guide to the Bible*, pp. 343-356. Ed. by R. Altar and F. Kermode. Cambridge: Harvard University Press, 1987.

Tanner, J.P. "The Literary Structure of the Book of Daniel." *BSac* 160 (2003): 269-282.

Taylor, J.B. *Ezekiel*. TOTC. Downers Grove, IL: InterVarsity, 1969.

Thomas, D. Winton, ed. *Documents from Old Testament Times*. New York: Harper and Row, 1958.

Thompson, J.A. *Jeremiah*. NICOT. Grand Rapids: Eerdmans, 1980.

Trever, J.C. "The Book of Daniel." *BA* 48 (1985): 89-102.

Tucker, Gene, and Christopher Seitz. "Isaiah 1-39, 40-66." *NIB*. Vol. 6. Nashville: Abingdon, 2001.

VanGemeren, Willem. *Interpreting the Prophetic Word*. Grand Rapids: Zondervan, 1990.

Vawter, Bruce, and Leslie J. Hoppe. *Ezekiel: A New Heart*. Grand Rapids: Eerdmans, 1991.

von Rad, Gerhard. *Old Testament Theology*. 2 vols. Trans. by D.M.G. Stalker. New York: Harper and Row, 1965.

Wahl, H.-M. "Noah, Daniel und Hiob in Ezechiel XIV 12-20 (21-23): Anmerkungen zum Traditionsgeschichtlichen Hintergrund." *VT* (1992): 542-553.

Waltke, B.K. "The Date of the Book of Daniel." *BSac* 133 (1976): 319-329.

Walton, John H., Victor H. Matthews, and Mark W. Chavalas. *The IVP Bible Background Commentary: Old Testament*. Downers Grove, IL: InterVarsity, 2000.

Watts, John D.W. *Isaiah 1-33; Isaiah 34-66*. WBC. Waco: Word, 1985, 1987.

Webb, Barry G. *The Message of Isaiah*. Downers Grove, IL: InterVarsity, 1996.

Weippert, H. *Die Prosareden des Jeremiabuches*. BZAW 132. De Gruyter, 1971.

Westermann, Claus. *Isaiah 40-66*. OTL. Philadelphia: Westminster, 1969.

_____ . *Lamentations: Issues and Interpretation*. Minneapolis: Fortress, 1994.

Wevers, J.W. *Ezekiel*. Grand Rapids: Eerdmans, 1969.

Whitcomb, J.C. *Darius the Mede: A Study in Historical Identification*. Grand Rapids: Eerdmans, 1959.

Whybray, R.N. *Isaiah 40–66*. NCB. Grand Rapids: Eerdmans, 1980.

Wildeberger, H. *Isaiah 1–12; Isaiah 13–27*. Minneapolis: Fortress, 1991, 1997.

Wilson, R.D. *Studies in the Book of Daniel*. New York/London: G.P. Putman's Sons/Knickerbocker, 1917. Cited 8 June 2004, online: http://www.home.earthlink.net/~ironmen/wilson/studies_chap17.htm.

Wilson, R.D., and R.K. Harrison. "Daniel, Book of." *ISBE²*, 1:859-866. Rev. ed. by G.W. Bromiley. Grand Rapids: Eerdmans, 1979.

Willis, Timothy. *Jeremiah*. College Press NIV Commentary. Joplin, MO: College Press, 2002.

Wiseman, D. "Chaldea." *ISBE²*, 1:630-633. Rev. ed. by G.W. Bromiley. Grand Rapids: Eerdmans, 1979.

Wiseman, D.J., et al. *Notes on Some Problems in the Book of Daniel*. London: Tyndale, 1965.

Wong, Ka Leung. *The Idea of Retribution in the Book of Ezekiel*. Leiden: Brill, 2000.

Woodard, B.L. "Literary Strategies and Authorship in the Book of Daniel." *JETS* 37 (1994): 39-53.

Wright, Christopher J.H. *The Message of Ezekiel: A New Heart and a New Spirit*. Downers Grove, IL: InterVarsity, 2001.

Yamauchi, E.M. "The Archaeological Background of Daniel." *BSac* 137 (1980): 3-16.

Young, E.J. *The Book of Isaiah*. 3 vols. Grand Rapids: Eerdmans, 1964–72.

_____ . *An Introduction to the Old Testament*. Grand Rapids: Eerdmans, 1964.

_____ . *Who Wrote Isaiah?* Grand Rapids: Eerdmans, 1958.

Youngblood, Ronald F. *The Book of Isaiah: An Introductory Commentary*. Grand Rapids: Baker, 1984.

Zimmerli, W. *Ezekiel*. 2 vols. Hermeneia. Philadelphia: Fortress, 1979, 1983.

Zimmermann, F. "The Aramaic Origin of Daniel 8–12." *JBL* 57 (1938): 255-272.

_____. "Some Verses in Daniel in Light of a Translation Hypothesis." *JBL* 58 (1939): 349-354.

Zuck, Roy B., ed. *A Biblical Theology of the Old Testament.* Chicago: Moody, 1991.

ISAIAH

HISTORICAL AND CULTURAL BACKGROUND

Isaiah's ministry spanned a considerable period of time. The superscript in Isaiah 1:1 mentions four kings: Uzziah, Jotham, Ahaz, and Hezekiah. Uzziah died in 742 B.C. (the date of Isaiah's call, Isa 6:1) and Hezekiah lived until 687. Isaiah preached during most of this period though the date of his death is unknown. Jewish tradition says he was martyred by Manasseh, Hezekiah's son.

The time from the death of Uzziah until Hezekiah's latter years was a period of political upheaval in the ancient biblical world, brought on by the resurgence of Assyria. During the period from about 810 until 750 both Israel and Judah had experienced peace and prosperity.[1] But Tiglath-Pileser came to the throne of Assyria in 745 and immediately began an Assyrian expansion program south, east, and west. He took the northern territory from Israel in 732, and his successor, Shalmaneser V, conquered Samaria and brought the northern kingdom to an end in 722 B.C. The Syro-Ephraimite war, the background of Isaiah 7, occurred in 733. Although King Ahaz (735–715 B.C.) escaped from that threat, his appeal to Assyria for help (2 Kgs 16:7ff.) doomed Judah's independence, and she became a vassal of Assyria. His son Hezekiah (715–687) tried several times to wrest Judah free of the Assyrians. He was encouraged by Babylonian rebellions in the southeast Assyrian empire and with Egyptian resurgence. A Babylonian general, Merodach-Baladan, led two revolts against the Assyrians in the last decade of the eighth century. Both times the revolts were put down, but each one encouraged nations in the west, including Hezekiah, to withhold tribute to Assyria and make an attempt at independence. Merodach-Baladan even sent envoys to Hezekiah (Isaiah 39), probably when Sargon died in 705.[2]

---

[1]See the chapter on Amos pp. 552-560 for other details.

[2]It is generally acknowledged that chapters 36 to 39 in the book of Isaiah

However, Assyria defeated the Babylonian uprisings and Egypt proved to be an unreliable ally which set the stage for Assyrian concentration on Judah. In 701 Sennacherib came against Judah. He destroyed Lachish, the second most heavily fortified city in Judah and threatened Jerusalem.[3] Sennacherib speaks in his own records of conquering 46 Judean fortified cities and shutting Hezekiah up in Jerusalem "like a bird in a cage."[4] Although Hezekiah, and Jerusalem, survived through the intervention of God, as Isaiah foretold (Isa 37:5-7), it cost him dearly in tribute and family (2 Kgs 18:6).[5]

TEXT AND AUTHOR

Isaiah was the son of Amoz (1:1), a person otherwise unknown to us. It is significant that Isaiah's name means "Yahweh is salvation," for his message underscores that truth.[6] He apparently lived in Jerusalem (ch. 7) and tradition holds that he had royal blood. He certainly seemed to have easy access to the kings (chs. 7 and 36–39). His call in the Temple (ch. 6) suggests one attuned to worship. His response to his call reflects spiritual maturity and humility. He was called to be a prophet in 742 B.C., the year King Uzziah died, and he preached at least until the Sennacherib crisis in 701 B.C., maybe even through the death of Hezekiah in 687. Isaiah was married to a "prophetess" (8:3) and had at least two sons, Shear-jashub (literally, "a remnant will return," 7:3) and Maher-shalal-hash-baz (literally,

---

are not in chronological order. The events in chapter 39 occurred before Sennacherib's invasion recorded in chapters 36–37 but are placed after the event in the book of Isaiah to provide a transition to chapters 40–66.

[3]Archaeologists have uncovered grim testimony to the defeat of Lachish, a mass grave with the remains of 1,500 bodies in it.

[4]This devastation could very likely be behind the descriptions in Isaiah 1:4-9. For a convenient source of the Assyrian record see D. Winton Thomas, ed., *Documents from Old Testament Times* (New York: Harper and Row, 1958), pp. 66-67.

[5]These events are recorded in both 2 Kings 18–20 and Isaiah 36–39. Sennacherib's account says that several of Hezekiah's daughters were taken to Nineveh as well as concubines, musicians, and much wealth. Sennacherib also created a room in the center of his palace at Nineveh and lined the walls with depictions of his conquest of Lachish. These can be seen in the British Museum in London. For a description of Sennacherib's palace and pictures of the reliefs see Hershel Shanks, "Destruction of Judean Fortress Portrayed in Dramatic Eighth-Century B.C. Pictures," *BAR* 9 (March/April, 1984): 48-65.

[6]The name Joshua comes from the same Hebrew root and has the same meaning. The root word for salvation or its derivatives occur 53 times in Isaiah.

"speed spoil, hasten prey," 8:3). Both sons were living testimonies of Isaiah's message to Ahaz in chapter 7. Shear-jashub reminded Ahaz that the crisis of his day was not the end of Israel, and the birth of Maher-shalal-hash-baz assured him that his enemies, Syria and Israel, would soon be destroyed (7:3-9; 8:1-4). The message of both names is reiterated in some of Isaiah's other sermons as well (9:2; 10:6,20, 21,22; 11:11; 33:23).

Isaiah is considered one of the greatest theologians in the Old Testament, presenting profound insights into the nature of God. He is also deemed one of the best poets of the Old Testament, master of image and metaphor, wordplay and pun, and rhetorical flourish.[7] He was creative and direct, yet mature and profound.

THE TEXT OF ISAIAH

The discovery of the Dead Sea Scroll Isaiah texts was a major step forward in textual study of Isaiah. The scroll moved the text fully 1000 years backward in history to pre-Christian times. Cave 4 yielded a complete text of Isaiah from the second century B.C. We now have three texts of Isaiah: the Hebrew Masoretic Text, the Septuagint, and the Hebrew 1QIsa[a]. Although there is hardly a verse in the Qumran scroll that is identical with MT, most of the variations are insignificant, characterized by differences between the defective and full writing of vowel letters.[8] The overwhelming agreement of Qumran with the MT restored confidence in the MT and eliminated scholarly propensity to emend the MT. A new respect for the careful work of the scribes has developed. There are, however, several places where the Qumran text has aided in understanding a difficulty in the MT and probably has preserved the original reading.[9] English translations differ on how many changes they make in the MT.[10]

---

[7]For example, reading chapter 24 in Hebrew reveals wonderful wordplays.

[8]Joseph Rosenbloom, *The Dead Sea Isaiah Scroll* (Grand Rapids: Eerdmans, 1970). For example, in 5:28 MT has *kṣr* and the Qumran scroll has *kṣwr*; or see 21:11 where MT has *mlylh* and Qumran has *mlyl*. The differences are merely whether or not certain vowel sounds are represented by consonants.

[9]John N. Oswalt, *Isaiah 1–39*, NICOT (Grand Rapids: Eerdmans, 1986), pp. 29-30. For example in 21:8 MT has "a lion called out" but Qumran has "a watcher called out." Qumran makes the most sense and many newer translations have accepted its reading.

[10]They range from 4 changes (JPSV) to 15 (RSV). Oswalt lists the verses (ibid.).

HISTORY OF INTERPRETATION

The nature and composition of the book of Isaiah is one of the most complex issues in Old Testament studies. Even the casual reader will notice a major shift in emphasis in the book at chapter 40. But the traditional view was that the Isaiah of 1:1 was responsible for the whole book, and this was not questioned until the late eighteenth century.[11] Similar words and themes that were scattered throughout the book, assumptions of inspiration, detailed predictions of the future, and the extensive use of Isaiah by the New Testament were the foundations for unquestioned acceptance of Isaiah as the author. Only when the Enlightenment questioned divine inspiration and detached the OT from the NT did questions arise about the origins of the book of Isaiah. It was then that J.G. Eichhorn in 1783 and J.D. Doderlein in 1789 advanced the theory of a dual authorship to the book.

The ensuing debate settled on three major factors for assigning chapters 40–66 to a different and later (sixth century) author:[12]

1. The historical setting of chapters 40–66 reflects the exilic period when Jerusalem was destroyed and the people were in exile. Chapters 1–39 presuppose the Assyrian dominance of the Near East and mention their presence in Palestine often. However, chapters 40–66 seem to presume the audience is in exile in Babylon (48:20) and looks forward to their release. Jerusalem and the Temple are in ruins (44:26; 58:12; 61:4) and are to be rebuilt (54:11-14). Babylon was not even a world power in Isaiah's day and Cyrus was still 150 years in the future (44:28; 45:1). Isaiah predicts an exile (11:11) but chapters 40–66 presuppose it. The content of the second half was therefore irrelevant to the late eighth century. Moreover, Jeremiah and other seventh-century prophets do not refer to Isaiah's prophecies of the exile, which one would expect since they lived near the time it was going to occur.

---

[11]Scholars debate the significance of the remarks of the twelfth-century Jewish scholar, Ibn-Ezra, who wrote of the secret of the second half of the book. But he made clear that he thought Isaiah wrote the whole book. The Babylonian Talmud, *Baba Bathra* 15:1a, stated that Hezekiah and his company wrote Isaiah, Proverbs, Song of Songs, and Ecclesiastes. This probably means they "edited" the books.

[12]The critical position is fully explained in a number of introductions. A standard, older work is Otto Eissfeldt, *The Old Testament: An Introduction*, trans. by Peter Ackroyd (New York: Harper and Row, 1965), pp. 303-346.

2. The striking differences in language, style, and concepts between the two halves can be accounted for only by positing two different authors. Scholars pointed out that Isaiah was not mentioned in the second half. Also God is conceived of in different ways. He was majestic and holy in the first, but Creator and Redeemer in the second. The ideas in the second half are more advanced and reflective. The Messiah is a Davidic king in the first half, but a suffering servant in the second. Many words and phrases occur in one part but not the other. These words include choose, praise, pleasure, goodwill, and rejoice.[13] Some words are used with different meanings in the two parts, words such as righteous and judgment. The vocabulary seems more "modern" in the second part. The style of writing seems different. It is more lyrical, flowing, and impassioned in the second half with repeated words and wordplays more often.[14] Though there are similarities between the two halves, it is the differences that carry the most weight.[15]

3. Since the Hebrew prophet first of all addressed the people of his day with God's word, it was unheard of that a prophet would address a people 150 years in the future. A prophet always speaks to his contemporaries and the message of 40–66 would be irrelevant to the eighth century. The prophet can speak of the future, but it is the near future. Just as Isaiah of Jerusalem spoke of the deliverance from Sennacherib in the near future, so the prophet of the second half speaks of release from exile in the near future. Since the Enlightenment concluded that the Bible was a purely human book, any divinely inspired knowledge of the distant future was impossible. Furthermore, by the analogy of prophecy, since no other prophet did such a thing, Isaiah could not have either.

When critical scholars turned to study chapters 1–39 and 40–66, they found a lack of unity within these sections as well. Chapters 1–39, the so-called First Isaiah, were divided up, on literary grounds, into several sections held to come from different periods and authors. For example, Eissfeldt lists all of chapters 15–16, 19, 23,

---

[13]S.R. Driver (*An Introduction to the Literature of the Old Testament* [1891; New York: Meridian Books, 1956; a recent printing of the second edition from 1897], pp. 238-240), has a lengthy list.

[14]The comments here are necessarily brief. One should consult Eissfeldt or Driver for the extended argument.

[15]Driver, *Introduction*, pp. 243-244.

24–27, and parts of chapters 2, 9, 11, 12 and 21 as non-Isaianic.[16] Others saw a basic core of Isaiah to which additions had been made, probably by his followers. Later, a form-critical analysis of various traditions was explored.[17]

Study of chapters 40–66 led to questions about its unity as well. Some saw many different oral sermons brought together. Others saw a literary composition that showed development and progress. The so-called servant songs (42:1-7; 49:1-6; 50:4-9; 52:13–53:12) also presented a problem for study. Were they originally independent and how did they fit into the overall context? These questions have not been answered but there is a tendency to no longer isolate them from their context.

Chapters 56–66 were also then isolated because of a supposed different historical setting and themes, and called Trito-Isaiah. It seemed to scholars that the point of view was that of exiles now returned to Palestine. There is a mood of disappointment after the return from exile, and the religious and economic problems of the returned community are reflected in chapters 56–66. A new Temple is presupposed and the eschatology is different. The polemic against idolatry is different as well. The view of God is not as lofty. Further study revealed to some that Trito-Isaiah itself was a composite work.[18]

From the beginning of the modern approach to Isaiah, conservative scholars defended the traditional view.[19] They advanced the following arguments:

1. The present canonical form attributes the whole book to Isaiah as do the New Testament and rabbinic authorities. If inspiration and authority of the New Testament means anything these facts should

---

[16]Eissfeldt, *Introduction*, pp. 317-328. See also Driver, *Introduction*, pp. 229-230.

[17]Gerhard von Rad, *Old Testament Theology*, trans. by D.M.G. Stalker (New York: Harper and Row, 1965), 2:155-175.

[18]Elizabeth Achtemeier, *The Community and Message of Isaiah 56–66: A Theological Commentary* (Minneapolis: Augsburg, 1982), pp. 11-16.

[19]Among conservative Christians see J.A. Alexander, *The Prophecies of Isaiah* (1846–47; repr. Grand Rapids: Zondervan, 1953, 1971); Oswald T. Allis, *The Unity of Isaiah* (Philadelphia: Presbyterian and Reformed, 1950); E.J. Young, *Who Wrote Isaiah?* (Grand Rapids: Eerdmans, 1958); from a Jewish perspective see R. Margalioth, *The Indivisible Isaiah* (New York: Yeshiva University, 1964). For recent work see: J. Alec Motyer, *Isaiah: An Introduction and Commentary*, TOTC (Downers Grove, IL: InterVarsity, 1999); and Oswalt, *Isaiah Chapters 1–39*.

carry some weight. The NT cites the book of Isaiah 20 times from both halves of the book. In one interesting case John 12:38-41 quotes Isaiah 6:10 and 53:1. Also, the complete scroll from Qumran contains the whole of Isaiah with no division between chapters 39 and 40.

2. There are many similarities in language and concepts between the two halves, and these support a unity of authorship. These include hundreds of words and phrases.[20] Conservatives suggest that arguments from style are subjective and somewhat circular. The differences between the two halves of Isaiah can be better explained by differences in subject matter, audience, age of Isaiah, circumstances, and intentions of the author. Isaiah's ministry lasted for more than four decades. It is unreasonable to hold him to one style of writing or one historical setting. The most striking similarity is Isaiah's unique designation for God, "the Holy One of Israel," which occurs an equal number of times in both halves. Furthermore, Babylon appears in both halves, Palestine is the assumed setting of both halves, Zion is a central focus in both sections, destruction language is similar in both, and the unity of theme and thought structure could have come from one individual. Critical scholars acknowledge that there are close resemblances in style between all proposed sections of Isaiah.[21] Motyer has suggested that the first half of Isaiah consists of Isaiah's sermons delivered early in his career. When the dark days of Manasseh arrived after the death of Hezekiah, Isaiah turned to pure literary activity, as found in the second half of the book.[22] Oswalt asserts that the nature of the message of chapters 1–39 "demands" that chapters 40–66 must be included to complete and validate Isaiah's message. He holds that the central theme of Isaiah is the nature and destiny of the people of God. How can a sinful people become the servants of God? The problem is set forth in chapters 1–6 and the rest of the book works out the solution. Chapters 7–39 repeatedly call for trust in God rather than the nations. Judah seemed to lack motivation, and so motivation is given

---

[20]R.B. Dillard and Tremper Longman III, *An Introduction to the Old Testament* (Grand Rapids: Zondervan, 1994), p. 271 (referencing the work of Margalioth). Critical scholars attribute the similarities to Isaiah disciples who generated the "non-Isaianic" material.

[21]William Sanford LaSor et al., *Old Testament Survey* (Grand Rapids: Eerdmans, 1982), pp. 373-374.

[22]Motyer, *Isaiah*, p. 31.

her in chapters 40–48. Although God delivered Judah from Assyria, he would not deliver her from Babylon. However, Judah could learn in exile that God was present. Further, it would be through the servant that Judah would learn servanthood (chs. 49–55). This would not solve all problems (chapters 56–66) but resolution awaited the revelation of God's glory.[23] Oswalt thus calls for future scholarship to focus on interpreting the book as a whole. Motyer affirms this perspective. If we did not have chapters 40–66 then Isaiah of the first half would be a failure. What he had said about trust in God and hope would not have been true. The Babylonian defeat would have been the end.[24] "The sustained polemic of Isaiah 40–66 is that Yahweh has announced the future and is able to bring it to pass (40:21; 41:4,21-29; 43:12-12; 44:6-8,24-28; 45:11-13)."[25] The exile and restoration were already anticipated in early Isaiah (Isa 6:11-12, Jerusalem depopulated; 7:3, "Shear-jashub" means "a remnant will return"), and the prophet understood his words to be for the distant future that was handed over to his disciples for safe keeping (8:16).[26]

Furthermore, it is difficult to see the circumstances under which the name of a great prophet, like the assumed author of chapters 40–66, could have been lost and his work attached to that of another great prophet, Isaiah. If the book has had several authors and editors over a period of hundreds of years, how did it come to have its present unity? Do committees produce great literature?

3. The third argument relates to provenance. If the second half was written during the exile in Babylon, why are there no details of Babylon?[27] Jeremiah, Ezekiel, and Daniel wrote just prior to and during the exile and their details are clear. If the exile cured Israel

---

[23]Oswalt, *Isaiah*, p. 21-23.

[24]Motyer, *Isaiah*, p. 33.

[25]Dillard and Longman, *Introduction*, p. 274. One must also consider the issue of genre. Could many of the verbal differences between the two parts of Isaiah come from the fact that many of the oracles in chapters 1–39 are judgment oracles and many in chapters 40–55 are salvation oracles? Genre requires its own style and language.

[26]Ibid.

[27]There is in fact important evidence, if one looks for it, to support a significant exilic experience for Israel and Judah in the late eighth century that could provide a background for the assumed exilic setting of the second half of the book. The 701 invasion of Sennacherib created dozens of destroyed cities and thousands of refugees. See Stephen Stohlmann, "The Judean Exile after 701 B.C.E.," in *Scripture in Context II: More Essays on the*

of idolatry, why does it come up again in Isaiah 57? Why do the sins of Isaiah 59 sound like Amos, Micah, and Isaiah 1–39? Why are the trees, geography, rainfall, climate, and sea that of Palestine and not of Mesopotamia?[28]

Modern scholarship on Isaiah has taken a different direction from the atomizing tendencies of the past. There is now a search for the major themes or links that hold the entire book together. Childs in 1979[29] pointed out no matter what critical scholars may think the background to Isaiah 40–66 is, the fact remains that for us it is joined to chapters 1–39 and attributed to Isaiah of Jerusalem. If there were historical references in the later chapters, they were taken out (!). We can only understand them from their present context. A careful study shows that chapters 40–66 are crucial to understanding chapters 1–39 and vice versa. There is a concern with prophecy and fulfillment in the book that is lost if it is separated into two sections. The "former things" of First Isaiah are confirmed by Second Isaiah. If the connection between the two sections is severed then the latter is only a "confused fragment." In contrast to the interests of previous scholars in investigating small units, some scholars now assume that there must have been reasons why some ancient scribe or school of scribes put the material together into one book.[30] However, this emphasis is not on authorial unity but redactional unity.

Several suggestions for the unity of the book have been made since the early 1980s. These include: 1) The fall of Jerusalem is the linchpin and unifying center; the first half predicted it, the second half offers words of new life and the reestablishment of God's rule in Jerusalem. 2) A social dynamic in which the text is interacting with the conditions of the day, to offer hope in situations that deny hope is obvious. 3) First and Second Isaiah share two fundamental themes: Israel's blindness and deafness and God's election of Israel.

Comparative Method, ed. by W.W. Hallo, J.C. Moyer, and L.G. Perdue (Winona Lake, IN: Eisenbrauns, 1983), pp. 147-175; J.B. Payne, "Eighth Century Israelitish Background of Isaiah 40–66," *WTJ* 29 (1966–67): 179-190; *WTJ* 30 (1967–68): 50-58, 185-193.

[28]Motyer, *Isaiah*, p. 32.

[29]Childs, *Introduction*, pp. 325-333.

[30]R. Clements observed that it is questionable whether the two sections ever existed as totally independent collections (*Isaiah 1–39*, NCB [Grand Rapids: Eerdmans, 1980], p. 2).

4) Second and Third Isaiah are held together by a school of Isaiah who held to the theology of Second in opposition to the leaders of their day. Third is a commentary on 56:1. 5) Certain texts are programmatic (ch. 1, 35:1–48:8, and 65–66) for an overarching structure. They have some macrostructural potential. 6) The whole book is structured as a covenant disputation genre. The objective of the book is to persuade the reader to repent and seek reconciliation with God. The author/compiler most likely comes from the sixth century.[31]

W.H. Brownlee advanced the thesis that Isaiah was a two-volume work (chs. 1–33 and 34–66) consciously edited into parallel sections, thusly:

1. Chs. 1–5 and 34–35 (ruin and restoration)
2. Chs. 6–8 and 36–40 (biography)
3. Chs. 9–12 and 41–45 (agents of blessing/deliverance and judgment)
4. Chs. 13–23 and 46–48 (anti-foreign/Babylonian oracles)
5. Chs. 24–27 and 49–55 (universal judgment/deliverance and universal redemption)
6. Chs. 28–31 and 56–59 (ethical sermons)
7. Chs. 32–33 and 60–66 (restoration of Judah and the glories of the new Jerusalem/heavens/earth)[32]

The modern interest in the redactional unity of Isaiah has been developed out of a new interest in the evolution of the written text, not the oral tradition. Scholars now assume that the written texts of the prophets evolved to meet new historical circumstances. For Isaiah there was a conscious effort to unite the book into a coherent whole. Scholars also see that as the book was shaped by the redactional process, the earlier material was reinterpreted by the later, and the later additions consciously echoed earlier parts of the text. This then can account for the unity of the book. The emphasis is then on this "Canonical" form of the book.[33]

---

[31]See David Carr, "Reaching for Unity in Isaiah," *JSOT* 57 (1993): 61-80.

[32]W.H. Brownlee, *The Meaning of the Dead Sea Scrolls for the Bible* (New York: Oxford, 1964), pp. 247-259.

[33]For this perspective see the newer commentaries on Isaiah: Brevard Childs, *Isaiah*, OTL (Louisville, KY: Westminster John Knox, 2001); and Walter Brueggemann, *Isaiah 1–39* (Louisville, KY: Westminster John Knox, 1998).

STRUCTURE

The structure of this complex book offers a challenge to the interpreter. Even those who agree on a macrostructure do not agree at many points of detail. Brownlee's suggestion above represents a minority position.[34] The popularity of dividing the book into the two halves of chapters 1–39 and 40–66 is seen in many of the major commentaries which are published in two volumes, even Oswalts'. Within this large picture the macrostructure seems to involve the following outline, presented here with a brief summary of each section.[35]

I. Chapters 1–6: earlier sermons on the sins of Israel (Judah) and God's judgment on her are capped with Isaiah's call that sets the stage for understanding many of the themes of the book.

II. Chapters 7–12: Judah's lack of trust demonstrated and the subsequent introduction of hope through the figure of a Davidic "Messianic" king (7:14; 9:1-7; 11:1-9); completed by a hymn of hope in chapter 12. This section is paralleled by chapters 36–39 where Hezekiah is contrasted with Ahaz of chapter 7.

III. Chapters 13–23: God's trustworthiness is demonstrated by his control over the nations as announced in a series of judgments against the nations, from east (Babylon) to west (Tyre).

IV. Chapters 24–27: General visions of destruction of the earth and the world's city (24) and songs of renewal of Judah's city (26) that demonstrate even further God's universal power and control.

V. Chapters 28–35: Another series of judgments on Judah and the nations announced as "Woes." Like chapters 1–12 it ends with a hymn of hope for the redeemed of Zion (35).

VI. Chapters 36–39: Hezekiah, in contrast with Ahaz of chapter 7, trusts in the Lord when the Assyrians threaten.

VII. Chapters 40–48: The proclamation of restoration and redemption for Judah provides the background for an attack on the idols of the nations and introduction of the theme of the servant. Cyrus becomes God's instrument, and Babylon's demise is promised.

VIII. Chapters 49–55: Restoration, deliverance, and the ministry of the servant are explained through and around the last three so-

---

[34]But supported also by John Goldingay, *Isaiah,* NIBCOT (Peabody, MA: Hendrickson, 2001), p. 6.

[35]Oswalt, *Isaiah 1–39,* p. 54; Willem VanGemeren, *Interpreting the Prophetic Word* (Grand Rapids: Zondervan, 1990), pp. 253-254.

called "Servant Songs." The section ends with an invitation to the abundant life for all peoples (55).

IX. Chapters 56–66: The community continues to struggle with a holy life and obedience to God. Ultimately they must still trust in God as he brings all things to fulfillment.

GENRE

Isaiah was a master of the Hebrew language. Therefore, his book is full of a variety of genres, extensive vocabulary, and vivid images. He created many wonderful metaphors and images, and liberally used wordplays, alliterations, and assonance. Besides the common prophetic speech forms of judgment speech, covenant lawsuit, vision reports, hymns, announcements, and proclamations of salvation, Isaiah used parables, taunts, woes, sarcasm, and images bordering on the apocalyptic. He, perhaps more than any other prophet, fully mined the richness of the Hebrew language to preach his message. Isaiah's descriptions of the Messianic king (ch. 9), or the peaceful kingdom (ch. 11), or the blessings on redeemed Zion (ch. 35), or the suffering of the servant (ch. 53) have created some of the most memorable passages in the OT.

THEOLOGICAL THEMES[36]

The message of such a complex book as Isaiah is difficult to summarize in a way that does justice to the depth and breadth of the major themes. A topical arrangement is a typical method, but this is always artificial in that no biblical book has a neat thematic outline arranged according to the demands of a systematic theological summary. Therefore, we will adopt here a chronological method, tracing themes and concepts in the book as they appear in the canonical form of the book, beginning with chapter 1. The book is marked by a theological unity that needs to be understood in any approach to the book.[37] Yet this unity is not a simple presentation. Many para-

---

[36]See Paul R. House, *Old Testament Theology* (Downers Grove, IL: InterVarsity, 1998), ch. 11; and Roy B. Zuck, ed., *A Biblical Theology of the Old Testament* (Chicago: Moody, 1991), ch. 8.

[37]Oswalt, *Isaiah 1–39*, p. 31. Typically Oswalt describes the theology of the book under the headings of: God, Humanity and the World, Sin, and Redemption.

doxes and contrasts are a part of the rich theological fabric of the book.

Chapters 1–6. Isaiah begins with a graphic depiction of Judah's sin, which he characterizes as "rebellion." In the form of a covenant lawsuit he describes their turning against God because of lack of knowledge and a despising of God (1:3-6). He also calls this sin, evil, and iniquity (v. 4). The nature of this sin is further defined as turning to false gods and other countries for security, and arrogant pride (2:5-11). Their sin is also one of injustice, not caring for the needy of the community and thus violating the righteous demands of the law. Because of this lack of compassion their formal worship is worthless, a mere going through motions (1:10-20). Therefore, Jerusalem is apostate, a whore (1:21). Judah's corrupt nature is evidenced in daily life, characterized by land grabbing, drunken carousing, a perverted sense of good, and pervasive injustice in the law courts (5:8-23). All of these charges can be summarized under the rubric of violations of the covenant (compare especially the demands in the book of Deuteronomy). Judah is an unproductive vineyard planted by a gracious and hopeful owner who reaps only bad grapes despite the best care (5:1-7). Therefore, God's decision to bring judgment on Judah is totally justified (1:24-31; 2:12–4:1; 5:5-6,24-30). He is not capricious or arbitrary but loving and caring, like a father or a vine grower. Yet they turned against him. He is the holy God who will show himself through judgment to be "holy in righteousness" (5:16).

But because he is a holy God there is hope and a possible future. Maybe the people will repent and turn back (1:18-20). Nevertheless, God will restore them (1:24-26) and they will once again become a faithful city. The time is coming when God will create a totally new fruitful branch and a new protection for Zion, but only after the majority has been destroyed (4:2-6). He will protect this new Zion like he did Israel in the wilderness (4:5). There will even be a time in the future when all nations will come to this restored Zion to find peace and hope (2:1-4). These rich themes are picked up throughout the book.

An account of Isaiah's call (ch. 6) appears at the end of this first section rather than at the beginning of the book as in Jeremiah and Ezekiel. In his call we see the origin of his passion for the holiness of God and his pessimism about Israel's spiritual condition. Isaiah sees the Holy God on his throne and is convicted of his sin (6:1-5).

Therefore, it is understandable that his favorite title for God is "the Holy One of Israel," which is distributed equally throughout chapters 1–39 and 40–66. Isaiah is harsh on Judah's sin because God is holy. She should be living in fear and obedience but instead is living in ignorance, arrogance, and outright rebellion. This should not be and could not last. The people were so hardened in their ways that Isaiah's preaching would only make them more determined to continue (6:9-12). Verses 9-10, with the negative references to seeing and hearing, generate an important double motif for the rest of the book. Israel and the idols are blind and deaf, but also Israel is summoned to hear and see (especially after ch. 40). The servant is the model of one who sees, hears, and obeys.[38]

Chapters 7–12. These chapters, set within a historical context, raise a critical theme: is God trustworthy and will Judah trust him? Chapter 7, following right after chapter 6, illustrates the hardness of the heart of Judah exemplified in king Ahaz. He refuses to trust God when threatened, refuses a sign, and earns the wrath of God. Yet God gives a sign and through a promised Immanuel (7:10-17; 8:5-8), a promised king (9:2-7), and a promised Davidic descendent (ch. 11), provides assurance that a remnant will survive and be restored to the land. These are the most important Messianic claims of the book. According to Isaiah the Messiah is: a descendent of David, filled with the Spirit of God, one who will bring in a new era of peace and righteousness, and one who will establish a new community. This is a clear criticism of the current king and the prevailing ideology of the court.[39]

The remnant theme is an important one, already in evidence in the book of Amos (5:3). It is an affirmation of God's grace even as he plans to deliver his wrath against the sinful nation. Even in the midst of the devastation wrought by the Assyrian army a remnant will survive (10:20-27).

Also in this section Isaiah's theology of history appears. God controls all the nations and can even use them, including Assyria, to carry out his plans (ch. 10). This is one reason why Judah can trust him. This theme is at the center of chapters 13–23. Yet Assyria herself will suffer the judgment of God because of her arrogance and cruelty.

---

[38]The root "hear" appears 106 times in the book, the root "see" 84 times.
[39]VanGemeren, *Prophetic Word*, pp. 262-263.

The section ends with a hymn of praise for the salvation that God has brought (ch. 12). These elements of praise appear often later.

Chapters 13–23. These chapters expand on Isaiah's theology of history. God not only holds Assyria accountable but all the nations within Judah's world. The nations addressed in order are: Babylon, Assyria, Moab, Damascus (Syria), Cush and Egypt, Babylon again, Edom, Arabia, Jerusalem (!), and Tyre. The lesson is clear: all nations rise and fall at the pleasure of God, and therefore each must answer to him. He is Lord of the universe and will establish justice by judging each for its deeds. Because of her apostasy, Judah (Jerusalem) is treated just like the nations. But even among this lengthy series of judgment speeches there are a few echoes of hope (14:1-3,32; 16:5; 19:18-25).

Chapters 24–27. These chapters are often called the "Little Apocalypse" and considered a late addition to the book. But a careful reading shows little of the apocalyptic genre. There is a continuation of the theme of judgment from the previous section but now expanded in general terms to all creation and its inhabitants in chapter 24. However, out of the ruins will spring hope and praise because the wicked are punished (24:14-16a). The rescued of the Lord will have a banquet spread for them (25:6-8) for their trust in the Lord is vindicated (25:9). They will be a new and strong city established for peace in which the dead will live (ch. 26). They will also be a fruitful vineyard (compare ch. 5) in which Israel will blossom once more after the shame of the exile (ch. 27). This is Isaiah's eschatology: the day is coming when God will restore and reinvigorate his people.

Chapters 28–35. These chapters continue the indictment of Israel and Judah for their pride, and their turning to politics, military alliances, and wealth for security rather than to their covenant Lord. These charges are delivered in the genre of six woe oracles (28:1; 29:1,15; 30:1; 31:1; and 33:1). Judah's machinations again are based in the lack of trust which was already condemned in 2:6-9 and reflected in the attitude of Ahaz in chapter 7.

Chapter 35 rounds off this section with a hymn (similar to how ch. 12 rounds off the first section). The hymn provides a vivid word picture of the restored land, people freed from handicaps, and the peace that comes because of God's grace and restoration of his people. This is the center focus of Isaiah's hope for the future.

Salvation, redemption, and restoration follow punishment and judgment. The redeemed will see the wonders of the Lord and shout for joy as all sorrow and sadness will flee (35:9-10). This theme is continued in chapters 40–66.

Chapters 36–39. Through a historical narrative these chapters return to a main theme: can God be trusted? Hezekiah, in time of national crisis, trusts God to deliver Jerusalem, and he does. This narrative concludes the first half of Isaiah and deliberately contrasts Hezekiah with Ahaz and his lack of trust in chapter 7. It also demonstrates the truth at 2:5,22. The Holy One of Israel is faithful, the Lord of all nations, and he can and will deliver his people despite seemingly overwhelming odds. The issue is not political, economic, or military power, but the power of God versus the power of the nations. Yet even in the midst of this power message Hezekiah receives the warning — everything will be carried off to Babylon (39:6). God can be trusted to deliver his people, but he can also be trusted to carry out his justice and threat of judgment for Israel's sin. He is a consistent and holy God, who inspires both hope and fear.

Chapters 40–48. Chapters 40 to 55 are dominated by the theme of servant. The major question seems to be whether Israel will become the servant of God or not.[40] Often the concept of servant has been studied from the four so-called "Servant Songs," 42:1-9; 49:1-6; 50:4-9; 52:13–53:12. But this is too narrow a focus. The whole section centers on the word and theme of servant.[41] The servant is sometimes Israel (41:8; 44:1,21; 49:3) and sometimes apparently an unnamed individual (42:1-4; 52:13ff.). The task of the servant is multiple: anointed by God to participate in the exercise of judgment, appointed to function as a prophet, sent to extend ministry to the Gentiles, appointed as a minister to Israel, chosen to be part of a worldwide revelation and salvation, and assigned to suffer as an innocent victim for the people. Christians are accustomed to understanding this servant in Messianic terms. The Messianic figure in the first half of Isaiah was, in contrast, a King after the model of David (Isa 9:6-7). Perhaps the transition between the two concepts is Isaiah 37:35 with a reference to "my servant David."

---

[40]Oswalt, *Isaiah 1-39*, p. 57.

[41]The word "servant" occurs 21 times in chapters 40–55, only one time in the plural. The word occurs in the plural nine times in chapters 56–66 but not in the singular.

Chapter 40 is noted for its announcement of comfort for the people. The time of Judah's troubles are past, and now is the time for the restoration of God's kingdom on earth (40:9-11). This introduces the many oracles of salvation that appear in chapters 40–48 with their typical "fear not" theme: 41:10,14; 43:1,5; 44:2; 54:4. The oracles seem to presuppose that the judgment of God promised in the first half of the book has occurred, Judah has experienced punishment and exile, and now is the time for her restoration.[42] This is in fact good news and the descriptions of what God is going to do remind us of the glorious vision of chapter 35.

The God who can do this is the incomparable creator God who has no rival (40:12-31). That is why Judah can trust in him and mount up like eagles. That is also why the people have nothing to fear, no matter what circumstances they may find themselves in. A corollary is that the pagan idols are nothing and have no standing before God. They are man-made, powerless, and a delusion (41:21-29; 44:9-20). They cannot prevent God from keeping his promises.

In this section we also have further proof of the sovereignty of God. He designates the great Cyrus as his shepherd and anointed one (44:28; 45:1). For the moment Cyrus is God's servant to deliver Israel from her captivity. This means the humiliation of the mighty Babylon, for God controls her future also. The theology of history is identical to what we saw in God's control of Assyria (chs. 10 and 36–37). A further example of God's power is that he can bring to pass what he said he would contrary to the idols who can doing nothing like that (41:22; 42:9; 43:9-13; 44:8; 45:21; 46:10; 48:3).

Chapters 49–55. The theme of restoration continues, especially through the ministry of the servant. The servant is Israel (the redeemed remnant?) whose task is to bring Israel back to God (49:1-5). God's grace toward Israel overflows in faithfulness and loyalty. He will not allow his covenant people to disappear from history. He ever renews his relationship with them. This restoration theme is a main focus of these chapters. Zion will flourish as her children return (49:8-26). Singing and celebration will mark the demonstration of God's covenant love (49:3; 52:9; 54:1). The desolate land will

---

[42]Though usually the assumed background is the Babylonian captivity, the initial audience could have been the thousands of refugees produced by the Assyrian invasion recorded in Isaiah 36–37. It was then reapplied to the devastating exile of 587 B.C.

be crowded with a population explosion. Royalty will bow to them, and they will never be put to shame again. The heavens and earth may vanish but God's salvation will endure (51:6). The good news of God's reign will be proclaimed (52:7).

But the mission of the remnant will extend beyond Israel to all the nations. The God of the universe could not be limited to just one nation. It was too small a thing (49:6). Israel was intended to be a light to the nations so that all may experience God's salvation.

On the negative side Isaiah describes God's wrath in a memorable image that Jeremiah expands (cp. Isa 51:17-23 with Jeremiah 25). God's wrath against sin is a cup from which the sinful must drink. Drinking will cause them to stagger and lose control, just as a drunken person has no control over his faculties, mental or physical. This is not a sidebar but central to the concept of God's holiness. Out of holiness comes a judgment on sin, for God is just and righteous and cannot let sin go unnoticed. God is not vindictive, but he will vindicate himself and his people by not letting sin go unpunished.

Ultimately salvation would come through the innocent suffering of the servant (52:13–53:12). In the most powerful statement of vicarious suffering in the Bible, Isaiah announced the intention of God to lay the sin of all on one person. Through the submissive, despised servant/lamb will come reconciliation. Christians recognize this servant as the Messiah, the Christ. No other could accomplish this mission. Through this suffering one will come God's new "covenant of peace" through which Israel will expand to include all nations (54:1-10).

This section closes with one of the most powerful invitations in the Bible, the invitation to come and feast on the riches that God freely offers to all (ch. 55). God's plans are beyond human comprehension but all can still rejoice in the generous, divine offer. Even all of nature will respond in joy (see also Psalms 96–98).

Chapters 56–66. The book of Isaiah closes out by repeating themes from the first 39 chapters of the book. The blessings of salvation in chapters 40–55 did not change the fundamental facts of life with God. Israel still needs to practice righteousness, and God still needs to manifest his glory.

The human condition remains in need of discipline. If this section is directed to the people after the exile, it demonstrates that nothing has changed. They must not take the gift of God's grace as permission to ignore their covenant obligations. The admonitions to Israel are contained in two large blocks, 56:1–57:13 and 58:1–59:14. Here we find that faithfulness in Sabbath keeping is still important (56:2,6), idolatry is still forbidden (57:1-13), religious observances cannot take precedence over seeing that justice is done (58), sin and iniquity prevent righteousness and justice from being done (59:1-14), and rebellion has brought God's judgment (63:10-14; 64:5b-12). These passages are grim reminders that in this age humans are still trapped in the consequences of the fall. Isaiah's solution to this human condition comes in a vision of a new heaven and earth (65:17-25).

The God portrayed in this section is also the same as portrayed in the early chapters. Israel is where God will display his glory so that all nations can come to live under his blessings (56:1-8; 60:1-3; 66:18-24). God chose Israel so that all nations would come to know him. Furthermore, God also holds the nations accountable. Edom will experience his fierce wrath against her sin (63:1-6) as a paradigm for the accountability of all nations before him. This is part of the vindication of Zion so that God's glory may be displayed through his works (ch. 62). Forgiveness is open to Israel because of God's nature: he will not be angry forever (57:14-21). It is the spirit of God that has anointed his messenger to bring this good news, which is the good news of liberty for the captive and vengeance on the sinner (61:1-4). The one new addition of thought is an important one. In order to finally provide a place for God's will to be perfectly done, he will create a new heaven and earth, a place where no human activity will be in vain, where at last all people will give delight to God, where all conflict and tears will vanish, and where all will worship God eternally (65:17-25; 66:22-23). God's peace will finally come to the contrite of spirit and humble of heart (57:14-21). The vision of 2:1-5 will be realized. Isaiah's eschatological projections will become a reality.

NEW TESTAMENT CONNECTIONS

The student of the New Testament will be familiar with many themes and texts from Isaiah because of the book's profound influence on Jesus' teaching and ministry and on Paul's thought. The New Testament contains over 40 direct quotes from and nearly 390 allusions to Isaiah. Isaiah accounts for nearly one-fourth of the quotes from the Old Testament in the New Testament. Over 60% of the quotes from and allusions to Isaiah come from chapters 40–66.

For the New Testament, understanding the ministry and teaching of Jesus required knowledge of Isaiah. Quotes from Isaiah explained

John the Baptist's ministry (Isa 40:3; Matt 3:3), the importance of Jesus' birth (Isa 7:14; Matt 1:23), the purpose of Jesus' ministry (Isa 61:1-2; Luke 4:18-19), the hard-heartedness of the Jewish people to Jesus' teaching, and why Jesus taught in parables (Isa 6:9-10; Matt 13:14-15; Mark 4:12; Luke 8:10; John 12:39-40; Acts 28:26-27; see also Isa 29:13 and Matt 15:8-9). Also Isaiah explained the beginning of Jesus' ministry in Galilee (Isa 9:1; Matt 4:15-16) and Jesus' role as quiet servant (Isa 42:1-4; Matt 12:18-21). Of course Jesus as the suffering Messiah could only be understood from Isaiah 53 (John 12:38; Matt 8:17; Luke 22:37, plus numerous allusions).[43] Jesus was indeed the Messiah of the Old Testament. For Peter, Jesus' suffering offered a paradigm for Christians (Isa 53:9; 1 Pet 2:18-24).

For Paul, Isaiah provided important ideas for his complex discussion of the relationship between Jews and Gentile Christians in Romans 9–11. The remnant idea provided for him understanding of how Jews could be saved (Isa 10:22-23; Rom 9:27-28). Isaiah's reflections on Zion explained why the Jews stumbled over belief in Jesus (Isa 28:16; Rom 9:33), but there was no shame in believing (Rom 10:11). It was Isaiah's universal understanding of God that helped Paul understand the Christian mission to the Gentiles (Isa 65:1; Rom 10:20), and Isaiah's understanding of God's incomparableness that helped him see the future possibility of Israel's salvation (Isa 59:20-21; Rom 11:26-27; Isa 40:13-14; Rom 11:34-35). Isaiah even anticipated the victory of Jesus over death (Isa 25:8; 1 Cor 15:54).

Of course quotations from Isaiah are not the only evidence of the influence of Isaiah. The New Testament's authors used the language of the Old Testament, for they were steeped in its teaching. Therefore, allusions to Isaiah are found throughout Luke–Acts, John, and Revelation.[44] John's wonderful metaphors for Jesus as light of the world, water of life, good shepherd, way, and vine all find their background in Isaiah. Isaiah's eschatology provides the source of a hundred allusions in Revelation (compare Isaiah 60 and 65 with Revelation 21–22). It is no wonder that Isaiah is respected by Christians and has been referred to as "The Gospel of Isaiah."

---

[43]James Flamming, however, remarks on the low numbers of quotes and allusions to Isaiah 53 given its importance for understanding the death of Christ. He suggests that maybe it was too nice of a fit and the early Christians could have been accused of making up the death of Christ to fit the text ("The New Testament Use of Isaiah," *SwJT* 11 [1968]: 99, n. 25).

[44]Ibid., p. 101.

JEREMIAH

HISTORICAL AND CULTURAL BACKGROUND

Historically the time of Jeremiah (approximately 640 to after 587 B.C.) was one of almost unparalleled political ferment in the ancient Near East. During this period mighty Assyria, who had destroyed the northern kingdom and ruled Mesopotamia, Palestine, and sometimes Egypt for over a century, collapsed. The neo-Babylonian empire rose to replace it and carried on almost constant battles with Egypt to control the Near East.

After Hezekiah came to the throne of Judah in 715, Assyria went through a period of weakness. Hezekiah, with others, decided the time was ripe to revolt. The able Assyrian king, Sennacherib, soon settled matters elsewhere in the empire and came into Palestine. Judah was devastated but Jerusalem was spared by the intervention of God (Isaiah 36ff.). This was pictured as a reward to Hezekiah for being a good and repentant king. However, his son Manasseh, having seen the devastation brought by Hezekiah's turning to God and away from Assyria, reversed that policy with a vengeance (2 Kings 21). He did all he could to eliminate covenantal faith and to force thoroughgoing paganism on Judah. The streets ran red with innocent blood (2 Kgs 21:16). He also maintained vassalage to Assyria and adopted many of her religious practices. The author of Kings lays at Manasseh's feet the blame for the eventual destruction of the nation and exile (2 Kgs 21:11-15). However, Josiah, Manasseh's grandson, had the character of Hezekiah and promoted widespread religious reform.

Josiah came to the throne at age eight in 640 following the assassination of his father Amon, and the subsequent execution of the assassins. Within eight years, by 631, he had begun a reform movement, and by his twelfth year he began to purge the country of pagan worship (2 Chr 34:3).

Ashurbanipal, the last great king of Assyria, died in 627, the year of Jeremiah's call. Assyria began to weaken and was unable to maintain control over Palestine, thus paving the way for Josiah to carry out his reform without interference. Other countries began to press in on Assyria or assert independence. These included the Cimmerians and Scythians of the Caucasus Mountains, the Medes of western Iran, the Babylonians under Nebopolassar to the south, and Egypt under Psammetichus.

In Josiah's eighteenth year, while the Temple was being cleaned as a part of the reform, a scroll of the law was found (probably part or most of the book of Deuteronomy, though this is strongly debated; 2 Kings 22; 2 Chr 34:8-21). This led to further reforms, including a magnificent celebration of the Passover (2 Kings 23).

The year 612 is an important peg date in the history of the ancient Near East. After struggling for years against the coalition of Medes and Babylonians, Nineveh, the capital of Assyria, fell. Survivors fled west to Haran, where Psammetichus and Egypt joined the coalition. In 610 Haran fell and Assyria came to an end. Psammetichus died that same year. Neco II succeeded his father, and, determined to assert Egyptian influence in Palestine, marched to Carchemish to try to help the remnant of the Assyrians against Babylon.

Josiah decided to intercede and met Neco at Megiddo (which Josiah now controlled), apparently to resist Neco's attempt to gain power. Josiah was killed, and his body was brought to Jerusalem (2 Kgs 23:28-30). His son, Jehoahaz II, took the throne, but he was removed within three months by Neco and taken captive to Egypt. (Neco, by the way, was too late to help the Assyrians.) Eliakim, Jehoahaz's brother, renamed Jehoiakim by Neco, was put on the throne as a vassal to the Egyptians. Egypt remained in control of Palestine and Syria for a few years as Babylon secured its eastern areas.

In 605 Neco advanced to Carchemish in the north of Syria apparently to consolidate his power, but he was completely routed by the Babylonians under Nebuchadnezzar II. In 604 Nebuchadnezzar marched into the Palestinian coastal plain and sacked Ashkelon. Jehoiakim submitted to Babylon. Later (601) Babylon marched to Egypt but was firmly resisted. Jehoiakim apparently used the occasion to renege on his pledge to Babylon (2 Kgs 24:1).

In 598/97 Babylon marched into Palestine. Jehoiakim died just before the attack on Jerusalem and Jehoiachin, his son, became king. He was king only three months when the Babylonians took him captive to Babylon, where he remained in custody for years, until released and given a stipend by the king of Babylon (2 Kgs 25:27-30). Nebuchadnezzar captured Jerusalem, carried off treasure and captives, and put Mattaniah, Jehoiachin's uncle, on the throne, renaming him Zedekiah.

Zedekiah was a weak ruler, afraid of his advisors and drawn to Jeremiah. His reign was a time of continuous political intrigue with pro-Babylon, pro-Egyptian, and pro-independence parties jockeying for influence. An insurrection in Babylon in 595/594 apparently led to a meeting of the foreign ministers of Edom, Moab, Ammon, Tyre, and Sidon in Jerusalem to plot revolt (Jer 27:1-3). It came to nothing but Judah decided to follow a course of seeking independence. Nebuchadnezzar returned in 588/87, besieged Jerusalem, and sacked it, carrying off numerous captives and more treasure, and destroying the city and Temple. Jeremiah, who had been under guard (Jeremiah 38), was freed by the Babylonians and treated kindly (Jer 39:11-14). The exile had begun, though captives had been taken to Babylon earlier (including Daniel and Ezekiel). Gedaliah was made governor and the capital moved to Mizpah. Jeremiah supported Gedaliah. Some Judeans assassinated him and then fled to Egypt, taking Jeremiah with them (Jeremiah 41–43). In 581 another deportation was taken to Babylon, and Judah was subsumed under the province of Samaria.

It is against this background that the book of Jeremiah is to be interpreted. Many of his sermons and events in his life are dated and can be firmly placed into their historical setting. This gives a concreteness to Jeremiah's message and life that is missing from some other prophets.

TEXT AND AUTHOR

Jeremiah the prophet stands in a long tradition of OT prophets distinguished by the fact that the word of the Lord came to him (Jer 1:2,4). Although often the name of the prophet carries a message of its own, the derivation of Jeremiah's name is unclear. It could come from a root meaning "to lift up" or a root meaning "loosen (the womb)" or "cast." In the book of Jeremiah his name is spelled two ways: יִרְמְיָהוּ (*Yirmᵊyāhû*, 114 times) and יִרְמְיָה (*Yirmᵊyāh*, 9 times, all within chs. 27:1 to 29:1). There are nine other Jeremiahs in the OT, three were King David's warriors (1 Chr 12:4,10,13) and two were near contemporaries of Jeremiah the prophet (2 Kgs 23:31; Jer 35:3).[1]

We have more biographical information about Jeremiah than any other figure in the OT outside of King David. We also have more insight into his heart from his "confessions" than for any other prophet. Therefore, we should be able to understand Jeremiah better than any prophet.[2]

Jeremiah's father was Hilkiah, a priest from the village of Anathoth (1:1). This was not the Hilkiah who found the book of the law in the Temple early in Josiah's reign (2 Kgs 22:3-10). Anathoth was a small village about three miles north of Jerusalem in Benjaminite territory (Josh 21:18) and the home of the priest Abiathar. Abiathar was David's high priest who was exiled to Anathoth by Solomon because he had supported Adonijah for king (1 Kgs 2:26-27). Hilkiah, and thus Jeremiah, was probably a descendant of Abiathar. Later the people of Anathoth opposed Jeremiah (Jer 11:18-23).

Jeremiah's call came in the thirteenth year of the reign of King Josiah (1:2), which would have been 627 B.C. His ministry continued through the reigns of several kings and through the fall of Jerusalem to the Babylonians in 586 B.C. After the fall of Jerusalem, Jeremiah was taken to Egypt against his will and apparently died there (Jeremiah 43). Thus Jeremiah's ministry spanned one of the most tumultuous and critical periods in Judah's history (see below). According to Jeremiah's testimony he was a young man at the time of his call (1:6), perhaps a teenager, which would put his birth somewhere around 640 B.C., near the time Josiah became king at age eight (2 Kgs 22:1).

Some scholars have doubted that 627 was the date of Jeremiah's call. Rather they think that 627 is the date of Jeremiah's birth. This

---

[1]"Jeremiah," *IDB*, p. 822. The name also occurs outside of the OT on three clay seals, two from the mid-eighth century and one from the mid-seventh century B.C., and on a Lachish ostracon (inscribed pottery sherd) from the late sixth century.

[2]I say "should" because there are a wide variety of opinions on how useful the material in the book of Jeremiah is for coming to an understanding of the real prophet. On the one hand William Holladay thinks we can know a lot about him (*Jeremiah*, Hermeneia [Minneapolis: Fortress Press, 1989], 2:25) and on the other R.P. Carroll thinks Jeremiah is a mostly fictional character created by postexilic writers (*Jeremiah* [Sheffield: JSOT Press, 1989], p. 75). See below under "History of Interpretation."

would then put the beginning of his ministry several years later, perhaps as late as 609 after Josiah's death.[3] Their reasoning is based on several arguments from silence. There are no oracles that can be confidently assigned to the time of Josiah, there is no explicit reference to the reform of Josiah, and there is no good candidate for the "foe from the north" of chapters 4 and 6 in 627 B.C. In addition the first datable event in the book of Jeremiah is the Temple sermon in chapter 26, which is dated to the first year of Jehoiakim in 609. However, none of these reasons is particularly strong. Most scholars have not been persuaded, and the traditional date is widely held.

Jeremiah's response to his call to prophesy was similar to others called by God — reluctance supported by an excuse (compare Moses, Exodus 3–4, and Isaiah, Isaiah 6). His age prevented him from knowing how to speak (1:6). But it was not just his age; his culture was against him also. In ancient Israel the task of the young people was to learn from the elders. The elders were the ones who deserved honor and respect when they spoke.

Jeremiah's objection was met and overcome (1:7-10). However, his call ends on a threatening note. He was commanded not to break down before the people or God would break him (1:17). God would make him strong so that he could prevail against the people (1:18-19). Such ominous words were verified by Jeremiah's experiences. He was often opposed, his life threatened, and he was imprisoned more than once (11:18-23; 18:18-23; 20:1-6; 26; 36; 37; 38). As a consequence we often see into Jeremiah's heart, for he did not suffer his persecution in silence. He cried out for the defeat of his enemies (12:1-4), wished for their death (18:19-23), railed against God for being deceived (20:7-12), and wished he had never been born (20:14-18).

Jeremiah's anguish both at his treatment and at what he saw happening to Judah (4:19) has earned him the title, "The Weeping Prophet." However, this is only partially true, for there is a great deal more in the book of Jeremiah than lament. Yet because of this material we learn that the life of a prophet was often punctuated by distress and persecution. It was an arduous task to be a faithful spokesperson for God.

---

[3]Holladay, *Jeremiah*, 2:25-26; J.P. Hyatt, "Jeremiah," *IB*, ed. by G.A. Buttrick et al. (New York: Abingdon-Cokesbury Press, 1951–57), 5:779-780.

THE TEXT OF JEREMIAH

The book of Jeremiah is unique in the OT in that it has been pre-served for us in two versions. The Hebrew text, or Masoretic text, is the text behind our English Bibles. The Greek text, or Septuagint, however, is much different. It is about one-eighth shorter and the chapters are arranged differently. It is missing many words or phras-es found in the Hebrew text, and sometimes whole verses or pas-sages, for example, 10:6-8; 33:14-26; and 39:4-13. Also the so-called "Oracles against the Nations" which appear in the Hebrew text as chapters 46–51 come after 25:13 in the Greek text and have a dif-ferent sequence. With the discovery of the Dead Sea Scrolls, which included fragments of the Hebrew text of Jeremiah, it became clear that there was a Hebrew text tradition that supported the Greek ver-sion.[4] The Greek version itself is uneven. The Greek of chapters 1–28 differs from chapters 29–52 and apparently represents differ-ent levels of revision.[5] Scholars have supported the opposite views that the shorter Greek text is more original (Janzen) and that the longer Hebrew text is more original (Althann).[6] However, for prac-tical purposes it would be precarious to base a study of the book of Jeremiah on only the Greek text since we have only a fragment of the apparent Hebrew text behind it. Thus, most scholars accept the Jewish and Christian canonical form of Jeremiah which is based on the Hebrew text.[7]

---

[4]The fragment that demonstrates this fact is called 4QJer[b]. It contains only part of Jer 9:22–10:18. It is one of 4 fragments found in caves 2 and 4 in the Qumran area. The other 3 fragments support the Hebrew text form. For a full discussion of the textual issues see J. Gerald Janzen, *Studies in the Text of Jeremiah* (Cambridge: Harvard University Press, 1973).

[5]Peter Craigie, Page Kelley, and Joel Drinkard, *Jeremiah 1–25*, WBC (Waco: Word, 1991), p. xlii.

[6]Robert Althann, *A Philological Analysis of Jeremiah 4–6 in the Light of North-west Semitic* (Rome: Biblical Institute, 1983).

[7]These two different text traditions perhaps reflect the fact that when Jeremiah and Baruch were taken to Egypt they took with them a copy of the material they had produced up to that point and left a copy in Judea. Subsequent editorial activity in the two isolated geographical locations pro-duced two different editions. From his study of chapters 4–6, Althann argued that the Greek translators produced the differences because they did not understand the nature of Semitic poetry and routinely omitted par-allelisms and other repetitions.

HISTORY OF INTERPRETATION

The book of Jeremiah offers one of the most complex challenges to the interpreter of any Old Testament prophetic book. The material is complex and some of the genres are unique to Jeremiah. In the last one hundred years scholars have offered many theories to explain the composition of the book, some complex, and some that contradict each other. The large differences between the Hebrew and Greek text of Jeremiah make the matter even more complex.

A brief summary of the apparent structure of the book will highlight some of the issues.

CHAPTERS 1–25:14

This section seems to be a unit from the earliest preaching of Jeremiah. Chapter 25 is a transition chapter to the next section, but the first 13 verses offer a conclusion to chapters 1–24 with key links to chapter 1 and other material in the early chapters. Verse 13 refers to the words uttered against the land that were written in "this book." Chapter 36 narrates the story of the scroll of Jeremiah's sermons that was composed by Baruch under the direction of God in the fourth year of Jehoiakim (605 B.C.). That this was much of the material in chapters 1–24 is a reasonable conclusion. But even within this section there are complex blocks of material that are interrelated and suggest smaller units. Chapters 2 and 3 are arranged around the theme of the marriage metaphor and are dated to the time of Josiah (3:6). They included a call for repentance (3:22–4:2). Chapters 4–6 carry the theme of the menacing "foe from the north" and suggest massive devastation of Judah under an invading army. Chapters 14–15:4 concern "the drought." Chapters 21:11–23:8 are addressed "To the royal house of Judah." Chapter 23:9-40 is addressed to the prophets. Scattered within chapters 11–20 are Jeremiah's "confessions" that recount his persecution and inner struggles. These occur in 11:18-23; 12:1-6; 15:10-21; 17:14-18; 18:18-23 and 20:7-18. Chapter 24 uses the figure of the good and bad figs to refer to those taken into captivity by Nebuchadnezzar in 598/97. This provides a fitting conclusion to the first section in the book.

This first section of the book is quite complex but seems concerned largely with judgment against Judah and Jerusalem. Yet there are hints of hope for the future that go beyond the judgment and look to a return of exiles. The good figs of chapter 24 are those in exile. Much of the material is probably from before 605.[8]

CHAPTERS 25:15–33:26

This section begins with a transitional passage aimed at foreign nations (25:15-38). Jeremiah is to make them drink the cup of God's wrath. In the Hebrew Bible this theme is not picked up again until chapters 46 through 51. However, in the Greek version, the Septuagint, the oracles against the nations follow immediately on 25:13 which is a more logical order and fits the pattern observed in the book of Isaiah. Chapters 26–33 juxtapose judgment and hope. Chapters 26 through 29 continue the theme of God's judgment on Judah and predict a lengthy stay for the exiles in a letter Jeremiah wrote to them (ch. 29). We see specific examples of opposition to Jeremiah. Chapter 26 completes the account of Jeremiah's Temple sermon in chapter 7. Chapters 27 and 28 take up the issue of the true prophet (from ch. 23) and demonstrate that a salvation message is not necessarily a mark of a true prophet. However, chapters 30–33 look beyond the exile to a return and restoration of Judah. These chapters of hope are often called "The Book of Consolation." These chapters include both poetry (chs. 30–31) and prose accounts of Jeremiah's symbolic actions (ch. 33). The poetic section contains the well-known promise of a new covenant (31:31-34).

CHAPTERS 34–45

These chapters cover Jeremiah's experiences and the last days of Jerusalem. The chronology of chapters 34–36 is not straightforward. Chapter 34 is during the final days of Jerusalem, which is covered in more detail in chapters 37 and following. However, chapter 36 goes back to early in Jehoiakim's reign, to 605 (the fourth year of Jehoiakim, 36:1) and provides incidental information about the origin of the written form of the early sermons of Jeremiah. However, the chapters are informed by a common theme — opposition to the word of Jeremiah.

Chapters 37 to 39 relate Jeremiah's imprisonments during the

---

[8]J.A. Thompson, *Jeremiah,* NICOT (Grand Rapids: Eerdmans, 1980), pp. 27-29; J.G. McConville, *Judgment and Promise: An Interpretation of the Book of Jeremiah* (Winona Lake, IN: Eisenbrauns, 1993), ch. 2.

last days of Jerusalem and its eventual fall to the Babylonians. Jeremiah's message is vindicated. Chapters 40–42 relate Jeremiah's adventures after the fall, his support of the new governor Gedaliah, the assassination of Gedaliah, and Jeremiah being taken to Egypt against his will. Chapters 43–44 are his message to the exiles in Egypt. Chapter 45 ends this section with a brief word to Baruch that he shall live through the coming disaster.

CHAPTERS 46–51

This section is the logical extension of 25:14-38 which introduced the word of the Lord to the nations. The nations around Judah all receive words of judgment for their behavior. Egypt and Moab receive the longest word with the exception of Babylon which is the subject of chapters 50 and 51. Yahweh, who through the use of these nations, brought judgment on Judah, now calls them to account for their own sins. Though God used them to conduct holy war against his own people, they still were held accountable for their actions and also stood condemned by God.

CHAPTER 52

The book of Jeremiah ends with a concluding summary about the final end of Jerusalem and the release of Jehoiachin from prison in Babylon many years later. This chapter is essentially a verbatim account taken from 2 Kings 24:18–25:30.

The above brief sketch shows the complexity of the arrangement of the material in Jeremiah. Though there is clear order in some sections, other sections challenge the interpreter. The variety of material is also seen in the great variation between poetry and prose in the book. The prose is of different kinds: biography, long prose sermons, and historical material.

Bernard Duhm was the first modern scholar to offer an explanation for the nature of the material in Jeremiah.[9] He saw the book as composed of authentic oracles of Jeremiah, biographical narratives from Baruch, and a large body of material from later editors influenced by the theology of the book of Deuteronomy. Authentic Jeremiah material was very small and almost all poetic.

---

[9]B. Duhm, *Das Buch Jeremia* (Tübingen, 1901).

Sigmund Mowinckel proposed that the book was composed of three major collections of material that underwent a long editorial process.[10] These three major blocks he labeled Types A, B, and C. For Mowinckel Type A was mostly authentic oracles of Jeremiah in poetic form and mostly in chapters 1–25. Yahweh was the principal speaker. These were transmitted orally for a time. An important subtype was Jeremiah's "confessions." Type B material was mostly biographical in nature and mostly in chapters 26–29 and 34–45. These were in the third person and contained historical data. There was also some autobiography. Scholars debated whether Baruch was the source of this material. Mowinckel believed the material did not come from Baruch but from Egypt sometime between 580 and 480 B.C. The third type of material has produced the most critical problem for the book. Type C is composed of prose discourses in monotonous, wordy, yet highly rhetorical style, and is close to Deuteronomy in thought and word. It is normally presented as autobiographical. This material is scattered throughout the book, within both poetic and biographical sections. Mowinckel did not think this material was from Jeremiah but composed by later editors and redactors.[11] John Bright later proposed a Type D material in autobiographical style in which Jeremiah either describes some experience through which the divine word came to him or engages in symbolic action and explains it.[12]

Considerable discussion has followed Mowinckel's proposals about the nature of the composition and date of the book of Jeremiah. E.W. Nicholson raised doubts about Baruch's connection with the Type B material.[13] He saw little difference between the Type B and Type C material and thought both came from a circle of men who produced the prose material in Jeremiah. This material represents the final expression of a tradition that developed around the ministry of Jeremiah in response to the needs of the surrounding community.[14] However, many have argued that Baruch is the most likely

---

[10]Sigmund Mowinckel, *Zur Komposition des Buches Jeremia* (Kristiana, 1914).

[11]Thompson, *Jeremiah*, pp. 33-37.

[12]John Bright, "The Prophetic Reminiscence: Its Place and Function in the Book of Jeremiah," *Biblical Essays, Proceedings: Die ou Testamentiese Werkgemeenskap* (1966), pp. 11-30.

[13]E.W. Nicholson, *Preaching to the Exiles* (New York: Schocken Books, 1970).

[14]Thompson, *Jeremiah*, p. 42.

source for the biographical material. Who else, especially in Egypt where Jeremiah was reviled, would have preserved it?[15]

Mowinckel's Type C material has also generated a great deal of debate. It appears to be written in a style that is close to the history books, Joshua through 2 Kings, and Deuteronomy. How can we account for this phenomenon? One position taken is that the book of Deuteronomy influenced a circle of scribes and others who during the exile produced the final edition of the history, and the final edition of the book of Jeremiah.[16] This would account for the shared style and themes in both works.

In this view the purpose of the Deuteronomic authors/editors, "preachers in the exile," was twofold. They sought to explain why the chosen people of God, Israel and Judah, had suffered the catastrophes of 722 and 587 B.C., and they sought to engender hope in the exiles.[17]

On the other hand there does not seem to be any good reason why Jeremiah, perhaps influenced by the book of Deuteronomy while growing up in Anathoth, could not have developed his own style. John Bright has attempted to show that the similarities between the diction of the prose material in Jeremiah and the Deuteronomy-influenced material in Joshua to Kings are not as strong as they seem. Many of the words and phrases in Jeremiah are unique or appear in Jeremiah poetry also.[18] W.L. Holladay argued that many of the so-called deuteronomistic phrases in Jeremiah have their prototype in Jeremiah poetry.[19] H. Weippert argued along the same lines. She pointed out that the language of the speeches was typical sixth-century prose, that the peculiarities of the language are typical of the period of Jeremiah, and that there is little difficulty in supposing the prophet used both poetry and prose in his sermons.[20]

In addition McConville has shown that Jeremiah and the books of Kings have a different perspective on the future of the nation.

---

[15]Eissfeldt, *The Old Testament*, p. 355; Thompson, *Jeremiah*, p. 39; John Bright, *Jeremiah*, AB (Garden City, NY: Doubleday, 1965), p. lxx.

[16]Nicholson, *Preaching to the Exiles*.

[17]Thompson, *Jeremiah*, pp. 48-49.

[18]John Bright, "The Date of the Prose Sermons of Jeremiah," *JBL* 70 (1951): 15-35.

[19]W.L. Holladay, "Prototype and Copies: A New Approach to the Poetry-Prose Problem in the Book of Jeremiah," *JBL* 79 (1960): 351-367; and "Style, Irony and Authenticity in Jeremiah," *JBL* 81 (1962): 44-54.

[20]H. Weippert, *Die Prosareden des Jeremiabuches*, BZAW 132 (de Gruyter, 1971).

Kings holds out little hope for the future but is only concerned about showing why the nations fell (contra Nicholson). Jeremiah, on the other hand, points ahead to a profound hope for the future. There will be a return from exile and a new covenant.[21]

However, there is a modern thrust in the other direction. Some scholars are so impressed by the complexity of the arrangement of the book and the inner inconsistencies that they cannot believe it could come mostly from one person. W. McKane speaks of a "rolling corpus" whereby he means that the book of Jeremiah was continually edited and added to over a period of time. Early editions of Jeremiah were expanded as new situations required reinterpretation and reapplication. These new situations included the fall of Jerusalem and experiences of the Judeans in exile, in Egypt, and in the postexilic time.[22] R.P. Carroll also believes that the book is essentially made up of disparate pieces that came from a variety of postexilic settings, even into the Persian period.[23] In fact Jeremiah is perhaps "more the creation of the tradition than the creator of it."[24]

This skepticism seems unnecessary. Even Carroll recognizes that the so-called deuteronomistic material in Jeremiah that is supposed to mirror that of Joshua–Kings has its own distinctive quality.[25] If that is so then how is it useful to speak of deuteronomistic language in Jeremiah? Arguments based on style and theology are slippery and inconclusive. After the similarities have been adduced what do they mean? A holistic reading of the book of Jeremiah could well provide other conclusions.[26]

---

[21]McConville, *Judgment and Promise*.

[22]W. McKane, *Jeremiah 1–25* (Edinburgh, T. and T. Clark, 1986), pp. l-lxxxiii.

[23]Carroll, *Jeremiah*, pp. 57-72.

[24]Ibid., p. 77. Carroll has expressed his views in two major books besides the small volume referred to here. See R.P. Carroll, *From Chaos to Covenant* (New York: Crossroad, 1981); and *Jeremiah: A Commentary*, OTL (Philadelphia: Westminster, 1986). Such skepticism of the book of Jeremiah does not answer the question of why all the biographical material is in the book in the first place. We hardly know anything about any of the other prophets and yet their sermons were preserved. Knowledge of Jeremiah is not necessary to understanding the book. Why then would all of the material about him have been created if it did not have some foundation in fact? See Craigie et al., *Jeremiah 1-25*, pp. xxxviii-xl.

[25]Quoted in McConville, *Judgment and Promise*, p. 22.

[26]Ibid., pp. 24-25.

Therefore, it seems reasonable that, although there was probably editorial activity on the book of Jeremiah, there is no reason not to conclude that the bulk of the book goes back to him. What we learn from the book of Jeremiah is that he was a towering figure who had a long ministry in a critical period of Judah's history. Such a person would have had a tremendous influence on the people of his day and the following era. It would be surprising if he did not make a strong impact on those who gathered around him and preserved his words, and those who took up the task of compiling a history of the nation. The exile proved that his words were true, and he gained great credibility and influence. His long ministry would mean that changing times and circumstances required him to address new and changing issues, even revising previous messages.[27]

STRUCTURE

    I. 1:1–25:14 — Prophecies of Doom
       A. 1:1-19 — The call
       B. 2:1–6:30 — Prophecies from the time of Josiah
       C. 7:1–20:18 — Prophecies from the time of Jehoiakim
       D. 21:1–25:14 — Against king and prophet
   II. 25:15-38; 46:1–51:64 — Prophecies against the Nations
  III. 26:1–33:26 — Destruction and Restoration (chs. 30–33 — book of consolation)
  IV. 34:1–45:5 — Jeremiah and the Last Days of Jerusalem
   V. 52:1-34 — Historical Appendix (cf. 2 Kings 25)

GENRE

Jeremiah has a rich variety of speech forms and genres of prophetic speech. Many of them have already been mentioned.[28] We will only summarize briefly here. The book Jeremiah is unique in the quantity of biographical information we have about the prophet. This is the so-called "Type B" material in parts or all of chapters 19–21, 24, 26–28, and 34–45. Jeremiah is also unique in the quantity of prose sermons it includes, the so-called "Type C" material in such chapters as 7, 11, 16, 18, and 23:25ff. Jeremiah is also unique

---

[27]McConville, *Judgment and Promise*, pp. 14, 24, 27.
[28]See above under "History of Interpretation."

in the amount of autobiographical material it has, the so-called confessions in which Jeremiah offers intimate insight into his struggles with God. This is what John Bright called the "Type D" material in 1:4-19; 13:1-11; 16:1-8; 18:1-18; 19:1-3; and 20:7-18.

Jeremiah also includes the common range of prophetic speech forms that are found in other prophets, the prophetic oracles in poetic form. These are the so-called "Type A" material. Chapters 1–25 have the largest amount. These common types include judgment speeches (5:1-6), covenant lawsuits (2:2-13), announcements of salvation (30:18-22; 31:1-6), disputations (3:1-5), symbolic acts (27), parables (18:1-11), and oracles against the nations (46–51). Chapters 30–34 contain a series of important promises of return and restoration and are called "The Book of Consolation."

THEOLOGICAL THEMES[29]

The prophetic books are not systematic expositions of the prophets' thoughts, but compilations of sermons hammered out in the context of inspiration, revelation, the life of the prophet, and the historical and social context of the nation. Major themes may be discerned but they are presented in a variety of contexts and settings. Therefore, a theological summary is artificial but can be useful in understanding the big picture.

1. God. An understanding of God is at the foundation of all prophetic discourse and is revealed in the major themes that follow, but a few things can be said directly about Jeremiah's concept of the divine.

Many of the major themes in Jeremiah are contained in chapter 1. This is true of the concept of God. He is the God of the whole world, for Jeremiah's first call is to be a prophet to the nations (1:5,10,15; cf. 25:15-26; 27:2-8). To be sure, this included Judah, but the prophetic task was for the whole world. The book thus includes a large section addressed to individual nations (chs. 46–51). God is a universal God because he is the creator of the whole world and everything in it (5:22; 8:7; 10:12-13; 27:5-6; 31:35-36). God is a God both near at hand (immanent) and above the earth (transcendent) (23:23-24). He therefore knows the hearts of everyone (11:20; 16:17;

---

[29]See House, *Old Testament Theology*, ch. 12; and Zuck, *Biblical Theology*, ch. 9.

29:23). He was also specifically the God of Israel, a fact that underlies the numerous expressions of the covenant in the book (see below). But he is also the Lord of history; all nations answer to him (chs. 46–51), and Nebuchadnezzar was even his servant (27:6). For Israel he is the fountain of living water (2:13), the God who chose them and led them into the land (2:1-7). He is her husband and father (2:2; 3:1-5,19; 31:9,32), for he loved her (31:3) and was steadfastly loyal to her (9:24; 31:3; 32:18; 33:11).

Therefore, the other "gods" were really no gods and entirely worthless (2:5,11). They were like broken cisterns and powerless to do anything (2:13,28).

2. Covenant. The prophets have been defined as covenant mediators. This is especially true of Jeremiah. The book everywhere assumes the covenant and is full of covenant language, especially from the book of Deuteronomy. Jeremiah knew Israel was chosen at the Exodus (2:2-7; 7:21-22; 16:14-15). His strong judgment theme can be understood only in the context of Deuteronomy 28 and the covenant curses (see below on sin). There are numerous references to law (2:8; 6:19; 8:8; 18:18), commandment (32:11; 35:14,16,18), chose/chosen (33:24), obey (3:13; 7:23; 11:4; 17:24), disobey ("did not listen," 7:24,26; 11:8; 19:15), and my people (2:11,13; 5:31; 8:7; 14:17) to name a few concepts. The covenant is specifically mentioned in 11:1-13 because they had broken it (see also 14:21; 22:9; 32:40; 33:20,21; 50:5; "this covenant," 11:1 occurs in Deut 5:3; 29:9,14). Jeremiah admired king Josiah who led in covenant renewal (22:15-16; 2 Kings 22–23). Jeremiah's vision for the future involved the new covenant (31:31-34, see below).

3. Sin and apostasy. Jeremiah's call included four verbs for judgment that were repeated throughout the book (1:10). The grounds for the judgment against Israel and Judah were covenant breaking. This covenant breaking involved a wide variety of sins that Jeremiah described in some detail. A general term would be apostasy, a turning against the covenant God and a turning to false gods. Judah rejected God's word (5:12-13; chs. 26; 34–36) which came through Jeremiah, and believed in lies and practiced lies (3:10; 5:31; 6:13; 7:4,8; 9:5,6; 27:17). They became involved in syncretism, confusing obedience to Yahweh with service to false gods or deliberately disobeying the covenant (chs. 2; 7:9,18-20,30-34; 8:12; 16:18). This included the abhorrent practice of child sacrifice (7:31; 19:5; 32:35). They trusted in physical structures and ceremonies while ignoring or violating the Ten Commandments (ch. 7). They apparently felt that Isaiah's promises that God would protect Zion were eternal and not tied to covenant faithfulness (ch. 26). All their leadership had failed. The priests were corrupt (2:8; 5:30-31; 6:13-15) and failed to fulfill their duties of teaching the law. The prophets spoke lies and preached peace when the times required calls to repent and announcements of judgment (see below). The kings oppressed the poor and thought only of themselves with no concern for God or the covenant (chs. 21–22; 23:1-8). Everyone could accurately be called foolish and stupid (4:22).

Therefore, the only possible divine response was judgment. Most of Jeremiah's messages include some sort of judgment statement. At times he holds out some hope of repentance and return (3:13-14,22-25; 4:1-4; 18:11). But by chapter 25 there is little hope left. It has become clear that the people will not repent. They will go into exile. The only hope is after exile.[30] The judgment will take the form of an enemy from the north coming in and destroying the nation (4:5-31; ch. 6). Awful scenes of doom are described in chapters 19 and 25:1-13. The good people are considered those who have already been taken captive to Babylon (ch. 24). Seventy years of exile await the people (25:1-14; 29:1-14). Chapters 37–45 detail the last years of Judah and Jerusalem in which Jeremiah was often opposed and imprisoned, but ultimately vindicated, for his word came to pass.

4. True Prophets. One of the struggles for Jeremiah was the issue of prophecy. There were always many prophets among the people. The issue was who was sent from God and who was an imposter (see 1 Kings 22). Jeremiah seemed to wrestle with this more than any other prophet. On the one hand he knew he was a prophet sent from God. On the other hand his message was not of peace and consolation but doom and destruction. Although Jeremiah knew this was the message for the day, he still questioned its unrelenting focus (20:7-8). All other prophets preached peace and well-being (23:17; ch. 28) and were loved by the people. Yet they were wrong and were denounced by Jeremiah (23:9-40). They were immoral, ungodly, followers of Baal, spoke from dreams, were a burden to the people and to God, and spoke lies originating in divination (14:14-16). Their message was not the word needed for the hour. Everything was not fine, and peace was not going to come.

---

[30]See McConville, *Judgment and Promise.*

They did not know this because they had not been a part of God's council (23:18). In one vivid case the false prophet Hananiah died within a year as punishment for his false message (ch. 28). On the other hand, in one case a prophet who spoke the truth and then fled for his life was hauled back from Egypt and executed (26:20-23). Jeremiah's conflict with the prophets and people was a life or death matter, for him and ultimately for the nation.

5. Repentance. Even though Jeremiah's main message was judgment and doom, he did hold out hope for the people. God would not bring the destruction planned (ch. 18) if they would repent and turn back to God (3:13-14,22-25). Through the use of the multifaceted word שׁוּב (*šûb*), Jeremiah encouraged Judah to take action that would reverse their fortunes. He also used the same word to speak of their apostasy, their turning away from God (3:14,22, "faithless," NIV; cf. 4:1-4; 8:4-5). They had turned their loyalty away from God; they could also turn it back. This double-duty covenantal usage of *šûb* occurs in Jeremiah more then any other prophet. This part of the message of Jeremiah demonstrated God's justice and compassion. Judah's fate was not set in stone (18:7-8). She could alter the outcome. Jeremiah even composed a confession Judah could use to make things right (3:22a-23; 14:7-10).

6. Future Hope. The message of doom predominates in Jeremiah. The destruction of Judah and Jerusalem is foretold in sometimes vivid terms. Yet there is hope for the people which was already anticipated in Jeremiah's original commission "to build and to plant" (1:10; cf. 24:6; 31:4-5,28). Exile is unavoidable and necessary, but it is not the end. Chapters 30–33 show Jeremiah's transformation to a prophet of salvation as he builds on Deuteronomy 30:1-6. However, there are many hints at the hopeful future before these chapters. Chapter 3:14-18 sees a future time when the people will be restored and multiplied, and the nations will flock to Jerusalem. It will be such a glorious time that the Ark of the Covenant will be forgotten. The pronouncement of a righteous branch of David reigning as a just and wise king raises the Messianic dream (23:5-6; 33:15-16). This promise was a clever play on the name of the last, hapless king of Judah, Zedekiah ("the lord is my righteousness" will become "the LORD is our righteousness," 16:6). The return from exile will be a new exodus (16:14-15). The exile itself will be long, but has a determined end, seventy years (25:12; 29:10-14). Jeremiah demonstrated his own confidence in the promises of the Lord by investing in the future of the nation (32:6-15). The exiles will return with joy and exuberant rejoicing (31:1-14). This future hope included one of the most significant promises for the church of any in Jeremiah, the promise of a new covenant that would involve the heart, not a written code on stone (31:31-34). This promise builds on the promise of a new heart in 24:7 (see Ezek 11:19; 36:26). This promise is an expression of God's grace and confirmation of his determination to always have a people called by his name (31:35-37).

7. **Jeremiah's Complaints.** One of the unique features of the book of Jeremiah is the many passages that are Jeremiah's personal complaints to God. We have deep insight into Jeremiah's struggles with his ministry. He suffered for his faithfulness in proclaiming the message of God, but he did not suffer in silence. His complaints are confined to chapters 11 to 20. He confronts God about the nature of his ministry and the opposition it raised, and he clashed with his opponents over their failure to respond to God's word (12:1-4; 15:10-11; 15:15-21; 18:19-23; 20:7-18). Jeremiah questions God's theodicy (12:1-4; 18:19-23), his own birth (15:10-11; 20:14-18), and the content of his message (20:7-12). His complaints are similar to the laments in the Psalms. God prepared Jeremiah for his tough ministry when he was commissioned (1:17-19), but it did not make it any easier to endure the persecution.

NEW TESTAMENT CONNECTIONS

Jeremiah is quoted several times in the New Testament and alluded to often. Many of the New Testament authors seem to have been nurtured on the language and thoughts of the prophet Jeremiah.

The New Testament teaches that the new covenant promised in Jeremiah 31:31-34 was established by Jesus Christ and confirmed by his death and resurrection. This new covenant is an essential component of the Kingdom of God as inaugurated by the incarnation of the Son of God. Therefore, Jesus refers to the new covenant when establishing the Lord's Supper at the last Passover meal (Luke 22:20).[31] Paul also refers to the "new covenant" when he gives instructions about

---

[31]The synoptic gospel passages all have textual variants. Matthew 26:28 and Mark 14:24 in the accepted text have only "covenant" but variants add "new." There are variants to Luke 22:20 that omit verses 19b-20.

the Lord's Supper (1 Cor 11:25). The writer of Hebrews is unambiguous about the importance of the promise of the new covenant and its realization in the Incarnation. He quotes all of Jeremiah 31:31-34 in Hebrews 8:8-12 and verses 33-34 in Hebrews 10:16-17. Jesus is the mediator of a better covenant because the first one was faulty. His perfect sacrifice annulled sins once and for all.[32]

Matthew 2:18 applies Jeremiah 31:15 to the weeping for the babies in Bethlehem killed by Herod. Jesus cleanses the Temple and quotes part of Isaiah 56:7 and Jeremiah 7:11 to authenticate his action. Jesus also chides his disciples' lack of faith and understanding by quoting Jeremiah 5:21 as a question. Paul quotes Jeremiah 9:24 twice, once to counter human arrogance and boasting (1 Cor 1:31) and once to defend himself against "super apostles" (2 Cor 10:17).

Matthew places Judas's death in the context of Old Testament prophecy with a reference to Jeremiah, although it seems more likely that the quote is from Zechariah (Matt 27:9). However, recent research has suggested that Matthew had in mind the larger text of Jeremiah 19:1-13 and used some phraseology from Zechariah 11:12-13.[33]

There are many allusions to Jeremiah in the New Testament as well, although allusions are somewhat slippery to pin down. Jesus' prayer in Gethsemane to be freed from the cup is an allusion to the Old Testament concept of the cup of God's wrath against sin as detailed in Jeremiah 25:15-29 and 51:7 as well as Isaiah 51:17-23. This cup is also mentioned in Revelation 14:10; 15:7; 16:19; 17:2,4; 18:3.

Scholars have said that the apostle Paul patterned his ministry after Jeremiah. They point to the connections between Jeremiah 1:5,7-8 and Galatians 1:15, Acts 26:17, and Acts 18:9-10. Paul was set apart before birth, was confident God would rescue him from danger, and was admonished not to be afraid.

Jesus and the apostles were educated in the Old Testament, and it is no surprise to find not only many quotes but numerous allusions in the New Testament. The book of Jeremiah had a profound impact on both the theology and language of the New Testament.

---

[32] See also the allusion in 2 Corinthians 3:3 (tablets of the heart and tablets of stone) and the reference to an eternal covenant in Hebrews 13:20 which is a citation of Jeremiah 32:40.

[33] See D.A. Carson, "Matthew," in *The Expositor's Bible Commentary*, ed. by Frank E. Gaebelein (Grand Rapids: Zondervan, 1984), 8:563.

LAMENTATIONS

HISTORICAL AND CULTURAL BACKGROUND

The setting is the destruction of the city of Jerusalem by the Babylonians in 587 B.C. (2 Kings 25; Jeremiah 39). The two decades from 609 to 587 were a calamitous series of misfortunes for the little state of Judah and her capital city. The good king Josiah who had led the state to independence and prosperity in his short reign was killed in battle with the Egyptians at Megiddo in 609 B.C. (2 Kgs 23:28-30). In an instant, Judah lost her independence and began a downward spiral. The Egyptians removed Josiah's son, Jehoahaz, who had succeeded him, demanded tribute, and put another son of Josiah, Eliakim (renamed Jehoiakim; 609–598 B.C.), as their own puppet on the throne. During Jehoiakim's eleven year reign the Babylonians became the ruling power in Mesopotamia. Nebuchadnezzar defeated Egypt at Carchemish in 605 and expanded his control into Palestine. In 601 when Egypt defeated Babylon, Jehoiakim turned to Egypt for assistance and rebelled against Babylon (2 Kgs 24:1). In 598 the Babylonian king, Nebuchadnezzar, arrived in Judah. Jehoiakim died three months before Jerusalem fell (on the way to exile? 2 Chr 36:6), and his son, eighteen-year-old Jehoiachin, was put on the throne. The hapless Jehoiachin was taken prisoner to Babylon where he remained in prison for 37 years (2 Kgs 24:10-12; 25:27). Nebuchadnezzar took booty and thousands of leading people (including Ezekiel) to Babylon (2 Kgs 24:13-14,16) and put his own puppet on the throne, the uncle of Jehoiachin, Mattaniah, whom he renamed Zedekiah. Zedekiah was a weak king, easily swayed by competing parties in Jerusalem. Within a decade he was persuaded to rebel against Babylon, despite Jeremiah's warnings. This time, 588–87, Nebuchadnezzar came with a vengeance and destroyed the city of Jerusalem and the Temple. He also carried all but the poorest of the land into exile. The once-favored city and the chosen people of God were abandoned and devastated. According to Jeremiah and other prophets this was God's judgment on Judah's apostasy and rebellion. Lamentations was written in this atmosphere of crisis, destruction, and loss of God's favor. Judah has lost her Temple, king, and land.

TEXT AND AUTHOR

The book, along with many other biblical books, is anonymous. Jewish tradition attributed authorship to Jeremiah (*Baba Bathra* 15a), and the Septuagint and Latin Vulgate followed suit. In 2 Chronicles 35:25 Jeremiah is said to have composed laments over the deceased king, Josiah, and these were written in the "Laments." Also, Jeremiah occasionally uttered emotional responses over the plight of the people (9:1), and lived through the destruction of Jerusalem. Therefore, it is not surprising that some would ascribe authorship to him. However, the text does not demand Jeremiah as the author.

The style of the book suggests it was written by one author who lived close to the time of the destruction of the city and was eyewitness to its ruins. The author was one who cared deeply about the city and was devastated by its collapse and destruction.

STRUCTURE

The book of Lamentations occurs in different places in the Jewish and Christian canons. In the Jewish canon it is placed in the third section, the "Writings," (Kethubim) after Qoheleth (Ecclesiasties) and before Esther, or fourth in what was known as the five Megilloth or Rolls.[1] These were the five books traditionally read in the synagogue at the festivals. Lamentations was read on the ninth of Ab (July/August) which commemorated the destruction of the Jerusalem Temple in 587 B.C.[2] The Septuagint (c. 250–200 B.C.) attributed the book to Jeremiah and placed it after his book. The Christian canon kept this arrangement. Its title in the Hebrew Bible

---

[1]The order is Ruth, Song of Solomon, Ecclesiastes, Lamentations, and Esther in the text behind the popular Hebrew Bible, *BHS*. Another Jewish tradition places it third.

[2]Zechariah 7:1-7 seems to reflect that this custom began soon after the fall of the city.

is אֵיכָה (*'êkāh*, "how" or "in what way") which is the first word in 1:1; 2:1; and 4:1. Later Jewish scholars called it *Qinoth* which means "Dirges" and the Septuagint followed with *Threnoi* ("Dirges").

Lamentations is a short book, only five chapters long. The organizing principle of the book is the poetic acrostic in which each line or group of lines in a poem begins with succeeding letters of the alphabet. Since the Hebrew alphabet has twenty-two letters, each chapter of Lamentations has twenty-two strophes, or stanzas (which match the verses; chapters 1, 2, 4 and 5), or sixty-six strophes (chapter 3). The chapters, however, are not uniform in length because of the way the acrostic structure is applied. Each strophe in chapters 1 and 2 has three lines with the first line in each strophe beginning with a letter of the alphabet.[3] In chapter 3 each strophe also has three lines but the lines of each strophe begin with the appropriate letter, not just the first line.[4] Chapter 4 follows the pattern of chapters 1 and 2 except that each strophe has two lines. Chapter 5 is not an acrostic but has twenty-two lines (verses), so it maintains the emphasis on twenty-two.

The reason for the popularity of the acrostic is not clear. It may have aided in memory, it may have intended to convey that the subject had been completely covered, from "A to Z," or it may have been an aesthetic or artistic way of imposing limits and form on the expression of grief.[5] Though this seems a rigid pattern, the poet was able to express himself in a vivid manner, and the acrostic serves to add further punch to his language.

Each poem (chapter) has its own individuality and emphasis. The first poem pictures personified Jerusalem mourning over her destruction, first in the third person (vv. 1-11) and then in the first person (vv. 12-22). The second poem continues the theme but from the perspective of the author as he describes the wrath of God against

---

[3] An anomaly occurs in that the Hebrew letters ע (*'ayin*) and פ (*pe*) in chapters 2, 3 and 4 are in reverse order.

[4] The 66 verses come from the fact that for some reason each line has been designated a verse. This chapter could also have been structured with just 22 verses as chapters 1 and 2. This seems to have been the intention of the author. Psalm 119 has eight line strophes for each letter and each of the eight lines begin with the appropriate letter. There are many acrostic Psalms, but none so elaborate as Psalm 119, or Lamentations.

[5] Norman Gottwald, *The Hebrew Bible: A Socio-Literary Introduction* (Philadelphia: Fortress, 1985), p. 541. Gottwald prefers a combination of the latter two reasons. See also Delbert Hillers, *Lamentations*, AB (New York: Doubleday, 1972), p. xxvi.

Jerusalem. It concludes with an admonition to the people to cry to God and an appeal to God to consider their plight (vv. 18-22). The third poem personifies the nation and speaks in the first person. It adds a reflection on the mercy and compassion of God. The fourth poem describes the condition of the people in the besieged Jerusalem before it fell and lays the blame for their plight on the prophets and priests. The last poem describes the destitute condition of the exiles and appeals to God for restoration. The fifth poem is marked by a much higher incidence of synonymous parallelisms than the other four. An analysis of the five poems suggests that the focus is on the third which includes the strong expression of hope in the middle.[6]

GENRE

The book is dominated by the lament form which apparently has its own style, the so-called *qinah*. This style is characterized by a special meter in which the second half of a parallel line is shorter than the first half, a phenomenon referred to as a 3:2 meter. This gives the line a definite rhythm, sometimes called a "limping" rhythm. But this form is also found in nonlament poetry.[7]

The most common style in Lamentations seems to be the funeral dirge, usually sung at the funeral of a person. The earliest examples are from David (2 Sam 1:17-27 — over Saul and Jonathan; and 2 Sam 3:33-34 — over Abner). In Lamentations the form has been applied to the city rather than the individual.[8] The prophetic books contain several examples of dirges as a part of declarations of judgment in which the dirge is ironic or mocking (Amos 5). The nation is considered as good as dead.[9]

The lament in Lamentations, though often depicted as from an individual, is communal in nature, representing the whole nation.

---

[6]Gottwald, *The Hebrew Bible*, p. 542; Dillard and Longman, *Introduction*, pp. 308-309.

[7]Scholars debate if there is such a thing as meter in Hebrew poetry. Some count syllables, some count accents. There is no consensus on the matter.

[8]The lament was not unique to Israel in the ancient world. See W.C. Gwaltney, "The Biblical Book of Lamentations in the Context of Near Eastern Lament Literature," in *Scripture in Context II*, ed. by W.W. Hallo, J.C. Moyer, and L.G. Perdue (Winona Lake, IN: Eisenbrauns: 1983), pp. 191-211.

[9]Hillers, *Lamentations*, p. xxvii doubts that the dirge genre fits Lamentations.

This lament style is popular in the Psalms (see Ps 44, 60, 74, 79, 80 which especially reflect defeat in battle). Psalm 137 reflects an exilic background. However, the Lamentations also include other types of expression, including expressions of trust (3:20-24), the meaning of suffering (3:25-39), and prayer (5:1,20-22).

THEOLOGICAL THEMES

The main theme of Lamentations is firmly grounded in covenant theology. The covenant demanded obedience that would bring God's blessing, as often stated in Deuteronomy. But disobedience would bring God's curses and ultimate destruction (Deut 28:15-68). Lamentations is a response to this consequence of Judah's disobedience. This struck the people of Jerusalem so hard because they had confidence in a Zion theology that seemed to counter Deuteronomy. This theology, based in Isaiah, held that all who trusted in Zion would be safe (Isa 14:32; 31:4-5; 33:20-22; 37:35). Jeremiah's message of the destruction of Jerusalem was met with strong opposition because of this Zion theology (Jeremiah 26). But when the covenant theology of Deuteronomy proved true, it seemed to some that God had not kept his word. Therefore, the people felt the laments were a proper response. God was fighting against Judah, not for her (Lam 2:4-5). Lamentations deals with the problem of national suffering, as opposed to Job which deals with individual suffering.

The awful fact that Jerusalem's suffering could have been avoided seems to have finally become clear. Judah had the example of the northern kingdom to reflect on, and Jeremiah's warnings were specific enough. God's word was vindicated, and it was left to the survivors to recognize that he was righteous (1:18). But it still was difficult to deal with this reality. However, this recognition led to a confession of sin, a recognition that the suffering was justified (1:5,6,14,18-19,22).

Lamentations gave form and shape to mourning for the Judeans (Zechariah 7). It provided a vehicle for bringing to God their grief, despair, and pain. This had the positive effect of negating self-righteousness and making it clear that they were under the judgment of God. The laments expressed the depths of anguish but were addressed to God. God may be the one who punishes, but he also is the only one who cares about their grief.

Therefore, there are sparks of hope in Lamentations. As in the laments in the Psalms, eventually lamenting to God leads one to reflect on the greatness and goodness of God and hope creeps in. So 3:22-33 expressed the assurance that God will not abandon those who turn to him for help. His mercies are fresh every day. Israel has sinned but God will forgive and restore her (see also 3:57,58; 4:22; 5:21,22).

NEW TESTAMENT CONNECTIONS

There are no quotes or apparent allusions from Lamentations in the New Testament, though there might be an allusion to 3:45 in 1 Corinthians 4:13. In the New Testament Jesus is the one who laments and suffers. He wept over Jerusalem (Luke 19:41-44), and he prayed in anguish that God's cup of wrath be taken from him (Luke 22:39-46). On the cross he cries out from a lament Psalm, Psalm 22:1. Otherwise, there is little about lamenting in the New Testament. Because Jesus takes on himself the wrath of God against sin, there is no more suffering for it. God has demonstrated once and for all that he will not abandon his people. The New Testament does talk about suffering, but it is the suffering of the followers of Jesus who suffer for their faith.

EZEKIEL

HISTORICAL AND CULTURAL BACKGROUND

The book of Ezekiel contains fourteen precisely dated passages including the opening verses. Ezekiel's vision in chapter 1 is dated to the thirtieth year, the fourth month, the fifth day of the month (1:1). This is further defined in verse 2 as the fifth year of King Jehoiachin's reign which would be 593 B.C. The thirtieth year is not explained further but the most reasonable interpretation is that it refers to the thirtieth year of Ezekiel's life.[1] This means that Ezekiel was born in 623 B.C. during King Josiah's reign and was a contemporary of Jeremiah in Jerusalem and Daniel in Babylon. He was born and lived through the chaotic last years of the kingdom of Judah. He was taken captive to Babylon in the second deportation in 597 B.C.[2] The date he received his first vision in 592 B.C. corresponds to the year after the events described in Jeremiah 27–28.

Josiah came to the throne at age eight in 640 following the assassination of his father Amon, and the subsequent execution of the assassins. Within eight years, by 631, he had begun a reform movement, and by his twelfth year he began to purge the country of pagan worship (2 Chr 34:3).

In Josiah's eighteenth year, while the Temple was being cleaned as a part of the reform, a scroll of the law was found (probably part or most of the book of Deuteronomy, though this is strongly debat-

---

[1] Some have suggested that it refers to the thirtieth year after Josiah's reform but, if so, certainly the author would have said so. Others have tried to emend the text to third year or thirteenth year. Still others have suggested it refers to the thirtieth year of Jehoiachin's reign and to the final editing of the book. But if this is so, then verse 2 contradicts verse 1. It seems unlikely an editor would leave such a glaring contradiction. See John B. Taylor, *Ezekiel*, TOTC (Downers Grove, IL: InterVarsity, 1969), pp. 36-39, for more details.

[2] There was an earlier deportation in 605/604 that included Daniel (Dan 1:1ff.).

ed; 2 Kings 22; 2 Chr 34:8-21). This led to further reforms, including a magnificent celebration of the Passover (2 Kings 23).

The year 612 is an important peg date in the history of the ancient Near East. After struggling for years against the coalition of Medes and Babylonians, Nineveh, the capital of Assyria, fell. Survivors fled west to Haran, where Psammetichus and Egypt joined the coalition. In 610 Haran fell and Assyria came to an end. Psammetichus died that same year. Neco II succeeded his father, and, determined to assert Egyptian influence in Palestine, marched to Carchemish to try to help the remnant of the Assyrians against Babylon.

Josiah decided to intercede and met Neco at Megiddo (which Josiah now controlled), apparently to resist Neco's attempt to gain power. Josiah was killed, and his body was brought to Jerusalem (2 Kgs 23:28-30). In one tragic moment Judah lost her independence and bright future. Josiah's son, Jehoahaz II, took the throne, but he was removed within three months by Neco and taken captive to Egypt. (Neco, by the way, was too late to help the Assyrians.) Eliakim, Jehoahaz's brother, renamed Jehoiakim by Neco, was put on the throne as a vassal to the Egyptians. Jehoiakim was a self-indulgent king who let the reforms of Josiah lapse and pagan cults returned to Judah. Jeremiah condemned the king for his selfish, grand ways (Jer 22:13-19). Egypt remained in control of Palestine and Syria for a few years as Babylon secured its eastern areas.

In 605 Neco advanced to Carchemish in the north of Syria apparently to consolidate his power, but he was completely routed by the Babylonians under Nebuchadnezzar II. In 604 Nebuchadnezzar marched into the Palestinian coastal plain and sacked Ashkelon. Jehoiakim submitted to Babylon. Later (601) the Babylonians marched to Egypt but were firmly resisted. Jehoiakim apparently used the occasion to renege on his pledge to Babylon (2 Kgs 24:1).

In 598/97 Nebuchadnezzar invaded Palestine. Jehoiakim died just before the attack on Jerusalem, and Jehoiachin, his son, became king. He was king only three months when the Babylonians conquered Jerusalem and took him captive to Babylon, where he remained in custody for thirty-seven years, until released and given a stipend by the king of Babylon (2 Kgs 25:27-30).[3] Nebuchadnezzar also carried

---

[3]Deciphered Babylonian documents from the 590s B.C., specifically a ration tablet from that time, refers to Ya'u-kinu king of the land of Yahudu', a clear reference to Jehoiachin.

off treasure and other captives, including Ezekiel, the queen mother, princes, mighty men, and smiths and craftsmen (2 Kgs 24:14). He put Mattaniah, Jehoiachin's uncle, on the throne, renaming him Zedekiah. However, Ezekiel 1:2 suggests that Ezekiel and the exiles still considered Jehoiachin the legitimate king.

Zedekiah was a weak ruler, afraid of his advisors and drawn to Jeremiah. His reign was a time of continuous political intrigue with pro-Babylon, pro-Egyptian, and pro-independence parties jockeying for influence. An insurrection in Babylon in 595/594 apparently led to a meeting of foreign ministers of Edom, Moab, Ammon, Tyre, and Sidon in Jerusalem to plot revolt (Jer 27:1-3). It came to nothing, but Judah decided to follow a course of seeking independence. Nebuchadnezzar returned in 588/87, besieged Jerusalem, sacked it, and carried off more captives and treasure. He also completely destroyed the city and Temple. In 581 another deportation was taken to Babylon, and Judah was subsumed under the province of Samaria.

Although Jeremiah and Ezekiel do not refer to each other, they were almost certainly acquainted with each other's preaching. Though Jeremiah was in Jerusalem and Ezekiel was in Babylon after 597, they addressed the same issues in similar ways.[4]

The referenced dates in Ezekiel mostly follow a chronological pattern as the following chart shows:

Reference	Event	Yr/mo/day	Modern date	Yr B.C.
1:1-2	Ezekiel's call	30(5)[5]/4/[6]5	July 31	593
8:1	Vision of idolatry in Jerusalem	6/6/5	Sept. 17	592
20:1	Deputation of elders	7/5/10	Aug. 14	591
24:1	Siege begins	9/10/10	Jan. 15	588
26:1	Oracle against Tyre	11/-/1[7]	Between Apr. and Apr.	587–586
29:1	Oracle against Egypt	10/10/12	Jan. 7	587
29:17	Babylon will get Egypt	27/1/1	Apr. 26	571

---

[4]See Taylor, *Ezekiel*, p. 35; Walther Zimmerli, *Ezekiel 1*, Hermeneia (Philadelphia. Fortress, 1979), pp. 11-15; and William L. Holladay, "Had Ezekiel Known Jeremiah Personally?" *CBQ* 63 (2001): 31-34. Holladay answers in the affirmative.

[5]The 30th year of Ezekiel's life was the 5th year of King Jehoiachin's exile as verse 2 explains. This was the basis of the rest of the dates in the book.

[6]Verse two does not list the month.

[7]No month is listed.

30:20	Oracle against Pharaoh	11/1/7	Apr. 29	587
31:1	Oracle against Pharaoh	11/3/1	June 21	587
32:1	Lament over Pharaoh	12/12/1	Mar. 3	585
32:17	Egypt to Sheol	12/(1)^8/15	Between Apr. and Apr.	586–585
33:21	News of the fall of Jerusalem	12/10/5	Jan. 8	585
40:1	Vision of the new Jerusalem	25/1/10	Apr. 28	573

If one sets apart the oracles against the nations in chapters 25–32, the other dates are in chronological order. Even in chapters 25–32 only 29:17 is out of order. So it looks as if there is an intentional, historical, and chronological plan to the book of Ezekiel. In this regard Ezekiel is similar to Haggai and Zechariah.

The geographical setting of the book is Babylon in Mesopotamia. Ezekiel reports that he was among the exiles in Babylon at the river Chebar (or Kebar, 1:3). Chebar is actually a canal off the Euphrates River north of the city of Babylon. It flowed sixty miles along the Euphrates before rejoining it near ancient Erech. It was a part of the vast canal system that extended the arable land in Mesopotamia beyond the two rivers and made life there possible. Specifically he was at Tel Abib (3:15) which literally means a mound of flood debris. Were the exiles located at a place which needed hard work to bring it back into productive use?[9] The exiles of this period numbered about 10,000 and included many political, military, and religious leaders, and craftsmen. It was Babylonian policy to settle exiles together in one place and it was certainly to Judah's exiles' advantage. In the later Persian period (fifth century) there is evidence that the exiles had succeeded in business and farming ventures.

The cultural background is also Mesopotamian. The creatures described in Ezekiel's vision in chapter one resemble winged creatures with human faces which are abundant in ancient Near Eastern art, especially from Assyrian sites. Many of these creatures were quadrupeds, winged bulls with human heads or lion bodies with human heads. These creatures usually represent lesser gods who

[8]Greek has "first month," Hebrew text does not list a month. It may assume the same date as 32:1.

[9]When the modern state of Israel established a new capital city on the Mediterranean coast they named it Tel Aviv (same name).

support the thrones of the greater gods. Also four-winged, eagle-headed human figures are attested. Some in the Persian period have human heads, four wings, and bull legs.[10] Four-faced creatures seem to be unique to the Ezekiel text however. The eyes in the wheels were probably sparkling gems to dazzle onlookers. Mesopotamian texts speak of levels in heaven, with each level formed of different colored stone. The middle heavens had stone of lapis lazuli (sapphire in many English translations). Therefore, the elements in the vision in chapter one can be understood within this Mesopotamian background. Many of the elements also reflect theophanies from other OT texts.[11] Ezekiel appropriated familiar motifs and symbols to explain the unexplainable, the appearance of God in Babylon.

TEXT AND AUTHOR

Ezekiel was the son of Buzi and a priest (1:3). Age thirty was when a priest entered service (Num 4:30), but Ezekiel would never serve in the Temple in Jerusalem.[12] He did, however, possess extensive knowledge of the Temple and its worship. His language also shows influence from the book of Leviticus, chapters 17–26.[13] His name means "God strengthens, makes strong," a most appropriate name under the circumstances.[14] Ezekiel and the exiles needed to know that God had not abandoned them in Babylon. He was married, but his wife died suddenly (24:15-18). He was forbidden to mourn her death, apparently as a symbolic action for the exiles that they should not mourn the fall of Jerusalem (24:1-3,22). The event was too tragic and stunning for any adequate expression of grief.

The book is very personal in nature. It is written entirely in the first person so that we participate with Ezekiel in his experiences.

---

[10]John H. Walton, Victor H. Matthews, and Mark W. Chavalas, *The IVP Bible Background Commentary: Old Testament* (Downers Grove, IL: InterVarsity, 2000), p. 690.

[11]Moshe Greenberg, *Ezekiel 1–20*, AB (New York: Doubleday, 1983), p. 58.

[12]This is perhaps the significance of the year 30 in 1:1. At an especially meaningful but unfulfilled time in his life when he should have anticipated serving in the temple in the presence of God, Ezekiel saw God in Babylon. This was a powerful manifestation for Ezekiel and all of the exiles.

[13] Zimmerli, *Ezekiel 1*, pp. 46-52, gives the details.

[14]The only other Ezekiel appears in 1 Chronicles 24:16 as the head of a priestly order.

Many of his messages required actions that involved strange behavior and personal suffering. He lay on his side for long periods of time (4:4-6), ate siege rations (4:9-17), shaved his head and beard (ch. 5), packed his bags and dug through a wall (12:1-7), set up a road sign (21:18-20), walked among bones of bodies in a valley (37:1-14), and joined two sticks together (37:15-17). Throughout, Ezekiel is addressed as "son of man," a term intended to point out his humanness in relation to God's holiness and glory.

Ezekiel has suffered at the hands of the critics also. For a time in the mid-twentieth century some scholars judged that Ezekiel exhibited behavior of someone with severe mental problems. He was variously described as psychotic, schizophrenic, epileptic, or paranoid. The most radical approach was a thorough analysis according to Freudian categories.[15] Others saw him as a mystic or as a physically sick person who eventually recovered.[16] Fortunately, this phase of interpretation has receded. Scholars recognize that other prophets exhibit some of the same behavior. They also point out that divinely directed symbolic actions are common among the prophets. Consequently, the cause of the action must be sought within the interchange between the prophet and God, and the intended result of the symbol, not in personality disorders.[17]

THE TEXT

The text of Ezekiel in the MT differs from the Septuagint. The latter is four to five percent shorter than the Hebrew text. The MT exhibits several pluses over the Greek, that is, short additions or glosses. Also the MT has a different arrangement of chapter 7 and a longer chapter 36. Whether this is because of common textual corruptions or different ancient editions is difficult to say.[18]

---

[15]Edwin C. Broome Jr., "Ezekiel's Abnormal Personality," *JBL* 65 (1946): 277-292. The well-known Karl Jaspers supported this diagnosis.

[16]See Zimmerli, *Ezekiel 1*, pp. 17-18, for a survey of views.

[17]The very idea that a modern scholar could analyze the personality of an author of an ancient text from a different culture is absurd.

[18]Though not a textual issue, it is interesting that a Jewish tradition suggested a different canonical order for the three major prophets. The Babylonian Talmud, *Baba Bathra* 14b, suggests the sequence: Jeremiah, Ezekiel, Isaiah. The reasoning is that "the book of Kings concludes with destruction, Jeremiah contains only destruction, Ezekiel begins with destruction and concludes with a promise of consolation, and Isaiah contains only promises

HISTORY OF INTERPRETATION

Until the early twentieth century Ezekiel escaped radical dissection by the critics. S.R. Driver observed that "No critical question arises in connexion with the authorship of the book, the whole from beginning to end bearing unmistakably the stamp of a single mind."[19] Further, he asserts that "[T]he literary style of Ezek. is strongly marked" and that "[T]he volume of his prophecies is methodically arranged, evidently by his own hand. . . ."[20]

This consensus was questioned in the first decade of the twentieth century by German scholars.[21] At first a few sections were assigned to another hand, but progressively more and more were considered not authentic to Ezekiel. Part of the reason was the fact that Ezekiel addressed at one time the exiles in Babylon and at another time the inhabitants of Jerusalem, and at times seemed to be observing events in Jerusalem (chs. 8–11). The many doublets in the book and the priestly rather than traditional prophetic emphases also were questioned. C.C. Torrey set the book in the third century B.C. and considered Ezekiel a fictional character. However, in the latter half of the twentieth century several scholars began to argue for a more traditional approach to the book and greater respect for the dates and references in the book. Work by C.G. Howie reversed the critical tide. Howie argued from archaeological and historical sources that the traditional date could be supported.[22] Greenberg argued for a holistic approach to the book. Zimmerli said that one must start with the dates in the book and that most are authentic. He finds only a few passages that were originally independent.

Greenberg observed that the unexamined assumptions of scholars have deeply influenced modern scholars. Some think only the poetic is original, some are controlled by the "universal prejudice" of original simplicity, and others have a prejudice that "equates authenticity with topical or thematic uniformity."[23] The proper way

---

of consolation: we thus join destruction to destruction and consolation to consolation."

[19]Driver, *Introduction*, p. 279.

[20]Ibid., p. 296.

[21]See Zimmerli, *Ezekiel 1*, pp. 6-8, for details.

[22]Carl Gordon Howie, *The Date and Composition of Ezekiel* (Philadelphia: SBL, 1950).

[23]Greenberg, *Ezekiel*, p. 20.

is to approach the text openly and listen to it humbly and patiently. The critic must not impose antecedent judgments on the text.

Given the setting of Ezekiel it is no surprise that he addresses both the exiles in Babylon and people in Jerusalem. The exiles in Babylon were the elite of Jerusalem and were intensely interested in what was happening there. Furthermore, Jeremiah 29 makes it clear that the exiles hoped for a rapid return to the Promised Land. Jeremiah goes to great lengths to emphasize that this is not the case. They must settle down for the long haul. Ezekiel addresses these same issues. Therefore, the explicit setting of the book in Babylon with its message for both the exiles and the city of Jerusalem must be taken seriously.[24]

STRUCTURE

The structure of the book of Ezekiel is easily discerned. It falls into three major sections with chapters in each section addressing different topics.

    I. Judgment on Judah and Jerusalem — 1:1–24:27
      A. Ezekiel's call — 1:1–3:27
      B. Symbolic actions and the destruction of Jerusalem — 4:1–5:17
      C. Judgment on idolatry — 6:1-14
      D. The end has come — 7:1-27
      E. The defiled Temple is abandoned — 8:1–11:25
      F. Parables and allegories of judgment — 12:1–17:24
      G. Individual responsibility — 18:1-32
      H. More parables and allegories of judgment — 19:1–24:27
    II. Oracles against the Nations — 25:1–32:32
      A. Ammon, Moab, Edom, Philistia — 25:1-17
      B. Tyre — 26:1–28:26
      C. Egypt — 29:1–32:32
   III. Restoration of Judah and Jerusalem — 33:1–48:35
      A. Ezekiel as watchman — 33:1-33
      B. The shepherds of Israel — 34:1-31
      C. Against Mount Seir (Edom) — 35:1-15
      D. Israel blessed and renewed — 36:1-38
      E. The valley of dry bones and the two sticks — 37:1-28
      F. Gog and Magog — 38:1–39:29

---

[24]Ibid., pp. 15-16.

GENRE

One reason the book of Ezekiel challenges the interpreter is because of its many different genres. Interpretation requires sensitivity to the picturesque language and style of the book. The book is full of vivid allegories.[25] We find allegories of the vine (ch. 15), Yahweh's unfaithful wife (ch. 16), eagles (ch. 17), a lioness (ch. 19), a vineyard (ch. 19), a sword (ch. 21), two sisters (ch. 23), and a caldron (ch. 24). Ezekiel engages in many symbolic actions (see above). We also find visions (chs. 1–3; 8–11; 37; 40–48) in which Ezekiel may be transported to a different location (Jerusalem or the valley of bones). Ezekiel includes a historical-theological survey of Israel's history (ch. 20), legal sayings (chs. 14; 18; 22), proverbs (ch. 18), priestly and ritual information (chs. 43; 44; 45), disputation oracles (ch. 33), and funeral laments (chs. 19; 27; 32).[26]

One outstanding characteristic of the style of Ezekiel is the repeated reference to the "son of man." It is God's favorite designation for him (see 2:1,6,8, etc.).[27] It apparently is God's way of stressing Ezekiel's human nature as his agent in contrast to God as the source of the message. Also, the phrase emphasized to Ezekiel that he was but a man and that anything he did for God was by the power of the Spirit.[28]

---

[25]Both allegory and symbolic actions are unusual among the prophets though not totally absent. This contributes to the difficulty of interpreting Ezekiel.

[26]See Daniel Block, *The Book of Ezekiel*, NICOT (Grand Rapids: Eerdmans, 1997), 1:15-16, for a more detailed listing.

[27]The phrase as a form of address to Ezekiel occurs over 90 times in the book.

[28]The phrase is used in Daniel 7:13 with special significance. There it refers to one who will be given everlasting dominion over all nations. In the New Testament the phrase is Jesus' favorite way of referring to himself. It was not a common Messianic title and Jesus seems to be stressing his humanity, but the ambiguity of the phrase made it possible for the spiritually astute to gain intimations of Jesus' Messianic mission.

THEOLOGICAL THEMES

The theology of Ezekiel is very complex as one might expect from a prophet who is intensely engaged in speaking God's message to God's people in such a chaotic time. The hopes for the continuation of the Davidic dynasty and the nation had collapsed, and the promises to Abraham seemed at an end. The people needed to hear a fresh message that God had not abandoned his promises, but the presentation took on a new form. In what has been called apocalyptic language, God asserted his rulership over all kingdoms and nations, and his plans to bring both Israel and all nations under that rulership.

Two major themes stand out: judgment and restoration. But they are presented in a variety of ways.

1. The first task Ezekiel faced was to establish the sovereign rule of God over Israel and the nations. Therefore, chapter one confronts the reader at once with a vision of God's overwhelming glory and the presence of his throne in Babylon. The cherubim, pictured as anthropoid beings, support the throne. Though many of the symbols in the vision come from the Mesopotamian culture, Ezekiel makes it clear that they are only representative of a spiritual reality. All that he can see is "the appearance of the likeness of the glory of the LORD" (1:28b). In a sense God and Israel have come full circle for it was in Mesopotamia that God appeared to Abram to call him to Canaan.

God's immanence is crucial to the exile's understanding of him. Though they are where they are because of sin, it does not mean God has abandoned them. They are still accountable to him, and he is still working on their behalf. He is not confined to the Temple nor is his power confined to the land of Israel. Thus, when Ezekiel sees the glory of God leaving the Temple (ch. 10), it is a message to Israel that the destruction of the Temple has nothing to do with God's lack of power, presence, or relevance. He withdraws because it has become a place of idolatry and is ripe for judgment. The fact that his glory returns to the new Temple shows that he expects once again to be worshiped there in obedience (ch. 43).

A favorite term of Ezekiel for God is "glory of Yahweh." This refers to Yahweh's splendor, and as a priest Ezekiel was likely influenced by the references to the appearance of Yahweh in the Pentateuch (1:28; 3:12,23; 8:4; 9:3; 10:4,18; 11:22-23; 43:2,4-5; 44:4; see Exod 24:16,17; 40:34-35; Lev 9:6,23; Num 14:10,21,22; 16:19,42). Everything that will be done will be for God's glory, including judgment and restoration. Both attest to the righteous and holy character of God that Israel and the nations must acknowledge.

God's desire is that the people know him. Everything that he is doing is aimed to produce an intimate relationship with him. Therefore, the phrase "that they may know that I am the Lord" occurs approximately sixty times in the book. This could be called the major theme of the book.[29] God's acts of divine judgment are designed to create this knowledge. God brings judgment on both Israel and the nations so that they will know (Israel, 6:7,10; 11:10,12; 12:15; 13:14; 17:21; 22:16; the nations, 28:22; 29:6; even Gog, 38:23). But he also will restore Israel to the land and to their former blessings, and rescue them from false leaders (34:27) so that they will know (20:42; 36:11; 37:6). For this reason also he will reestablish his covenant with them (16:62).

2. Israel is described in vivid ways as a sinful people ripe for punishment because they have broken the covenant. Even though language of the covenant is sparse in Ezekiel the covenant is in the background. All the announcements of judgment presuppose the covenant and its demand for obedience. In three passages, chapters 16, 20, and 23, Ezekiel demonstrates that historically Israel has persisted in unfaithfulness and rebellion. In chapter 16 Israel is the foundling whom God rescues, raises, and at the proper age enters into a covenant relationship (marriage) with. In return Israel played the harlot with other gods and nations; that is, she violated covenant faithfulness. In chapter 20 Ezekiel suggests that Israel had continually cycled through times of rebellion and disobedience. From the beginning they had rebelled and refused to forsake the idols of Egypt (v. 8). Even in the wilderness after receiving the law and the Sabbath as a sign, they rebelled (vv. 13,21). When they received the gift of the land, they insisted on worshiping in the Canaanite fashion rather than remaining obedient (v. 28). In chapter 23 Israel is also seen as sinful from the beginning. She played the harlot even while in Egypt. Judah might have thought that since Israel went into captivity years earlier she was better than her sister. But she was not (v. 11). The same spirit of unfaithfulness controlled them both. Some of the expressions Ezekiel uses are vivid and vulgar, but they leave no doubt of Judah's guilt. They should have been shamed but were not.

---

[29]Eugene H. Merrill, "Ezekiel," in *A Biblical Theology of the Old Testament*, ed. by Roy B. Zuck (Chicago: Moody Press, 1991), p. 367.

Chapter 8 details the deviations that were going on in the Temple. Syncretism and idolatry were rampant. In secret rooms images were worshiped, at the gate of the Temple the Babylonian goddess of fertility was worshiped, and even in the inner court of the Temple pagan rites to the sun were practiced (vv. 8ff.,14,16). These pagan acts were abominations to the holy God. But the idolatry was not just external, the people had "set up idols in their hearts" (14:3). This was apostasy in its worst form, and God raised up Ezekiel, and other prophets, to confront the people. But there were other prophets in Ezekiel's time who tried to cover over the grave abominations of the people. They did not speak for God but spoke from divination, itself an abomination (13:1-16). They had no clue what the true message was, preaching the totally inappropriate message of peace (v. 16; cf. Jer 23:17).

Ezekiel also lists specific covenant violations besides idolatry. They have treated parents with contempt, oppressed the poor and alien, profaned the Sabbaths, committed incest and adultery, taken bribes, and charged interest (22:6-12). Breaches of the covenant could not be more obvious. God had no choice but to implement the curses of Deuteronomy 28:15-68.

3. Ezekiel shares with the other prophets messages of judgment on the nation. The only response God could make to sin was to execute punishment on the sinners. Though portrayed in many ways, the judgment was focused on the destruction of Judah and Jerusalem and the subsequent exile. As noted above there was a strong tendency among the exiles to downplay their circumstances and wish for a rapid return to the land. Jeremiah dealt severely with this issue (ch. 29), but there were apparently prophets predicting swift return. The first word of Ezekiel is judgment (4:1-3), the sign of a siege of Jerusalem. The king of Babylon was the sword of the Lord, his instrument to carry out the purpose of God (21:19). The image of fire is also used throughout the OT to suggest the devastating destruction that God would bring. This too suggests armies and sieges, for a fallen city was customarily burned (ch. 15; 20:45-49). These images make it clear the coming destruction was sure (ch. 12) and complete. The actual fall of Jerusalem is recorded about halfway through the book (33:21).[30]

---

[30]If one removes the oracles against foreign nations and considers only the material addressed to the covenant people.

Exile was the consequence of the Babylonian invasion. The city was a pot from which the people would be taken and given to the sword and to exile (11:4-13). Judah was a vine planted in fertile ground but uprooted, transplanted, and struggling to survive in barren soil (19:10-14). The end had come (ch. 7). This part of the message is no surprise, for the whole book is addressed to the exiles.

4. Ezekiel articulated in clear terms the concept of individual responsibility, though he did not invent the idea.[31] Apparently the exiles were quoting a popular proverb so they could claim they were innocent sufferers, "The fathers eat sour grapes, and the children's teeth are set on edge" (18:2; see also Jer 31:27-30). However, Ezekiel counters, "It is only the person who sins that shall die."[32] Ezekiel makes his case by two hypothetical cases: a person who obeys the law in everything but has a son who does not, and a person who has a lawbreaking father, but who keeps the law. In each case the person who is disobedient suffers the punishment and no one else. A wicked son of a righteous father will be punished, but an obedient son of a wicked father will not be (chs. 19–20; in fact not even a Noah, Daniel, or Job could save their children, 14:14-16). Therefore, the exiles cannot say they are suffering unjustly. In fact, God is a gracious and merciful God, and if the wicked will repent, God will forgive them (chs. 21–22). The OT has a place for the collective sense of the people but that is not in view here.

5. But judgment and punishment were not the end of the matter. Precisely because God was gracious and merciful, he provided for the survival of a remnant. This concept goes back as early as Isaiah 10:20-23. In passages that detail the terrible judgment that God was initiating, Ezekiel includes messages of hope. God will spare some so that they may know he is the Lord (6:8-10). After decimating Judah with sword, famine, beasts, and plague, God will allow survivors (14:21-23). This concept laid the foundation for the theme of restoration.

6. Other prophets had looked beyond the exile to restoration as a consequence of God's mercy and grace. The paradigm was God's salvation first exhibited in the Exodus event (see Isaiah 40–66). In the future God would provide a new exodus. Ezekiel also uses the

---

[31]Compare, for example, all the laws in Exodus that hold individuals responsible for their actions, or that protect individuals from maltreatment.
[32]NRSV translation. The traditional "soul" here means "person."

Exodus experience as a paradigm. In 20:33-40 Ezekiel uses language directly from the book of Exodus to describe what God is going to do for the exiles. Specifically he will bring them out with "a mighty hand and an outstretched arm" and he will "bring you into the wilderness" (vv. 34b-35a). Further he will renew the covenant with them and bring them back to the land of Israel (vv. 37,42). So they will experience a new cleansing and a new beginning. As a shepherd God will search far and wide for his scattered flock (34:11-16), return them to the land, and make a covenant of peace with them there (34:25-31) which will be an everlasting covenant (16:60). More importantly God will bring them back to the land, purify them, and give them a new heart and a new spirit (36:25-26; 11:19). That is, he will establish a new covenant with them and a new relationship that will overcome the weaknesses of the old covenant (cf. Jer. 31:31-34). The restored people will have the inclination and the will to obey God. They will live in a restored land as well, like a new Eden (36:30,35). This restoration will involve new life and a new union of the nation (ch. 37).

7. God is the lord of foreign nations also. Therefore, Ezekiel, like many of the other prophets, addresses some of the other nations (chs. 25-32) and details the sins for which they will receive judgment. He is interested in those closest to Israel: Ammon, Moab, Edom, and Philistia (ch. 25) who mistreated Judah during the Babylonian crisis. But he is most interested in Tyre (chs. 26-28) and Egypt (chs. 29-32). Tyre is marked by pride, pride in its beauty and wealth (ch. 27). This pride seems to know no boundaries, for the king takes on godlike pretensions and elevates himself beyond all human limits (ch. 28). He worships himself. Therefore, Tyre and Sidon's power will be taken away.

Egypt will meet a similar fate for the same reasons. She and her rulers are arrogant, and the Pharaoh considers himself god (ch. 29). She venerates numerous idols but they will not save her from the one God of the universe (chs. 30; 31). Missing from the list is Babylon, who at the present is being used as God's sword to punish Israel. But from the other prophets, like Jeremiah (chs. 50-51), we know that God will execute justice on her as well.

8. Ezekiel has a dramatic eschatology (chs. 38-48). His view of the future has created some of the most varied interpretations of any OT passages. The messages of chapters 38-39 and 40-48 seem clear enough. Chapters 38-39 are similar to the oracles against the

nations in that they picture the nations coming against the land of
Israel, suffering defeat under God's judgment, and ending with
Israel restored to the land. Chapters 40–48 counter chapters 8–11.
They look forward to the destroyed Temple being perfectly rebuilt,
the priesthood, offerings, Sabbaths, and festivals being restored, and
the glory of God returning to the Temple. Refreshing water will flow
from the Temple to the desert, and new boundaries of the land and
the tribes will be established. Like chapters 1–3, chapters 40–48
come from a vision. These visions form an envelope around the
book of Ezekiel.

Scholars have offered several interpretive models for chapters
38–48. A purely literal model seems precluded by the location of the
new Temple on a very high mountain, the lack of many details for
the Temple, the difficulty of aligning the territory of the tribes with
real places in the land, and the unreality of the flowing water in
chapter 47. The symbolic Christian model which sees the vision fulfilled symbolically in the church is supported by the language from
these chapters used by the New Testament authors (see below). But
if this model precludes any real meaning for Ezekiel's contemporaries, then it must be adjusted. The dispensationalist model made
popular in the Schofield Reference Bible provides a combination of
a literal and futurist approach. It applies the passage to a Millennial
age following the so-called Church age when a literal Israel will once
again live in the land, rebuild the Temple, and observe the sacrifices
and rituals. But this model seems to misread the New Testament's
teaching on the work of Jesus Christ, the significance of his sacrificial death, and his atonement for the sins of all. It casts doubt on
God's consistent and progressive dealings with mankind and his
plan for the redemption of Jew and Gentile together. It falters on
attempting a literal interpretation of highly metaphorical passages.

An apocalyptic model recognizes the chapters as featuring symbolism, numerical symmetry, and highly figurative language that
attempts to portray truth about the future. Chapters 38–39 are clearly of this style, and chapters 40–48 should be understood in a similar way. This model fits the many allusions to Ezekiel in the eschatological passages of the New Testament, especially the book of
Revelation. God's plans for the future of Israel were formulated in
language and symbols that would be meaningful to Ezekiel the priest
and to his audience. In this model the message for the future is summarized as: the perfection of God's plan for his people, the central-

ity of worship in the new age, the abiding presence of the Lord in the middle of his people, the blessings that will flow from God's presence, and the orderly allocation of duties for God's people.[33]

When interpreting any of the prophets, we must be careful to adopt a model that begins with the original setting and genre of the text and progresses carefully to the New Testament. It is never legitimate to bypass the New Testament which over and over portrays Jesus Christ as the Messiah who fulfilled the OT. Modern newspapers do not make an effective interpretive grid for the OT.

NEW TESTAMENT CONNECTIONS

The book of Ezekiel is alluded to numerous times in the New Testament though there are no actual quotations. Well over half of the allusions occur in the book of Revelation.[34] Jesus is clearly the faithful shepherd and the Davidic Messiah of Ezekiel 34. He is also the source of life-giving water from whom streams of living water flow (John 4; 7:38-39). He was greater than the Temple (Matt 12:6) and the temple that could be built in three days (John 2:19). Jesus was the full glory of God revealed (John 1:14) and the radiance of God's glory (Heb 1:3).

Some of the numerous parallels between Ezekiel and Revelation can be noted in chart form.[35]

Ezekiel	Topic	Revelation
37	Resurrection	20:4-9
38–39	Battle with Gog and Magog	20:7-10
39:21-29	Judgment	20:11-15
40–48	New temple and new Jerusalem	21:1–22:5
47:1	River flowing	22:1
47:12	Stream with fruit trees	22:1-5
48:16-17	Measurements of the city	21:16-17

---

[33]Taylor, *Ezekiel*, p. 253.

[34]Allusions are difficult to count. Does one word or symbol constitute an allusion or must we have at least two words, or three? LaSor, Hubbard, and Bush (*Survey*, p. 478) count 65 allusions and quotes in the NT with 45 in Revelation. The UBS edition of *The Greek New Testament* lists 141 allusions with 84 in Revelation.

[35]There are many other allusions in Revelation also. For example, the figures in Ezekiel 1 have influenced verses in Revelation 4; 5; 6; 7; 18; and 21. The language of Ezekiel 26–27 has many influences in Revelation 18.

| 48:30-34 | Twelve gates | 21:12-13 |
| 48:35 | Name: Lord is there | 21:23; 22:4-5 —
God and lamb
are there |

But note these differences:

40–42	*Temple*	*21:22 – no need for one*
43:13-27	*New altar and sacrifices*	*None*
44	*New priesthood*	*None*
45	*Land divided*	*None*

John's vision for the future is structured in much the same way as is Ezekiel's. The only differences are those that involve worship, priesthood, and the specifics of land. They are missing because they were types fulfilled in Jesus and the church. The eschatology of John owes much to the book of Ezekiel, but his model of interpretation is to read it as apocalyptic and through the focal point of Jesus Christ as the center of God's redemptive plan.

DANIEL

The book of Daniel is named for its principal character who was exiled in Babylon with others of the nobility in 605 B.C. "Daniel" (דָּנִיֵּאל, *dānîyē'l*) means "God is my judge." The book's two languages (Hebrew/Aramaic) and genres (history/story; prophecy/apocalyptic) inspire both young and old and perplex the most audacious scholars, making it one of the most disputed books of the Old Testament.[1]

HISTORICAL AND CULTURAL BACKGROUND

"In the third year of the reign of King Jehoiakim of Judah, King Nebuchadnezzar of Babylon came to Jerusalem and besieged it" (1:1, NRSV). This precise dating (605 B.C.) sets the stage for all that follows and reflects the geopolitical dynamic extant for much of the ancient Near East's history. Syria-Palestine's location between Mesopotamia and Egypt along the trade route dictated that Mesopotamia and Egypt compete for control of the region, forcing its inhabitants to choose between the two powers. Understanding this process clarifies many of the actions taken by the biblical characters. Prophetic admonitions to trust God often went unheeded as the various kings attempted to play one nation off against the other (cf. Isa 30:1-2), as the Rabshakeh's speech to the inhabitants of Jerusalem illustrates.

---

[1]R. Rendtorff, *The Old Testament: An Introduction* (Philadelphia: Fortress, 1986), p. 273. For a survey of the issues see: A.B. Rhodes, "The Book of Daniel," *StudBib* 6 (1952): 436-450; R.D. Wilson and R.K. Harrison, "Daniel, Book of," *ISBE*[2], rev. ed. by G.W. Bromiley (Grand Rapids: Eerdmans, 1979), 1:859; R.K. Harrison, *Introduction to the Old Testament* (Grand Rapids: Eerdmans, 1969), pp. 1105-1106; Dillard and Longman, *Introduction*, p. 329; E.J. Young, *An Introduction to the Old Testament* (Grand Rapids: Eerdmans, 1964), p. 360; G.L. Archer Jr., *A Survey of Old Testament Introduction* (Chicago: Moody, 1964), p. 365.

On what do you base this confidence of yours? Do you think that mere words are strategy and power for war? On whom do you now rely, that you have rebelled against me? See, you are relying on Egypt, that broken reed of a staff, which will pierce the hand of anyone who leans on it. Such is Pharaoh king of Egypt to all who rely on him. But if you say to me, "We rely on the LORD our God," is it not he whose high places and altars Hezekiah has removed, saying to Judah and to Jerusalem, "You shall worship before this altar"? Come now, make a wager with my master the king of Assyria: I will give you two thousand horses, if you are able on your part to set riders on them. How then can you repulse a single captain among the least of my master's servants, when you rely on Egypt for chariots and for horsemen? Moreover, is it without the LORD that I have come up against this land to destroy it? The LORD said to me, "Go up against this land, and destroy it" (Isa 36:4b-10 = 2 Kgs 18:19b-25, NRSV).

This problem of "Whom shall we trust?" repeated itself in the life of the various kings of Israel, specifically coming into play just prior to the Babylonian captivity.

When the Assyrian Empire began to crumble, Nabopolassar, king of Babylon, revolted against Assyria in 626 and established Babylon as the heir apparent to Assyria. Nineveh fell in 612, leaving the way open for the growth of Babylonian power. Egypt attempted to limit Babylon's influence by placing Jehoiakim on the throne as its vassal (2 Kgs 23:34-35). Judah remained under Egyptian control until 605. Nebuchadnezzar came against Jerusalem, besieged it, made Jehoiakim his vassal, and took to Babylon some of the Temple vessels and representatives of the royal family, including Daniel, Hananiah, Mishael, and Azariah (Dan 1:1-6). Jehoiakim submitted to Babylon for three years before he rebelled, believing Egypt would come to his aid (2 Kgs 24:1,7). Nebuchadnezzar responded in force, conquering Jerusalem in 598/7 and, upon the death of Jehoiakim (2 Kgs 24:6; Jer 22:19; 36:30), appointed a new king. Jehoiachin succeeded his father and surrendered (2 Kgs 24:12; 2 Chr 36:10; Ezek 17:12). Zedekiah became king (2 Kgs 24:17). Early in his reign Zedekiah maintained his vassal status serving Nebuchadnezzar (2 Chr 36:13; Ezek 17:12-14) but rebelled in 589/8 (2 Kgs 24:20). Nebuchadnezzar responded, destroying Jerusalem and exhiling its inhabitants (2 Kings 25).

Daniel served both Babylonian and Persian kings — Nebuchadnezzar (1–4), (Nabonidus)/Belshazzar (ch. 5), and Cyrus (10:1). Three Babylonian kings reigned between Nebuchadnezzar and (Nabonidus)/Belshazzar — Amel-Marduk (562–560, "Evil-Merodach" of 2 Kgs 25:27-30), Neriglissar (560–556), and Labashi-Marduk (556) — none of which Daniel mentions. Nebuchadnezzar's reign provides the background for chapters 1-4, Belshazzar and Darius the Mede's reigns provide the background for 5–8 and 9, while Cyrus's rule provides the background for 10–12. Cyrus, a Persian vassal, rebelled against his Median king Astyages in 550 and began the expansion of what would become the Persian empire. By 539, the dissatisfaction of Babylon's powerful Marduk priesthood (and probably the populace) with Nabonidus's devotion to the moon god Sin paved the way for Cyrus's general to take Babylon without a struggle, though Belshazzar was killed (5:30). One "Darius the Mede received the kingdom" (5:31).

From this foundation Cyrus launched the Persian empire which ruled the Near East for the next two centuries. Cambyses succeeded his father, expanding the empire, ultimately conquering Egypt. Cambyses' death provided opportunity for Persian vassals to revolt until Darius Hystaspes brought order and reorganized the empire. His son, Xerxes, expanded into Greece, but was ultimately defeated at Salamis in 479. Persian influence began a slow decline. Darius III became king in 336 when Greece was on the rise (Dan 7:5-6). Alexander the Great became master of the area by 327. In 323 Alexander died in Babylon leaving four generals to fight over his empire. Four kingdoms came into existence: Thrace, Macedonia, Ptolemaia, and Seleucia. The Seleucids and the Ptolemies fought for the next two centuries for control of Palestine each exerting power — Ptolemies, 301–200; Seleucids, 200–163 — until the Maccabean revolt against Antiochus Epiphanes IV, whose Temple desecration Daniel designated the "abomination of desolation" (9:27; 11:31; 12:11).[2]

HISTORY OF INTERPRETATION

Prior to historical criticism's rise in the late nineteenth century, most scholars accepted the historical and cultural background described in the book, which portrays people and events during the

---

[2]Cf. Dillard and Longman, *Introduction,* pp. 338-341.

days of the Babylonian Exile of the sixth century B.C. The beginning of the twentieth century witnessed the erosion of this view. Scholars embracing the new criticism believed the book's contents indicated a compositional date of the second century B.C. This second-century date suggested the book to be a fictional story, inaccurate in its historical statements referring to the sixth century, but reflecting the politics and theology of the Maccabean Revolt. This cleavage continues today and demands the following summary.

Critical scholars cited Porphyry's (A.D. 233–304) ancient argument as the forerunner of the new view, contending Daniel "to be a work that was actually composed in the second century B.C. and is thus a pseudonymous work that employs 'prophecy after the fact' (*vaticinium ex eventu*)."[3] This new interpretation opened the door for a host of prospects, one of the latest being "the author-compiler of Daniel was indeed the founder and Right Teacher of the Qumran-Essene community"![4] Evangelical scholars defend[ed] the traditional view against this new interpretation because it presupposes the impossibility of predictive prophecy (a miracle of words). Scholars who adopt the critical view must put their "faith" in prophecies written as history after the fact, believing the book contains numerous errors. Such "faith" (a) places the sovereignty of God at risk, (b) challenges divine inspiration, and (c) disputes the nature of Christ (cf. Matt 24:15-16; Mark 13:14; Luke 21:20).[5] These philosophical issues intensify the rhetoric of this ongoing debate, as Davies' comments illustrate.

> . . . [S]ome scholars . . . resort to suggesting that all this material [chaps. 7-12] is intended to vindicate the genuine predictions of the book by demonstrating the accuracy of the "predictions" already fulfilled. This is a sorry verdict on the book of Daniel as largely a deliberate fraud perpetrated on a (supposedly) gullible audience to serve, as it were, a meritorious end by untruthful means. For this assessment "liberal" scholarship is

---

[3]Dillard and Longman, *Introduction,* p. 331; cf pp. 330-332. See also Eissfeldt, *Introduction,* p. 520; S. Talmon, "Daniel," in *The Literary Guide to the Bible,* R. Altar and F. Kermode, eds. (Cambridge: Harvard University Press, 1987), p. 344.

[4]J.C. Trever, "The Book of Daniel," *BA* 48 (1985): 101.

[5]B.K. Waltke, "The Date of the Book of Daniel," *BSac* 133 (1976): 320, 329.

heavily criticised by conservative commentators, and here at least I would agree with them. It seems to me unlikely that the lively and varied presentations of the history can be explained in such a simple way; their bulk suggest that they serve a more important purpose than a mere show of feigned clairvoyance; and furthermore, I find it difficult to ascribe such gullibility to the original readers of the book. If there is gullibility in this case, it is more probably on the part of rationalistic critics.[6]

Therefore, "Until more is known about the psychic factors . . . involved in foresight and foretelling," the critical scholar should refrain from dismissing "out of hand the claim of the author to have experienced the visionary material recorded in the work."[7] The following represent the most significant areas of discussion.[8]

DANIEL 1:1 AND JEREMIAH 25:1

According to Daniel 1:1 Nebuchadnezzar came against Jerusalem "in the third year" of Jehoiakim's reign, while Jeremiah 25:1,9 and 46:2 state this event occurred in the "fourth year" of Jehoiakim. Recognition of the two methods of dating in the ancient Near East — accession/nonaccession year — resolves the problem.[9] Assuming Jeremiah used the nonaccession method harmonizes the two passages making the "third year" of Daniel 1:1 equal to the "fourth year" of Jeremiah 25:1,9 and 46:2. Further, Daniel records the taking of certain royal family members but does not mention the capture of Jerusalem in 605, thus agreeing with Jeremiah in which the city was still standing.[10]

---

[6]P.R. Davies, "Eschatology in the Book of Daniel," *JSOT* 17: (1980): 43.

[7]Harrison, *Introduction*, p. 1131.

[8]See also: Young, *Introduction*, pp. 362-364; J.E. McKenna, "Daniel," in *Old Testament Survey: The Message, Form, and Background of the Old Testament*, 2nd ed., ed. by W.S. LaSor, D.A. Hubbard, and F.W. Bush (Grand Rapids: Eerdmans, 1996), pp. 574-576; G.L. Archer Jr., "Modern Rationalism and the Book of Daniel," *BSac* 136 (1979): 129-130.

[9]D.J. Wiseman, "Daniel 1:1," in *Notes on Some Problems in the Book of Daniel*, ed. by D.J. Wiseman et al. (London: Tyndale, 1965), pp. 16-18; G.F. Hasel, "The Book of Daniel: Evidences Relating to Persons and Chronology," *AUSS* (1981): 47-49.

[10]See also: E.M. Yamauchi, "The Archaeological Background of Daniel," *BSac* 137 (1980): 3-4; Dillard and Longman, *Introduction*, pp. 333-334; Wilson and Harrison, "Daniel, Book of," *ISBE²*, 1:862-863; Harrison, *Intro-*

DANIEL'S USE OF "CHALDEAN"

Early critical scholars argued that Daniel's use of "Chaldean" in an ethnic sense (5:30), as well as the more restrictive "wise men" (1:4; 2:2,10; 3:8; 4:7; 5:7,11), occurred nowhere else and therefore reflects a date much later than the sixth century. This runs counter to the evidence: (a) Herodotus used the terms with both nuances (*His.* 1.181-83); (b) Isaiah (23:13; 43:14) and several Assyrian kings (Ashurnasirpal II [883–859 B.C.], Adad-Nirari III [811–783 B.C.]) used the term ethnically; (c) the use in 5:30 "may have derived from a completely differing origin . . . sounding like the name of the Chaldean nation."[11] So these two uses in Daniel accord with ancient Near Eastern usage of the ninth to the fifth centuries.[12]

NABONIDUS AND BELSHAZZAR

Early critical scholars denied the historicity of Daniel because the book mentions Belshazzar as a king of Babylon (5:1,2,9,22,29,30; 7:1; 8:1), but ancient Near Eastern documents refer to Nabonidus as the "King of Babylon" and Belshazzar as his son: "As for me, Nabonidus, king of Babylon . . . and as for Belshazzar, the eldest of my offspring."[13] Such texts indicate that Belshazzar ruled as king in his father's absence, thus harmonizing Daniel with known ancient Near Eastern facts and agreeing with Belshazzar's promise to make the successful interpreter of the writing "third in the kingdom" (5:7,16).[14]

---

duction, pp. 1112-1113; Archer, *Survey*, pp. 369-370; Young, *Introduction*, pp. 364-365.

[11]Archer, "Rationalism," pp. 136-137; cf. R.D. Wilson, *Studies in the Book of Daniel* (New York/London: G.P. Putman's Sons/Knickerbocker, 1917), pp. 319-341. Cited 8 June 2004.
Online: http://www.home.earthlink.net/~ironmen/wilson/studies_chapt17.htm.

[12]See also Wilson and Harrison, "Daniel, Book of," *ISBE²*, 1:864; Harrison, *Introduction*, pp. 1113-1114; Young, *Introduction*, pp. 365-366; Archer, *Survey*, p. 370; D.J. Wiseman, "Chaldea," *ISBE²*, 1:630-633; Yamauchi, "Background," pp. 5-6.

[13]P.-A. Beaulieu, trans., "Nabonidus' Rebuilding of E-Lugal-Galga-Sisa, The Ziggurat of Ur," *The Context of Scripture*, ed. by W.W. Hallo (Leiden: Brill, 1979–2003), 2.123B:313.

[14]See also: Dillard and Longman, *Introduction*, p. 333; Wilson and Harrison, "Daniel, Book of," *ISBE²*, 1:863; Harrison, *Introduction*, pp. 340-341, 1120; Young, *Introduction*, pp. 367-368; Archer, *Survey*, pp. 370-371; id. "Rationalism, pp. 134-135; Talmon, "Daniel," p. 344; Kitchen, *Reliability*, pp. 73-74; Waltke, "Date," pp. 328-329; Yamauchi, "Background," p. 6.

DARIUS THE MEDE

When Babylon fell, Belshazzar was executed and the sixty-two-year-old "Darius the Mede" became king (Dan 5:30-31[Heb 5:30–6:1]; 9:1). Though a major character in the book of Daniel, Darius's identity has no counterpart in the extrabiblical records, making his identification one of the thorniest problems found in Daniel research.[15] Four proposals have gained prominence. *(1) Rowley* argued no historical character known as "Darius the Mede" ever existed. Daniel's account of this individual, written much later, represents a "conflation of confused traditions."[16] The first "conflation" occurred when Darius Hystaspes reconquered Babylon in 520. A second "conflation" occurred when this information merged with Cyrus who was approximately sixty-two years old when Babylon fell. A third "conflation" occurred because passages such as Jeremiah 51:11,28 anticipated Babylon's destruction at the hands of the Medes, even though neither Cyrus nor Darius Hystaspes were Medes. To Rowley, therefore, the author of Daniel lived much later and did not have a proper understanding of the history of the Persian period. *(2) Whitcomb* argued Smith's translation of the Nabonidus Chronicle correctly differentiated between one "Ugbaru," who was associated with the fall of Babylon but died a few days after its capture, and one "Gubaru," who was appointed governor and is probably the individual designated "Darius the Mede."[17] *(3) Wiseman* identifies Darius with Cyrus, arguing that Darius took the name "Cyrus" as king of Babylon.[18] Using the analogy of 1 Chronicles 5:26, he translates Daniel 6:28 explicatively: "Daniel prospered into the reign of Darius, *even*

---

[15]For a detailed history of research see B.E. Colless, "Cyrus the Persian as Darius the Mede in the Book of Daniel," *JSOT* 56 (1992): 113-126; cf. J.M. Bulman, "The Identification of Darius the Mede," *WTJ* 35 (1972–73): 247-267.

[16]H.H. Rowley, *Darius the Mede and the Four World Empires in the Book of Daniel* (Cardiff: University of Wales, 1934), p. 54, see also pp. 55-60; cf. Dillard and Longman, *Introduction*, pp. 334-335.

[17]J.C. Whitcomb, *Darius the Mede: A Study in Historical Identification* (Grand Rapids: Eerdmans, 1959), pp. 10, 17, 21-22, 43-46; see also S. Smith, *Babylonian Historical Texts Relating to the Downfall of Babylon* (London: Methuen and Co., 1924), pp. 110ff.; Dillard and Longman, *Introduction*, pp. 335-336.

[18]D.J. Wiseman, "Darius the Mede," in *Notes*, pp. 12-16; cf. Dillard and Longman, *Introduction*, p. 336.

[rather than *and*] the reign of Cyrus the Persian."[19] *(4) Shea* identifies Darius with the general in the Persian army who conquered Babylon.[20] This individual died, not a few days after the battle (contra Whitcomb), but over a year later, allowing time for the general to serve as vassal king over Babylon. Though each of these historical probabilities contain difficulties, new discoveries may yet clarify the issue.[21] For now the extant evidence indicates "that 'Darius the Mede' was a real historical personage, whatever his true identity."[22]

NEBUCHADNEZZAR'S DISEASE

This disease (ch. 4), probably *boanthropy*, the delusion that one is an ox or cow,[23] does not occur in neo-Babylonian sources, although the Qumran document, "The Prayer of Nabonidus,"[24] preserves the view that Nabonidus suffered with this disease and that the author of Daniel substituted the name of Nebuchadnezzar for Nabonidus. This idea fails to explain (1) "why the author of Daniel . . . employed the material found in 4Q as the basis for ch. 4, and then . . . changed the entire nature of the disease as well as altering the names and the locale,"[25] (2) the lack of Near Eastern materials that describe Nabonidus as mentally ill, or (3) why the Prayer of Nabonidus "contains pathological aspects . . . unfamiliar to modern scientific medicine," but in Daniel "Nebuchadrezzar's madness is a well-attested psychotic condition."[26] So the identification of Daniel 4 with the Prayer of Nabonidus remains extremely unlikely. Evangelicals argue the Near

---

[19]Colless, "Cyrus the Persian," pp. 114-115, emphasis added.

[20]W.H. Shea, "Darius the Mede: An Update," *AUSS* 20 (1982): 236, 240-243; cf. K. Koch, "Dareios, der Meder," in *The Word of the Lord Shall Go Forth*, ed. by C.L. Myers and M. O'Connor (Winona Lake, IN: Eisenbrauns, 1983), pp. 289-299; Dillard and Longman, *Introduction*, pp. 336-337.

[21]Dillard and Longman, *Introduction*, p. 337.

[22]Wilson and Harrison, "Daniel, Book of," *ISBE²*, 1:863. For summaries of the problem see: Harrison, *Introduction*, pp. 192-193, 341-343, 1121-1123, 1128-1129; Talmon, "Daniel," p. 344; Yamauchi, "Background," pp. 8-9; Dillard and Longman, *Introduction*, pp. 334-337; Archer, *Survey*, pp. 371-374; id., "Rationalism," pp. 135-136; Young, *Introduction*, pp. 370-371.

[23]Wilson and Harrison, "Daniel, Book of," *ISBE²*, 1:863-864; cf. Harrison, *Introduction*, pp. 1114-1120.

[24]Cf. B.A. Levine and A. Robertson, trans., "The Prayer of Nabonidus," *COS*, 1.89:285-286.

[25]Wilson and Harrison, "Daniel, Book of," *ISBE²*, 1:864.

[26]Ibid.

Eastern materials' silence derives from the society's refusal to mention it except "in the vaguest way," while Hebrews such as Daniel would be free to circulate the story.[27] Three centuries of silence before Berossus (Josephus, *C. Ap.* 1:20) mentioned the issue seem to corroborate this interpretation.[28]

DANIEL AMONG THE "WRITINGS" AND BEN SIRA'S OMISSION

The Hebrew Bible locates Daniel among the writings rather than the prophets, indicating to critical scholars a Maccabean date. Evangelical scholars argue Daniel's social location as a court official took precedence over his function as a classical prophet. Ben Sira, writing about 180 B.C., omits Daniel from his catalogue of famous Israelites (Sir 49:1ff.), motivating critical scholars to argue Daniel was unknown by him.[29] The fact that Ben Sira does not mention other famous Israelites — Asa, Jehoshaphat, Ezra, Mordecai, etc. — *does not prove* these people did not exist; neither does Daniel's absence prove he did not exist. Finally, this argument does not account for the process by which within fifty-to-one-hundred years Daniel moved from an unknown individual to one who was famous enough to be mentioned in three of the four Maccabean books (1 Macc 2:60; 3 Macc 6:7; 4 Macc 12:11; 16:3,21; 18:13).[30]

LINGUISTIC DATA

These data focus on the characteristics of both the Hebrew and Aramaic and the influence of supposed foreign loanwords. Early critical scholars (e.g., Driver and Rowley) believed the Persian and Greek loanwords, together with the Hebrew and Aramaic language,

---

[27]Ibid., 1:863.

[28]See also Young, *Introduction,* p. 367; Talmon, "Daniel," p. 345; Yamauchi, "Background," pp. 7-8.

[29]K. Koch, "Is Daniel Also among the Prophets?" *Int* 39 (1985): 117-130; Koch is the exception; he dates the book in the Maccabean age, but shows it had a prophetic connection prior to its canonization.

[30]See also Young, *Introduction,* pp. 207, 369-370; Archer, *Survey,* pp. 368-369; id., "Rationalism," pp. 132-133; McKenna, "Daniel," p. 575; Talmon, "Daniel," pp. 344-345; D.E. Fox, "Ben Sira on OT Canon Again: The Date of Daniel," *WTJ* 49 (1987): 344-345.

established a date subsequent to Alexander's conquest of Palestine in 332.[31] New understandings of such Persian loanwords as *satrap* — derived from the Old Persian *kshathrapān* and *shatarpān* prior to Cyrus's conquest[32] — indicate Greek culture influenced the ancient Near East before the Neo-Babylonian Empire, making the argument that the Greek names for the musical instruments (Dan 3:5,7,10,15) pointed to the Maccabean period invalid.[33] The Hebrew of Daniel is very similar to that of Ezekiel, and the Aramaic closely resembles royal court Aramaic, which originated in the seventh century and ultimately spread throughout the ancient Near East.[34] Finally, Daniel's Aramaic specifically resembles the Elephantine Papyri (fifth–fourth centuries[35]), as well as the Aramaic of Ezra 4:7–6:18 and 7:12-26.[36]

DANIEL AND DAN'EL

In Ezekiel 14:14 and 20 God states that "Noah, Daniel, and Job . . . would save only their own lives by their righteousness," while 28:3-4 states the king of Tyre is "a mortal, and no god" though "wiser than Daniel." Evangelical scholars[37] believe Ezekiel's "Daniel" refers to the same individual as found in the book of Daniel. Cooke accepts this, but identifies the biblical Daniel as "a Jew who, by his

---

[31]Driver, *Introduction*, p. 508; H.H. Rowley, *The Aramaic of the Old Testament: A Grammatical and Lexical Study of Its Relations with Other Early Aramaic Dialects* (London: Oxford University, 1929), pp. 23ff.; H.H. Rowley, "The Bilingual Problem of Daniel," *ZAW* 50 (1932): 256-268.

[32]G.L. Della Vida, "The Phoenician God Satrapes," *BASOR* 87 (1942): 29-32.

[33]W.F. Albright, *From the Stone Age to Christianity* (Garden City, NY: Doubleday, 1957), p. 475.

[34]F. Rosenthal, *Die aramaistische Forschung seit Th. Nödeke's Veröffentlichungen* (1939; repr., Leiden: Brill, 1964), pp. 66ff.; H.L. Ginsberg, "Aramaic Studies Today," *JAOS* 42 (1942): 229-238; H.H. Schaeder, *Irainische Beiträge* (Halle, Saale: Max Niemeyer verlag, 1930–), 1:253.

[35]Archer, *Survey*, pp. 374-379; cf. id., "Rationalism," pp. 142-144.

[36]K.A. Kitchen, "The Aramaic of Daniel," in *Notes on Some Problems in the Book of Daniel*, ed. by Wiseman et al. (London: Tyndale, 1965), pp. 31ff., 59. See also Young, *Introduction*, p. 371; Wilson and Harrison, "Daniel, Book of," *ISBE²*, 1:860-861; Harrison, *Introduction*, pp. 1124-1127; McKenna, "Daniel," p. 574; Talmon, "Daniel," p. 343; P.W. Coxon, "The Syntax of the Aramaic of *Daniel*: A Dialectal Study," *HUCA* 48 (1977): 107-108, 121-122.

[37]Archer, "Rationalism," pp. 133-134; D.I. Block, *The Book of Ezekiel*, NICOT (Grand Rapids: Eerdmans, 1997–98), 1:447-450.

integrity and wisdom (28³. . .), rose to a high position at the Babylonian court," living "near the time of Ezekiel," whose "story" was "used by the author of *Daniel* to edify a later age."[38] Most critical scholars agree that "Daniel" refers to "Dan'el" of the fifteenth-century Ugaritic *Aqht* legend.[39] Because Job and Noah represent "devout men belonging to foreign nations."[40] Ezekiel employs them to move from the "sphere of the covenant people into one of world-wide range,"[41] to heighten "the picture of Jerusalem's guilt,"[42] or the like. Such interpretations remain problematic.[43] (1) "*Dny'l* and *dn'l* are variant spellings of the same name, and the fuller form *Da-ni-èl* is attested in the eighteenth-century-B.C. Mari Letters."[44] (2) The assertion that Ezekiel refers to the ancient Dan'el rather than his contemporary because Noah and Job are ancient figures runs counter to the fact that "Ezekiel does not attach much importance to exact patterns for enumeration."[45] For example, "the triad 'sword – famine – pestilence' (Ez. v 12, 17, vi 11, xii 16, xiv 12ff, 21) is so irregularly used that neither climax nor elevation can be established," indicating "the position of the name does not allow any clear-cut deductions."[46] (3) The interpretation of "an Israelite Daniel flanked by a pre-Israelite and a non-Israelite" remains "an equally satisfying theological construction" (Dressler), as Eichrodt's and Zimmerli's "worldwide view" interpretation.[47] (4) Because ". . . several thousands of years must have elapsed between the time of Noah and the appearance of the patriarch Job . . . there remains no problem whatever with the inclusion of a sixth-century Daniel as third paragon of piety a thousand years later than Job."[48] Perhaps these

---

[38]G.A. Cooke, *The Book of Ezekiel* (1936; repr., Edinburgh: T. & T. Clark, 1970), p. 153.

[39]W. Eichrodt, *Ezekiel* (Philadelphia: Westminster, 1970), pp. 188-189; Zimmerli, *Ezekiel 1*, p. 314; J. Day, "The Daniel of Ugarit and Ezekiel and the Hero of the Book of Daniel," *VT* 30 (1980): 174-184.

[40]Eichrodt, *Ezekiel*, p. 188.

[41]Zimmerli, *Ezekiel 1*, p. 314.

[42]Cooke, *Ezekiel*, p. 153.

[43]H.H.P. Dressler, "The Identification of the Ugaritic Dnil with the Daniel of Ezekiel," *VT* 29 (1979): 155-158.

[44]Block, *Ezekiel*, 1:448; cf., E. Lipiński, "Review of André Lacoque, *Le Livre de Daniel*," *VT* 28 (1978): 233.

[45]Dressler, "Identification," p. 156.

[46]Ibid.

[47]Ibid., p. 157; cf. Eichrodt, *Ezekiel*, p. 188; Zimmerli, *Ezekiel 1*, p. 314.

[48]Archer, "Rationalism," p. 133. See also: Block, *Ezekiel*, 1:449; H.-M. Wahl,

reasons influenced Rendtorff to identify the biblical Daniel with Ezekiel's Daniel (14:13-14,20; 28:3), but remain "uncertain whether there is any connection with the Dn'il mentioned in the texts from Ugarit."[49] Exactly why scholars make the Daniel/Dan'el connection remains a mystery, other than the supposition they desire to avoid any identification with the biblical Daniel.[50]

TEXT AND AUTHOR

Neither the philosophical challenge nor the supposed historical errors provide sufficient evidence to reject Daniel's traditional date and authorship. Exegetical/theological evidence for Danielic authorship exists also. (1) The "abomination of desolation" language of Daniel 9:2, 11:31, and 12:11, employed in Matthew 24:14-15, points to Danielic authorship. (2) The connection of the first person vision reports in 7–12 (7:2,4,6,28; 8:1,15; 9:2; 10:2) with the third person narrative accounts in 1–6 points to Danielic authorship in much the same way as older prophetic books combined vision reports with narrative accounts to produce the prophetic book (cf. Amos 7:1–9:15). (3) Four theological themes in Daniel have more in common with earlier prophets than the later apocalyptic material of the second century — prominence of angels, the last judgment, the resurrection of the dead, and the establishment of the Messiah's kingdom on the earth. In fact, none of these occur in such books as 1 Maccabees, the Greek additions of Daniel, Baruch and Judith.[51] (4) The specific personalities of Daniel's angels (8:16; 9:21; 10:13,21; 12:1) demonstrate a greater complexity than earlier works, which

---

"Noah, Daniel und Hiob in Ezechiel XIV 12-20 (21-23): Anmerkungen zum Traditionsgeschichtlichen Hintergrund," *VT* (1992): 551-552; Dressler, "Identification," pp. 157-158.

[49]Rendtorff, *Introduction,* p. 276.

[50]See also G.A. Barton, "Daniel, a Pre-Israelite Hero of Galilee," *JBL* 60 (1941): 213-225; P. Joüon, "Trois noms de personnages bibliques à la lumière des textes d'Ugarit," *Biblica* 19 (1938): 280-285; J. Lewy, "*Nāh et Rušpān*" in *Mélanges syriens offerts à M. René Dussaud* I (Paris: Geuthner, 1939), pp. 273-275; M. Noth, "Noah, Daniel and Hiob in Ezechiel 14," *VT* 1 (1951): 251-260; S. Spiegel, "Noah, Danel and Job, Touching on Canaanite Relics in the Legends of the Jews," *Louis Ginzberg Jubilee Volume* (New York: American Academy for Jewish Research, 1945), pp. 305-355 [English Section].

[51]Archer, *Survey,* p. 380.

picture them as "impersonal divine messengers"[52] (cf. e.g., Gen 16:7; Exod 14:19; Num 20:16; Judg 2:1; 13:3; 2 Sam 24:16; 1 Kgs 19:5; 2 Kgs 1:3; 1 Chr 21:12; 2 Chr 32:21; Job 33:23). Further, in Zechariah (1:11-14,19; 2:1-3; 3:1-6; 4:1-5; 5:5-10; 6:4-5; 12:8) angels play so similar a role to those in Daniel as "to warrant the deduction that either Zechariah had influenced Daniel or Daniel had influenced Zechariah."[53] (5) The last judgment (7:10,22,26) and the resurrection of both righteous and wicked (12:2), while more advanced than the view of the resurrected righteous nation Israel (Hos 6:1-2; Ezek 37:11-14) or the resurrection of righteous individuals in the nation (Isaiah 24; 27), "does not appear as advanced as that of the New Testament, which proclaimed a general resurrection of all mankind at the end of the age, prior to final judgment."[54] (6) Taken together these facts indicate the possibility of observing "some kind of progression in the development of these doctrines during the history of God's revelation to Israel," but they contain nothing "radically new in any of the four areas under dispute."[55] (7) Such evidence indicates that Daniel himself authored the book in the sixth century, or its compilation occurred "shortly thereafter, and . . . was extant not later than the middle of the fifth century B.C."[56]

STRUCTURE

Daniel exhibits two genres (historical/apocalyptic), two languages (Hebrew/Aramaic), and two numbers of speech (1st/3rd persons).

Historical	1–6	Apocalyptic	7–12
Hebrew	1:1–2:4a; 8:1-13	Aramaic	2:4b–7:28
3rd person speech	1–6	1st person speech	7–12 (framed by 3rd person speech, 7:1; 10:1)

---

[52]Harrison, *Introduction*, p. 1131; cf. Wilson and Harrison, "Daniel, Book of," *ISBE*[2], 1:865.

[53]Archer, *Survey*, p. 380.

[54]Harrison, *Introduction*, p. 1131; cf. Wilson and Harrison, "Daniel, Book of," *ISBE*[2], 1:865.

[55]Archer, *Survey*, p. 381.

[56]Harrison, *Introduction*, p. 1127. For other discussions relating to authorship, text, and date see also Dillard and Longman, *Introduction*, pp. 330-331; McKenna, "Daniel," pp. 574-576.

The bifid structure facilitates memorization and allows the narratives to serve as the sociopolitical background out of which the prophetic visions were revealed.[57] Scholars have made the general observation that Hebrew comprises those sections which deal with God's people and their destiny while Aramaic embodies those sections describing the great empires.[58] They do not believe the Aramaic represents a translation from a Hebrew *Vorlage*, though some have postulated the original was in Aramaic and that chapters 1:1–2:3 and 8–12 were subsequently translated into Hebrew to facilitate the book's canonical recognition.[59]

These structural issues fed the debate relative to the book's unity. Critical scholars, stressing a late date and citing these structural issues as evidence of disunity, argue[d] the book was written "after the fact."[60] Evangelical scholars, stressing an early date and the book's unity, argue[d] the book consists of predictive prophecy.[61] As modern scholarship engages in more holistic approaches these issues begin to blur.[62]

Marked advances in the structural understanding of the book have occurred in recent years. Lenglet observed, in addition to the commonality of Aramaic, chapters 2–7 exhibited a chiastic structure in which chapter 7 develops further the themes of chapter 2.[63]

---

[57]Wilson and Harrison, "Daniel, Book of," *ISBE*[2], 1:860; cf. Harrison, *Introduction*, pp. 1107, 1127

[58]E.g., Wilson and Harrison, "Daniel, Book of," *ISBE*[2], 1:860; Young, *Introduction*, p. 362; Archer, *Survey*, p. 378.

[59]E.g., L.P. Hartman and A.A. DiLella, *The Book of Daniel* (Garden City, NY: Doubleday, 1978), p. 14; Ginsberg, "Aramaic Studies," p. 231; F. Zimmermann, "Some Verses in Daniel in Light of a Translation Hypothesis," *JBL* 58 (1939): 349-354; id., "The Aramaic Origin of Daniel 8-12," *JBL* 57 (1938): 255-272. See also: Davies, "Eschatology," p. 33; Dillard and Longman, *Introduction*, pp. 345-346; McKenna, "Daniel," pp. 570-572; Talmon, "Daniel," p. 343.

[60]E.g., H.L. Ginsberg, "The Composition of the Book of Daniel," *VT* 4 (1954): 246-275.

[61]Wilson and Harrison, "Daniel, Book of" *ISBE*[2], 1:862. Cf. Rowley, the exception, who argues for the late date and defends the unity; H.H. Rowley, "The Unity of the Book of Daniel," *HUCA* 23 (1950–51): 233-273; repr. in *The Servant of the Lord and Other Essays* (London: Lutherworth, 1952), pp. 237-268; H.H. Rowley, "The Composition of the Book of Daniel: Some Comments on Professor Ginsberg's Article," *VT* 5 (1955): 272-276.

[62]For a summary of the compositional discussion see A.B. Rhodes, "The Kingdoms of Men and the Kingdom of God," *Int* 15 (1961): 413-414.

[63]A. Lenglet, "La structure littéraire de Daniel 2–7," *Bib* 53 (1972): 169-

Chapter 2	Chapter 3	Chapter 4	Chapter 5	Chapter 6	Chapter 7
4 Gentile kingdoms rule Israel	Divine deliverance of Hananiah, Mishael, and Azariah from the fiery furnace	Divine humbling of the Babylonian King, Nebuchadnezzar	Divine humiliation of the Babylonian King, Belshazzar	Divine deliverance of Daniel from the lion's den	4 Gentile powers rule over Israel
A	B	C	C'	B'	A'

The visions of the four kingdoms (2, 7) provide the framework for the material in between. The stories of deliverance (3, 6) share a parallel structure: "command to worship the king as god, refusal, denunciation, enforcement of the penalty, miraculous deliverance . . . acknowledgment of the God of the Jews by the pagan king."[64] Chapters 4 and 5, the center of the composition deal with "the divine judgment on a king, which is announced in a mysterious way (in *4.2* by a dream, in 5.5 by the writing on the wall), but first has to be interpreted by Daniel (*4.5ff*.; 5:13ff.) and is finally fulfilled (*4.5ff*., 5.30)."[65] All of this focuses on the pagan king as he moves from an expression of "faith in Daniel's God as 'God of gods' (2:47), 'Most High' (4:34), 'the living God, enduring forever' (6:26[MT 27])," to the issuance of "a decree that no one speak against this God (3:29)," to an order for "everyone to tremble and fear 'before the God of Daniel' (6:26)."[66] Chapter 7 develops further chapter 2's visions. The fourth kingdom of 2 is replaced by an eternal kingdom, while in 7 "the main interests are in the 4th kingdom, its evil acts and fate (vv. 7ff.)."[67]

Gooding suggests a different structural pattern. He argues the major transition occurs between chapter 5 and 6 rather than chapters 6 and 7.[68] This pattern "has the advantage of being more intricate," displaying the "binding relationships within each of the two cycles," as well as the "relationships between the paralleling mem-

190; cf. J.P. Tanner, "The Literary Structure of the Book of Daniel," *BSac* 160 (2003): 273; Rendtorff, *Introduction*, pp. 273-275.

[64]Rendtorff, *Introduction*, p. 274.

[65]Ibid.

[66]McKenna, "Daniel," p. 572.

[67]Rendtorff, *Introduction*, pp. 274-275. For discussions of Daniel's structure see W.H. Shea, "Daniel 1-6," *AUSS* 23 (1985): 277-295; G.R. Beasley-Murray, "The Interpretation of Daniel 7," *CBQ* 45 (1983): 53-54; Dillard and Longman, *Introduction*, pp. 347-348.

[68]D.W. Gooding, "The Literary Structure of the Book of Daniel and Its Implications," *TynBul* 32 (1981): 43-79.

bers of each cycle," yet fails "to explain the Aramaic section in chapters 2–7."[69]

Chapters 1-5	Chapters 6-12
Chapter 1: Daniel and his friends refuse to eat the king's food and are vindicated	**Chapter 6**: Daniel refuses to obey the king's command regarding prayer and is vindicated
Two Images	**Two Visions**
Chapter 2: Nebuchadnezzar's dream image	**Chapter 7:** Daniel's dream/vision of 4 beasts coming out of the sea
Chapter 3: Nebuchadnezzar's golden image	**Chapter 8:** Daniel's vision of a ram and a goat
Two Kings Humbled	**Two Writings Explained**
Chapter 4: The humiliation and restoration of Nebuchadnezzar	**Chapter 9:** Daniel understands the captivity is over (Jer 25:11-12; 29:10)
Chapter 5: Belshazzar warned and punished.	**Chapters 10-12:** the "book of truth" (10:21), destruction of "the king" (11:36-45)

Perhaps Tanner offers the best explanation of the structure to date. Building off Gooding's observations, Tanner argues for an overlapping structure in which chapter 7 functions as a hinge.

|——*Sovereignty of God over Gentile Kingdoms* ——|—*Visions of Daniel*—| |
|—*Hebrew*—|——————*Aramaic*——————|——*Hebrew*——|

1	2	3	4	5	6	7	8	9	10–12
						Vis. 1	*Vis 2*	*Vis. 3*	*Vis. 4*
	A	B	C	C′	B′	A′			
His. Setting	4-part Image	Refusal to Worship Image	Neb. Humbled	Bel. Humbled	Refusal to Cease Praying	4 Beasts	Ram and Goat	70 Weeks	Final Visions
3rd per	3rd per	3rd per	3rd per	3rd per	3rd per	3rd/1st per	1st per	1st per	3rd/1st per

This organization accounts for most of the structural markers. (1) It takes advantage of the book's linguistic divisions. (2) It recognizes the overlapping nature of chapter 7 which "serves as a hinge to both major sections of the book."[70] (3) Chapter 7 functions as a

---

[69]Tanner, "Literary Structure," pp. 274, 276.
[70]Ibid., p. 282.

"hinge" by restating "the succession of ancient Gentile kingdoms," while providing "more detail about the 'latter days' when the Antichrist will arise."[71] (4) Chapter 7:25-27 contains dual motifs — "the exaltation" of Daniel/God and "the opposition and defeat of the future ruler."[72] The ending of each chapter in *1–6 closes with this honoring and exalting motif* (cf. 1:18-21; 2:46-49; 3:28-30; 4:36-37; 5:29-30; 6:25-28), while the endings of chapters *8–12 close with the opposition and defeat motif.* (5) Though these visions begin as first-person vision reports (7:2), they are bracketed by the introduction of the third person: "In the first year of King Belshazzar of Babylon, *Daniel* had a dream and visions of *his head as he lay in bed.* Then *he wrote down* the dream: *I, Daniel*, saw in my vision by night the four winds of heaven stirring up the great sea" (7:1-2, emphasis added, cf. 10:2). This blending of the third and first person indicates the report is a summary of the vision and serves to link chapter 7 with what preceded as well as pointing to the material that follows. Chapter 10:1-3 continues the process begun in 7:1-2, linking 10ff. with 7. (6) All of this is linked by the terms "dream[s]" (1:17; 2:1,2,3,4,5,6,7,9,26, 28,36,45; 4:5,6,7,8,9,18,19; 5:12; 7:1), "vision[s]" (2:19; 4:5,13; 7:1,2, 7,13,15; 8:1,2,13,15,16,17,26,27; 9:21,23,24; 10:1,7,8,14,16; 11:14), and the introductory datings (2:1; 7:1; 8:1; 9:1; 10:1).[73] In this way, "the sixth-century prophet composed the book, creating a unified artistic narrative of historical events theologically critiqued by a highly crafted ironic vision."[74]

GENRE

The historical/apocalyptic, Hebrew/Aramaic, and third/first person accounts all come into play in a discussion of the book's genre. (1) The supernatural/antisupernatural cleavage among scholars determines the definition of the genres. Critical scholars type nonhistorical chapters 1–6 using ahistorical terms and designate 7–12 "apocalyptic visions," or the like, while evangelical scholars choose historical terms for 1–6 and label 7–12 "apocalyptic prophecy," or the like. (2) The Hebrew and Aramaic divisions of the book reflect the

---

[71]Ibid., p. 278.

[72]Ibid., p. 279.

[73]Rendtorff, *Introduction,* p. 274.

[74]B.L. Woodard, "Literary Strategies and Authorship in the Book of Daniel," *JETS* 37 (1994): 40.

author's tendency to employ Hebrew for those sections "addressed [to] the nation of Israel" and Aramaic for those sections "pertain[ing] to the Gentile nations in their relationship to Israel's exile."[75] (3) The first-person speech of 7–12 gives that section a more personal and emotional nuance (cf. e.g., the phrase "Daniel, greatly beloved," 10:11) than the more detached third-person speech of 1–6. As such, the book exhibits a "unity in diversity" quality which allows the author to employ materials from one genre in the other genre. This fluidity must be kept in mind in any discussion of genre.

COURT NARRATIVE

Critical scholars, date the book late and type chapters 1–6 as "Märchen, Legend, Court Tale, Aretalogical Narrative, and Midrash,"[76] "Diaspora Novel,"[77] "comedy,"[78] or the like, all of which implies "a lack of historical intent."[79] Evangelical scholars describe these chapters as "court narrative,"[80] or the like, perceiving these chapters to be a historically accurate account of specific events in the lives of Daniel, Hananiah, Mishael, and Azariah. Therefore, both groups of scholars may compare Daniel to the biblical stories of Joseph and Esther[81] as well as the extrabiblical text of Ahikar, Tobit and 3 Ezra 3.[82] The fact that there exists "little difference (at the genre level) between historical narrative and fiction" allows both critical and evangelical scholars to "utilize the same methods to tell the story: plot, characters, dialogue, dramatic tension,"[83] but readers should not be blinded to the fact of the great philosophical gulf separating these two groups of scholars.

---

[75]Tanner, "Literary Strucrure," p. 281.

[76]J.J. Collins, *Daniel with an Introduction to Apocalyptic Literature*" (Grand Rapids: Eerdmans, 1984), p. 42.

[77]Talmon, "Daniel," pp. 353, 355.

[78]E.M. Good, "Apocalyptic as Comedy: The Book of Daniel," *Semeia* 32 (1985): 41.

[79]Dillard and Longman, *Introduction,* p. 341

[80]Ibid., pp. 341-342.

[81]W.L. Humphreys, "A Life-Style for Diaspora: A Study of the Tales of Esther and Daniel," *JBL* 92 (1973): 211-223.

[82]Collins, *Daniel,* p. 42; cf. Dillard and Longman, *Introduction,* p. 341.

[83]G. Osborne, *The Hermeneutical Spiral: A Comprehensive Introduction to Biblical Interpretation* (Downers Grove, IL: InterVarsity, 1991), p. 153.

APOCALYPTIC PROPHECY

Apocalyptic prophecy consists of two genres: apocalyptic and prophecy. The secondary literature is replete with definitions of apocalyptic literature indicating no consensus regarding the genre's definition.[84] While scholars do not agree specifically regarding the inherent traits comprising the apocalyptic genre, one of the most prominent definitions of the genre is, *"revelatory literature with a narrative framework, in which a revelation is mediated by an otherworldly being to a human recipient, disclosing a transcendent reality which is both temporal, insofar as it envisages eschatological salvation, and spatial insofar as it involves another, supernatural world."*[85] Apocalyptic prophecy contains several differences from classical, Hebrew prophecy.[86]

Prophetic Texts	*Apocalyptic Texts*
Broad Eschatology	*Narrow Eschatology*
Looked to the near future and the messianic age.	Looked past the near future to the end of time.
Human Mediator	*Heavenly Mediator*
The prophet served as the mediator ("The word of the Lord was to X") who revealed that word to the people, Jeremiah 12.	The heavenly messenger (angel) served as mediator to the individual (Daniel) who sealed up the message till the end, Dan 12:4.
Unusual Imagery	*Bizarre Imagery*
Heavenly imagery derived from this world (Jeremiah's almond branch and pot, 1:11,13; Ezekiel's valley of dry bones, 37:1ff.	Imagery bordered on the bizarre, grotesque terms (beasts of all kinds, worldly and otherworldly, rooted in pagan mythology), Daniel 7.

---

[84]Dillard and Longman, *Introduction,* p. 342.

[85]J.J. Collins, *Apocalypse: The Morphology of a Genre,* Semeia 14 (Missoula, MT: Scholars, 1979), p. 9. For discussions of apocalyptic see P.D. Hanson, *The Dawn of Apocalyptic* (Philadelphia: Fortress, 1975), pp. 430ff.; R.N. and R.K. Soulen, *Handbook of Biblical Criticism,* 3rd ed. rev. (Louisville, KY: Westminster John Knox, 2001), pp. 8-10, 142-145.

[86]Dillard and Longman, *Introduction,* pp. 343-345; McKenna, "Daniel," pp. 567-570.

Prophet Afflicts the Comforted . . .	*Seer Comforts the Afflicted . . .*
by warning the people that outside oppression (whether Babylon, Persia, or the like) would come due to their sins, including their oppression of a subclass in their midst.	by revealing an apocalyptic message of comfort to those oppressed by an outside force (Babylon and Persia, Greece, Antiochus Epiphanes, and Rome).
Judgment Proclaimed Was. . .	*Judgment Proclaimed Was. . .*
uncertain, postponed, or averted with repentance.	certain, in terms of deliverance for the oppressed.
Prophetic Authorship and Predictions Disputed	*Danielic Authorship and Predictions Disputed*
The books claim both prophetic authorship and predictions; Daniel contains authorship information and visions similar to that of other prophets.	They are said by critics to be written after the fact because many apocalyptic texts are written in that format (Enoch, Zephaniah, Ezra).[87]

The above reenforces the connection between prophecy and Daniel's apocalyptic.[88] The oppression out of which it arose dictated its in-tension characteristics of concealment and revelation. Apocalyptic sought to reveal the hope of a better day to the oppressed in a manner that would conceal the same information from their oppressors. For this reason "The heavy use of imagery will . . . discourage a literalistic reading of the so-called apocalyptic timetables (e.g., Dan. 9:25-27). To compute the time of the end from Daniel's seventy weeks is to misuse the text. . . ."[89] These are part and parcel of the symbols used to reveal truths in the context of concealment.[90] Because of the close affiliation of prophecy and apocalyptic, students of Daniel should study intertestamental apocalypses, but should also give specific attention to similar material such as Isaiah

[87]Cf. J.H. Charlesworth, ed., *The Old Testament Pseudepigrapha: Apocalyptic Literature and Testaments* (Garden City, NY: Doubleday, 1983), 1:3-772.
[88]J.J. Collins, "Apocalyptic Genre and Mythic Allusions in Daniel," *JSOT* 21 (1981): 89-90.
[89]Dillard and Longman, *Introduction*, p. 345.
[90]A.B. Mickelsen, *Daniel and Revelation: Riddles or Realities?* (Nashville: Thomas Nelson, 1984), p. 196.

24-27 and Zechariah. These texts and comparative studies in the ancient Near East indicate that Daniel's apocalyptic material has antecedents as far back as the thirteenth century, even as it possesses analogues in the Seleucid era.[91]

THEOLOGICAL THEMES

Several theological themes permeate the book. The sovereignty of God flows through every chapter, whether Daniel and his friends' choice regarding their diet (1), Nebuchadnezzar's dream or Daniel's visions (2, 7), deliverance from fiery furnaces or lions' dens (3, 6), God's rule over kingdoms (4-11), or the resurrection of the dead (12). Such stories illustrate proper conduct for the oppressed who look to God for deliverance and furnish a backdrop to prepare God's oppressed people for future oppression (7-11), and reassure that God's sovereignty extends beyond death (12). These lessons are far more valuable than the determination of the numerology of 9:25-27 or 12:11-12,[92] the establishment of "historical details," or "the times and seasons."[93]

NEW TESTAMENT CONNECTIONS

Several direct connections with Daniel occur in the New Testament. The book of Revelation perhaps has the most in common with Daniel. Both are apocalyptic in type. Both make use of beasts of the sea (Daniel 7; Revelation 13). Both emphasize the sovereignty of God as a comfort for the oppressed and encourage distressed Christians to persevere in their faith. Revelation 1:7,13,18 and 14:14 make use of "coming in the clouds" imagery of Daniel 7:13. Jesus makes use of the "abomination of desolation" imagery of Daniel to predict the turmoil accompanying the destruction of Jerusalem (Dan 9:27; 11:31; 12:11; Matt 24:15; Mark 13:14; Luke 21:24). Daniel 12:2 anticipates the New Testament doctrine of the

[91]Dillard and Longman, *Introduction*, p. 345; cf. Tremper Longman III, *Fictional Akkadian Autobiography* (Winona Lake, IN: Eisenbrauns, 1991); A.K. Grayson, *Babylonian Historical-Literary Texts* (Toronto: University of Toronto, 1975).
[92]Dillard and Longman, *Introduction*, p. 351, cf. pp. 348-350.
[93]McKenna, "Daniel," p. 582; Davies, "Eschatology," p. 44.

resurrection (Matt 22:29-32; 28:1ff.; Mark 16:1ff.; Luke 24:1ff.; John 11:23-26; 20:1ff.; 1 Cor 15:20-22,51-54; 1 Thess 4:14; Rev 20:12).[94]

---

[94]Dillard and Longman, *Introduction,* pp. 351-352. For an excellent survey of the impact of the book of Daniel on Christian theology see J.G. Gammie, "A Journey through Danelic Spaces: The Book of Daniel in the Theology and Piety of the Christian Community," *Int* 39 (1985): 144-156.

MINOR PROPHETS

GARY HALL

BIBLIOGRAPHY FOR
THE MINOR PROPHETS

Achtemeier, Elizabeth. *Minor Prophets I.* NIBCOT. Peabody, MA: Hendrickson, 1996.

_____ . *Nahum–Malachi.* Int. Atlanta: John Knox, 1986.

Alexander, T.D. "Jonah and Genre." *TynBul* 36 (1985): 35-59.

Allen, Leslie. *The Books of Joel, Obadiah, Jonah, and Micah.* NICOT. Grand Rapids: Eerdmans, 1976.

Allis, O.T. "Nahum, Nineveh, Elkosh." *EvQ* 27 (1955): 67-80.

Anderson, F.I., and D.N. Freedman. *Amos.* AB. New York: Doubleday, 1989.

_____ . *Hosea.* AB. Garden City, NY: Doubleday, 1980.

_____ . *Micah.* AB. New York: Doubleday, 2000.

Archer, Gleason, and Gregory Chirichigno. *Old Testament Quotations in the New Testament.* Chicago: Moody Press, 1983.

Armerding, Carl E. "Habakkuk." In *The Expositor's Bible Commentary,* 7:493-534. Ed. by Frank E. Gabelein. Grand Rapids: Zondervan, 1985.

_____ . "Nahum." In *The Expositor's Bible Commentary,* 7:449-489. Ed. by Frank E. Gabelein. Grand Rapids: Zondervan, 1985.

Baker, D.W. *Nahum, Habakkuk and Zephaniah.* Downers Grove, IL: InterVarsity, 1988.

Baldwin, Joyce. *Haggai, Zechariah, Malachi.* TOTC. Downers Grove, IL: InterVarsity, 1972.

Ball, I.J. *Zephaniah: A Rhetorical Study.* Berkeley: Bibal Press, 1988.

Barker, Kenneth L., and Waylon Bailey. *Micah, Nahum, Habakkuk, Zephaniah.* Nashville: Broadman and Holman, 1998.

Barton, John. *Joel and Obadiah: A Commentary.* Louisville, KY: Westminster John Knox, 2001.

Ben Zvi, E. *A Historical-Critical Study of the Book of Obadiah.* Berlin: BZAW, 1996.

_____ . *Micah.* Grand Rapids: Eerdmans, 2000.

Berlin, Adele. *Zephaniah: A New Translation with Introduction and Commentary.* AB 25A. New York: Doubleday, 1994.

Bright, John. *A History of Israel.* 4th ed. Philadelphia: Westminster, 2000.

Brown, William. *Obadiah through Malachi.* Louisville, KY: Westminster John Knox, 1996.

Bruce, F.F. *New Testament Development of Old Testament Themes.* Grand Rapids: Eerdmans, 1968.

Brueggemann, Walter. *Tradition for Crisis: A Study in Hosea.* Atlanta: John Knox, 1969.

Carson, D.A. "Matthew." In *The Expositor's Bible Commentary.* Ed. by Frank E. Gaebelien. Grand Rapids: Zondervan, 1984.

Cathcart, K.J. "Nahum." *ABD,* 4:999.

Childs, B. *Introduction to the Old Testament as Scripture.* Philadelphia: Fortress, 1979.

Christensen, Duane. "Andryej Panufuik and the Structure of the Book of Jonah: Icons, Music, and Literary Art." *JETS* 28 (1985): 133-140.

_____. "Zephaniah 2:4-15: A Theological Basis for Josiah's Program of Political Expansion." *CBQ* 46 (1984): 669-682.

Coggins, Richard J. *Haggai, Zachariah, Malachi.* OTG. Sheffield: JSOT Press, 1987.

_____. *Joel and Amos.* Sheffield: Sheffield Academic Press, 2000.

Coggins, R.J., and S.P. Re'emi. *Israel among the Nations: A Commentary on the Books of Nahum, Obadiah, Esther.* Grand Rapids: Eerdmans, 1985.

Cook, Stephen L., and S.C. Winter, eds. *On the Way to Nineveh: Essays in Honor of George M. Landes.* Atlanta: Scholars Press, 1999.

Craig, Kenneth. "Jonah in Recent Research." *Currents in Research* 7 (1999): 97-118.

Dillard, R.B. *Joel.* Grand Rapids: Baker, 1992.

Dillard, R.B., and Tremper Longman III. *An Introduction to the Old Testament.* Grand Rapids: Zondervan, 1994.

Dodd, C.H. *The Old Testament in the New.* Philadelphia: Fortress, 1963.

Eissfeldt, Otto. *The Old Testament: An Introduction.* Trans. by Peter R. Ackroyd. New York: Harper and Row, 1965.

Ellul, J. *The Judgment of Jonah*. Trans. by G.W. Bromiley. Grand Rapids: Eerdmans, 1971.

Ferguson, Paul. "Who Was the King of Nineveh in Jonah 3:6?" *TynBul* 47 (1996): 301-314.

Finley, T.J. *Joel, Amos, Obadiah*. Chicago: Moody, 1990.

Floyd, Michael H. *The Minor Prophets*, Part 2. Grand Rapids: Eerdmans, 2000.

Fretheim, T.E. *The Message of Jonah: A Theological Commentary*. Minneapolis: Augsburg, 1977.

Hall, Gary. "Origin of the Marriage Metaphor." *HS* 23 (1982): 169-171.

Hanson, Paul. *Dawn of the Apocalyptic*. Philadelphia: Fortress, 1975.

Harrison, R.K. *Introduction to the Old Testament*. Grand Rapids: Eerdmans, 1969.

Hasel, Gerhard F. *Understanding the Book of Amos*. Grand Rapids: Baker, 1991.

Hays, John H. *Amos, His Time and Preaching: The Eighth Century Prophet*. Nashville: Abingdon, 1988.

Hiers, Richard H. "Day of the Lord." *ABD*, 2:82-84.

Hill, Andrew. *Malachi*. AB. New York: Doubleday, 1987.

Hillers, Delbert R. *Micah*. Philadelphia: Fortress Press, 1984.

House, Paul R. *Old Testment Theology*. Downers Grove, IL: InterVarsity, 1998.

_____. *The Unity of the Twelve*. Sheffield: Almond Press, 1990.

_____. *Zephaniah. A Prophetic Drama*. Sheffield: Almond Press, 1988.

Hubbard, David. *Joel and Amos*. Downers Grove, IL: InterVarsity, 1989.

_____. *With Bands of Love: Lessons from the Book of Hosea*. Grand Rapids: Eerdmans, 1969.

Hugenberger, Gordon P. *Marriage as a Covenant: Biblical Law and Ethics as Developed from Malachi*. Grand Rapids: Baker, 1998.

Janzen, J. Gerald. "Eschatological Symbol and Existence in Habakkuk." *CBQ* 44 (1982): 394-414.

_____. "Habakkuk 2:2-4 in the Light of Recent Philological Advances." *HTR* 73 (1980): 53-78.

Jeremias, Jorg. *The Book of Amos*. OTL. Trans. by D.W. Scott. Louisville, KY: Westminster John Knox, 1998.

Johnson, D.E. "Fire in God's House: Imagery from Malachi 3 in Peter's Theology of Suffering (1 Pet 4:12-19)." *JETS* 29 (1986): 285-294.

Judisch, Douglas. "The Historicity of Jonah." *CTQ* 63 (1999): 144-157.

Kaiser, Walter. *Malachi: God's Unchanging Love.* Grand Rapids: Baker, 1984.

_____ . *Micah–Malachi.* WBC. Dallas: Word, 1992.

Kidner, Derek. *Love to the Loveless: The Story and Message of Hosea.* Downers Grove, IL: InterVarsity, 1991.

King, Greg A. "The Day of the Lord in Zephaniah." *BSac* 152 (1995): 16-32.

_____ . "The Remnant in Zephaniah." *BSac* 151 (1994): 414-427.

King, Philip J. *Amos, Hosea, Micah: An Archaeological Commentary.* Philadelphia: Westminster, 1988.

_____ . "The Eighth, the Greatest of Centuries?" *JBL* 108 (1989): 13-15.

Knight, G.A.F. *Hosea: Introduction and Commentary.* London: SCM Press, 1960.

Kobayashi, Y. "Elkosh." *ABD*, 2:476.

Kselman, J.S. "Zephaniah, Book of." *ABD*, 6:1077-1080.

Landes, G.M. "The Kerygma of the Book of Jonah." *Int* 21 (1967): 3-31.

Leslie, E.A. "Habakkuk." *IDB*, 2:503-505. Ed. by G.A. Buttrick. Nashville: Abingdon, 1962.

Limburg, James. *Hosea–Micah.* Int. Atlanta: John Knox, 1988.

_____ . "Sevenfold Structures in the Book of Amos." *JBL* 106 (1987): 217-222.

Maier, W.A. *The Book of Nahum.* St. Louis: Concordia, 1959.

Mason, R.A. *Micah, Nahum, Obadiah.* Sheffield: Sheffield Press, 1991.

Mauch, T.M. "Zechariah." *IDB*, 4:941-943.

Mays, James L. *Amos.* OTL. Philadelphia: Westminster, 1969.

_____ . *Hosea.* OTL. Philadelphia: Westminster Press, 1969.

_____ . *Micah.* OTL. Philadelphia: Westminster, 1976.

McComiskey, Thomas E., ed. *The Minor Prophets: An Exegetical and Expository Commentary.* 3 vols. Grand Rapids: Baker, 1992–1998.

McKane, William. *The Book of Micah: Introduction and Commentary.* Edinburgh: T. & T. Clark, 1998.

McKenzie, S.L., and H.N. Wallace. "Covenant Themes in Malachi." *CBQ* 45 (1983): 549-563.

Merrill, Eugene. *An Exegetical Commentary: Haggai, Zechariah, Malachi.* Chicago: Moody Press, 1994.

Meyers, Carol L., and Eric M. Meyers. *Haggai, Zechariah 1–8.* AB. New York: Doubleday, 1987.

——————. *Zechariah 9–14: A New Translation with Introduction and Commentary.* AB. New York: Doubleday, 1993.

Miller, Stephen. *Nahum, Habakkuk, Zephaniah, Haggai, Zechariah.* Nashville: Broadman and Holman, 2004.

Motyer, J.A. *Amos: The Day of the Lion.* Downers Grove, IL: Inter-Varsity, 1974.

Ogden, G.S. "The Prophetic Oracles against Foreign Nations and the Psalms of Communal Lament: The Relationship of Psalm 137 to Jeremiah 49:7-22 and Obadiah." *JSOT* 24 (1982): 89-97.

Parker, R.A., and W.H. Dubberstein. *Babylonian Chronology 626 B.C.–A.D. 45.* Chicago: University of Chicago Press, 1946.

Parrot, A. *Nineveh and the Old Testament.* New York: Philosophical Society, 1955.

Patterson, Richard D. "A Literary Look at Nahum, Habakkuk, and Zephaniah." *GTJ* 11 (1990): 17-27.

——————. "The Psalm of Habakkuk." *GTJ* 8 (1987): 163-194.

Paul, S.M. *Amos: A Commentary on the Book of Amos.* Minneapolis: Fortress, 1991.

Peckham, Brian. "The Vision of Habakkuk." *CBQ* 48 (1986): 617-636.

Peterson, David. *Haggai and Zechariah 1–8.* OTL. Philadelphia: Westminster, 1984.

——————. *Zechariah 9–14 and Malachi: A Commentary.* OTL. Louisville, KY: Westminster John Knox, 1995.

Prinsloo, W.S. *The Theology of the Book of Joel.* BZAW 163. Berlin: Walter de Gruyter, 1985.

Prior, David. *The Message of Joel, Micah and Habakkuk: Listening to the Voice of God.* Downers Grove, IL: InterVarsity, 1998.

Proctor, J. "Fire in God's House: Influence of Malachi 3 in the NT." *JETS* 36 (1993): 9-14.

Raabe, P.R. *Obadiah: A New Translation with Introduction and Commentary.* New York: Doubleday, 1996.

Redditt, Paul. *Haggai, Zechariah, Malachi*. Grand Rapids: Eerdmans, 1995.

Roberts, J.J.M. N*ahum, Habakkuk, Zephaniah*. Louisville, KY: Westminster/John Knox 1991.

Robertson, O. Palmer. *The Books of Nahum, Habakkuk, and Zephaniah*. NICOT. Grand Rapids: Eerdmans, 1990.

Ryken, Leland. "Amos." In *A Complete Literary Guide to the Bible*. Ed. by L. Ryken and T. Longman III. Grand Rapids: Zondervan, 1993.

_____ . *How to Read the Bible as Literature*. Grand Rapids: Zondervan, 1984.

Sandy, D. Brent, and Ronald L. Giese Jr. *Cracking Old Testament Codes*. Nashville: Broadman and Holman, 1995.

Sasson, Jack. *Jonah*. AB. New York: Doubleday, 1990.

Shank, Harold. *Minor Prophets I: Hosea–Micah*. College Press NIV Commentary. Joplin, MO: College Press, 2001.

Simon, Urial. *Jonah*. JPS Commentary. Philadelphia: Jewish Publication Society, 1999.

Smith, Billy, and Frank S. Page. *Amos, Obadiah, and Jonah*. Nashville: Broadman and Holman, 1995.

Smith, Gary V. *Amos: A Commentary*. Grand Rapids: Zondervan, 1989.

_____ . *Hosea, Amos, Micah*. NIV Application Commentary. Grand Rapids: Zondervan, 2001.

Smith, Ralph L. *Micah–Malachi*. WBC. Waco: Word, 1984.

Spronk, Klaas. *Nahum*. Kampen: Kok Pharos, 1997.

Stuart, Douglas. *Hosea–Jonah*. WBC. Waco: Word, 1987.

Stuhlmueller, Carroll. *Rebuilding with Hope: A Commentary on the Books of Haggai and Zechariah*. Grand Rapids: Eerdmans, 1988.

Sweeney, Marvin A. "A Form-Critical Reassessment of the Book of Zephaniah." *CBQ* 53 (1991): 407-408.

_____ . "Habakkuk." *HBC*. San Francisco: Harper Collins, 1988.

_____ . "Habakkuk, Book of." *ABD*, 3:1-2.

_____ . "Structure, Genre and Intent in the Book of Habakkuk." *VT* 41 (1991): 63-83.

_____ . *The Twelve Prophets*. Vol. 1. *Hosea, Joel, Amos, Obadiah, Jonah*. Ed. by David W. Cotter. Collegeville, MN: Liturgical Press, 2000.

_____ . *The Twelve Prophets*. Vol. 2. *Micah–Malachi*. Ed. by David W. Cotter. Collegeville, MN: Liturgical Press, 2000.

_____ . *Zephaniah*. Hermeneia. Minneapolis: Fortress, 2003.

Szeles, Maria Eszenyei. *Wrath and Mercy: A Commentary on the Books of Habakkuk and Zephaniah*. Grand Rapids: Eerdmans, 1987.

Tsumura, David T. "Ugaritic Poetry and Habakkuk 3." *TynBul* 40 (1989): 24-48.

Unger, Merrill. *Zechariah*. Grand Rapids: Zondervan, 1963.

VanGemeren, Willem. *Interpreting the Prophetic Word*. Grand Rapids: Zondervan, 1990.

Verhoef, Pieter A. *The Books of Haggai and Malachi*. NICOT. Grand Rapids: Eerdmans, 1987.

von Rad, Gerhard. *Old Testament Theology*. Trans. by D.M.G. Stalker. New York: Harper and Row, 1965.

Waltke, Bruce K. "Micah." In *Obadiah, Jonah and Micah*. Ed. by D.W. Baker, T.D. Alexander, and B.K. Waltke. Downers Grove, IL: InterVarsity, 1988.

Walton, John, et al. *The IVP Bible Background Commentary: Old Testament*. Downers Grove, IL: InterVarsity, 2000.

Ward, J.M. *Hosea: A Theological Commentary*. New York: Harper and Row, 1966.

Watts, J.D.W. *Obadiah: A Critical Exegetical Commentary*. Grand Rapids: Eerdmans, 1969.

Whiting, J.D. "Jerusalem's Locust Plague." *National Geographic* 28 (1915): 511-550.

Wiseman, D.J. "Jonah's Nineveh." *TynBul* 30 (1979): 29-52.

Wolff, Hans Walter. *Haggai: A Commentary*. Trans. by Margaret Kohl. Minneapolis: Augsburg, 1988.

_____ . *Hosea*. Hermeneia. Trans. by G. Stansell. Philadelphia: Fortress Press, 1974.

_____ . *Joel and Amos*. Hermeneia. Trans. by W. Janzen et al. Philadelphia: Fortress, 1977.

_____ . *Micah: A Commentary*. Trans. by G. Stansell. Minneapolis: Augsburg, 1990.

_____ . *Obadiah and Jonah: A Commentary*. Minneapolis: Augsburg, 1986.

Yamauchi, Edwin. "The Scythians: Invading Hordes from the Russian Steppes." *BA* 46 (1983): 90-97.

Young, E.J. *An Introduction to the Old Testament*. Rev. ed. Grand Rapids: Eerdmans, 1960.

Zorn, Walter. "The Messianic Use of Habakkuk 2:4a in Romans."
    SCJ 1 (Fall 1998): 213-230.
Zuck, Roy B., ed. *A Biblical Theology of the Old Testament*. Chicago:
    Moody, 1991.

HOSEA

HISTORICAL AND CULTURAL BACKGROUND

Hosea was a contemporary of Amos, Isaiah, and Micah.[1] Hosea and Amos are the only two writing prophets who preached to the northern kingdom, but Hosea is the only one who lived in the north. Under Jeroboam the son of Joash (1:1) Israel experienced a period of prosperity and expansion (2 Kgs 14:23-29). Assyria was in a period of decline, Syria had been defeated, and there was peace with Judah to the south. Hosea's ministry is dated by four Judean kings but only one in Israel, which gives the book a Judean orientation. Hosea's ministry apparently covered the last days of Jeroboam, who died in 746 B.C., and the reign of several kings who followed. Since Hezekiah of Judah began his reign in 715 (1:1), Hosea can be assigned to the years from the 750s to the 720s.[2] It was a period of political chaos in Israel after the peace and prosperity of Jeroboam's reign.

Hosea's first child's name, Jezreel (1:4), spoke to the judgment on the Jehu dynasty for Jehu's violent overthrow of Ahab's family (2 Kings 9-10). Jeroboam's son who succeeded him, Zechariah, was assassinated by Shallum after six months, and the Jehu dynasty ended. Four of the six kings who followed Jeroboam's reign were assassinated, and three reigned less than two years.

After 745, Assyria was on the rise under Tiglath-Pileser III who was determined to expand the Assyrian empire. This spelled trouble for all the nations to the west, including Israel.

Shallum reigned one month and was assassinated by Menahem. Menahem had to pay heavy tribute to the Assyrians (2 Kgs 15:17-22). Pekahiah succeeded his father, Menahem, and was immediately assassinated by Pekah (737) who organized an anti-Assyrian coalition. Pekah and Syria attacked Ahaz and Judah (Isaiah 7; 2 Kgs 16:5), and Ahaz

---

[1]For more information on this historical setting see the chapter on Amos.
[2]Douglas Stuart, *Hosea–Jonah*, WBC (Waco: Word, 1987), p. 9.

appealed to Assyria for help. In 733 Tiglath-Pileser invaded Israel, devastated the land, deported Israelites, and took most of the land, leaving only Samaria and the hill country of Ephraim. Hoshea murdered Pekah and submitted. But eventually he grew restless and withheld tribute from Tiglath-Pileser's successor, Shalmaneser V. Shalmaneser invaded in 724, and Samaria fell to the Assyrians in 722.

Hosea seems to allude to this chaos in leadership and internal disintegration. The first chapters would reflect the prosperous and peaceful time of Jeroboam that was filled with religious syncretism and idolatry. The chaotic rise and fall of the following kings is reflected in 7:7 and 8:4. Vacillation between Egypt and Assyria is mentioned in 7:11 and 8:9. The war between Judah and Israel-Syria seems reflected in 5:8-11.[3] The devastation at the hand of the Assyrians and ultimate destruction of Samaria and exile is anticipated in chapters 10, 13, and 14.

Hosea shared with Amos a concern for the oppression of the poor and the perversion of injustice (e.g., 12:7-8). But he was more focused on the idolatry of the nation and its ramifications for Israel's relationship with God.

TEXT AND AUTHOR

We know little about the man Hosea. We do know he was married and had three children. We know that his marriage was stained with his wife's apparent infidelity and that his wife left him. But we do not know his occupation before becoming a prophet or his home town. He is the son of Beeri who is otherwise unknown.

Hosea's name comes from a root which means "to rescue, deliver, save, help."[4] Hosea's name reflects the causative form of the verb which can be translated, "he has saved, delivered." In this sentence "he" is understood as Yahweh and the omitted object is understood to be "us." This was also the original name of Joshua (Num 13:8,16; Deut 32:44), and the name of the last king of Israel (2 Kgs 17:1-4).[5]

---

[3]Or maybe an earlier attack by Uzziah on Benjamin (F.I. Anderson and D.N. Freedman, *Hosea* [New York: Doubleday, 1980], p. 34).

[4]The root is ישׁע, *yš'*, from which the name Isaiah is also derived.

[5]A person by that name is also mentioned in Jeremiah as the father of Azariah. Azariah was one of the leaders in Judah after the fall of Jerusalem who ignored Jeremiah and led the survivors to Egypt (Jer 42:1; 43:1-2).

The name sometimes occurs with the theophoric short form "yah" at the end, explicitly citing Yahweh as the subject.

Scholars have extensively debated the nature of Hosea's marriage and the character of his wife, Gomer. On the surface Hosea 1:2 seems to be saying that God commanded Hosea to marry a prostitute, a morally questionable demand. Both Gomer and the future children are designated by the same word, "harlotry" (זְנוּנִים, z³nûnîm; see also 2:4[Heb 6] of the children). This same word is used in the phrase describing the people of Israel in 4:12 and 5:4: they have a "spirit of harlotry." Z³nûnîm is a masculine plural abstract noun. Does it refer to an ethical or social status defined by real, individual acts of sexual infidelity, or does it refer more to a social atmosphere or spirit of the age? Stuart holds to the latter view.[6] Gomer and the children shared the trait of Israel as a nation. It was faithless and committed spiritual prostitution through its idolatry and therefore had a spirit of prostitution (4:12; 5:4). Thus the designation had nothing to do with Gomer's character or personal action. She and the children, and even Hosea, were a part of the spirit of the age. Women who actually practiced prostitution were called זֹנָה (zōnāh), "prostitutes."[7]

Some scholars prefer a straightforward reading of the text. God did demand Hosea to marry a promiscuous woman because his marriage was a symbol of God's relationship to idolatrous Israel whose idolatry was conceived of as religious adultery.[8] Others think Gomer was somehow involved in Canaanite fertility practices. Since she participated in the fertility cult of Baal she was already a prostitute.[9] Wolff thinks Gomer was a typical Israelite woman who had submitted to the bridal rites customary among the Canaanites.[10]

---

[6]Stuart, *Hosea–Jonah*, pp. 26-27.

[7]A feminine participle form of the verb, "practice prostitution." See Gen 34:31; 38:15; Lev 21:7; Judges 16:1; Prov 6:26; Jer 2:20; Hos 4:14; etc. On the verb *znh* see Gary H. Hall, "זנה," *NIDOTTE*, 1:1122-1125. The English translations differ widely in their rendering of Hosea 1:2.

[8]Raymond B. Dillard and Tremper Longman III, *An Introduction to the Old Testament* (Grand Rapids: Zondervan, 1994), p. 357.

[9]Elizabeth Achtemeier, *Minor Prophets I*, NIBCOT (Peabody, MA: Hendrickson 1996), p. 5; James L. Mays, *Hosea*, OTL (Philadelphia: Westminster, 1969), p. 3.

[10]Hans W. Wolff, *Hosea*, Hermeneia, trans. by G. Stansell (Philadelphia: Fortress, 1974), p. xxii.

Others think that Gomer became unfaithful after the marriage and the implications were not realized until years later.[11]

Whatever position one takes, two items must be kept in mind. The meaning of the story is symbolic, and its implications are clear. God's relationship to Israel was like that of a husband to an unfaithful wife. If that is so, then it would seem that the actual marriage of Hosea and Gomer would have to mirror the history of the divine relationship in some way. Thus it would seem most likely that Gomer was not promiscuous at the time of the marriage but became so later. She had a deep-seated spirit of harlotry not evident until later. This would mirror the fact that Israel was not idolatrous in her early relationship with God but soon became so (2:14-15; see Jer 2:2-3). In this interpretation it would be questionable whether all the children were Hosea's.

Who was the woman of chapter 3, Gomer or another woman whom Hosea took for a wife? It seems most logical that she was Gomer, who eventually left Hosea's home and followed her inclinations. However, in a display of extraordinary grace and forgiveness, Hosea took her back. This too symbolized God's forgiving nature hinted at in 2:14-15.[12] However, others think this was another, unnamed woman.[13] Again, for the symbolism to be meaningful, it would seem that the woman would have to be Gomer.

STRUCTURE

The macro structure of the book of Hosea is simple: chapters 1-3, Hosea's marriage experience and application; chapters 4–14, Hosea's other sermons. The structure of the second section is difficult to determine and several suggestions have been offered. Mays makes no attempt at an outline but suggests 37 units.[14] However, Anderson and Freedman offer a cogent microstructure of 23 units, three in chapters 1-3 and 20 in the rest of the book. Chapters 4–14 are divided into three divisions: chapters 4-7, The State of the Nation; chapters 8–11, The Spiritual History of Israel;

[11]Anderson and Freedman, *Hosea*, p. 116.

[12]Achtemeier, *Minor Prophets*, p. 6; Wolff, *Hosea*, p. xxii; Anderson and Freedman, *Hosea*, p. 292.

[13]Mays, *Hosea*, p. 3; Stuart, *Hosea–Jonah*, p. 27.

[14]Mays, *Hosea*, pp. v-vi; E. Achtemeier lists 32 pericopes (*Minor Prophets I*, pp. vii-viii).

and chapters 12–14, Retrospect and Prospect: Jacob-Israel in History and Prophecy.[15]

Hosea's sermons are characterized by vivid language and metaphors. The marriage metaphor is only one of many. The father-son metaphor of chapter 11 is also an important formulation and points to another way to see the covenant relationship. The richness of the language of Hosea is captured by Mays:

> In his help to Israel Yahweh is physician (14:4; 7:1; 11:3) and shepherd (13:5). In his judgment he is hunter (7:12), carnivore (5:14; 13:7f), wound and infection (5:12). As Savior he is like dew (14:5) and fruitful tree (14:8). Yahweh looks on Israel as herd (13:5-8), heifer (10:11), vine (10:1), grapes and early fig (9:10). In her sin and suffering Israel is like the sick (5:13); a fickle bird (7:11f); a stubborn cow (4:16); an unborn child (13:13); a cake of bread (7:8); morning mist (6:4); chaff, smoke and dew (13:3). In restoration Israel is compared to the flourishing plant life of Lebanon (14:5-7) and sown ground (2:21ff).[16]

Hosea's command of language, his style of vivid metaphors and pithy sayings, and his fervor in presentation provide the student with challenges of interpretation. Hard study will repay many dividends. At the same time, the Hebrew text of Hosea causes the translator difficulty. There are many unsolved problems of understanding the text. It is often suggested that the reason for the textual difficulties is that since Hosea was from the north he used a dialect not well known in the south. Though possible this has not been confirmed.

GENRE

Hosea is a master of genre. He uses a wide variety of speech forms in his message. The most common language is divine speech when Yahweh speaks in the first person, but this often alternates with Yahweh spoken of in the third person (see 4:1-9). A vivid genre

---

[15]Anderson and Freedman, *Hosea*, pp. xi-xii. Dillard and Longman agree that a division in chapters 4–14 comes after chapter 11 (*Introduction*, p. 359). Some see chapters 4–13 composed of 3 sections based on the 3 words in 4:1b. There is no "faithfulness," 4:2–6:3; no "loyalty," 6:4–10:15; and no "knowledge of God," chapters 11–13. Chapter 14 is then the conclusion, a call to repent.

[16]Mays, *Hosea*, pp. 9-10.

is the legal dispute in which Yahweh brings a legal charge against his people, for they have violated the covenant. The key word is רִיב (*rîb*), "charge, indictment" (4:1; 12:2). This sets the stage for the judgment speeches that announce punishment for breaking the covenant (4:1-3; 8:1-3; 13:1-3). The court proceeding against the unfaithful wife also fits this category (2:2-15). The background would be the gathering of the people at the city gate where the elders sat to dispense justice (see Ruth 4). Hosea calls God's people to account to answer the charges against them.

We also find laments and complaints (4:6; 5:11; 7:8-9; 8:8) and the influence of the wisdom genre (4:11,14b; 8:7). There are also assurances of God's response to his people (6:1-3; 14:5-9) and didactic calls to listen (5:1). The salvation oracles of 1:10-11 and 2:16-23 occupy an important place in the theology of the book.

THEOLOGICAL THEMES[17]

The book of Hosea has a rich theology, but only a few themes can be highlighted here. The book revolves around two foci: Yahweh as the God of Israel and Israel as the people of Yahweh.[18]

1. The relationship between Yahweh and Israel was grounded in the event of the Exodus from Egypt. Hosea 11:1-11, a summary of Israelite history, begins "Out of Egypt I called my son" (cf. Exod 4.22). This history was important, for it marked the beginning of the covenant between Yahweh and Israel and countered the myth of Baal. God had chosen Israel as his people and delivered them from bondage. This act of grace and faithfulness to his promises underscored the covenant as a gift. Israel lived under the generous blessing of the covenant in the Promised Land, receiving the wonderful produce of the land (2:8-9,15,22). Tragically Israel had mistaken this blessing as a gift from Baal. It was in history, not nature, where God acted, but Israel forgot that crucial fact. Israel's rebellion went back as far as Jacob (12:2-4). They seemed to always reject God and his gifts, even in the wilderness period (11:2-4; 13:5-6). Judgment would involve a reversal of this history (2:14; 11:5; 12:9). History was

---

[17]See Paul House, *Old Testament Theology* (Downers Grove, IL: Inter-Varsity, 1998), pp. 346-354, and Roy B. Zuck, ed, *A Biblical Theology of the Old Testament* (Chicago: Moody, 1991), pp. 397-413.

[18]Mays, *Hoses*, p. 7.

important because it was in that precise arena where God worked out his covenant.

2. Hosea's most innovative expression of the covenant was the development of the marriage metaphor to convey Israel's terrible apostasy. The metaphor expressed the covenant so well because both marriage and the covenant expected loyalty, faithfulness, and purity.[19] The foil for the metaphor in Hosea was the Canaanite religious cult and mythology of Baal. Israel learned from the Canaanites that Baal, a dying and rising god in the myth, was the giver of fertility and crops (2:5,12) and that the way to ensure fertility was to participate in cultic prostitution (4:12-14). But this was apostasy, gross unfaithfulness, a tragic breaking of the covenant, pure rebellion. Hosea discovered in his own life that the strongest possible way to express this grave sin was through the use of the language of harlotry and adultery.[20]

This was a brave and incisive direct assault on the Canaanite system and the syncretism of his day. "By this strategy Hosea achieves a fresh modernism that plunges into the contemporaneity of his audience."[21] It also gave a new dimension to the understanding of the relationship between Yahweh and his people. God's love for his people was brought to the foreground. It suggested an intimacy that could not be expressed in any other way. It allowed for the concepts of adultery and harlotry to be used in graphic and symbolic ways. But it also raised the danger that the Israelites would begin to think of Yahweh in sexual terms as they did of Baal. This was a risk Hosea, and God, were willing to take.

Hosea also used an old tradition of conceiving of the covenant relationship in father-son terms (11:1). This led to very tender language (11:2-3). It too emphasized faithfulness, loyalty, obedience, and carried with it the obligation to honor God (implied in 4:7).

3. Hosea not only spoke in metaphors, but he charged Israel with straightforward violation of the Decalogue. Covenant and law are paralleled in 8:1b, but the violation of one or more of the Ten Commandments is made explicit in 4:2,12a,13-14; 7:4,13; 10:4; 13:2 and elsewhere. In several of his accusations he deepens and broad-

---

[19]Gary Hall, "Origin of the Marriage Metaphor," *Hebrew Studies* 23 (1982): 169-171. The first mention of religious harlotry is in Exodus 34:14-16 and Leviticus 19:29.

[20]Hall, "זנה," *NIDOTTE*, 1:1122-1125; and "נאף," *NIDOTTE*, 3:2-5.

[21]Mays, *Hosea*, p. 8.

ens the implications of the commandments. It is not just that Israel broke the commandments. Their lawlessness exhibited a far more serious defect of character and spiritual insight. She had failed in every way.

4. What God demanded was covenant loyalty that was expressed by the terms "knowledge of God," "devotion/commitment," and "faithfulness/integrity" (4:1). God expected Israel to be reliable and carry out their responsibilities to him and to each other. He expected them to exhibit a quality of life based on a positive attitude toward the covenant. They were expected to enthusiastically embrace their relationship with him spelled out in the covenant. Knowledge of God was Israel's main deficiency (4:1). God demanded knowledge rather than sacrifice (6:6). This was not a pious confession or enthusiasm for worship, but a full understanding and positive response to everything that God had done for Israel in the Exodus and wilderness wanderings. They must know their history and know that it was God who gave them the good things of the land (2:8; 11:3). Knowledge involved a personal response to God's salvation acts and obedience to the covenant.

5. Because of Israel's apostasy God would punish her. Justice demanded it. Punishment would take two forms: God would take away his good gifts of the produce of the land (2:9-13). Even the people would be barren (4:3,10; 8:7). Famine, hunger, and childlessness would replace God's blessings. Secondly, military defeat and collapse of the country would ensue (7:16b; 8:3,13-14; 10:6-10; 11:6; 13:15-16) by the hands of the Assyrians (10:6; 11:5). This was not the end, but discipline to entice Israel to return to God (2:14-15; 11:10-11). This reveals a tension between God's anger and his passion for reconciliation (11:8-9; 13:14).

6. Judgment was not the last word. Hosea offered an opportunity for return (14:1-3). But return must be based on confession and repentance. Hosea even formulated a confession for Israel to use (cf. Jeremiah 3:22b-23). The punishment would leave Israel with no recourse but to turn to God, for they would be totally desolate. Restoration would be a new engagement and marriage (2:16-23), and the land would be restored. No longer would they confuse Baal with God. The old history of election and compassion would be revived as the old terms would be taken up again (2:21-23). God never gave up on his desire to save his people (14:4-8).

NEW TESTAMENT CONNECTIONS

Hosea provided a fruitful text for the New Testament. Matthew considered God the Father leading Israel the son out of Egypt (11:1) a type of Jesus Christ, who also as the one, true Son (and true Israel) came out of Egypt (Matt 2:15). Jesus found in Hosea 6:6 a text to force his opponents to reflect on what it really meant to do the will of God (Matt 9:13; 12:7). Paul found in Hosea 1:10; 2:1a; and 2:25 a profound formulation about Israel's restored relationship to God that he could apply to the Gentiles being brought into the church (Rom 9:25). Paul also found the questions of Hosea 13:14 answered in the resurrection of Jesus. Jesus seemed to allude to or perhaps quote Israel's despondent words in his words to the mothers as he stumbled toward his crucifixion (Luke 23:30 and Hos 10:8). The many references to Jesus rising on the third day have been connected with Hosea 6:2 (Matt 16:21; Luke 9:22; 24:7,46; 1 Cor 15:4). Besides the quotes there are many thematic connections between Hosea and the New Testament. Paul carries on the marriage image with the church as the bride of Christ (Eph 5:23,32). The new Jerusalem, the church, is the bride of Christ according to Revelation 21:2,9 (cf. 19:7-11). God's love for Israel is paralleled in the New Testament by God's love for the church and the world. Knowledge of God in the New Testament comes through Jesus Christ. God's compassion, his new covenant through Christ, and repentance and restoration are other important themes developed in the New Testament.

JOEL

HISTORICAL AND CULTURAL BACKGROUND

Often the introductory information to a prophetic book indicates something of the historical background by listing the kings under whom the prophet preached. Joel is one of the few that does not give us that information. Therefore, the historical setting of the book is unknown and must be discerned from internal evidence.[1] This makes the setting speculative, and we can only talk about probabilities. We also must be careful we do not deduce evidence from what is not mentioned in the book. For example, often it is concluded that since no kings are mentioned in the book, it was written in a time when there were none.

Four dates or periods have been proposed. The earliest date proposed is that Joel preached in the time of Joash of Judah (837–800 B.C.).[2] Support is drawn from the fact that the enemies mentioned in the book are not Assyrians and Babylonians of the later time but the Philistines, Phoenicians, Egypt, and Edom, all enemies in the ninth century (3:4,19; cf. 2 Kgs 8:20-22).[3] Priests and elders are mentioned but not a king because Joash, put on the throne at age seven by the priest Jehoida and his followers, was under their tutelage (2 Kings 11). References to the Temple and worship would not fit a postexilic date well. Further, the placement of the book between Hosea and Amos in the canon suggests an early date.

A late postexilic date, down to the fourth or even third century has been proposed also. Support is drawn from the developed apoc-

---

[1] Compare Hosea 1:1, Amos 1:1, and Micah 1:1 with Joel, Jonah 1:1 and Obadiah 1 for example.

[2] E.J. Young, *An Introduction to the Old Testament*, rev. ed. (Grand Rapids: Eerdmans, 1960), pp. 255-256.

[3] The chapter divisions are different in the Hebrew text and English translations. English 2:28-32 are chapter 3 in Hebrew, and English chapter 3 is chapter 4 in Hebrew. English chapter and verse divisions will be followed here.

alyptic ideas of the Day of the Lord in chapters 2 and 3 which could only come after the exile. The presupposed exile in 3:2, the mention of Greeks in 3:6, and relatively large number of Aramaisms also point to a late date.[4] The late date would also explain why a king is not mentioned and would account for the references to priests and daily sacrifices (1:9; 2:14) after the Temple was rebuilt. Joel's apparent heavy dependence on previous prophets also is considered evidence for a late date.[5]

A middle position is that Joel was active sometime in the Persian period, probably after the time of Nehemiah (445 B.C.) and before the fall of the Persians to the Greeks, that is, sometime around 400 B.C.[6] Others suggest an earlier postexilic period in the late sixth to mid-fifth century, prior to the time of Nehemiah and closer to the time of Haggai and Zechariah.[7]

Allen, following Jacob Myers and Gosta Ahlstrom, supports a date shortly after 520 B.C. The mention of Greeks in 3:6 is not necessarily late since the Greeks had already established a trading center in the Eastern Mediterranean by the middle of the sixth century. The reference to the Sabeans in 3:8 would have to be before the end of the sixth century when they lost control of the eastern trade routes. The references in 3:4 could reflect the late sixth century when the Phoenicians and Philistines were in control of the Mediterranean ports on the coast. The reference to the wall of Jerusalem in 2:7 does not have to be post-Nehemiah since the wall was not totally destroyed in 588 and Nehemiah only rebuilt the destroyed portions, not the whole wall. The references to the Temple and to sacrifices suggest a post-515 date after the Temple was rebuilt. The quote in 2:17 from Obadiah 17 suggests a date after Obadiah who is usually dated in the exilic or early postexilic period.

On the other hand Stuart opts for a time just after one of the

---

[4]Otto Eissfeldt, *The Old Testament: An Introduction*, trans. by Peter R. Ackroyd, (New York: Harper and Row, 1965), p. 394.

[5]Scholars who posited a late date tended to hold a negative view of the theological value of the book. See Brevard Childs, *Introduction to the Old Testament as Scripture* (Philadelphia: Fortress, 1979), p. 388.

[6]R.K. Harrison, *Introduction to the Old Testament* (Grand Rapids: Eerdmans, 1969), p. 878-879; H.W. Wolff, *Joel and Amos*, Hermeneia, trans. by W. Janzen et al. (Philadelphia: Fortress, 1977), pp. 4-6.

[7]L. Allen, *The Books of Joel, Obadiah, Jonah and Micah* (Grand Rapids: Eerdmans, 1976), pp. 22-24; Dillard and Longman, *Introduction*, p. 367.

invasions of the Assyrians in 701 B.C. or the Babylonians in 598 or 588 B.C.[8]

The variety of opinions on the date of Joel illustrates the difficulty of certainty when explicit evidence is lacking. In this case the historical background, as important as it is for the prophets, must remain elusive. However, sometime in the exilic or early postexilic period (550–500 B.C.) seems to fit well. The power of Joel's message fortunately is not tied to a precise era. His allusions to and quotes from several of the prophets illustrate the ongoing power of the prophetic message.

TEXT AND AUTHORSHIP

Very little is known of Joel the prophet except that his father was Pethuel. The name Joel means "Yahweh is God" and was a popular name in the Old Testament. There are at least twelve other Joels, most listed in the postexilic books of Ezra, Nehemiah, and Chronicles.[9] Its etymology probably accounts for its popularity. Joel is not called a prophet in the book, but the fact that his words are among the prophetic collection indicates that he was considered a prophet.

STRUCTURE

The book is developed in two sections, with each section having two parts. Each of the four sections is almost equal in length.

    Superscription — 1:1
  I. The Coming Disaster, Call to Repent, and Day of the Lord — 1:2–2:17
    A. The coming disaster and call to repent — 1:2-20
    B. The day of the Lord — 2:1-17
 II. A Word of Hope, Promise of the Spirit and Judgment on the Nations — 2:18–3:21
    A. Blessings of restoration and sending of the spirit — 2:18-32
    B. Judgment on the nations and the glory of Judah — 3:1-21

---

[8]Stuart, *Hosea–Jonah*, p. 226.

[9]"Joel," s.v. *IDB*. The name "Elijah" is an interesting variant name in which the same two theophoric elements are reversed and a first person suffix added to yield "My God is Yahweh."

GENRE

Joel is a mixture of prophetic styles of preaching. He opens with a call to lament because of the devastation caused by a locust plague (see especially 1:5,8,11,13). This is patterned after lament Psalms. He follows with a call to flee patterned after the warning given for an invading army (2:1ff.). But there is also an oracle of salvation with the familiar charge, "Do not fear" (2:21,22) and a promise of a future bursting with food and water (3:17-18). Joel is also noted for his apocalyptic element when he describes the day of the Lord (2:1-11), the coming of the spirit (2:28-32), and the judgment of God on the nations in the "valley of Jehoshaphat" (3:9-16). This is not a full-blown apocalyptic as found in Ezekiel 38–39 however. It is grounded in the covenant curses of Deuteronomy 28 and the Song of Moses in Deuteronomy 32.[10]

Some see the book as a liturgical poem that was to be used in worship at the Temple.[11] This would make Joel a prophet of the cult. However, several references in the book seem too historically specific to fit well a liturgical text.

THEOLOGICAL THEMES

The rich message of Joel has several important themes. The dominant theme is the Day of the Lord (1:15; 2:1,11,31; 3:13). This theme was already an established concept by Joel's day. Amos introduced the theme (5:18-20) and was followed by Isaiah (2:6-22) and Zephaniah (chapters 1, 2). The Day of the Lord refers to a time in the future when God will intervene in the world and establish his reign. Everyone who has sinned against God, Gentiles or Israel, will be exposed and punished. But this vindication of God's holiness and justice had a positive side, for it also meant vindication for those loyal to him. In Joel, the Day has two aspects, a present time and a future day. In chapter 1, Joel applies the negative side of the theme. The Day of the Lord has come upon Judah like a plague of locusts that destroyed the land and caused wailing and weeping. The covenant curses of Deuteronomy were being applied. In chapter 2 Joel builds on this theme with even more vivid eschatological references: dark-

---

[10]Stuart, *Hosea–Jonah*, p. 228.
[11]Dillard and Longman, *Introduction*, p. 368.

ness, gloom, devouring fire, invading armies, earthquakes, darkening of the sun and moon. No one could stand before this onslaught.

The proper response to the judgment on the people and land was repentance with weeping and fasting (2:12-17) in the hope that the Lord would extend mercy and spare his people. Joel's emphasis on fasting and solemn assemblies (1:14; 2:12) indicates his interest in and the importance of the cult. Earlier prophets like Hosea, Amos, and Jeremiah had criticized the cult, but they were attacking its misuse, when the heart was not right with God and worship was only an act.

Joel, like Jonah, was well aware of the compassionate side of God as revealed in Exodus 34:6-7. But unlike Jonah he found this concept to be one of encouragement and hope. For if God was compassionate, perhaps he would relent, forgive them, and restore their fortunes with covenant blessings again (2:12-14).

Joel was not disappointed in this hope. The covenant promises of rain and grain were restored (2:18-27). The land would once again receive moisture and be fruitful, and the people could rejoice in the presence of the Lord. This was a powerful message about the importance and efficacy of repentance in the covenant relation with God.

The other side of the covenant faithfulness of God was the implications for the nations who had participated in the destruction of Judah and Jerusalem that produced the exile. Even though the exile was the result of God's judgment on the sin of his covenant people, those who were his instruments were not guiltless. Thus Joel saw that the restoration of Judah meant also justice and judgment for the nations (3:1-16). How could the nations, who had carried Judah off into exile and sold her into slavery, expect to escape accountability to the Lord of the universe? Their own actions would be turned back on them as God vindicated himself and his people.

Joel ends his book with a glorious conclusion to the day of the Lord. It will be a future day of profusion of plenty in the holy city. God will dwell there in Zion, and Jerusalem and Judah would be inhabited forever (3:17-21).

One of the most famous prophecies of Joel, because of the New Testament usage, is the outpouring of the spirit on everyone (2:28-32). This passage also has eschatological implications with its references to drastic changes in the heavens, and salvation centered in Zion. The presence of God's spirit is noted throughout the Old Testament, but Joel takes it an important step further. Whereas elsewhere the spirit was given at certain times to selected individuals, Joel looks for the day when it will be given to all, young and old, male and female, slave and free. This fulfilled the desire of Moses (Num 11:29) and pointed to significant changes in the way God would work among his people.

NEW TESTAMENT CONNECTIONS

Joel 2:28-32 is quoted verbatim by Peter on the day of Pentecost (Acts 2:17-21) in defense against accusations that he and the others were drunk. Peter announces to the astonished audience that the great Day of the Lord of the Old Testament had arrived. The proof was the outpouring of the spirit that enabled them to speak in tongues. That wonderful, glorious time was now here. Then Peter preached the first gospel sermon showing the centrality of Jesus' death and resurrection to God's plan of redemption. Three thousand were convicted and were baptized and the church, the new Israel, was established and on the move. The future kingdom had broken into human history. The activity of the spirit throughout the book of Acts confirms Peter's words. Jesus' promise of the Holy Spirit in John 14 must be understood in this context also.

Joel's vision of the future when all barriers would be removed by the coming of the spirit is confirmed by Paul also in Galatians 3:28, for in the church all are free and equal under God. Paul affirms this point further in Romans 10:13 when he cites Joel 2:32 that "everyone who calls on the name of the Lord will be saved."

"Calling on the name of the Lord" is a common theme in the New Testament (Acts 4:9-12; 9:14,21; 22:16; 1 Cor 1:2; 2 Tim 2:22). Peter affirms that that means calling on the name of Jesus who is the only name through whom salvation comes (Acts 4:11-12).

AMOS

HISTORICAL AND CULTURAL BACKGROUND

The time in which Amos preached was one of the best times in Israel's history, one of the greatest centuries politically and economically. It has been called a Golden Age in Israel, or at least a Silver Age.[1] Jeroboam the son of Joash (1:1; Jeroboam II) reigned from 786 to 746 B.C. and was an astute and able king (2 Kgs 14:23-29). This auspicious time was made possible because Assyria was in a period of decline, with inept rulers. She was also involved defending her northern borders from expanding Urartu. Damascus to the north had been destroyed by Assyria in 801 B.C. and was later involved in a long and debilitating struggle with Hamath further to the north.[2] The Arameans had been subdued (2 Kgs 14:25-28). Egypt and Babylon were in decline. The long wars with Judah had ended.

Because of these factors Jeroboam was able to restore Israel's previous northern and southern borders east of the Jordan. International trade expanded and produced new wealth. Large scale urbanization resulted, and the merchant class gained power. Farmers were forced from the land, and a poor class grew that could be oppressed by the wealthy (5:10-12; 8:4-6). A leisure upper class grew decadent in its lifestyle (2:8; 4:1; 6:1-6), idolatry (8:14), and sexual immorality (2:7). The result was judicial corruption and a breakdown in justice. Judah in the south under Uzziah (783–742 B.C.) experienced similar conditions. The prosperity of the period has been demonstrated from the archaeological record. Excavations at Tirzah have revealed that in the tenth century the houses were of the same size. But in the eighth century there was a section of the city

---

[1]Gerhard F. Hasel, *Understanding the Book of Amos* (Grand Rapids: Baker, 1991), p. 12. Phillip King, "The Eighth, the Greatest of Centuries?" *JBL* 108 (1989): 3-15.

[2]James L. Mays, *Amos*, OTL (Philadelphia: Westminster, 1969), p. 2

that had large, expensive houses, and a section that had close-ly built houses.[3]

Amos also mentions an earthquake (1:1) which was remembered by Zechariah in the late sixth century (Zech 14:5). Excavations at Hazor and Samaria have produced evidence of an earthquake dated to about 760 B.C. This is perhaps the one to which Amos referred.[4] These dates place Amos somewhere between 780 and 760 B.C. Hosea, Isaiah, and Micah were later contemporaries of Amos, Hosea per-haps overlapping with him in the northern kingdom.

Despite the apparent affluence at this time, there were dark clouds on the horizon for in a few years Assyria would begin a resur-gence that would spell the doom of Israel (8:2). In fact, Amos speaks of the coming destruction in earthquake-descriptive terms (8:8; 9:1,5). In 745 Tiglath-Pileser took the throne of Assyria and soon led it to control of the ancient Near East once again. Samaria and Israel fell to the Assyians in 722, just 30 or so years after Amos's ministry.

TEXT AND AUTHOR

Amos is believed by most scholars to be the earliest "writing" prophet although not the earliest prophet.[5] That is, he is the first prophet whose sermons have been recorded and saved for posteri-ty. This marked a major shift in the importance accorded the prophet and his words. His sermons now took on a permanence and relevance for future generations. Amos also marks a shift from prophets who preached to individuals, usually kings, to prophets who addressed the whole nation.

The book begins with the formula, "The words of Amos," an introduction shared with Jeremiah (Jer 1:1). Most prophetic books specify that the contents are the "word of Yahweh" which came to the prophet (Hos 1:1; Joel 1:1; Micah 1:1; Zeph 1:1; Mal 1:1). How-ever, Amos makes it clear elsewhere that what he speaks are the words of Yahweh (1:2,3,6,9,11; 3:1; 4:1; 5:1; 7:16; 9:1; etc.).

---

[3]Mays, *Amos,* p. 2. Other sites exhibit the same phenomenon.

[4]Earthquakes were common in Palestine because it was on a major fault line (Num 16:31; 1 Sam 14:15). The prophets often used earthquake lan-guage to picture God's coming judgment: Joel 2:10; 4:16[Eng 3:16]; Isaiah 24; 29:6; Micah 1:4; Nahum 1:5.

[5]He was preceded by such prophets as Samuel, Nathan, Gad, Elijah, Elisha, and Micaiah to name a few.

We do not know a great deal about the man Amos. There apparently is little significance to his name.[6] From 1:1 we learn his occupation and the era in which he prophesied. The biographical section in chapter 7:10-14 tells us a bit more. Amos was a shepherd from Tekoa, a small village ten miles south of Jerusalem, about five miles southeast of Bethlehem in the southern kingdom of Judah. Amaziah the priest used that fact against Amos when he told him to go back home (7:12), implying that he had no right or authority in the northern kingdom since he was from the south.

Amos was also a "dresser of sycamore trees" (7:14). This probably means that he worked on the sycamore figs to help them ripen more quickly. The traditional understanding has been that Amos was of humble origins and occupation, from the lower level of society since sycamore figs were the food of the poor. However, in recent years some scholars have suggested that Amos was probably from at least the middle class, if not the upper class, of society. The term נֹקֵד (nōqēd, "shepherd," 1:1) is now understood as referring to an owner of flocks with some social status, not just a humble shepherd.[7] In this understanding he also owned sycamore groves and was thus a person of some means. Consequently, he probably traveled about the country in pursuit of his business interests. That is how he knew so much about the justice system and the geography of the country. However, since he says that he "followed" the flock, which would indicate common shepherd activity (7:15), some commentators still think he was a person of humble means and occupation.[8]

Amos claims that he was not a prophet nor the son of a prophet (7:14) when Amaziah called him a "seer" (חֹזֶה, ḥōzeh; 7:12). These verses have caused considerable discussion.[9] The phrases in the Hebrew text are verbless clauses so that the time element is not clear. If Amos was saying he was not (past tense) a prophet, then he was saying that God had called him out of another occupation and

---

[6]It comes from a root that means "to carry" or "to load." No use is made of this root or idea in the book. This is not the same Amoz as the father of Isaiah (Isa 1:1). In Hebrew the two names share only one letter.

[7]Hasel, *Understanding the Book of Amos*, pp. 35-40. *Nōqēd* is used in 2 Kings 3:4 to refer to the King of Mesha. In Ugaritic texts the term refers to high official functionaries.

[8]F.I. Anderson and David N. Freedman, *Amos* (New York: Doubleday, 1989), pp. 187-188, 777-779.

[9]Hasel, *Understanding*, pp. 41-47.

he had no hereditary relationship to the prophetic office.[10] If Amos was saying that he is not (present tense) a prophet, then he was disassociating himself from any of the current prophets, of whom there were many in the northern kingdom. It seems most probable that the term "seer" and "prophet" were considered synonymous. Amos was saying that he did not come from a line of prophets, but Yahweh had called him from life as shepherd and caretaker of sycamores to be a prophet. Certainly Amos preached and saw visions as prophets did, and both Amaziah and Amos used the verb "to prophesy" of Amos's activity (7:12,14; see 3:7-8).

STRUCTURE

Prophetic books often seem to be put together haphazardly with little thought given to order or logic. However, it is becoming increasingly clear that this impression is in error. It is true with the book of Amos. Careful study has revealed a coherent structure that can be analyzed in several ways. Anderson and Freedman suggest a three-part macro structure. Part I is the Book of Doom, 1:1–4:13. Part II is the Book of Woes, 5:1–6:14. Part III is the Book of Visions, 7:1–9:6. An Epilogue of 9:7-15 finishes the book.[11]

James Limburg suggests seven sections to the book, each section centered in the number seven.[12] The oracles against the nations in 1:2 to 2:16 have 14 divine speech formulas, a repeated three plus four equal seven formula, and indict seven nations before getting to Israel. Chapter 3 has seven divine speech formulas. Chapter 4 has seven "says the Lord." Chapters 5 and 6 have seven "says the Lord." Chapters 7:1 to 8:3 have seven divine speech formulas. Chapters 8:4 to 9:15 have seven divine speech formulas. Clearly, Amos (or an

---

[10]From the time of Samuel prophets were paid and many occupied an official position in the society and at the court of the king (1 Kgs 18:19; 20:35; 22:6; 2 Kgs 9:1).

[11]Anderson and Freedman, *Amos*, pp. xxv-xlii. Stuart thinks the structure is simple and sees three sections: 1:2–6:14; 7:1–8:3; 8:4-9:15 (Stuart, *Hosea–Jonah*, p. 287). Hubbard and Smith see a somewhat similar threefold structure (David Hubbard, *Joel and Amos* [Downers Grove, IL: InterVarsity, 1989], pp. 118-119; Gary V. Smith, *Amos: A Commentary* [Grand Rapids: Zondervan, 1989], pp. 7-9).

[12]James Limburg, "Sevenfold Structures in the Book of Amos," *JBL* 106 (1987): 217-222.

editor) put the book together with some careful thought in order to convey a coherent message. The focal point is judgment on Israel, but Amos used a unique way of working up to his point by concentrating on foreign nations in chapters 1 through 2:6. This was a clever psychological ploy to get the audience's attention and approval. Then he turns to his main subject and pierces the heart of the listeners with the grim truth of their transgressions and sins.[13] The rest of the book focuses on Israel's covenant failure and rebellion. At the center of the book stands the lament, or funeral dirge, over Israel in 5:1-17. It begins and ends with a mourning note (5:1-2,16-17). It contains two calls to seek God and live (5:4-7,14-15) and focuses at the center on a hymn to God (5:8-9). Amos also records five visions that speak of judgment to come (7:1-9; 8:1-3; 9:1-6). The words of the restoration of the tent of David at the end (9:11-15) is so different from the rest of the book that many deny Amos would have preached such words.[14] However, this is to put the prophet into a genre straitjacket that he does not deserve. Most prophets have a word of hope from Yahweh, why not Amos?

GENRE

The short book of Amos is full of a variety of genres. Although the prevailing mood is judgment and doom, Amos chose several ways to express his views. He is the first to have an extensive section condemning the nations around Israel. These oracles have a set formula and list only a few of the sins of each nation (1:2–2:6). Other prophets followed Amos's example with their own extensive collection of these types of oracles (Isaiah 13–23; Jeremiah 47–51; Ezekiel 25–32). Amos's most common form is the judgment speech, which details the accusations and then the judgment which will follow (ch. 4). He also used woe or funeral lamentation (5:1-17; 6:1-7), vision reports (7:1-9; 8:1-3; 9:1-6), wisdom style (3:2-8; 6:12), and hymn fragments (5:8-9; 9:5-6). Included is a third-person account in 7:10-17 with a judgment speech. Ryken has provided a fresh perspective by analyzing the entire book under the rubric of satire. This would

---

[13]Note that Judah is included in the "foreign nation" category to make the number seven.

[14]Mays, *Amos*, p. 165.

explain the sometimes very bitter and pointed condemnations of the people (2:6-7; 4:1-2,4-5; 5:18-20).[15]

THEOLOGICAL THEMES[16]

Though a small book, Amos has a profound understanding of God in relationship to his covenant people and to the world.

1. **The Lord is the God of the universe**. He was not just a national deity, comparable to the foreign countries' national deities, but he controlled all the nations and they were accountable to him (1:2–2:16). If they violated international treaties or universal standards of morality, they would be punished. He treated the nations as if they were under covenant to him. He moved other nations about as he willed, just like he moved Israel about (6:14; 9:7). His deliverance of Israel from Egypt exhibited his control over that world power (2:10; 3:1). He was Creator and sustainer of the world (4:13; 5:8; 9:5-6). Nature could be his instrument to carry out his judgments such as famine and drought, etc. (4:6-12; 7:1-3). Therefore, he can depose kings (7:9) and destroy his own people (8:1-3). So he was the God of history and nature.

2. **God revealed his secrets to the prophets**. Though he may act in history and nature, that must be interpreted and he did so through the prophets (3:7-8). Amos was called to be a prophet, a spokesman for God, even though he had no training and no family background in prophecy (7:10-14). Amos's ministry was product of God's sovereignty, not Amos's desire.

3. **Worship and justice go together**. There was a resurgence in worship during the eighth century, but it concentrated on form (4:4-5; 5:21ff.; 8:14). Since there was also a breakdown in social morality (4:1; 5:11; 8:4ff.), God rejected this superficial devotion. If worship was to have any meaning, then the moral claims of the covenant law must be observed. God desired justice and righteousness. Justice was defined in economic terms and was reflected in treatment of the poor. It was clear that in Israel the economic prosperity of the eighth century was accompanied by exploitation of the poor. Merchants

---

[15]Leland Ryken, "Amos," in *A Complete Literary Guide to the Bible*, ed. by Leland Ryken and Tremper Longman III (Grand Rapids: Zondervan, 1993), pp. 337-347.

[16]See House, *Old Testament Theology*, pp. 357-363.

were dishonest, and excess consumption and leisure were the goals (4:1; 5:11; 6:1; 8:4-6). Therefore, the rich are roundly condemned (4:1ff.; 6:1ff.; 8:4ff.). The needy and the poor are equated with the righteous (2:6; 5:12). To seek God was not to go to the shrines, but to do justice (5:4-7). Worship must include identification with the character and purpose of the One worshiped. God had required of Israel sacrifice and festival worship, but the circumstances in Israel in the eighth century provoked his censure. Now he hated these sacred times and acts (5:21-24), for it was mere noise. What the just, loving, merciful God (Exod 34:6-7) required was compassion and justice. "But let justice roll down like waters, and righteousness like an ever-flowing stream" (5:24) has echoed down through the centuries as a clarion call to seek what God's heart seeks.

4. **Israel was elected for a purpose**. To be chosen as God's people implied responsibility, and failure to carry out this responsibility meant judgment (3:2). All that God was doing was intended to prompt his people to return to him and to their purpose for which he chose them (ch. 4), but it was a failure ("yet you did not return to me").

Election was grounded in the covenant made with Israel through Moses at Sinai. Amos was not an innovator as some have supposed. His accusations and promised judgments come right out of the covenant demands and curses of the Pentateuch, especially Deuteronomy. Amos's concern for the poor echoed many of the laws in Deuteronomy (see Deut 5:19; 15:4-11; 16:19; 24:7,14-15). Deuteronomy 4:21-31 preached many of the themes preached by Amos. The punishments to be visited on Israel fit the covenant curses of Deuteronomy 28 (see especially verses 21,22,30,39-40,48,62,64 and 29:27; 31:17-18,21; 32:30).

5. **The essence of sin was a condition of the heart** which led to pride and to rebellion against God. Israel had a distorted view of God and his purpose. Even other nations were caught up in sin. However, since they did not know Israel's God, they were judged on the basis of integrity and fairness in international relations (ch. 1). Idolatry had made inroads into Israel (2:8; 5:26; 8:14), and the worship at Bethel, Dan, and Gilgal was condemned (3:14; 4:4-5; 5:4-5; 7:10-14; 8:14). The people may have thought their worship was proper, but it wasn't. Syncretism, the old nemesis of Israel, was at work. Perhaps the people were unable to distinguish between proper worship of God and seemingly innocent practices they had adopted

from other nations. However, no matter how heartfelt the worship was, it was hateful to God.

6. **Spiritual renewal was emphasized**. God was to be sought through carrying out his will in daily life. The worship centers were only useful if community life matched God's desire (5:4-6,21-24).

7. **For Amos the near history of Israel was mostly doom**. The people had violated the covenant and so could expect famine, destruction, even exile. Amos was aware of the events in other nations and condemned injustice and treaty violations among them also (ch. 1). However, Amos's view of the distant future (9:11-15) was that God would restore Israel's former glory and elevate her to a position of prominence in the world. God would "restore their fortunes" (9:14, see Deut 30:3). This phrase occurs only once in Amos and Deuteronomy but Jeremiah makes extensive use of it (Jer 30:18; 32:44; 33:11,26, etc.). God would restore the "booth of David" (9:11), a promise based on the promise to David in 2 Samuel 7. Therefore, ultimately Amos viewed the future with hope. The God of the universe, of the world, and of Israel, who held all accountable, would not allow his people to be utterly destroyed.

NEW TESTAMENT CONNECTIONS

Amos 5:25-27 is quoted by Stephen in his sermon in Acts 7:42-43. In the context of relating the long idolatrous history of ancient Israel, Stephen supports his argument that idolatry was early by referring to Amos's assertion that Israel followed foreign gods in the wilderness. Stephen refers to "the book of the prophets," perhaps alluding to the fact that what we call the minor prophets had been collected already into one "book."

Amos 9:11-12 is quoted by James in Acts 15:16-17.[17] For James the future envisioned by Amos has come to pass in the conversion of the Gentiles to Christianity and the ensuing composition of the

---

[17]Both quotes follow the Greek translation of the Old Testament, the Septuagint, in which the Septuagint differs in several places from the Hebrew text. These differences have been explained in several ways. See Gleason Archer and Gregory Chirichigno, *Old Testament Quotations in the New Testament* (Chicago: Moody Press, 1983), pp. 151-155. Most probably the Greek translators misread the Hebrew text or supplied some interpretation. Actually the Septuagint version fits James's point better in Acts 15 than the Hebrew text, although the overall thrust of the Hebrew text is not violated.

church. This is a rebuilding of the Davidic kingdom. The conclusion of the Jerusalem conference based on James's reasoning has had far-reaching implications for the worldwide expansion of the church.

Paul alludes to Amos 5:15 in Romans 12:9. Part of his instructions to Christians on living a growing and mature Christian life includes the admonition to hate evil and seek good.

Other New Testament connections with Amos are thematic. Luke, Paul, and James share Amos's strong concern for social justice and the compassionate treatment of the poor and oppressed (Luke 4:18; 6:20; 7:22; 11:41; 14:13,21; Acts 9:36; 10:4,31; 1 Cor 11:22; Jas 2:1-10). Amos is not quoted in these passages, but his spirit is behind them.

OBADIAH

HISTORICAL AND CULTURAL BACKGROUND

From clues in the brief book it seems that Obadiah preached after the destruction of Jerusalem in 587 B.C. (vv. 10-14). The main accusation is that the Edomites took advantage of the Babylonian attack on Judah and Jerusalem and participated in the destruction. Other texts reflect this alleged participation by Edom in the event (Ps 137:7; Ezek 25:12-14; 35:1-15). The early postexilic period seems to be the best fit for Obadiah.

The name Edom refers either to the name given Esau after he sold his birthright (Gen 25:30; 36:1,8) or to the land of Edom and its inhabitants. The land was also called Seir in the Old Testament (Gen 36:8).[1] The land of Edom was bordered on the north by the wadi Zered, a deep canyon going east from the south end of the Dead Sea, and on the south by the Gulf of Aqabah. It also included the Arabah valley directly south of the Dead Sea. The land was marked by high cliffs on the west (up to 3400 feet), deep canyons, and high plateaus on the east that quickly gave way to desert. In Old Testament times the King's Highway, a major trade route between Egypt and Mesopotamia, passed through its eastern section. In modern times the area is best known for its ancient city of Petra.

Israel and Edom had a long history of conflict, warfare, and subjugation. Esau moved to Edom before Jacob's return from Haran (Gen 32:3), and his descendents inhabited the land. The Edomites refused Israel permission to cross their land via the King's Highway after the Exodus (Num 20:14-21). Saul had battles with the Edomites and David conquered them with considerable slaughter, putting garrisons in the land (2 Sam 8:13-14). Solomon had trouble with them,

---

[1]Both names are wordplays in the Hebrew. Esau was born red and the "pottage" that Jacob gave to Esau is called "red stuff" in Hebrew (אָדֹם, 'ādōm). Also Seir has the same Hebrew consonants (שֵׂעָר) as the word "hairy" (Gen 26:25) which is itself a play on the name Esau.

and in Jeshoshaphat's time the Edomites joined the Ammonites and Moabites for raids on Judah. But the allies ended up fighting each other (2 Chronicles 20). Edom gained her freedom for a time from Jehoram (2 Chronicles 21). Amaziah took control again and killed 20,000 soldiers (2 Chronicles 25). During Ahaz's reign Edom invaded Judah and carried off captives (2 Chr 28:17). Edom retained her freedom from Judah but became a vassal state of Assyria in 736 B.C. After the fall of Jerusalem some Edomites were able to settle south of Hebron in Judah. During the fifth century Edom fell to the Arabs, and in the third century it was overrun by the Nabataeans and more Edomites fled to Judah. In the second century B.C. the Jewish rulers were able to gain control over southern Judea again and compelled the residents to be circumcised. In New Testament times southern Judah was called Idumea and the old Edom territory was called Nabatea. The notorious King Herod was part Idumean.

TEXT AND AUTHOR

We know nothing about the author except his name.[2] There is some uncertainty about the spelling of his name. The Hebrew text reads עֹבַדְיָה (*'Obadyāh*) which means "worshiper or devotee of Yahweh." However, the Septuagint has *Abdiou* and the Latin Vulgate *Abdias*. This indicates a different original Hebrew spelling that would mean "servant of Yahweh." Perhaps they are two different spellings of the same name.

Obadiah and its shorter form, Obed, are very common names in the Old Testament. There are twelve Obadiahs and five Obeds.[3] The most famous Obadiah is the steward in charge of Ahab's palace who hid 100 prophets of Yahweh from Jezebel's purge (1 Kgs 18:3-16). Attempts to identify the author of our book with this Obadiah are unconvincing.[4] The most famous Obed is the grandfather of David (Ruth 4:17,21-22).

The most we can know about our Obadiah is that he was a prophet of God who lived in the sixth century B.C.[5] He was prob-

---

[2]As is the case with Malachi also.

[3]See s.v. "Obadiah" and "Obed," in *NBD*[2], ed. by J.D. Douglas and N. Hillyer (Downers Grove, IL: InterVarsity, 1982).

[4]See the Babylonian Talmud, *Sanhedrin* 39b.

[5]Although some would push his date to later, near the time of Malachi in the fifth century. See s.v. "Obadiah, Book of," in *NBD*[2].

ably knowledgeable of prophets who preceded him, especially Jeremiah.

STRUCTURE

The book of Obadiah is the shortest in the Old Testament although it has caused considerable comment. It focuses its attention on one topic, the denunciation of the nation of Edom and the implications for Israel. Its structure is simple:
1. The judgment on Edom – 1-14
2. The day of the Lord on all nations – 15-16
3. The salvation and restoration of Israel – 17-21

The book of Obadiah is only one of many prophetic denouncements and judgments on Edom, but it is the only one that is a whole book. The other prophetic books include Edom among other nations who are denounced (see Isa 34:5-17; 63:1-6; Jer 49:7-22; Lam 4:21-22; Ezek 25:12-14; 35; Joel 3:19; Amos 1:11-12. See also Mal 1:2-5). Obadiah 1-9 shares many identical phrases with Jeremiah 49:7-22, which suggests some literary connection between the two passages. However, the two texts have a different order of phrases so they were perhaps quoting an earlier oracle against Edom. There are also some close similarities to phrases in Joel. It is probable that Joel is quoting Obadiah 17 in Joel 2:32 ("as the Lord has said").

GENRE

Obadiah fits the prophetic oracle against the nations. Obadiah uses the prophetic perfect tense to describe a judgment that is yet to be fulfilled, but is as good as done. The style is marked by vivid poetry and metaphors. The full intent of the denunciation of Edom is revealed in the last section that looks to the restoration of Israel. This shows that the intended audience was Israel and that the announcement of judgment against a foreign nation was fundamentally a message of hope for God's people.

THEOLOGICAL THEMES

God's universal reign and moral judgment on all nations is the focus of Obadiah. All nations are accountable to God for how they treat others (see Amos 1). Edom's grave sin was her inhumanity toward Judah and Jerusalem when the latter were already suffering severe attack. Edom's fate was sealed by her actions. There is just retribution.

But Obadiah looks beyond the present and the future judgment of Edom to see the permanent establishment of the reign of God (21). This reign will be demonstrated in a concrete way by the restoration of Israel and her possession of the land of her enemies. The righteous were thus assured that those who oppose God will meet their rightful end, and those who remain faithful will ultimately be rescued and exalted.

NEW TESTAMENT CONNECTIONS

The book of Obadiah is brief and specific and has had little influence on the New Testament. Paul quotes from other Old Testament books but reflects the conviction of Obadiah that God will bring just retribution on all people (Rom 12:19). The book of Revelation shares the conviction that the kingdom of God will be established forever (Rev 11:15). This in itself is a profound and sustaining idea.

JONAH

HISTORICAL AND CULTURAL BACKGROUND

Jeroboam II reigned from 786 to 746 B.C. which puts Jonah in the mid-eighth century B.C. Jeroboam II is described by the author of Kings as an evil king, but his reign was marked by remarkable political and economic expansion. It was a time of Assyrian weakness which enabled the Israelite king to expand his borders north and east. International diplomatic and military losses coupled with uprising and famine marked the mid-eighth century in Assyria. However, in 745 B.C. Tiglath-Pileser III came to the Assyrian throne and embarked on an immediate and highly successful expansion of the Assyrian empire. By 738 he had expanded control south and west and exacted tribute from most of the states of Syria and Palestine, including Israel. After the death of Jeroboam, Israelite politics became a disaster with coup and countercoup and rebellions against Assyria. In 722 the Assyrians destroyed Samaria, deported thousands, and established Israelite territory as a province in the empire. Therefore, the anti-Assyrian attitude of Jonah is no surprise.

Nineveh was an ancient city whose occupation goes back to 4500 B.C. The city gained prominence during the first Assyrian empire under Shalmaneser I (c. 1260 B.C.). It was an alternate royal residence under Tiglath-Pileser I (1114–1076 B.C.), and later kings built palaces there. In its heyday Nineveh was enclosed by an inner wall seven and one-half miles in circumference though in Jonah's day it was perhaps only three miles. It is estimated that it could have held 175,000 people. The book of Jonah gives the population as 120,000 (4:11).

Two notices about the city in the book of Jonah have cast doubt on the historicity of the book. Jonah 3:3 refers to the size of the city as a "three days' walk across"[1] and 3:6 refers to the "king of Nineveh."

---

[1] NRSV. This is the traditional translation. NIV has "it took three days to

From what is known of the size of the city, even at its largest, it seems unlikely that it would take three days to walk through it. Therefore, 3:3 may be an exaggeration to express the great size of the city,[2] or be based on a hazy memory,[3] or the Hebrew phrase may be understood as an idiom referring to the length of the visit.[4] There is much in favor of this latter interpretation. The reference to a "great city for God" immediately preceding the phrase likely refers to the importance of the city from God's perspective, not the size of the city.[5] Also the word usually understood as the length of time to go through the city and thus refer to its width (מַהֲלַךְ, *mahălak*) is used in Nehemiah 2:6 to refer to the length of the visit of Nehemiah to Jerusalem, not the distance from Babylon to Jerusalem.[6] There is evidence that ancient protocol required a visitor to a city to follow certain rules of introduction to the authorities that would have required at least three days.[7] Furthermore, if we understand that Jonah preached his sermon more than once, then he would have spent at least a day or two visiting various places in the city.[8]

The reference to the "king of Nineveh" is not a serious issue if one understands that Assyrian kings occasionally resided in Nineveh,[9] and that the term could easily be understood as a reference to the Assyrian king. First Kings 21:1 refers to Ahab as the "King of Samaria" but clearly means the King of Israel. The story focuses on Nineveh so the narrator is interested in that city not the empire. On the other hand, evidence has been uncovered that the word "king" can also refer to governors of cities or provinces.[10]

Scholars have also questioned the repentance of the Assyrian king. Why would such a monarch pay attention to a visitor from a

---

go all through it" which is a free rendering of the Hebrew. The Hebrew literally says "from walking three days."

[2]Allen, *Joel, Obadiah, Jonah, and Micah*, pp. 221-222.

[3]Achtemeier, *Minor Prophets I*, p. 257.

[4]Stuart, *Hosea–Jonah*, pp. 483-484.

[5]Ibid., p. 487.

[6]Ibid.

[7]Ibid.

[8]John Walton et al., *Bible Background Commentary: Old Testament* (Downers Grove, IL: InterVarsity, 2000), p. 779.

[9]Tiglath-Pileser I, Ashurnasirpal II (883–859 B.C.), and Sargon II (722–705 B.C.) all used the city as royal residences.

[10]Paul Ferguson, "Who Was the King of Nineveh in Jonah 3:6?" *TynBul* 47 (1996): 301-314.

little nation in the far west? It must be remembered that the ancient cultures were superstitious, syncretistic, and easily influenced by natural disasters. During the reign of Assur-Dan III (773–756) several events happened that could have produced a heightened sense of anxiety and openness to a "prophet." For example, a total solar eclipse occurred on June 15, 763 B.C., an earthquake occurred about the same time, armies were invading from the north, and famine and epidemics were rampant. Earthquakes and eclipses especially were bad omens and indicators of divine wrath.[11]

TEXT AND AUTHORSHIP

Jonah is introduced as a prophet and as the son of Amittai. Nothing else is known about him from the book. He is no doubt to be identified with Jonah the son of Amittai of 2 Kings 14:25 who prophesied that Jeroboam II would reexpand the borders of Israel to mirror David's empire. There we are told Jonah was from Gath-hepher, a village in the territory of Zebulun (Josh 19:13) west of the Sea of Galilee and a few miles northeast of New Testament Nazareth.

Jonah's name means "dove" but it probably has no significance.[12] We learn from the book that Jonah was strongly anti-Assyrian which is not surprising given Israel's experience with that nation. The book is written in the third person, but we do not know who the narrator was. Therefore, the date of the book is uncertain.[13]

STRUCTURE

Most agree that the book of Jonah is a unit. It is a coherent narrative about an episode from the life of Jonah. Generally only chapter two's place in the book has been questioned. It is poetic, first person, reflects a different attitude of Jonah than is seen in the rest of

---

[11]Stuart, *Hosea–Jonah*, pp. 491-492.

[12]Some claim it is an allegorical reference to Israel used as a common endearing term. However, a survey of the word for "dove" in the Old Testament (32 occurrences) shows that it is never used in that sense for Israel. The closest are three references in the Song of Solomon where "dove" is a word expressing affection (2:14; 5:2; 6:9). Once Ephraim is referred to as a "silly dove," which is hardly an affectionate term (Hos 7:11).

[13]See discussion below.

the book, and thus suggests contradictory viewpoints in the book.[14] On the other hand, if the chapter is original, it gives us insight into the complex character of Jonah, who is on the one hand disobedient but on the other grateful to God for his grace. Its thanksgiving style is proper for one who was rescued from certain death by God. A careful analysis suggests that the poem fits well with the overall purpose of the book.[15]

The structure follows the chapter divisions:

1. God's commission and Jonah's flight — 1:1-17
2. The Psalm of thanksgiving — 2:1-10
3. Re-sending, preaching, and repentance — 3:1-10
4. God's lesson for Jonah — 4:1-11

GENRE

The genre of the book is the most controversial issue for understanding the book. Conclusions about genre affect many of the other aspects of the book including the identity of Jonah and the historical background covered above.

First of all the book of Jonah is a prophetic narrative. It begins with the typical "Now the word of the Lord came to. . . ." However, it differs from all of the other prophetic books in that it focuses on a narrative from the life of Jonah, not on his prophetic messages. It is more akin to the narratives of the prophets Elijah and Elisha that we find in the books of Kings. We have narratives from the lives of other prophets in prophetic books, like Jeremiah and Ezekiel, but they form only a minor part of the book.

The book has been designated as history, parable, midrash, allegory, and didactic story. The most radical approach calls it a combination of two legends and a mythological, fairy-tale motif (referring to the great fish that swallowed Jonah).[16]

The book is clearly didactic. The narrative builds toward the end where it focuses on the divine speech of God (4:4,10-11). When the point of the narrative has been made, the story ends. We do not learn the outcome of the repentance of the people nor anything more about Jonah. We may surmise from other parts of the Old

---

[14]Childs, *Introduction*, pp. 422-424.
[15]Stuart, *Hosea–Jonah*, pp. 438-439.
[16]Eissfeldt, *Old Testament*, p. 405.

Testament, for example Nahum, that if Nineveh did repent, it was not permanent. But Jonah disappears entirely.

Stuart also calls the book "sensational literature."[17] By that he means that several things are included in the narrative to excite the imagination and emotions of the reader, especially the storm at sea, the fish story, and the plant story.

Jonah is not an allegory. Allegory is highly symbolic and fictional, designed at every juncture to point beyond itself to a deeper meaning. Allegories are extended analogies and the audience must recognize at every point the intended reference. There are few allegories in the Old Testament though one thinks of Jotham's ironic story in Judges 9:7-15 or Nathan's story for David (2 Sam 12:1-15) or Job's story about his friends (Job 6:15-21).[18]

Jonah is not midrash. This designation has been made mostly by Jewish scholars. Midrash is a commentary on biblical texts and is didactic. It analyzes key texts and attempts to apply them. There is none of this in Jonah. In fact Jonah looks more like a primary text that would have midrash written about it.[19] On the other hand Jonah 3:9 and 4:2 are almost verbally identical to Joel 2:13-14. Therefore, some see Jonah as midrash on Joel. This seems unlikely. The concepts of Joel 2:13 are very common, based on Exodus 34:6-7. This was a common teaching both books could draw on.

Jonah is structured like a parable. The narrative proceeds step by step up to the climax at the end of chapter 4. When the point is made, the book ends abruptly. One is reminded of New Testament parables like the parable of the Good Samaritan. Details from real life that include real cities and reflect real social conditions are made into a story to illustrate a teaching of Jesus. When the point is made, the story ends. Allen supports the view that the book is "a parable

---

[17]Stuart, *Hosea–Jonah*, p. 435.

[18]Years ago Leland Ryken called for understanding parables in the Bible as having allegorical elements. He was not advocating a return to the fantasies of medieval exegesis but a common sense interpretation based on Jesus' own interpretation of selected elements of his parables. See *How to Read the Bible as Literature* (Grand Rapids: Zondervan, 1984), pp. 145-148, 199-203.

[19]Stuart, *Hosea–Jonah*, p. 436. There are two references to midrash in the Old Testament, 2 Chr 13:22, the "*midrash* of the prophet Iddo," and 2 Chr 24:27, the "*midrash* of the Book of Kings." The NIV translates the word as "annotations" in both places; the NRSV as "story" and "Commentary on" respectively.

with certain allegorical features."[20] He understands the literary "tone" to be parody or satire. Jonah is a "ridiculous figure" whom no one would defend. He is self-centered and self-righteous. Therefore, the function of the book is to challenge the attitude of some group in Israel that Jonah represents. Allen sees the book as a parallel to Jesus' parable of the Prodigal Son. God's great love and forgiveness are demonstrated while a misunderstanding of God's nature is challenged.[21] If the book of Jonah is a parable, it is the longest one in the Bible. Four chapters seem quite long for the genre.

Many are convinced that Jonah is a historical narrative. It is presented as historical and is connected with an historical figure, the Jonah of 2 Kings 14:25. Real historical places are mentioned. Objections to its historicity, in addition to some alluded to above, are the great fish that swallowed Jonah and the reported repentance of the king and city of Nineveh. Aside from arguments based on the possibility of someone surviving three days in the belly of a large fish or whale (apparently it has happened),[22] the narrative of Jonah is close to the narratives about Elijah and Elisha in 1 and 2 Kings. Their stories too are full of miraculous events, especially the narratives about Elisha. In their stories, placed in the dark days of Ahab and Jezebel, these men of God needed the divine validation of their ministries to rescue the nation from certain spiritual suicide. In the case of Jonah the miracle of the great fish was needed to rescue Jonah from the consequences of his disobedience and turn him back to God. Therefore, if the only objection to the big fish is because of an antisupernatural bias, the objection can be ignored. Miracle can be an integral part of biblical historical narrative.[23]

The New Testament would also seem to argue in favor of real history. Jesus' reference to the sign of Jonah indicates that he understood Jonah as a real person and his three days in the fish as a real event (Matt 12:38-42). However, the force of this argument is lessened somewhat when one observes that today we refer to New Testament parable characters as though they were real. Thus one often hears references to the Good Samaritan as though he were a real person even though everyone knows he is not. It is possible Jesus was doing something similar.

---

[20]Allen, *Joel, Obadiah, Jonah, Micah*, p. 181.
[21]Ibid., p. 178.
[22]Harrison, *Introduction*, p. 907.
[23]Stuart, *Hosea–Jonah*, p. 440.

The simplest view is to understand Jonah as an historical narrative. However, it is more than that for it is a narrative with a didactic purpose, and that purpose is made clear at the very end. In this way it differs from the narratives of Elijah and Elisha. The latter are a part of a larger narrative, and the meaning of individual stories about these prophets are derived from the larger context. Not so with Jonah. The brief story is a self-contained unit and is to be understood as it stands. This is why the parabolic interpretation has been popular.

In fact it is difficult to decide between history and parable. Either interpretation will give the same meaning. Neither is a denial of the inspiration of Scripture. Both lead the interpreter to the same understanding of the meaning of the story and to the same insight into the nature of God.[24]

A second element of genre is the nature of chapter 2. It is a poetic hymn with many similarities to the Psalms. It is closest to a thanksgiving Psalm (vv. 1,6,9). Under the circumstances one might expect a lament, for Jonah is trapped in the belly of the fish. But the fish was the means God used to save him from death in the sea, so a thanksgiving psalm is appropriate. The psalm contains the elements usually associated with thanksgiving: introduction (v. 2), description of distress (vv. 3-6a), appeal to God for help (v. 7), reference to God's rescue (v. 6b), and vow of praise (vv. 8-9).[25] Though of a different genre the poem is integral to the narrative of Jonah and is understandable only in its context.[26]

THEOLOGICAL THEMES

The message of the book focuses on God's compassion that extends to all people. God's commission to go to Nineveh challenged Jonah's comfort zone. We know from other prophets that God was Lord of the universe and had messages for many nations. Jonah's refusal to go illustrates a narrow perspective that was perhaps shared by many in Israel. The fact that Nineveh was an Assyrian

---

[24]Dillard and Longman, *Introduction*, pp. 392-393.

[25]Stuart, *Hosea–Jonah*, pp. 471-472. English versification differs from the Hebrew. English 1:17 is Hebrew 2:1 and English 2:1 is Hebrew 2:2, etc. through chapter 2.

[26]Ibid.

city, and part of that sometimes powerful, wicked empire that endangered Israel so often, placed Jonah in a difficult position. He did not respond well. In fact the sailors in the boat were more sensitive than Jonah. While they were terrified at the storm and sought God's intervention, Jonah, the cause of the trouble, slept soundly in the bottom of the ship.

The response of the Ninevites is also juxtaposed with Jonah. They repent when they hear Jonah's message and utter a penetrating understanding of God. Perhaps he will relent, accept their repentance, and turn away the predicted punishment (3:7-10). This profound sentiment parallels Jeremiah 18. But it was not a sentiment that pleased Jonah. His response in 4:2-3 reveals the real issue for Jonah. He understood God's compassion well enough, but he was selective in how he wanted it applied. Jonah seems to represent those elect of God who appreciate the grace God shows them, but interpret it to mean they can be the only recipients. Or at the least, they may understand God's grace is larger than their world, but they don't want to hear about it or see it applied. They see election as a privilege not as an act of grace.

The key text for Jonah's understanding of God is Exodus 34:6-7. This is a text that is reflected throughout the Old Testament in the Psalms and prophets. It expressed a truth that Jonah knew but did not want to see applied. The lesson of the growing and dying plant was a simple way to express this truth (4:6-11). If Jonah could be concerned about a little plant, then how much more could God be concerned about a city full of repentant people. This is one of the clearest statements in the Old Testament of the universal nature of God's grace. Israel was chosen for the purpose of witnessing to God's grace in the world. If they abandoned that purpose, then they were not faithful to God. The narrative ends abruptly after the point is made. The reader is left to reflect on the simple truth of God's statement. The narrow human viewpoint that focuses only on present personal comfort will not be able to understand the mind of a compassionate God. He does not see the world as humans do. If his people are to reflect his will for the world, they had better break out of their narrow provincialism and begin to see the world, even enemies, through the eyes of God. Yes, God is a gracious and compassionate God. That is a truth applicable not just to the elect but to all who seek God. God is a merciful, loving God who will respond to repentance, even from the worst sinners.

NEW TESTAMENT CONNECTIONS

Jesus' reference to Jonah is the only direct use of the book in the New Testament. When confronted by the Pharisees with a request for a sign, Jesus promised them only one sign, that of Jonah — three days in the earth. This was a reference to his burial, but the Pharisees had no way of knowing that (Matt 12:38-43; Luke 11:29-32). Jesus extends the reference even further and compares the Pharisees to the people of Nineveh. At least Nineveh repented, but even though a prophet greater than Jonah is here, the people are unwilling to repent (implied). This would have been a great insult.

The New Testament builds on the Old Testament concern for all nations. The gospel is for the whole world, not just a few (Matt 28:19-20; John 3:16-17; Acts 10–11; etc.). In Christ all ethnic groups become one. There is no Jew and Gentile (Gal 3:28). God is patient and does not want anyone to be lost (2 Pet 3:9). Many Christians need to hear God's word to Jonah.

MICAH

HISTORICAL AND CULTURAL BACKGROUND

The time frame of Micah's ministry (1:1) is during the reigns of Jotham (742–735 B.C.), Ahaz (735–715 B.C.), and Hezekiah (715–687 B.C.). This makes him a contemporary with Isaiah and near to the time of Hosea and Amos.[1] Therefore, the historical setting is the same as that of Isaiah (see the details under Isaiah). The references to Samaria (1:1,6), Omri, and Ahab (6:16) suggest that he began his ministry before the fall of Samaria in 722 B.C. A reference to Micah 3:12 in Jeremiah 26:18 shows that he prophesied during the time of Hezekiah after 715 B.C. Some have suggested that 1:10-16 describe the advance of Sennacherib toward Jerusalem in 701.

The reign of king Jotham ushered in significant changes in the fortunes of Judah and Israel. The reigns of Uzziah (783–742 B.C.), Jotham's father, and Jereboam II (786–746 B.C.) in the north were marked by territorial expansion and prosperity. The mighty nation of Assyria was in decline and the small states in Palestine had their freedom once more. But the death of Uzziah coincided with the rise of the soon-to-be-powerful king of Assyria, Tiglath-Pileser III (745–727 B.C.). Because of inept leadership Israel soon felt the brunt of his power, and Samaria fell to Assyria in 722 B.C. Judah protected her independence for awhile, but in the time of Ahaz she became a vassal of the expanding world power. King Hezekiah was encouraged by regime change in Assyria and rebellions in Babylon and led his own rebellion in 701 B.C. This drew the wrath of Sennacherib who, after gaining control in Babylon, advanced into Palestine. He subdued the little kingdoms there, invaded Judah, destroyed Lachish and numerous other cities, and surrounded Jerusalem. Through divine intervention Hezekiah and Jerusalem were delivered from certain destruction (Isaiah 36–37; 2 Kings 18–19).

---

[1] In fact in the Septuagint version the book of Micah is placed immediately following Hosea and Amos.

Micah's ministry covered these tumultuous years, and he preached destruction on both Samaria and Jerusalem. But he also preached hope and restoration, a message very much like his contemporary Isaiah.

TEXT AND AUTHORSHIP

We know little about Micah the prophet. He was from Moresheth (1:1), probably the Moresheth-gath of 1:14. This Moresheth was about twenty miles southwest of Jerusalem at the edge of the Shephelah, near Lachish. It is on the road from Azekah to Lachish and was fortified by Rehoboam, Solomon's son (2 Chr 11:5-10). It was therefore more than a small pastoral town and would have been visited by government officials. We do not know Micah's parents or where exactly he preached, but internal evidence suggests he worked in Jerusalem (he seems to know well the misconduct of government officials, 2:1-2,8-9; 3:1,5,9,11). Like Amos, his hometown is given, perhaps because he did not live or preach where he grew up.

Micah was a popular name in the Old Testament and appears in two other variations, Mica and Micaiah. It means "Who is like Yahweh?"[2] His name is appropriate for the book for a focus of its theology is on the sovereignty of God. There is probably a wordplay on the name in 7:18, "Who is a God like you . . . ?"

STRUCTURE

The structure of the book of Micah is complex and scholars have questioned how much of it actually comes from Micah of Moresheth. The chief obstacles to the unity of Micah seem to be the sharp contrast between judgment and hope, and the apparent references to the sixth-century destruction and restoration of Jerusalem.

Most scholars are willing to accept that the first three chapters are from Micah but after that there is little agreement on the origin of the material. Chapters 6 and 7 have been assigned to the exilic and postexilic period. Chapters 4 and 5 sometimes have been attached to

---

[2]The most well-known other Micah is the Ephraimite in Judges 17–18 whose ephod, idols, and private priest are taken to Dan by some Danites. The most famous Micaiah is the prophet who predicted Ahab's death in 1 Kings 22.

chapters 1–3 and sometimes have been assigned to later times. The fate of Micah at the hands of the critics is at present unclear.[3] Nevertheless, it is not necessary to take this negative view of the book of Micah in order to understand its structure and theology.

Micah apparently does contain a few verses that represent preaching that comes from an earlier, independent source. Micah 4:1-3 is identical to Isaiah 2:2-4. The consensus is that both Micah and Isaiah are quoting another popular source. But Micah gives his own flavor to the quote by adding verse 4.[4]

Careful analysis of the book shows that Micah shifts back and forth between pronouncing judgment and announcing hope in a patterned way. There are two cycles, chapters 1 to 5 and chapters 6 to 7.

> Superscription — 1:1
> I. First Cycle — 1:2–5:15
>   A. God's judgment on sin and apostasy in Samaria and Judah — 1:2–3:12
>   B. God's message of hope to Israel — 4:1–5:15
> II. Second Cycle — 6:1–7:20
>   A. God's dispute and reproach — 6:1–7:7
>   1. God's dispute and required action — 6:1-8
>   2. Israel's social sin denounced — 6:9-16
>   3. Micah's lament over the evil in Israel — 7:1-7
>   B. Words of Hope and Restoration — 7:8-20[5]

Such careful arrangement could be the result of later editors, but there is no good reason why Micah could not have arranged his own sermons when they were written down. Little is actually known about the composition of the prophetic books so that speculation often takes on a life of its own. The one account we do have shows the

---

[3]Childs' conclusion about modern studies of the Old Testament, and especially Micah, is that "few books illustrate as well as Micah the present crisis in exegetical method. In spite of many good insights and interesting observations of detail, the growing confusion over conflicting theories of composition has increasingly buried the book in academic debris. Needless to say, no general consensus of the book's form or function appears in sight" (Childs, *Introduction*, p. 431).

[4]Allen, *Joel, Obadiah, Jonah and Micah*, p. 243-244.

[5]See Dillard and Longman, *Introduction*, p. 400. Leslie Allen proposes a more detailed, nuanced approach with three sections, 1:2–2:13; 3:1–5:15; and 6:1–7:20. The first and third sections parallel each other and the center section has a chiastic arrangement. Each smaller section has the interplay of "doom" and "hope" (Allen, *Joel, Obadiah, Jonah and Micah*, pp. 260-261).

prophet used a scribe and was responsible for the material (Jeremiah 36). Rationalistic assumptions that at the outset eliminate inspiration, revelation, and predictive prophecy do not lend themselves to open-minded study of the prophets. The prophets in fact claim that they operate under divine direction and all three concepts are at work.

GENRE

The genre of Micah contains two typical styles, announcements of doom and destruction, and announcements of hope. For example, 1:2-7 is a typical announcement of judgment. It begins with a call to listen (1:2) and description of God's coming (vv. 3-4), a description of Samaria and Jerusalem's sin (v. 5), and an announcement of the judgment introduced by "therefore" (vv. 6-7). Chapters 4 and 5 are typical announcements of hope with several units that follow the pattern. There are several references to "the latter days" (4:1) or to "that day" (4:6; 5:10). The topics include all nations coming to Jerusalem, the reign of Yahweh, the destruction of the nations, and the survival of the remnant.

Micah also included a covenant lawsuit section using the technical word רִיב (*rîb*, "legal charge, dispute, case, controversy") in 6:1-3. God as judge and offended party called Israel to account in a courtroom setting to lay out his case against her.

Micah's style is often brilliant. Chapter 1:10-16 is a fine example with its detailed play on words. Each city named is matched with a verb that is related to the city name in some way to describe the judgment that is coming. These are difficult to produce in English. For example, "Gath" and the verb "tell" (v. 10a) share similar consonants in reverse order. "Beth-leaphrah" (literally "house of dust") will roll in the "dust" (v. 10b). "Shaphir" is the beautiful city that will go in "nakedness" (v. 11a). The "house of Achzib" (literally "house of deceit") is a "deception" (v. 14b).

THEOLOGICAL THEMES

Micah mixes two major themes throughout the book, God's judgment on the people's sin and hope for the future. The sins of the people fit two main categories, social injustice and idolatry. All levels of society were involved in social inequities. The people were full of greed (2:1-2; 6:10-12), the rulers oppressed the people (3:1-4), bribery occurred at all levels even among the priests and prophets (3:9-11; 7:3), and there was total family breakdown (7:5-6). Idolatry included illegitimate altars (1:5), idols and images (1:7; 5:13-14), trust in military might (5:10-11), and divination (5:12). These charges parallel Isaiah's in Isaiah 2:6-8. The people had abandoned trust in the invisible but powerful God for the visible but powerless works of their own hands. The special people of God had become like the nations and would be treated in the same way.

Because of the people's rebellion, judgment in the form of destruction was certain. The land would be devastated (1:6), the cities destroyed (1:8-16). War will bring distress, disgrace, and darkness (3:5-7; 5:1) and make labor useless (6:14-16). Exile will be the ultimate result and only a remnant will be left (4:10; 5:7-9).

In this context Micah's famous formulation of what God really desires is remarkable (6:1-8). It is placed in the context of a covenant lawsuit (vv. 1-2). God brings Judah into court and proclaims his innocence. He had not done anything to deserve the way they had treated him (vv. 3-5). Then Micah reminds the people of what God's basic requirements were: "to do justice, to love kindness, and to walk humbly with your God" (v. 8). In other words they were to do all the things they were not at that time doing. He also condemned sacrifices that were made for their own sake. He did not condemn the cult as such but a cultic life that was undertaken apart from a holy life lived out with compassion and a burning desire to treat everyone with fairness and equity (see also Isa 1:10-20).

Despite the destruction that was coming on the nation, Micah emphasized that it was not the end. A gracious God would not let his people totally disappear from the earth. They still had a purpose to carry out. Therefore, after the exile there would be restoration and blessing under the reign of God (4:6-7; 7:11-20). Furthermore, the time would come when all nations would flock to Jerusalem to learn the ways of the Lord and peace and justice would reign (4:1-4). This is one of the most magnificent visions of the future in the Old Testament (cf. Isa 2:2-4).

Micah also looked to the future reign of God that would come in the form of a ruler who came out of Bethlehem to defeat the foes and establish peace (5:2-6). Not only did Micah urge the people to walk in humility, he understood that the might of God could be manifested in the small things as well (v. 2).[6]

---

[6]English 5:2 is 5:1 in the Hebrew text.

NEW TESTAMENT CONNECTIONS

The vision that Micah had for the future importance of Bethlehem is reflected in the New Testament. In Matthew 2:1-6 it was the scribes and chief priests who quoted Micah 5:2 to King Herod. In other words it was not Matthew introducing a proof text for his argument that Jesus fulfilled the Old Testament, but the Jews themselves who interpreted the Micah text in a Messianic manner. It is remarkable that despite this evidence the Jewish leaders did not accept Jesus as Messiah.

Jesus condemned the cultic perfectionism of the Pharisees (Matthew 23) and reminded them of what Micah required (v. 23). The weightier matters of the law were justice, mercy, and faith. It was hypocrisy to be fastidious about obedience to the law and ignore its foundational principles.

Micah's vision of the future gathering at Zion and the ensuing peace (4:1-4) evoked a picture of the future that unfolded in several ways. Judah did indeed return from exile and rebuild the Temple, but the new edifice did not approach its previous glory. Then the Messiah came and declared that he was the true Israel and temple and more important than either. Through him the earthly types were done away. Through Jesus all nations would have access to God and his unique gift of peace (John 14:27; 16:33). The New Testament also points to the end of time when ultimately the nations will flock to the new Jerusalem to experience the glory of God (Rev 21:22-27).

NAHUM

HISTORICAL AND CULTURAL BACKGROUND

Evidence from the book suggests the parameters for the date of the book. The fall of the Egyptian city Thebes (Hebrew — "No-Amon") in 3:8-10 suggests Nahum was written after 663 B.C. when Ashurbanipal and the Assyrians conquered Thebes. The predictions of the fall of Nineveh (2:1ff.; 3:1ff.) suggest a date before 612 when that city fell to the Medes and Babylonians.

Assyrian dominance over Israel and Judah began in the middle of the eighth century under Tiglash-Pileser III (745–727) and continued through the fall of Israel (722 B.C.) and through the reigns of the Judean kings Ahaz (735–715, see Isaiah 7), Hezekiah (715–687, see Isaiah 36–37) and Manasseh (687–642).[1] The Assyrian king, Ashurbanipal, dominated the middle of the seventh century (668–627). He attacked Egypt and extended his control as far south as Thebes in 663. However, by 650 the Egyptians were able to break free and the Assyrian hold over the Middle East began to slip. The Babylonians also rebelled under Ashurbanipal's brother but were reconquered in 648. It was perhaps in this period that Manasseh began to make some independent moves as suggested by his building activities in 2 Chronicles 33:14-16. Despite his military activity Ashurbanipal had time to renovate both Nineveh and Babylon and collect an enormous library at Nineveh. There was a general feeling of security and well-being. But it did not last long. After his death (627) Assyria collapsed with astonishing speed. Babylon soon gained its freedom, and for the next fifteen years the Medes and Babylonians put increasing pressure on Assyria until in 612 B.C. the capital, Nineveh, fell to the combined forces.

It was during this turbulent period that Nahum offered a message of hope to Judah by delivering a prediction of the collapse of

---

[1]See 2 Kings 15:29–21:18.

the wicked city, Nineveh (and by extension the Assyrians). It is most likely that he wrote during the early part of this period rather than toward the end. The fall of Thebes was still fresh, and its rebuilding was not known. The Assyrians were still powerful and in control (1:12). Therefore, sometime around 650 would be a reasonable date.[2] If this is the time, then Nahum would have encouraged Manasseh's attempts at independence and Josiah's reforms.[3]

TEXT AND AUTHOR

Nahum the man is mentioned only in 1:1. His name comes from the Hebrew verb that means "to comfort or have compassion" (compare Isa 40:1, "Comfort, comfort my people."). Other names come from the same Hebrew root: Nehemiah ("Yahweh is comfort," Neh 1:1; Ezra 2:2), Nahamani and Nehum (Neh 7:7), Naham (1 Chr 4:19), Menahem (2 Kgs 15:14), and Tanhumeth (Jer 40:8). The name Nahum has also been found on a seventh-century seal from Lachish.

Nahum is called an Elkoshite, which means he was from the village of Elkosh. The site has not been identified though many scholars agree that it was probably in Judah, just north of Lachish and near Moresheth (see Micah 1:1, "Micah the Moreshethite"), possibly the modern Beit Jebrin.[4] Other suggestions have been: Al-Qush in northern Assyria, about 50 miles north of the ancient site of Nineveh; a village in northern Galilee; the New Testament village of Capernaum ("village of Nahum").[5] One scholar has suggested a wordplay, a combination of the Hebrew words for God (אֵל, 'ēl) and severe (קָשֶׁה, qšh), which then introduces the message of the book.[6]

---

[2]W.A. Maier, *The Book of Nahum* (St. Louis: Concordia, 1959), p. 36. Others who would agree are Robertson, Spronk, Baker, Armerding (see the bibliography). Others have suggested at least before 627 and the death of Ashurbanipal. Others have suggested just before 612 and the fall of Nineveh.

[3]Klass Spronk, *Nahum* (Kampen: Kok Pharos, 1997), p. 13, believes Nahum is a pseudonym for a court official of Manasseh who had access to royal treaty documents and knew Akkadian. That was one reason he was so well informed about world events.

[4]Ralph Smith, *Micah–Malachi*, WBC (Waco: Word, 1984), p. 63.

[5]See Y. Kobayashi, "Elkosh," *ABD*, 2:476.

[6]Spronk, *Nahum*, p. 32. Spronk expands on an idea advanced earlier by O.T. Allis, "Nahum, Nineveh, Elkosh," *EvQ* 27 (1955): 67-80.

STRUCTURE

Nahum's work is called an "oracle," a "book," and a "vision" (1:1). "Oracle" is a translation of the Hebrew מַשָּׂא (*maśśā'*), which is sometimes understood as "burden." The word occurs often in the prophet Isaiah's words against the nations (Isa 13:1; 14:28; 15:1; 17:1; 19:1; etc). Nahum is the only prophetic book referred to directly as a "book." Therefore, some have suggested that the material never existed in oral form but was intended from the first to be read since it was an "underground" document.[7]

Nahum is recognized for its elevated literary and poetic style. Often expressions are short and crisp as in the descriptions of the attackers advancing on Nineveh (2:3-6; 3:2-3). Imagery and figures of speech abound. For example, Nineveh is a lion about to be killed (2:11-13), a prostitute about to be exposed (3:3-6), a ripe fig about to fall into the mouth (3:13).[8] Some scholars have found a partial acrostic in 1:3-7, expanded by some to verses 2-10. However, the evidence for even half an alphabetic acrostic seems weak.[9]

Nahum is closely related to the book of Jonah. Both address Nineveh. Both end in a question. Both are grounded in the character of God described in Exodus 34:6-7. Jonah emphasizes the positive side. Nineveh repents and is forgiven, for God is merciful and compassionate (Jonah 3:10; 4:2; Exod 34:6).[10] Nahum shows the other side. God is slow to anger but will not leave sin unpunished (Nahum 1:3; Exod 34:7). Both perspectives are needed to fully understand the nature of the biblical God.

Scholars do not agree on the structure of the book, but there do seem to be some internal clues which Elizabeth Achtemeier has seen.[11] This is an adaptation of her insights.

   I. Superscription — 1:1
   II. Opening Hymn on the Character of God — 1:2-11
   III. Five Judgment Oracles against Nineveh — 1:12–3:19

---

[7]Kenneth Barker and Waylon Bailey, *Micah, Nahum, Habakkuk, Zephaniah* (Nashville: Broadman and Holman, 1998), p. 161.

[8]See Barker and Bailey, *Micah, Nahum, Habakkuk, Zephaniah*, pp. 144-145 for many examples.

[9]See Spronk, *Nahum*, pp. 22-26, for a survey of the voluminous discussion.

[10]The Hebrew verb *nhm* appears in Jonah 4:2 translated as "relent" in NIV.

[11]Elizabeth Achtemeier, *Nahum–Malachi*, Int. (Atlanta: John Knox, 1986), p. 6.

A. First Oracle: Nineveh cut off, good news for Judah — 1:2-15[12]
B. Second Oracle: an army invades the city — 2:1-13
C. Third Oracle: woe to the debauched city — 3:1-7
D. Fourth Oracle: a case study — Thebes — 3:8-13
E. Final Oracle: nothing can be done to escape — 3:14-19

The five oracles are introduced by "Thus says the Lord" in 1:12. The word "wickedness" in 1:11 and 3:19 (NIV, "cruelty") form an inclusion around the five oracles. The first four oracles end with a call to pay attention (הִנֵּה, *hinnēh*, "look" or "see" in English) in 1:15; 2:13; 3:5,13.

Although the book is a collection of oracles against Nineveh, Judah is addressed also (1:13,15; 2:2). Bad news for Assyria is good news for Judah. Judgment on the former means salvation for the latter.

Nahum exhibits many verbal parallels with the book of Isaiah. Most notable is 1:15a which appears in Isaiah 52:7. Nahum 1:15b is also close to Isaiah 52:1b. The emphasis on God's wrath in 1:2-11 parallels Isaiah 51:17-23 including the recurring phrase "no more." Nahum 3:7 has several parallels with Isaiah 51:19. There are numerous terms and expressions that occur in Nahum and Isaiah 51–52.[13] Armerding links the following passages: Nahum 1:2 and Isaiah 59:17-19; 1:3-6 and 29:6; 1:4 and 33:9; 1:4-5 and 42:15; 1:15 and 52:1,7; 2:9-10 and 24:1,3; 2:10 and 21:3-4; 3:5-7 and 47:2-3; 3:7 and 51:19. There is also the "shared pattern of oppression, deliverance, and judgment experienced specifically in relation to Assyria."[14]

GENRE

The major type of prophetic speech is an oracle of judgment against Assyria. However, this is formulated in several different ways. There is a hymn of praise in 1:2-8 which places the book in the

---

[12]The English versification of chapter 2 differs from the Hebrew. English 1:15 is Hebrew 2:1 and English 2:13 is Hebrew 2:14. The English versification is followed here.

[13]These parallels have led Carl Armerding to conclude that there is "specific literary interdependence" between the two books ("Nahum" in *The Expositor's Bible Commentary*, ed. by Frank E. Gabelein [Grand Rapids: Zondervan, 1985], 7:455). See also the chart in Barker and Bailey, *Micah, Nahum, Obadiah, Zephaniah*, p. 146.

[14]Armerding, "Nahum," p. 455. He lists verses from 16 chapters in Isaiah. The most extensive Isaiah passages are 10:5-34 and 51:17–52:7.

context of God the creator. Nahum 1:12-13 and 15 are salvation oracles for Judah. Nineveh is mocked and taunted in 2:3-10,11-13; 3:8-
13,14-17. These taunts are full of satire. A disputation occurs in 1:9-
11. Nahum has used a variety of ways to declare the downfall of the
"great" Assyria.

THEOLOGICAL THEMES

The book of Nahum develops almost exclusively the theme of the
wrath of God (1:2-7). Many find this idea repugnant from a Christian
perspective and wish to ignore the book. Others have accused Nahum
of a narrow nationalism, especially since he seems to totally ignore
the sins of Judah. One has even accused him of being a false
prophet.[15] Such evaluations are subjective and do not do justice to
the biblical idea of God. They also ignore the New Testament.

Nahum's theology is grounded in Exodus 34:6-7 and in the character of God. God is holy and just. Therefore evil cannot be allowed
to stand. Furthermore God loves his people, and therefore his zeal
for their faithfulness and well being will not allow others to oppress
them without consequences. God's wrath and vengeance is the biblical way of expressing his just judgment on sin and evil. God is long
suffering toward sin, but he will not let it go unpunished (Exod
34:7). Nahum announces that the time has come for this judgment
to be carried out on the Assyrians who had dominated Israel and
Judah, and the Middle East, for centuries. Their arrogance and cruelty was unsurpassed. Isaiah had explained that God could use
Assyria as his instrument to punish Israel (Isaiah 10), but that did
not absolve them from responsibility for their evil. Jonah had
announced destruction on Nineveh for her sin. But when she
repented, God stayed the destruction. However, now the time had
come for justice to be done.

God was the sovereign God of the universe and of nations. He
was the avenging God, great in power, before whom no one could
stand (1:2,3,6). He could use others to do his work if he wished
(2:1,3ff.). Therefore Judah was to understand that the coming fall of
Assyria at the hands of the Medes and Babylonians was the work of
God. This view of God is threatening "only to those who want to be
their own gods and rule the earth in their own ways, but to those

---

[15]See K.J. Cathcart, "Nahum," *ABD*, 4:999.

who trust in God it is a comfort and an affirmation that he is truly sovereign."[16]

The other side of the picture is that God who exacts vengeance on his enemies is a protector for his people. He is their stronghold (1:7). His action is good news (gospel) to his people (1:15). That means the yoke of servitude Judah had experienced since the days of Ahaz would be broken. Therefore, the Lord was good (1:7). His goodness was defined both by his being slow to anger and his not clearing the guilty (1:3). There were certainly times when the Judeans doubted his goodness as they suffered under the Assyrians, but God was willing that even Nineveh have a chance to repent (Jonah). God's anger is slow because he is great.[17]

NEW TESTAMENT CONNECTIONS

Nahum is not quoted in the New Testament though Paul quotes Isaiah 52:7 (a verse almost identical to Nahum 1:15) in Romans 10:15. However, the Christian will recognize many thematic and verbal similarities to Nahum in the New Testament. Jesus affirms that no one is good but God (Luke 18:19; Nahum 1:7). Paul instructs Christians to leave vengeance to God (Rom 12:19; cf. Heb 10:30; 1 Thess 4:6), a theological truth grounded in the Old Testament. Furthermore, Paul points to the terribleness of evil and sin and God's wrath upon it in Romans 1:18–2:11 (see also Rom 4:15; 5:9; 9:22; 12:19; 13:4; Eph 2:3; 1 Thess 2:16). John in Revelation sees the powerful of the earth trying to hide from the wrath of the Lamb (6:16-17), and from the seven plagues and the seven bowls of the wrath of God (chs. 15–16). Ultimately the wicked will be destroyed as the Word of God treads out the winepress of the fury of the wrath of God Almighty (Rev 19:11-15). The New Testament is one with Nahum in understanding this aspect of God's character. Yet the New Testament also attests to God's long suffering, wishing that all be saved (2 Pet 3:9).

---

[16]Achtemeier, *Nahum–Malachi*, p. 8. For other images of God's wrath see Isa 51:17-23 and Jer 25:15-29.

[17]Ibid., p. 11.

HABAKKUK

HISTORICAL AND CULTURAL BACKGROUND

The one concrete historical reference in the book of Habakkuk is the mention of God raising up the Chaldeans (כַּשְׂדִּים, *kaśdîm*) in 1:6. This would point to a time when the Neo-Babylonian Empire was coming to prominence. Babylon gained independence from Assyria in 626 B.C. Assyrian power weakened in the coming decade under pressure from the Medes and Babylonians. Finally in 612 Nineveh fell to their combined power and the great Assyrian hegemony over the ancient Near East ended forever. This decline of a controlling power in Mesopotamia aided Josiah's religious and political reform which began in 632. Babylon's final ascendancy to dominance in the ancient world was assured by her defeat of Egypt at the Battle of Carchemish in 605. This spelled trouble for Judah and because of folly and inept leadership she was invaded by Babylon in 597 and 587 B.C. The last invasion resulted in complete defeat, wholesale deportation of Judeans, and the end of the nation as a political entity.

Since Habakkuk sees the Babylonians still on the horizon but on the march, some time between 626 and 597 would seem to fit best for his ministry. Numerous scholars suggest sometime between 609 and 605 as the most likely time. The reference to destruction and violence, lack of justice, and slackness of the law in Judah in Habakkuk 1:3-4 would seem to fit best the period between the death of Josiah and battle of Carchemish. Josiah's reform collapsed with his death and his son Jehoiakim reverted to the religious syncretism of Manasseh (2 Kgs 23:36-37). The five woes of 2:6-19 also suggest a date after Babylon had had some time to establish her reputation as a destroyer of nations.[1]

---

[1]Some scholars think the reference to the wicked in 1:4 is not to Judeans but must match the wicked in verse 13. This seems unlikely since the wicked

TEXT AND AUTHOR

We know nothing concrete about Habakkuk. The superscription to his book contains neither an indication of time nor a reference to a heritage that we often find in other prophetic books. Even his name offers little assistance. Some suggest it comes from a Hebrew root meaning "embrace" but this is not clear.[2] In the second half of the twentieth century many scholars concluded Habakkuk's name was derived from an Assyrian word for a garden plant, *habbaququ/hambaququ*, and exhibited an Assyrian cultural influence on seventh-century Judah. Achtemeier thinks it might be a nickname.[3]

Perhaps this lack of information is what has led to Jewish legends about Habakkuk. In the apocryphal "Bel and the Dragon" (second century B.C.), one of the later additions to the canonical Daniel, Habakkuk is carried by an angel from Jerusalem to Babylon to feed Daniel in the lion's den. In the first-century-A.D. pseudepigraphic *Lives of the Prophets* he is identified as from the tribe of Simeon.[4]

Some scholars have tried to establish that Habakkuk was a cultic prophet. The psalm in chapter 3 and the musical term in 3:1 (שִׁגְיֹנוֹת, *šigyōnôth*) are the only evidence for this conclusion. The most we can say is that the prophet used cultic forms for his larger purpose as he did other forms (see under Genre).

STRUCTURE

The book of Habakkuk seems to be united by theme and repetition of key words. The development of the dialogue with God leads toward the conclusion in 2:3-4. The woes that follow in 2:6-20 build on that conclusion and show further the character of the Babylonians. The psalm of chapter 3 celebrates the Creator and looks to the future with hope, based on the promise of 2:3-4.

Nevertheless the unity of Habakkuk has been questioned. The

---

in 1:4 ignore justice and the law. For a full discussion of this debate and the variety of dates offered see Barker and Bailey, *Micah, Nahum, Habakkuk, Zephaniah*, pp. 257-260.

[2]Based on this etymology a Jewish tradition developed that Habakkuk was the son of the Shunammite who befriended Elisha (2 Kgs 4:16 uses the word "embrace."). However, Elisha lived in the mid-ninth century B.C.

[3]Achtemeier, *Nahum–Malachi*, p. 34.

[4]Marvin A. Sweeney, "Habakkuk, Book of," *ABD*, 3:1.

new superscription in 3:1 suggests a separate composition and maybe a later addition to chapters 1 and 2. Furthermore, the fact that the commentary on Habakkuk found among the Qumran scrolls contained only chapters 1 and 2 led some to believe chapter 3 was later. However, the Qumran sectarians had a specific agenda and the material in chapter 3 may not have fit their purpose well. Also a manuscript from the caves at Murabba'at from the same period as the Qumran scrolls does contain chapter 3.

The structure of the book seems clear. After the superscription in 1:1 the first part of the book develops in a two step dialogue between Habakkuk and God. A) 1:2-11 — first complaint and divine response; B) 1:12–2:5 — second complaint and divine response; C) 2:6-20 — five woes against the oppressor; D) 3:1-19 — psalm of praise and hope for the future. Chapter 3 is integral to the book for it shows that Habakkuk heard and understood the importance of God's second response. Even in the dark days that were coming Habakkuk knew that living by faith in a faithful God provided hope for the future.

GENRE

Habakkuk demonstrates a mastery of several genres and a freedom to intermingle them for his purposes. Chapters 1:2–2:5 take the form of a dialogue between the prophet and God in which Habakkuk uses the familiar complaint form from the Psalms ("How long, O Lord," Psalm 13). But the dialogue also seems to include some wisdom terms and themes, for example, the concern for justice, and the contrast of the righteous and wicked in chapter 1. Chapter 2:6-20 adopts woe oracles to show the sure judgment on the oppressor. Chapter 3 has the typical elements of a hymn of creation that extols the greatness of God through reflection on his creation. It ends with an expression of trust.

THEOLOGICAL THEMES

At first glance the book seems to be about theodicy. How does a righteous God deal with great evil?[5] It also seems to address human doubt, for Habakkuk is not afraid to confront God about the nature

---

[5]M.A. Sweeney, "Habakkuk," *HBC,* ed. by J.L. Mays et al. (San Francisco: Harper Collins, 1988), p. 739.

of his actions.[6] However, a deeper look suggests these are not the main themes. The main issue is not about how God rewards the righteous and punishes the wicked. Nor is Habakkuk a doubter. He has a deep faith in God.[7] The book is more concerned about the providence of God. How will God keep his promises to Israel and to the whole world?[8]

Habakkuk's first question is prompted by his observation of the lack of justice and concern for the Torah among the covenant people (1:4). All he sees is violence. Because he knows the nature of the covenant God, he knows that God would not allow such a situation to persist. But he is surprised by the fact that God seems not to have done something about it already ("How long . . ." 1:2). He has complete confidence that God should and would do something. Habakkuk had grown weary with the way the world was and wished God's order to be established.[9]

The answer both delights and confounds Habakkuk (1:5-11). He is assured that God is already at work, but it is not how Habakkuk would have envisioned it. The answer comes out of an older perspective already stated in Isaiah 10. God was using a powerful Mesopotamian nation to do his will and bring justice on Judah. God will use their justice (1:7) to fix Judah's justice. God's answer is witness to the fact that the existence of chaos, evil, and violence in the world may not be because of God's absence but because he is at work. This is an unsettling claim that seems to run counter to what God's people would expect.[10] But this is a claim also made by Habakkuk's contemporaries, Jeremiah (Jeremiah 12) and Ezekiel (Ezekiel 5). God was using Babylon to execute his judgment on his covenant people.

Therefore, the second question was how long could this go on (1:17)? Habakkuk positioned himself to receive another response (2:1). The answer that came has provided grounds for profound theological reflection through the centuries, including becoming a basic text for the New Testament (see below), "The righteous will

---

[6]D.W. Baker, *Nahum, Habakkuk, Zephaniah* (Downers Grove, IL: Inter-Varsity, 1988), p. 43.

[7]Achtemeier, *Nahum–Malachi*, p. 31.

[8]Ibid., p. 32.

[9]Ibid., p. 36.

[10]Ibid., p. 38.

live by his faith/faithfulness" (2:4, NIV). God will act in his own time and in the meantime God's people are to trust in God.[11]

The rest of the book expresses this fundamental trust. The five woes of chapter 2 reflect the confidence that God will treat the unrighteous Babylon with justice. Those who rely on themselves and not on God cannot sustain their life.[12]

The psalm of chapter 3 confirms what Habakkuk learned from his vision of 2:1. God had proven himself in the past by showing his complete mastery of creation and the nations. He had conquered chaos before and he would do so once again. God will triumph and evil will fall. Therefore, even though present times looked bleak (3:17), Habakkuk will trust in the LORD (3:18-19). The providence of God over the world calls for faithfulness from God's people under all circumstances.

NEW TESTAMENT CONNECTIONS

Habakkuk 2:4 appears in Paul's writing twice in discussions about the importance of faith (Rom 1:17; Gal 3:11). In Romans the quotation is a part of Paul's larger argument in chapters 1–5 on the sinfulness of mankind and the faithfulness of God. It is part of the genius of the gospel message that the righteous can live by faith (1:17). In Galatians the quote appears as a part of Paul's argument that obedience to the Law cannot justify. Justification comes only through faith. Paul's quote in Romans differs slightly from both the Septuagint and the Hebrew.[13] Therefore, the quote is ambiguous. Is he referring to the faithfulness of the believer, or to God's faithfulness as shown through Jesus Christ? Many scholars hold that the righteous one in Paul's letter is the believer who lives by faith in Christ. On the other hand some scholars understand that Paul is interpreting Habakkuk

---

[11]The Jewish rabbis recognized the importance of this declaration. The Talmud Tractate *Makkot* (23b-24a) states that God revealed 613 commandments to Moses, which were reduced to eleven by David, six by Isaiah, three by Micah (6:8), and to one by Amos ("Seek me and live") and Habakkuk ("The righteous shall live by faith").

[12]Achtemeier, *Nahum–Malachi*, p. 48.

[13]The Hebrew text has "The righteous shall live by *his* faithfulness." The Greek has "The righteous shall live by *my* faithfulness." The Hebrew implies the faithfulness of the righteous one, the Greek implies God's faithfulness. Paul does not use a pronoun.

messianically. Therefore, the righteous one is a reference to Christ. Christian are saved by the faithfulness of Christ.[14]

Like Habakkuk, Christians who live by faith through troubled times will be ultimately vindicated. God will come in triumph to deliver his people from evil (Rev 19:11-16).

---

[14]See Walter D. Zorn, "The Messianic Use of Habakkuk 2:4a in Romans," *SCJ* 1 (Fall 1998): 213-230.

ZEPHANIAH

HISTORICAL AND CULTURAL BACKGROUND

The prophet Zephaniah ministered during the reign of King Josiah (1:1) who came to the throne in 640 B.C. at the age of eight (2 Kgs 22:1). Josiah reigned until 609 when he was killed by the Egyptian Pharaoh Neco at Megiddo (2 Kgs 23:29). If Zephaniah prophesied during the early years of Josiah (see below), he would have been born during the dark days of Manasseh, the long-reigning and evil son of Hezekiah.

The second half of the seventh century B.C. was a time of extreme political turmoil in the ancient Near East.[1] The powerful Assyria, which had controlled the land of Mesopotamia, Palestine, and ultimately Egypt for nearly a century, began to crumble. The long reign of King Ashurbanipal (668–627) came to an end. He had enlarged Assyrian control to its greatest extent ever when he reconquered Thebes in Egypt in 663 B.C. However, in the 650s Egypt broke away and in the southeast the Babylonians rebelled. Ashurbanipal regained control of Babylon, but shortly after his death the Babylonians drove the Assyrians out of Babylon (625). The collapse of Assyria was unexpectedly rapid. Asshur was captured by the Babylonians and Medes in 614 and Nineveh fell in 612. The remnant of Assyrians retreated to Haran which fell in 609. Pharaoh Neco rushed to Assyria's aid but arrived too late. In 605 the Babylonian's defeated the Egyptians at Carchemish, and Babylonian control over the Near East was complete.

Events in Judah were profoundly impacted by the rise and fall of the Mesopotamian powers. During Assyria's heyday Manasseh (687–642), the son of Hezekiah, ruled Judah. He was a vassal to the

---

[1]See John Bright, *A History of Israel*, 4th ed. (Philidelphia: Westminster, 2000), pp. 310-331, for a description of the era.

Assyrians and used the situation to completely reverse his father's religious reforms. His vigorous promotion of all sorts of pagan practices earned him the title of the most evil king that Judah ever had (2 Kgs 21:1-18). His conduct was even worse than the Canaanites who inhabited the land before Israel (2 Kgs 21:9). Manasseh was a vigorous promoter of Assyrian religions (2 Kgs 21:3) and even practiced child sacrifice (2 Kgs 21:6). His evil extended beyond the religious sphere to active persecution of innocent people, probably Judeans loyal to Yahweh (2 Kgs 21:16). This perhaps included killing any prophets that may have attempted to preach. We know of no prophets who prophesied during his evil reign. Some of Manasseh's actions were no doubt dictated by his vassalage to Assyria, but he seemed quite willing to go beyond those demands. If Zephaniah was born in the last decades of Manasseh's reign, his name would indicate faithful parents who perhaps yearned for God's intervention.

Twenty-two year old Amon (642–640) followed his father to the throne, but he was assassinated after two years by his own officials. The reason for the palace coup is not clear, but it did not succeed as the "people of the land" rose up and executed the plotters (2 Kgs 21:19-24). Josiah, at the time only eight years old, was made king in 640 B.C. Thus began a hopeful time in Judah, who by default experienced a brief period of freedom.

As early as his eighth year Josiah, perhaps under the tutelage of wise advisors, began a religious reform (2 Chr 34:3). This was coupled with vigorous political expansion that was made possible by the rapid decline of Assyria (2 Kings 22; 2 Chronicles 34). Josiah's control eventually extended as far north as Megiddo, and Judah enjoyed a time of independence, expansion, and peace. It was short lived, for Josiah was killed in an ill-advised battle with the Egyptians at Megiddo in 609 (2 Kgs 23:29-30).

Josiah's extensive religious reforms, which included the expulsion of all pagan practices, the cleaning of the Temple, and the finding of the book of the Law, died with him. The exact dates of Zephaniah's ministry are debated. The tone of Zephaniah 1 and 3 suggests that he prophesied early in Josiah's reign, before the reforms. Zephaniah describes a country and city full of foreign cultic practice (1:4-6,8-9) and injustice (3:3-5), a state of affairs that would ill fit Judah after Josiah's discovery of the book of the law in 622 (2 Kgs 22:3ff.).

Zephaniah seems to anticipate that God's judgment will be carried out by the imminent invasion of a foreign army (1:4,10-13; 2:1; 3:1-4). Scholars have suggested the army in view was the Scythians,[2] the Assyrians,[3] or the Babylonians. The latter seems the most likely.[4]

TEXT AND AUTHOR

The book of Zephaniah is ascribed to a man by the name of Zephaniah (1:1). The theophoric name, Zephaniah, means "Yahweh has hidden, protected, treasured." It is a combination of an abbreviated form of Yahweh ("yah") attached to a verb (see also the names Gedaliah, Amariah, and Josiah[5] in verse 1). The verb root צָפַן (*sāphan*) occurs in other names also (Elzaphan and Elizaphan — Exod 6:22; Lev 10:4; and Num 3:30; 34:25; 1 Chr 15:8; 2 Chr 29:13). Zephaniah was born during the evil days of King Manasseh (see above). "The word of the LORD that came. . . ." means that Zephaniah was a prophet in line with other OT prophets like Hosea, Micah, Joel, and Jeremiah whose books have similar headings.

There are three other Zephaniahs in the OT: a priest who was an intermediary between King Zedekiah and the prophet Jeremiah (Jer 21:1; 29:25,29; 37:3; 2 Kgs 25:18), the father of a Josiah in the time of Zechariah (Zech 6:10,14), and an ancestor of Samuel (1 Chr 6:36). The name also occurs on a seal impression from the early sixth century found at Lachish.

We know little about the man Zephaniah, for he is mentioned only in verse 1. However, the genealogy of verse 1, in an unusual move, traced his ancestry back to the fourth generation. This immediately draws attention to the first person in the list, Hezekiah. It is highly probable he is King Hezekiah who reigned in Judah in the late eighth century and who undertook an important religious reform (2 Kings 18-20; Isaiah 36-39). Thus Zephaniah had royal blood, was a relative of King Josiah, and perhaps had a significant impact on Josiah's reform (see below).

Cushi, another ancestor of Zephaniah, has aroused interest. It appears related to the Hebrew word for Ethiopia, Cush. But it seems

---

[2]Based on a brief reference in the Greek historian Herodotus. However, their incursion into Palestine was probably brief and had no effect on Judah.

[3]The Assyrians seem unlikely since they are the subject of one of the threats in 2:13-15.

[4]Dillard and Longman, *Introduction*, pp. 417-418.

[5]Josiah's name is spelled with the longer form of the abbreviation, "yahu."

unlikely that the name means Zephaniah's father was an African. Cushi is also a proper name in Jeremiah 36:14.

STRUCTURE

Scholars traditionally find in the book a threefold structure: 1:2–2:3, threats against Judah and Jerusalem; 2:4–3:8, threats against foreign nations; 3:9-20, promises of salvation and restoration.[6] Others find a threefold structure with a different placement of 2:1-3 and 3:1-8.[7] The major weakness of the traditional analysis is the placement of 3:1-8. Since it addresses the wickedness of Jerusalem, how can it be included with 2:4-15 that focuses on the destruction of four of Judah's enemies? A twofold structure has also been suggested: 1:2-18, announcement of the day of Yahweh, and 2:1–3:20, an exhortation to seek Yahweh.[8]

Redaction critics have concluded that chapter 3 is mostly exilic or postexilic, for it contains eschatological elements and presupposes a remnant that will be brought back from exile.[9] This extends also to 2:7,8,9a,10-11. Recently many scholars have rejected such an approach as unfounded and subjective. There seems little reason to suppose that a prophet could or would only preach judgment or that he could not conceive of a remnant surviving before the fact.

Careful analysis has found that Zephaniah is replete with repetitions of key words and ideas and characterized by inclusion, chiasm, and parallel grammatical structures.[10] The unity of the book is demonstrated by the presence of key words at the beginning and

---

[6]Childs, *Introduction*, p. 458. Many evangelical scholars agree: Dillard and Longman, *Introduction*, p. 418; J. Alec Motyer, "Zephaniah," in *The Minor Prophets; An Exegetical and Expository Commentary*, vol. 3, *Zephaniah–Malachi*, ed. by Thomas E. McComiskey (Grand Rapids: Baker, 1998), p. 901; Willem VanGemeren, *Interpreting the Prophetic Word* (Grand Rapids: Zondervan, 1990), p. 174.

[7]O. Palmer Robertson suggests 1:2-18; 2:1-15; and 3:1-20 (*The Books of Nahum, Habakkuk, and Zephaniah* [Grand Rapids: Eerdmans, 1990], pp. 45-46), whereas Waylon Bailey prefers 1:2–2:3; 2:4-15; and 3:1-20 (Barker and Bailey, *Micah, Nahum, Habakkuk, Zephaniah*, p. 403).

[8]Marvin A. Sweeney, "A Form-Critical Reassessment of the Book of Zephaniah," *CBQ* 53 (1991): 407-408.

[9]Childs, *Introduction*, p. 458.

[10]Motyer, "Zephaniah," pp. 901-904; Sweeney, "A Form-Critical Reassessment."

end. "The face of the earth" in 1:2-3 matches "all the earth" in 3:19-20. "The word of the LORD" in 1:1 matches "says the LORD" in 3:20. The false king "Milcom" (מַלְכָּם, *malkām*) in 1:5 contrasts with the true king, "the king (מֶלֶךְ, melek) of Israel, the LORD" in 3:15. The "warrior" of 1:14 contrasts with the "warrior" of 3:17. The cut off "name" of 1:4 contrasts with the honored "name" of 3:19,20 (NIV, "honor"). The presence of "deceit" in 1:9 contrasts with the city free of "deceit" in 3:13.[11] There are many parallels within smaller sections of the book as well. The charge of failure to seek the LORD in 1:6 is balanced by the threefold call to seek him in 2:3. The repetition of the "day of the LORD" or "day" or "time" bind the whole book together (see below).[12] Grammatically chapter 1 is dominated by first person singular verbs when Yahweh speaks and third person singular verbs that mark the prophet speaking on Yahweh's behalf. Chapters 2 and 3 are dominated by second person plural imperative verbs, second person plural active verbs, and second person personal suffixes.[13] This suggests a subtle unity to chapter 1 and chapters 2 and 3.

The book of Zephaniah reflects a coherent address to Judah and Jerusalem which in its present form shows an intricate unity. Its intent was to encourage the reformation of Josiah[14] by calling for renewal, demonstrating God's sovereignty over Judah's enemies, and providing hope for the future. All of this has been formed around the critical theme "the day of Yahweh."[15]

I. Superscription — 1:1
II. Judgment on Judah — 1:2–2:3
    A. God will sweep away Judah and Jerusalem — 1:2-6
    B. God's punishment is near — 1:7-13
    C. The day of the Lord is near — 1:14-18
    D. Call to seek the Lord — 2:1-3
III. Judgment on Judah's Closest Enemies — 2:4-15
    A. West — Philistines — 2:4-7
    B. East — Moab and Ammon — 2:8-11

---

[11]Motyer, "Zephaniah," pp. 903-904.

[12]For "day" see 1:7,8,9,10,14,15(6×),16,18; 2:2,3; and 3:8,11,16. For "time" see 1:12 and 3:19,20 (Motyer, "Zephaniah," p. 902).

[13]Sweeney, "A Form-Critical Reassessment."

[14]Ibid., p. 406; Barker and Bailey, *Micah, Nahum, Habakkuk, Zephaniah*, 396.

[15]Childs, *Introduction*, p. 459.

GENRE

The book of Zephaniah, apart from the superscription, is written entirely in poetry. It is marked by first person speeches from God (e.g. 1:2-6,8-13,17-18) and prophetic announcements on God's behalf (e.g. 1:14-16; 2:1-3,4-7,13-15). Chapters 1 and 2 and part of 3 contain threats and judgment speeches. There are also promises of the return of a remnant in the future (3:9-13) and a call to sing for joy (3:14-18). It ends with a promise of restoration for Judah (3:19-20).

THEOLOGICAL THEMES

Zephaniah is noted for his concentration on the theme of the "day of the Lord." He has other concerns, but they are all integrated into his major theme. However, it will be useful to look at the themes separately.

1. **The day of the LORD is a central feature of the prophetic message.**[16] The concept is first mentioned in Amos and Isaiah in the eighth century, but it seemed to have already been a part of the common thought. Apparently the community visualized a day of blessing and Yahweh's favor. Amos shattered that idea, pointing out it was a day of judgment, gloom, and death (Amos 5:18-20). Zephaniah developed the idea in several important directions. First, it was a day of Yahweh's wrath (1:18; 2:2,3), a day of God's punishment on Judah and Jerusalem for their failure to seek God and for their syncretism (1:7-9,12b,14-18; 3:1-7). This judgment would begin with the merchants (1:10-11 — Jerusalem's Wall Street[17]) and result in wailing and death (1:10). It was a day that was near (1:7,14). Zephaniah's warning of its coming was intended to produce repentance (2:2-3).

---

[16]Richard H. Hiers, "Day of the Lord," *ABD*, 2:82-84; Greg King, "The Day of the Lord in Zephaniah," *BSac* 152 (1995): 16-32; Achtemeier, *Nahum–Malachi*, pp. 66-67.

[17]Achtemeier, *Nahum–Malachi*, pp. 70-71.

Secondly, it was a day when Yahweh would establish his sovereignty over the nations by bringing judgment on Judah's enemies (2:4-15). The listed nations were those especially in conflict with King Josiah. Therefore, Yahweh's universal reign as "King of Israel, the LORD" (3:15) would be firmly established. This meant, as Amos had affirmed earlier (Amos 1), that all nations were accountable to God, not just Israel and Judah. Thirdly, the covenant foundation for Zephaniah's preaching is emphasized by the application of the covenant curses of Deuteronomy (cf. Zeph 1:13,15-16 and Deut 28:29-49). Fourthly, there was a positive side to the day for it would result in salvation and restoration for God's people. It was a day of rejoicing (3:16-17), deliverance (3:19), and restoration (3:20). The restoration also has a Deuteronomy flavor (for "restore fortunes" [2:7; 3:20] see Deut 30:4,9). Therefore, God's people could wait in confidence (3:8) as he acted to reverse Genesis 11 and bring all nations to himself (3:9-10).

2. **The remnant.**[18] The power of God to destroy the wicked and wickedness in Judah and among the nations paved the way for a remnant to emerge who would enjoy intimacy with God and live under his protection (3:20). Thus the remnant idea is closely tied to the Day of the Lord theme. The remnant concept has three elements (see 1:4-6; 2:1-3,4-7,8-11; 3:9-13,14-20). First, it presupposes divine judgment on the community will result in complete destruction until only a few are left (3:11-12). It is not an arbitrary judgment, for Judah's sins require the covenant curses. However, by God's grace and mercy a few will remain (see Isa 10:20-23 — God's judgment is "destruction overflowing with righteousness"). Secondly, the remnant are those fully committed to the Lord, those righteous and humble before him (2:3; 3:13). They heed the call to seek the Lord, obey him, and provide a nucleus for the continuation of God's people. They are a people after God's heart, honest and upright (3:13). Thirdly, because of God's grace the remnant have a hopeful future as his righteous ones. They will occupy their enemies' land (2:7,8), live securely, sheltered by God in his presence (3:12-13,15) with their fortunes restored (2:7; 3:20). The outcast and oppressed will be saved and their shame removed (3:19).

3. **The sin of Judah.** Zephaniah condemned the syncretistic spirit adopted under the reign of Manasseh. The Assyrian religious cults

---

[18]Greg A. King, "The Remnant in Zephaniah," *BSac* 151 (1994): 414-427.

were not acceptable (1:5-6,8-9; see 2 Kings 23) for they ran counter to the requirements of the law (Lev 18:1-5; Deuteronomy 7). The practical outcome was injustice, corruption, and violence (1:9b; 3:3-7b). The other practical outcome was a deistic self-centeredness (1:12b).[19] Their thinking had become polluted until they treated Yahweh just like an idol or pagan god. He existed but did nothing, and therefore no one needed to take him seriously. The idols could do nothing (Isa 41:23-24; Jer 10:5), and to treat Yahweh in the same way was to consider him powerless and false. This was worse than active rebellion which at least took his existence seriously. Such a mind-set was the ultimate mark of self-centered pride (Gen 3:5). This attitude also describes modern Western culture and perhaps many in the church.

4. **A future promise of universal salvation.** Much has been made of Zephaniah's eschatology, especially for dating purposes.[20] However, his view of the future is an important outgrowth of the Day of the Lord and remnant theology. After the judgment God will work to bring all nations under his redemptive umbrella (3:9-10). He is not concerned only for Judah but for all nations. Thus, the essential elements in the promise to Abraham (Gen 12:1-3) will come to fruition.

NEW TESTAMENT CONNECTIONS

Zephaniah is not quoted in the New Testament, but Christians will recognize that important themes recur. The "day of the Lord"[21] of Zephaniah with its multifaceted focus in the New Testament centers on the coming of Jesus Christ to inaugurate the kingdom of God. The phrase itself occurs in only three places (1 Thess 5:2; 2 Thess 2:2; 2 Pet 3:10), but there are many related words and phrases used: the day of Christ/Jesus Christ (Phil 1:6,10; 2:16; 1 Cor 1:8; 5:5; 2 Cor 1:14), that day (1 Thess 5:4; 2 Thess 1:10; 2:3; 2 Tim 1:12; 4:8), or the day (Rom 2:16; Heb 10:25). Jesus sometimes referred to "the day" or "that day" when the kingdom of God would come and the day of judgment would ensue (Matt 7:22; 26:29; 25:13; Luke 21:34; etc). This coming judgment was also referred to as the "day of wrath" (Rom 2:5; Eph 5:6; Col 3:6; 1 Thess 1:10; 2:16; Rev 6:16-

---

[19]Achtemeier, *Nahum–Malachi*, pp. 68-69.

[20]Childs, *Introduction*, pp. 458-462.

[21]Richard H. Hiers, "Day of Christ," *ABD,* 2:76-79.

17; 14:10,19; 15:1,7; 16:1,19). This reflects the eager anticipation for the return of Christ, the final judgment, and introduction of the new heaven and new earth.

Zephaniah's anticipated reversal of Genesis 11 and the offering of salvation to all nations (3:9) were actualized on the day of Pentecost in Acts 2. The joining of Jew and Gentile in the church made God's plan a reality.

The distrust of the faithful action of God reflected in the deism of Zephaniah 1:12 is reflected in the attitude of the scoffers in 2 Peter 3:3-7.

Paul recognizes that only a remnant of Israel has survived her disobedience (Rom 9:27), but it is a remnant chosen by grace (Rom 11:5). Therefore Gentiles are grafted into the people of God, but Jews will be saved through faith also.

HAGGAI

HISTORICAL AND CULTURAL BACKGROUND

Haggai's book is set within a worldwide context, in the postexilic era, by the reference to Darius in verse 1. The great king Cyrus, who had defeated the Babylonians, established the Persian Empire, and allowed the Jews to return to Palestine, died in battle in 530 B.C. He was followed by his son Cambyses (530–522). Cambyses died without a child. He had assassinated his brother, so the way was open for a relative to succeed him. This relative was Darius the son of Hystaspes. A usurper named Gaumata attempted to take the throne but was quickly eliminated by Darius. Darius also had to put down other rebellions in the empire, but by his second year he had taken total control. He reigned until 486 B.C.

Darius's second year was 520, so Haggai's precisely dated messages were given within a four and one-half month period in 520 B.C. Specifically his first message was on August 29, his second on October 17, and his last two on December 18.[1] Zechariah 1:1, dated in October 520, illustrates the overlap between the two prophets. Haggai's career was brief, and we do not know what became of him. Zechariah came to the fore to carry on his mission, and Haggai faded from view.

The first exiles had returned to Jerusalem after Cyrus's decree in 539 B.C. One might have expected a mass return, but most Jews chose to stay in Babylon where they had settled in (see Jer 29:4-9). About forty-three thousand chose to return (Ezra 2:64). When they arrived in Jerusalem, they found nothing but ruins, devastation, fal-

---

[1]These precise dates are possible because of the evidence from numerous Babylonian texts that have enabled scholars to match up the old lunar calendar with our Julian calendar. See R.A. Parker and W.H. Dubberstein, *Babylonian Chronology 626 B.C.–A.D. 45* (Chicago: University of Chicago Press, 1946).

low land, and opposition from the Samarians and the local popula-tion. They rebuilt the altar and laid the foundation for the Temple but did nothing more. Only because of the encouragement of Haggai and royal support was the task taken up again sixteen years later in 520 (Ezra 1–6). The Temple was finally finished in 516 B.C. This inaugurated what has become known as the "Second Temple Era" which lasted until the destruction of Jerusalem and Herod's Temple in 70 A.D. by the Romans.

TEXT AND AUTHORSHIP

Very little is known about Haggai the prophet. We do not know his age or his father. We do know he prophesied in Jerusalem for about four months, but we do not know if he was a native or grew up in exile. We do know that he was considered a prophet, for he is described as one five times in his book (1:1,3,12; 2:1,10) and twice in the book of Ezra (Ezra 5:1; 6:14). He may have been an old man who had seen the old Temple before it was destroyed by the Baby-lonians (2:3). His name comes from the word חַג (ḥag), which is the Hebrew noun for "festival" that in turn comes from the root חָגַג (ḥāgag), "celebrate a festival." Perhaps he was born on a feast day.[2] His name could mean "my feast." It is interesting that the Septua-gint, the Greek version of the Old Testament, prefaces Psalms 138 and 146–149 with references to Haggai and Zechariah.

STRUCTURE

The structure of the book is simple, following the four precisely dated messages of Haggai. Haggai 1:1-15 — Haggai's first message, get to work and rebuild the Temple, was followed by the immediate response of the people. Chapter 2:1-9 — the second message was directed to Zerubbabel, Joshua, and the people to encourage them to continue working, for the Lord would bring splendor to the Temple. Chapter 2:10-19 — the third message taught the lesson of cleanness

---

[2]A few other names related to the root appear in the Old Testament: Haggi (Gen 46:16; Num 26:15), Haggith (2 Sam 3:4), and Haggiah (1 Chr 6:30). Haggai was a somewhat popular name in the Old Testament world, occurring on some Hebrew seals, in Phoenician and South Arabian texts, and in Aramaic papyri from the fifth century B.C. For a similar name for-mation see the name Shabbathai from the word for Sabbath (Ezra 10:15).

and uncleanness. Chapter 2:20-23 — the fourth message assured Zerubbabel that he was God's chosen signet ring. The four messages are a part of a twice-repeated pattern: accusation, response, assurance. The first cycle is accusation — 1:1-11, response — 1:12-14, and assurance — 2:1-9. The second cycle is accusation — 2:10-17, response — 2:18-19, and assurance — 2:20-23. In this pattern we see a balancing of negative and positive messages, of warnings and assurances.[3]

GENRE

The genre is mixed as the structure above shows. Prophetic accusations are followed by assurances of God's blessing or triumph. The accusations contain announcements of God's judgment (1:5ff., 10ff.; 2:14ff.). The assurances have the familiar "Do not fear" (2:5) preceded and followed by statements of encouragement (2:4,23).

THEOLOGICAL THEMES

Haggai's message is focused on one theme: the Jews must rebuild the Temple. This may seem an uninspiring theme and in fact seems to run counter to the prophets who condemned Temple worship (Isaiah 1, Jeremiah 7). But Haggai was convinced that his message was the right one for his time. God had raised up a foreign king to facilitate the Jews' return from exile so that the Temple and city could be built. Dereliction in this task was indicative of a lack of obedience to God and a lack of trust in him.

God was the controller of nature and provided all their necessities which he could also withhold (1:10-11; 2:17-19). Neglect of the Temple was neglect of God. Ezekiel had shown the glory of God leaving the Temple prior to the fall of Jerusalem and the destruction of the Temple (Ezekiel 10). Haggai's vision was for the glory of God to return to the holy mount, but it could not without the Temple. Ezekiel had also looked forward to the reconstruction of the Temple (Ezekiel 40–48). Haggai was determined that Ezekiel's vision should be fulfilled.

Haggai drew a direct line between neglect of the Temple and lack of provisions for the people. Their conduct and lack of obedience

---

[3]See Joyce Baldwin, *Haggai, Zachariah, Malachi*, TOTC (Downers Grove, IL: InterVarsity, 1972), p. 31.

had consequences. They were in want because they had not kept their commitment (1:6; 2:16-17). The ruined Temple was like some contamination in the city, ruining everything else also (2:10ff.).

God's ultimate goal in history could be reached if they obeyed him. He had the power to once again bless them with provisions. He had the power to adorn the new Temple with the finest gold and silver (2:8-9). He could overthrow all nations (2:22). He had already chosen his own servant through whom to work (2:23). The future was God's, and the returned exiles could join him in that future.

NEW TESTAMENT CONNECTIONS

There appears to be one brief quote from Haggai 2:6 in Hebrews 12:26. It appears in a passage in which the writer of Hebrews is warning his readers not to reject the grace of God. As he had "shaken the earth" before, he can do so again to separate the obedient from the disobedient.

Jesus' teaching on the Temple in the New Testament stands in contrast with Haggai. The Temple will no longer be important, for the place of worship will not be important (John 4). Jesus identified himself with the Temple (John 2:21; Matt 26:61) and taught that he was greater than the Temple (Matt 12:6). Jesus as the fulcrum of God's redemptive plan made the Old Testament priests and sacrifices obsolete. He also made the Temple obsolete. For Paul the Christian and the church were the temple of God (1 Cor 3:16-17; 2 Cor 6:16). For John the new heaven will have no temple because God and the Lamb are the temple (Rev 21:22).

Furthermore, the glory of God that filled the first Temple, the "Shekinah glory" (Exod 40:34-38; 1 Kgs 8:10-11), did not appear in the second Temple despite Ezekiel's vision (Ezek 43:1-7). This visible presence of God would finally appear when Jesus the Messiah "became flesh and lived (tabernacled) among us, and we have seen his glory . . ." (John 1:14). Jesus was "the reflection of God's glory and the exact imprint of God's very being . . ." (Heb 1:3).

ZECHARIAH

HISTORICAL AND CULTURAL BACKGROUND

The historical background is the same as that of Haggai. Like Haggai, some of Zechariah's messages are precisely dated, the first one coming "in the eighth month, in the second year of Darius" (1:1) which would be October of 520 B.C. This places the beginning of his ministry in the middle of Haggai's four oracles. Zechariah's second message was on the "twenty-fourth day of the eleventh month," that is February 15, 519 B.C. The last date in the book is in 7:1, the "fourth day of the ninth month" in the fourth year of Darius, that is, December 7, 518 B.C. There are no dates in Zechariah 9–14, and scholars differ on the background for these chapters (see below).

In 520 B.C. Darius was just beginning a long and prosperous reign over Persia. He followed Cambyses, the son of the great Cyrus. Darius in his first year had to put down opposition, but he soon established control. His long reign ended in 486 B.C.

The first exiles returned in 538 to rebuild the Temple, but soon ceased work because of discouragement and opposition. However, Haggai and Zechariah gave them the impetus they needed, and with Zerubbabel's leadership they finished the job in four years (Ezra 6:15).

TEXT AND AUTHOR

According to 1:1, Zechariah was the son of Berechiah and the grandson of Iddo. He was a contemporary of Haggai and joined with him in encouraging the rebuilding of the Temple (Ezra 5:1; 6:14). His name apparently means "Yahweh remembers," a fitting meaning given the circumstances of the returned exiles who were very discouraged. Zechariah was a popular name in the Old Testament. One scholar has counted 30 different Zechariahs.[1] We do not know the

---

[1] T.M. Mauch, "Zechariah," *IDB*, 4:941-943.

age of Zechariah but he could be the young man referred to in 2:4. Zechariah was also a contemporary of Zerubbabel (4:6,7,9) who was appointed governor by the Persian king, Darius I, and who, inspired by Haggai and Zechariah, led in the rebuilding of the Temple (Ezra 2:2; 3:2-13; Hag 1:1-2:9; Zech 4:8-10).

Zechariah's paternity is not clear. He is called the son of Berechiah only in 1:1. He is called the son of Iddo in Ezra 5:1; 6:14 (cf Neh 12:4,16[2]). Some scholars have suggested that Berechiah in 1:1 is a corruption of Jeberechiah of Isaiah 8:2 where a Zechariah is a witness for Isaiah. These scholars suggest a scribe has confused the two Zechariahs, a clear chronological blunder.[3] Since "son" can also mean descendent, the simplest solution is to understand that Berechiah was the father and Iddo the grandfather of Zechariah.[4] Perhaps Ezra listed the grandfather because he was better known.

It is possible that Zechariah was a priest. He shows considerable interest in priestly things, such as the Temple, the responsibilities of the high priest (ch. 3), respect for Joshua the high priest (6:10-11), cleansing of the land and removal of defilement (3:9; 5:3,6-11).

Zechariah also was informed by the message of the preexilic prophets. Many of the imperatives that burst out are similar to other prophets; imperatives such as "cry out," "flee," "escape," "sing and rejoice," and "be silent" (1:14; 2:6,7,10,13). Scholars have counted over twenty allusions to the eighth-century prophets Isaiah, Hosea, Amos, and Micah, and the seventh-century prophets Jeremiah and Ezekiel.[5]

HISTORY OF INTERPRETATION

The book of Zechariah seems to naturally divide into two halves, chapters 1–8 and 9–14. The first half is marked by eight visions and precise dates. The second half does not mention Zechariah or the Temple, and has no dates. Consequently, for a long time, many scholars have suggested two different authors for the book of Zechariah: Zechariah the prophet for chapters 1–8 and someone else for chapters 9–14. Several reasons have been given for different author-

---

[2]However, these may not be the same people at all.

[3]Smith, *Micah–Malachi*, p. 168.

[4]See a similar situation for Jehu who is called the son of Nimshi (1 Kgs 19:16; 2 Kgs 9:20) and the son of Jehoshaphat, son of Nimshi (2 Kgs 9:2,14).

[5]Baldwin, *Haggai, Zechariah, Malachi*, p. 61-62.

ship. These include the following: the first half is dominated by prose, the second half by poetry; characteristic phrases like "thus says the LORD" occur in the first half but not the second half; there are differences of vocabulary between the two halves; and some of the references in the second half seem to point to a time later than the sixth century, for example, the reference to the Greeks in 9:13.

One of the earliest efforts to deny Zechariah's authorship of chapters 9–14 was based on a defense of the accuracy of the New Testament. Matthew 27:9 contains an Old Testament quotation and attributes it to Jeremiah, but the words are a free translation of Zechariah 11:13. Therefore, Joseph Mede (1586-1638) concluded that Zechariah 9–11 was written by Jeremiah.[6] Other scholars suggested a preexilic date for the material in chapters 9–14. Support was found in the references to the Northern and Southern Kingdoms (9:10,13; 10:6), the references to Assyria and Egypt, and the portrayal of Syria-Palestine in chapter 9.

In the eighteenth century, others argued that the chapters came from the late postexilic era, even the second century and Maccabean times. Some argued for the Greek period, in the fourth century. Chapter 9:1-8 were seen as a reference to the advance of Alexander the Great in 332 B.C. The references to Egypt in 9:11; 10:10-11; and 14:18-19 reflected the third century in Egypt. The reference to Greece (9:13) was dated to sometime after the death of Alexander.[7] The supposed development in theological concepts, especially in the apocalyptic nature of the material, was also posited in favor of a later date.

More recently a few have swung back to the preexilic era for chapters 9–14.[8] It is clear that scholarship is unable to achieve any kind of unanimity on the date and background for the second half of the book of Zechariah.

Despite the prevailing views on the disunity of the book of Zechariah, several lines of evidence suggest a basic unity to the book. Even if chapters 9–14 are from a different time and different author(s), there must have been some reason why the material was joined to chapters 1–8. There is what Childs calls a "surprising compatibility between the two books of material."[9] Both sections speak

---

[6]Ibid., p. 63.
[7]Ibid., pp. 65-66.
[8]Childs, *Introduction*, p. 476.
[9]Ibid., p. 482.

of: 1) Jerusalem's special security and blessing (2:5; 9:8; 14:11), 2) the return of fertility and water (8:12; 14:8), 3) the restoration of the covenant relationship with God (8:8; 13:9), 4) removal of the curse of 5:3 in 14:11, 5) divine judgment on the nations (1:18ff.[Heb 2:1ff.]; 14:12), 6) conversion of the nations and worship of Yahweh (2:11[Heb 2:15]; 8:20,22; 14:16), 7) the regathering of the exiles (8:7-8; 10:9ff.), 8) the new age that will result in a change in the cultic rites (8:18ff.; 14:20), 9) the outpouring of the spirit (4:6; 12:10), 10) the clearing away of those who swear falsely in the name of God (5:4; 13:3), and 11) a messianic figure who triumphs through humility (3:8; 4:6; 9:9).[10]

In light of the evidence can one still hold to a single authorship for Zechariah? Several scholars think so. The differences between the two halves are explained by suggesting that, like any good author, Zechariah could have arranged the material by topic and shared ideas. He also could have functioned as a prophet over a long period of time and the material from the second half could be from his later years. In that case one would not expect the material to be identical in style, subject matter, or vocabulary.[11] The reference to the Greeks in 9:13 is explained by the fact that Greek influence in the Near East predated Alexander by several centuries. Assyrian inscriptions show Greek traders in Mesopotamia as early as the eighth century.[12] The thematic unity of the book is recognized by everyone and is most easily explained by unity of authorship. Could not the redactor who is often credited with the unity of the book be Zechariah himself? The issue is inconclusive but the evidence does not compel one to opt only for multiplicity of authorship.[13]

---

[10]Ibid., pp. 482-483. Despite these observations Childs does not believe the two halves come from the same author. He thinks the similarities are due to dependence on the same prophetic books, Jeremiah, Isaiah, and Ezekiel.

[11]Dillard and Longman, *Introduction*, p. 430.

[12]Ibid., p. 431.

[13]Ibid. Childs cites the multiplicity of ideas about the historical context of chapters 9–14 as "further evidence of the breakdown of method within the discipline" of critical scholarship. Despite the "danger" of another approach he comes at the issue from the perspective of the "canonical approach" (Childs, *Introduction*, p. 476).

STRUCTURE

The structure of the first half of the book is easier to see than that of the second half although there are markers there as well.

I. Dated Messages — 1:1–8:23
   A. Introduction and call to repentance — 1:1-6
   B. Eight visions — 1:7–6:8
      1. The four horsemen and the promise of restoration of Jerusalem and Temple — 1:7-17
      2. The four horns struck down by the four blacksmiths — 1:18-21 (Heb 2:1-4)
      3. The measuring line and great repopulation of Jerusalem — 2:1-13 (Heb 2:5-17)
      4. The cleansing of Joshua and the people — 3:1-10
      5. The seven-branched lampstand, two trees, and rebuilding of the Temple by Zerubbabel — 4:1-14
      6. The flying scroll and judgment on those who swear falsely — 5:1-4
      7. The wickedness in a basket in the form of a woman which is removed to Babylon — 5:5-11
      8. The four chariots that patrol the earth — 6:1-8
   C. Coronation of Joshua as the Messianic Branch — 6:9-15
   D. Question on fasting and promise of restoration — 7:1–8:23

II. Undated Messages — 9:1–14:21
   A. The first burden — 9:1–11:17
      1. Judgment on Israel's enemies — 9:1-8
      2. The coming of the king and freeing of the captives — 9:9-17
      3. The restoration of Judah and Joseph from exile — 10:1-12
      4. The parable of the deposed shepherds and the rejected shepherd — 11:1-17
   B. The second burden — 12:1–14:21
      1. The victory of Jerusalem and Judah — 12:1-9
      2. Mourning for the one pierced — 12:10-14
      3. Idols cut off and prophets shamed — 13:1-6
      4. The shepherd struck and one third of the flock rescued — 13:7-9
      5. The final victory of Jerusalem and the gathering of all nations to worship there — 14:1-21

GENRE

The variety of genres within the book and the obscure nature of the origin of the apocalyptic genre have contributed to the question of the unity of the book. In general the book is written in prose, but there is some poetry, especially in chapters 9 and 10. The first half is dominated by vision reports in chapters 1:7–6:8. There are also exhortations marked by imperatives in 1:2-6 and as a part of the vision reports in 2:6,7,10, and 13. Symbolic action is reported in 6:9-13. Chapters 7 and 8 are presented in sermonic fashion with reflection on fasting and other topics. Chapters 9–11 and 12–14 are called "Oracles" or "Burdens" (מַשָּׂא, maśśā').

A widely debated genre issue is whether Zechariah contains apocalyptic material, and if so, how much. The debate centers on the definition of apocalyptic and the history of its development. Some conclude that apocalyptic was a late development and since Zechariah is apocalyptic, chapters 9–14 are late.

Most see the apocalyptic genre as a development out of prophetic eschatology. There are two major dissenters. Paul Hanson associates its development with postexilic conflicts over leadership in Israel between prophets and priests. The priests won, so the successors of the prophets created a vision of a final cosmic intervention of Yahweh on behalf of his people.[14] G. von Rad finds the origins of apocalyptic in the wisdom literature and asserts that it is completely incompatible with the prophetic view of history.[15]

The best example of apocalyptic in the Bible is the book of Revelation. From this we learn that the apocalyptic perspective sees the present situation as evil and hopeless. God will intervene to judge the world and bring in the end. In the meantime the people of God are to remain faithful and pure, and persevere. The perspective is of this world and the world to come. The genre is marked by visions, heavenly interpreters, fantastic animal and nature images, and cosmic chaos. The language is highly figurative and stylized.[16] This literature requires careful attention to the stereotypical language that is used.

---

[14]Paul Hanson, *Dawn of the Apocalyptic* (Philadelphia: Fortress, 1975).

[15]Gerhard von Rad, *Old Testament Theology*, trans. by D.M.G. Stalker (New York: Harper and Row, 1965), 2:303.

[16]D. Brent Sandy and Ronald L. Giese Jr., *Cracking Old Testament Codes* (Nashville: Broadman and Holman, 1995), pp. 178-181.

Based on the above definition there does seem to be apocalyptic in Zechariah. The visions show some of the elements in incipient form. Chapters 9–14 show further elements. There are connections with earlier prophecy. However, Zechariah does not appear to be dualistic and does not reach the developed form of the genre found in the book of Daniel. Smith concludes that Zechariah is at least a forerunner of the genre.[17]

THEOLOGICAL THEMES[18]

The message of Zechariah 1–8 is concerned with both the wide perspective of concern for the Gentiles and a narrow focus on the Temple. The eight visions, arranged in a somewhat "loose chiastic structure,"[19] clarify these concerns.

But first Zechariah begins with a traditional prophetic note, a call to repentance (1:2-8). The returned exiles should not imitate their late ancestors and turn against God. This was futile, for although the prophets were no longer around, God's word stood forever (vv. 5-6).

A multifaceted theme in both halves of Zechariah is the deliverance of the people, the promise of the return of the people of God to Jerusalem and Judah, and the nations joining Israel in worship of God. These are not separate ideas but are closely connected. The breaking of the yoke of exile (1:18-21) naturally leads to the restoration of Jerusalem and return of exiles to fill it up again (ch. 2). This promise of the third vision would have provided tremendous hope for those struggling to rebuild the Temple. This is the theme of 10:6-12 also. A part of this larger theme is the overcoming of the nations or the judgment on the nations for it was the nations who had held control over Judah and the land (9:11-15; 12:1-9; 14:1-11). Stated in apocalyptic-like language the message of hope to the returned exiles was powerful. The very nations who controlled them for so long would be under the power of God's people as he executed justice on the world. An equally powerful part of this theme was the repeated assertion that the nations would come to worship and glorify God (2:11; 8:20-23; 14:16-19). This was also the message of Isaiah and

---

[17]Smith, *Micah–Malachi*, p. 175. Compare, however, Achtemeier who asserts that "the Book of Zechariah, as a whole . . . is not apocalyptic" (*Nahum–Malachi*, p. 145).

[18]See House, *Old Testament Theology*, pp. 386-393.

[19]Dillard and Longman, *Introduction*, p. 433.

other prophets (Isa 2:2-4). God's glory would not be vindicated until all nations could acknowledge that he was God.

Part of the promise to the returned people was the assurance that the Temple would be rebuilt (1:16; 4:7-10; 6:9-15). God's supremacy would once again be visible in the reality of the Temple where he could reside. Two individuals are highlighted for leading in this rebuilding, Zerubbabel and the high priest Joshua. This emphasized that restoration of the Temple required priestly sanction. The Temple would not only be rebuilt but it would have a proper priesthood to carry out the holy duties.[20] It was therefore crucial that the priesthood be pure and undefiled. Thus the fourth vision assures Zechariah and his audience that Joshua will be cleansed and the accuser (*satan*) rebuked. In fact the whole nation was cleansed as their wickedness was removed to the far reaches of the earth (5:5-11).

This restoration and cleansing however did not exempt the redeemed community from giving vigilance to holy living. God's answer to the question about continuing to fast for the fall of Jerusalem reiterated the ancient covenant obligations to care for the oppressed of the land (ch. 7).[21] If they could do this, the joy of fasting to the Lord would return (8:18-19).

A significant messianic figure comes from the pages of Zechariah, the coming of the servant Branch (3:8; 6:12). In 6:12 this is Joshua the high priest who will help rebuild the Temple. This concept is taken up from Isaiah 4:2; 11:1; and Jeremiah 23:5; 33:15. Perhaps here Zechariah intends to blend the concept of a kingly messiah of Isaiah and Jeremiah with that of a priestly figure, a Priest-King.

The messianic figure of the Shepherd-King comes to the fore in chapters 9–14. He is a shepherd rejected by his people, pierced and smitten, and sold for thirty pieces of silver. This would seem to be counter to a Davidic kingly figure, but Zechariah seems to have combined the Davidic ideal with the servant figure of Isaiah 42:1-4; 49:1-6; 50:4-9 and 52:13–53:12. The appropriation by the New Testament of these passages provides an interpretive grid for the Christian (see below).[22]

---

[20]Scholars often do not recognize this twofold approach and suggest that the name "Joshua" in 6:11 would have originally read "Zerubbabel."

[21]Zechariah is firmly grounded in the moral theology of Deuteronomy and the eighth-century prophets here.

[22]See the treatment by F.F. Bruce, *New Testament Development of Old Testament Themes* (Grand Rapids: Eerdmans, 1968), pp. 100-114.

The eschatological (apocalyptic?) message of chapters 9–14 can be best summed up by comparing chapters 9, 12, and 14. The nations who have subjugated Judah will be destroyed (9:1-8), and Judah and Jerusalem will experience the victory (12:1-9). After a decisive and perhaps final battle between the nations and Jerusalem in which God comes in power to win the victory, Jerusalem will be inhabited in security (14:1-5,11). That great day will be marked by significant changes in nature (eternal light), living water flowing out of Jerusalem, the acknowledgment by the whole world that the Lord is One (14:6-9; cf. Deut 6:4), and universal worship of God (14:16-19). It will be a day beyond any that the returned exiles had ever experienced or imagined. This ultimate victory and glorification of God in the whole world realizes the victory anticipated throughout the Old Testament.

The message of Zechariah to the returned exiles seems to be twofold. They are assured that God will raise up the necessary leadership to rebuild the Temple. They are also assured that the nations that have caused them so much suffering will ultimately be defeated and Jerusalem will dwell in peace. But the message is expanded further to include the great vision that the nations will ultimately be converted to the one, true, living God and come to Jerusalem to acclaim his glory and holiness. Zechariah's message is not just for Judah but for the whole world.

NEW TESTAMENT CONNECTIONS

The New Testament makes extensive use of Zechariah through both quotes and allusions. Jesus and the church apparently reflected deeply on the eschatological message of Zechariah and saw his vision of the future come to fruition in the life of Jesus, especially in the events in the last week of Jesus' life. Quotations include Zechariah 9:9 in Matthew 21:5 and John 12:15 (cf. v. 16 — the disciples did not at first understand); 11:13 in Matthew 27:9[23] (cf. 26:15); 12:10 (cf. Isa

---

[23]Matthew ascribed the quote to Jeremiah though the phraseology seems more near Zechariah. Perhaps Matthew had Jeremiah 19:1-13 with its many obvious parallels to the account and Zechariah 11:12-13 in mind, but used mostly phrases from Zechariah. He then credited Jeremiah with the blended quote because he was a more important prophet. See D.A. Carson, "Matthew," in *The Expositor's Bible Commentary*, ed. by Frank E. Gaebelein (Grand Rapids: Zondervan, 1984), 8:563.

53:5) in John 19:37 and Revelation 1:7; 13:7 in Mark 14:27. Zechariah
14:8 is alluded to in John 7:38. When the contexts of the quotes from
Zechariah are considered, the connections become even deeper. For
example, the context of Zechariah 13:7 includes the pronouncement
in 13:9, "they will be my people," a clear covenantal promise. The
connection is that the rejected and smitten shepherd is the suffering
Messiah, that is Jesus. F.F. Bruce has found the concept of "Shepherd-
King" to be a fruitful connecting theme.[24] He notices the thematic connections to the New Testament from Zechariah 9:9-10,16; 11:12; 12:10;
13:7-9; 14:4 and 21. Of course many of these are based on the actual
quotations.[25]

These quotes and allusions show that the New Testament found
in Zechariah 9–14[26] a powerful witness to the coming of the Messiah
and his rejection and death at the hands of his own people. But
beyond this the fact that the book of Revelation picked up the language and symbols of Zechariah also shows that the New Testament
found in them fruitful images for its picture of the second coming
of the Messiah. For example compare the following chart:

Revelation		Zechariah
6:4,5,6; 19:11	colored horses	1:8; 6:2,3,6
12:10	the accuser	3:1
7:1	four spirits/angels	6:5
1:7	the pierced one	12:10,14
21:25; 22:5	light	14:7
22:1	living water	14:8
11:15; 19:6	king reigns	14:9
22:3	secure city	14:11

Some suggest numerous other parallels to even the present
times. It is wise, however, to restrain our enthusiasm for the images
of Zechariah and not go beyond what the New Testament offers as
parameters for interpretation.

---

[24]The connection between shepherd and leader is a major theme in the
Old Testament. Moses and David were shepherds, and one thinks of Psalm
23, Ezekiel 34 and Jeremiah 23:1-6, as well as numerous other texts.

[25]Bruce, *New Testament Developments*, pp. 100-114.

[26]C.H. Dodd included Zechariah 9–14 among his list of Old Testament
texts used most often by the New Testament authors (*The Old Testament in
the New* [Philadelphia: Fortress, 1963]). Bruce calls the passion narratives of
the first and fourth Gospels a midrash (commentary) on Zechariah 9–14
(Bruce, *New Testament Developments*, p. 114).

MALACHI

HISTORICAL AND CULTURAL BACKGROUND

The book gives no explicit information on the historical setting. What we can know about the historical background must be extracted from clues in the text. The mention of a governor in 1:8 suggests a postexilic date when there was no king. Zerubbabel and Nehemiah both are given this title (Hag 1:1; Neh 5:14; the word is a Persian loan word). The references to the Temple in the book (1:10; 3:1,10) suggest a post-Haggai date after the Temple was rebuilt. It was long enough after the rebuilding so that the worship taking place seems to have degenerated into mere routine. The social conditions reflected in the book seem to be closest to that reflected in Ezra–Nehemiah. For example, there are references to the marriage of pagan wives (Mal 2:11-15; Neh 13:23-27), neglect in paying the tithe (Mal 3:8-10; Neh 13:10-14), corruption of the priesthood (Mal 1:6–2:9; Neh 13:7-9), and social oppressions (Mal 3:5; Neh 5:1-13).[1] If Malachi preceded Nehemiah, then he would probably have lived between 500 and 444 B.C.[2] or perhaps he was prior to Ezra's time (458 B.C.).[3]

TEXT AND AUTHOR

We know nothing about the author of the book of Malachi. Apart from the reference in 1:1 there is no mention of him in the rest of the Old Testament. The book does not mention his father or the time in which he preached.

The name means "My messenger," but not everyone agrees on its

---

[1]Walter Kaiser, *Malachi: God's Unchanging Love* (Grand Rapids: Baker, 1984), p. 16.

[2]Smith, *Micah–Malachi*, p. 298.

[3]Baldwin, *Haggai, Zechariah, Malachi*, p. 213.

significance. Some take the word to be a noun and not a proper name. These scholars also suggest that since the phrase "Oracle, the word of Yahweh" occurs only three times in the Old Testament (Zech 9:1; 12:1; and here) our book of Malachi is an anonymous book and is to be understood with Zechariah 9–11 and 12–14 as three anonymous prophecies at the end of the Book of the Twelve.[4] "My messenger" in Malachi 1:1 then should be identified with the reference in 3:1 to "my messenger," an unnamed prophet of God.[5]

The traditional view that Malachi is the proper name of a prophet is more probable for two reasons: Zechariah 9–14 are intricate parts of the book of Zechariah and should not be isolated out as anonymous pieces, and there is evidence elsewhere in the Old Testament that a noun with a first person suffix can be a proper name. Thus we find Abi ("my father," 2 Kgs 18:2), Ethni ("my gift," 1 Chr 6:41), and Beeri ("my well," Gen 26:34). Some suggest that Malachi is a shortened form of Malachijah which would mean "Yahweh is my messenger" but such a name seems unlikely.[6]

STRUCTURE

The book of Malachi is a unit. It is bound together by the disputation style which was perhaps taken from Jeremiah and other prophets. Six disputations form the core of the book. It then concludes with two exhortations.

1. Superscription — 1:1
2. Dispute about God's love — 1:2-5
3. Dispute about God's honor and fear — 1:6–2:9
4. Dispute about faithfulness — 2:10-16
5. Dispute about God's justice — 2:17–3:5
6. Dispute about repentance — 3:6-12
7. Dispute about speaking against God — 3:13–4:3
8. Two exhortations — 4:4-6[7]

---

[4]Eissfeldt, *Old Testament*, pp. 440-441.
[5]The LXX apparently understood the word this way and translated it in 1:1 as "his messenger."
[6]Compare Abi with Abijah in 2 Chr 29:1.
[7]Smith, *Micah–Malachi*, p. 299. The Hebrew Bible has only three chapters for Malachi while our English versions have four. English chapter four is 3:19-24 in the Hebrew text.

The placement of the book in the canon differs in the Hebrew and English versions. In the Hebrew canon Malachi is the last of the Book of the Twelve and appears last in the second major section called the Nebiim. This places it immediately preceding the first book of the third section, the book of Psalms. In our English Bible it is the last book of the Old Testament which gives the last exhortation about the coming of Elijah (4:5-6) special significance. This means that for Christians the Old Testament ends looking ahead to the great coming day of the Lord.

GENRE

The genre is prophetic speech but especially the disputation style. Prophetic disputation is marked by the prophet directly challenging popular thinking. He does this by quoting something said, or were thinking, and responding directly to it. This style is previously found in Micah 2:6-11 and Jeremiah 2:23-25,29-32; 3:1-5; 8:8-9. The statements of dispute are found at 1:2,6; 2:10,14,17; 3:7,13. Each dispute is structured a little differently, but each has common elements: a statement from the prophet, a response from the people that indicates innocence or ignorance, and a response from Malachi with either a word of salvation, an exhortation, or a threat. The response of the people may not be their direct words, though one can imagine the words of hecklers who heard Malachi preach. Some of the responses may be Malachi's own words as he accurately reflects the reaction he sees in the people.

THEOLOGICAL THEMES

The message of Malachi has to be understood within its historical context. The decades after the rebuilding of the Temple were a discouraging time for the returned exiles. Apparently the restored Temple did not bring the glory they had anticipated. Famine, poverty, oppression, moral laxity, and skepticism were endemic. Malachi tried to reassure them and call them back to obedience.

The covenant is the focal point of Malachi's message. It is implied in 1:2-5 and stated clearly in 4:4. Yahweh, the covenant God, is the one who speaks to them, and he is in the right to expect certain levels of behavior. We find the covenant term, God as Father (1:6; 3:17 [see 2:10]), which implies that Israel is his son. As the

Father he desires to bless his children. His covenant with the priests (2:4-7) was a part of the larger covenant and was for the good of the people. The priests were to be examples of covenant faithfulness but had failed. The people had also broken the covenant (2:10). They despised God (1:6) and were not obedient, robbing God of what was his (1:14; 3:8) as specified in the covenant law.

The people were also unfaithful in human relationships, breaking the covenant of marriage (2:14) and marrying foreigners (2:11). God hated divorce and desired godly children, which was possible only through marriage faithfulness (2:3-16). The close connection between marriage faithfulness and covenant faithfulness had been made long ago by Hosea and Jeremiah. In the postexilic period God still expected the same faithfulness.

God presented himself as the great King (1:6,14) as well as the Father of the covenant people. They should not forget he was Master and Lord and deserved fear and respect (3:16; see also 1:6,11,14; 2:2,5; 4:2). This also meant he was the great King over all the nations. How could his own people then neglect him?

Malachi knew obedience to God was recognizable in life and worship. Justice was required (3:5). His admonitions were very much in line with the teaching of Deuteronomy (see 4:4). Lax offerings were also condemned for they were a sign of a deeper spiritual problem. Malachi was not a legalist but he understood the deeper meaning of obedience to the covenant law. Obedience brought significant blessings just as promised in Deuteronomy (3:17-18).

Malachi also held out hope for the future. The day of the Lord was coming. It would be preceded by a messenger (3:1). Specifically the prophet Elijah would come to prepare the way by turning the people to the Lord (4:5-6). Through countering every objection of the people, assuring them of God's covenant love, and promising the coming of the day of the Lord, Malachi gave fresh hope to the people.

NEW TESTAMENT CONNECTIONS

The New Testament use of Malachi is varied. Jesus regarded John the Baptist as Elijah and therefore the one foretold by Malachi (Mal 4:5-6; Matt 11:14; 17:10-13; Mark 9:11-12; Luke 7:24-30). This was one of the indirect ways that Jesus claimed to be the Messiah. John the Baptist was also the messenger of Malachi 3:1 who was to prepare the way for Jesus (Luke 1:76). Mark 1:2 collates Malachi 3:1

with Isaiah 40:3. The Gospel writers make it clear that the eschatological hope of Malachi was fulfilled in Jesus the Messiah.

Paul quotes Malachi 1:2-3 in Romans 9:13 in support of his argument that God is free to choose whom he wishes. It has nothing to do with works.

There are several apparent allusions to various verses in Malachi. Jesus probably has in mind Malachi's statement on divorce from 2:15 when he defines marriage and divorce (Matt 19:4-5). Paul speaks of one father in 1 Corinthians 8:6 (Mal 2:10) and of polluting the table of the Lord in 10:21 (Mal 1:12). James asserted that God does not change (Jas 1:17; Mal 3:6). There are several references to judgment coming like fire (Mal 4:1; Matt 3:10; Luke 3:9; 2 Thess 1:8) or refining by fire (Mal 3:3; 1 Pet 1:7). The book of Revelation questions who can stand before the Lord (Mal 3:2; Rev 6:17). It also refers to the names of the faithful in a book (Mal 3:16; Rev 20:12). For a little book Malachi seems to have had significant impact on the thinking of Jesus and the New Testament authors. The Elijah connection validates Malachi's place as the last book of the Old Testament in the Christian Bible.